OHIO IS MY DWELLING PLACE

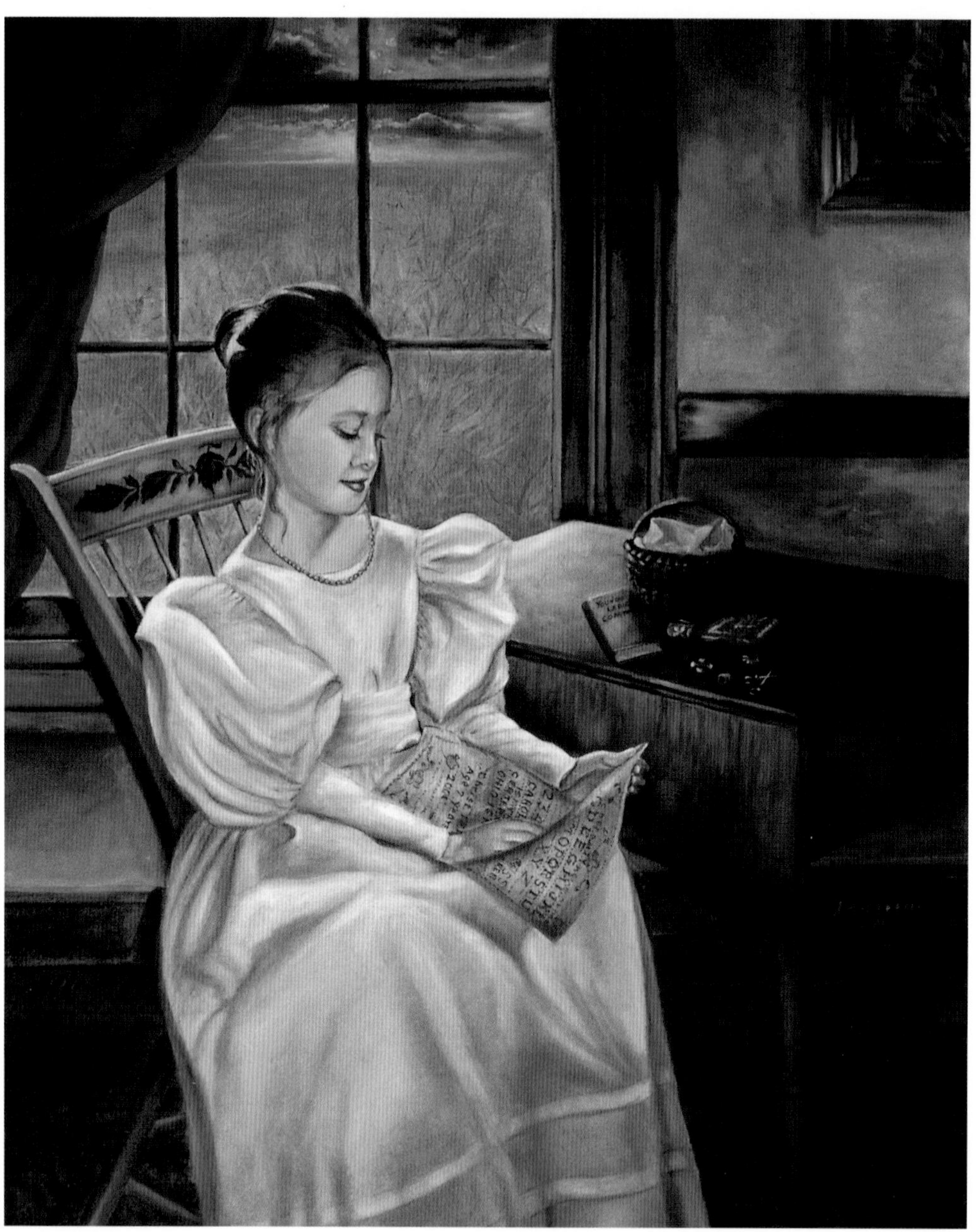

With my needle and my thread,
Which now appears so neat,
Before I was quite nine years old,
I did this work complete.
It still will show when I am old,
Or laid into the tomb,
How I employed my little hands,
While I was in my bloom.

OHIO IS MY DWELLING PLACE

schoolgirl embroideries
1800–1850

Sue Studebaker
with a foreword by Kimberly Smith Ivey

ohio university press
athens

To the Ohio pioneer girls and their teachers who with their endless hours of stitching have left a tangible and enduring legacy of our state's history in their needlework.

The publication of this volume has been made possible in part by the generous contributions of Kent D. Anderson, Mrs. John B. Greene, Mrs. Lewis Hughes, Mrs. Virginia W. Kettering, Burnell R. Roberts, and Dr. Richard B. and Sue Studebaker.

Ohio University Press, Athens, Ohio 45701

Printed in Hong Kong

Ohio University Press books are printed on acid-free paper ∞ ™

09 08 07 06 05 04 03 02 5 4 3 2 1

Frontispiece: "Caroline," by C. L. Creager
Maps were created by Kenneth Gruver.

Library of Congress Cataloging-in-Publication Data

Studebaker, Sue.
Ohio is my dwelling place : schoolgirl embroideries, 1800-1850 / Sue Studebaker.
p. cm.
Includes bibliographical references and index.
ISBN 0-8214-1452-6 (alk. paper) — ISBN 0-8214-1453-4 (pbk. : alk. paper)
1. Samplers—Ohio—History—19th century. 2. Children's art—Ohio. 3. Ohio—History—1787-1865. I. Title.

NK9112 .S779 2002
746.44'041'09771—dc21

2002025800

contents

Part Two. Central Ohio 129

Part Three. Northern Ohio 203

maps

foreword

> *Almost priceless to-day, and but yesterday the work of little girls, the sampler presents perhaps the most charming story in all the history of needlework. How frightened and stage struck those same children of long ago would be if they could but come back to us to-day, and see with what awe and veneration we handle their childish efforts! What a justification of maternal admonitions toward industry and the reward of virtue! For this almost universal form of needlework, so unassuming in purpose and so naïve in execution, is no less a form of art as are the famous Elgin marbles or the treasures in our own museums.*[1]

So wrote Florence Yoder Wilson in the November 1929 issue of *Needlecraft: The Magazine of Home Arts*. Recognizing samplers as an art form, Wilson also believed that samplers could teach us many things. Eight years earlier, Ethel Stanwood Bolton and Eva Johnston Coe voiced a similar belief in their book, *American Samplers*. A monolithic list of twenty-five thousand American samplers between the years 1630 and 1830, the book is still an essential resource today for sampler scholars.

Some seventy years later the subject of samplers and schoolgirl needlework maintains its popularity with scholars, collectors, and needleworkers. Even more so today, we appreciate samplers as a window to the past. Curators systematically examine sampler stitches, techniques, and design elements in the process of identifying a sampler's origins. Researchers scour dozens of documents in the attempt to locate the vital statistics of stitchers. Samplers and schoolgirl art continue to attract collectors and bring record prices at auctions. Modern-day needleworkers, eager to learn more about the history of their craft, seek out information from publications, exhibits, and symposiums. Students of material culture turn to samplers to provide a glimpse of a group of people seldom mentioned in the history chronicles.

A host of books written in the past twenty-five years discuss the important role of samplers and needlework in women's lives. One of the leading and earliest contemporary authors on the subject is Susan Burrows Swan, whose 1977 book, *Plain and Fancy: American Women and Their Needlework, 1700–1850*, tells the story of early American women by tracing needlework trends and their relationship to changes in society. *New England Samplers to 1840*, Glee Krueger's important compilation of samplers and teachers, serves as a model for researchers. Betty Ring's exhaustive research on the often anonymous needlework teachers changed forever the way samplers are perceived. No longer do we think of a sampler as simply child's work, but rather as an adult woman's art executed by a child's hands. Many recent books and catalogs provide in-depth studies of samplers from specific geographic regions or schools, usually in New England or the Middle States. However, relatively little has been written about girls and their needlework from the southern or western states until now.[2]

Sue Studebaker's comprehensive book covering the development of female education and the role of needlework in a young lady's life in Ohio significantly contributes to the study of regional styles in American needlework and samplers. Sue is an expert in the field of Ohio samplers and needlework. A highly respected author, scholar, and connoisseur, she has immersed herself in this study since 1986. Each needleworker has been meticulously researched to verify her Ohio residence and to learn more about her life and family. Literally hundreds of teachers and schools have been identified in addition to the documentation of more than 290 pieces of needlework. This checklist of Ohio samplers, teachers, and schools is an invaluable aid to needlework researchers.

Samplers reveal much about their makers' world, often providing details of their creators' names, ages, families, and locations. Because they are products of a particular society, samplers reflect attitudes, expectations, and changes within that culture. Thus, samplers are essential guides to a better understanding of the societies in which these Ohio girls and women lived and of how these societies differed from place to place and over time. By documenting Ohio samplers and the girls and women responsible for them, *Ohio Is My Dwelling Place* illuminates the lives of people often overlooked in written history—the girls and women who lived in Ohio during the years 1800 to 1850. Sue Studebaker uses the samplers to weave together a story of the roles played by the needleworker, her family, and her teacher in Ohio's early history. In a clever example of this technique, Sue employs Marion W. Edison's 1844 sampler to narrate the account of the Edison family, including Marion's youngest brother, the renowned Thomas Edison.

Samplers also reveal much about the aesthetics of a time period. The reader has only to flip through the pages of this book to be captivated by the charm and beauty of many Ohio samplers. As Florence Yoder Wilson wrote, samplers prove "that art flourishes sometimes in unexpected places, and springs from the most humble hands."[3]

Kimberly Smith Ivey
Associate Curator of Textiles, Colonial Williamsburg

preface

My first publication about Ohio samplers made its debut in 1988 at an exhibition at Warren County Historical Society Museum at Lebanon, Ohio. It was a wonderful place to begin my research and show the results of the work, because many beautiful samplers were produced in this part of southwestern Ohio. One hundred and eighteen documented samplers were listed in that catalog, and more than one hundred were exhibited.[1]

A considerable amount of new information has trickled in during the ensuing years, especially about needlework teachers and schools in the state before 1850. Many have never before been catalogued. More important, the documented samplers that are attributed to Ohio girls now number 290 and represent fifty-seven of Ohio's eighty-eight counties.

Some of the new discoveries are beautifully stitched and sophisticated, while others are simple marking samplers. Research efforts were not diminished, however, because a sampler was plain and simple. Sometimes the stitchers of the less sophisticated practice samplers came from families who made significant contributions to the history of the state and our expanding nation, and their stories add interest and importance to the needlework.

As a native of Ohio, my mother's family having come from Virginia to settle in Ohio in 1809, I have a great interest in the state's history. My approach to Ohio samplers is primarily from a historical point of view, rather than focusing on the needlework techniques and the vocabulary of stitches that young stitchers used. I have attempted to weave together a brief story of the stitcher, her family, and the circumstances that surrounded her life.

acknowledgments

When the Ohio sampler research began never could it have been anticipated that the project would be a "work in progress" for so many years. Akin to a giant jigsaw puzzle, it has pieces that have eluded our search for more than a decade. One bonus to this labor of love has been the friendships I have formed with kindred souls who are as excited about trying to find these pieces as I have been. Many people have encouraged me and generously given of their time, and they have my sincere appreciation.

First I want to thank the authors of other books and scholarly articles about early American needlework. Their support, knowledge, enthusiasm, and advice have guided me in the Ohio sampler work. These authors include Susan Burrows Swan *(Plain and Fancy)*, Glee Krueger *(New England Samplers to 1840)*, Betty Ring *(Girlhood Embroidery)*, Kimberly Smith Ivey *(Virginia Samplers—In the Neatest Manner)*, Gloria Seaman Allen *(Family Record)*, and Patricia T. Herr *(The Ornamental Branches*, about Moravian needlework). All have my admiration. Their books have taught me much and have been inspirations for the Ohio project. All of these generous women have encouraged me over the years and have shared every tidbit of new information about Ohio needlework wherever they discovered it.

Three longtime friends—Beverlee Cooper, Delores Klaber, and Jan Thomas—also deserve special mention and words of appreciation, for they have tirelessly helped with finding the genealogical information necessary to document the Ohio origins of the stitchers. Without their expertise, dedication, and hours of research, the book would have taken *another* decade for me to finish alone.

Beverlee Cooper, a talented interior designer by profession, who has a bent for searching the Ohio public and genealogical records on her computer, has also helped with many other aspects of the project. Her creativity and optimism about the book inspired me to "just do it."

Delores Klaber, an ardent antique collector and voracious reader, has a wonderful personal library of books on early history and family genealogies at her fingertips. With her computer

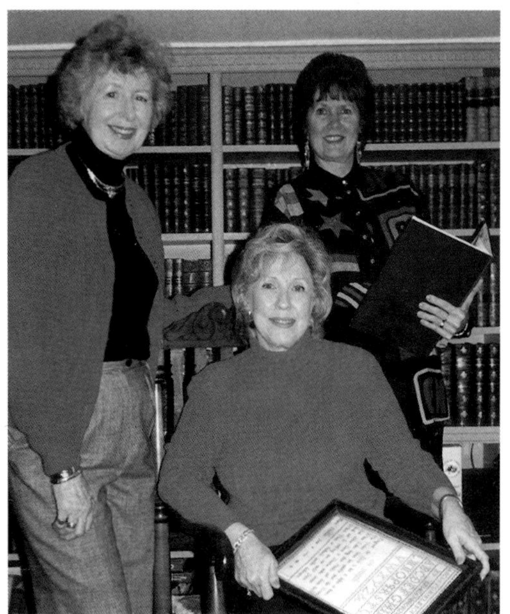

Klaber (*left*), Thomas, and Cooper (*seated*).

knowledge, she knows what is available at "private" historical society libraries around Ohio and is an incredible sleuth.

Jan Thomas's primary interest has always been early textiles and costumes. She served for an extended period as the Curator of Textiles at Warren County Museum in Lebanon. Jan searched diligently for information about female education, so that a pioneer teachers and schools chart could be assembled. This particular part of the project was an enormous effort that just kept growing.

I am also indebted to several special contributors to the book who unselfishly furnished material that added immeasurably to the contents. They include Jane Collins, who shared the Eunice Rice memoirs; Dennis Dalton, for his research about the Waynesville School and Academy; Michael McAfee, for giving me the 1880 *Harper's Monthly* article on "Needleart Revival"; David Sheley, for the 1839–40 Granville Female Seminary Catalog; Mary Allen for sharing the letter written by Sister Jennie M. Wells about the Shaker "Marks" box; and Adriene St. Pierre, who shared her insight and research of the Ann Hulme Price letters.

The success of the Ohio sampler project relied wholly on the owners of the samplers and their willingness to share their treasured needlework with us. Many of them had done considerable research on their samplers, and they were eager to participate in what we were doing. There are far too many names to list here, but the owners' names *are* listed with the list of documented Ohio samplers. I give them my wholehearted thanks for their unwavering confidence and support. I hope they are pleased with the book.

The completion of this publication also depended on the cooperation and valuable assistance of museums and historical societies and their kind and capable staff. My thanks to Mary Payne, director, Mary Klei, curator, and all the staff of the Warren County Museum in Lebanon; Brian Hackett, director, and the staff of the Montgomery County Historical Society in Dayton; President James B. Briley and Kim McGrew of the Campus Martius Museum in Marietta; Tom Kuhn, director, and James Bliven, curator, of the Ross County Historical Society Museum, and Pat Medert, archivist of the McKell Library in Chillicothe; H. William Lawson, director of the Mahoning County Historical Society in Youngstown; Barbara Warmelink, formerly of the Education Department of Cleveland Museum of Art; Ellice Ronsheim and Thomas Burke of the Ohio Historical Society; Sylvia Reid of the Cincinnati Historical Society; Dean Zimmerman, former director of the Western Reserve Historical Society Museum in Cleveland, and the staff of Western Reserve Historical Society Library; Linda Smucker, director of the Pioneer and Historical Society of Muskingum County in Zanesville; Jane Lightner, director of the Preble County Historical Society Museum in Eaton; Jean Kaufman, curator of the Salem Historical Society of Columbiana County; Jean McDaniel, archivist of the Robbins-Hunter Museum in Granville; Dorothy Justus, president of the Scioto County Historical Society in Portsmouth; Anita Ellis, chief curator of decorative arts at Cincinnati Art Museum; Helen Pinkney, textile curator of the Dayton Art Institute; Marjorie Brown, curator of Benninghofen House Museum of Butler County Historical Society in Hamilton; Laurence J. Russell, curator of the Edison Birthplace Museum in Milan; Reverend Vernon Nelson, archivist of the Moravian Archives in Bethlehem, Pennsylvania; Lorraine Mootz, docent at the Stickmuster (Sampler) Museum of Celle, Germany; Marilyn Cryder, curator of the Delaware County Historical Society Museum in Delaware; Barbara Sour of the Champaign County Historical Society in Urbana; Marilou Creary, curator of the Firelands Museum in Norwalk; Henry R. Timman, a historian in Huron County; Sister Agnes Geraldine and Sister Anna Catherine Coon, SCN, of Nazareth Academy in Bardstown, Kentucky; Lynn Russell, former director of Walton House Museum of Centerville-Washington Township Historical Society in Centerville; Deborah DeCurtins, former curator of Overfield Tavern Museum in Troy; Monica Wisener of the Randolph County Museum in Winchester, Indiana; Lois Wolf, collections manager of the Milan Historical Museum; Charles Griffin of the Warren County Genealogical Society; Valerie Elliott, head of the Smith Library of Regional History in Oxford; Karen Campbell, genealogist and reference librarian at the Mary L. Cook Public Library in Waynesville; Carole Medlar, genealogy librarian at the Dayton-Montgomery County Public Library; Lois Helton and Debra Eisert, reference assistants at Kettering-Moraine Library; the staff of the Middletown Public Library; and Mary Brooks, of the Archives Department of the Friend's Westtown School in Chester County, Pennsylvania.

Since more than three hundred samplers were examined and researched, a myriad of people all over the state were called upon to search out needed information about samplers from their counties. They helped in a variety of ways, and their inquiries and assistance played an important part in the progress, and ultimate completion, of this book. My heartfelt thanks to Kent Anderson, Betsey Bond, Roger Boone, Katie and Megan Borgert, Shirley Brubaker, Karen Buckley, Ricky Clark, Jane and John Diehl, Pastor Marilyn H. Doyle, Celia Elliott, Sarah and Katie Granson, Barbara and Ken Gruver, Jane Sikes Hageman, Jane and George Harold, Dr.

M. Donald Hayes, Sylvia Hess, JoAnn Hill, Margriet Hogue, Stephen Kelley, Ralph Krueger, Peg LeVert, Kathy Liston, Emilou McDorman, Larry Mosteller, Melvin and Connie Porcher, Rebecca Rogers, Judy Rose, Suzanne Smith, Marilyn Strickler, Jane Telfair, Margaret Tichnor, and Jenny and Carl Withers.

Many dealers through the years have found Ohio needlework and have kindly put me in touch with collectors and sampler owners. Some have also generously provided photographs for the book. My thanks go especially to Susie and Rich Burmann, Bea Cohen, Amy Finkel of M. Finkel & Daughter, Tim and Barbara Martien, Joyce Rivers, Debbie Shafer, Joan Townsend, and Susie and Jim Widder. Tom Porter of Garth's Auctions and Charles Muller of the Antique Review have also given liberal support to the Ohio sampler search.

My sincere gratitude extends to Kimberly Smith Ivey, associate curator of textiles at Colonial Williamsburg, for writing the foreword to this book. A scholar and friend, Kim willingly gave of her time and expertise. I am also indebted to the staff of Ohio University Press for their enthusiasm and confidence in this project.

Finally, I want to express my appreciation to my husband, Richard, who took the majority of the photographs and researched the beginning history of Ohio and each county. With endearing enthusiasm and patience, he has always served as my "best listener."

introduction

The Early Settlement of Ohio

The golden age of Ohio samplers coincided with the years of rapid expansion of the Ohio Country between 1803 and 1850. By the midpoint of the nineteenth century, Ohio's population had risen to almost two million. We can gain insights into where our young Ohio stitchers and their families lived when we examine the migration patterns to the new territory.

Once the Northwest Territory was opened for settlement, the lands northwest of the Ohio River were very enticing. Among those most eager to migrate were the soldiers of the Revolutionary War who had been promised land for their military services. Tough and hardened by the war, these men were ready to tackle the dangers and burdens of the frontier wilderness. To them, the "land of promise" became a reality fulfilled. Many settlers from Kentucky came north across the wide Ohio River, but the majority of immigrants came from areas that were part of the thirteen original colonies. (See map 1.)

The Seven Ranges

This area is the easternmost section of Ohio, next to Pennsylvania and a narrow strip of Virginia. It was the only land surveyed by government agents under the Continental Congress. Their surveying work commenced in 1785, and two years later these lands were offered for public sale in New York City. Because of the proximity to Pennsylvania, the first migration to this land was mostly from New York and Pennsylvania. The survey of "The Seven Ranges" established the foundation of the American Land System, which led to the orderly surveying, sale, and settlement of public lands in the United States all the way to the Pacific Ocean.[1]

Today this first survey of 1.5 million acres comprises the counties of Columbiana, Carroll, Harrison, Belmont, Monroe, Jefferson, and parts of Guernsey and Washington.

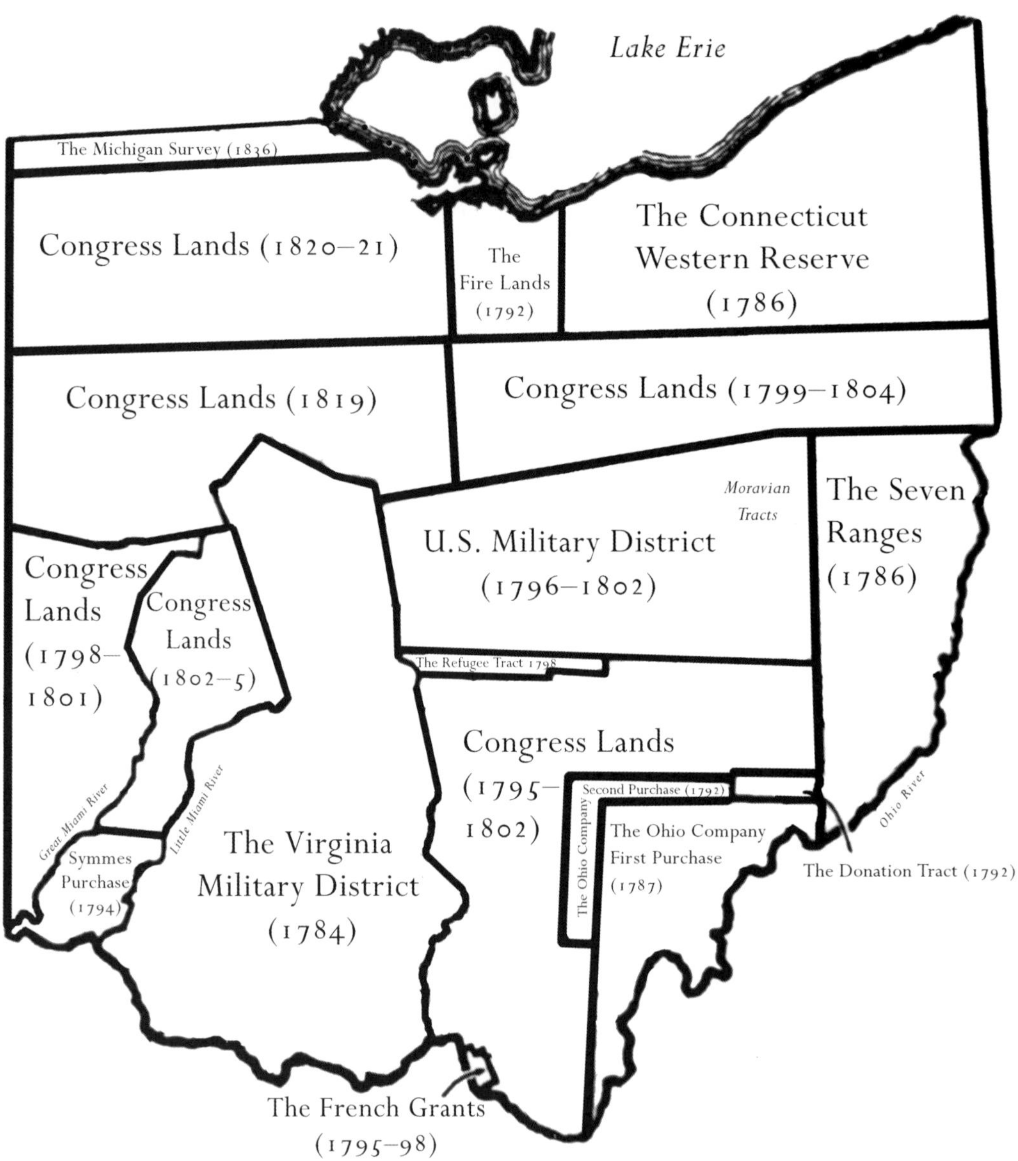

Map 1: The Building of Ohio

This map shows several separate areas, including The Seven Ranges, The Ohio Company Purchase, The Virginia Military District, The Connecticut Western Reserve, the U.S. Military District, and the Congress Lands. The Land between the Miamis was made up of the Congress Lands (1802–5) and the Symmes Purchase.

The Ohio Company Purchase

The Ohio Company Purchase was formed by a group of land speculators in Massachusetts. Composed of 1.5 million acres, this was the first large land sale made directly by the Continental Congress. The promotional sales in Massachusetts brought about a predominance of emigrants from that state and the rest of New England.

The Ohio Company could not examine this piece of real estate from Massachusetts, and the body of land they selected from a map turned out to be, with only a few exceptions, the most hilly and untillable of any tract of similar size in the state.[2] This poor land was not quickly settled and to this day is sparsely populated. A large number of the disappointed emigrants moved down the Ohio River to better agricultural lands.

The Ohio Company tract today comprises the counties of Washington, Athens, Meigs, and parts of Gallia and Morgan.

The Virginia Military District

This tract of land was promised to the Revolutionary War soldiers who served from the State of Virginia. They were given generous awards of 100 to 15,000 acres each, depending on rank and length of service.[3] The area consisted of all the lands between the Scioto and Little Miami Rivers. Large numbers of abolitionists came to this area of Ohio, especially the Quakers of Clinton and Warren Counties. These Quakers were quick to establish meeting houses and schools, and a significant number of samplers were produced in the region.

Today the Virginia Military District includes thirteen counties: Scioto, Adams, Brown, Clermont, Highland, Pike, Clinton, Fayette, Ross, Greene, Pickaway, Madison, and Union, plus parts of Warren, Clark, Champaign, Logan, Harden, Delaware, and Franklin. Many of these counties have some of the best farmland in the state.

The Land between the Miamis

More early Ohio samplers have survived from this section of the state than from any other area. This land was settled earlier and more densely than surrounding counties. In the booming settlements of Cincinnati, Lebanon, and Dayton, many schools were established for both male and female students, and dozens of needlework teachers advertised regularly.

Most of the initial land purchases in this area were made by citizens from New Jersey.

These settlers were influenced to come to the Ohio Country by Judge John Cleves Symmes, a native of their state. He had purchased some 300,000 acres there, and was eager to sell parcels of his land. One of those eager to buy was General Jonathan Dayton, namesake of the tiny settlement situated at the confluence of the Great Miami, Stillwater, and Mad Rivers.

The Connecticut Western Reserve

The vast area known as the Connecticut Western Reserve was sold to the Connecticut Land Company in 1795, with shares owned by forty-eight individuals, including Moses Cleaveland, namesake for that new settlement. At this early stage, some envisioned a new state called "New Connecticut," with Cleveland as its capital.[4] War veterans from Connecticut were given special preference in the purchase of lands and soon brought their families west to settle.

This large area, which bordered Lake Erie to the north and Pennsylvania to the east, comprised the present counties of Trumbull, Ashtabula, Geauga, Portage, Summit, Cuyahoga, Medina, Lake, and Lorain. Samplers from this area often show influences from New England schools.

"The Firelands," or "Sufferer's Lands," were set aside by the Connecticut legislature for supporters of the American Revolution who lost their homes to fire during the war. In September 1781, the British and Tories destroyed by fire the Connecticut towns of New London, Greenville, Fairfield, Danbury, Ridgefield, Norwalk, East Haven, New Haven, and Groton. A tract of 500,000 acres at the west end of the Connecticut Reserve was set aside to compensate these two thousand families. The "sufferers" formed the Ohio Corporation in April 1802 to manage their Ohio lands. Today this area comprises all of Erie and Huron Counties.

The United States Military District

The U. S. Military District, established in June 1796, was an area reserved to satisfy a 1776 resolution by the Continental Congress authorizing that bounty lands be granted to Continental Army officers and soldiers in lieu of cash payment. The government was rich in land but poor in money. These 2.5 million acres of good land are found in the present-day counties of Franklin, Delaware, Knox, Licking, Morrow, Noble, Marion, Holmes, Coshocton, Muskingum, Tuscarawas, and Guernsey. By the time of statehood in 1803, the tract had been surveyed and, for the most part, settled by war veterans from all thirteen colonies.[5]

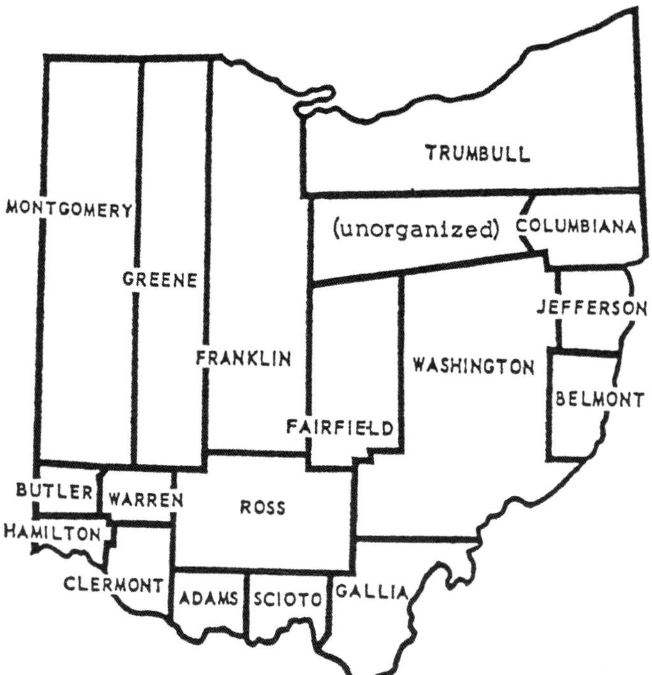

Map 2: Ohio in 1803

Shows the configuration of the state when it was admitted to the Union.

The Moravian Tracts

The Moravian Tracts were established by the Continental Congress in May 1785 for the sole use of the Christian Indians who formerly had settled there. Years earlier, three towns had been established by the Moravian Missionaries for the Indians: Schoenbrun (1772), Gnadenhutten (1772), and Salem (1780), all situated on the Tuscarawas River. These Christian Indians suffered a horrendous attack on March 8, 1782. On that day, white settlers murdered many Indian women and children in retaliation for Indian attacks on them. In an attempt to compensate for this massacre, the Continental Congress donated two thousand acres in trust to the Moravian Brethren at all three towns to encourage the Christian Indians' return.[6] Few ever returned.

One of the most beautiful pieces of needlework associated with Ohio history has Moravian ties. The story and needlework of Amelia McIntire appear on pages 181–83.

The Congress Lands

By far the largest area of this new state consisted of the Congress Lands, which were sold by the Federal Land Offices, established in May 1800, at Steubenville, Marietta, Chillicothe, and Cincinnati. They immediately began a booming "land-office business" in opening up the frontier.

The final sales of Congress Lands were made in the northwest quadrant of the state, beginning in 1819.

The migration to the Northwest Territory was so rapid that between the years of 1788 and 1802, the population of the state reached fifty thousand, the requirement for statehood. On March 1, 1803, Congress admitted Ohio as the seventeenth state, with seventeen designated counties.[7] One third of the state at this time was still Indian Territory, comprising the entire area north of the 1795 Greenville Treaty Line and west of the Connecticut Western Reserve.

Settlers flocked to the new state, and during a period of only seven years, one hundred eighty thousand more people were added to the population rolls. The pioneers continued to arrive in spite of constant conflicts with the British and Indians in the northwestern quadrant.[8] Not until the War of 1812 was formally concluded in the summer of 1813 did the State of Ohio secure all of its land from the British and Indians. Five years later, in 1818, a treaty was signed with the Miami Indians at St. Marys, allowing conclusive and indisputable settlement of the last twenty-two of the counties that make up the state today.

Why Samplers Were So Important

Some of the first Ohio settlers left behind substantial homes and considerable wealth to come to the Ohio Country. Their young daughters wore pretty clothes, enjoyed gay social events, and had all the amenities that "families of the better sort" were accustomed to. For them, adjustment to frontier life may have been tedious and uncomfortable. Letters sent back home to friends, however, usually sounded hopeful and happy. Their parents, after all, were the prominent men and women of the little towns and hamlets and often owned huge tracts of land. The majority of the sampler stitchers, however, came from ordinary families who had just "adequate" homes. Their parents worked hard and were attempting to carve out a life in this untamed territory. They looked at Ohio as a rewarding land of opportunity.

One could hardly overemphasize the importance of needlework skills for a young girl in the eighteenth and early nineteenth centuries. Making certain that their daughters learned how to sew well was a considerable duty for every parent, regardless of the family's economic status. A quaint verse seen with some frequency on samplers tells this succinctly: "This I have done that you may see, What care my parents took of me." Little girls might begin to sew when they were

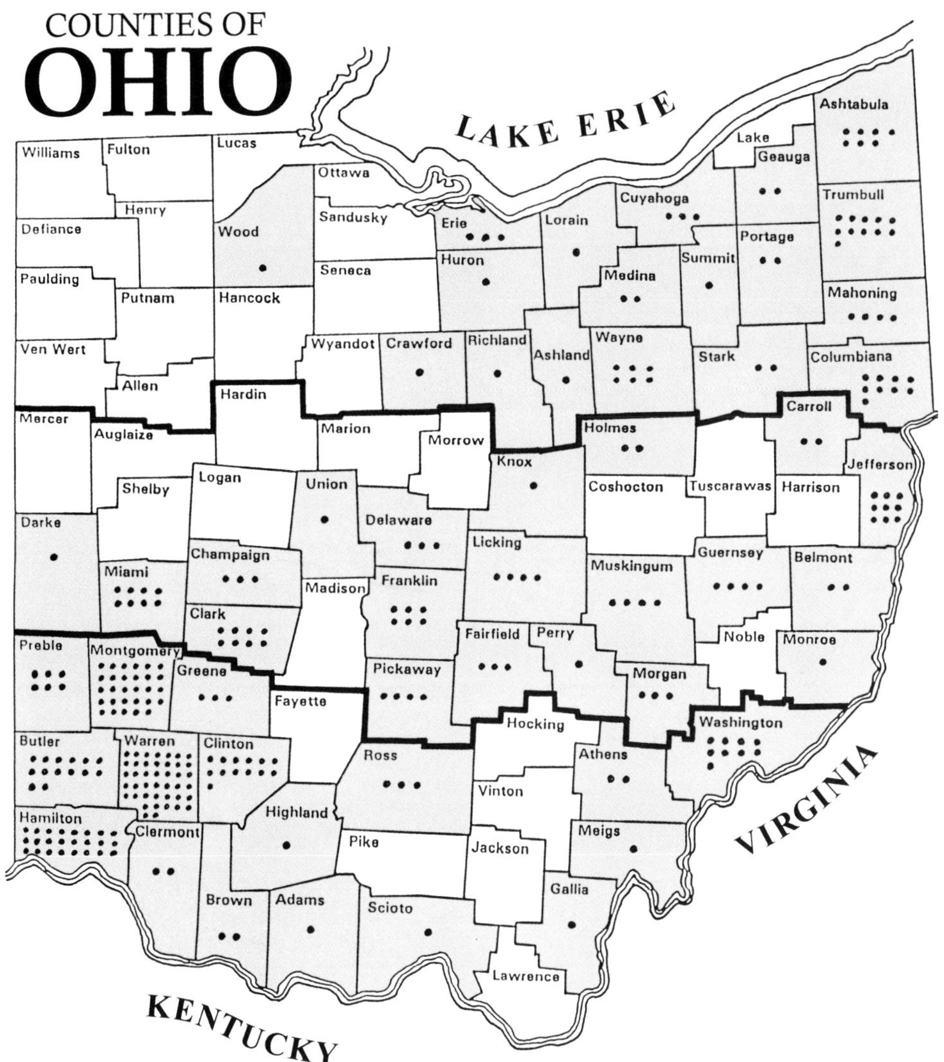

Map 3: The Three Sampler Regions of Ohio

Shows the number of samplers found in each county.

Adams - 1
Ashland - 1
Ashtabula - 7
Athens - 2
Belmont - 2
Brown - 2
Butler - 14
Carroll - 2
Champaign - 3
Clark - 8
Clermont - 2
Clinton - 13
Columbiana - 9
Crawford - 1
Cuyahoga - 3
Darke - 1
Delaware - 3
Erie - 2
Fairfield - 3
Franklin - 6
Gallia - 1
Geauga - 2
Greene - 3
Guernsey - 4
Hamilton - 24
Highland - 1
Holmes - 2
Huron - 1
Jefferson - 9
Knox - 1
Licking - 4
Lorain - 1
Mahoning - 4
Medina - 2
Meigs - 1
Miami - 8
Monroe - 1
Montgomery - 29
Morgan - 3
Muskingum - 4
Perry - 1
Pickaway - 4
Portage - 2
Preble - 6
Richland - 1
Ross - 3
Scioto - 1
Summit - 1
Stark - 2
Trumbull - 11
Union - 1
Warren - 42
Washington - 9
Wayne - 6
Wood - 1

five or six years old, and by the time they were seven or eight, it was not unusual for them to make a simple marking or practice sampler. When that was completed they were expected to learn a variety of stitches and to commence work on a larger and more complicated sampler.

Antique collectors often discover an unfinished canvas for sale, which certainly suggests that not every little girl enjoyed the long hours spent with her needle and embroidery frame. Can you imagine the little girls you know today sitting for hours and hours with "thus their little hands employed"? A sampler was not easily and quickly made, nor was making one just an exercise in stitching. In a curious way, it was a form of discipline. The young stitchers were given very little choice as to the overall design, the verse used, the thread colors, or what stitches they put on their sampler. Almost without exception, the "instructress" or needlework teacher would make those decisions for her students.

Cultural and religious preferences significantly influenced where a girl was to receive needlework instruction. For example, Catholic families were likely to patronize the female seminaries that were established by the Church. Plain and ornamental needlework was always an important part of the curriculum of parochial schools. Ohio's many German settlers, however, usually were not eager to send their daughters to any type of needlework school or teacher to learn to stitch. Instead, the "Duch" girls, many of whom were still speaking German in their homes, received their training at mother's knee. There they were taught the traditional Germanic motifs found on their samplers and hand towels.

Even though the Age of Enlightenment brought welcome changes in the education of young women, learning to read, write, and "cipher" were not considered the most important accomplishments for a young lady. Learning the art of housewifery and proficiency in sewing, however, was of major concern to every young girl. A little book entitled *Means and Ends or Self Training,* published in Boston in 1840, gave the following advice to its young readers:

> *Nothing will aid you so much in the practice of economy in your dress, as expertness with your needle. No American woman, let her speak all the tongues, and play on all the instruments invented, can be said to be* educated, *if she is not a good needle-woman.*
>
> *The time may come when all young women will find more advantageous occupations than embroidery and other fine needle-work; when female education shall be given to drawing from nature; to designing, painting, sculpture, etc. Fine needlework harmonizes with female employment; it may be classed among pleasant recreations. It is a convenient employment for a social circle. It is a branch . . . though perhaps the lowest . . . of the fine arts. And a stronger argument than all these in its favor is that it furnishes a valuable gift to bestow, and a most gratifying one to receive.*[9]

Without doubt, young stitchers often gave needlework projects as cherished gifts to parents or other family members. Framed samplers not only were treasured decorations for the home, but, when hung in a public room, also served as courting tools. This was an era when young men knew the value of a wife and mother who was proficient with the needle and thread. A girl's handwork was likely to be noticed and admired by a visiting suitor.

In *The Young Lady's Own Book,* Edward C. Biddle wrote: "It is also to be wished that mothers in those ranks where income is usually small, would initiate their daughters well in the art of repairing (clothing etc.). It is an indispensable part of female economy, and its humble trophies would be in reality more honorable, as well as more useful, than the finest piece of embroidery ever sent in from a boarding school; much comfort, in families that are not affluent especially, depends upon the 'stitch in time.'"[10] Clearly, not every family had the means to send their daughters to formal schools or small dame schools. For these families, "plain" needlework could be taught at home; "ornamental" needlework was an unnecessary luxury.

Early accounts, diaries, and letters written by females to distant relatives are difficult to find, but they most always have certain things in common. Time and again they reflect the importance of the church in women's lives, and they reveal how many family members died at very young ages. The women faced these tragedies and took comfort that their loved ones were now with God and "had been called to a better home." This was usually written in a simple, almost terse way. Men found new wives, more babies were born into the family, and grief had to be passed over quickly. Another common element in their lives is that they rarely spent a day without doing some form of needlework. Over and over they noted "I worked on the quilt today," or "my petticoat is nearly ready for hemming," or "William's shirt needs repair."

Young girls were rarely mentioned in early history books, journals, and letters. A sampler, along with an ancient tombstone, is often the only reminder that a young girl even existed.

What Makes It Ohio?

There are no characteristics, unusual stitches, distinctive borders, or patterns that are unique to Ohio samplers, except perhaps the steamboat motif. There are, however, a few elements of design that turn up regularly, providing quick clues that Ohio may be the origin of the piece. If a sampler has those four letters, *O-H-I-O*, stitched on it, or a familiar Ohio teacher or school name appears on the canvas, its origin is almost certain. When genealogical research proves that the stitcher's parents were living in Ohio at the time the sampler was produced, we also assume that the needlework was done in Ohio. We know, however, through old letters, family diaries, and school records that girls from affluent families were occasionally sent to boarding schools in the East and to nearby Kentucky seminaries and schools. Their needlework has been included in this book because they and their families were living in Ohio.

Surprisingly, the least dependable information about samplers is contributed by well-meaning owners who have inherited the family heirlooms. Family provenance may point research in the right direction, but it usually does not provide enough proof to document the sampler as being produced by a girl then living in Ohio.

Identifying and documenting each stitcher was an important part of the Ohio sampler project. Public records of all kinds were searched and reliable sources are listed in the bibliography. Sources for research included, but were not limited to, census records; marriage records; death, land, and tax records; probate and court records; church records; published obituaries; and cemetery records. Because samplers are personal items, no two are exactly the same. Just as each piece of needlework is unique, so are the stories of the girls who made them. When the "bits and pieces" of the stitcher's family history can be put together, they often provide a new perspective and more sensitive appreciation of her sampler.

If convincing evidence was not found that the stitcher's family was living in Ohio when the needlework was executed, the sampler was excluded from the listing of Documented Ohio Samplers. Some of the family stories of these "lost girls" were intriguing and historically important, but, with regret, they had to be excluded from the project.

Providing footnotes for every genealogical fact written about each stitcher would have been possible but of limited interest to most readers. It was not my intent to provide a complete genealogical study of the stitcher or her family but to offer enough family history to "bring her back to life" for a few moments as readers study her sampler.

Note: Unless otherwise indicated, all illustrated samplers and associated needlework have a linen canvas embroidered with silk thread.

part one

SOUTHERN OHIO

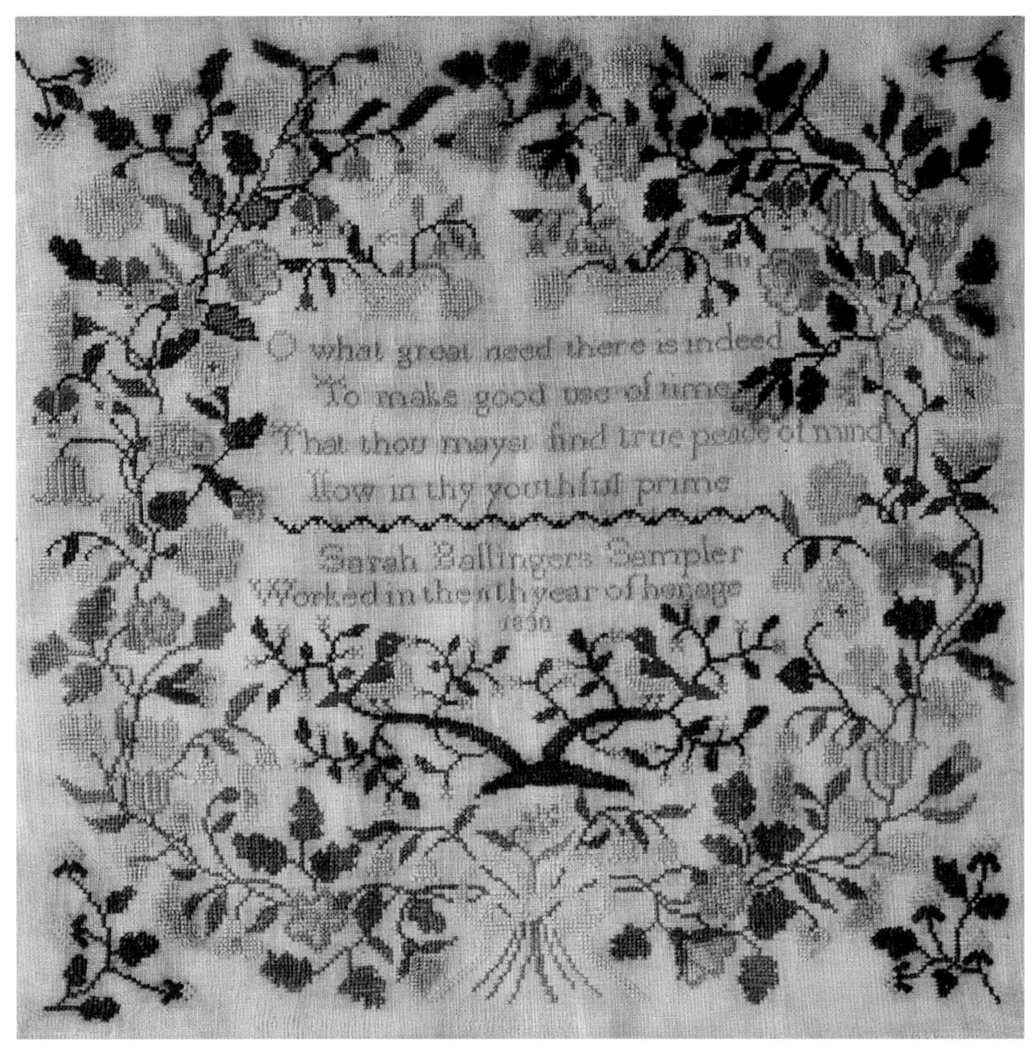

Washington County

In November 1787, a meeting of the directors of the Ohio Company was held in Boston at Bracket's Tavern. That evening General Rufus Putnam, who had served with honor in the Revolution, was appointed superintendent of the group, and the men of the Ohio Company began to make clear plans for their venture to the Ohio lands. The company, composed of forty-eight men mostly from New England, was an outgrowth of an effort on the part of Revolutionary officers to secure the bounty lands due them for service in the war.[1]

With all preparations made, the following month General Putnam and two companies of men headed west. Despite weeks of horrendous hardship and winter cold, both groups made their way to Sumrell's Ferry in Westmoreland County, Pennsylvania. From there, the final part of their expedition was a five-day journey down the Ohio River to their destination of Fort Harmar, situated at the confluence of the Ohio and Muskingum Rivers. On April 7, 1788, the expedition reached the site that became the first permanent white settlement in the Northwest Territory—Marietta. Three months later, on July 26, Washington County was formed.

Among those courageous men of the Ohio Company was Oliver Dodge, whose granddaughter Mary Wing Dodge executed the sampler shown in figure 1.

The Marietta pioneers turned their attention to the education of their children very soon after their arrival in Ohio. In the summer of 1789, Bathsheba Rouse, the daughter of John Rouse from New Bedford, Massachusetts, established the first school in the Northwest Territory in nearby Belpre, just fourteen miles below Marietta. By the 1820s, there were likely a number of teachers in the area offering instruction in needlework. One such teacher advertised in several issues of the popular Marietta newspaper, *American Friend*: "Notice of the opening of a young ladies school in one of the apartments of the Academy [Muskingum Academy]. The school opened Monday, Dec. 3, 1821. It will be taught by Miss Goldthwaite, recently from New England, . . . who has taught young ladies there, before coming to Ohio. Students may board nearby. Cost of tuition for 'regular' subjects: $3.00, $5.00 extra for drawing, painting, embroidery, etc."[2]

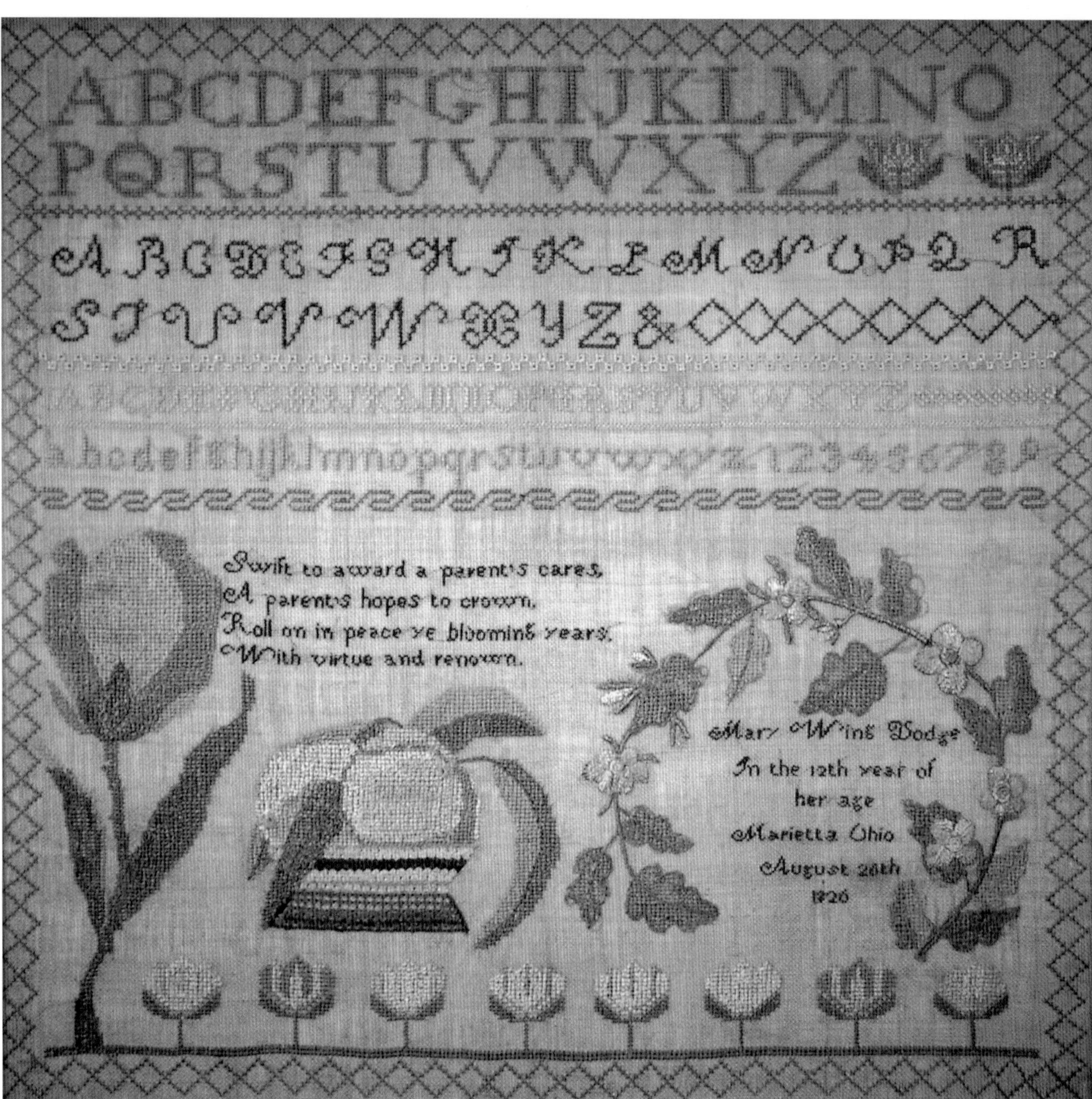
ABCDEFGHIJKLMNO
PQRSTUVWXYZ
Swift to award a parent's cares,
A parents hopes to crown.
Roll on in peace ye blooming years,
With virtue and renown.
Mary Wing Dodge
In the 12th year of
her age
Marietta Ohio
August 28th
1826

« Fig. 1: Sampler of Mary Wing Dodge. 1826.

Size: 18½" L x 19½" W. Collection of Larry and Sarah Mosteller.

Mary Wing Dodge was born in Marietta, Washington County, on March 5, 1815, to Oliver and Eudocia (Wing) Dodge. Her sampler, dated 1826, is very different in design from any other Ohio sampler. The lower half of the canvas displays unusual designs of a large tulip-like flower and a bowl of fruit. Like the stiff row of small open tulips along the bottom, they seem to be drawn by an unschooled hand. All four sides of Mary's sampler are framed by a diamond border.

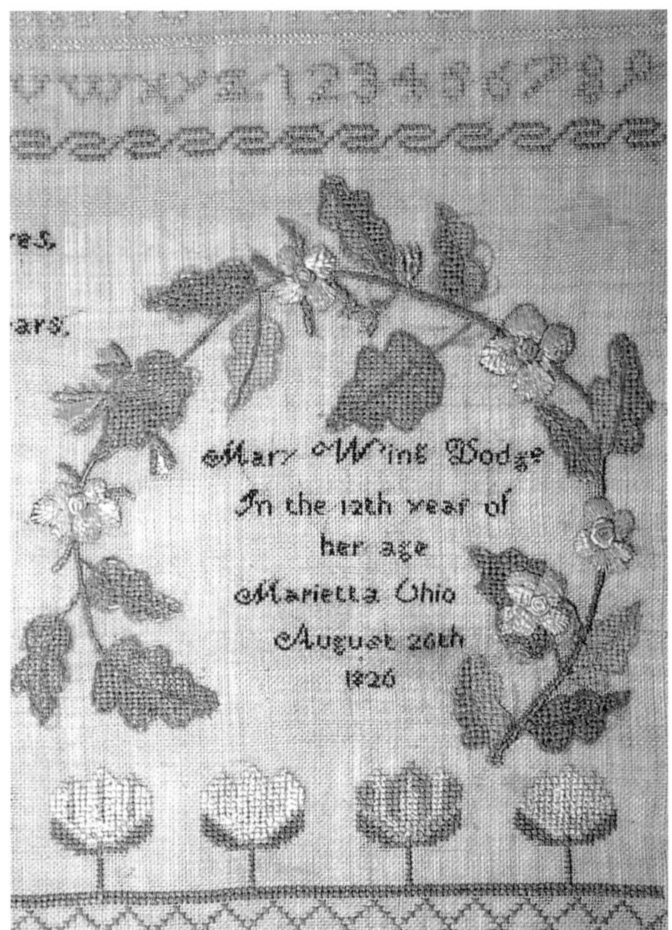

Fig. 2: Detail of Dodge Sampler.

In contrast to the sampler's childlike designs, the flowering wreath that encircles the reserve area where Mary stitched her name is artfully done. The inscription reads: "Mary Wing Dodge—In the 12th year of her age—Marietta Ohio—August 26th—1826."

Fig. 4: Stone Homestead.

Colonel John Stone's large frame home stands today not far from the banks of the Ohio River. The house has had few exterior changes since it was built in 1798. The scene of many antislavery activities, it was originally situated much closer to the river. Early in the nineteenth century, the large house was moved back from the floodplain by oxen teams.

The cornfields around Colonel Stone's farm provided safe hiding places for slaves and their families. During the daylight hours, even the escaping slave children would be quiet so as to not be discovered. When night fell, John Stone could then load the fleeing families into his wagon and move them on a few miles to another safe house farther inland. There they could finally "board" the underground railroad that would eventually lead them north to freedom.[3]

« Fig. 3: Sampler of Melissa Barker Stone. 1830.
Size: 13½" L x 21" W. Collection of Larry and Sarah Mosteller.

Colonel John Stone, a strong abolitionist, and his wife, Charlotte (Loring) Stone, reared eight children. Young Melissa, their second child, completed this sampler in 1830 when she was eight years old. Apparently Melissa felt strongly about slavery, too, because historical accounts tell about her in the following incident: "At one time two young ladies in Belpre, Melissa Stone and Abbie Browning, took provisions across the Ohio in a skiff and left them on a hill a little ways below Parkersburg (then part of Virginia) for a slave who was afterwards caught, flogged, and put in jail!"[4]

Melissa went on to graduate from Putnam Female Seminary in Zanesville, Ohio, in 1844, when she was twenty-two years old.

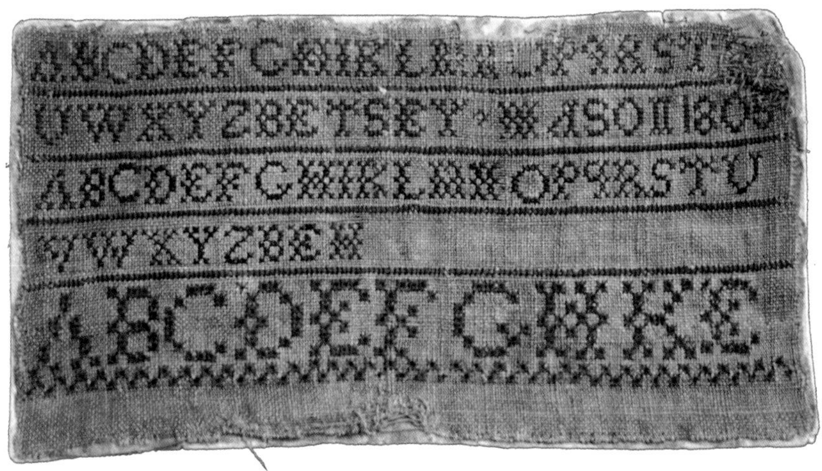

Fig. 5: Sampler of Betsey Mason. 1805.
Size: 5" L x 10" W. Author's collection.

The earliest Ohio sampler discovered is the small marking sampler of Betsey Mason. Betsey was just six when she executed this sampler in Adams Township. Her parents, William and Rebecca (Sharp) Mason, came from Philadelphia to the Northwest Territory in 1797 and settled in the village of Lowell, a few miles north of Marietta on the Muskingum. Elizabeth (Betsey), the sixth child, was born in the Northwest Territory in 1799, four years before the area achieved statehood.

William and Rebecca Mason did not set out for Ohio, but ended up there quite by accident. Betsey's father and his father and brothers built boats near Redstone, Pennsylvania, and moved their families on board to float to a Western future home. Their destination was Kentucky. Just above Marietta, however, the boat with William and Rebecca's family was wrecked, and this branch of the Mason family stayed in Ohio. The rest of the family continued on down the Ohio River and settled in Kentucky.[5]

Betsey married William Morris on April 7, 1819, in Marietta and spent the remainder of her life in Washington County. This small sampler is a significant document even though, regrettably, someone has cut off the lower part of the canvas.

Fig. 6: Sampler of Elvira Howe. 1818.
Size: 3½" L x 8½" W. Collection of Delores and Lowell Klaber.

Just a few miles west of Marietta is the tiny settlement of Barlow where Benajah Howe settled with his second wife, Salley Betsey (Brown). Benajah and Salley came from Poultney, Vermont, and arrived with their children in Ohio early in the nineteenth century. Two of their daughters, Lucy and Elvira, made samplers that have survived, both using the same sampler verse: "It is education formes the mind. / Just as the twig is bent the tree's inclin'd." Elvira's 1818 marking sampler was done in her twelfth year. She married Samuel Collis in Marietta in June 1828. The mother of four children, she died in April 1855 and is interred at the Newcomers Cemetery in Springfield, Ohio.

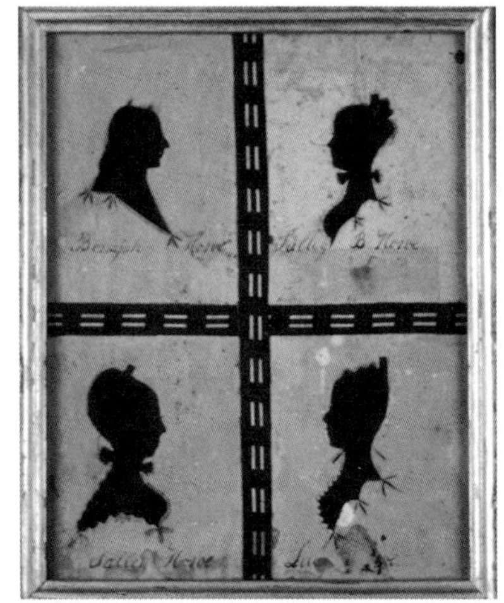

Fig. 7: Silhouettes of the Howe Family.

The silhouettes of the Howe family were found with Elvira's sampler, along with early family letters, a wood-and-ivory flute, and other memorabilia. The silhouettes of the parents, Benajah and Salley B., appear on the left and the likenesses of their daughters Salley and Lucy are on the right.

Fig. 8: Sampler of Eliza Ann Reckard. 1823.
Size: 16" L x 16" W. Collection of Mrs. Ardis Postle.

Eliza Ann Reckard's needlework is well stitched and colorful. It is one of the most attractive samplers found from Washington County. Eliza Ann was born in Marietta on September 10, 1810, the daughter of Calvin and Rhoda (Bordon-Westgate) Reckard. She married Junia Jennings and the couple resided in the village of Marietta. She is interred in Oak Grove Cemetery.

Fig. 9: Detail of Reckard Sampler.

The white building is probably a church, but the steeple has an enormous bird perching on the cross—a pleasing whimsical touch.

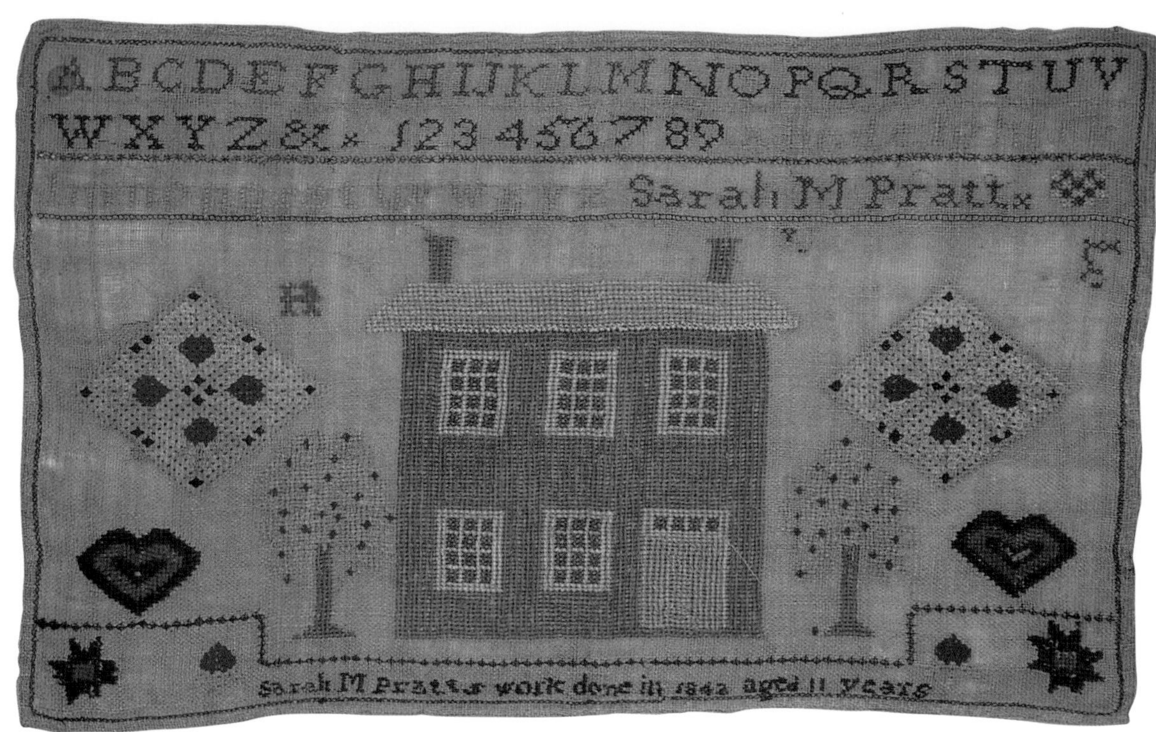

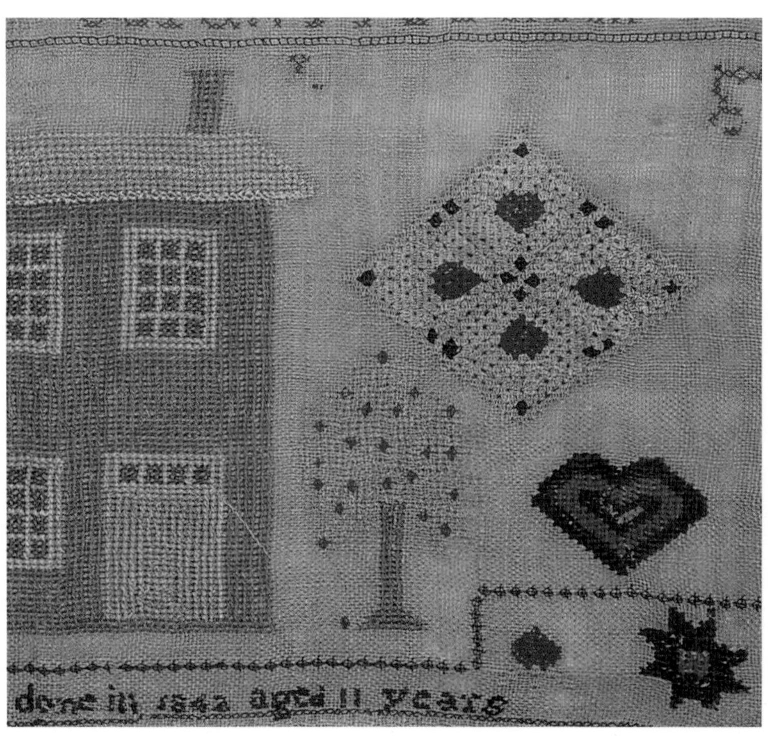

Fig. 11: Detail of Pratt Sampler.

The diamond motifs on either side of the building are done in queen stitch, which required skill and considerable time to execute. This complex diamond-shaped stitch was usually confined to small items or used as an accent stitch.[6] Sarah put hearts and geometric stars on the bottom corners, distinctive designs that add real charm to this sampler.

« Fig. 10: Sampler of Sarah M. Pratt. 1842.
Size: 10" L x 16" W. Collection of the Campus Martius Museum, Ohio Historical Society.

Sarah Pratt's grandfather, Azariah Pratt, came to Marietta in 1788, one of the first forty-eight settlers to arrive in Marietta. He married Sarah Nye, by whom he had ten children. His son Elisha, who was born in the block house at Fort Marietta in 1798, was the father of this young stitcher. Her mother was Lydia Smith, who was born in 1800 in Marietta. Sarah was their only child. She completed the sampler when she was eleven. Sarah's canvas has the proportions that we often see in samplers of the 1840s—less square and wider than they are long.

Sarah left an interesting letter that was written to a friend after her mother's death. Sarah was twenty years old at this time; below is a portion of the letter:

> *Oct. 5th, 1851*
>
> *We, that is Pa and myself, are in good health at present, but you cannot think what a great change has come over Marietta since you left. It has been very sickly this summer and there has been a great many deaths, more than ever before in one summer within my memory. Our neighborhood does not seem like the same that I lived in last winter. There seems to be a change in every house. The prevailing disease was the flux but very different from the common disease, the physicians could do but little with it,—never had such extreme cases before. It has now abated or I might say almost entirely left. Some of the persons who have died of the disease you may perhaps know, but the most of them were children. . . .*
>
> *You wished me to give the particulars of my mother's death, but I do not know where to begin it was such a mysterious death giving a shock to this neighborhood not soon forgotten. Ma was taken sick with a violent cold caused by coloring [dyeing wool or clothing] out of doors in the wind, was very sick for two days, had a doctor who said she would get over it, and she did seem better, and the next two days sat up a great deal, but had no appetite. . . . She was not in reality sick more than one day. . . . She became cold and died at 8:00 March 2nd. She was buried the next day at 2:00, one week from the time she was coloring. You may imagine it left a large break in a family so small, but you cannot imagine the isolation and loneliness visible in every corner and made by so sudden and unexpected death. . . . Now six months have passed, and it does not seem possible that I have no mother! . . .*
>
> *I expect to have a very lonesome winter, although we have the cleverest neighbors that could be wished. They are so kind to me I cannot be grateful enough. Accept all of you the affections of a true heart and remember me ever as your friend.—Sarah M. Pratt.*[7]

Sarah married the following year, and the loneliness must have begun to lessen. Life was difficult, there is no doubt.

Hamilton County

Hamilton County was the second formed in Ohio. Situated between the Great and Little Miami Rivers, it was the scene of fierce battles with the Indians in the 1780s. Fort Washington, built in the autumn of 1789 where Cincinnati now stands, was the most important and extensive military fort then in the Territories. In the early years, the fort served to protect the pioneers who ventured to the area. Cincinnati grew slowly at first, and as new families settled the little village, the site became more secure. By 1808, Fort Washington had been torn down and the land on which it stood divided into town lots.[8]

As early as 1792, however, there were enough inhabitants in Cincinnati that the citizens "asked subscribers to erect a house of pubic worship."[9] The Reverend James Kemper, who had brought his wife and children north from Kentucky in the autumn of 1791, served as the minister of this first Presbyterian church. The sampler of their grandniece Isabella hangs today in the restored Kemper log house in Cincinnati's Sharon Woods Village.

By the time Isabella made her sampler in 1830, many female academies and needlework teachers were advertising in the Cincinnati newspapers. The earliest announcement of a school for young ladies in Cincinnati appeared in both the *Western Spy* and *Hamilton Gazette:* "July 1802. Mrs. Williams begs to inform the inhabitants of Cincinnati that she intends opening a school in the house of Mr. Newman, saddler, for young ladies on the following terms: Reading, 250 cents; Reading and Sewing, $3.00; Reading, Sewing, and Writing, 350 cents per quarter."[10]

In 1800, just two years before Mrs. Williams's notice was published, the population of the village numbered about 750. Three decades later, the Census of 1830 showed nearly 25,000 inhabitants, and immigrants continued to arrive. To serve these new Ohioians, Cincinnati had at least fifty private or subscription schools. One of the earliest was started by Mrs. Wozencraft, who advertised in the April 2, 1811, issue of *Liberty Hall* newspaper. She offered to teach "Plain Sewing, Embroidering, Tambouring, Lace work, and Flowering," along with an impressive list of academic subjects, and she gives notice that "country produce will be taken in part pay, at the market price." As early as January of 1805, *Liberty Hall* and the *Cincinnati Mercury* carried the following advertisement: "SARAH & MARY ANN BROWNE RESPECTFULLY inform their friends that they continue their SCHOOL in Sycamore street, near the Recorder's office; where, young ladies are taught Reading, Writing, Arithmetic, Sewing, Marking, Embroidery and Drawing. Terms, two dollars per quarter, for Reading, Writing and Sewing, the other branches on a very reasonable advance. They can accommodate a few boarders, for which produce will be received at market price. Fine Sewing work will be received and punctually attended to."

Another popular early school, the Young Ladies Seminary, was opened near the northwest corner of Fourth and Walnut in 1820 by David Cathcart, who came to Cincinnati in 1812. His advertisement announced that a lady would be employed to teach "Drawing, Painting, Embroidery, etc."[11] Also advertised regularly were the Cincinnati Female Academy, established in 1823 by Dr. John Locke, and the Cincinnati Female Institution, operated by Albert, John, and I. W. Pickett in the 1830s, but these schools' curriculum announcements did not specifically mention needlework. They often mentioned things like "musick, drawing, & all ornamental branches belonging to female education." Needlework from these schools may survive, but it is difficult to document which school a stitcher attended.

Although she may not have advertised in the newspapers, Ann Hulme Price, a Quaker woman, was also teaching sewing in Cincinnati between 1824 and 1836. She wrote home to relatives living in New Jersey, and her letters make fascinating reading. They tell of her life and her impressions of her new surroundings. The family had just moved to Cincinnati from Lebanon, a much smaller town, and she begins by giving an account of why they left Lebanon:

> *You will perhaps be surprised to hear of our leaving the country. Many circumstances concurred to effect the change wich we have made and wich I think we will never regret . . . the loss of society, distance from (church) meeting, and the want of suitable schools for the children were our principal inducements to leave the country. . . . I am still more than ever pleased with this Country and I suppose that any family with even a little money may live better and cheeper in this town (Cincinnati) than in any other in the United States. . . . [T]here is a market held every day in the week abounding with every thing except Oysters wich can be had any where. . . . [W]e dined one day last week on the best perch I ever eat, the largest one was the size of a small shad and very fat. We have had apples all winter from the market and they have been brought to the door in April for 25 cents a bushel. . . . [A]ll kind of dry goods very low; the Ladies are as fine as Butterflies on tulips. Gapsy [gypsy] Leghorns loaded with ribbons and Artificials [flowers, and even fruits, were fashionable trimmings]. Poor creatures, they appear as if they did not know they have a Soul that must live for ever and ever when their poor Bodies are mouldering in the grave and food for worms, what a Humiliating thought. . . ."*[12]

As a Quaker, Ann had been advised to follow a "plainness in dress and simplicity in manners,"[13] and she obviously felt she had little in common with some of the Cincinnati ladies.

Several church-affiliated schools like the one opened by the Presbyterians were established as early as 1815. The Presbyterian church was offered for use as a schoolhouse, and within a few weeks of being opened, on April 15, 1815, enrollment was so great and the building so crowded that students were turned away. The following year a second school was started for females only.[14]

The Catholics founded St. Peter's Female Academy in 1829, listed in the Cincinnati Directory of 1836–37 as "For the support of female orphans, under the care of the Sisters of Charity . . . and they have under their charge 200 others, regular attendants of the school."

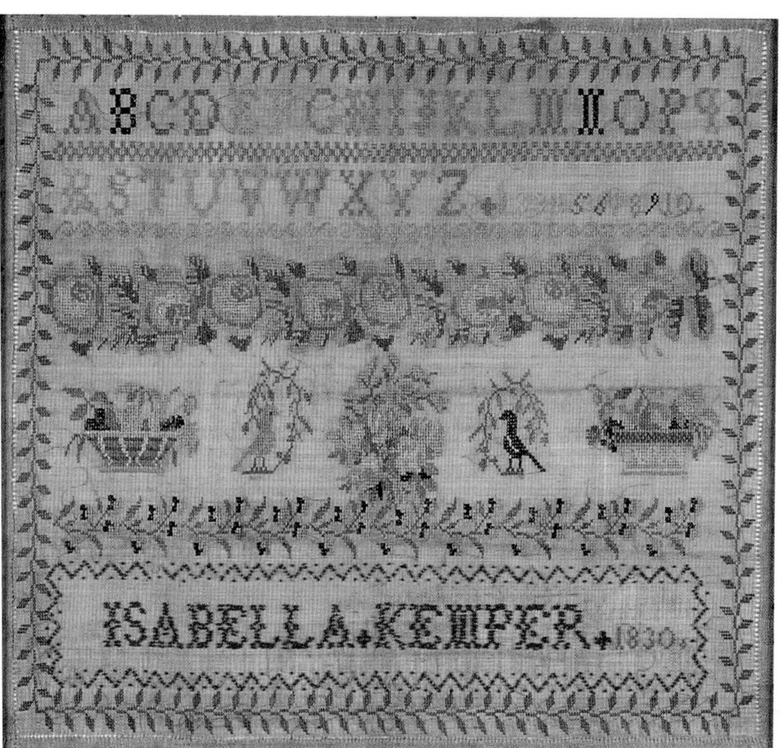

FIG. 12: SAMPLER OF ISABELLA KEMPER. 1830.
SIZE: 16½" L x 18" W. COLLECTION OF NATIONAL SOCIETY OF COLONIAL DAMES OF AMERICA IN THE STATE OF OHIO.

Isabella, the daughter of Presley and Mary (Menshaw) Kemper and grandniece of the Reverend James Kemper, was born in 1819, in the Walnut Hills area of Cincinnati. She made her sampler at age eleven. Her name and the frame surrounding it are executed in red glass beads. Many little girls at this time were making beaded bags to carry or to give as valued gifts, but Isabella decided to display her beadwork on a sampler.

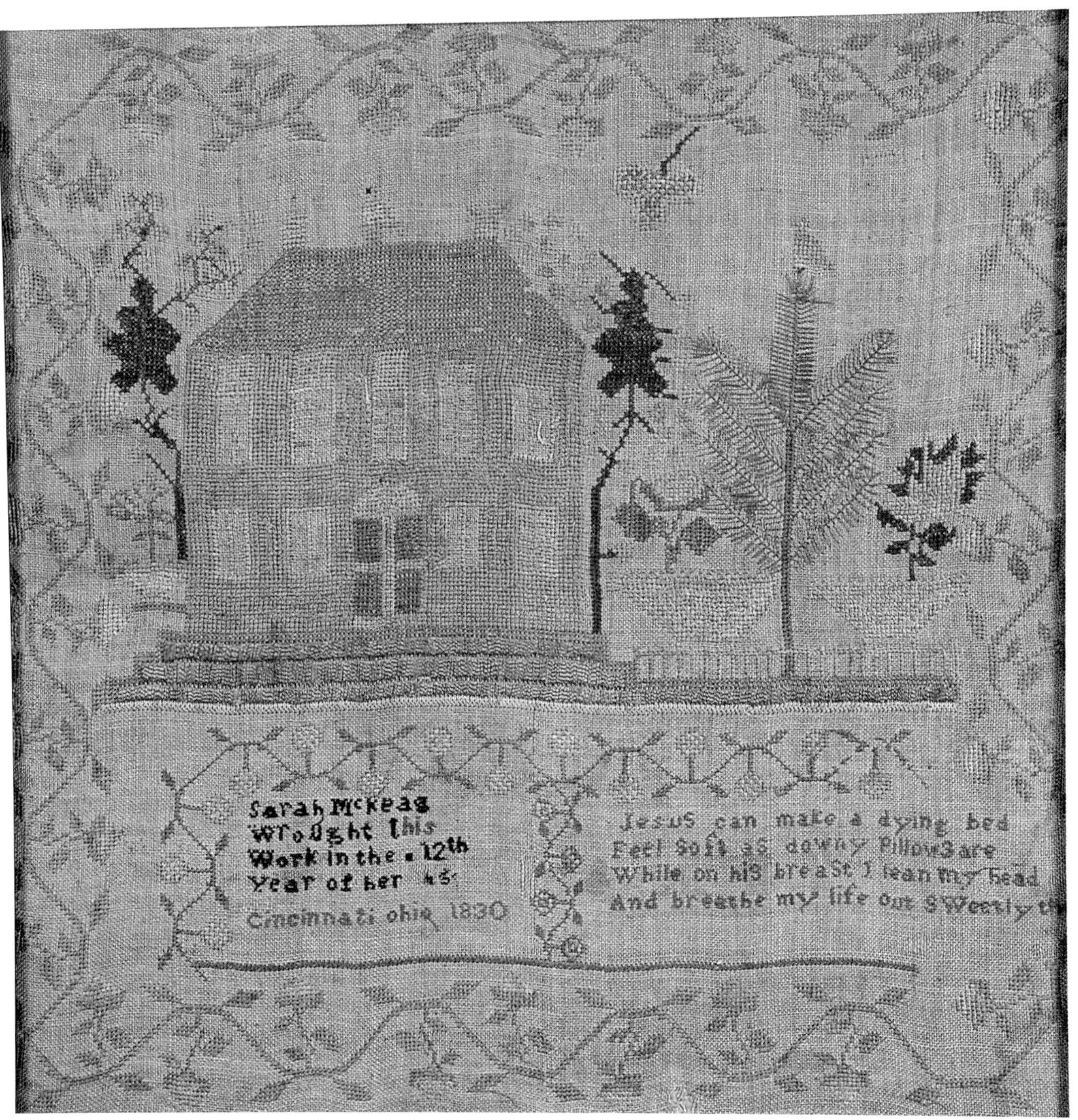

Fig. 13: Sampler of Sarah McKeag. 1830.
Size: 16" L x 16" W. Collection of Larry and Sarah Mosteller.

Sarah McKeag's sampler was stitched the same year that Isabella Kemper did her needlework, but these two Cincinnati samplers seem to have little else in common. These young stitchers certainly were not tutored by the same teacher. The naïveté of this sampler adds to its charm. The huge house set on a grassy lawn, is flanked by unusual trees, and the verse is one that has not been used on any other documented Ohio sampler. It reads: "Jesus can make a dying bed / Feel soft as downy pillows are / While on his breast I lean my head / And breathe my life out sweetly."

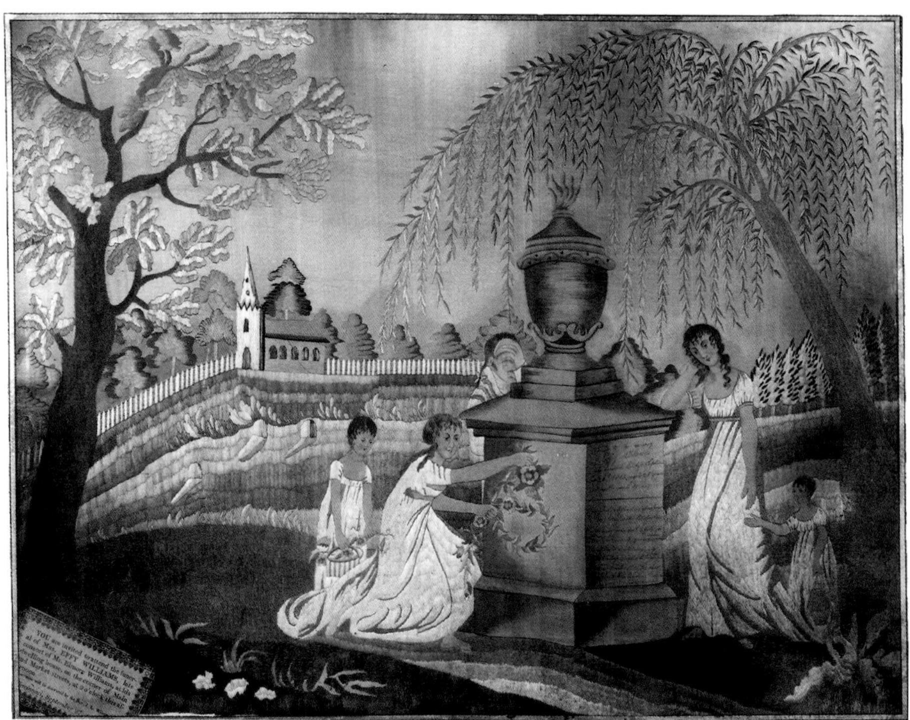

Fig. 14: Mourning Embroidery of Martha Williams. 1816.
Size: 20" L x 26" W. Silk on silk. Collection of
Cincinnati Art Museum, gift of Julia Sayre.

The memorial picture executed by Martha Williams to commemorate her mother's death is a sophisticated needlework that took considerable skill. We do not know where Martha learned to stitch so beautifully; it may have been under a local teacher's guidance, or possibly she attended an out-of-state academy. Elmore and Effy Williams were Martha's parents. Effy died in the autumn of 1813, and a card of invitation to her funeral is tucked into the corner of the picture. It announces that her funeral will be held at their "dwelling house, at the corner of Main and Market Streets. . . . September 27, 1813." Martha later married Samuel R. Allen and is buried in Spring Grove Cemetery in Cincinnati.

Fig. 16: Sampler of Sarah Alice Devoe. Undated. »
Size: 13½" L x 19½" W. Collection of Linda Gottschalk.

This sampler has a naive perspective and charm and is unlike any other Ohio sampler documented. Sarah framed the carefully stitched house very well, adding rather ominous clouds at the top and a large-scale flowering vine around the sides and bottom of the canvas. Sarah Alice Devoe's sampler is not dated, but she stitched beside her name the words "work done at the Catholic School in Cincinnati." Harriet Looker's sampler, completed at St. Peter's, looks very different from this sampler. The school that Sarah attended undoubtedly was not St. Peter's Female Academy, but it may well have been the Sixth Street Academy, organized in 1840 by eight members of the Sisters of Notre Dame.

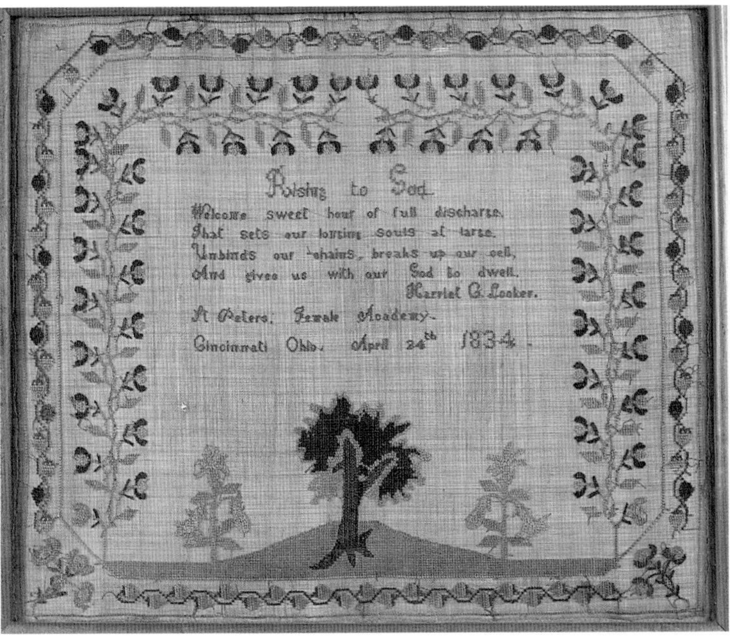

Fig. 15: Sampler of Harriet Looker. 1834. Size: 18" L x 21¼" W. Collection of Allan and Linda Cobourn.

Harriet Looker lived in Harrison, Ohio, and completed this needlework in 1834. She was the daughter of Samuel B. Looker, and the granddaughter of Othniel Looker, a Revolutionary War soldier under George Washington. He was appointed to serve for a short period as the fifth governor of Ohio in 1815. Since her family was a prominent one, it is not surprising that Harriet was sent to school in Cincinnati. A large city would have more schools, which could offer a broader curriculum. The name St. Peter's Female Academy is stitched on the canvas, which also displays a somber religious verse. The tree of life on Harriet's canvas is flanked by large lily flowers. The symbolism of the lily, the traditional flower of purity, reflects the spiritual teachings of the Sisters. Two samplers have been found from this school.

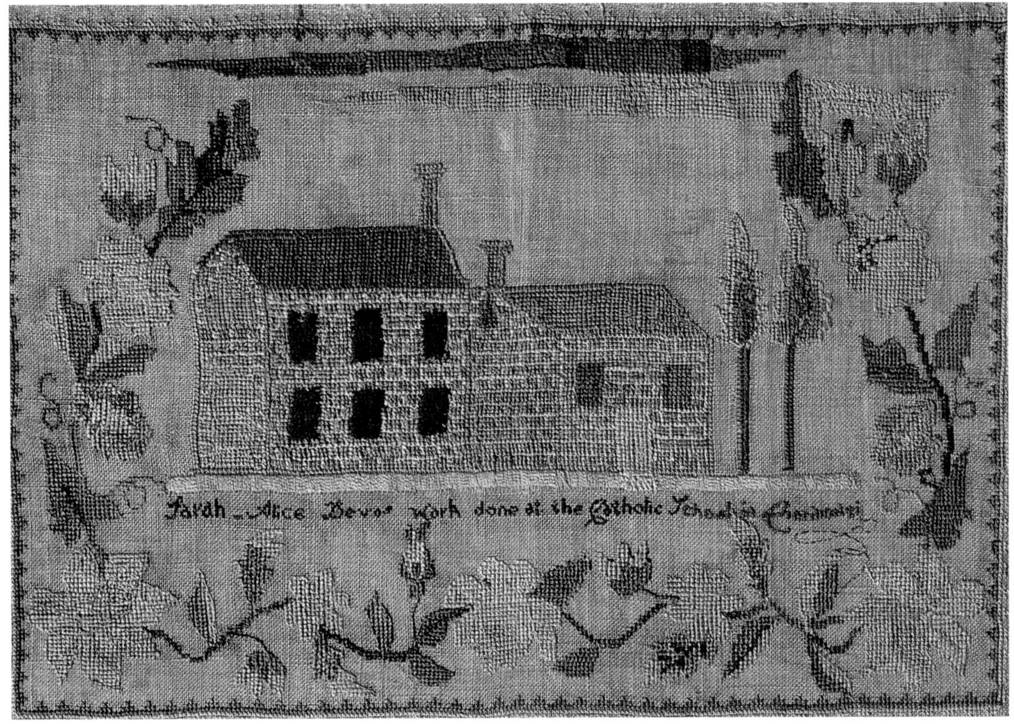

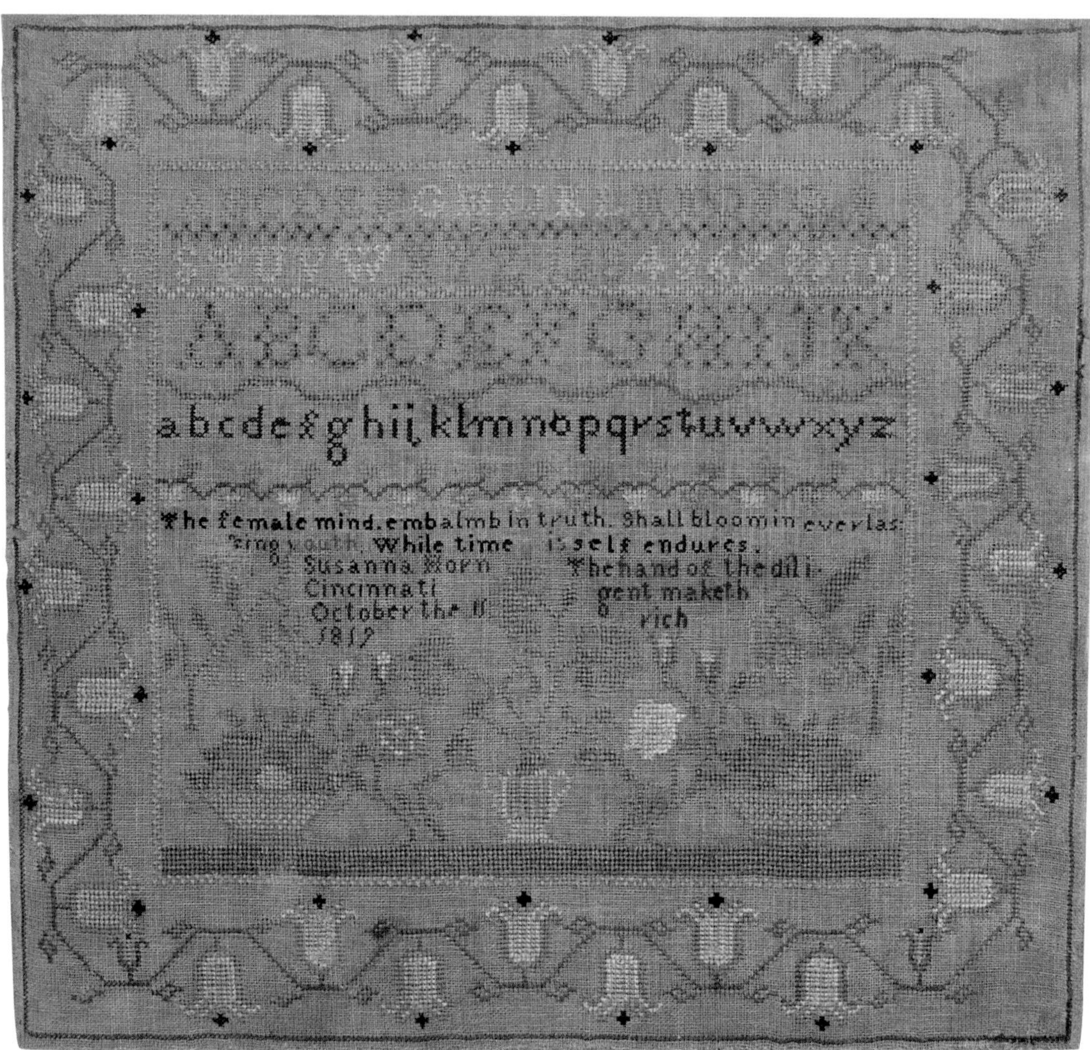

Fig. 17: Sampler of Susanna Horn. 1819.

Size: 17" L x 18" W. Collection of Cincinnati Museum Center.

The framed center of Susanna Horn's needlework is surrounded by a wide border of stylized tulips. The design of her canvas is well planned, though it is rather restrained and tightly constricted. The sampler is clearly marked with the date of completion and the stitcher's city of residence, Cincinnati.

Fig. 18: Portrait of Susanna Horn. Collection of Cincinnati Historical Society Library.

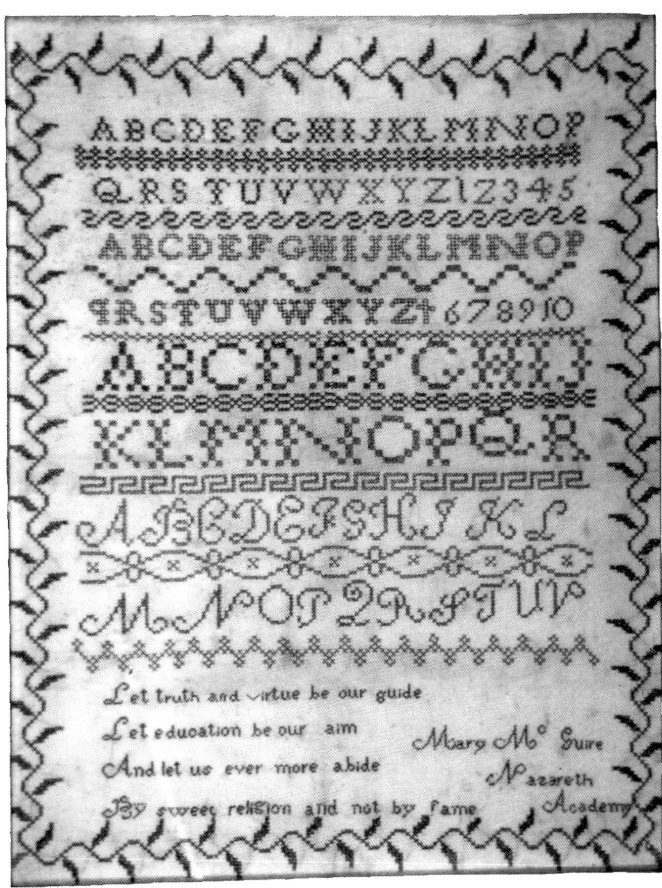

Fig. 19: Sampler of Mary McGuire. c. 1838.
Size: 15" L x 11½" W. Anonymous collector.

Mary McGuire's sampler verse is a well-known one: "Let truth and virtue be our guide / Let education be our aim / And let us ever more abide/ By sweet religion and not by fame." Next to the verse she stitched "Nazareth Academy," the name of the school where her carefully stitched plain sampler was executed.

Nazareth Academy was founded in 1812 by a community of Catholic sisters, in Kentucky, two miles north of Bardstown. Between 1820 and 1850, school records reveal the names of sixty girls from Ohio, both Catholic and non-Catholic, who attended Nazareth Academy. Mary McGuire, a Catholic girl from Cincinnati, entered the school on July 17, 1838, at the age of thirteen. There were a dozen or more girls from Cincinnati there at the same time.[15] It is believed that they came by way of the Ohio River to Louisville, and from there by stagecoach to Bardstown and Nazareth Academy.

The fact that needlework was always an important part of the curriculum at the Academy is indicated in early school records and the school's Annual Examination, Catalogue of Students, Awards of Premiums, and Commencement Exercises booklets. In the 1858 catalogue, the curriculum included "Embroidery and Needlework, Tapestry and Mat-work; Marking and Braiding."[16] Thirty years later they were offering even more needlework, but they probably were not still requiring the students to make the kind of sampler that Mary McGuire had executed decades earlier.

The German Influence

Many German immigrants settled in Cincinnati early in the first half of the nineteenth century and played important roles in the town's colorful history. By the mid-1840s, nearly one fifth of the adult population of Cincinnati was German. Reluctant to give up their old customs and language, they had their own German language newspapers and social circles.[17] The German language was being taught in the public schools, but we know of no organized needlework schools for the German girls. They probably were taught by their mothers, or some other family members, to do the traditional Germanic motifs that are seen on their samplers. Some, like Ammalia Frank (see fig. 20), seem to blend "der English" and German together on their handwork, and their sampler designs suggest that they did attend a private or public school to learn their stitches.

FIG. 20: SAMPLER OF AMMALIA LOUISE FRANK. 1841. »
SIZE: 15½" L x 12½" W. COLLECTION OF NANCY KOCH HOLTERHOFF.

Ammalia's parents, Jacob Benedict and Catherine (Hecker) Frank, both born in 1786, emigrated from Germany and came to Cincinnati about 1800. Jacob established a grocery business on the corner of Sixth and Race Streets. Ammalia, born in Cincinnati in 1826, married Dietrich Koch and was the mother of six children.

Her sampler was stitched when she was fifteen years old. The German influences can be seen in the scattered motifs in the lower half of the needlework and in the script-style alphabet letters at the top of the canvas. Notice that Ammalia, in all four alphabets, does not include the letter *j*. In printed alphabet needlework patterns before about 1785, the letter *i* is used in place of the letter *j*. Ammalia's instructress, working in the 1840s, apparently was still teaching her students with those early patterns for marking. In Ammalia's alphabets, as in the early German alphabet, the letter *i* resembles a *j*.

A classical scene with a Grecian temple is centered on the canvas, probably copied from a popular print of the day. Two other examples of Ammalia's handwork remain with her sampler. They show interesting motifs and designs that Ammalia stitched in Berlin woolwork, the type of needlework particularly in vogue in the 1840s and 1850s.

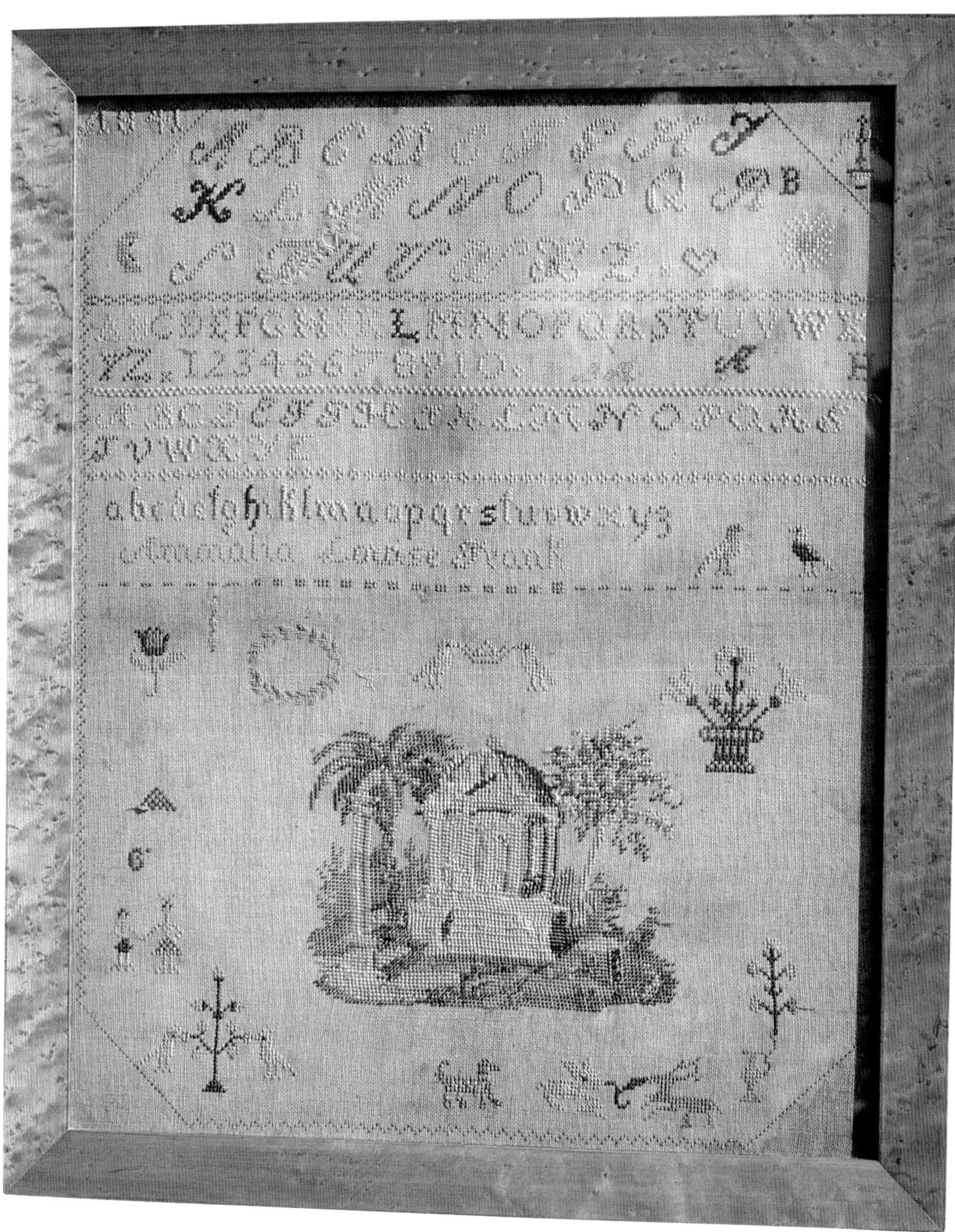

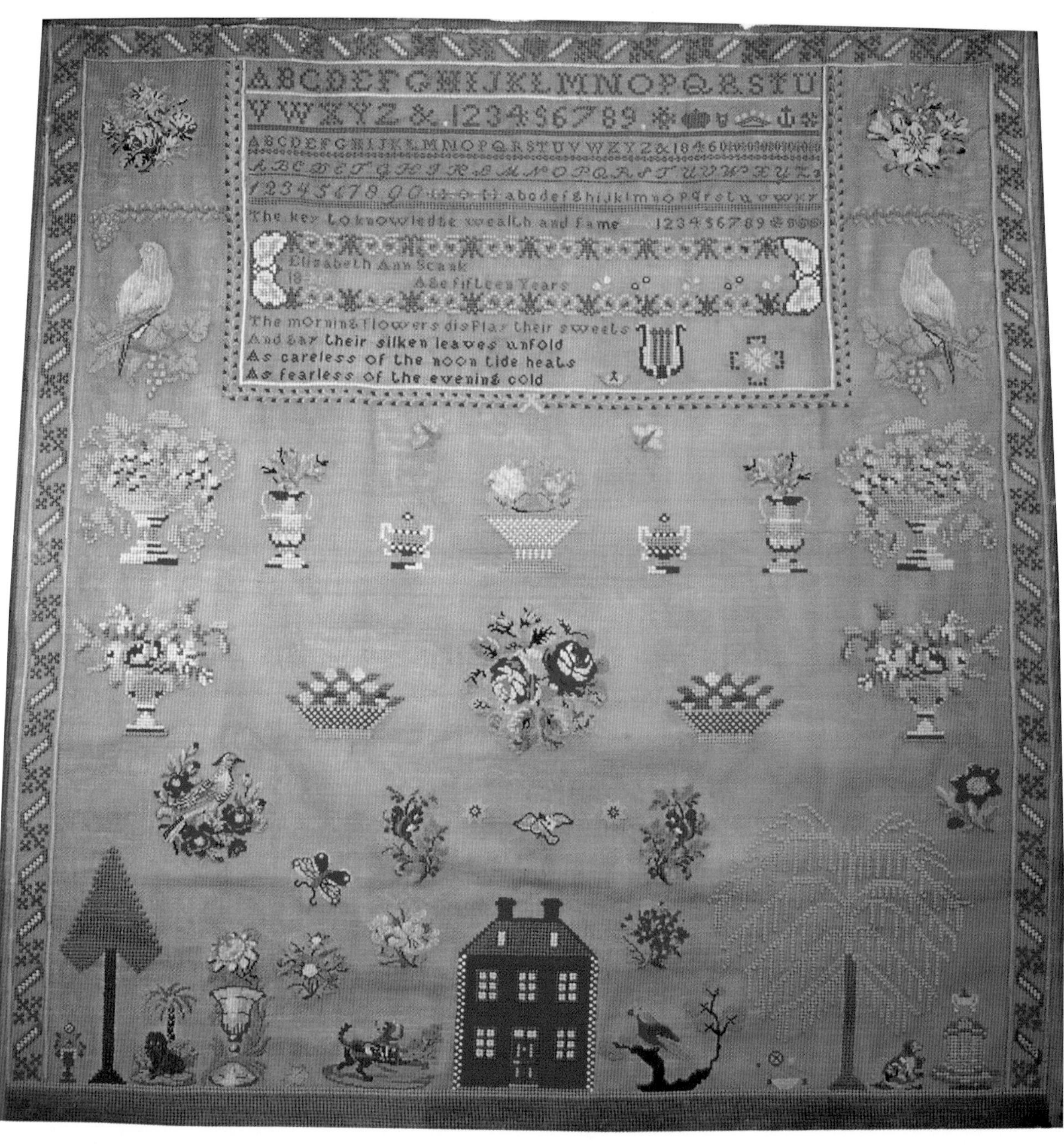

Fig. 22: Detail of Scank Sampler. »

« Fig. 21: Sampler of Elizabeth Ann Scank. 1846.

Size: 28½" L x 27½" W. Wool on linen. Collection of Marilyn K. Jinks.

Elizabeth (Lizzy) Ann Scank was born in Mount Healthy in Cincinnati on March 26, 1831, the daughter of John and Elizabeth (Hoel) Scank (Schenck). Lizzy married a young widower, Westley Lee, and took responsibility for the care of his three children. The couple then had six more children of their own. Her sampler and gold watch, along with many early photographs, remain in the family today.

Lizzy's colorful Berlin wool-work sampler, completed when she was fifteen, shows the variety of designs that were readily available in pattern books of the day. The unrelated small spot motifs are symmetrically placed in rows, and float in pairs on the oversized canvas. Lizzy's teacher may have encouraged her to use so many different patterns and designs so that her student could refer back to them later. Some of the same motifs were stitched on Martha Dorn's sampler (fig. 23), but they have been enlarged to accommodate the big canvas. The scene at the bottom of both samplers is charming and balances the overall composition of these very decorative embroidery projects. Her verse reads:

"The Key to knowledge, wealth and fame"
The morning flowers display their sweets
And say their silken leaves unfold
As careless of the noontide heats
As fearless of the evening cold.

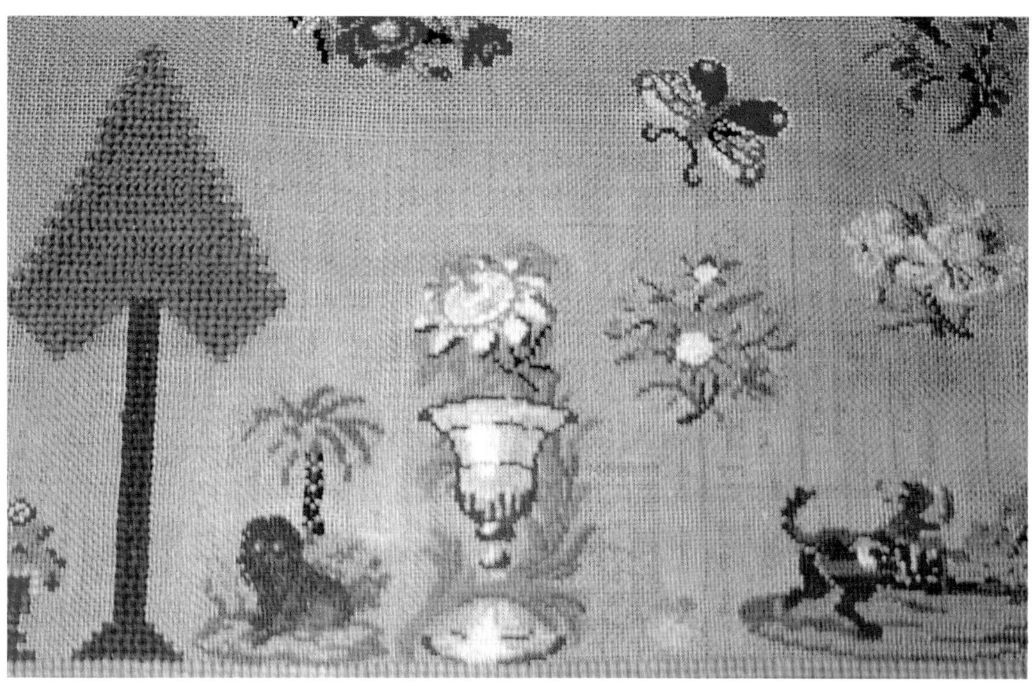

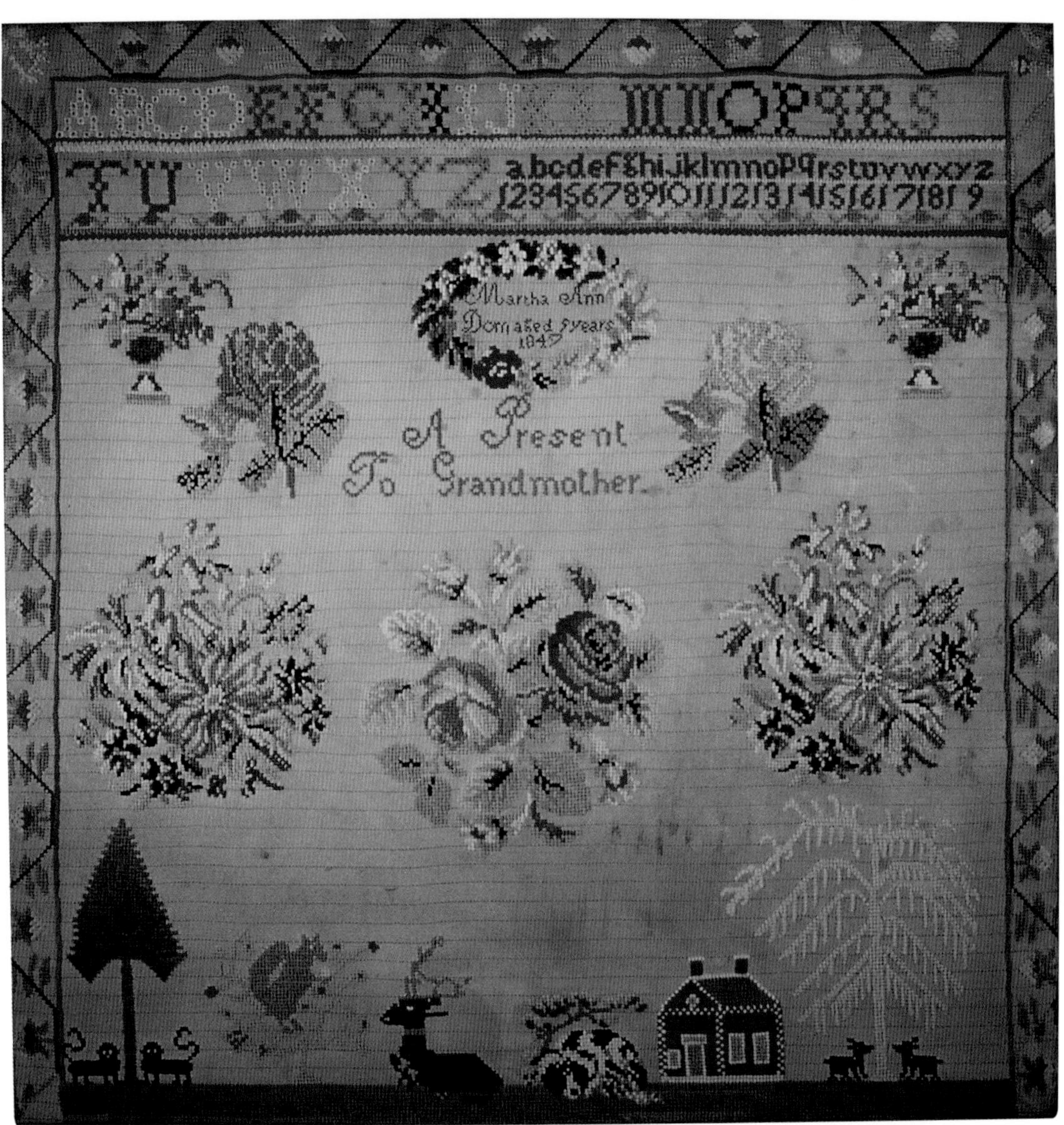

Fig. 23: Sampler of Martha Ann Dorn. 1847.
Size: 24" L x 24" W. Wool on linen. Collection of Mr. Frank W. Stout, grandson of the stitcher.

Martha Ann Dorn was the daughter of Phillip and Katharine (Lowe) Dorn and married Ephriam Brown Stout in Butler County, Ohio. She and Elizabeth Scank (fig. 21) must have attended the same school in Mount Healthy, near Cincinnati, though the identity of their teacher has not been determined. Both canvases are large, and the girls used many of the same motifs. Martha, who completed the sampler at age nine, did not place a verse at the top of her sampler, but instead stitched an inscription just below her name: "A Present To Grandmother." This would have been a prized gift, and the sampler remains with the family to the present day. Martha's father was a blacksmith by trade, a talented craftsman and an astute businessman. He became successful in the manufacture of carriages and wagons, and was one of the most prominent men in the county.

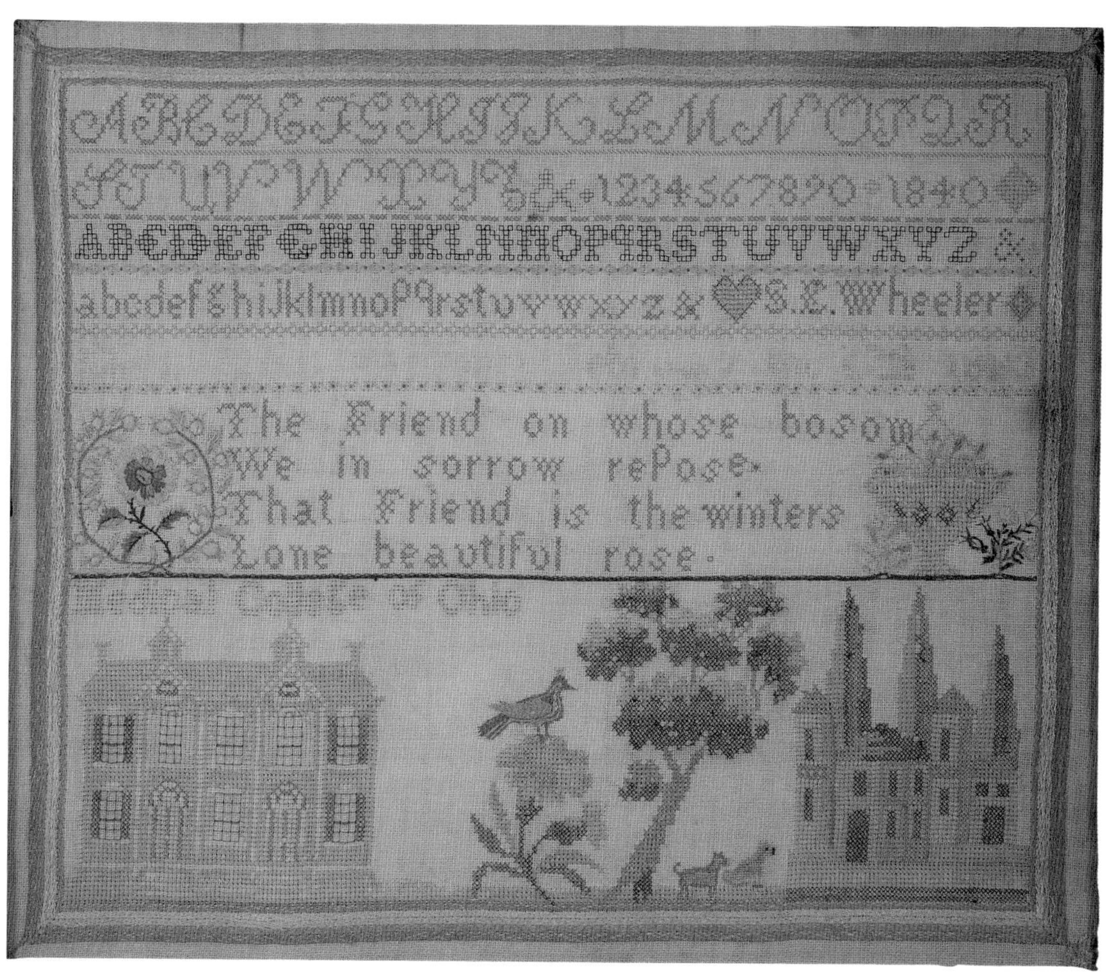

Fig. 24: Sampler of S. E. Wheeler. 1840.
Size: 15" L x 17½" W. Collection of William and Joyce Subjack.

The canvas worked by S. E. Wheeler is one of Ohio's most unusual samplers. Early sketches of the Medical College of Ohio, the structure seen on the left side of the canvas, verify that the stitcher executed a realistic and accurate rendition of the building. Young girls often searched with their teachers or parents for important buildings to put on their canvases, and there were good sketches of the Medical College of Ohio available to copy in needlework. The exact identity of the stitcher has not been determined, nor has the origin of this verse been found: "The Friend on whose bosom / We in sorrow repose. / That Friend is the winters / Lone beautiful rose."

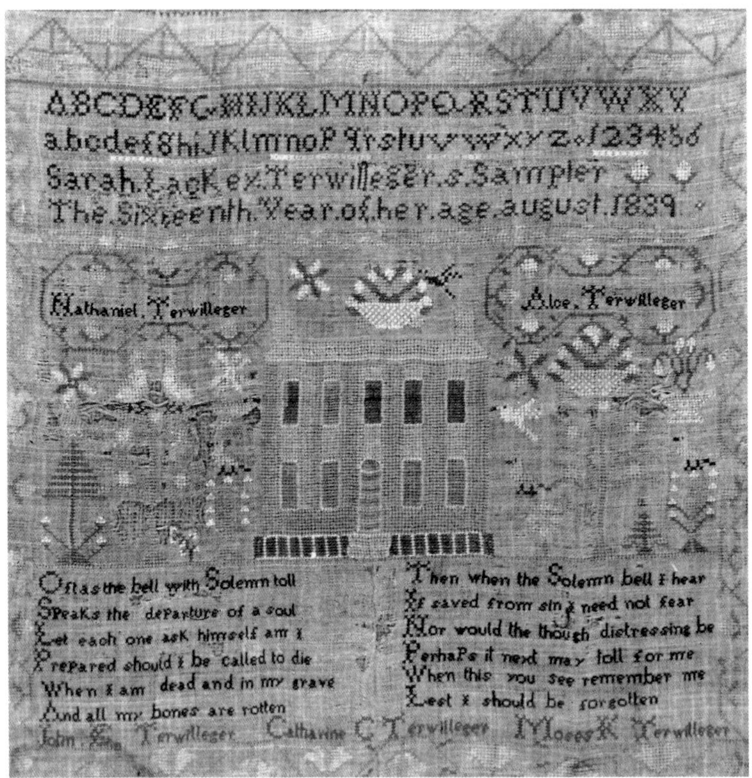

Fig. 25: Sampler of Sarah Terwilleger. 1839.
Size: 16" L x 16" W. Collection of Robert Elliott McGowan.

When sixteen-year-old Sarah Lackey Terwilleger worked this sampler, she must have felt that she was making an important family document. Her intuition was right, for well over a century and a half have passed since Sarah completed the last stitches, and her handwork is still hung with pride by her descendants. Not only is her needlework decorative, but she has left a wonderful rendition of her grandfather John Elliott's large stone home on the canvas.[18] In the upper part of the canvas are the names of her parents, Nathaniel and Alce (Elliott) Terwilleger. Along the bottom, Sarah has listed her older siblings, John Elliott, Catharine Crist, and Moses Kitchell Terwilleger. Perhaps she ran out of room to continue the names of other siblings, for there were nine children in all. Records tell us that by the time this was stitched, Sarah's father and siblings Moses and Catharine had already died, so she may have felt that it was especially important to have their names on her sampler.

The Terwilleger and Elliott families both played important roles in the development of Hamilton County. Sarah's paternal grandfather, Nathaniel Terwilleger, served in the Revolution and emigrated to Ohio from Ulster County, New York in the closing years of the eighteenth century. The father of a large family of nine children, he first settled in Sycamore Township. By 1802, Nathaniel Terwilleger owned sufficient land to lay out the plan for the town of Montgomery, and he is considered to be one of the founders of the town.

Sarah's maternal grandfather, pioneer settler John Elliott, came to Hamilton County, Ohio, before 1800. Sarah Lackey Terwilleger married Ebenezer Crist in the autumn of 1842 and had two daughters and three sons. She died on July 26, 1897, at the age of seventy-four and was buried in Hopewell Church Cemetery in Montgomery.

Warren County

In September 1795, barely a month after the peace treaty with the Indians had been signed at Fort Greenville, William Bedle of New Jersey set out from near Fort Washington to establish a new settlement. Known as Bedle's Station, it was the first settlement in what was to become Warren County.

The county, formed from Hamilton County, was officially organized on May 1, 1802. Named in honor of General Joseph Warren, who fell at the Battle of Bunker Hill, the county's population grew steadily and by 1820 numbered almost eighteen thousand. Lebanon, the county seat, was pleasantly located in the beautiful Turtle Creek Valley. Settlers from New Jersey, Pennsylvania, Maryland, Kentucky, and virtually all of the southern states, were attracted by its gently rolling hills and fertile farmlands.

Many journeyed without definite goals, but not so with Rev. William Van Horne, a Baptist minister from New Jersey. Van Horne had served as a chaplain in the Continental Army, and had been granted, in return for his services, a section of land east of Lebanon, Ohio, some thirty miles northeast of Cincinnati. With him journeyed his wife, six unmarried daughters, and his only son, Thomas. Daughter Elizabeth was thirty-one when she began the journey to Ohio on October 8, 1807. She had promised "valued friends" to keep a day-by-day diary as they traveled. The greatest misfortune of the long expedition was the death of Rev. Van Horne, who became ill and died during the journey. His family, disheartened but resolute, continued westward.

Elizabeth's remarkable journal gives insight into the hardships they endured and her impression of the tiny town of Lebanon upon her arrival: "It was a great undertaking to remove a family from Jersey State to the State of Ohio, and strength, fortitude, resolution, and a good share of Patience was absolutely necessary. None of the family are dissatisfied with the country, but the reverse."[19]

An extraordinary sampler associated with this family survives. It was worked by Catharine Sophia Van Horne, Elizabeth's niece (fig. 26).

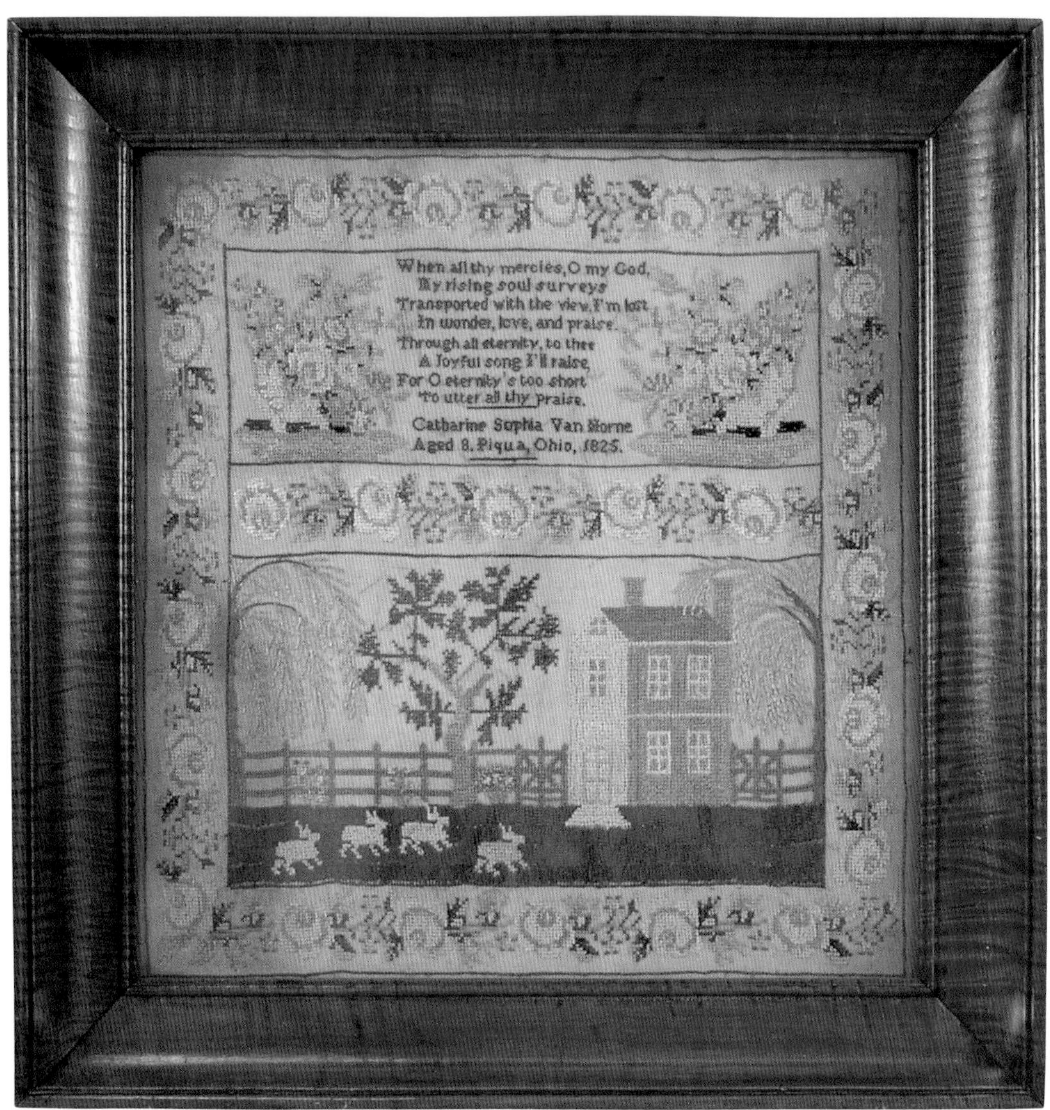

Fig. 26: Sampler of Catharine Sophia Van Horne. 1825.
Size: 17" L x 16½" W. Collection of The Dayton Art Institute.
Gift of the Estate of Elmer R. Webster and Robert A. Titsch, 1997.1.

Catharine Sophia Van Horne stitched her sampler when she was eight years old. The naïveté of her composition, with the shaded house situated on a grassy lawn and sheep grazing nearby, has enormous appeal. This sampler is one of the prettiest Ohio samplers discovered. The tiger-maple frame that surrounds the canvas is original, and nearly identical frames have been found on four other samplers from this area.

Catharine was the fourth child of Thomas B. and Sophia (Carmichael) Van Horne. Her father was appointed in 1820 by President Monroe to serve as land agent in Miami County at the Land Office in Piqua. His family apparently went with him for a period of time because Catharine stitched "Piqua" on her needlework. Records show that between 1826 and 1830, Catharine's father was back home working on his family farm in Warren County. Catharine's needlework shows a strong relationship to other Warren County samplers. We cannot be certain who her teacher was, but she was probably located in Lebanon, where several needlework teachers were advertising for students.

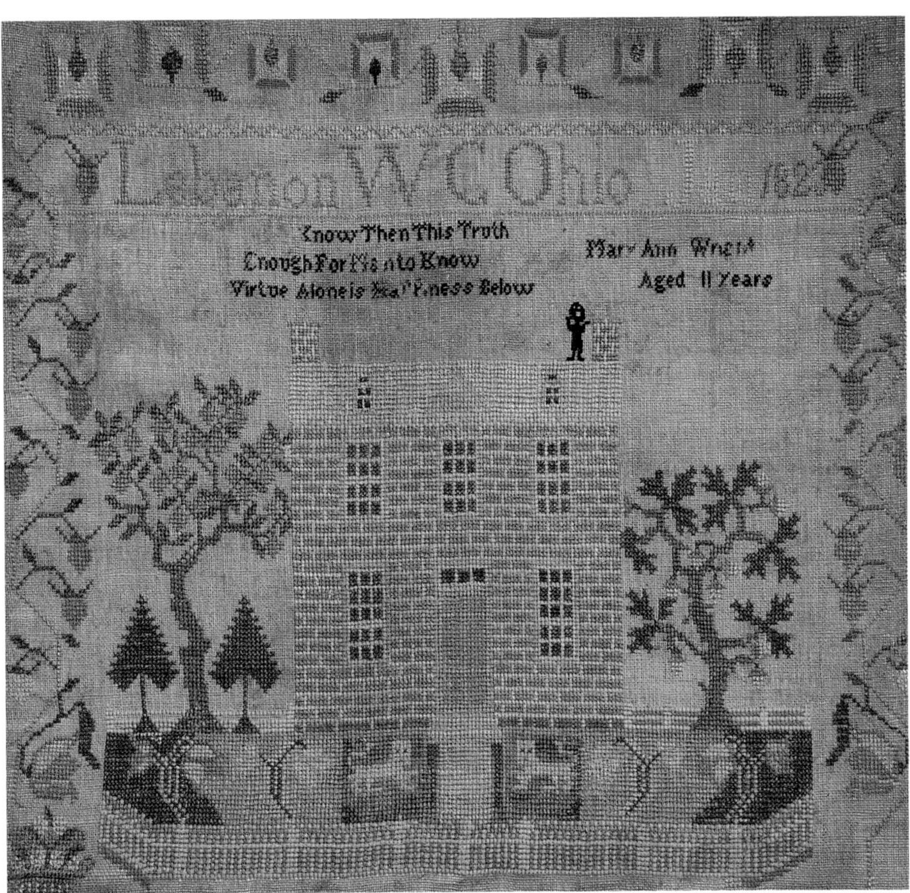

Fig. 27: Sampler of Mary Ann Wright. 1823.

Size: 18" L x 19" W. Collection of Wildwood Manor House, Metro Park District of Toledo.

The sampler of Mary Ann Wright is charming and well executed. It is boldly marked "Lebanon W C [Warren County] Ohio 1823." Mary Ann's parents were Allen and Sarah (Chadbourne) Wright. Born in 1812, Mary Ann was eleven when she completed her canvas. The Wrights were members of the Society of Friends, and they were part of a large extended family, all of whom, as Quakers, were active abolitionists. Mary Ann was living in an area where the Underground Railway was well organized. "Conductors" were everywhere, and the Wright family had connections with other "stations" in neighboring counties. Hundreds of slaves and their families were led on that trail to freedom. Mary Ann probably included her own antislavery statement when she stitched a black man standing precariously on top of the house. It may never be known for certain why that little figure leaning against the chimney was put there, but it is unique and eye-catching.

The Wright family originated in England and had moved to Castleshane, Monaghan County, Ireland, by the beginning of the eighteenth century. Her great-grandparents were born there and emigrated to Adams County, Pennsylvania, about 1740 with their young family. Perhaps early family ties to England are reflected in the two lions guarding the front steps of her house. Those lions, like the black figure, have never been found on any other Ohio samplers. The oak tree on the right, with its twisting trunk and limbs, however, has been found on other southern Ohio samplers and was used by several teachers.

In 1840 Mary Ann Wright married Horace Stokes, and they had one daughter. Both Mary Ann and her little girl died in 1843.

The Village of Lebanon

By the time Warren County stitcher Mary Ann Wright (figure 27) was old enough to take formal lessons in stitching, her parents had at least four teachers to choose from in Lebanon. Miss M. McMahan's offer to "teach Needlework and embroydery" appeared in Lebanon's *Western Star* dated July 27, 1819; Mrs. Catherine Forman's ads appeared in April of 1822 and 1823, offering "Plain Sewing and Needlework"; and Miss H. A. Adamson advertised in the *Western Star* on July 24, 1824, that she was teaching "plain and variegated needlework."

Ann Hulme Price (see page 13) was also teaching girls to stitch in Lebanon. A letter from Ann Price, dated May 2, 1824, written to her relatives in New Jersey, tells of her work in Warren County: "I was solicited while in Lebanon to teach a few girls plain sewing and marking which I did, having a girl all winter to do my [house]work, and I think I had completed in that quarter some of the handsomest samplers I ever had a hand in making. Rebecca [her daughter] made a small sampler of yellow canvass. she took every stitch at first showing. She afterwards began a large white one and has the border part done. She sends her love to cousin Sarah, as she says she has beat you, for she made her sampler in her 6th year and you made yours in your 9th, as her mother has told her."[20]

Ann Price also wrote: "Ann chatters every day about cousin Sarah. She gets my spectacles frequently when she cannot see to thread her nedle, and says Uncle John must send her a pair, her eyes are so weak. She is one of the best children and asks surprising questions for one her age." In studying the packet of letters left by Ann Price, we find that little Ann was only three and a half years old when this letter was written—and was already learning to thread a needle.

The letter continues: "Perhaps for the advantage of the children, I may teach another quarter and would thank you if you have an opportunity by any private hand, to send me the pattern of the border on your sampler, and the little blue bird wich I think is on it."[21] This trading of patterns from teacher to teacher can be seen in many instances, and the oak tree design in figures 26 and 27 is a good example.

Another local needlework teacher, Mrs. Williams, established Lebanon Female Seminary in 1830. She advertised on a regular basis not only in Lebanon but in Columbus and Xenia. Upon the opening of her school in Lebanon, the *Western Star* published the following welcoming notice:

Female Seminary—Saturday, April 20, 1830.

> We congratulate our citizens upon the prospect of establishing a permanent Female Seminary in this place. Mrs. Williams, whose advertisement appears in this days paper, has been satisfactorily recommended to a number of our citizens as amply qualified for possessing considerable experience as an instructress. Her school is to be opened in a few days and we trust she will receive such encouragement as to induce her to make Lebanon her permanent residence.[22]

Evidence shows that Mrs. Williams *was* very successful there. Her advertisements of the next few years reveal that she offered a curriculum of advanced subjects as well as "plain and ornamental work." They state that "having received the advantages of a liberal education in one of the first seminaries in Europe, and also studied under the most approved masters there, she trusts she is not incompetent to the charge; she therefore solicits a share of the public patronage. Mrs. Williams has made arrangements to receive a few boarders, to whose health, morals and intellectual improvement the most unremitting attention will be paid."[23] With these qualifications, one can understand why the townspeople must have urged her to establish her home there, and why she had the patronage of influential families like the Skinners (see fig. 28). She subsequently advertised that she had added another teacher to help her and would welcome additional boarding students.

Although the town was small, the citizens of Lebanon were successful all through the first half-century of settlement in attracting good teachers. The reason perhaps can be found in an excerpt from the Lebanon Academy Catalogue of September 1, 1845:

> The town of Lebanon is, in many respects, a favorable location for a school. It is one of the most healthy places in Southern Ohio, and is almost entirely free from many of the diseases common to this latitude. Its citizens are composed principally of the early settlers and their descendants, and it is not subject to those evils which usually result from a transient and floating population. It is believed that there are but few, if any, places, in this part of the country, where so few temptations are offered to lead the young and inexperienced astray.[24]

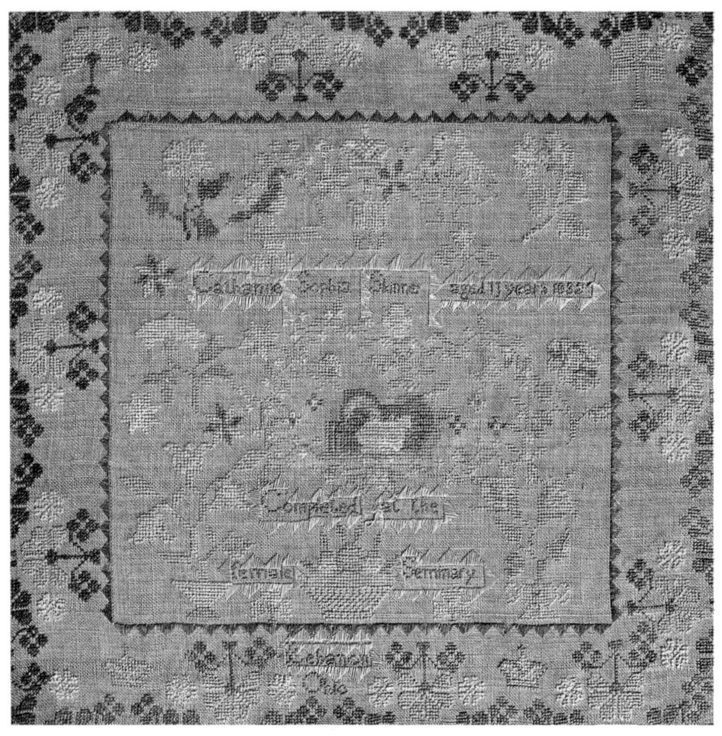

Fig. 28: Sampler of Catharine Sophia Skinner. 1832.
Size: 17½" L x 17½" W.
Anonymous collector.

Catharine Sophia Skinner was the daughter of a Presbyterian minister, Rev. Richard Skinner, and Catherine C. (Hurin) Skinner. Her family was a prominent one, and her maternal grandfather, Silas Hurin, was one of the founders of the town.

Catharine Sophia's attendance at the Lebanon Female Seminary is documented not only by the sampler she stitched but by a notice published in the September 3, 1831, edition of the *Western Star* about the activities of the school operated by Mrs. Williams, showing that Catharine was an excellent student who won awards for her good grades. Catharine Sophia died shortly after her fourteenth birthday in 1835 and is buried in Lebanon's Pioneer Cemetery.

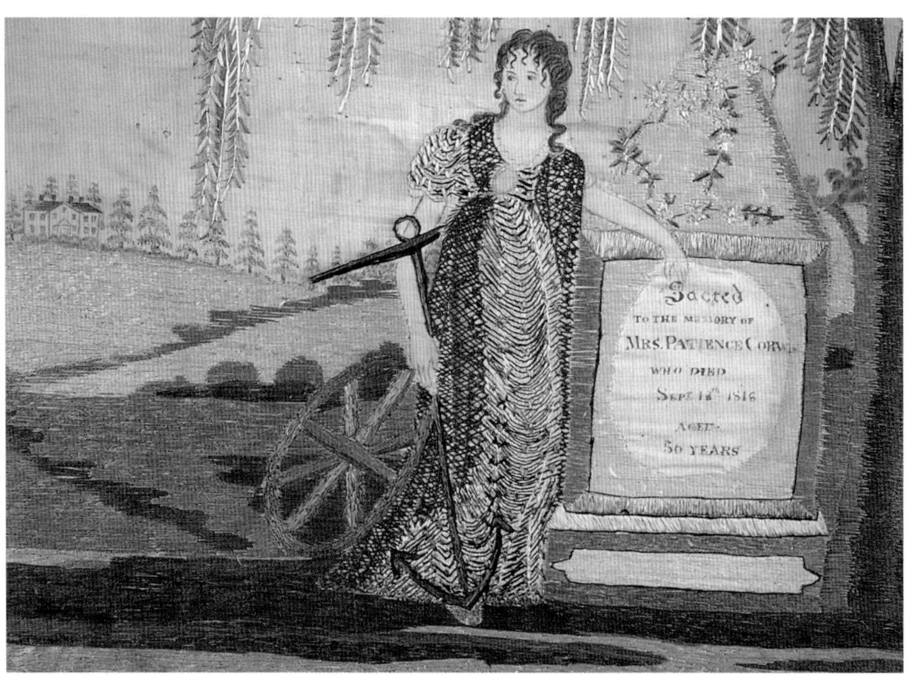

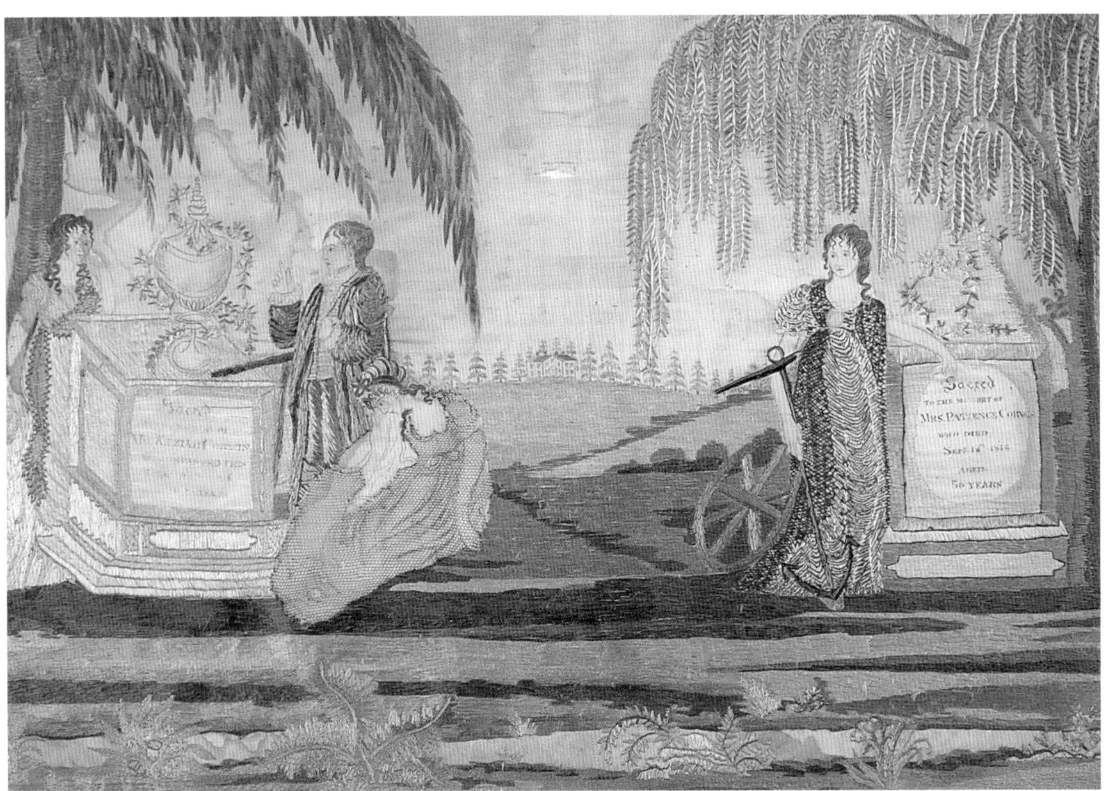

Fig. 29: Corwin Mourning Embroidery.

Size: 17" L x 22½" W. Silk on silk. Collection of Warren County Historical Society.

One of the most important embroideries associated with Ohio is the spectacular Corwin mourning picture, a memorial to Keziah (Case) Corwin and Patience (Halleck) Corwin. Patience and her mother-in-law, Keziah, died within two years of each other and are both buried in Lebanon's Pioneer Cemetery. As is often the case with mourning embroideries, this piece was neither signed nor dated by the stitcher. The silk canvas, with painted accents, exhibits a variety of stitches, including French knots and long, short, feather, and netting stitches.

Patience Halleck and Matthias Corwin were married in 1782 and were the parents of nine children. At the time of Patience's death in 1818, three teenage daughters, Rhoda, Phoebe, and Amelia, were still at home, and any one of the three girls could have made the elaborate memorial. It would have required a remarkably accomplished stitcher, however. The needlework was passed down through the family of Elvira (Corwin) Bryant, Keziah's granddaughter and a niece of Patience and Matthias Corwin. It is possible that Elvira, also in her teens when the mourning picture was executed, may have stitched this outstanding needlework. The identity of the stitcher is a mystery our research has been unable to solve.

« Fig. 30: Detail of Corwin Mourning Embroidery.

A wide variety of stitches are exhibited, including some intricate netting stitches on the gown of this female figure that needlework authorities have not seen before.

A Kentucky Connection

In 1806, a Presbyterian minister, Rev. John Lyle, opened the Bourbon Academy, a school in Paris, in Bourbon County. It had an enrollment of about two hundred students, both boys and girls. Rev. Lyle's School flourished until 1810, when he set about establishing an independent girls' school. At the time the Corwin needlework (fig. 29) was executed, probably between 1818 and the early 1820s, Rev. Lyle's school was just one of the choices open to the Corwin family where girls could have received a "worthy" education.

Another potential teacher might have been employed at Mrs. Beck's School in Lexington. It is noted in the writings of *Early Western Travels* by Thwaites in 1806 that there are "three good boarding schools for girls in Lexington, Kentucky, having over a hundred pupils in attendance . . . one being Mrs. Beck's, an English lady of high reputation." Her rates were two hundred dollars a year, a substantial amount for those days. A wide variety of academic subjects were offered at this school, as well as "musick, vocal and instrumental, drawing, painting, and embroidery, artificial flowers, and any other fashionable fancy work, plain sewing, marking, netting, etc."[25] "Mrs. Beck" was likely Mary (Menessier) Beck, the wife of George Jacob Beck. Before moving to Lexington, she lived in Cincinnati. Mr. Beck, an Englishman who came to the Northwest Territory in the late 1790s, was a noted landscape artist and sign painter. Mary Menessier Beck was also a talented artist in her own right.[26] Either one of them could have drawn the needlework picture on the silk canvas for the young Corwin girl to stitch.

Despite Lebanon's success at attracting teachers, some families sent their daughters south of the Ohio River for their educations, which included instruction in needlework. The large, well-to-do Corwin family had previously lived in Bourbon County, Kentucky, and retained strong ties there. Research is inconclusive, but it is probable that they sent one of their daughters to a fashionable female academy there, where she executed the extraordinary Corwin mourning picture. Several schools were operating in Kentucky at the time that might have attracted students from Ohio.

The Shakers of Union Village

The story of the religious sect commonly known as the Shakers began with a small group of dissident Quakers who left their home in England to come to America. Their leader, Mother Ann Lee, and her followers converted many and eventually succeeded in establishing nineteen communities. At their peak in the 1850s, the Shakers numbered about six thousand.

The Western Movement began when Shaker missionaries arrived in Kentucky and Ohio with hopes of forming new communities and converting others to their beliefs. Nowhere did they find conditions so favorable for carrying out the purpose of their mission as in the Turtle Creek Valley of Warren County, Ohio.

Union Village near Lebanon, organized May 25, 1805, became the largest Shaker community west of the Alleghenies. Some who joined the sect owned considerable tracts of land, which they consecrated to the use of the church. The Society eventually held in possession four thousand acres. Many of the people of "the World," however, looked at the Shakers with disdain. An excerpt from the 1807 diary of Elizabeth Van Horne says, "How many in this state are under strange delusions with respect and forms of Worship. . . . [T]he Shaking Quakers for one sect . . . it is awful to behold them. I have been to see them once but can give you no idea of my feelings at beholding them in their wild Indian powwow, and dancing. . . . [S]ome spectators faint . . . some shed tears . . . and others tremble, while some laugh and ridicule them."[27]

Shakers did not encourage young girls to make colorful decorative samplers and needlework pictures. This explains why Shaker samplers are so rare today. Only four Ohio Shaker samplers have been found.[28] While the young ladies of "the World" considered their samplers a source of pride and accomplishment, and framed canvases showing their needlework skills were prominently displayed, the young Shaker stitchers were not recognized in such a fashion. Probably Elcey Patterson never saw her sampler hanging on a wall, nor did any of her contemporaries.

Elcey's sampler (fig. 31), worked with blue thread, served as a good example of how to sew with precise stitches, so that her students could help with basic needlework chores required by the community. Clothes were rarely discarded, but were passed along to be redone and marked for another's use. Skills in the marking of linens were particularly important because when sent to the communal washhouse, these items could be identified as to which "family" house they belonged to and when they should be rotated into use. A marking sampler was usually kept in the stitcher's sewing basket, serving as a learning and reference tool.

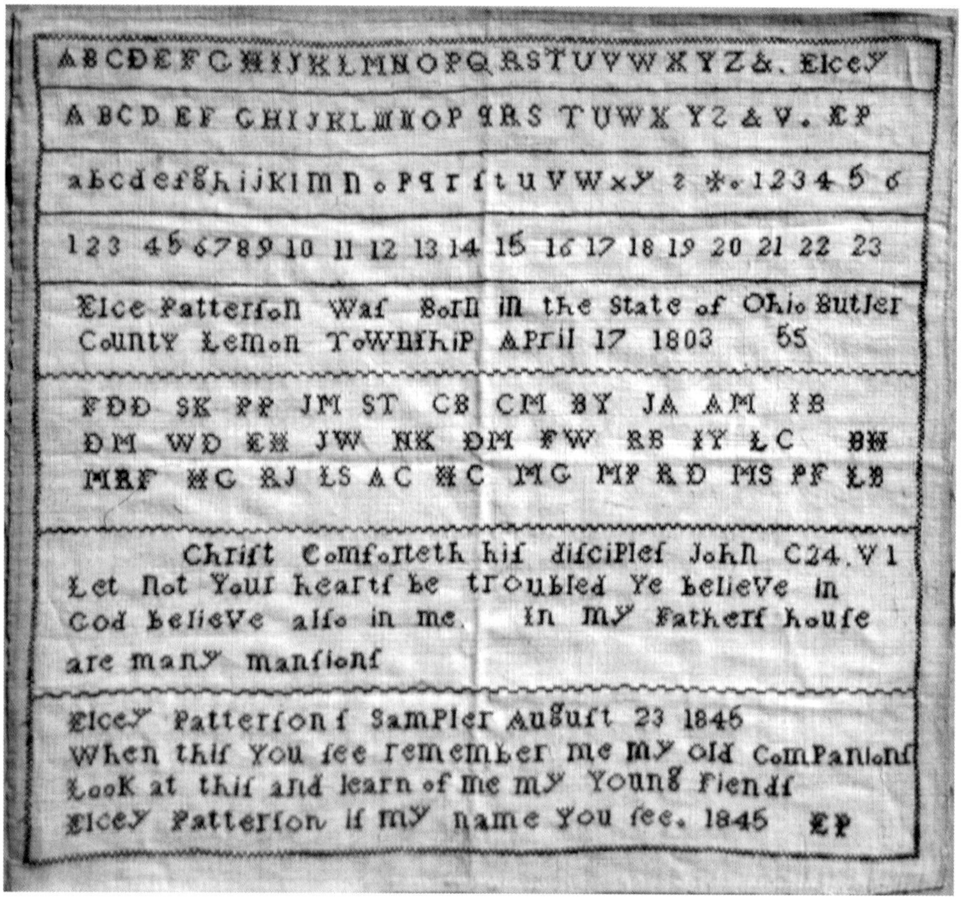

Fig. 32: Shaker "Marks" Box. »

Size: 5" L x 3" W x 1¾" D. Wooden. Collection of Mary and Patrick Allen.

This tiny Shaker box, with its one "finger" construction, is a rare find. Its lid still bears the label for its use, "Marks." Sister Jennie M. Wells, a member of the North Family Shakers at New Lebanon, New York, sent it to a friend as a gift in 1943. The accompanying note explains its importance: "I was so pleased to hear you liked the antique boxes. I presume this will sound odd to you but the label 'Marks' on the smaller one simply meant that in olden times we marked our clothes with our initials on small pieces of cloth and sewed them on to the garments . . . and as we took a great deal of time and patience to do those marks in cross stitch we saved the marks and used them over again. I would have taken that off but I wanted to send them along as soon as possible. I did not take the time to refinish the top. . . . I am sincerely yours, Sister Jennie M. Wells."[29] It is fortunate that Sister Jennie did not take time to remove the box label. Her letter gives us interesting information about the resourceful Shaker sisters.

« Fig. 31: Sampler of Elcey Patterson. 1845.
Size: 9⅛" L x 10⅛" W. Collection of Larry and Sarah Mosteller.

Elce Patterson was born in the State of Ohio
Butler County Lemon Township April 17, 1803
Elcey Pattersons sampler August 23, 1845
When this you see remember me my old companions
Look at this and learn of me my young friends
Elcey Patterson is my name you see 1845 E. P.

Elcey Patterson was three years old when her family left their home in Butler County and moved to neighboring Warren County to become members of the United Society of Believers (Shakers). Her parents, Joseph and Mary (Polly) (Van Kirk) Patterson, emigrated from New Jersey to Ohio before 1795.[30]

Elcey was raised and educated at Union Village near Lebanon, and completed this plain sampler when she was forty-two. The Shaker records mention her name with some frequency, listing it as Elce, Elcey, or Alcy. Elcey herself spelled her name two different ways on the sampler. Union Village Shaker journals also reveal that she "cared for the little girls."[31] She was entrusted with the responsibility of teaching them all manner of things, including needlework.

The top section of the sampler canvas is filled with three alphabets and rows of numbers, following the form of a myriad of samplers done in the 1840s. The midsection, however, was puzzling. A study of Shaker records revealed that the first two rows of letters are the initials of influential and founding elders of the faith, and the bottom row contains the initials of Shaker eldresses. These Shaker leaders were greatly revered, and by commemorating them on this sampler, Elcey could teach students their names and encourage them to remember and respect them. The Bible verse that follows the rows of initials typifies what was appropriate for a sampler produced in the pious religious setting. The verse at the bottom of Elcey's needlework mentions the "old companions" and "young friends" (misspelled as "fiends") found in a communal society.

The Shaker journal of Union Village noted on November 5, 1862: "Sister Elce Patterson departed this life at 1 o'clock + 25m Aged 59Y, 6M. + 20d."[32]

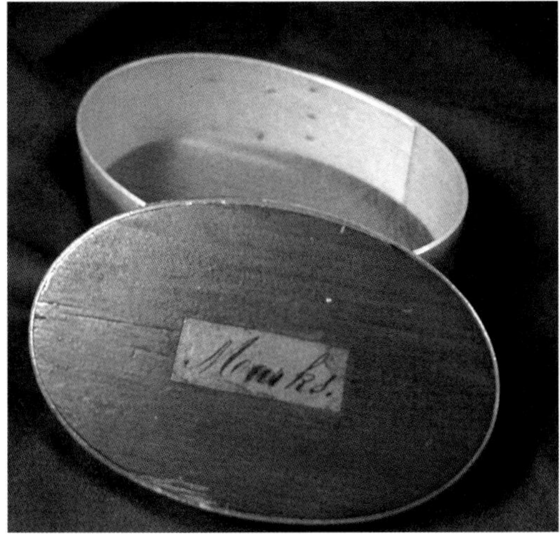

The Waynesville School

The founding members of the Miami Monthly Meeting of the Society of Friends who left their homes to come to the wilderness area of the Ohio lands could not have anticipated the phenomenal growth their congregation would enjoy. Nor could they have imagined how quickly that growth would happen. A few families had settled in Ohio's "Miami Country" at Waynesville as early as 1797. The Miami Monthly Meeting was formally organized on October 10, 1803. Barely two years later it had at least twenty-two hundred members, making it the largest Quaker Monthly Meeting in the United States.[33] The members wasted little time in establishing their first school, and as early as 1802, Roland Richards began teaching children of the village in the home of a church member. Waynesville was the center from which Quakerism spread throughout southwestern Ohio and Indiana.

One reason Ohio was enticing to the members of The Society of Friends was that it offered cheap, fertile land. Quakers from the South, where slavery was the predominant form of labor, had found it increasingly difficult to prosper in the slave economy without slaves.[34] The Ohio Country beckoned them to leave the institution of slavery that they found repugnant in the South and gave them an opportunity to join, and in some cases become actively involved in, the Abolitionist movement.

By 1805, a log structure was erected on Friends' property; it not only was used for a Meeting House but also accommodated the first school. That log structure has long ago disappeared, but the Friend's White Brick church and the small brick school nearby, both built in 1811, still stand. Originally built with just one room, it had two fireplaces, one at each end. The floor was constructed on an incline in order that the teacher could sit at the head of the class and see each student. The windows were noticeably graduated. The school was probably used until 1857, when the public Union School was opened.[35]

In the log school that opened in 1805, the first teachers were Elizabeth Wright and Susan (Mrs. Jonathan) Wright. It has not been determined exactly how long these two women taught school, but their initials appear on Leah Pugh's sampler, completed in 1811, indicating they served at least eight years.

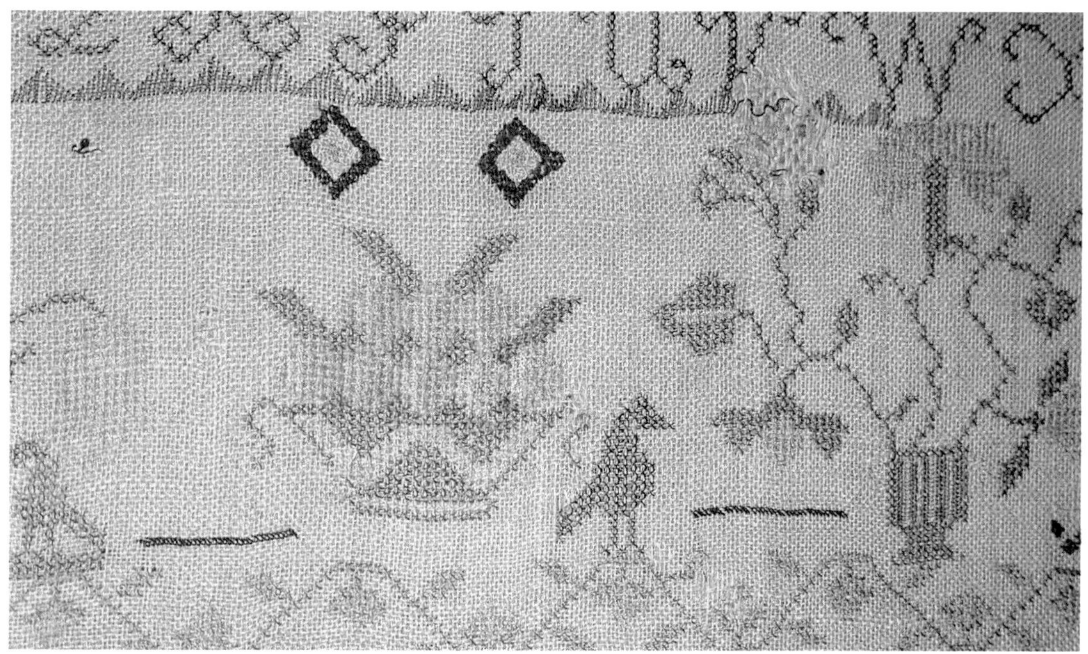

Fig. 33: The "W" Basket.

Eighteen samplers believed to have been stitched at the Waynesville School have been discovered. One identifiable motif is the "W" basket. It has five shaded pieces of fruit on the bottom layer, three more shaded pieces of fruit piled on the top, four leaves stiffly sticking out, curvaceous handles, and a *w* worked into the basket. This motif has been found on Quaker samplers done at Westtown School in Pennsylvania as early as 1803, but when it is found on an Ohio sampler, research invariably leads to Waynesville. That *w* may be merely a decorative design, or it may have first stood for "Westtown." The transferred motif has been found on a few Virginia samplers, but it worked especially well for Waynesville School in Ohio.

The Waynesville Academy

The Waynesville Academy, established in 1843 for advanced studies, was patronized by Quakers and non-Quakers. It closed its doors in 1857. As Friends migrated from Waynesville to other places in Ohio and Indiana, they eagerly established Monthly Meetings in their new territories. Most new Monthly Meetings quickly organized a school for their children. Evidence suggests that it was not uncommon, however, for families to continue to send their daughters back to the Waynesville School. It had a well-deserved reputation for teaching young women not only academic subjects, but also good needlework skills.

Fig. 34: Sampler of Mary Kelly. 1807. »
Size: 17" L x 12" W. Collection of Michael McAfee.

Mary Kelly's sampler is beautifully marked with the Waynesville School name. Stitched in the school's beginning years, it exhibits the typical Quaker motifs. The half-medallions at the bottom of the canvas are not often seen on Ohio Quaker needlework; they were faithfully copied from patterns that were used much earlier in Quaker schools elsewhere. Mary's sampler exhibits sprigs of flowers that we usually see on Quaker needlework, but she has made them much larger than those on most samplers.

Mary's parents were Samuel and Hannah (Pearson) Kelly, who immigrated to the Ohio Lands from South Carolina. She was born in 1789, the oldest of eight children. In June 1814, she married Andrew Whitacre.

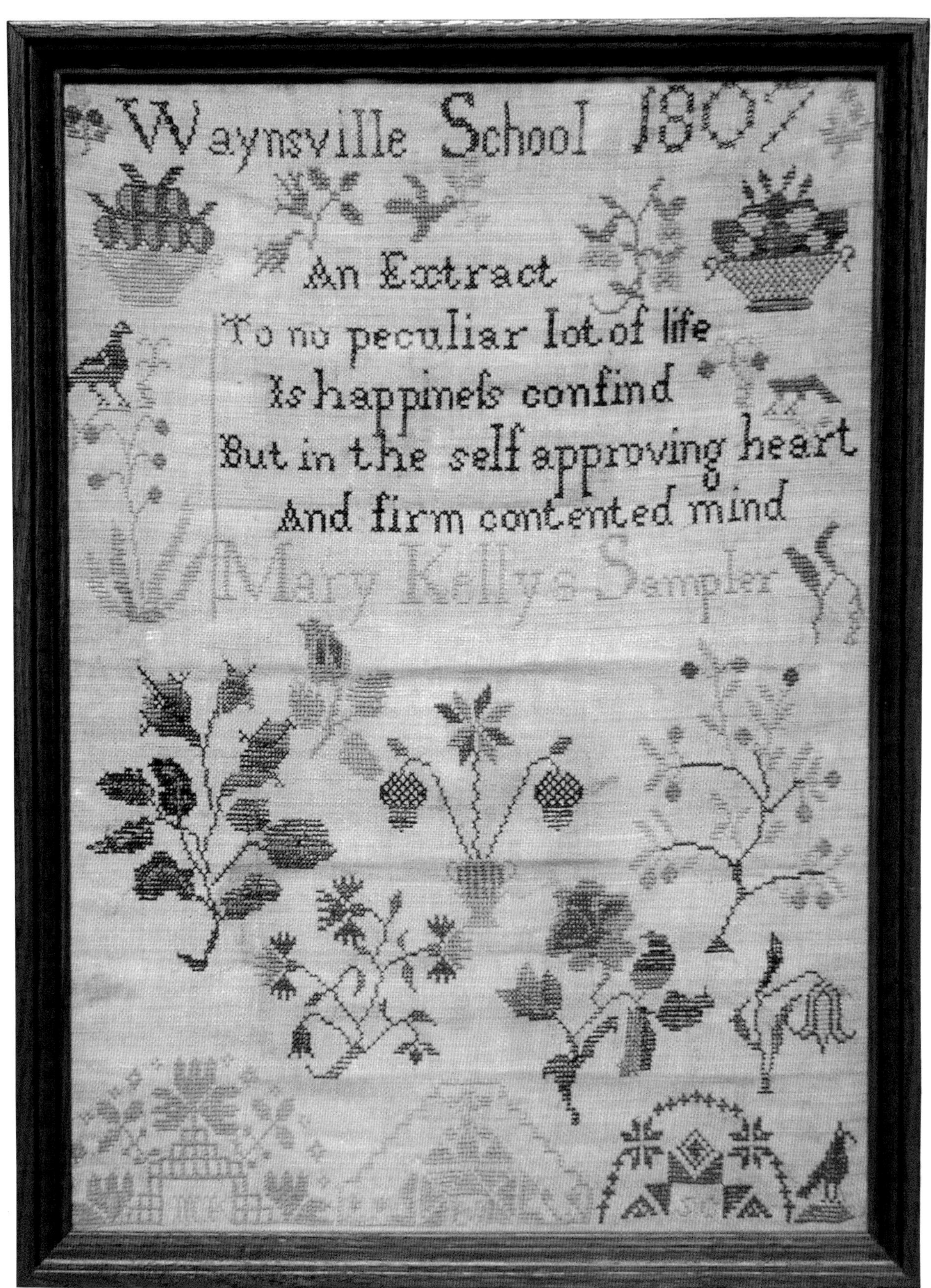
Waynsville School 1807
An Extract
To no peculiar lot of life
Is happiness confind
But in the self approving heart
And firm contented mind
Mary Kelly's Sampler

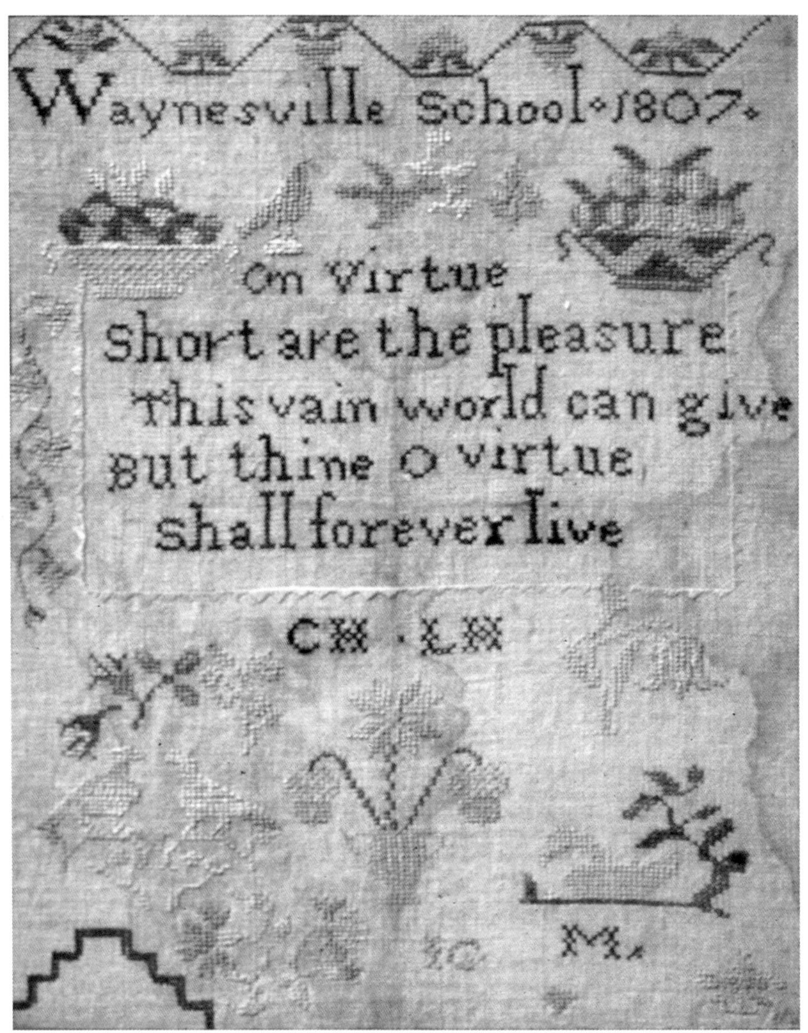

Fig. 35: Sampler of Mary Ann Hussey. 1807.
Size: 14" L x 11" W. Collection of Mr. and Mrs. Richard Johnson.

Even though Mary Ann Hussey placed only her initial "M" on this needlework, her sampler is well documented. She was the daughter of Christopher and Lydia (Grubb) Hussey and was born on November 28, 1797. Their initials appear on the canvas along with those of her grandfather, John Grubb.

The composition of this sampler matches that of Mary Kelly's 1807 needlework, except that Mary Ann chose not to stitch those repetitious medallions. She has included one design that was left out of Mary Kelly's needlework, a swan and an overhanging branch. This particular motif is repeatedly found in Quaker work. Even without the school name at the top, the beautiful "W" baskets on both this and Mary Kelly's sampler are clues that lead us to Waynesville.

Mary Ann Hussey married Mahlon Patterson. She died of smallpox on April 1, 1865.

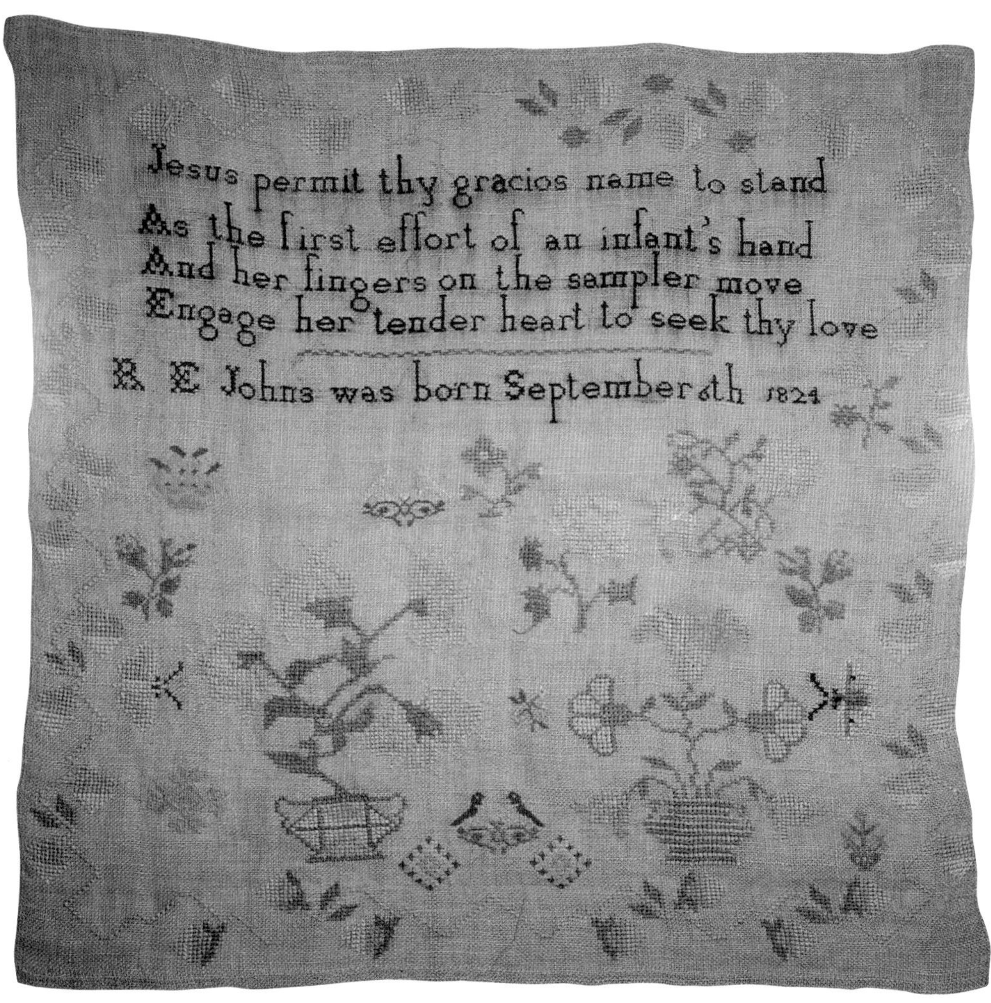

Fig. 36: Sampler of Rhoda Emily Johns. c. 1834.

Size: 17" L x 16" W. Collection of Monroe County (Indiana) Historical Society.

Rhoda Emily Johns did not date her sampler, but she tells us that she was born on September 6, 1824. It is curious that she used just the initials "R. E." instead of her full name, when she took the time to stitch the long word "September." Those initials are enough, however, to help us determine that she was the daughter of Quakers Isaac and Rhoda (Littell) Johns (John).

This sampler, c. 1834, has a verse that was a favorite of many young sampler workers and their teachers, and her canvas displays two motifs that were also favorites, the paired birds and the butterfly. The "W" basket used so often at the Waynesville School is stitched just under her name. No early records of teachers' or students' names have been found for the Waynesville School, but a "Friendship Book" kept by Rhoda Emily Johns, who later attended the Waynesville Academy in the 1840s, still accompanies the sampler.[36] The remembrance album is signed by sixty-five of Rhoda's friends, young women and men, some of whom listed the dates they apparently attended Waynesville Academy, ranging from 1844 to 1850. Some students listed their hometowns in Ohio as well as in other states. Both the early Waynesville School and the Waynesville Academy had numbers of boarding students, who likely stayed in the homes of local Quaker families.

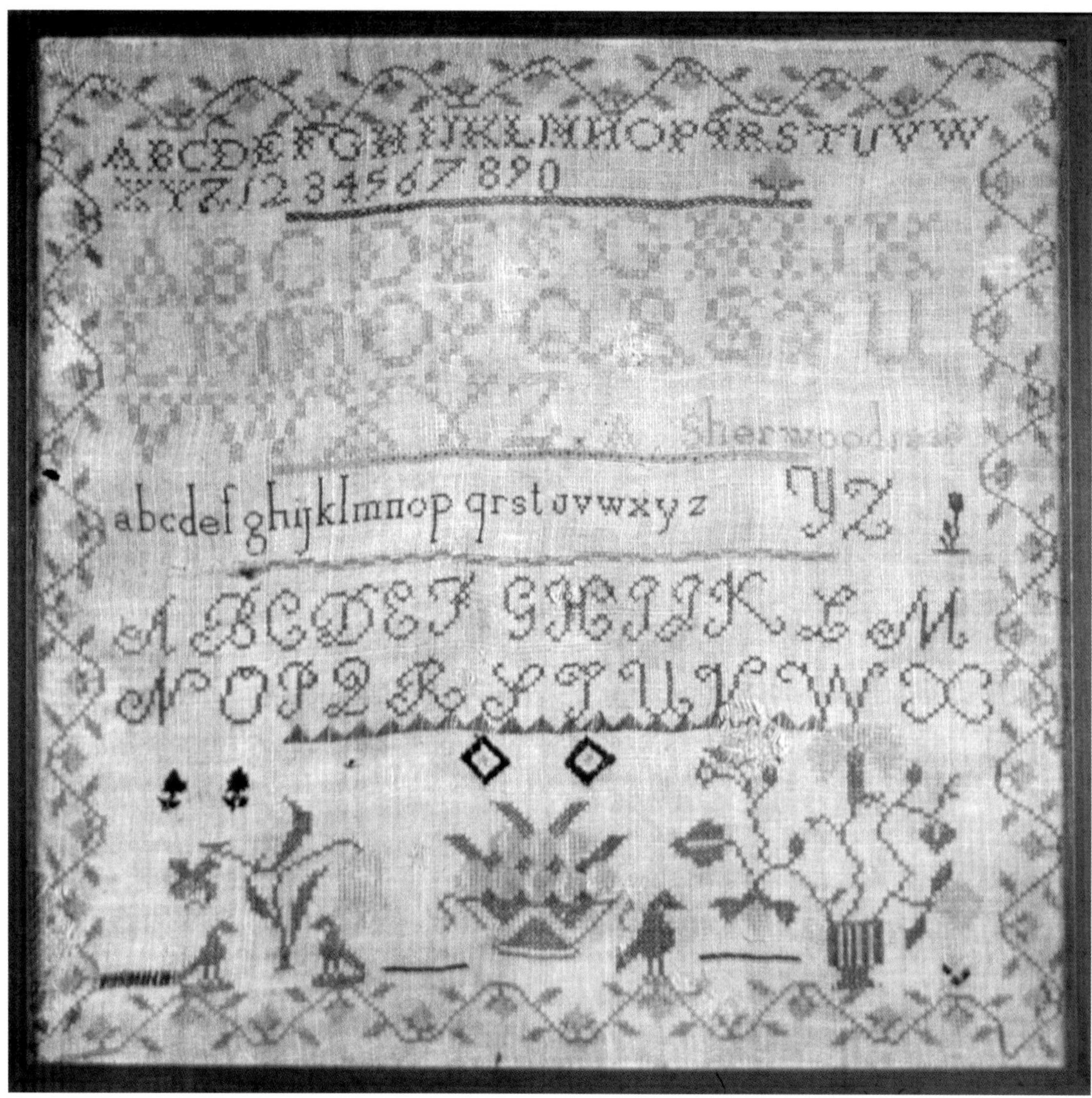

Fig. 37: Sampler of Abigail Sherwood. 1838.
Size: 17" L x 17" W. Collection of James and Helen Miller.

This large sampler exhibits a row of numbers, and four full alphabets. The lower part of the canvas is filled with motifs that were so often used at the Waynesville School. A big "W" basket is prominently centered in the canvas surrounded by pairs of birds, sprigs of flowers, and a striped urn. Abigail Sherwood, who completed this needlework when she was fifteen, then marked the sampler simply "A. Sherwood," almost as if she had not really planned to sign and date the work at all. Surrounded by a tight strawberry border, the composition of the sampler is well balanced.

Abigail was the eighth child born to Thomas and Dorcas Sherwood of Warren County. Born on October 23, 1823, she died just five years after she finished the work. The sampler remains with descendants of the family.

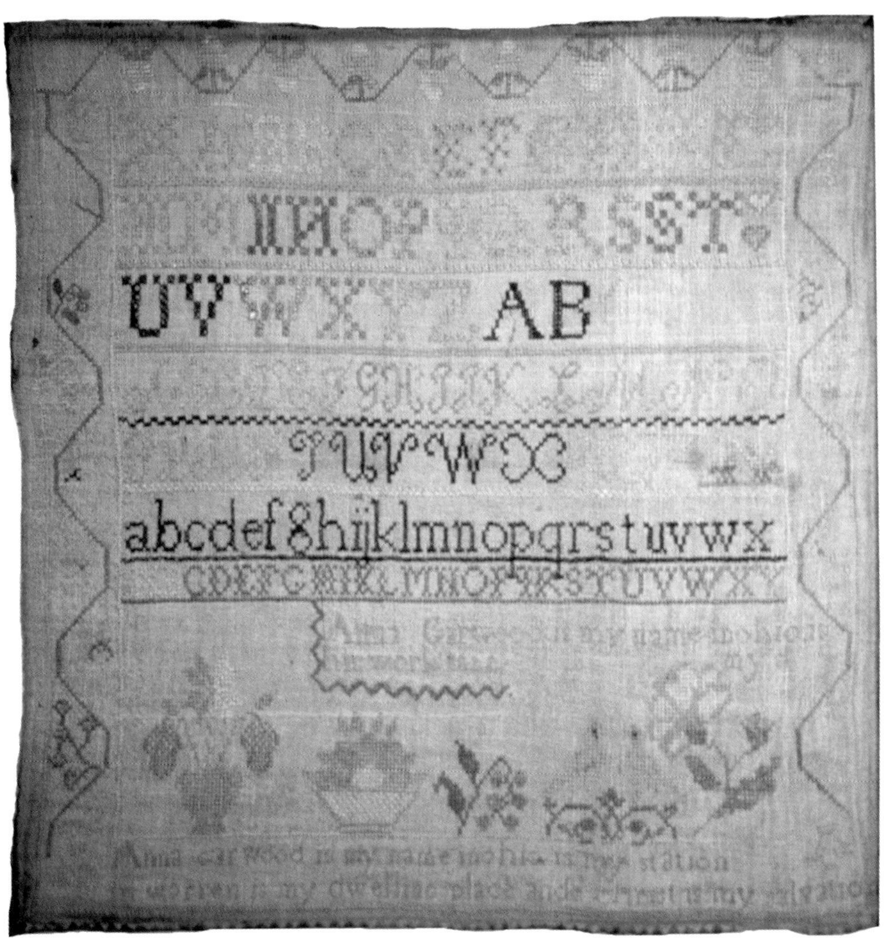

Fig. 38: Sampler of Anna Garwood. 1822.
Size: 16" L x 16" W. Collection of Victoria A. Kramb, Ph.D.

Anna Garwood's sampler features a verse that is a favorite of sampler collectors:

Anna Garwood is my name,
in Ohio is my station,
in Warren is my dwelling place
and Christ is my salvation.

The motifs stitched near the bottom of the canvas, along with the wide block style Roman letters of her alphabet give broad clues that Anna had attended a Quaker school. Anna made two attempts to fit her verse correctly on the canvas, but she did not succeed. Such childish efforts are appealing to many sampler collectors.

Anna was born in Ohio in 1810, the daughter of Jonathan and Priscilla (Evans) Garwood. Her grandfather, Daniel Garwood, and his family came to Ohio early in the nineteenth century from Virginia, and settled in Clear Creek Township near Waynesville, where they were members of the Crooked Creek Monthly Meeting. Upon their arrival in Warren County about 1810, Quaker records show that they soon "transferred their certificates" to the Miami Monthly Meeting at Waynesville.[37]

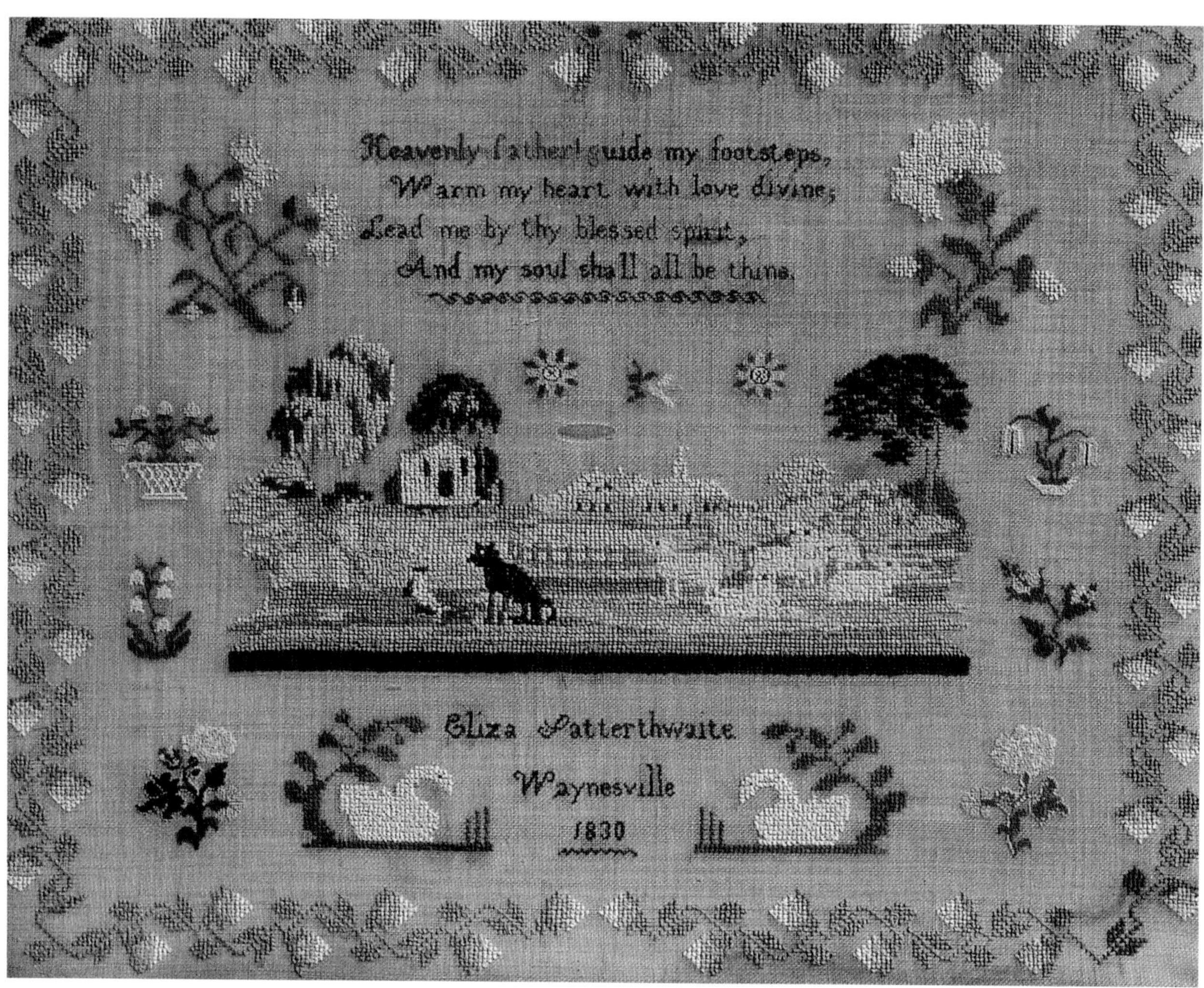

Fig. 39: Sampler of Eliza Satterthwaite. 1830.
Size: 17" L x 21" W. Anonymous collector.

The needlework of Eliza Satterthwaite exhibits some typical Quaker designs that were popular with the teachers at Waynesville School. But this sampler is strikingly different from others from that school. The familiar sprigs of flowers and the swans can be found on the canvas, but the center scene is far more sophisticated than others stitched at Waynesville. Eliza stitched "Waynesville" on her canvas because she lived there. She did not, however, learn to stitch there. Her parents sent her to a needlework teacher in nearby Wilmington, Clinton County.

Eliza's parents, John and Elizabeth Satterthwaite, came to Warren County, Ohio, from Buck's County, Pennsylvania, in 1802, a year before statehood. She was born on June 20, 1820. Eliza Satterthwaite Evans is interred in a Waynesville cemetery.

FIG. 40: PRACTICE SAMPLER OF ELIZA SATTERTHWAITE. 1830.

SIZE: 14" L x 11" W. COLLECTION OF ANNA S. MORRIS AND THELMA SUMMER.

The practice or marking sampler of Eliza Satterthwaite was done to prepare her for the stitching skills she would need to complete the large and beautiful canvas she executed later that same year. It is also marked "Waynesville."

The Village of Franklin

The *Western Star* newspaper, in June of 1822, ran a lengthy advertisement for the opening of a new school in Franklin. Hoping to attract parents from far and wide to patronize the school, the author of the notice described the town as follows: "It is beautifully situated on the East Bank of the Great Miami river, and considered as healthy as any town in the state, and inhabited by a moral people."[38] Founded by William Cortenus Schenck, in 1796, Franklin was just a few miles downriver from Dayton.

At age nineteen, William Cortenus came to the Northwest Territory, to the newly established village of Cincinnati. The young man had devoted himself to the study of civil engineering, and found abundant employment in the unsettled region. Many of the older towns in Ohio were surveyed and laid out by him. In 1798, Mr. Schenck returned to his father's home in Huntington, Long Island. There, he married Sarah Rogers and immediately brought her back to the Ohio lands. In 1803, having laid out the town of Franklin, he moved his family there. He recognized that schools must be established with little delay, so in August 1803, he placed the following notice in the *Western Star* and *Hamilton Gazette*: "School—A schoolmaster is much needed in this place. A person to teach an English school will find employment. W. C. Schenck—Franklin."[39]

William Schenck was commissioned as General of the Ohio Militia in the War of 1812. Eventually he brought his parents and eight brothers and sisters to Franklin.[40] Traveling from

Long Island with his father, Rev. William Schenck, were three unmarried sisters, Anna, Eliza, and Catherine Van Brough Schenck. Shortly after their arrival in 1817, they helped their father establish the First Presbyterian Church in Franklin. Catherine organized a Sunday School for young ladies, which attracted students even before the official church dedication of May 20, 1818. It was the first Sunday School in Warren County and probably the second one in all of Ohio. She wrote: "We have come to a determination to call on the inhabitants of Franklin to know how far they will assist in establishing a Sunday-school for females who are desirous of learning to spell, and read, also committing the Catechism and portions of Scripture to memory."[41]

No mention is made in this announcement that the girls will occupy part of their time with plain and ornamental sewing. It is likely that Catherine's students learned to stitch at the day school she organized, which was located in a house at the northeast corner of Main and Second Streets. Never married, Catherine was a devoted teacher who operated the school undoubtedly for an extended period of time. She died in 1878 at age ninety-seven. She taught school before coming to Ohio, and the samplers produced under her supervision at the Huntington Academy on Long Island look very much like those executed at her school in Franklin.[42] Nine samplers from C. V. B. Schenck's School in Franklin have been discovered. (Fig. 43 shows the one produced by Catherine's niece, Anna Cumming Schenck.)

Fig. 41: Drawing of the Schenck Home.

The Schenck family was one of the most influential in southern Ohio. Anna's home is shown here as it appeared in the 1875 Warren County atlas.

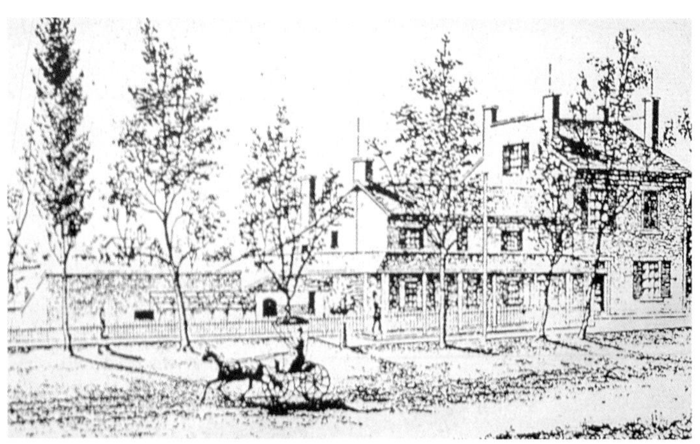

Fig. 42: Detail of Church. »

This church appears on every sampler that has been discovered from C. V. B. Schenck's Franklin school. Perhaps she used this design because her father was a minister and she wanted the girls to keep their religious training in mind as they diligently practiced with their needle and thread.

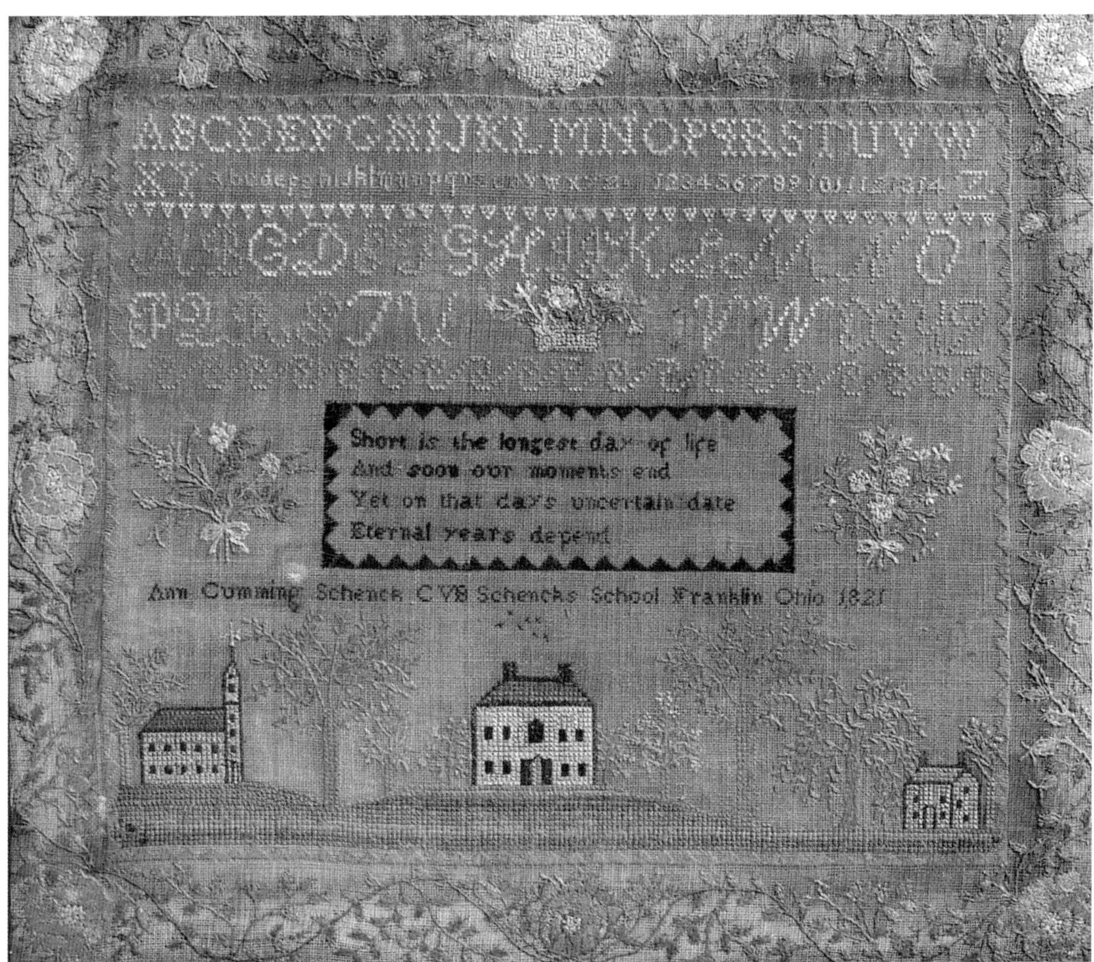

Fig. 43: Sampler of Anna Cumming Schenck. 1821.
Size: 17" L x 20" W. Collection of Harding Museum, Franklin Area Historical Society.

Anna Cumming Schenck's sampler is perhaps the prettiest of the nine samplers documented from C. V. B. Schenck's School in Franklin. Typically the canvases executed at this school show a steepled church and a commodious house with double chimneys, both situated on a green lawn. A flock of birds fly overhead. The sampler's luxuriant border is beautifully stitched, and the overall design of the canvas is more intricate than the others from Catherine Schenck's school. Anna was the daughter of John Noble Cumming Schenck and his first wife, Sarah Tapscott. She completed the canvas in her thirteenth year and precisely marked the name of her Aunt Catherine's school.

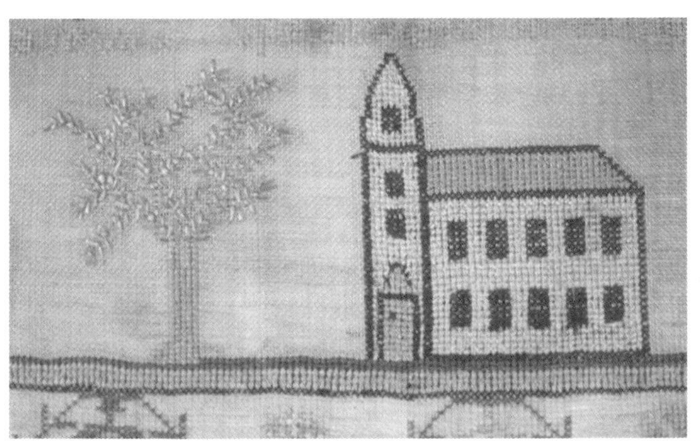

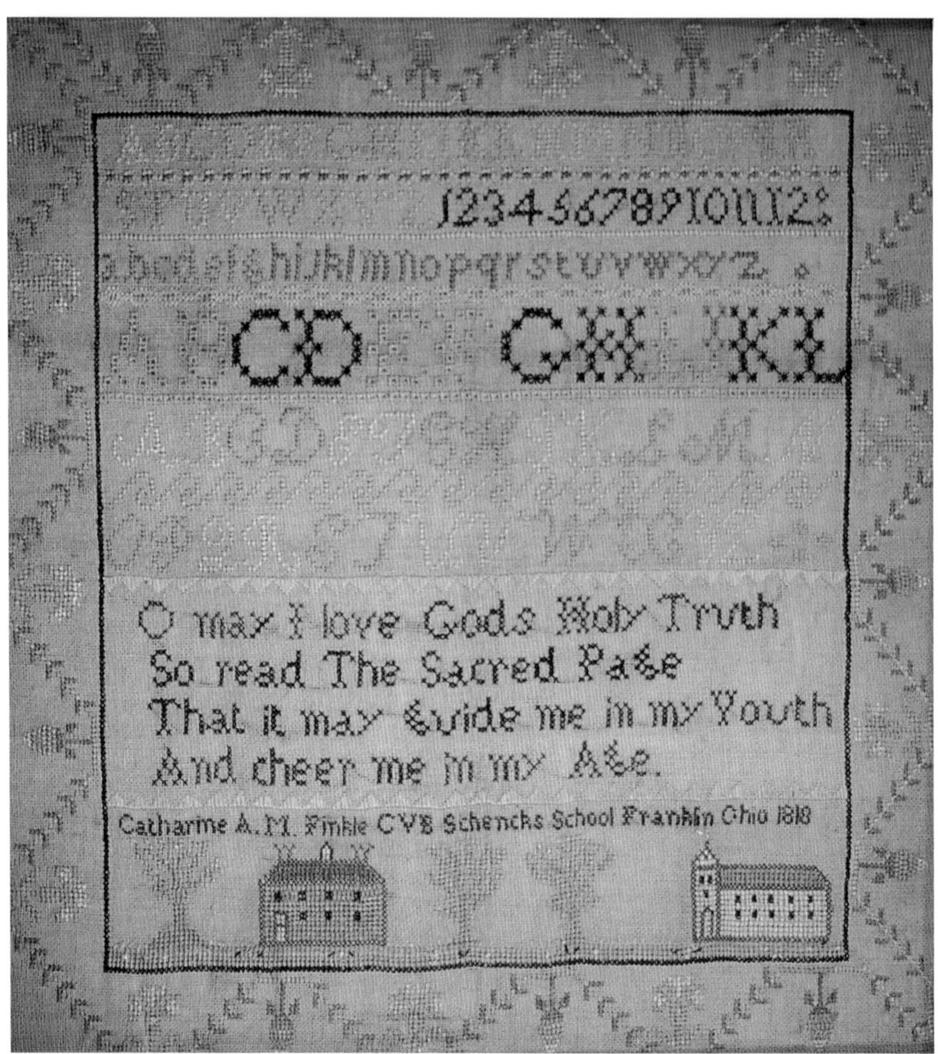

Fig. 44: Sampler of Catharine A. M. Finkle. 1818.
Size: 16" L x 15" W. Collection of Dr. John R. Ribic.

Catharine Ann Marie Finkle must have known that she would not have space for her whole name on the canvas if she included the school's lengthy name. Her teacher probably made the decision to feature the school, knowing that it would serve as a good advertising tool. Catharine Finkle was among the first students in 1818 to complete a sampler at Miss Schenck's newly organized school. This sampler closely resembles the one completed by Eliza Swain under Miss Schenck's guidance in 1829 (see fig. 54).

Catharine Finkle was born in Warren County, c. 1800–1805. Ohio marriage records show that she was married in 1822 in neighboring Butler County to Lewis P. Sayle.

Fig. 46: Detail of Ladd Sampler. »
The building Ann Maria stitched is large and nicely executed. The unusual trees are supported by trunks firmly embedded in the grassy lawn.

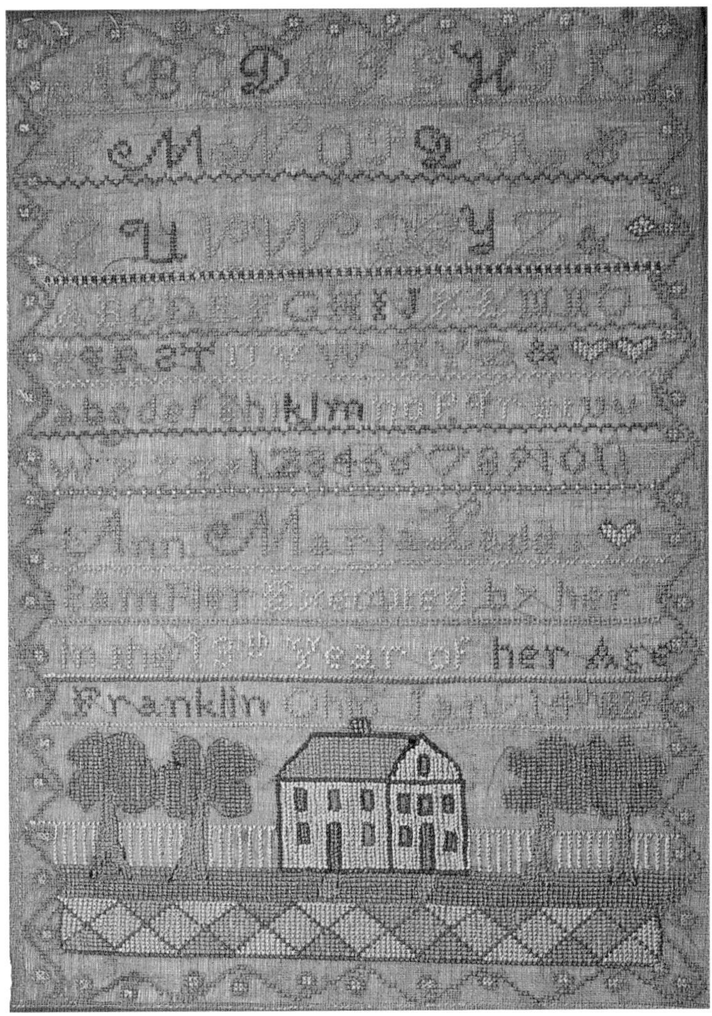

Fig. 45: Sampler of Ann Maria Ladd. 1829.
Size: 18" L x 13" W. Collection of Doris and Kyle Fuller.

Although it is marked "Franklin, Ohio," Ann Maria Ladd's sampler is very different from those done at Catherine Van Brough Schenck's school. Records show that several good schools were situated in the town at this time, but Ann Maria's teacher has not been identified. Stitched when Ann was thirteen, the canvas displays a colorful large diamond border at the bottom and distinctive clover-like trees. Two samplers like this have been discovered. The second was stitched a decade after the Ladd sampler by ten-year-old Elizabeth Stewart in 1839. No school name is on either canvas, but we know that the teacher, whoever she was, taught needlework for at least ten years.

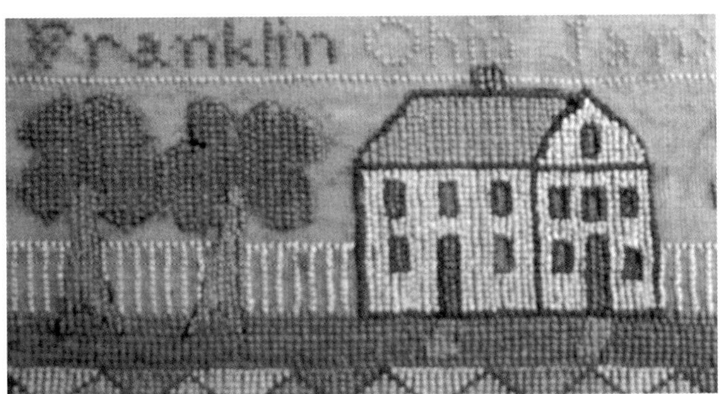

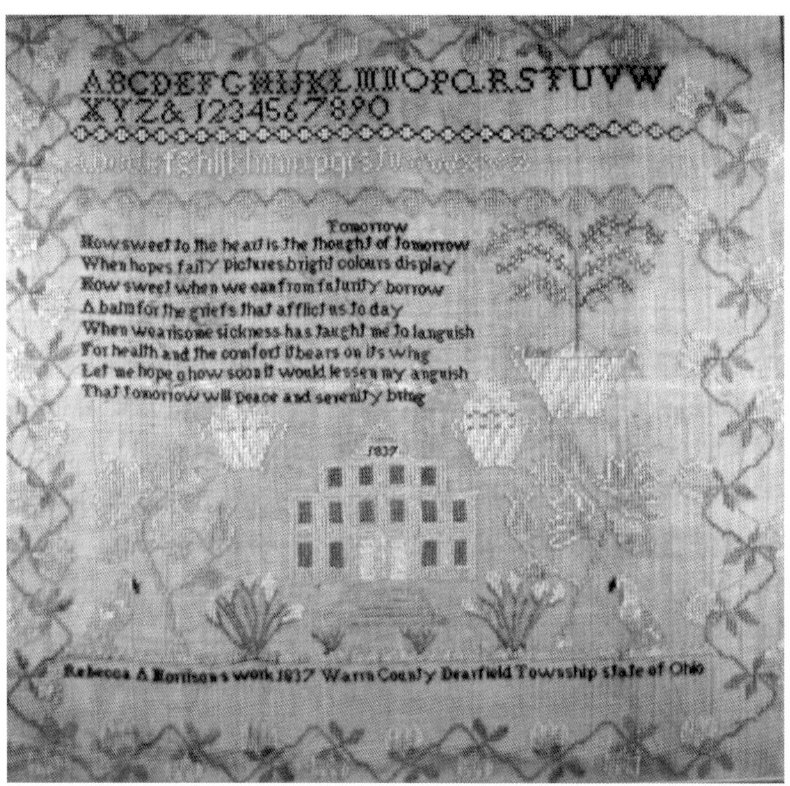

Fig. 47: Sampler of Rebecca A. Morrison. 1837.

Size: 16" L x 17" W. Anonymous collector.

When the 1837 sampler of Rebecca A. Morrison was discovered, it confirmed that an important needlework teacher worked over a long period of time in southern Warren County. Her school was probably in the small town of Mason, in Deerfield Township, the location Rebecca stitched on the canvas. The sampler of Mary F. Moore (fig. 49) was undoubtedly done under the tutelage of the same teacher.

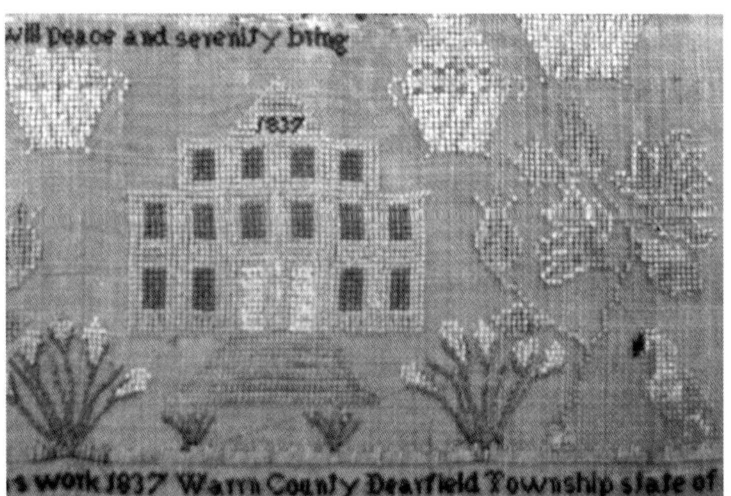

Fig. 48: Detail of Morrison Sampler.

The huge building in the center of the sampler is marked with the date in the peak of the roof. It is not known whether that structure really existed or was just a design that the teacher admired. This sampler shares many other key elements with that of Mary Moore: the floral zigzag border, the sprigs of small flowers embroidered at the bottom of the canvas, and the huge "parrots" on either side of those sprigs. Distinctive striped pots hold plants and flowers.

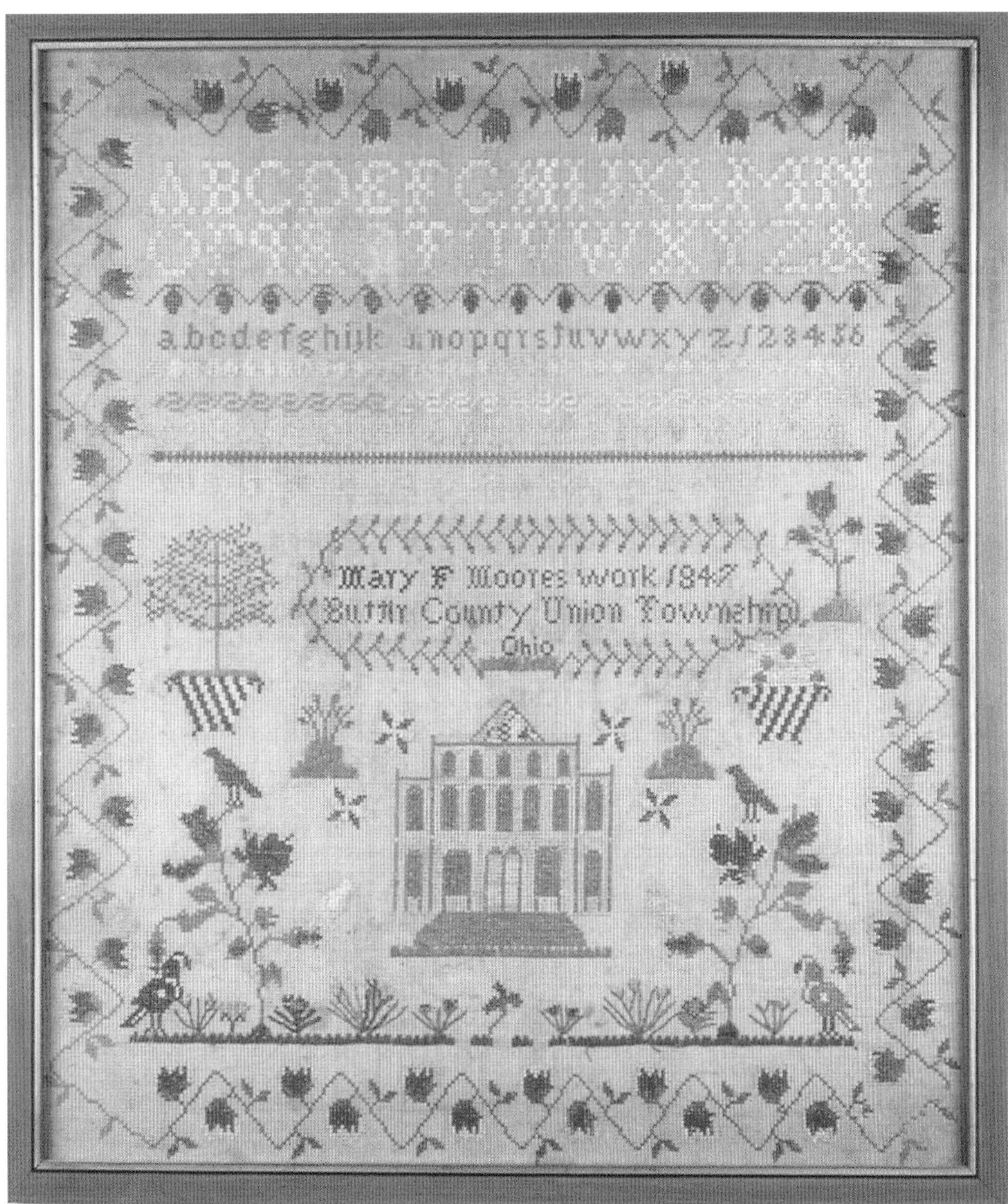

FIG. 49: SAMPLER OF MARY F. MOORE. 1847.

SIZE: 19" L x 17" W. COLLECTION OF MRS. A. W. RUMER.

This needlework shows strong color and pretty stitching. Rarely are samplers found in such good condition. Stitched by Mary F. Moore, the sampler is clearly related to Rebecca Morrison's needlework executed ten years earlier at the same school. Mary had a hard time fitting the 1847 date into the peak of the building. Samplers like these give evidence that teachers made subtle changes in the designs they taught but that their "signature" motifs did not change *significantly* over the years. Mary's sampler tells us that she lived just across the county line in Union Township of Butler County and that she finished her sampler in 1847.

The Village of Springborough

The earliest settlers of Springborough (now spelled "Springboro") arrived in 1796, and most of those first pioneers were members of the Society of Friends. The small village was a lively one with many industries. It played a major part in the Underground Railroad, and the Clearcreek Township area was perhaps the most intense in the country for harboring slaves on their escape.[43] At least eighteen village sites, and nine more in the township, directly aided runaways.

The Springborough Monthly Meeting of Friends was established in 1824. It continued for half a century until 1875, when it once again merged with the Miami Monthly Meeting in Waynesville, just eight miles away. The small Springborough congregation included Hannah Thomas, whose sampler appears in this volume (fig. 52). Perhaps Hannah's teacher was Emily Welding, a young Quaker woman from Philadelphia, whose advertisement for her Springborough school appeared in Lebanon's *Western Star* newspaper in March 1833. Welding, who apparently was unmarried, lived at Eli P. Hurst's Boarding School in Springborough for at least three years. Hurst also advertised in the *Western Star,* and his 1839 notice offered needlework, along with academic subjects, to prospective students.

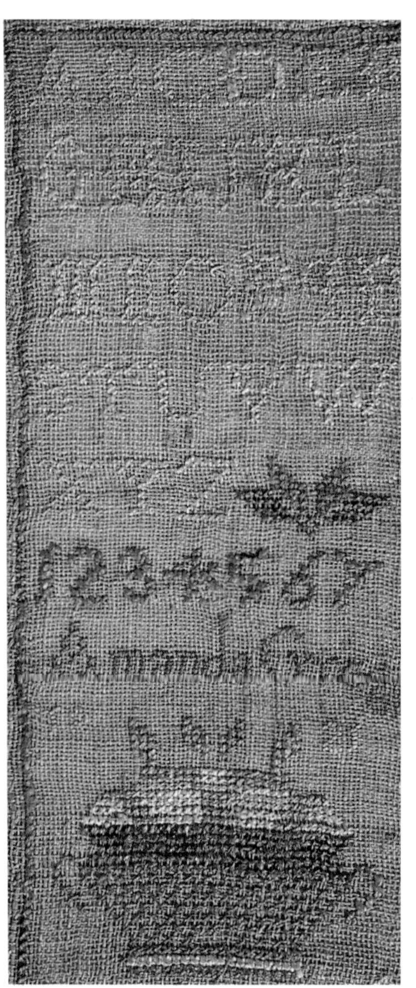

FIG. 50: SAMPLER OF AMANDA GREGG. 1821.
SIZE: 8" L x 3" W. COLLECTION OF WARREN COUNTY HISTORICAL SOCIETY.

Samuel Gregg, one of the first settlers, was a birthright Quaker born in 1773. He came to Ohio from Loudoun County, Virginia, with his wife Nancy (O'Brien) in about 1797. The Greggs had seven sons and six daughters. Their tenth child, Amanda, was born on November 23, 1814, and her marking sampler was completed in 1821. She executed the stitches well for someone so young, but failed to plan ahead to allow space for her numbers and her name.

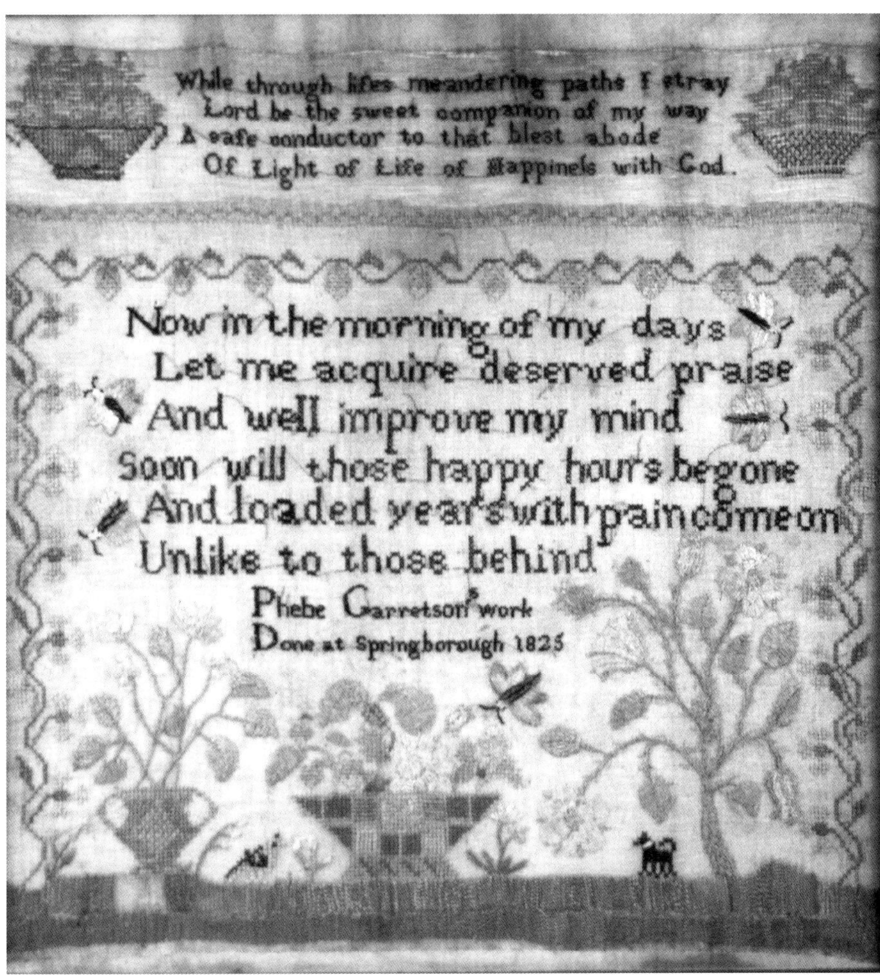

Fig. 51: Sampler of Phebe Garretson. 1825.
Size: 17" L x 17" W. Silk on linen. Collection of Annette Anderson Quebe.

The attractive sampler of Phebe Garretson was executed at Springborough in 1825, when she was just nine years old. The composition of her needlework does not look like that of any other Ohio Quaker sampler. The teacher who designed this canvas included two unusual verses, flowers and baskets of fruit, and a bevy of butterflies flitting about.

Phebe was born in Springborough on June 1, 1816, the daughter of John and Rebecca Garretson. In 1839 she married Joseph N. Taylor, who was also a native of Warren County, but who had moved to Monrovia, Indiana, with his parents in 1833. The newlyweds were active in Quaker affairs. Joseph and Phebe served as superintendent and matron for a time at Earlham College, where all five of their children eventually enrolled as students. Phebe died in 1898, just before her eighty-second birthday, and is buried with her husband at West Union Friends Cemetery near Monrovia.

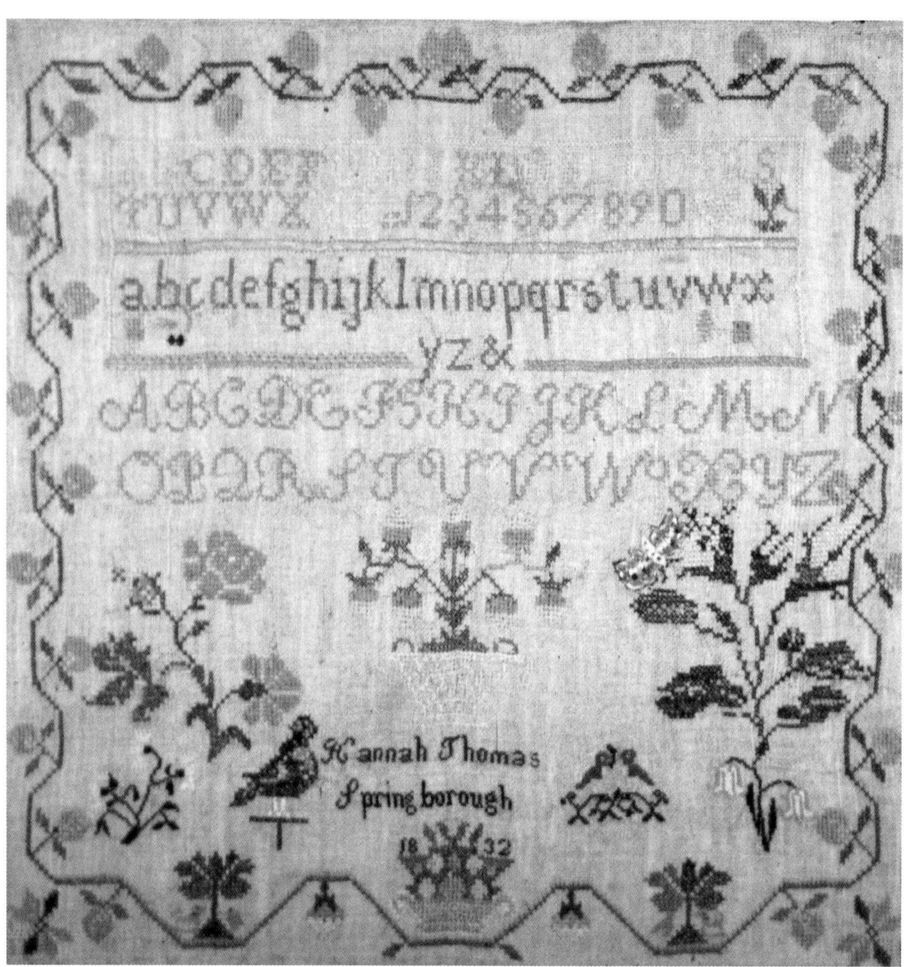

Fig. 52: Sampler of Hannah Thomas. 1832.
Size 17" L x 17" W. Collection of Glee Krueger.

Hannah Thomas stitched this sampler in Springborough, including many Quaker motifs on the canvas. Though she filled the canvas with just cross-stitch work, the sampler is well planned and executed. Her parents, Jonah and Elizabeth Thomas, joined the Springborough Monthly Meeting in 1829, with their four children. Jonah owned and operated a harness shop; the business and their home were situated on Main Street. The brick structure still stands today. During the years before the Civil War, the Thomases were active participants in the Abolitionist movement. By 1832, when this was stitched, Hannah had left the Quaker church and is recorded as "disowned" in 1829.[44]

Montgomery County

The story of the settlement of Montgomery County and the town of Dayton begins in the spring of 1796. Rivers were the highways of immigration, making this point at the confluence of three major rivers very important. Here the Stillwater, the Mad River, and the Great Miami joined. The founding families and their leaders had traveled from points near Cincinnati, making their way northward in three separate parties. Two groups traveled overland, and the third party came up the Great Miami River. All three parties must have found the trip to be an incredibly difficult trek. The early days were ones of great hardship and privation, but by summer, the pioneers were joined by other eager settlers, and they began the slow task of establishing a prosperous little village.

Dayton

During the summer of 1799, the inhabitants of the settlement became fearful of an Indian attack and decided to build a large blockhouse for their defense. The attack never came, and so the building, constructed on the Main Street bank of the Miami, was never used as a fort. The citizens soon converted it into a schoolhouse, where twenty-six-year-old Benjamin Van Cleve served as the first teacher of Dayton children. He likely offered only academic courses to the local children in the tiny town. Historical records indicate that fifteen years would pass in the pioneer village before girls had the opportunity to attend an organized local school that offered instructions in needlework and the "ornamental branches."

Records of private or subscription schools established for young ladies are sketchy, but the first one seems to have been Doninecia Sullivan's School for Girls, opened March 1815 on Main Street just south of Third.[45] Little is known about Miss Sullivan and her school, or any other Dayton girls' schools, until the 1840s. The Lancasterian Seminary put notice in the *Dayton Watchman* in February 1822 that "persons in this town and its vicinity, who are unable to pay for the education of their children, may, by applying at this school, have them taught gratis."[46] It is probably a safe assumption that in 1822 young girls were given some "plain needlework" instruction so that they could at the very least learn to mark linens and help with household sewing chores.

Documented samplers, however, give us evidence that by the 1830s locally run "dame" schools and private teachers were instructing young ladies in needlework. The Cooper Female Seminary, situated on First Street, opened in 1845. Named for Daniel C. Cooper, the school flourished for forty years, attracting girls from Dayton and the surrounding areas. Cooper, who surveyed the area and settled in Dayton in 1796, gave money as well as land for schools, churches, and a commons area downtown.[47]

Several Montgomery County samplers with "Dayton" stitched on the canvas show us, either with stylistic designs or school names included on the canvas, that the girls went to schools elsewhere. The school of Catherine Van Brough Schenck in Franklin was easily accessible to Dayton girls because it was a bit closer than Waynesville. Since it was situated on the Great Miami River, Dayton students would have had easy transportation to the school. C. V. B. Schenck's School and the Friends' Waynesville School, both in neighboring Warren County, were large enough to accommodate boarding students and were patronized by Dayton families.

FIG. 53: SAMPLER OF LEAH JANE ASHTON. 1833. »
SIZE: 21" L x 17½" W. COLLECTION OF SUSAN AND JON AIREY.

When Leah Jane Ashton completed this sampler, she marked that it was done "in her 12 year at Mrs. R. A. Cooper's School Dayton AD 1833." Mrs. Cooper encouraged Leah to fill the entire canvas with all sorts of beautiful motifs, and Leah has successfully squeezed in pretty designs wherever she could. The reserve area encircled by a vine wreath contains the following words: "I will no more despise / My dear Redeemers love / Nor turn away my soulful eyes / Nor from his paths remove." The large central basket filled with three pieces of fruit has not been seen on other Ohio samplers.

Leah was born in Cincinnati in 1821 to David and Olivia (Terrill) Ashton. Their initials (DOA) are prominently placed in this sampler. The family came to Ohio from Baltimore, Maryland, and by 1827 had made their way to Dayton. Leah married a young widower, Thomas Morrow, on April 19, 1851, in Miami County, and had six children. She died on February 11, 1894, at age seventy-two.

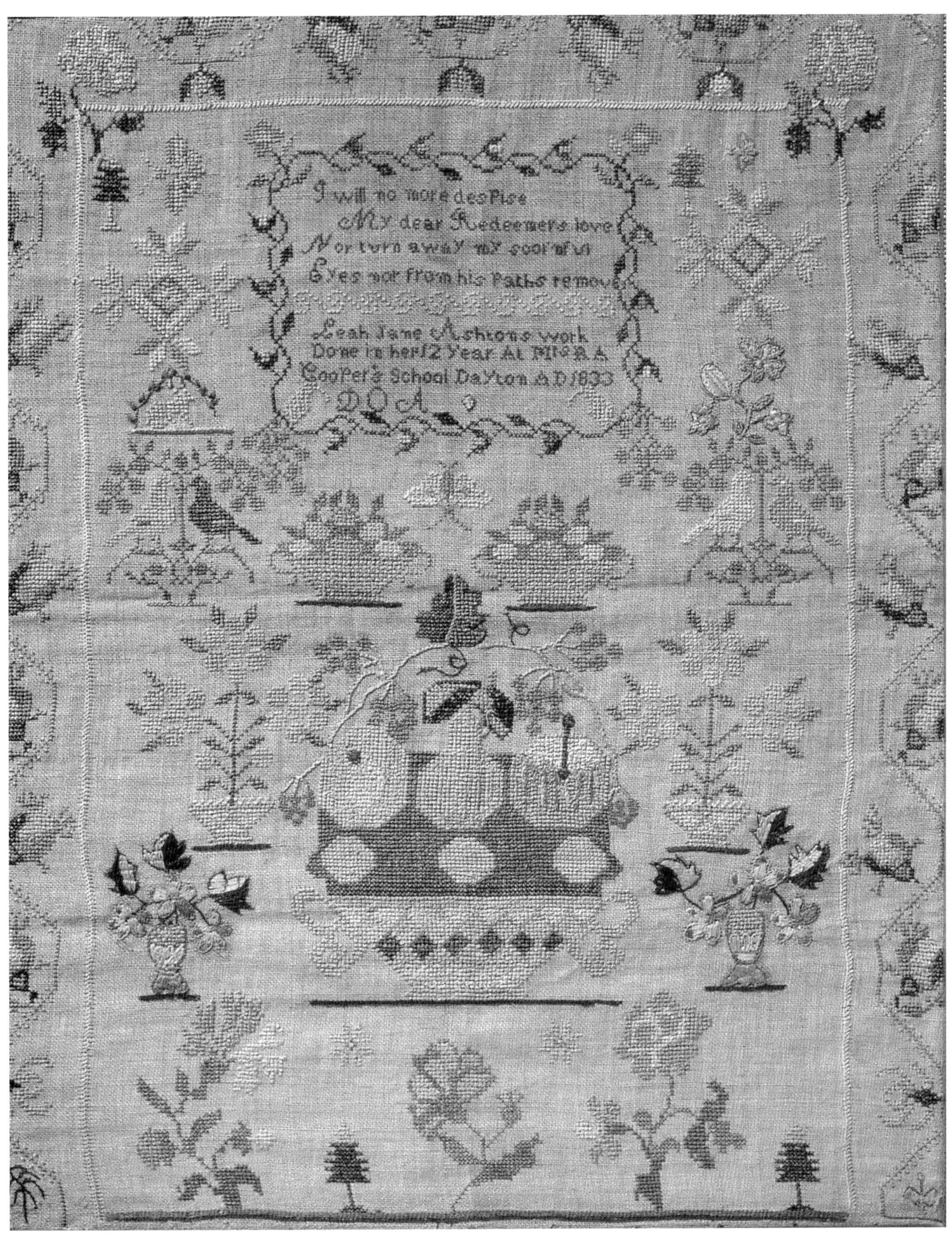
I will no more desPise
My dear Redeemers love
Nor turn away my
Eyes nor from his Paths remove
Leah Jane Ashtons work
Done in her 12 Year At Mrs A
Cooper's School DaYton AD 1833
D O A

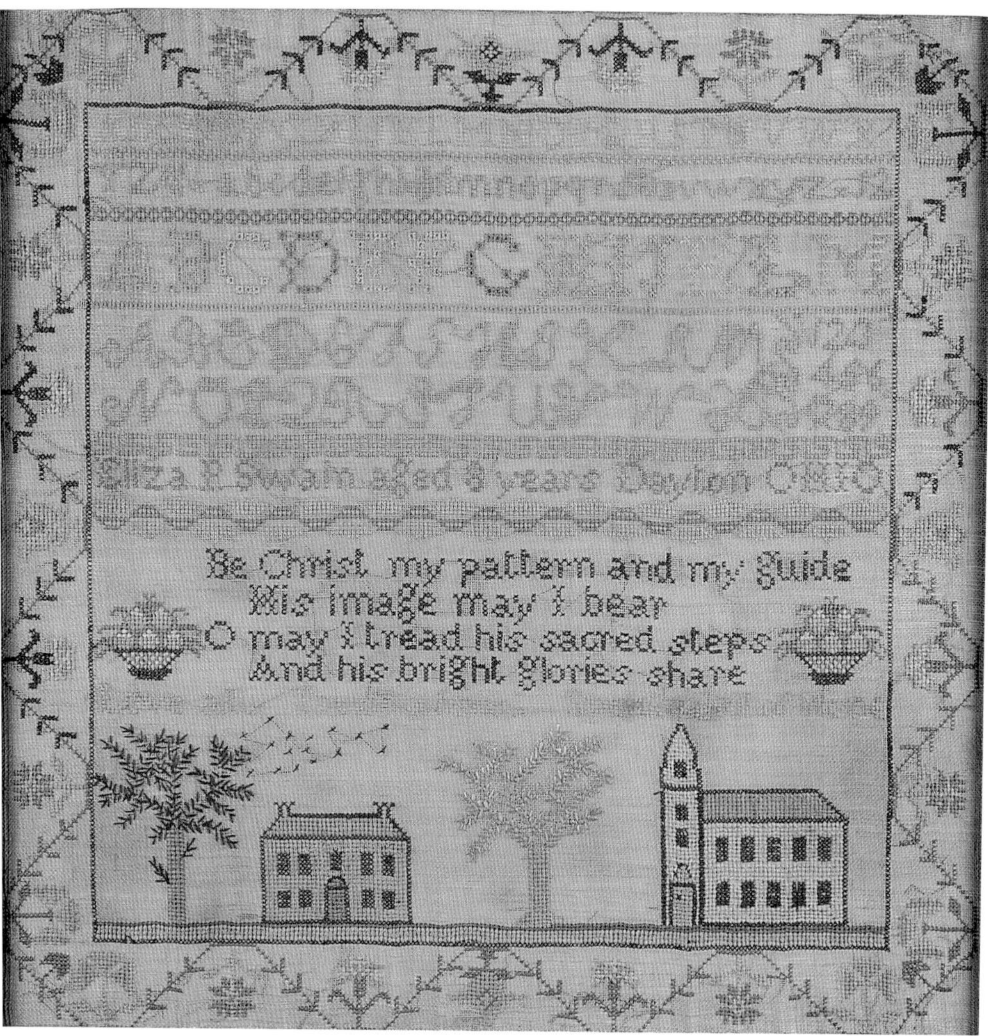

Fig. 54: Sampler of Eliza P. Swain. c. 1829.

Size: 17½" L x 17½" W. Collection of the author.

When Charles G. Swain and his wife, Alice, left Nantucket, Massachusetts, to come to Ohio in the first quarter of the nineteenth century, they probably had already formulated plans for making a good living in their new surroundings. Mr. Swain was active in civic affairs and owned a grocery in Dayton near the head of the State Basin called "The Sign of the Yellow Cask." The family lived near the Great Miami River, in a section that was then known as Miami City.

Even though they were members of the Methodist Church, rather than the Presbyterian, the Swains did not hesitate to send their young daughter eight miles downriver to Franklin in neighboring Warren County to attend Miss C. V. B. Schenck's School (see pages 48 and 49). Eliza's sampler reads: "Aged eight years—Dayton Ohio."

Eliza was born in 1821. In 1844, she married the minister of her church, Rev. William Herr, who was fifteen years her senior. She spent her life in Dayton and died at age eighty-four. Her grave is in Dayton's Woodland Cemetery.

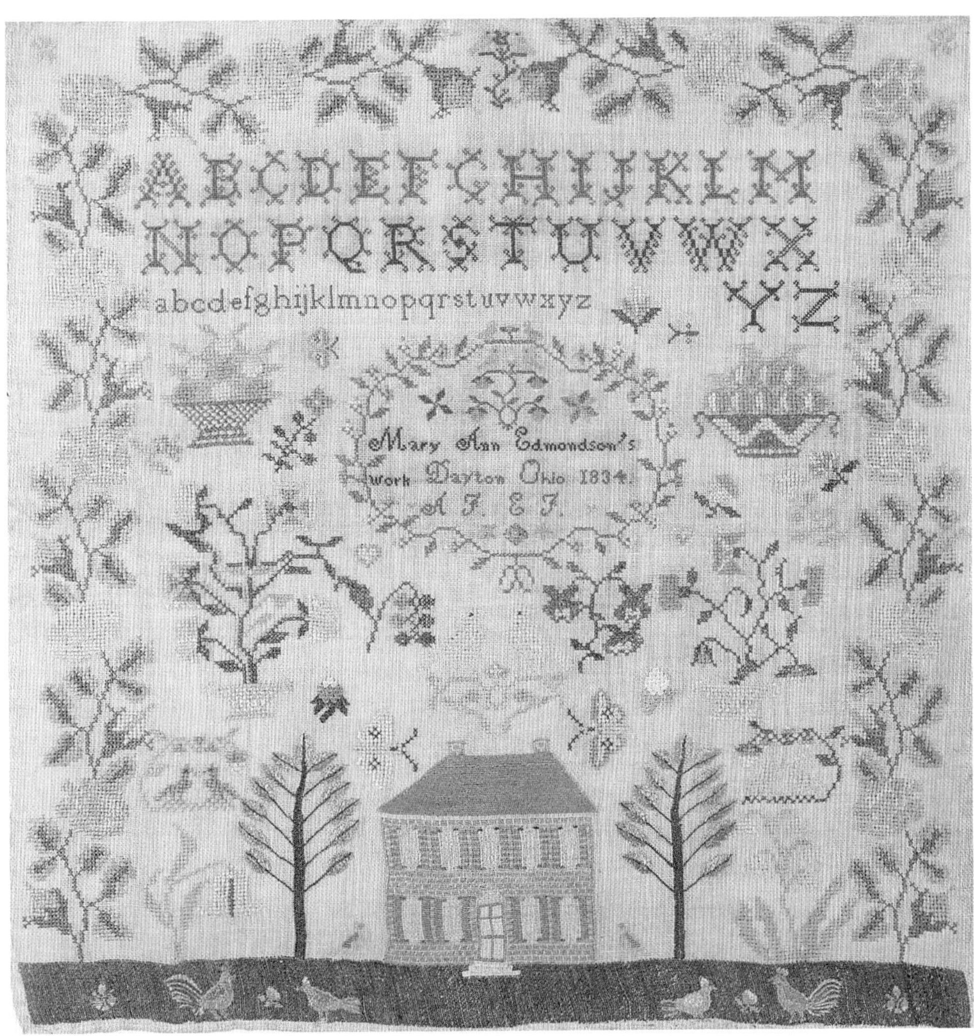

Fig. 55: Sampler of Mary Ann Edmondson. 1834.
Size: 18" L x 17½" W. Collection of the Ohio Historical Society.

Mary Ann Edmondson's sampler includes many Quaker design elements. The first clue that she attended the Waynesville School is the "W" basket on the right side of the large sampler (see fig. 33). The brick house flanked by trees is stitched with careful attention to architectural details, and it is situated on a "lawn" filled with fanciful butterflies, birds, and chickens. A rosebud vine encloses three sides of the canvas. The reserve area reads: "Mary Ann Edmondson's / work Dayton—Ohio 1834. / A F. E F." The initials may be those of her teachers at Waynesville School.

The alphabet at the top of the canvas is not the typical Quaker plain Roman alphabet that is usually displayed on Waynesville School pieces. Instead, each letter has a peculiar seraph. This style of lettering is also displayed on the sampler of her sister Hannah Edmondson (fig. 56) and is often found, with variations, on Scotch samplers. The sampler of another Edmondson sister, Ruth, also appears in this book. To find the samplers of three sisters is most unusual, especially since they were discovered in different sections of the state and in different collections. In 1842, Mary Ann married Rev. Daniel R. Biddlecom (Biddlecombe). She is interred in Woodland Cemetery in Dayton.

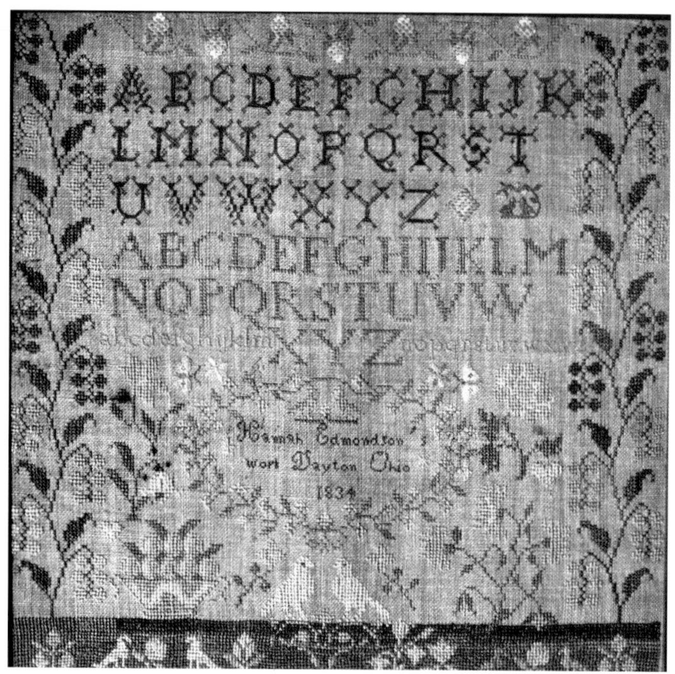

FIG. 56: SAMPLER OF HANNAH EDMONDSON. 1834. SIZE: 17" L X 17" W. COLLECTION OF PENNSYLVANIA HOUSE MUSEUM, SPRINGFIELD, OHIO, DAUGHTERS OF THE AMERICAN REVOLUTION.

Even though the samplers of the three Edmondson sisters (figs. 55, 56, and 57) have very different borders, their overall designs are similar, and they share many of the same motifs. A practice sampler done by Hannah, dated 1833, accompanies this sampler.

Hannah and Mary Ann Edmondson were both born in 1824 to Edward and Ruth Ann Edmondson. Hannah was born in Reading, Ohio, near Cincinnati, and Mary Ann was born after the family moved to Dayton. The Edmondsons were Quakers, and Mr. Edmondson was a tanner by trade. Hannah married Marion Monroe on May 29, 1851. Hannah, like her sister Mary Ann, is interred at Dayton's Woodland Cemetery.

FIG. 57: SAMPLER OF RUTH ANNA EDMONDSON. 1842. SIZE: 15½" L X 16¾" W. COLLECTION OF NATALIE RUTH DALL.

The sampler of the youngest Edmondson sister, Ruth Anna, also survives in good condition. It bears a resemblance to the work of her two older sisters, but she seemingly did not share the same enthusiasm for embroidery that their samplers exhibit. By the 1840s, Ruth Anna and her teacher were probably interested in doing the new Berlin wool-work pictures that were so popular to stitch. She created the same panel stitching at the bottom that Hannah had used, and the same vine cartouche surrounds her name in the center, but she stopped short of creating a pleasing, fully-worked sampler like those Mary Ann and Hannah executed.

Ruth Anna was born September 15, 1828, in Dayton and graduated from the Cooper Female Seminary. On October 19, 1848, she married James J. Rossell. She died just before her eighty-third birthday in September 1911.

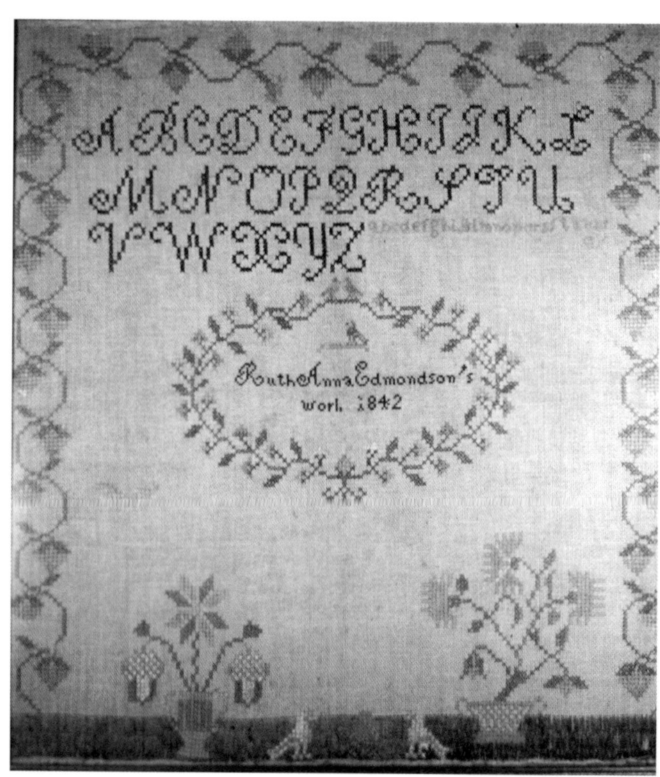

Fig. 58: Sampler of Anna A. Anderson. 1835. Size: 20" L x 20" W. Collection of Colleen Dignan.

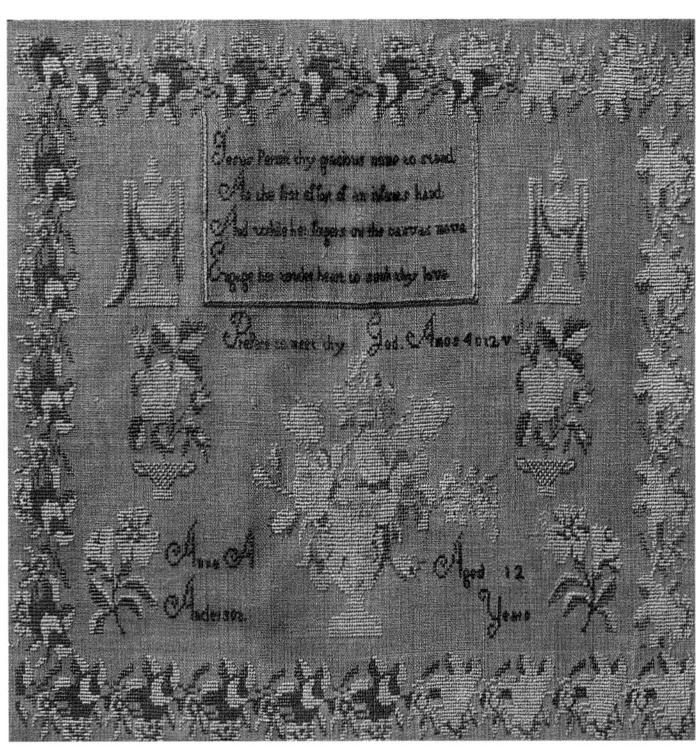

Anna Anderson was born in Norfolk, England, in 1823 to Robert and Ann (Hull) Anderson. They arrived in Philadelphia in 1829 and settled that same year in Ohio. They soon purchased one hundred acres of land in Montgomery County, near Miamisburg, where Anna finished her fine sampler. The carefully balanced composition of this canvas, with the fashionable draped neoclassical urns, gives an initial impression of an English sampler. Perhaps Anna was a student of Mrs. Thomas E. Thomas, "lately from England," who was teaching needlework in Butler County.[48]

Anna's father, Robert, established an ironworks and specialized in making architectural iron and cast-iron garden furniture. When Anna married Adam McHose about 1850, he joined his father-in-law in the business. One can still see their beautiful iron decorative accents on homes and stores around the area today.

Anna died just before the beginning of the Civil War at the age of thirty-eight, leaving two daughters. She is buried in Woodland Cemetery in Dayton, in the McHose family plot.

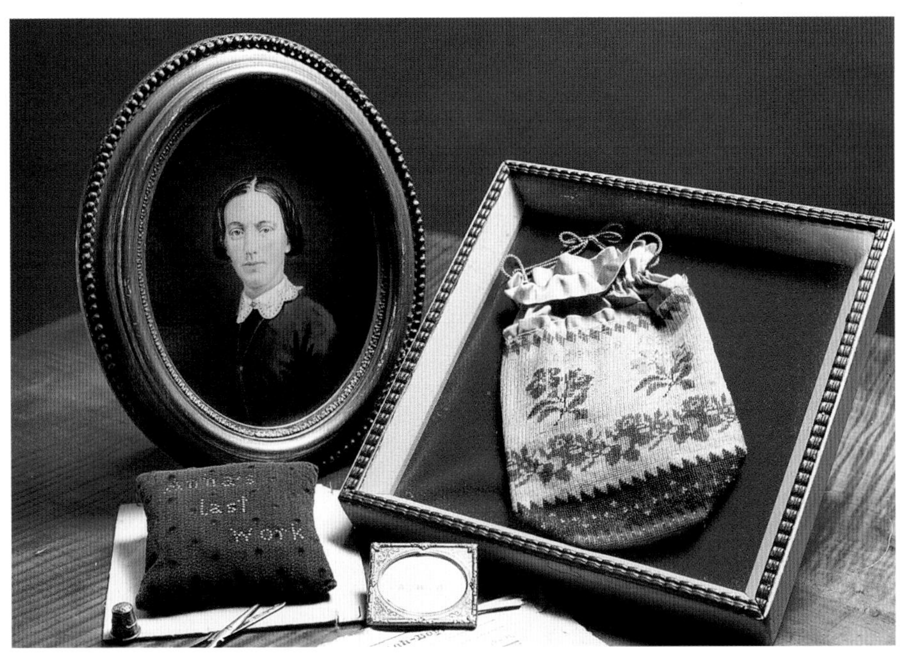

Fig. 59: Mementos of Anna A. Anderson. Anonymous collector.

Many related mementos survive that can be directly associated with Anna's needlework (fig. 58). Accompanying her sampler are two beaded bags, one inscribed with "A. Anderson 1832"; a simple cross-stitched "A. A. A." that she once marked on a pillowcase; and her portrait. The most poignant artifact, however, is her pincushion, with "Anna's Last Work" boldly patterned with pins.

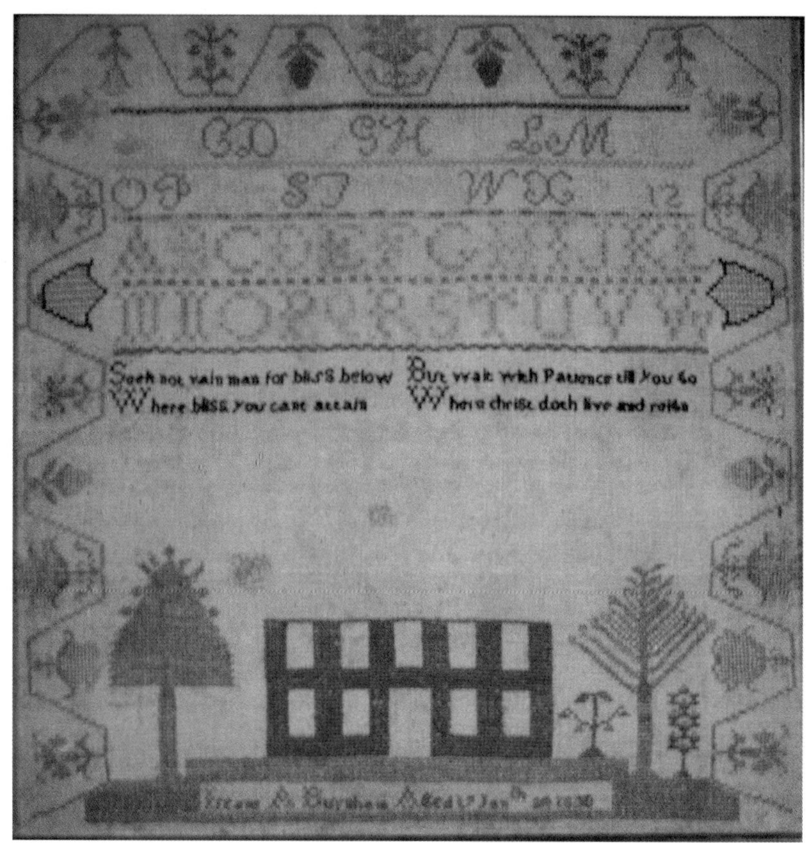

Fig. 60: Sampler of Ireana A. Burnham. 1830.

Size: 16½" L x 16½" W.
Collection of Centerville-Washington Township Historical Society.

Ireana Burnham was the daughter of John and Elizabeth (Huston) Burnham, who came to Washington Township in Montgomery County about 1800. Unfortunately, she did not complete her canvas, with its large house and unusual border. Ireana was seventeen when she worked on the sampler in 1830. Not long after that, in August of 1832, she married Caleb William Nutt. She was his second wife and the mother of fourteen of his sixteen children. Ireana Burnham Nutt died in April 1864 and is buried in Sidney, Ohio.

The Village of Germantown

Germantown was settled early in the nineteenth century, mostly by immigrants of German descent from Pennsylvania. Thirteen miles southwest of Dayton, it is situated in a pretty valley surrounded by productive farmlands, and many early homes survive. In 1842 at the time Adaline Taylor's sampler was made (see fig. 61), Germantown did not have a female seminary for young ladies of the community to attend. Sometime in the 1840s, however, a coeducational school was established that was touted as being "fair to equal any other in the West."[49] The age of students admitted and whether needlework instruction was offered at the school are unknown.

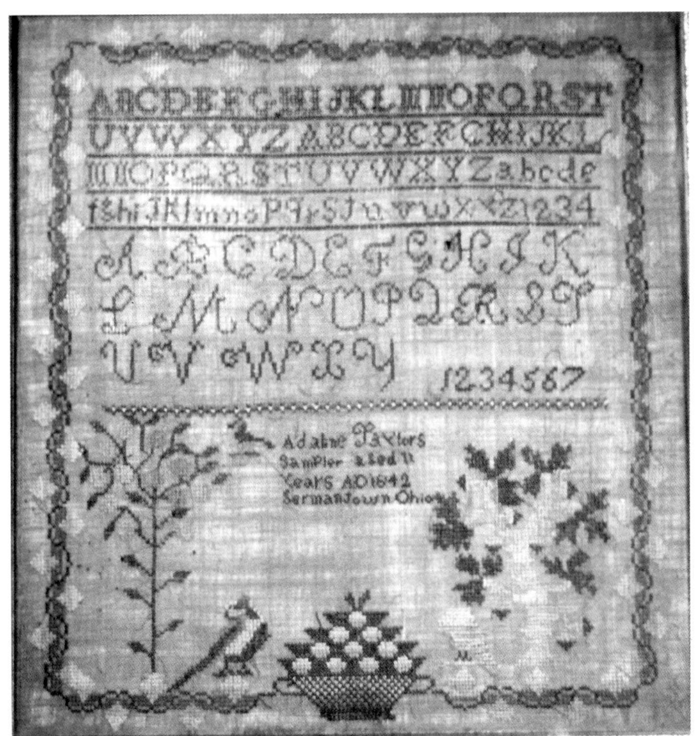

FIG. 61: SAMPLER OF ADALINE TAYLOR. 1842.

SIZE: 17½" L x 17½" W. COLLECTION OF THE AUTHOR.

Adaline Taylor's is the only known sampler to name the village of Germantown, Ohio. It was completed in 1842 when she was eleven years old. Adaline probably intended to put something in the empty space just above the basket heaped full of fruit, but may have been reluctant to add more stitching. She started with her numbers in two places but never succeeded in fitting them all in, and one of the large birds at the bottom of the canvas has no head. The daughter of Richard and Sarah (Heck) Taylor, Adaline, who never married, spent most of her seventy-eight years on the farm with her widowed mother and her brother Lewis and his family.

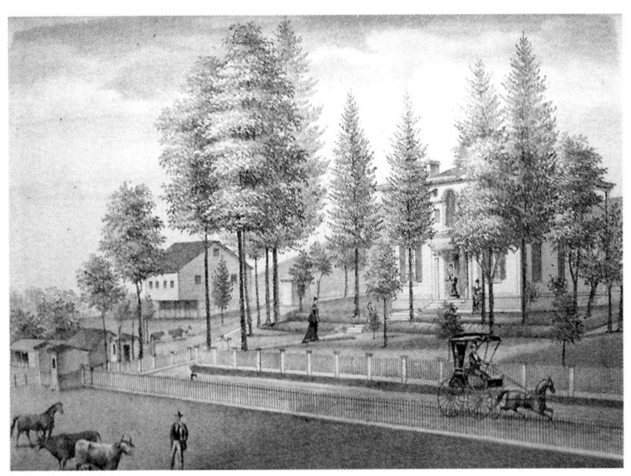

FIG. 62: THE TAYLOR HOME.

The Lewis Taylor home stands today near the edge of Germantown, looking very much as it did in the nineteenth century. A stately home, it remains today with descendants of the family, and the farm seems undisturbed by urban sprawl. The Taylor family donated land for the Germantown Cemetery just west of the house. When Adaline Taylor (see fig. 61) died in 1919, she was buried in the family plot just a few yards from her birthplace.

The "Duch" Transplanted

Many German families flooded into the Ohio Lands early in the nineteenth century and quickly took up some of the best farmlands in the new state. Most started out from points in Maryland and Pennsylvania. They loaded up their wagons, harnessed their mules and horses, and headed over the Appalachians with their families and meager possessions. An industrious, religious group of people, they were bound together by both heritage and language. Needlework by German American girls does not turn up often in the search for early Ohio embroideries. When a piece with a German folk-art look is found in some trunk or at a farm sale, people usually assume that it must have been done in Pennsylvania, although this may not necessarily be the case.

Because they spoke little or no English and were living on isolated farms rather than in urban settings, the "Duch" girls did not attend the "dame" schools or formal schools that were patronized by "der English" families. Though larger cities like Cincinnati by the 1840s had begun to assimilate German-speaking children into public schools, not much effort was being made to accomplish this in rural villages and farming areas.

German girls, however, knew the importance of needlework skills. They learned to sew at home, sitting at "mother's knee," instead of in formal schools. Mothers, or perhaps other talented stitchers in the family, showed them how to re-create traditional German motifs that had been passed down from one generation to the next, from the Old World to the New. The hand towels, or *handtuchen,* and samplers they produced have an entirely different look from the needlework produced by English, Scotch-Irish, and Welsh girls living on the neighboring farms. The embroidery of the German girls, with few exceptions, was sewn with cotton thread on a linen ground and confined to cross-stitch.

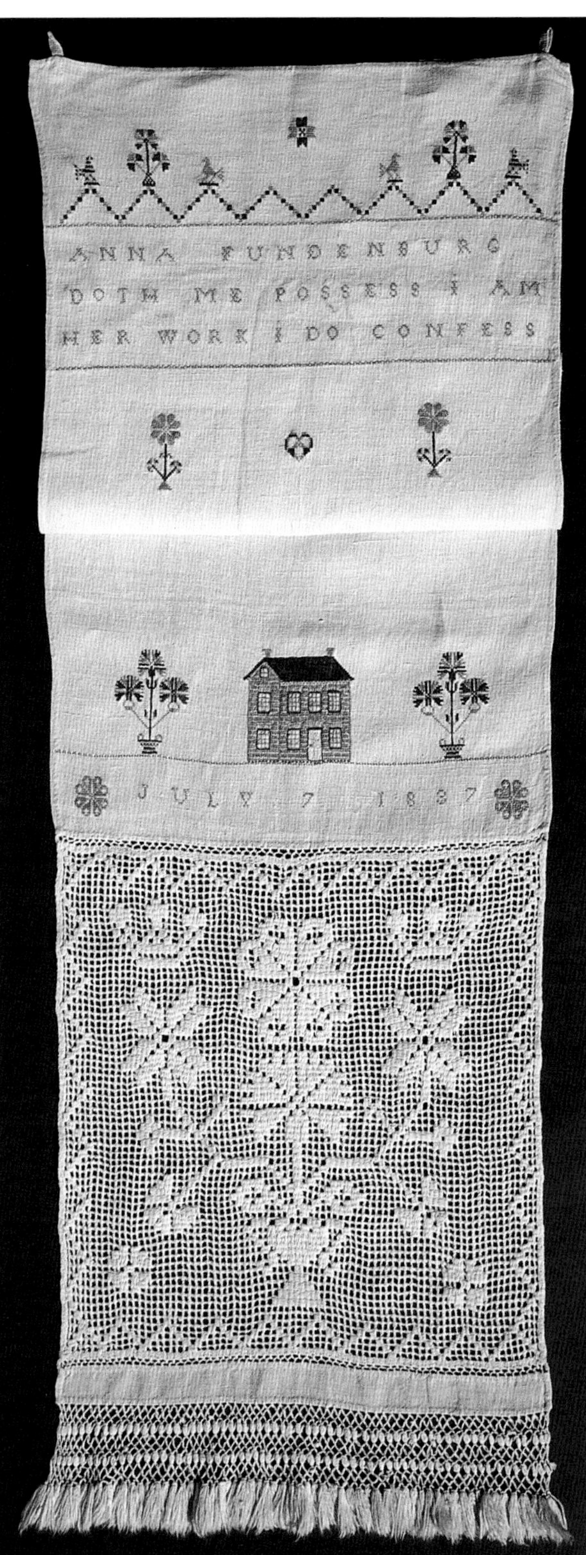

Fig. 63: Anna Fundenburg Towel.
Size: 51" L x 14¼" W.
Cotton on linen.
Collection of Eldon Studebaker.

This hand towel or "show towel" is one of three made by Anna Fundenburg. It is dated 1837 and was completed before her marriage to Simon Huffer. A young woman of twenty-five, Anna was living with her parents, John and Margaret (Shank) Fundenburg. The tabs sewn at the top of the towel were attached so that her handwork could be hung on a door somewhere in the house. Tradition dictated that nearly every door in a German home be decorated with an embroidered towel. Hung "for show," they were definitely not to be used to wipe one's hands. Two of Anna's towels have the following inscription: "Anna Fundenburg doth me possess, I am her work I do confess." The intricate crochet work at the bottom of the towel further served to show off her "domestic skills."

Fig. 64: Marking Sampler (1828) and Mementos of Anna Fundenberg.

Size: 7" L x 5" W (towel). Collection of the author.

The marking sampler done by Anna Fundenburg is dated 1828. Beneath it is another hand towel made by Anna in 1836, featuring crochet work at the bottom similar to the crochet border on her 1837 towel.

Anna was born near Frederick County, Maryland. Her family came to Ohio in 1828 at the urging of relatives who were already settled there. An excerpt from a letter to Anna's family is indeed persuasive:

> *October 29, 1827—Dear Friends and all Relations: You must not think that you are going to the back woods if you every start to come hear . . . not to the Back woods, but only to the garden of Paradise, and you will not meet neither wolfs nor Indians. David Shank, Sir, I think if you ever leave that place, you should come out hear, all of you, as you are there. It is always land for sale hear, and to rent, and such land you never seen in this world . . . so rich, and "levil," and settled as thick as in Maryland, and as many fruits of every kind as in them mountains, and a plenty of girls out hear, too!*
>
> *Now I must tell you the truth . . . I seen more pleasure since I am out hear than I ever seen in Maryland . . . and I will tell you why. . . . Because the people are more sociable than in Maryland and particular, young people . . . and chiefly all "Duch" people.*

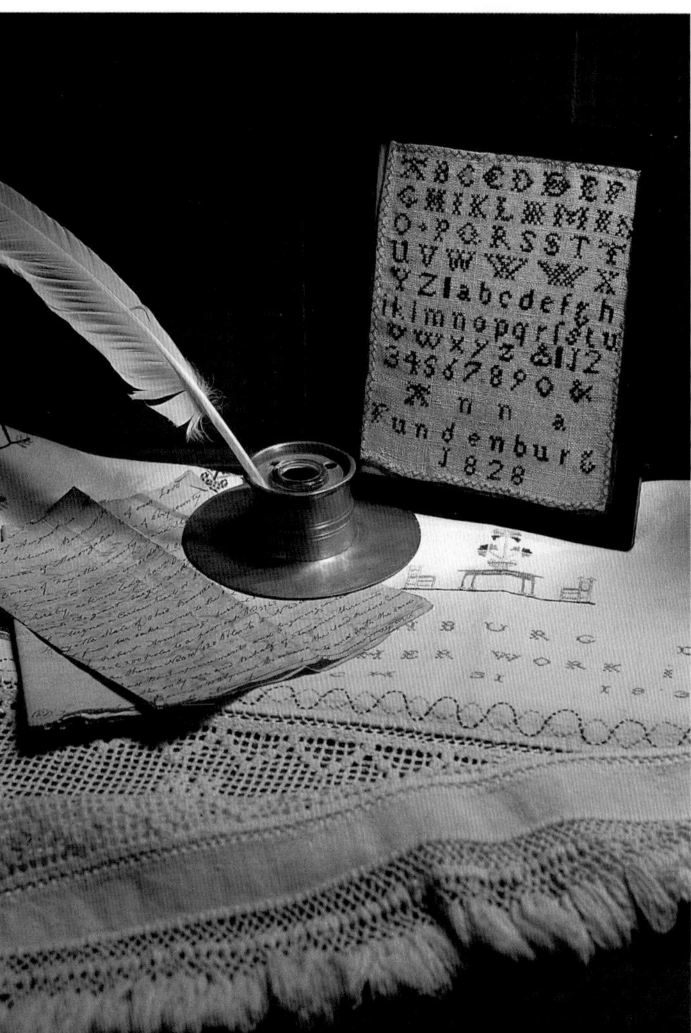

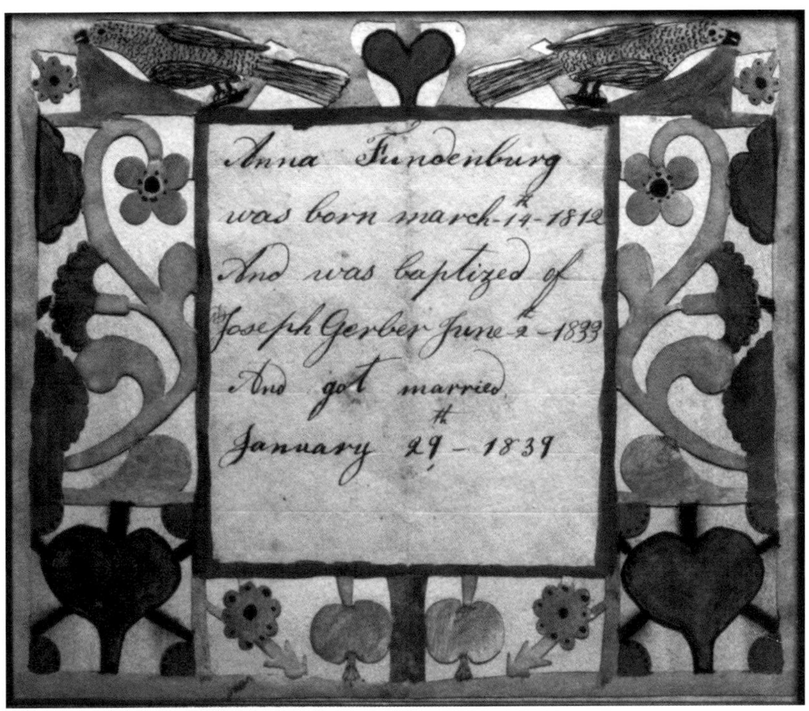
Anna Fundenburg
was born march 14th 1812
And was baptized of
Joseph Gerber June 2 1833
And got married
January 29 1839

Fig. 65: Fundenburg Fraktur.
Size: 6" x 7" W. Collection of the author.

Ohio frakturs are a rarity. This one features a *schrenschnitte* (scissor cut) border of stylized flowers, birds, and hearts on hand-tinted paper. It reads: "Anna Fundenburg was born march 14th—1812 and was baptized of Joseph Gerber June 2—1833 and got married January 29—1839."

Anna married Joseph H. Huffer, was an active member of the Lower Miami Church of the Brethren (Dunkard), and died at age seventy-five in 1887. She is buried in the church cemetery, very near the home whose likeness she had carefully stitched onto her hand towel years before.

The Village of Centerville

Two samplers from Centerville, in Washington Township, have been discovered and they look nothing alike. Centerville and Dayton, just ten miles apart, were both founded in 1796, but Centerville was still a tiny town by mid-nineteenth century, while Dayton, situated at the confluence of the three large rivers, had grown to well over ten thousand people by 1840. With the building of the Miami and Erie Canal, which became operational between Cincinnati and Dayton in April, 1830, travelers no longer needed to come over land through Centerville, and the sleepy little town was forgotten.[51]

Anna Mary McCracken (fig. 66) and Philena Doolittle (fig. 67) were most likely friends—their homes were only a block apart in tiny "Centreville"—but they must have had different needlework teachers. Research has not yielded the name of either girl's instructress, nor the name of any female academy located in the town. (The early spelling of the village name was changed in 1879.)

Fig. 66: Sampler of Anna Mary McCracken. 1840. »
Size: 17¼" L x 16¾" W. Collection of Centerville-Washington Township Historical Society.

Anna Mary McCracken was born in Pennsylvania in 1827 and came with her parents to Centerville in the 1830s. The verse on her sampler is perhaps the most popular one found on American samplers, but the scene that Anna Mary stitched is not a common one. The naïveté of the design makes this needlework very appealing. Appropriately centered on the canvas is an important house, situated on a sloping grass-covered hill. The first thing that draws our eye, though, is the perspective view Anna stitched of the fanciful walkway. She filled it with flowers, a large butterfly, birds, and animals.

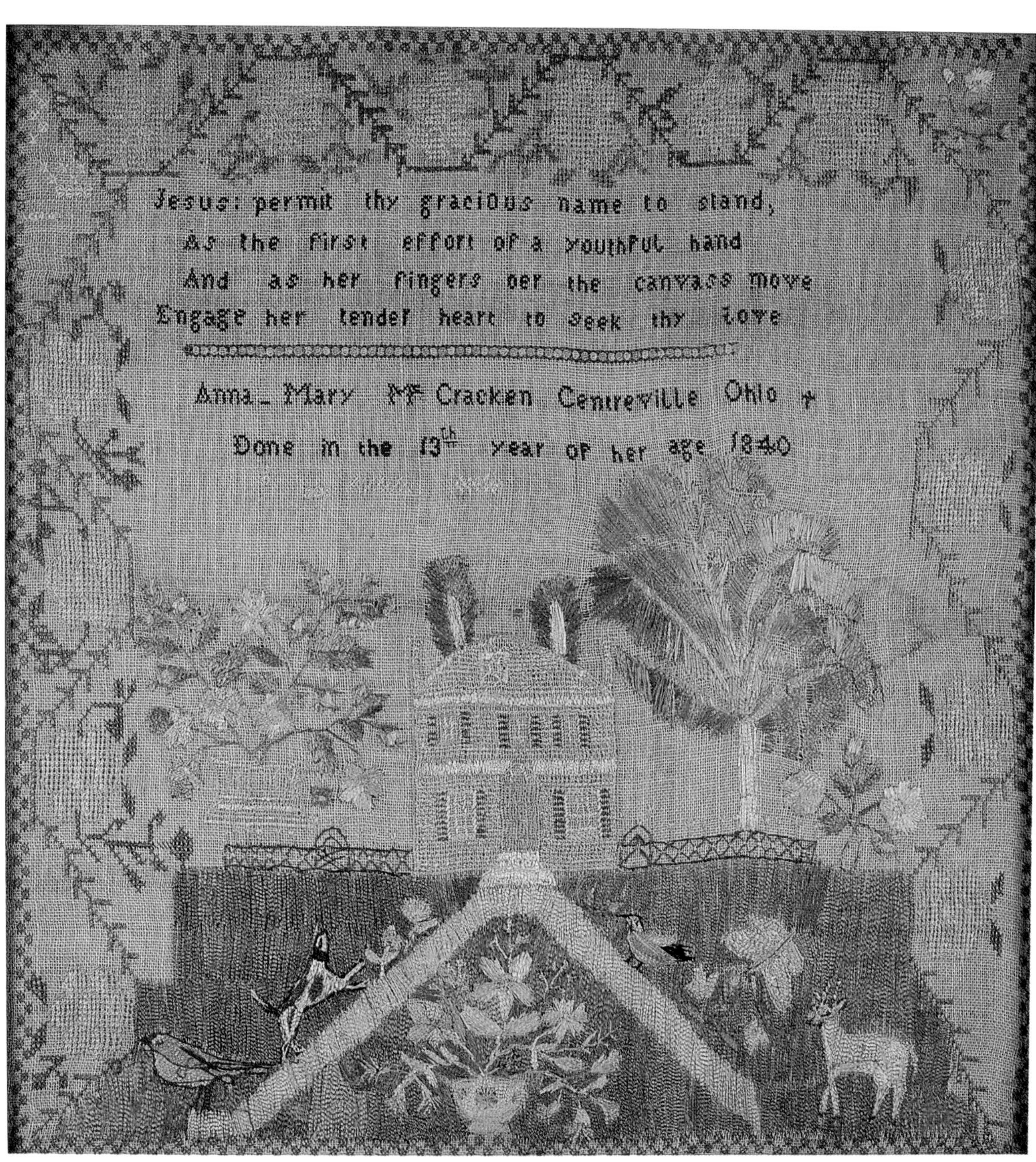
Jesus: permit thy gracious name to stand,
As the first effort of a youthful hand
And as her fingers oer the canvass move
Engage her tender heart to seek thy love
Anna_ Mary McCracken Centreville Ohio +
Done in the 13th year of her age 1840

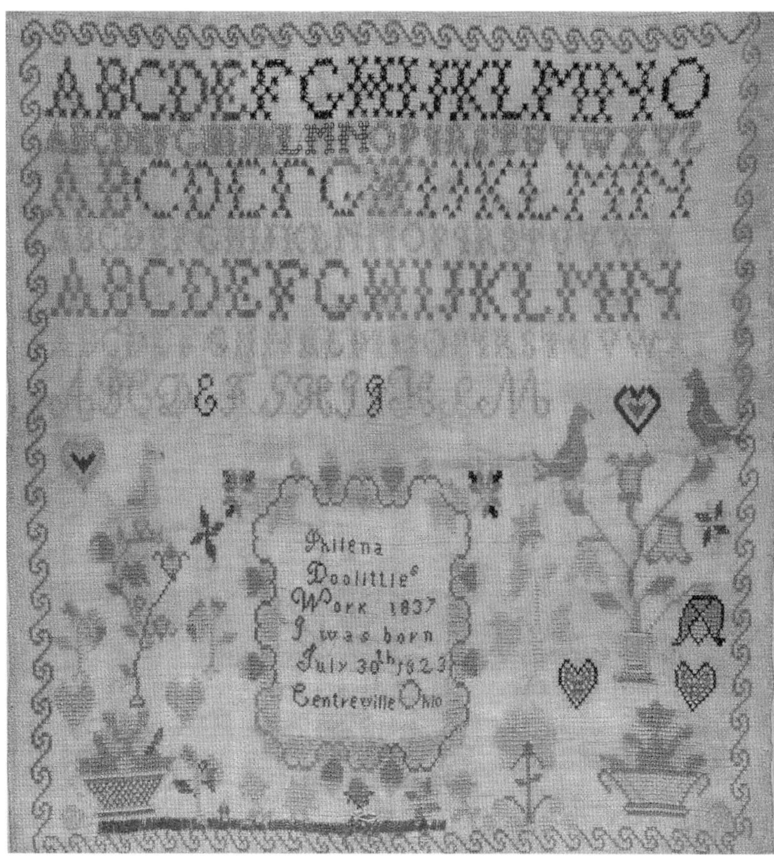

Fig. 67: Sampler of Philena Doolittle. 1837.
Size: 18" L x 16½" W.
Collection of M. Rolander.

Philena Doolittle's sampler is neatly stitched, but she had a difficult time planning the spaces for her alphabet. The lower half of the canvas was abundantly filled as Philena scattered several decorative designs around the reserve area in the center. Her sampler says: "Philena / Doolittles / work 1837 / I was born July 30th 1823 / Centreville Ohio." A "wave" border surrounds the canvas. Curiously, this sampler was discovered in England.

Philena was the daughter of Enos Doolittle, a Yankee peddler who came to Centerville in 1820. He married Bathsheba Robbins, the daughter of Benjamin Robbins, one of the founders of the village. Enos ran the once-famous Doolittle Tavern, reportedly one of the finest taverns west of the Alleghenies.

Fig. 68: Photograph of Doolittle Tavern.
Collection of Centerville Historical Society.

Doolittle Tavern, built in 1832, was a social center for the town's activities. It featured a large dining room that was sometimes used as a ballroom. Family quarters, where Philena Doolittle likely stitched her sampler (fig. 67), were also in the building. After his wife's death, Enos Doolittle sold the tavern and left Centerville. The large old stone building was torn down to make way for a new Washington Township Hall.[52]

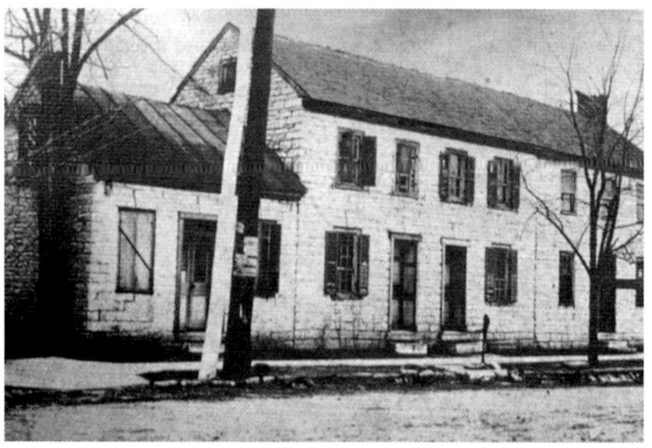

Clinton County

The whole of what was to become Clinton County lay within the designated Virginia Military Reservation, so many Virginians who had served in the Revolution came to the area to claim bounty lands due them for their service. Not until February 19, 1810, however, did the General Assembly of the State of Ohio formally vote that lands "be taken in about equal parts from the (neighboring) counties of Warren and Highland" to form this new county.[53]

Education of the children was one of the first priorities of the area's new settlers. Robert Way, a native of York County, Pennsylvania, arrived in Ohio early in the nineteenth century, and in 1813 he established the Dutch Creek Schoolhouse in Union Township. By the autumn of 1822, he had moved on, and his advertisements in Lebanon's *Western Star* were soliciting for his Springborough Boarding School in neighboring Warren County.[54]

The Society of Friends began streaming into the Ohio Lands from the South to settle Warren County even before 1800, and large numbers of those Quakers soon took up lands in the section that eventually became Clinton County. Breaking from the large Miami Monthly Meeting, the Center Monthly Meeting was formally organized by 1807. It was located just three miles from the county seat of Wilmington.[55]Some of the most beautiful samplers produced in Ohio came from young Quaker girls in that congregation.

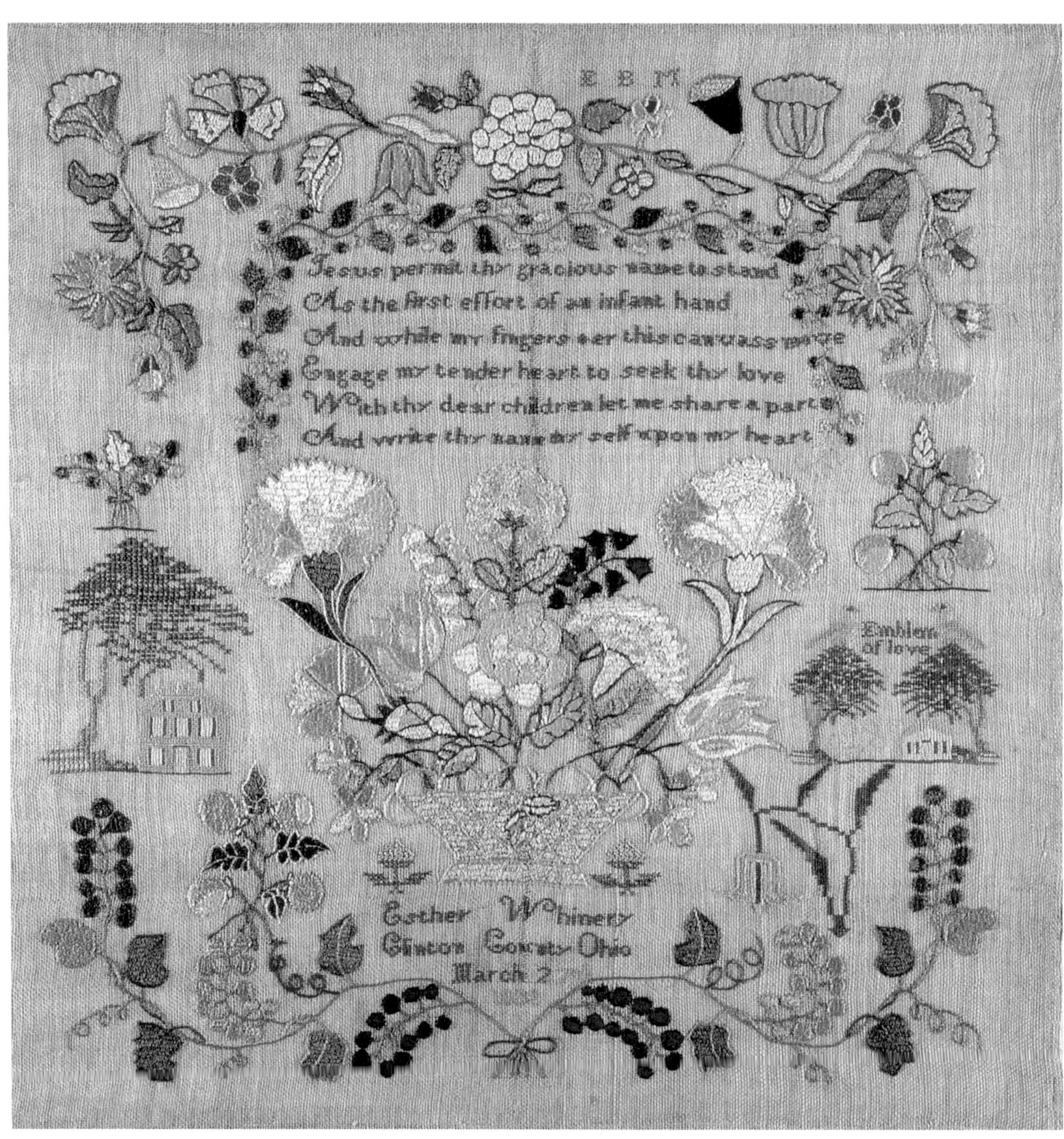
E E M
Jesus permit thy gracious name to stand
As the first effort of an infant hand
And while my fingers oer this canvass move
Engage my tender heart to seek thy love
With thy dear children let me share a part
And write thy name thy self upon my heart
Emblem of love
Esther Whimery
Clinton County Ohio
March 2

« Fig. 69: Sampler of Esther Whinery. 1838.
Size: 17" L x 17" W. © The Cleveland Museum of Art, 2001, Gift of Louise M. Dunn TR11517/51.

Several members of the large Whinery Family came from York County, Pennsylvania, to Liberty Township, Clinton County, in 1813, just three years after the county was formed. Not until 1832, however, did Thomas and Lydia (Perkins) Whinery arrive in southern Ohio to join the Center Monthly Meeting of the Friends' Society. Their daughter, Esther, stitched this colorful needlework and included her teacher's initials at the top of the canvas: "E. B. M." Though no positive proof has been discovered, there is a good chance that these initials stand for Elizabeth Mendenhall, whose sampler is shown in fig. 70.

Esther's sampler features a virtual garden of flowers that includes carnations, tulips, bell flowers, daisies, and roses. The clusters of grapes and the ivy leaves and vine that surround the verse are seen on several of the samplers produced by Clinton County girls who were members of the Center Monthly Meeting. The small buildings with overhanging trees are also typical designs found on their canvases. Even though the samplers vary in the colors used, and each sampler is unique, the stitching techniques indicate that the same instructress must have tutored these girls. The larger designs, like the carnation flowers and the basket, are executed in an encroaching satin stitch. Other stitches used are satin, tent, stem, and cross.[56]

By the 1840s Esther is recorded as being a teacher at the "old brick schoolhouse" in nearby Chester Township. We have no list of what was taught, but with her considerable skill with the needle, she may well have been teaching young ladies to work samplers.

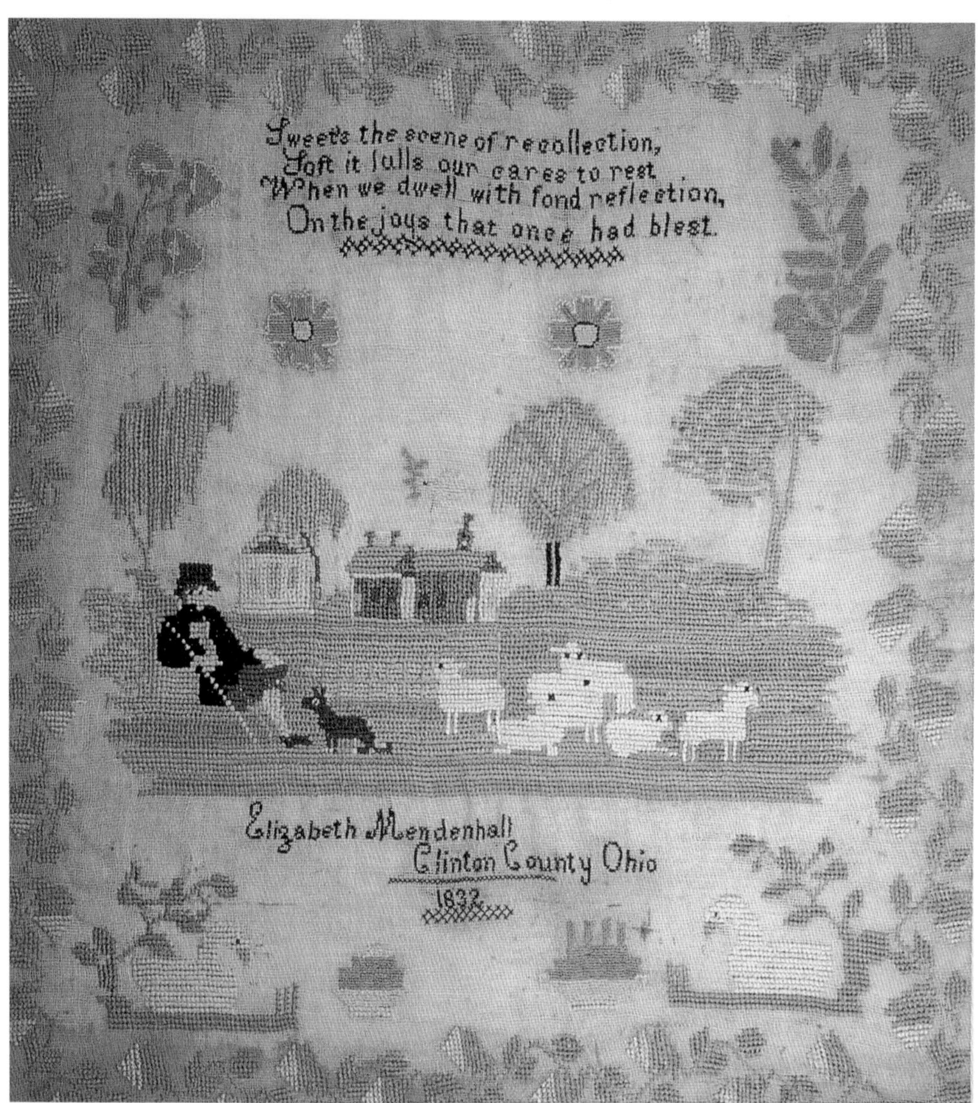

Fig. 70: Sampler of Elizabeth Mendenhall. 1832.
Size: 16" L x 16½" W. Collection of Randolph County Historical Society, Winchester, Indiana.

The center scene on Elizabeth Mendenhall's sampler shows a shepherd resting from his work with a staff in hand and his dog attentively waiting at his feet. Nearby sheep graze on the lawn. The two swans with the over-hanging branch are seen on almost every Quaker sampler discovered in the southern and southwestern parts of the state.

Elizabeth Mendenhall was twenty-five years old when she stitched this elaborate sampler in 1832. It may have served as an example for her students to see, since three other samplers from the area exhibit the same scene in the center of the canvas. Elizabeth was of an appropriate age to teach, and she was an accomplished needlewoman. Born in 1806 to Nathan and Ann (Harlan) Mendenhall, she remained unmarried and living in Ohio until she was forty-three years old. She married Walter Ruble in Randolph County, Indiana, in 1857, and spent the rest of her life in that state.

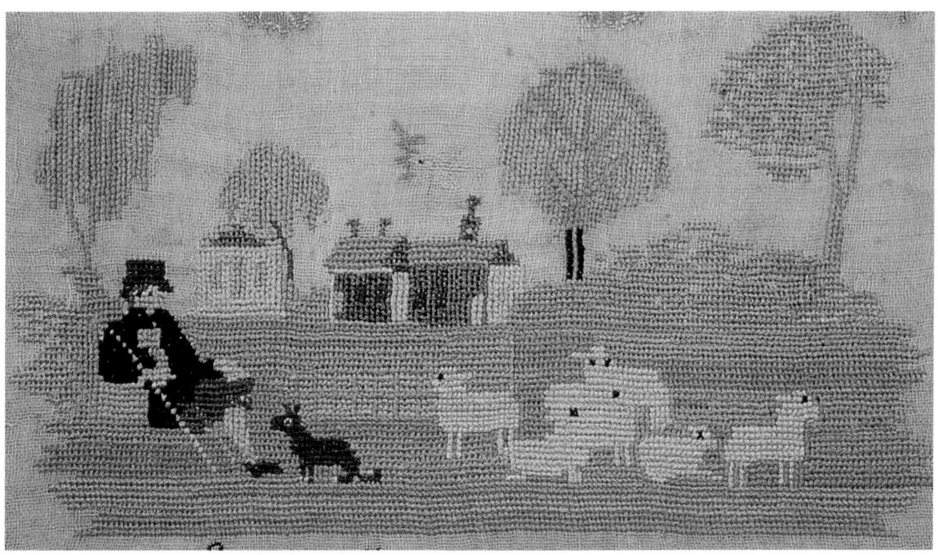

FIG. 71: DETAIL OF MENDENHALL SAMPLER.

A popular print of the day may have served as the inspiration for this pastoral scene. It has been found on four Wilmington samplers.

FIG. 72: SAMPLER OF PHEBE DOAN. 1834.
SIZE: 16¾" L x 16¼" W.
COLLECTION OF KELLY GEER AUSTIN

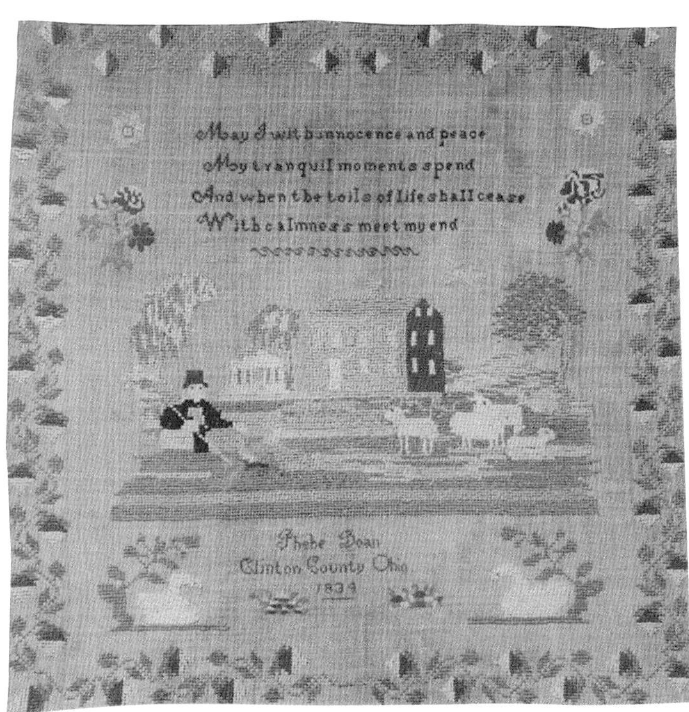

Phebe Doan was thirteen years old when she completed this sampler. Her teacher, probably Elizabeth Mendenhall (see fig. 70), designed a sampler very much like her own, but Phebe's flock of sheep has dwindled to just four, instead of the seven that Mendenhall stitched on her own canvas. The sampler is marked "Clinton County, Ohio," where she was a member of the Center Monthly Meeting, as was Miss Mendenhall. The canvas includes a large building with one shaded side, a design element not seen on the other Clinton County samplers.

Phebe was born May 6, 1821, to Joseph and Elizabeth (Carpenter) Doan. In 1839 she married Alfred Timberlake, and the couple had eleven children. She died in 1901 in her eightieth year and is interred near Richmond, Indiana.

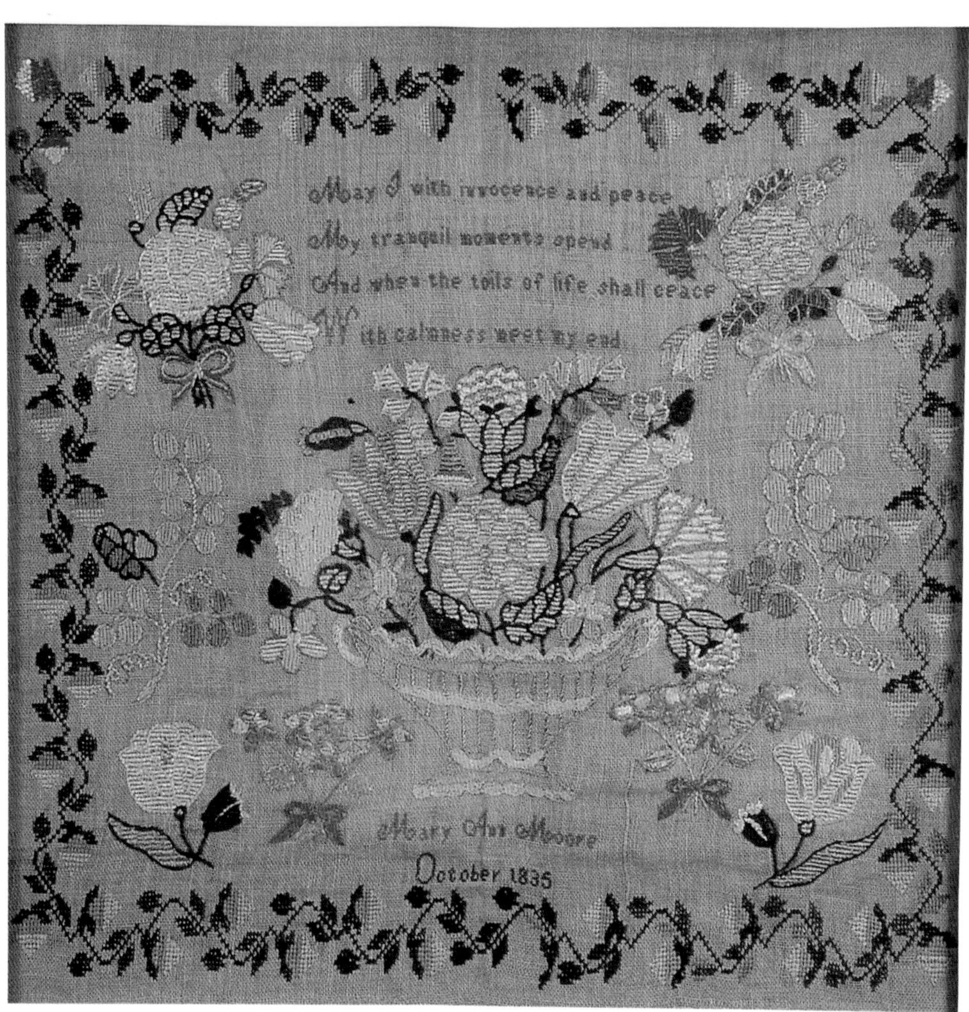

Fig. 73: Sampler of Mary Ann Moore. 1835.

Size: 16½" L x 16½" W. Collection of Susan Hazard Douglass and Rebecca Hazard Rauch.

Another Wilmington sampler that exhibits a relationship to that of Esther Whinery (fig. 69) is the needlework of Mary Ann Moore. Mary Ann produced not one, but two beautiful samplers, an unusual accomplishment for a young girl. This sampler has a border that is the same as the leaf-and-vine motif that surrounds the verse on the Whinery sampler. Several other motifs have also been duplicated.

Mary Ann Moore was the first of eight children born to Haines and Elizabeth (Antrim) Moore. Her father came to Clinton County, from Pennsylvania, c. 1813, and his marriage to Elizabeth Antrim caused her to be disowned in 1822 by the Society of Friends for marrying "out of unity." Haines was an energetic and talented cabinetmaker and farmer, and he operated a successful cabinetmaking shop on Main Street in Wilmington for many years.[57]

Mary Ann married Lewis M. Walker, also a native of Clinton County, and she spent her entire life there. She died in 1864 and is buried in the Haines Moore Family lot in Wilmington's picturesque old Sugar Grove Cemetery.

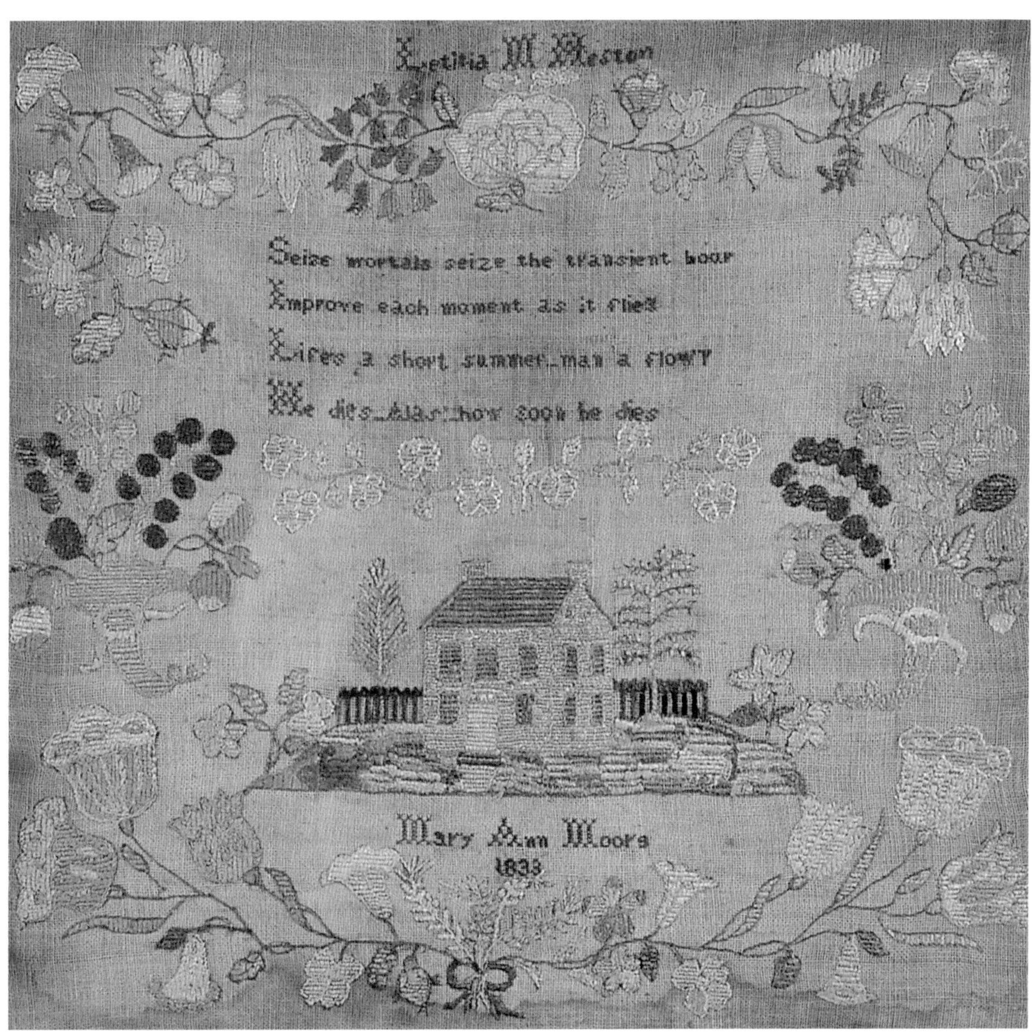

Fig. 74: Sampler of Mary Ann Moore. 1833.
Size: 17" L x 18" W. Collection of Susan Hazard Douglass
and Rebecca Hazard Rauch.

The first sampler that Mary Ann Moore produced was finished in 1833, under the guidance of Letitia M. Heston. A member of the Society of Friends, Letitia Heston came to Ohio from Baltimore, where she had been a teacher before coming west.[58] Even though this sampler was done in more muted shades, the flowers, grapes, and overall design match well with the samplers still being produced several years later by Wilmington girls. The carefully stitched house, with a picket fence, is situated on a little hillock, and the whole composition is well planned and executed.

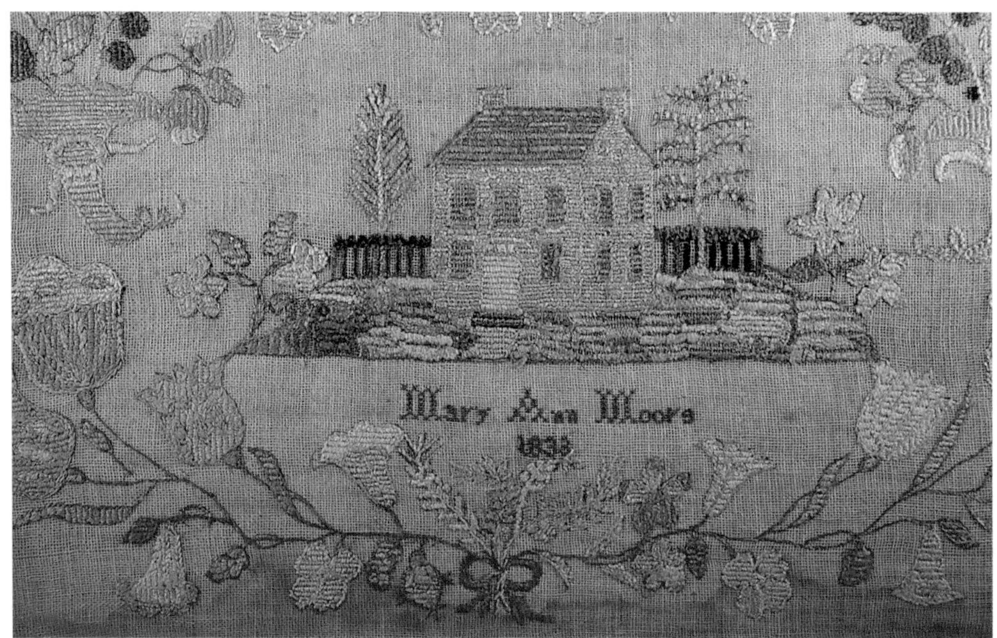

Fig. 75: Detail of Mary Ann Moore Sampler. 1833.

Although it is difficult to tell what kind of animals Mary Ann stitched in the yard, the large flowers that surround the pretty house are realistic and attest to her needlework skills. She was eleven years old when this sampler was completed.

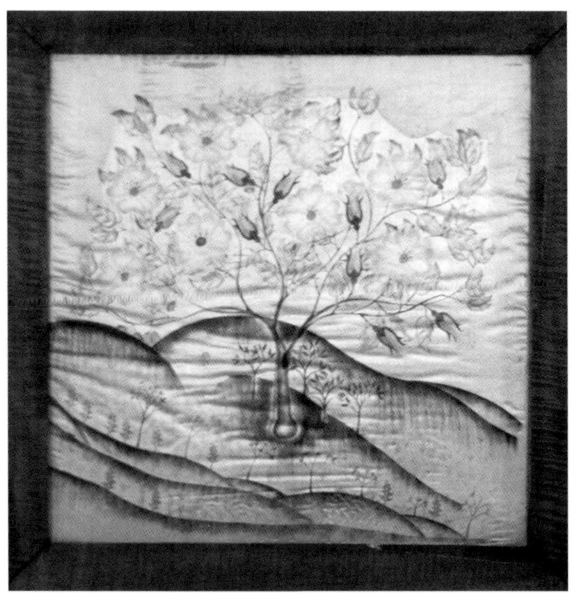

Fig. 76: Painted Silk Picture.

Size: 17¾" L x 17¾" W. Collection of Susan Hazard Douglass and Rebecca Hazard Rauch.

Accompanying the two samplers, and still with Mary Ann Moore's descendants, is a curious picture painted on a silk ground. Though it is unsigned, it, too, was most likely done by Mary Ann. All three pieces have the same original tiger maple frames.

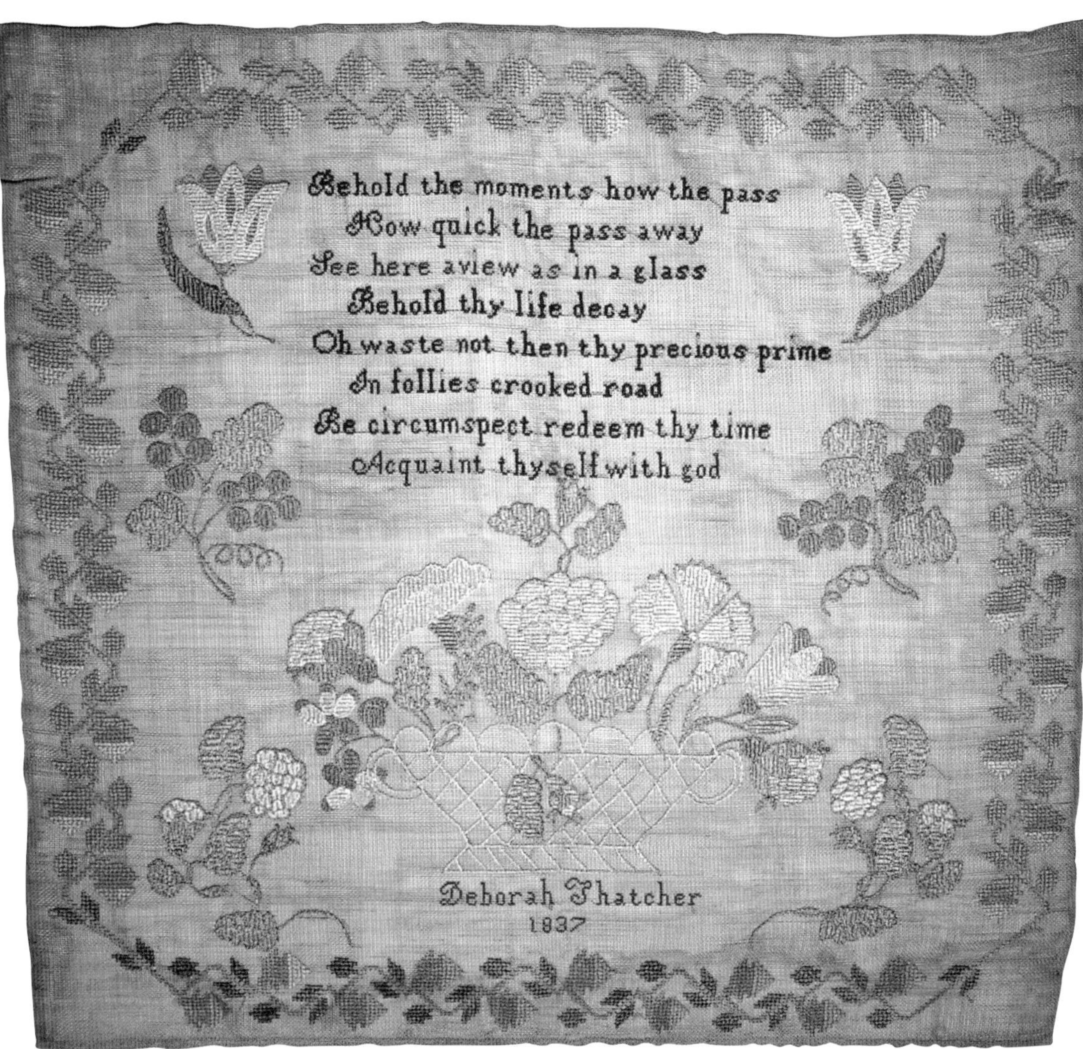

Fig. 77: Sampler of Deborah Thatcher. 1837.
Size: 17" L x 17½" W. Collection of Janet E. Hiatt,
great-great-granddaughter of stitcher.

Deborah Thatcher's sampler is clearly related in style and stitching technique to the samplers produced by members of the Center Monthly Meeting of the Society of Friends. Undoubtedly the same needlework teacher tutored Esther Whinery (fig. 69) and Deborah Thatcher. Both students produced beautiful needlework. The Bible records for this family tell us that Deborah (Hadley) Thatcher was born on April 14, 1817, which would have made her twenty years old when the sampler was stitched. She married Joseph Thatcher just after her seventeenth birthday, on May 15, 1834. This sampler is the only one we have discovered that was stitched by a young lady after her marriage. By the time this sampler was completed, Deborah already had two babies. Somehow she made the time to do ornamental stitching.

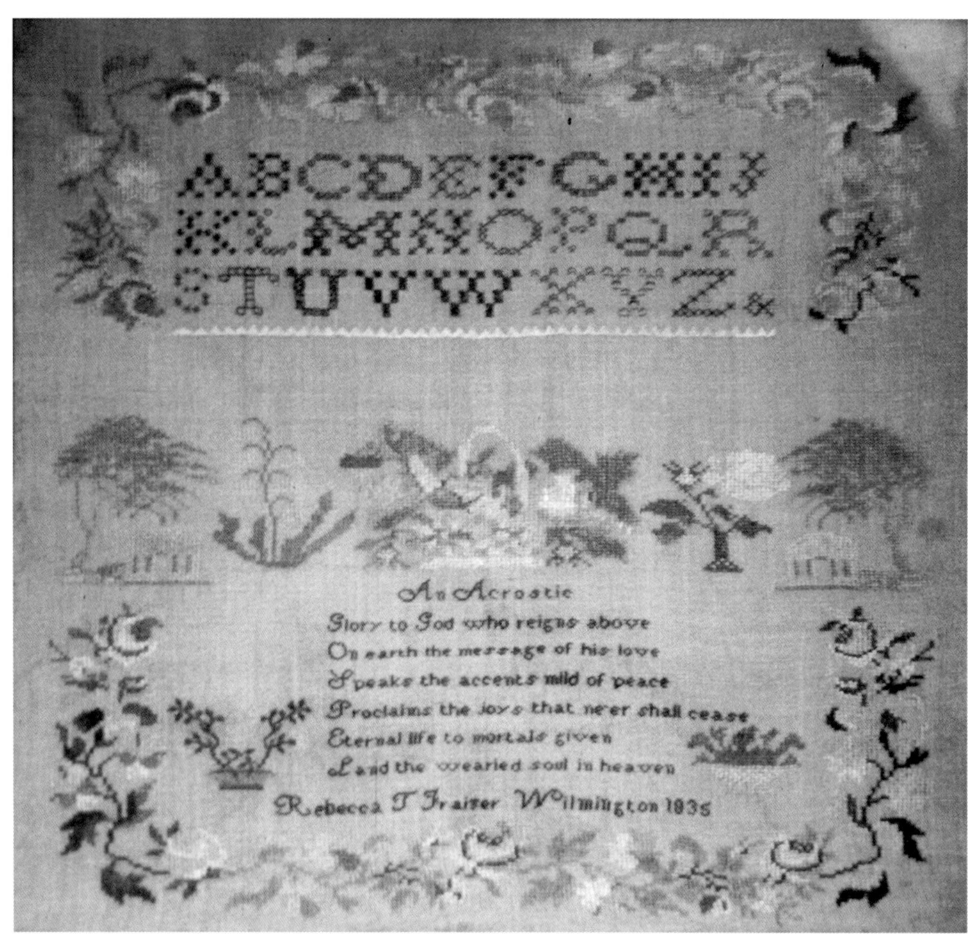

Figure 78: Sampler of Rebecca T. Frazier. 1835.
Size: 20" L x 20" W. Anonymous collector.

Rebecca T. Frazier's sampler, inscribed "Wilmington," was completed in her fourteenth year. Her family came to Ohio from the South about 1810, in the vanguard of the great Quaker migration.[59] A devout Quaker, she spelled the word *gospel* in block letters as she stitched a verse, line by line, down the canvas. In addition to this sampler, her practice sampler, some of her quilts, and a stuffed whitework dresser scarf or "splasher" that she stitched survive.

Rebecca was born to Jonah and Mary (Hadley) Frazier, their only child to survive infancy. In 1842 she married Jonathan Bailey and began to raise a family. Jonathan, a public-spirited man, involved himself in many religious and educational causes, and Rebecca shared her husband's enthusiasm and excitement in his ventures. They eventually moved to Whittier, California, where they were the very first settlers. The Bailey House Museum there contains a replica of her sampler and other memorabilia belonging to Rebecca. She died in Whittier on April 17, 1898.[60]

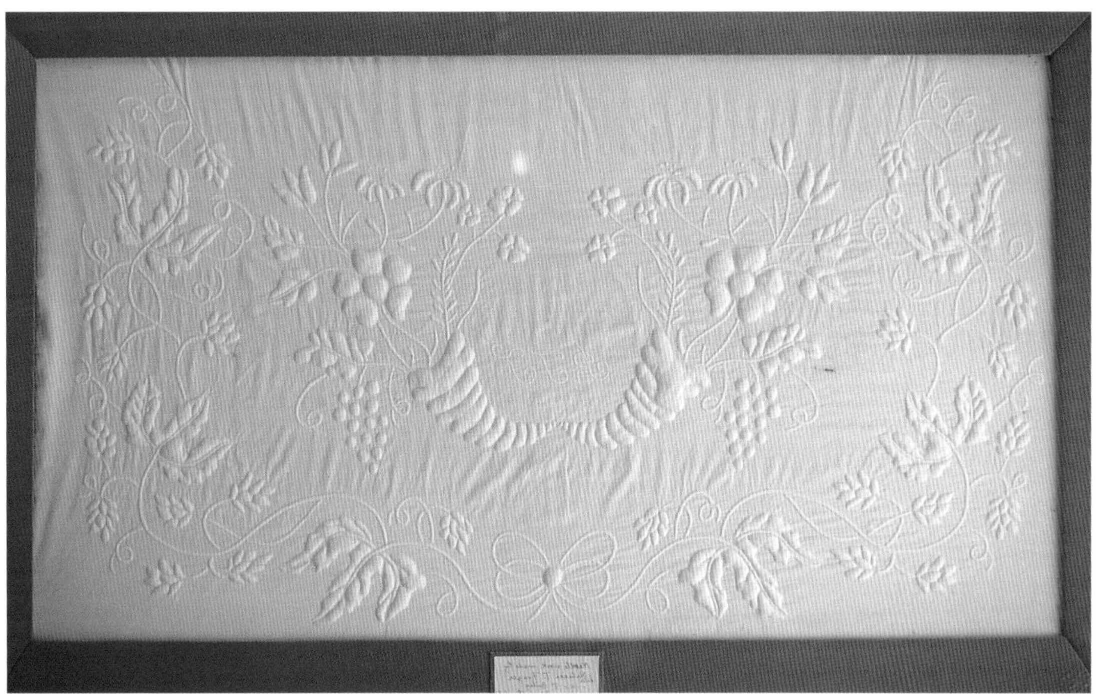

Fig. 79: Stuffed Whitework Dresser Scarf of Rebecca T. Frazier.
Size: 42" L x 23" W. Stuffed and quilted cotton. Collection of Margaret C. Smith.

This stuffed-whitework dresser scarf (toilette cover) is plainly marked with Rebecca's initials. When this was shown by Rebecca's descendants to an elderly relative, she said that she remembered her grandmother talking about the embroidered "splasher," a colloquial expression. This piece was hung on the wall behind the bed-chamber washstand to protect the wall, according to the relative. It looks very much like the one produced by the Quaker teacher Letitia M. Heston.

The terms "Marseilles," "whitework," and "stuffed work" all refer to the technique of quilting that Rebecca Frazier executed. In the early eighteenth century, Marseilles quilting was entirely handmade, but by 1760 machine-made Marseilles (loom or "mock") quilted products were widely imported to America from Europe. Both handmade and loom Marseilles quilted clothing and household linen items were popular until about the 1830s.[61] Rebecca's work was hand-stitched and demonstrates that she had excellent needlework skills. She complemented the stuffed-work elements of the splasher, with delicate white embroidery.[62]

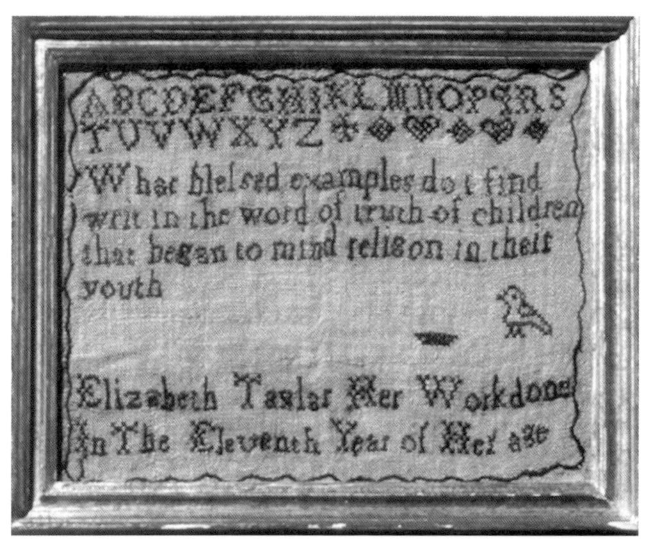
ABCDEFGHIKLMNOPQRS
TUVWXYZ
What blelsed examples do i find
writ in the word of truth of children
that began to mind relison in their
youth
Elizabeth Taslar Her Workdone
In The Eleventh Year of Her age

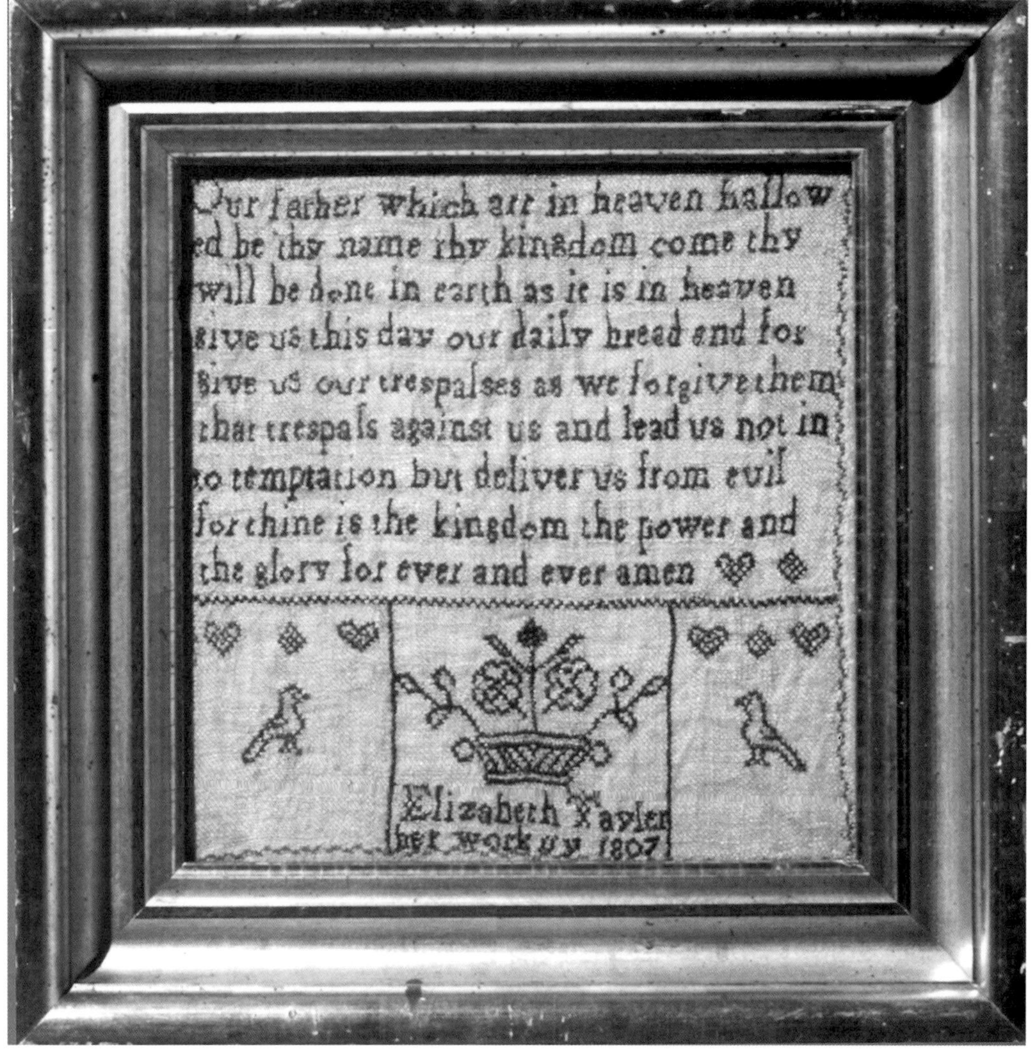
Our father which art in heaven hallow
ed be thy name thy kingdom come thy
will be done in earth as it is in heaven
give us this day our daily bread and for
give us our trespalses as we forgive them
that trespals against us and lead us not in
to temptation but deliver us from evil
for thine is the kingdom the power and
the glory for ever and ever amen
Elizabeth Tayler
her work ... 1807

« Figs. 80 and 81: Samplers of Elizabeth Taylor. 1807.
Sizes: 9½" L x 7½" W; 10½" L x 10½" W.
Collection of Delores and Lowell Klaber.

Elizabeth Taylor's two samplers were finished when she was eleven years old. Executed in blue silk thread, they are simple in design. The plainness of her work is somewhat puzzling because Elizabeth was a member of the Center Monthly Meeting of the Society of Friends. As the decades passed and teachers changed, samplers executed by girls from that congregation were very colorful and displayed a myriad of designs and stitches.

Elizabeth came to eastern Warren County with her parents, Jacob and Hannah Taylor, in 1806. Wilmington's Center Monthly Meeting church records reveal that Elizabeth married Joel Wright on June 15, 1815. A third sampler of Elizabeth Taylor, made in 1810, accompanies these two.

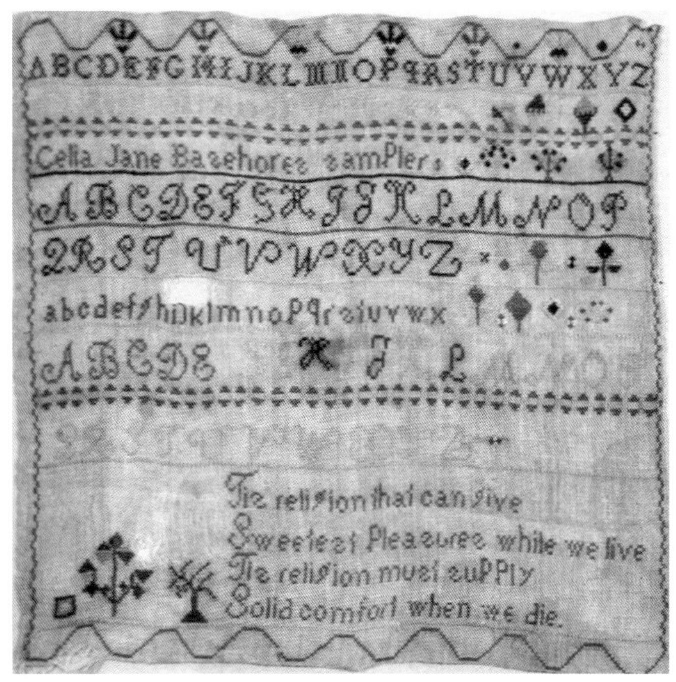

Fig. 82: Sampler of Celia Jane Bashore. c. 1835.
Size: 16½" L x 17½" W.
Collection of Karen Buckley.

This sampler was produced at New Antioch in Green Township. The township was organized as early as 1807, while it was still a part of Highland County. Executed by Celia Jane Bashore, the needlework was completed about 1835. Celia Jane's pioneer family had come to New Antioch about 1800, and they were among the founding settlers of this small community.

Celia Jane was born in 1825, the child of Barnett and Mary (Harvey) Bashore. She died when she was thirteen years old. Her older sister Susannah kept the sampler until her death many years later, and the needlework remains in the family today. A treasured memento of Celia Jane's short life, it reads: "Tis religion that can give / Sweetest pleasures while we live / Tis religion must supply / Solid comfort when we die."

Butler County

Butler County, formed in 1803, was named to honor the distinguished Revolutionary War officer General Richard Butler. In 1791 the important outpost of Fort Hamilton was erected, and today this is the site of Hamilton, Butler County's largest city. Once the Indian Wars were over and the area was safely opened to white settlers, the Great Miami River offered a "roadway" for those who wanted to acquire some of the black, rich bottomlands that lay on either side. So productive was that land that it soon became known as the "Garden of Ohio," famous for its immense crops of corn, grains, and vegetables.[63]

Early settlers lost no time in establishing schools for their children. In 1819, the first woman to establish a subscription school in Hamilton was Miss Ellen A. McMechan, the daughter of the Presbyterian minister Rev. James McMechan. The school opened at the northeast corner of Third and Buckeye Streets. She was said to be a woman of unusual accomplishments for her time and had the patronage of many prominent families in Hamilton. About seventy students attended the school, where Ellen taught for eight years. After leaving the profession, she married the Honorable Charles R. Smith.[64]

About the time that Ellen McMechan's school opened in Hamilton (see figure 83 caption, facing page), the Select School of Rev. Thomas E. Thomas was established at Paddy's Run, or "New London." Close to the Indiana border and founded mostly by Welsh settlers, the village is today called Shandon. Rev. Thomas's story is one of importance, for he devoted his life to preaching and teaching in various towns in southern Ohio.

The son of a Presbyterian minister, Rev. Thomas E. Thomas immigrated to America with his parents and siblings in 1818. Both he and his wife taught in the village of New London from 1820 to 1827. Their school attracted boarding students from as far away as Dayton. Rev. Thomas instructed the older students in advanced academic subjects, while Mrs. Thomas trained the girls in plain and ornamental sewing. The school was a large two-story building of hewn logs.[65] The interior partitions suggest that it may have been built specifically as a schoolhouse. An earlier log schoolhouse was built in 1807 at Paddy's Run by the members of the Congregational Church. Miss Polly Wiley taught some twenty-two students there for a period of one year.

(following page)

FIG. 83: SAMPLER OF MARGARET MCMECHAN. 1819.

SIZE: 16" L x 10" W. COLLECTION OF PREBLE COUNTY HISTORICAL SOCIETY.

The McMechans immigrated to America from Ireland. Margaret was born in Ireland in 1806, and her parents, David and Sara McMechan, brought their family to Collinsville, Ohio, sometime before 1815. Margaret married Samuel Baldridge Gilmore in 1828. Her daughter, Sarah Gilmore, also stitched a sampler that has been treasured by her family (see fig. 100). Completed in 1849, it clearly demonstrates how much needlework styles changed in the thirty years since her mother stitched this sampler. Margaret died September 5, 1881, and is buried at Fairhaven, Ohio.

This Ohio needlework is the only one we have discovered that has blocks of pattern darning on the canvas. Margaret McMechan executed this sampler when she was thirteen and marked the town of Hamilton near the bottom. A sewing exercise like this would have taken a great deal of time to complete. It is not known how she was related to Ellen McMechan, a teacher who established a school in Hamilton the year Margaret completed this sampler, but it is probable that she was Miss McMechan's pupil.

FIG. 84: DETAIL OF MCMECHAN DARNING SAMPLER.

Margaret McMechan would have kept this sampler to use as a reference tool when she needed to work on sewing chores. A young homemaker was expected to make garments for the family, hem and mark household linens, and mend and remake clothing that was passed down as children grew.

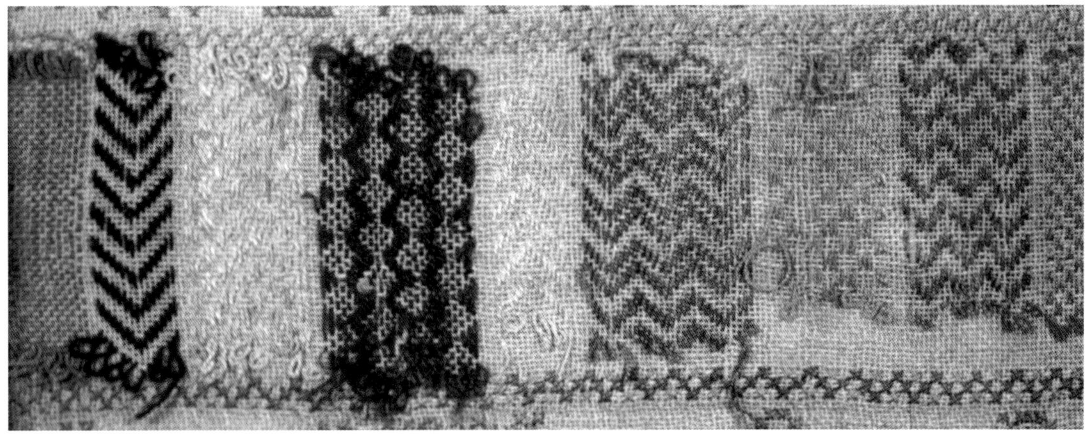

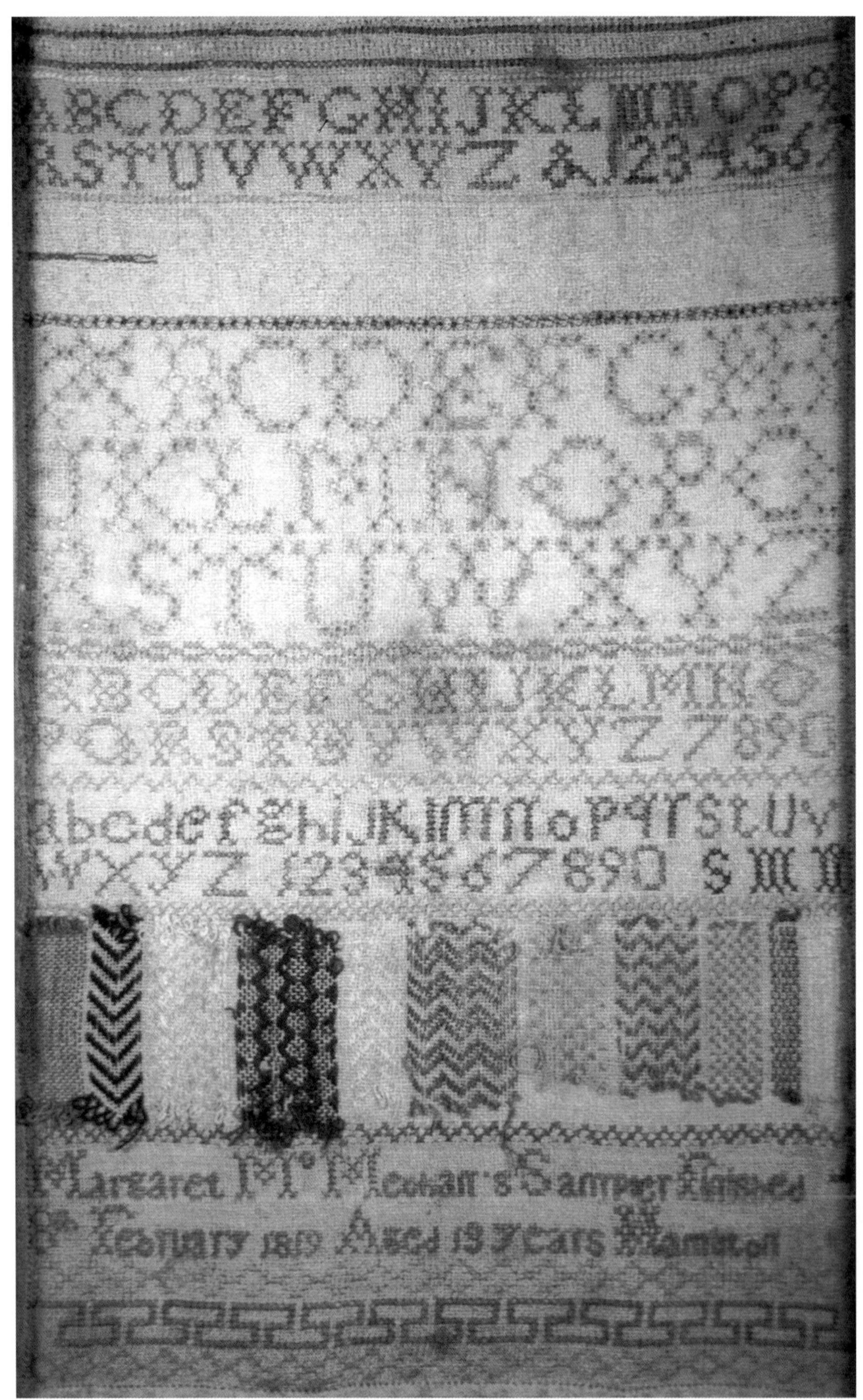

Fig. 83

The town of Oxford was well established when Miami University opened its doors in 1824. Seven years later Bethania Crocker began her well-known high school or "academy." Located in a brick house on Main Street, it had the support of the town's most illustrious citizens. Among those who endorsed her school in newspaper advertisements were Miami University president R. H. Bishop and professor William H. McGuffey, author of *The McGuffey Reader.* Both men demonstrated their support by sending their own daughters to Crocker's school.

Miss Crocker's fame spread, and the school flourished, attracting students from at least three states. On March 3, 1833, her *Western Star* advertisement gave an impressive list of academic subjects offered by the school. It noted that: "Instructions will be given in Needlework in connexion with any of the above branches, without additional charge. Board may be obtained in respectable families at $1.25 per week."[66]

Miss Crocker was apparently a marvelously mature young woman. Her father, Rev. Peter Crocker, a Congregationalist minister, his wife, and eighteen-year-old Bethania had migrated from Massachusetts to Indiana in 1830.[67] Bethania had been tutored by her father and further educated in New York City. She did not teach long at her academy, for in 1834 she became the wife of Rev. George Bishop, a son of the Miami University president. The school continued to prosper for many years under the direction of capable teachers like Abigail Clark and Jane, Lucy, and Anna North. It seems each young instructress would teach a short time and leave when she would find a suitable young man to marry. The school continued and was the nucleus for what was to become, in 1849, the Oxford Female Institute.[68]

Some puzzles are just not meant to be solved, it seems. This appears to be the case with the "Lemon Township Mystery Teacher." For more than a decade her identity has eluded researchers. Six exceptional samplers have been discovered (figs. 85, 88, 89, 91, 93, and 95) that are undeniably linked by overall design, common motifs, and stitching techniques. But who designed the canvases on which these young ladies stitched, and who was their instructress? Not one of the samplers gives even a small clue. Each sampler has a distinctive look, though they share certain elements. The most important tie is that the stitchers all lived in Lemon Township, Butler County. All completed their samplers between 1824 and 1840.

The largest nearby town was Middletown. No advertisements for a school or needlework teacher have been found in the local newspapers that help to identify this instructress. Unrelated, however, one historical account of the area notes: "Nathaniel Furman, assisted by his wife and Lucretia Williamson, opened his private academy/high school in Middletown in 1833."[69]

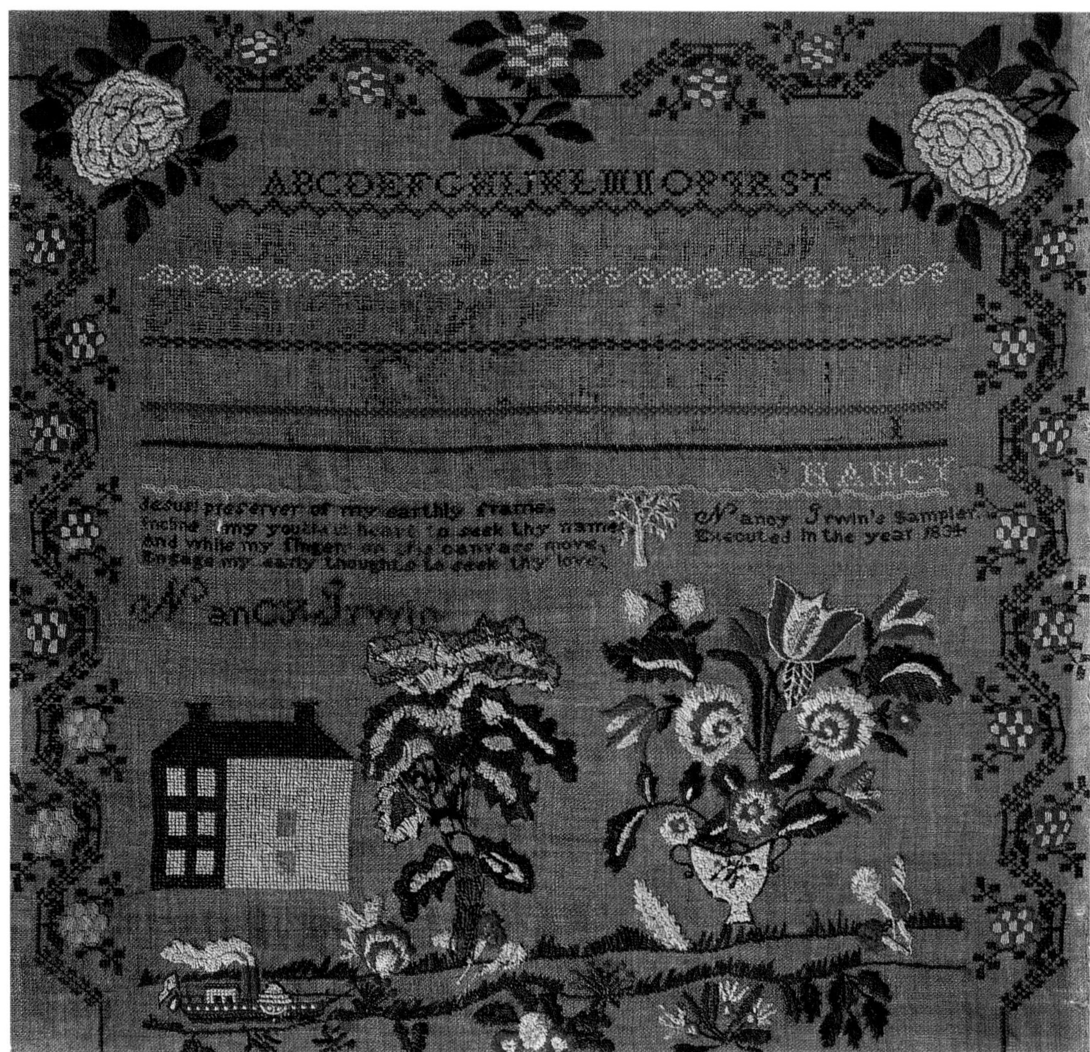

FIG. 85: SAMPLER OF NANCY IRWIN. 1834.

SIZE: 21" L X 22" W. COLLECTION OF WARREN COUNTY HISTORICAL SOCIETY.

One of the most attractive Ohio samplers documented is that of Nancy Irwin, completed when she was seventeen. Nancy was born June 2, 1817, the fourth child of Thomas Irwin and his second wife, Ann (Cunningham) Irwin. Thomas Irwin, one of Ohio's first settlers, arrived in Cincinnati sometime before 1793 and soon made his way to Lemon Township, Butler County. Records show that the family eventually included fourteen children.

Nancy's inclusion of the little steamboat, a motif seldom seen on samplers, makes this needlework especially appealing. Even though the threads of Nancy's alphabet have suffered deterioration, the sampler is still striking for its brilliant color, bold design, and variety of precise stitches. The identity of Nancy Irwin's needlework tutor is unknown, but similarities with five other samplers discovered suggest that the same Lemon Township, Butler County, teacher supervised their needlework lessons.

Nancy Irwin never married. She died on June 24, 1843, three weeks after her twenty-sixth birthday.

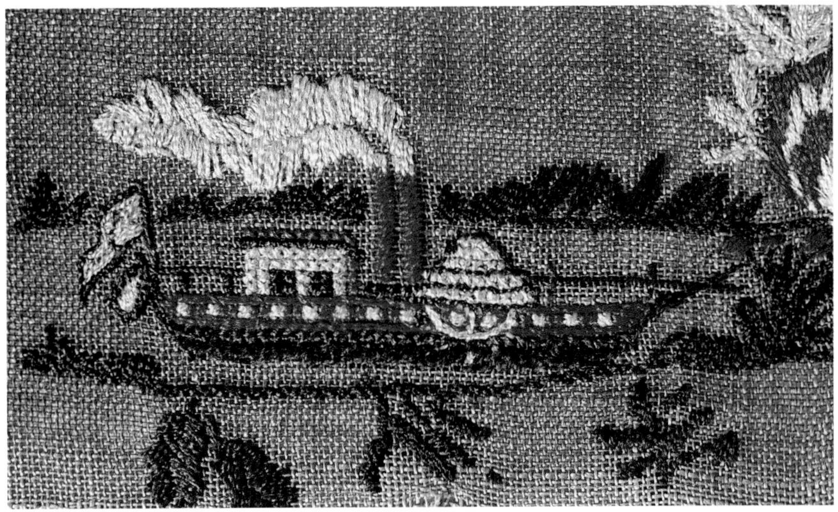

Fig. 86: Detail of Steamboat.

Two Lemon Township samplers featuring a steamboat have been discovered. Nancy Irwin did not live where she could see steamboats, but her teacher must have been familiar with them for this boat looks just like the ones that were plying up and down the Ohio River in the first half of the nineteenth century. The steamboat motif may well be unique to Ohio samplers. A third piece of needlework executed later in West Manchester on the Ohio River also exhibits this design (see figs. 224 and 225).

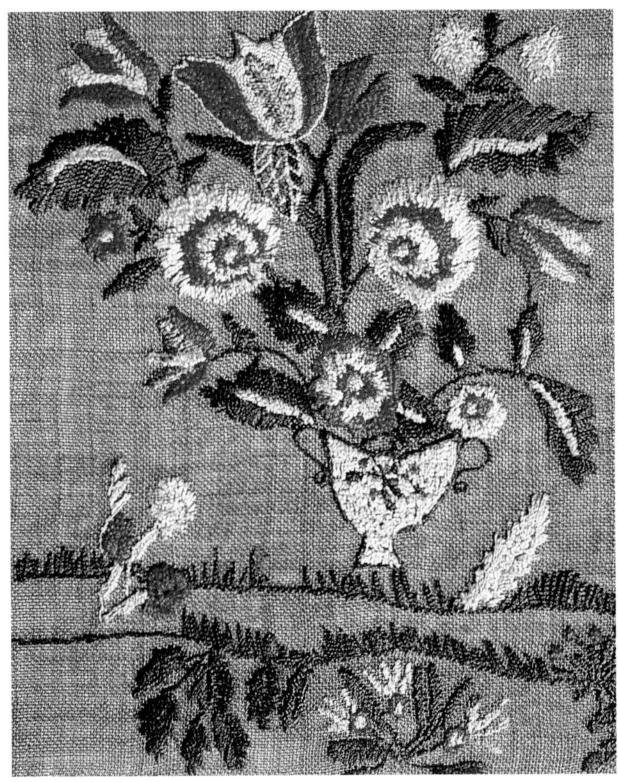

Fig. 87: Detail of Vase and Flowers.

This lopsided little vase filled with flowers is one of the motifs usually found on Lemon Township samplers. Notice that the vase is much too small to hold all those flowers. Our "mystery teacher" had a strange sense of scale and proportion when she drew the designs for the girls to stitch. The results have an appealing folk-art quality. What is small should be big, and what is big should be small.

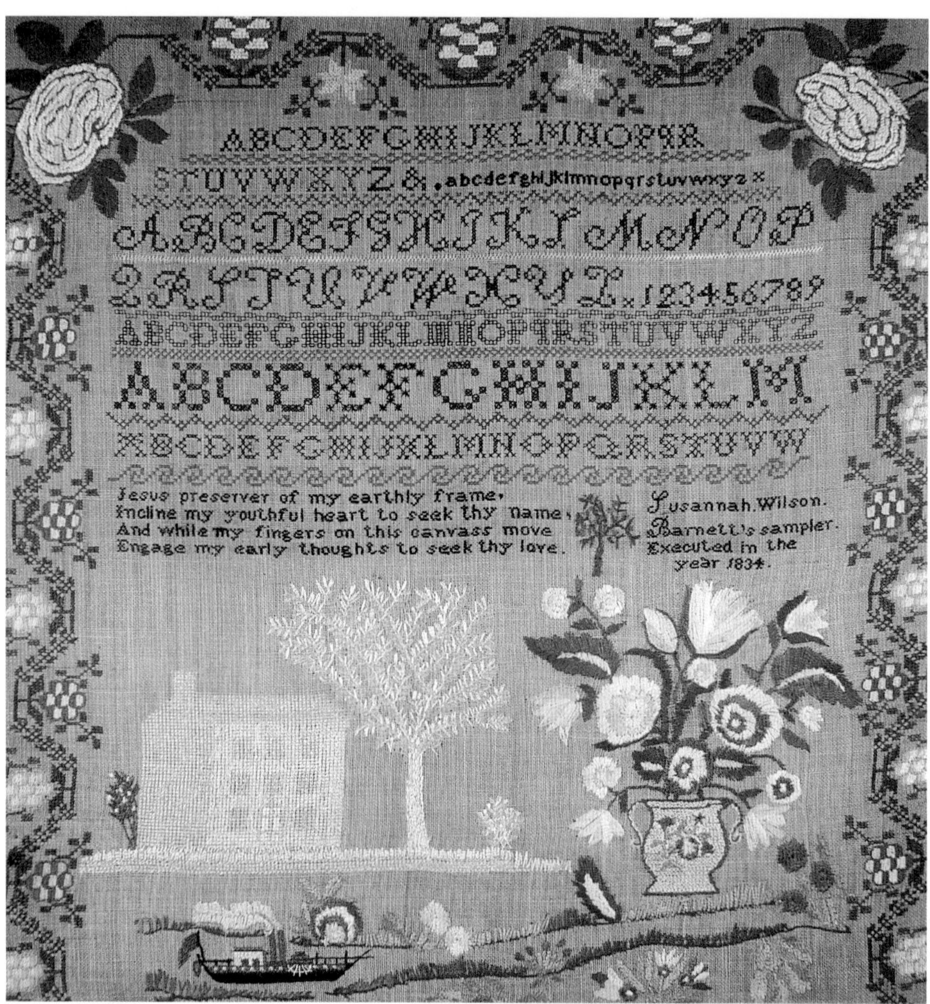

FIG. 88: SAMPLER OF SUSANNAH WILSON BARNETT. 1834.
SIZE: 24¼" L x 23¾" W. COLLECTION OF HUGH BARNETT.

Susannah Wilson Barnett was also seventeen years old when she stitched this sampler the same year that Nancy Irwin was working on her canvas. Their samplers are so similar that we can surmise that these two girls knew each other and were probably good friends. Notice how the buildings on both samplers are stitched with a shadowed effect.

Susannah was born on December 17, 1817, in Dauphin County, Pennsylvania, the second child of Samuel and Mary (Mitchell) Barnett. She was born just before the family moved to Butler County. By the 1830s the Barnetts had moved to Lemon Township, and records reveal that the family eventually included ten children. Susannah was married to William L. Crothers in 1835. The couple had nine children before her death at age fifty-five in 1873.

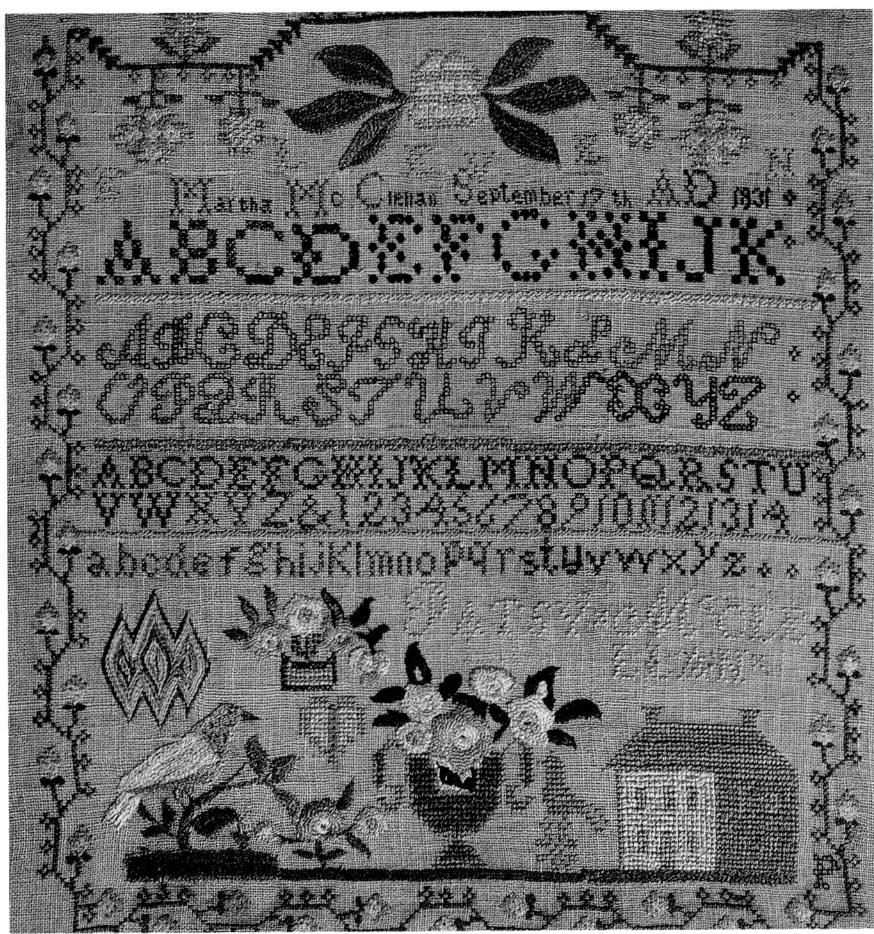

FIG. 89: SAMPLER OF MARTHA MCCLELLAN. 1831.
SIZE: 17¼" L x 17½" W. ANONYMOUS COLLECTOR.

Martha McClellan was eleven years old when she stitched this beautiful sampler. Her nickname, "Patsy," appears in faded stitches just above the shaded building. Notice that she has scattered *e-l-e-v-e-n* in block letters across the top. The border with the large white flower and leaves at the top of the canvas is often a part of the design vocabulary of Lemon Township samplers. James McClellan, Martha McClellan's grandfather, came to Ohio from Kentucky early in the nineteenth century. In 1807 he purchased land in Lemon Township, and his son, James Jr., settled his family nearby in 1820, the year Martha was born.

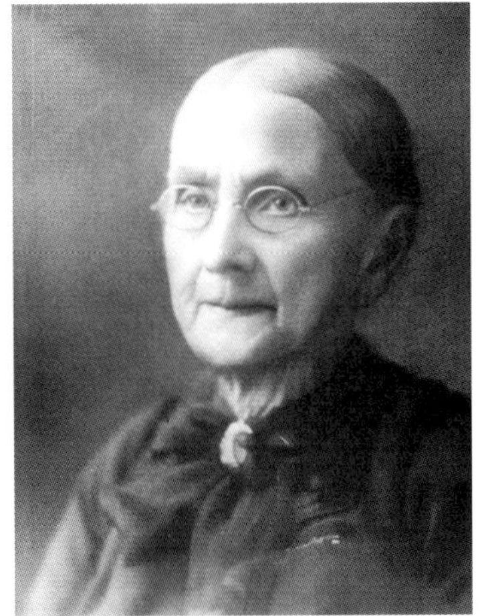

FIG. 90: PHOTOGRAPH OF MARTHA MCCLELLAN.

Martha Phillips McClellan married Enoch Drake Compton of Springdale (Cincinnati) in 1841 and later moved to a farm in Warren County. Unlike so many of the young stitchers featured in this book, she lived to the advanced age of eighty-seven, and died in Warren County in 1907.

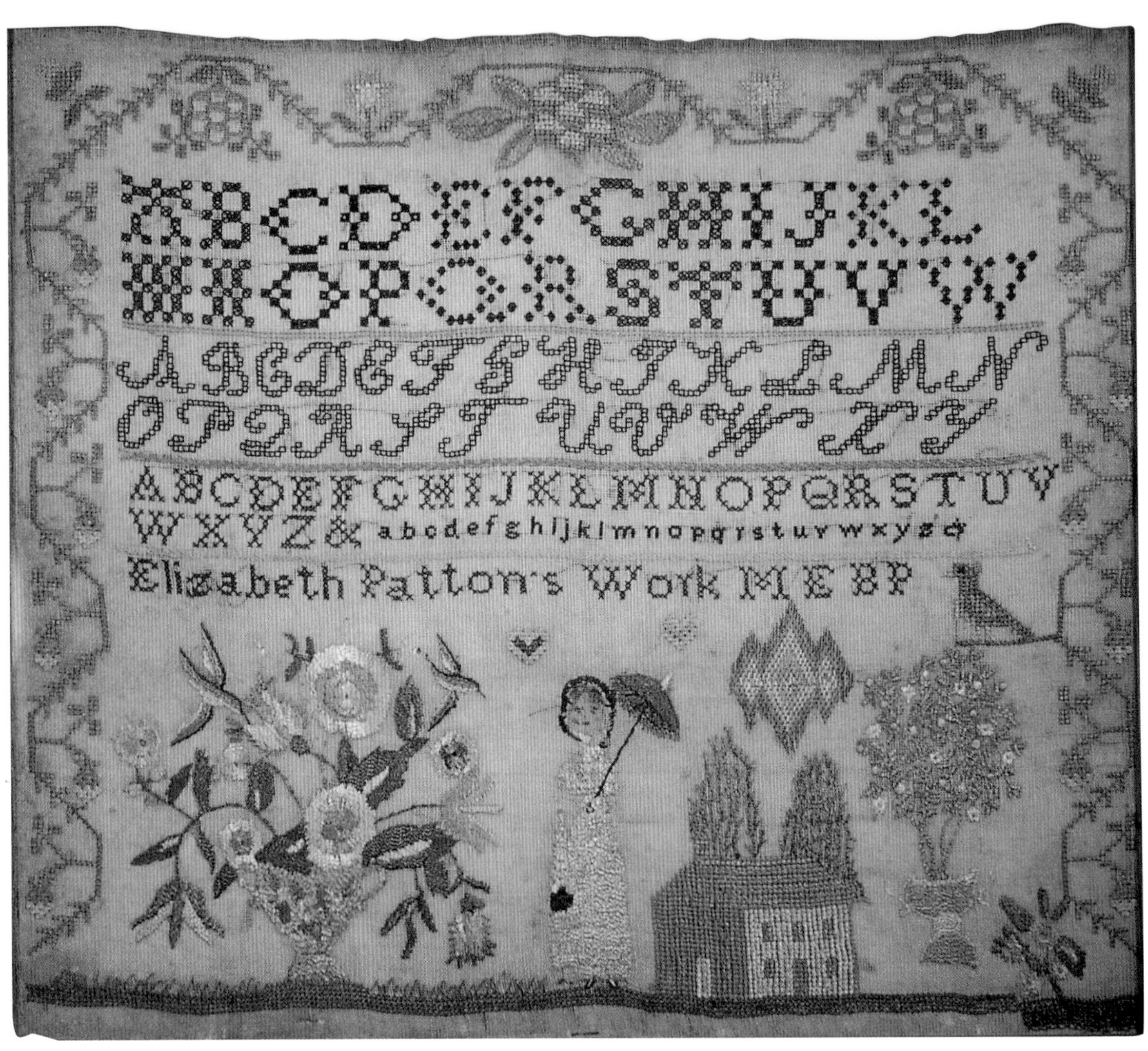

Fig. 92: Detail of Patton Sampler. »

This stylish lady, with her parasol, pretty dress, and handbag, is twice the size of her house. Elizabeth Patton's work provides another good example of the folk-art characteristics that the Lemon Township samplers exhibit.

« Fig. 91: Sampler of Elizabeth Patton. Undated.
Size: 14½" L x 17" W. Collection of the Overfield Tavern Museum.

When this beguiling sampler was discovered, there was no doubt that it was made in Lemon Township. Even though Elizabeth Patton's work is undated and gives no location or her age, the elusive Lemon Township teacher *had* to be her instructress. This sampler displays the same design elements that are found on the others from that location. The lopsided vase of large flowers, the three-diamond motif, and the border that surrounds the canvas are signatures of this teacher. It is the prim, fashionable figure next to the house, however, that catches our attention.

The smiling young lady with the parasol, handbag, and tiny feet is identical to the "headless" lady stitched on the sampler of Catherine Megie (fig. 93). Elizabeth Patton embroidered the head and face on the figure, while Catherine Megie attached a painted paper face, which has been lost from the canvas. Elizabeth Patton's needlework is well executed but exhibits a naïveté in composition when compared with Catherine Megie's work.

There were three Elizabeth Pattons in the immediate area who were of an appropriate age to execute this sampler. The fact that the needlework had remained in the stitcher's family until it found its present home enabled us to determine that the stitcher was the daughter of John and Mary Anne (McCormick) Patton. Elizabeth was born in Warren County in 1812. John Patton came to the Northwest Territory c. 1797–1800. He settled in Warren County on Section 34 in Deerfield Township, a few miles from Lemon Township in neighboring Butler County. When Elizabeth's parents inherited a quarter section of land in Clark County, c. 1832, the family "pulled up stakes" and moved there. Elizabeth married Andrew D. Small on July 5, 1847. She died in her seventy-eighth year on December 31, 1890, and is interred in Ferncliff Cemetery in Springfield, Ohio.

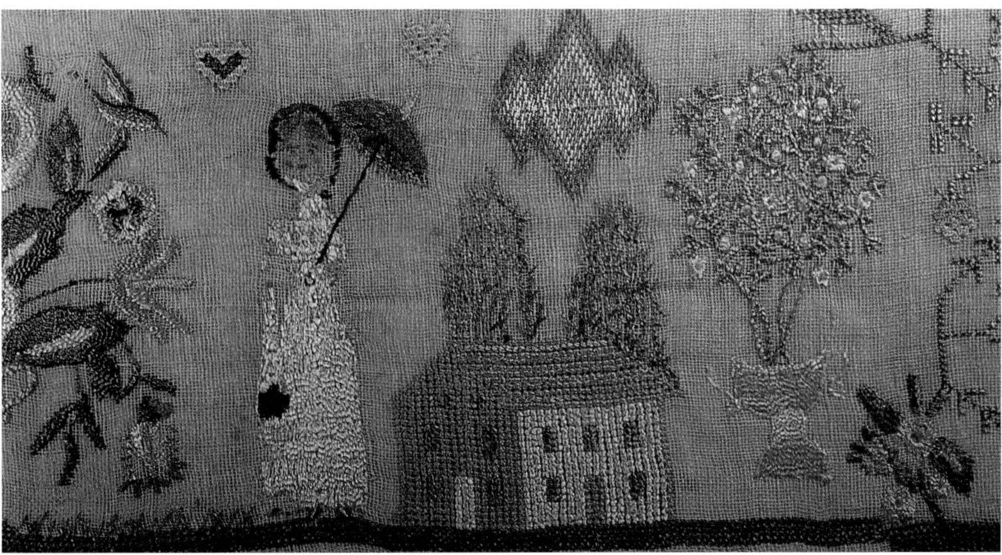

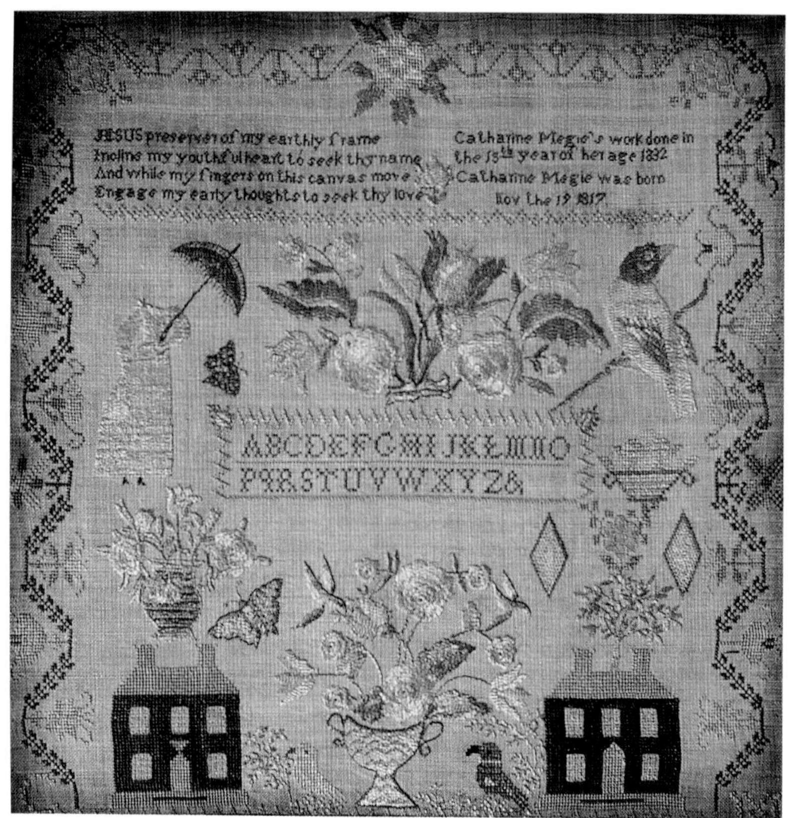

Fig. 93: Sampler of Catherine Megie. 1832.
Size: 17½" L x 17½" W. Collection of Mrs. Thomas J. Hancock,
great-great-granddaughter of the stitcher.

This sampler is well documented as having been done in Lemon Township, near Monroe, where Catherine Megie lived on a large, prosperous farm. Completed in 1832, when Catherine was fifteen years old, it is one of the most complex designs we have found in Ohio. The matching houses on either side, the butterfly, birds, subtly shaded flowers, and the female figure are all well executed. This is always true of the Lemon Township pieces of needlework. Their teacher, whoever she was, taught these young ladies to do excellent stitching. The only element that seems a bit careless in design is the rather lopsided little vase that holds the beautiful tulips and other flowers.

At first glance this sampler does not seem to fit with the other Lemon Township pieces. The composition of the canvas as a whole is more sophisticated and the colors more muted compared with the other samplers. This is partially true because too much light has taken its toll and faded the silk embroidery threads. There is little doubt that this stitcher was tutored by the "mystery teacher."

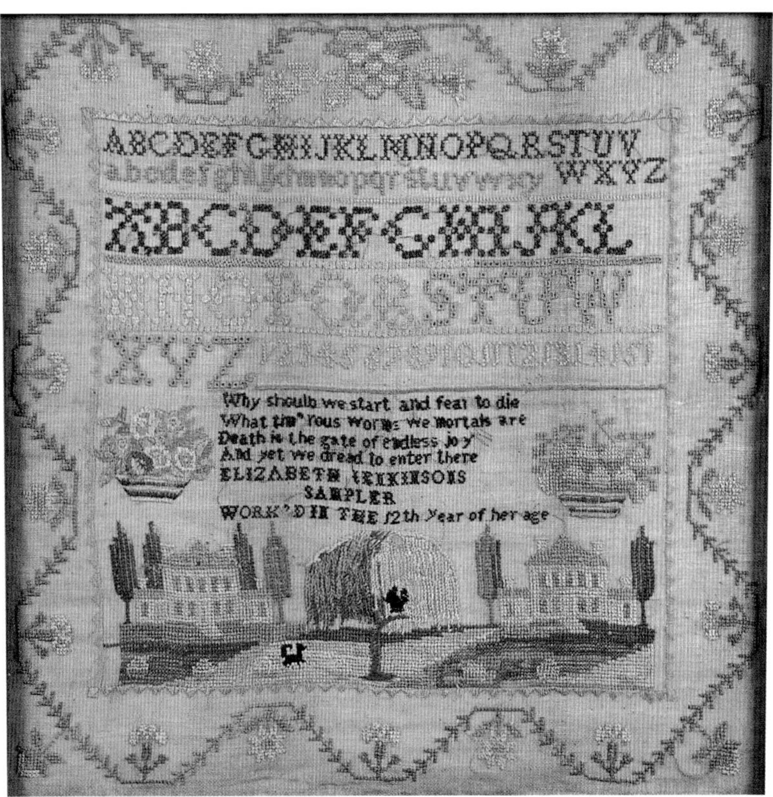

Fig. 95: Sampler of Elizabeth Jenkinson. 1824.

Size: 11½" L x 16½" W. Collection of Tim and Barbara Martien.

Elizabeth Jenkinson's sampler, completed when she was twelve years old, appears to be related to the sampler of Catherine Megie (fig. 93), done some six years later. Both girls have ties to Lemon Township. The border with the large white flower at the top is common to all six of the Lemon Township samplers, but this one and the needlework of Catherine Megie are the only ones that exhibit two important houses stitched at the bottom of the canvas. Elizabeth decided to liven up the scene with a little dog chasing a squirrel up a tree.

Elizabeth was the daughter of Major Joseph and Sally (Vail) Jenkinson, who were married in September 1807 in Butler County. He served under General John S. Gano as a major, First Regiment of the Ohio Militia, in the War of 1812.[70]

« Fig. 94: Portrait of Catherine Megie.

Catherine was a descendant of John Macghie (Megie) who came from Scotland in 1680 and settled in Elizabeth, New Jersey. Her parents, Benjamin and Sara (Brown) Megie, left New Jersey for Ohio in 1813 and eventually settled near Monroe. The family was a prominent one. On September 26, 1840, Catherine married Joseph Curtis on the family farm. She died in 1866 at the age of forty-nine. Her portrait is still with descendants of the family.

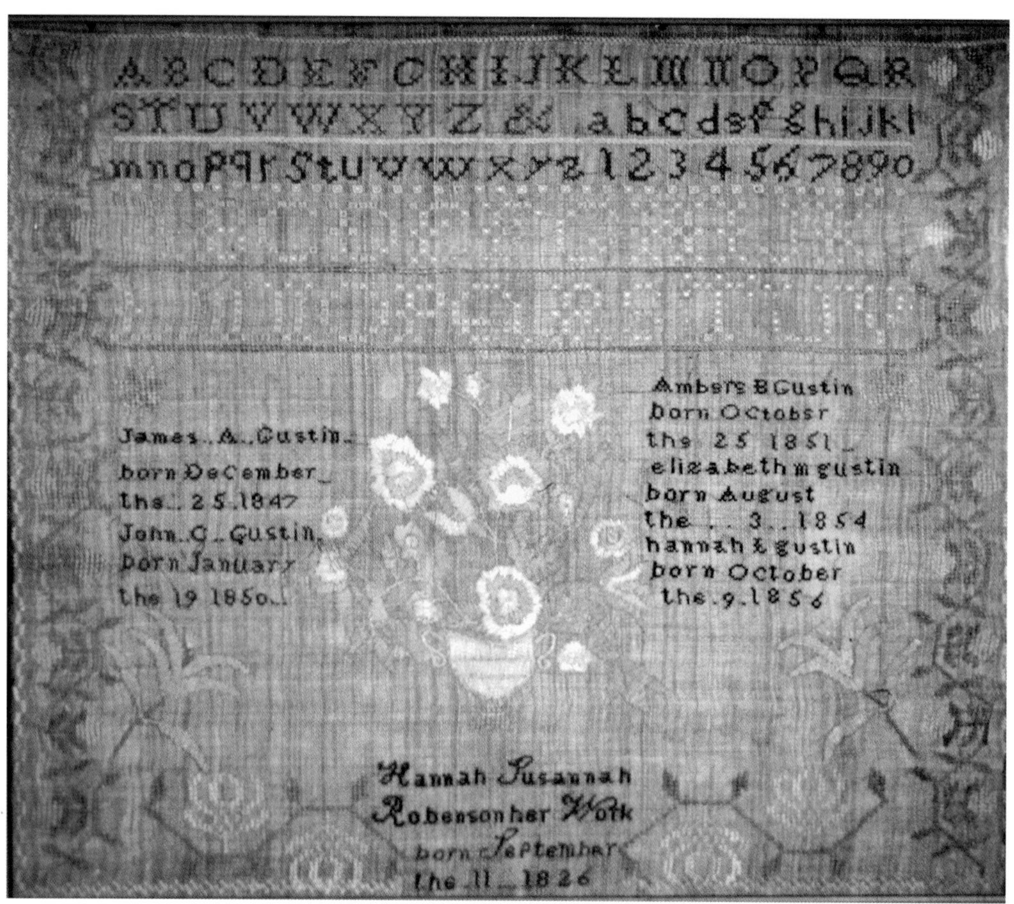

Fig. 96: Sampler of Hannah Susannah Robenson. c. 1840.
Size: 18½" L x 21" W. Collection of Connie and Melvin Porcher.

Unlike the other five Lemon Township samplers, the sampler of Hannah Susannah Robeson (c. 1840) features family genealogical information carefully stitched on the canvas. The clue that immediately showed the relationship to Lemon Township, however, was the vase of flowers in the center of the canvas. Hannah Susannah lived in Lemon Township and, as her sampler notes, was born on September 11, 1826. On November 24, 1845, at age nineteen she was married there to William Gustin. Hannah Susannah continued to stitch after her marriage and listed the births of her three daughters and two sons on this sampler. All of them are interred at Piqua in Miami County.

Fig. 97: Mourning Embroidery of Elizabeth Keely. c. 1844–45.
Size: 21¼" L x 18¼" W. Collection of Larry and Sarah Mosteller.

John W. and Ann (Iddings) Keely of Butler County were the parents of five sons and six daughters. The samplers of two of their daughters, Mary J. and Ann Elizabeth, have survived and, after being apart for many years, hang side by side today. The memorial sampler done by Elizabeth is unlike anything else found in the Ohio sampler search. Three years younger than her sister Mary, Elizabeth was born in Ohio in 1814. She stitched this mourning sampler, a type that most stitchers, young or old, were no longer doing, in tribute to her younger brother. The embroidery is executed in black silk threads.

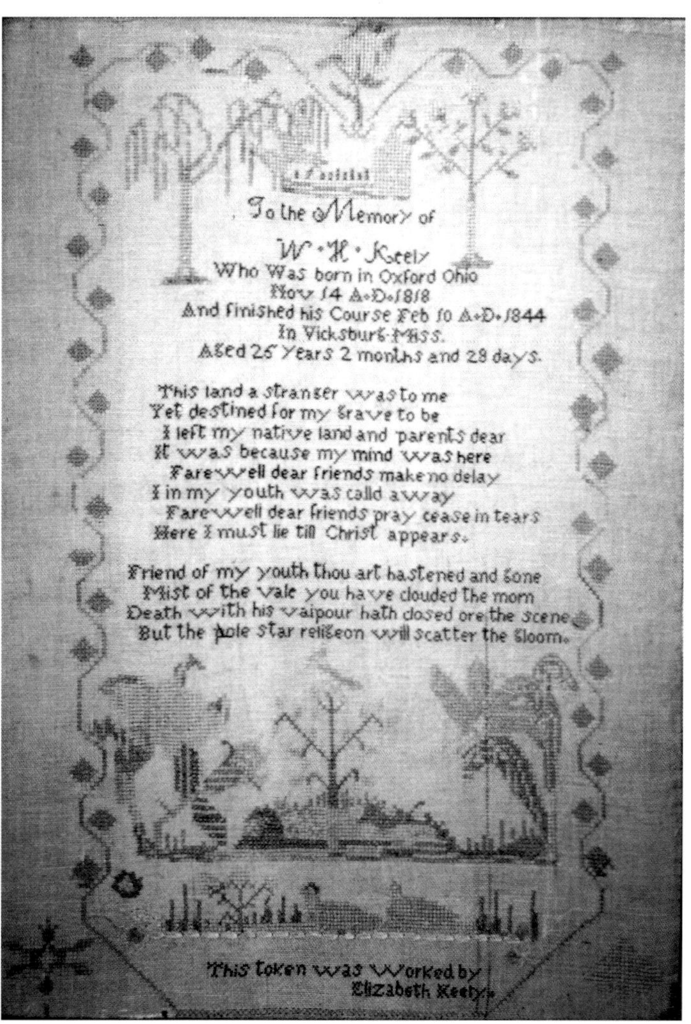

To the Memory of W. H. Keely
Who was born in Oxford Ohio Nov. 14 a.d. 1818
And finished his Course Feb. 10 a.d. 1844
In Vicksburg, Miss.
Aged 25 years, 2 months and 28 days

This land a stranger was to me
Yet destined for my grave to be
I left my native land and parents dear,
It was because my mind was here.
Farewell dear friends, make no delay
I in my youth was called away
Farewell dear friends, pray cease in tears
Here I must lie till Christ appears.

Friend of my youth art hastened and gone
Mist of the vale you have clouded the moon
Death with his vaipour hath closed ore the scene
But the pole star religion will scatter the gloom.

This token was worked by
Elizabeth Keely

Preble County

The history of the area that was to form Preble County begins in the late eighteenth century, when Fort St. Clair was built during the severe winter of 1791-92. The old fort, which has long since disappeared, was erected to guard communications between Fort Hamilton and Fort Jefferson. The brave Indian chief Little Turtle and his men were an ever-present threat to the soldiers and early settlers. The history books are filled with stories of their encounters.

The flat, rich lands of Preble County were part of the Congress Lands. Once the area was made safe, it did not take long for pioneer settlers to purchase land and bring their families to this part of the new state. The county, which borders Indiana, is still primarily farmland.

Little has been discovered about female education in the area, and it is likely that the girls learned to sew at informal, church-affiliated schools. The Scotch-Irish settlers established a Presbyterian congregation as early as 1806, and the Quakers (Society of Friends) organized the Elk Monthly Meeting in 1809. Beautiful needlework has been found that was produced by young girls whose families were associated with these denominations.

In the years 1806 and 1807, several families, most of whom were of Scotch-Irish descent and members of the Associate Reformed Presbyterian Church, opposed to slavery, left their homes in South Carolina and immigrated to Israel Township in Preble County. They held church services in their homes at first and in 1808 built the first Hopewell Church building of logs. The name was chosen because many of the settlers came from Hopewell, South Carolina. By 1825 the flourishing congregation needed a new and larger building. The men of the congregation did most of the labor, constructing a 45-by-70-foot church of Scotch architecture. Bricks were made and burned in a kiln near the front of the church. The floor was paved with brick, everyone paving under his own pew. This building was stitched on Martha Agnes Ramsey's sampler (fig. 98).

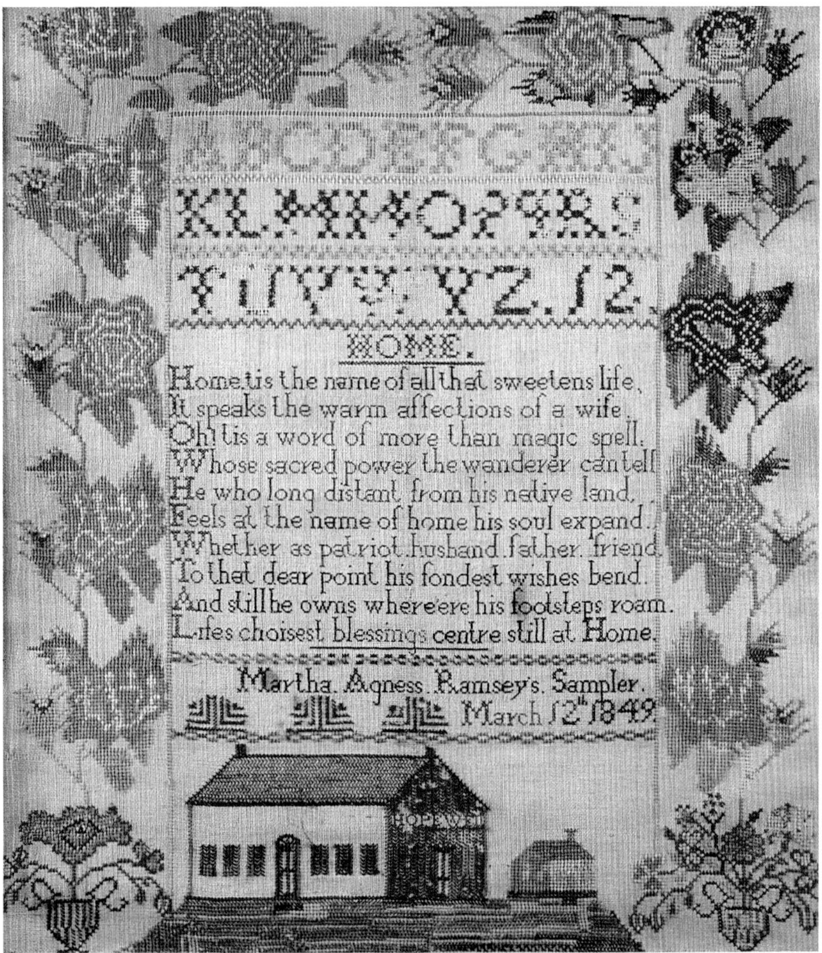

Fig. 98: Sampler of Martha Agnes Ramsey. 1849.

Size: 20" L x 18" W. Wool and silk on linen. Anonymous collector.

Martha Agnes Ramsey was twenty-three years old when she stitched this colorful canvas. She and Sarah Gilmore (see fig. 100) were first cousins, and their samplers were completed the same year. Martha was born July 11, 1826, to William and Sabine (Gilmore) Ramsey. Four years older than her cousin, Martha was a member and teacher at Hopewell Church, where both the Gilmore and Ramsey families attended.

The wide border of roses on Martha's sampler is done in wool thread on a linen ground. By the mid-nineteenth century, Berlin wool work was the most popular type of embroidery for young ladies to do. It required a rather monotonous stitch and was the forerunner of today's needlepoint work. The composition of Martha's canvas is well planned and executed. The building bears a sign that reads "Hopewell," and this is a good rendition of the brick church. The sampler verse, a long poem entitled "Home," is precisely stitched with silk thread.

Martha Ramsey never married and remained active in the church until her death in May 1900. Her needlework is a precious artifact that has been passed down through the Ramsey family.

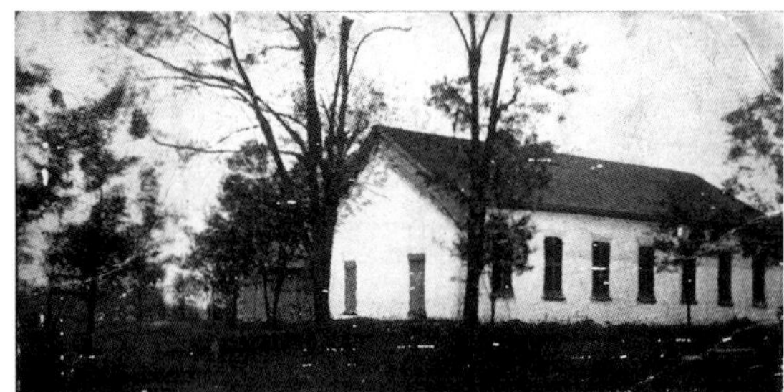

Fig. 99: Historic Hopewell Church.

Fig. 100: Sampler of Sarah H. Gilmore. 1849.

Size: 18" L x 19" W. Collection of Preble County Historical Society.

This sampler was completed when Sarah Gilmore was nineteen years old. She and Martha Agnes Ramsey (see fig. 98) were cousins and undoubtedly worked on their canvases as they visited with each other. The sampler of Sarah Gilmore's mother, Margaret McMechan Gilmore, also appears in this book (fig. 83). These mother-daughter samplers make an interesting study of how much needlework styles can change in both composition and stitching in a relatively short period of time.

Sarah's canvas is marked with a blue thread to help guide her work. This type of canvas was available early in the nineteenth century. First produced in Germany, it helped when counting and transferring Berlin wool work patterns. Called Penelope canvas, it was usually a plain woven fabric of cotton or linen that had a colored thread every tenth warp yarn.[71] Samplers of the 1840s often exhibit a predominance of Berlin wool work, and Sarah's border of large roses is typical. Within the framed center, a verse titled "The Rose" is neatly stitched with silk thread, which was more suited to the fine stitches required for the long poem.

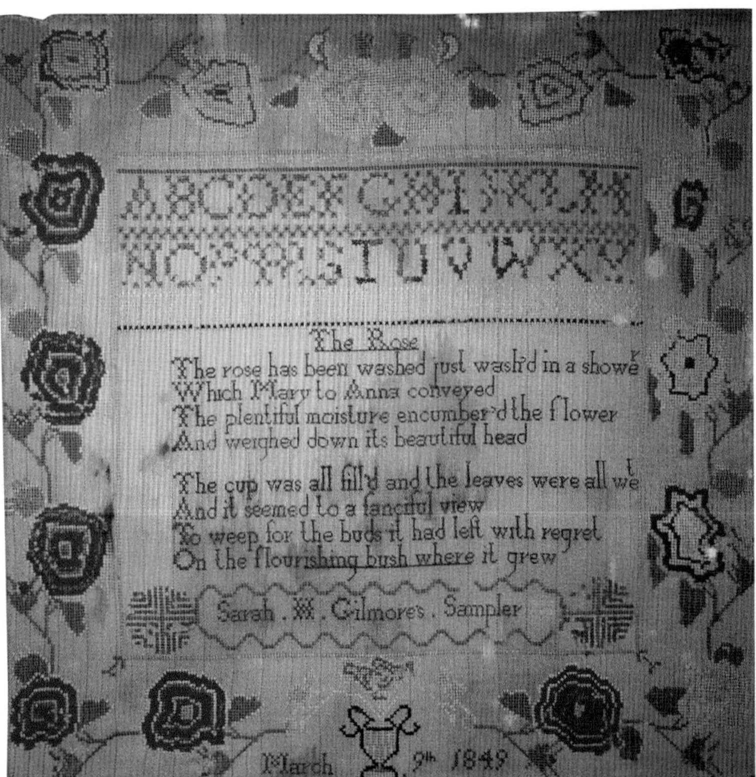

In 1862, when she was thirty-two years old, Sarah became the fourth wife of John Patterson Smith, a widower fourteen years her senior with four young children. By 1874 four more children were added to the family. When Bertha, their last child, was born, Sarah was forty-four years old. She died in 1892 and is buried by her husband in the Hopewell Church Cemetery.

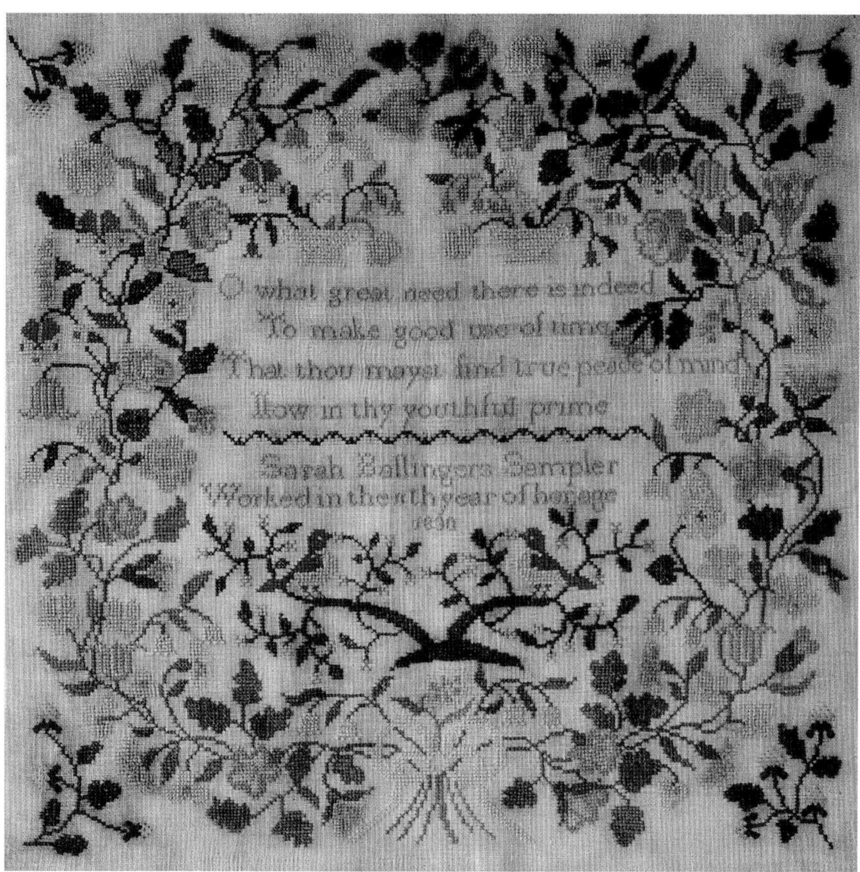

Fig. 101: Sampler of Sarah Ballinger. 1830.
Size: 17" L x 17" W. Anonymous collector.

Sarah Ballinger was eleven years of age when she completed this colorful sampler. An energetic and talented stitcher, she filled her canvas with a wide variety of bright, beautiful flowers. A ribbon bow holds her "bouquet" together at the bottom of the needlework. The verse is one that is not often seen. It reads: "Oh what great need there is indeed / To make good use of time / That thou mayst find true peace of mind / Now in thy youthful prime."

Sarah was born in Ohio on September 4, 1819, the sixth child of Isaac and Hannah (Haines) Ballinger. Her parents and grandparents came to Ohio from New Jersey, where they were members of the Burlington Monthly Meeting of the Society of Friends. By January of 1820, Isaac and Hannah had moved their young family to Preble County and transferred their certificates of membership to Elk Monthly Meeting. Sarah married William V. Brown on December 17, 1838, in Preble County, where the couple spent the rest of their lives.

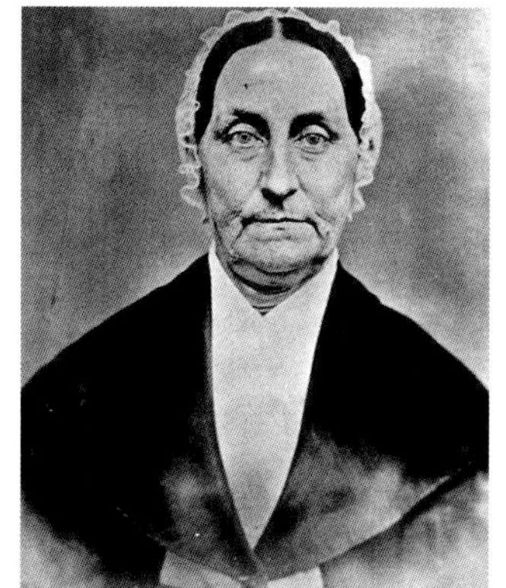

Fig. 102: Photograph of Sarah Ballinger Brown.

The exquisite needlework of Sarah Ballinger remains with her descendants today. The family treasures not only her sampler, but this photo, the family Bible, and other mementos.

Greene County

General Nathaniel Greene of the American Revolution never saw the Ohio Lands that were named for him, but those lands have wondrous Indian stories to tell. During the first explorations of white men into the area "between the Miamis," all of these lands were being used by the Indians for hunting grounds. The earliest maps show just two Indian towns: Old Chillicothe (in Greene County) on the Little Miami River and Picawillany (in Clark County) on the Mad River. These sizable Shawnee villages were located about fifteen miles apart.

Old Chillicothe, still referred to as "Old Town," was located three miles north of the present-day city of Xenia. When the celebrated Daniel Boone was taken prisoner in Kentucky in February 1778 during the Revolutionary War, he was held for a short time at Old Chillicothe before being taken northward to the British at Fort Detroit. The Shawnee, allies of the British, took such a fancy to Boone that they took him back to Old Chillicothe and adopted him into their tribe.[72]

Daniel Boone had been held captive there for several months when he witnessed 450 Shawnee Indian warriors planning to attack and destroy Boonesborough, Kentucky. He made a daring escape and was able to make his way back to Kentucky to give warning. That bold and brave effort undoubtedly helped to save the Boonesborough outpost and the frontier parts of Kentucky from devastation.

The Indians continued to make raids, and in mid-1779 Colonel John Bowman and his Kentucky militia knew they must stop the attacks. Bowman and his men marched northward and destroyed one hundred acres of Indian vegetable and corn crops and most of the village of Old Chillicothe. Still undaunted, the determined Shawnee regrouped and fortified their village of Picawillany on the Mad River.

On March 29, 1797, James Galloway arrived with his family from Lexington, Kentucky, to settle in Greene County. The land they chose along the banks of the Little Miami was the exact site where the former Shawnee Indian village of Old Chillicothe had been located. Perhaps

Galloway chose this spot because it was the same area he had come to fifteen years earlier in 1782 with George Rogers Clark's Kentucky Militia to destroy the Indian town.[73]

Tecumseh, the young chief of the Shawnee, returned to this site at the very time Galloway arrived, and they soon began to establish a close friendship. Accounts of the time tell us that Tecumseh visited the Galloway family many times during the next ten years. Tecumseh and James Galloway's daughter Rebecca, who was only five years old when the family first arrived in the Ohio lands, eventually fell in love. Tecumseh was forty years old and Rebecca sixteen when he asked for her hand in marriage. Rebecca accepted his proposal on the condition that she would be his only wife and that he would adopt her people's way of living and dress. Tecumseh considered the idea but finally decided he could not marry her, for if he did as she wished, he would lose his leadership role and the respect of his people. Just five years later Tecumseh was killed in battle.

The Galloway log cabin, a replica of the young girl's home, can be visited in Xenia today, but none of the needlework that must have been produced by the girls of the family has been found. Rebecca Galloway's niece, also named Rebecca Galloway, left a wonderful diary that she penned over a three-year period from January 1, 1840, through December 1842. Her diary details the "enjoyable evenings" they had, the young men who visited her and her friends, taking the sleigh to church, cutting apples and peaches, and nights spent visiting friends and relatives. She also wrote of the terrible toothaches that plagued her. Her stories of sickness and the treatments offered by the doctor are sad accounts of those days when so many died at an early age.

Rebecca wrote no delicious notes or direct references in her diary about making a sampler, but she relates how much time she spent doing sewing chores: "completed the blue silk bonnet," "mended my petticoat," "cut out a pair of corsets and worked at them till supper," "cut and made the skirt of Sarah's dress," "mended one pair of stockings," and "sewed at my dress and Mary Ann read to me." Never a day went by, it seems, without her picking up her needle and thread.[74]

Only two Greene County samplers have been discovered, both made in Xenia, the county seat. Several schools were operating there before 1850, and most of them were taught by women. Hannah Wright's school, located for a number of years in a "fine brick building on the hill south of the Pennsylvania station," was known for its excellence.[75] This boarding school, erected by her husband, Lewis Wright, attracted students from a wide area. Hannah Wright was teaching as early as the 1840s and probably earlier.

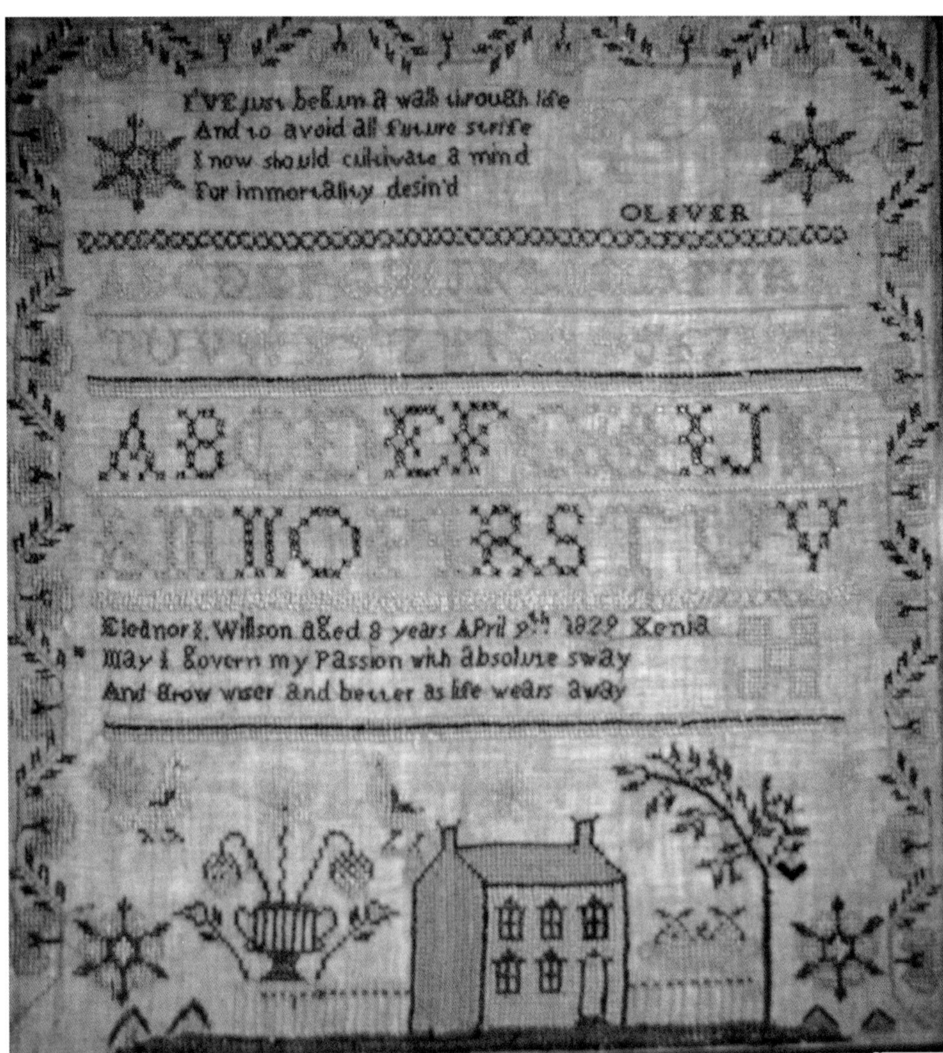

Fig. 103: Sampler of Eleanor I. Wilson. 1829.

Size: 17¾" L x 16¾" W. Collection of Dr. John R. Ribic.

When Eleanor Isabella Wilson stitched her canvas, she plainly marked that she was eight years old. Her work is neatly done, and the large building with the chimneys on either end may very well be a rendition of the school she attended. The same building appears on the Xenia sampler of Jane W. Jackson (fig. 104). The compositions of the two Xenia samplers match well, but there are subtle differences in the fence, building, trees, flowers, and in the surrounding border.

Eleanor's family members were among the first settlers in Greene County. She was born on April 9, 1821, to John and Sarah (Buckles) Wilson. In 1845, Eleanor married William Truesdale Hubbell, and the couple made their home in Shelby County. She died on March 31, 1909, in Sidney, Ohio.

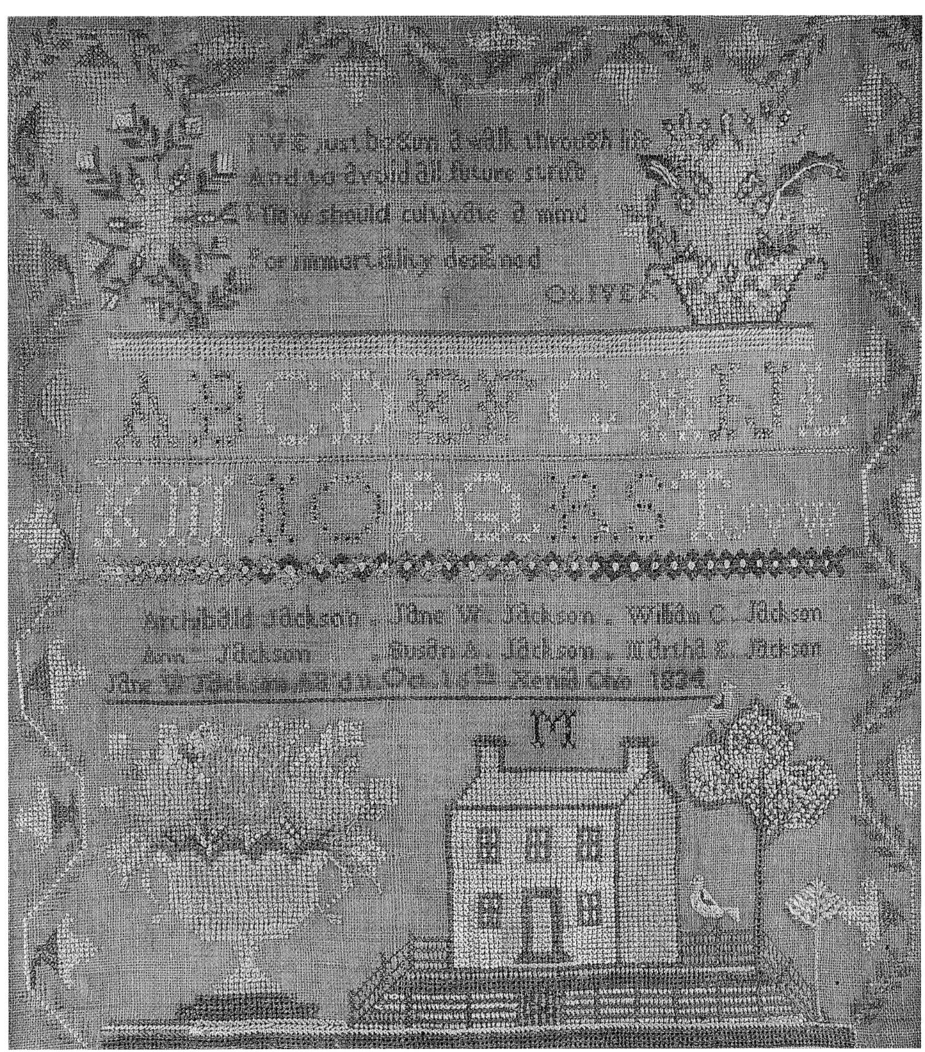

FIG. 104: SAMPLER OF JANE W. JACKSON. 1834.

SIZE: 15¼" L x 14¼" W. COLLECTION OF SHARI KNIGHT EURBANK.

Jane White Jackson's needlework was completed in Xenia in 1834 when she was eleven years old. Despite the considerable genealogical information on the canvas, very little is known about this girl and her family. Marriage records tell us that she married Daniel McMillan in April 1846 and that they lived in the Cedarville area.

Some pictorial elements on the lower section of this attractive sampler, like the tree beside the house and the huge scallop-rimmed urn filled with flowers have not been discovered on any other Ohio sampler. Jane's proficiency with the needle is demonstrated in the various stitches on the canvas, including cross, whip, herringbone, satin, and tent stitches. When we examine the overall design of the sampler, it is apparent that it was created at the same school that Eleanor Wilson (fig. 103) attended, though they may have had different instructresses. Both girls used the verse written by Oliver: "I've just begun a walk through life, / And to avoid all future strife, / I now should cultivate a mind / For immortality designed."

Brown County

The southern boundary of Brown County is defined by the wide Ohio River, and the town of Ripley was settled along its banks about 1812. This small village played a strategic role during the abolitionist movement in the first half of the nineteenth century. Undeniably the most important figure of this social upheaval was the Reverend John Rankin. It was his daughter Julia who stitched the sampler seen in fig. 105.

Julia's father, a Presbyterian minister and educator, is referred to in history books as the father of abolitionism. In 1825 he helped to organize and served as conductor of the famous Underground Railroad. Through his work in behalf of the fugitives, Ripley became the principal station of the secret slave escape route to Canada. It was John Rankin who personally told author Harriett Beecher Stowe the stirring episode of the young slave, Eliza, who carried her children to freedom over the treacherous ice of the Ohio River. This story, told by Stowe in her 1852 book *Uncle Tom's Cabin,* had such a strong emotional impact in dividing public opinion that it helped precipitate the Civil War.[76] Despite the risks involved, Julia and her family helped more than two thousand slaves to gain their freedom.

Although the village of Ripley was never large, good educational opportunities were available there. In 1829 John Rankin successfully opened Ripley College, and many students, particularly from the South, enrolled. The Ripley Female Seminary opened four years later, in 1832. Established under the direction of William C. Bissell and a "lady," records show that by 1846 it had forty students.[77] We have not discovered who the "lady" was who was teaching at the seminary, nor do we have a list of students' names. A second Ripley sampler, however, closely resembles Julia's work, indicating that these young girls were tutored by the same needlework instructress.

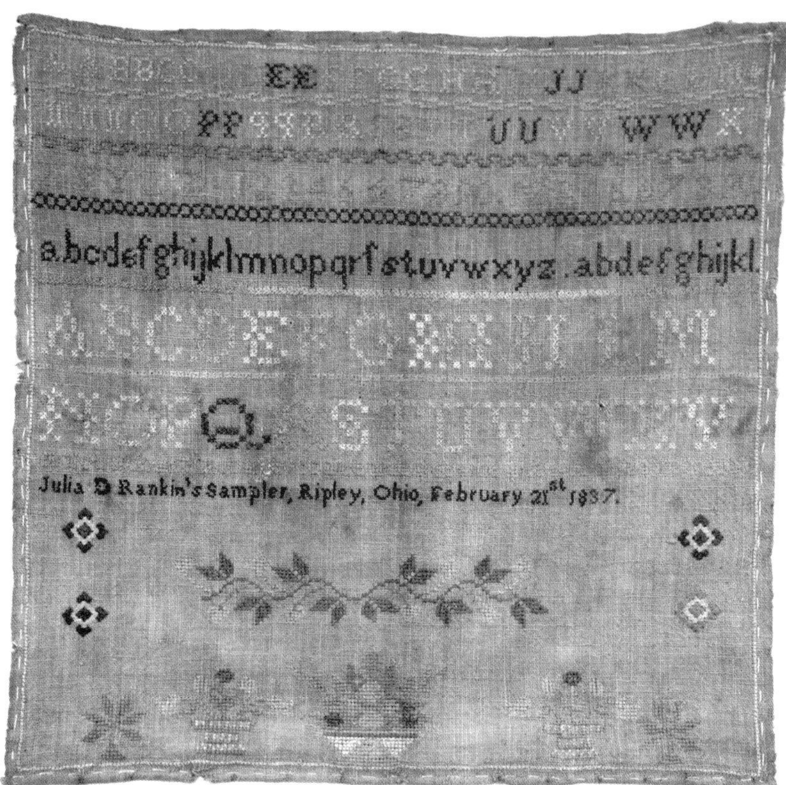

Fig. 105: Sampler of Julia Doak Rankin. 1837.
Size: 15½" L x 15½" W. Collection of Rankin House State Memorial, Ohio Historical Society.

Julia Doak Rankin, born on November 2, 1824, was the daughter of John and Jean (Lowry) Rankin. She completed this rather somber and plain sampler when she was thirteen years old and clearly marked the canvas with the words "Ripley, Ohio." Julia's parents had thirteen children born to them between the years 1816 and 1834 and one adopted child.

Fig. 106: The Rankin House.

The Rankin House, located on Liberty Hill in Ripley, is a state memorial today. Situated high on a cliff above the Ohio River, it served as a beacon of hope for slaves escaping to freedom. A small lantern hung in an upstairs window acted as a signal for those waiting to cross the Ohio from Kentucky. Once across, the runaway slaves were protected from the slave hunters and their masters. The house contains much of the original woodwork and a number of personal Rankin items, including the family Bible and pieces of original furniture. Julia's sampler is hung in a prominent spot in the dining room of this historic home.

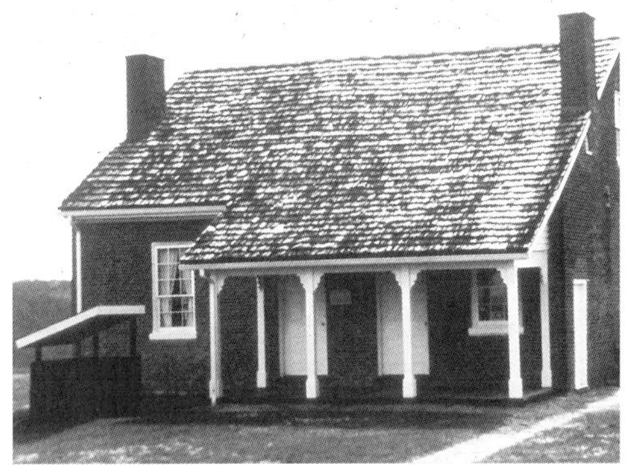

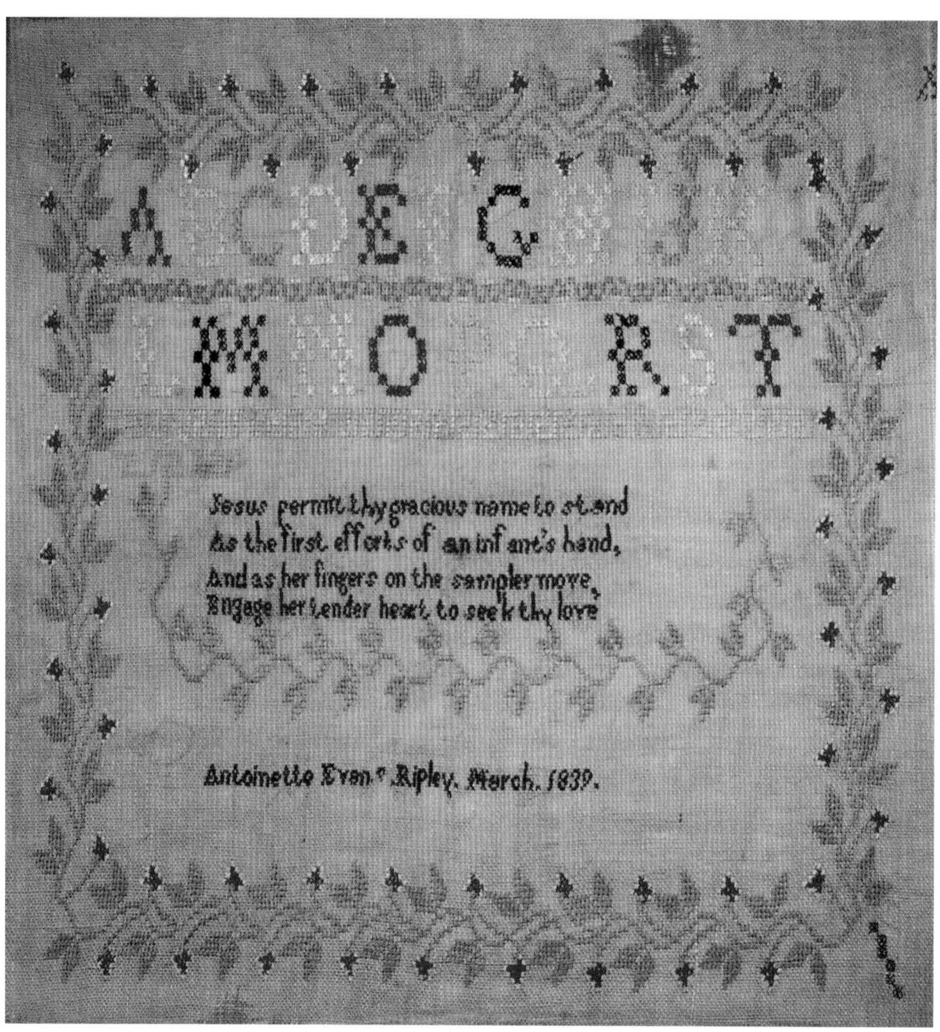

Fig. 107: Sampler of Antoinette Evans. 1839.
Size: 16" L x 16" W. Collection of Nancy Antoinette Noland DeCamp, great-granddaughter of the stitcher.

Antoinette Louise Evans's canvas, neatly marked with the town of Ripley, was completed when she was ten years old. When compared to Julia Rankin's sampler (fig. 105), the alphabet pattern and type of stitches used by the two girls are nearly identical, although the overall design of Antoinette's sampler is much more complex. Notice the exuberant vine border Antoinette executed so beautifully displays the same peculiar diamond-shaped leaves that can be seen on the Rankin sampler. This little girl's handwork has been treasured and conserved as it passed down through the family.

Antoinette (a name that has also been passed down from generation to generation) was the daughter of David Parker Evans and Nancy Curry Humphes. Antoinette married James Smith Campbell, whose grandfather Thomas Kirker served as the second governor of Ohio from 1807 to 1809. She died in Ohio in 1912.

Scioto County

The names of several Ohio counties—including Wyandot, Ottawa, Tuscarawas, and Scioto—originated with the American Indians. The densely forested county of Scioto, the Wyandot word for "deer," was formed in 1803. Among the first settlers in the area were Aaron and Mary Clingman Kinney, whose granddaughter Elizabeth Kinney stitched the sampler seen in fig. 108. This sampler is the only one discovered from Scioto County.

Portsmouth, the principal town and county seat, was laid out at the mouth of the Scioto River, where it flows directly into the Ohio. The village was platted by Henry Massie, and his town map clearly shows the Aaron Kinney tracts.[78] The Kinney family homestead built in 1810 is the oldest house in Portsmouth and still stands not far from the banks of the Scioto. Today it serves as a museum and the headquarters of the Scioto County Historical Society.

Portsmouth citizens did not have public schools available to them until 1838,[79] but there were several subscription or private schools in operation during the first years of settlement. One of the earliest established for young women was Mrs. Ashley's Seminary, begun in 1827, and local advertisements mention that she was teaching ornamental needlework. Two years later in 1829, Miss Dupuy advertised that she was "opening a school at her mother's residence" (in Portsmouth) and that students would be taught "ornamental needlework and painting on velvet."[80] Miss Dupuy's school would have been the type known as a "dame" school and limited to a very few students. Other schools like the Portsmouth Young Ladies Seminary (or Female Seminary) would have offered academic subjects as well as needlework instruction. This school was established sometime before 1832. The following appeared in the local newspaper in November of that year: "Mary Sharp wishes to give notice of a Young Ladies Seminary to begin November 26 in the room formerly occupied by Mrs. Kelsey."[81]

Elizabeth Kinney likely attended one of these private schools, as the first public school opened in 1838, three years after she made her sampler.

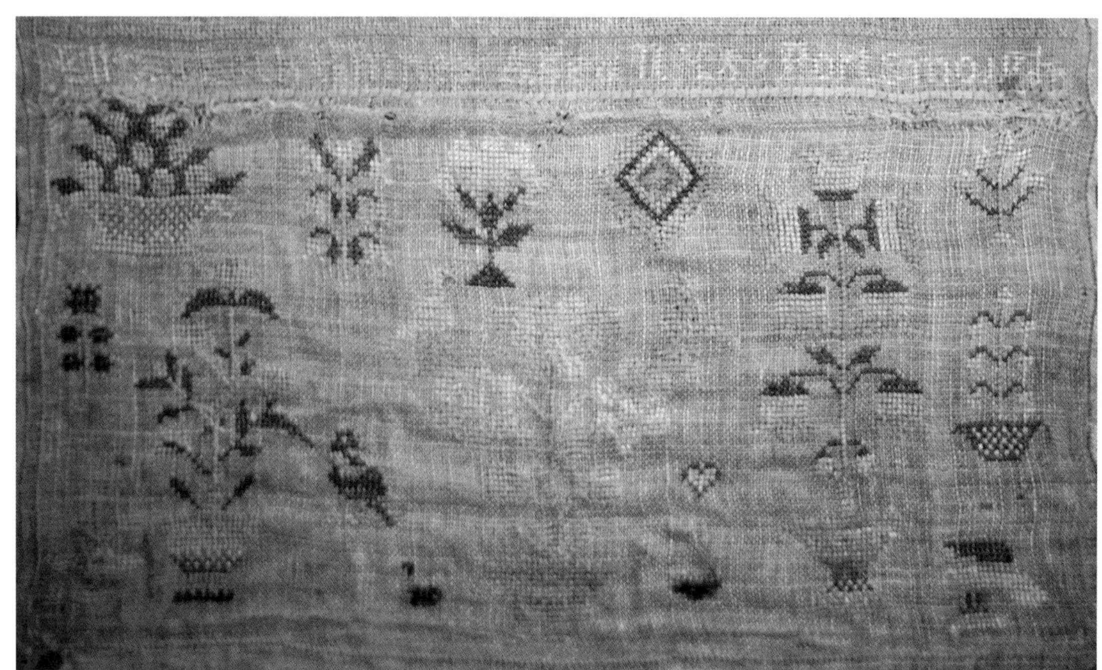

Fig. 108: Sampler of Elizabeth Kinney. 1835.
Size: 17" L x 17" W. Collection of Scioto County Historical Society.

Though the upper half of this sampler is difficult to read, the town name of Portsmouth can clearly be seen. The bottom half of the canvas exhibits a variety of stitches and scattered designs that are well executed and colorful. Elizabeth Kinney was born in Portsmouth and completed this needlework when she was eleven years old. She was the daughter of George Washington Kinney and Mary Waller. Her paternal grandfather, Aaron Kinney, brought his family to Ohio from Pennsylvania at the beginning of the nineteenth century and purchased nearly three hundred acres of land on the outskirts of the little village. He owned a tannery, and his son Washington Kinney continued in this business. Ohio marriage records tell us that Elizabeth Kinney married Samuel Randall Ross September 7, 1847.

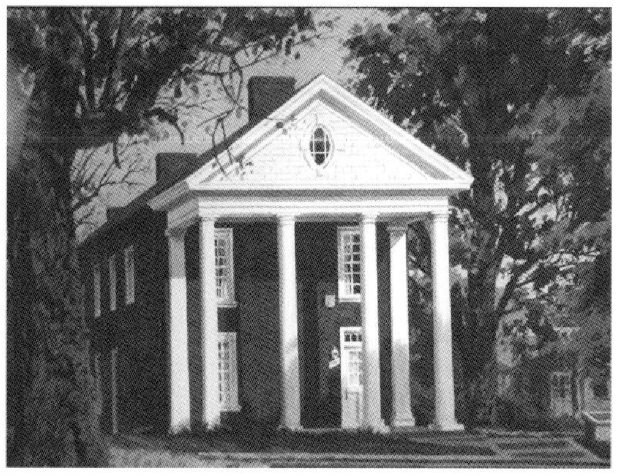

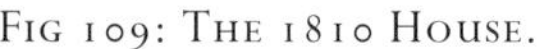

Fig 109: The 1810 House.

The Kinney homestead as it appears today. It is on the National Register of Historic Places.

Ross County

Ross County was formed in 1798 by order of General Arthur St. Clair, governor of the Northwest Territory. The county seat of Chillicothe was laid out in August 1796 along the west bank of the Scioto, and is today one of Ohio's most historic cities.

The opening of Zane's Trace in 1799 promoted settlement in the frontier town. Zane's Trace, a wagon trail that connected Zanesville with Maysville, Kentucky, passed through Chillicothe, and with its opening came a great change in the course of travel into the Ohio Country. Before this time, travel had been principally only via the Ohio River keelboats, but now settlers and their families could come overland. Not only was Chillicothe the seat of government for Ross County, and for the Northwest Territory, but eventually it was selected as the site for the first capital of the new State of Ohio. It was this first capitol building that Charity Trimble (fig. 111) likely stitched on her sampler.

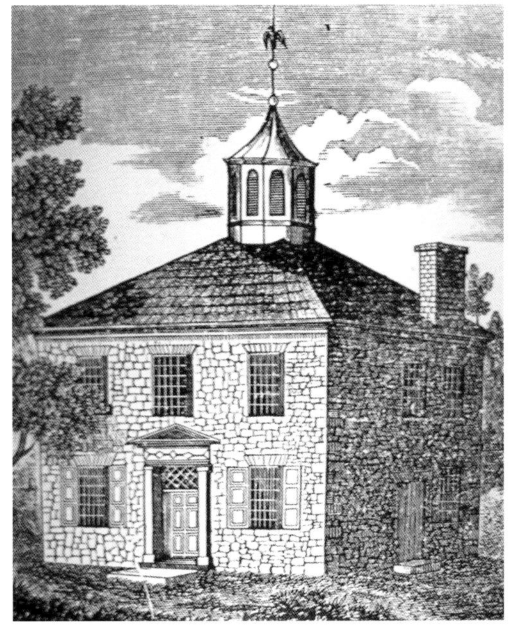

Fig. 110: First Ohio Capitol Building. Courtesy of Ross County Historical Society.

In 1800, construction of the new stone statehouse was commenced; it was finished a year later. A foursquare building with a beautiful cupola, it was the only governmental stone structure in the Territory. In November 1802, the territorial legislature met in this new building and drew up the State Constitution in anticipation of statehood the following year. The building served as the seat of government for Ohio until 1810, when the capital was moved to Zanesville.[82] This historic structure was demolished in 1852. The local newspaper later built a replica of the old stone building, and today the offices of the Chillicothe Gazette are there.

Fig. 111: Sampler of Charity Trimble. 1807. »

Size: 11" L x 13" W. Collection of Emilie B. Savage.

Charity Trimble's sampler is a beauty and is very different from any other Ohio sampler. Stitched on the canvas are these words: "When This You See Remember Me / And Bare Me In Your Mind / Let All The World Say What They Will / Speak of Me As You Find." Charity also included the initials of her parents and two sisters.

The design of Charity's sampler is divided into three distinct scenes or panels. The prim female figures, two with parasols, two without, the vases of stiff flowers that resemble strawberries, the striped basket of fruit—all of her motifs have triangular forms that contribute to the symmetric composition of the canvas. An exception, however, is the curious handled jar with one small blossom. The unusual little building on the right side of the canvas is a rendition of Noah's Ark. The bird with the twigs in its beak is bringing a sign to Noah that the ark is at long last approaching land. Note the waves of water under the floating boat.

It is probable that the large building centered in the bottom scene is her interpretation of the newly built first Ohio Capitol Building. This building, which was of such importance to the Northwest Territory, Ross County, and the new state government, would have provided a good subject for a young lady's needlework. Charity's rendition of the building does not show a cupola, but it is otherwise a faithful copy.

Charity was born on February 10, 1789. She was eighteen years old when she stitched this sampler. She was one of nine children fathered by John Trimble; her mother was Rachel Ridgeway, John's second wife. The Trimbles and their children emigrated from Virginia and settled for a short time in Pennsylvania, where they are listed as being members of the Redstone Monthly Meeting of the Society of Friends. About 1804, the family moved westward to make their home in Ross County.

Research did not reveal what school she went to, but the only one recorded at this early date in Chillicothe was the female academy that was opened in 1802 in a log house on Water Street. It was operated by Mr. John Hutt, who "provided academic instruction while his wife taught the fine art of needlework."[83]

On March 14, 1811, Charity married James McClintock, a promising young merchant. They were lifelong residents of Ross County and the parents of seven children. Charity died in 1868 and is buried in the Grandview Cemetery in Ross County beside her husband and two children who died in infancy.

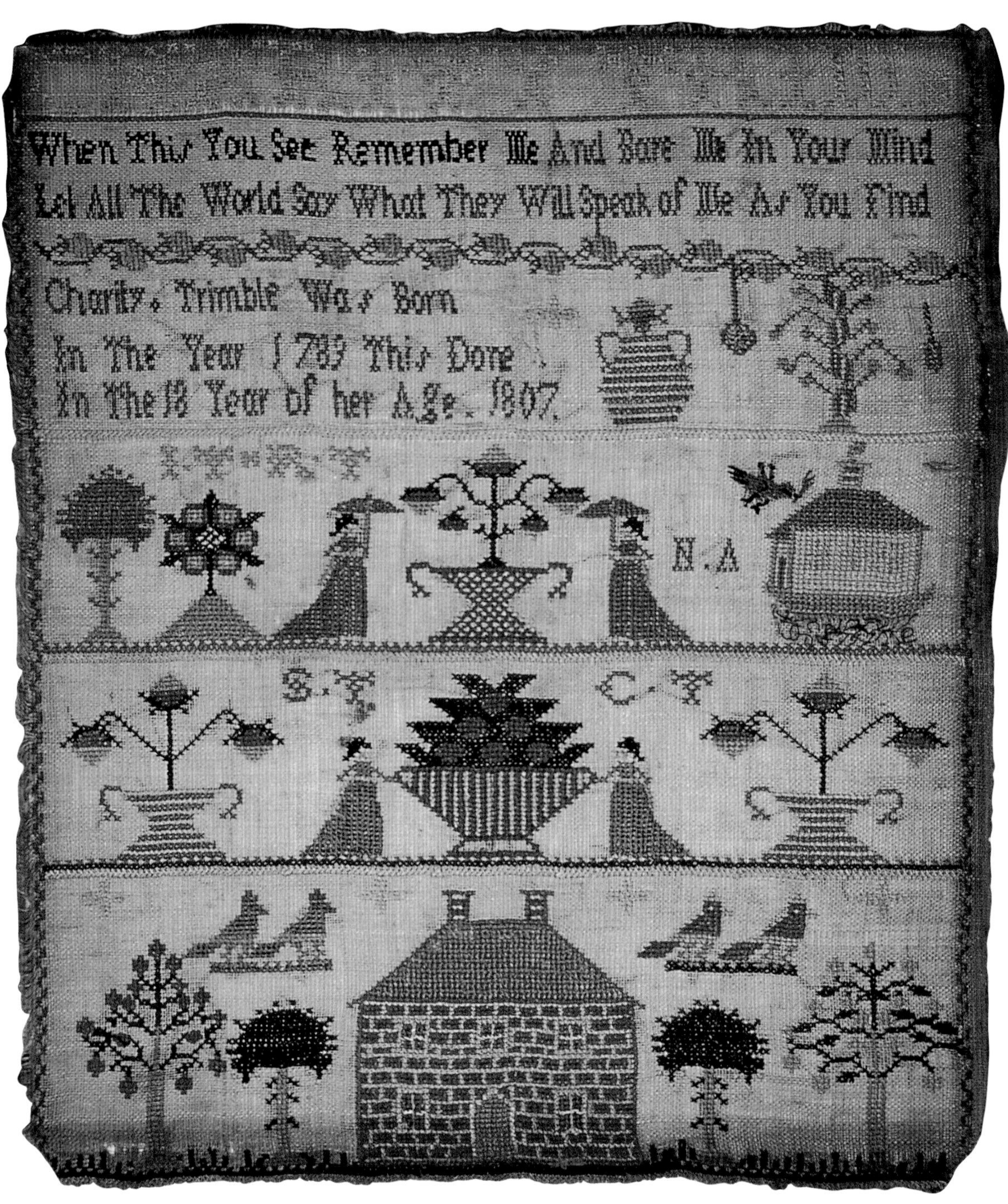
When This You See Remember Me And Bore Me In Your Mind
Let All The World Say What They Will Speak of Me As You Find
Charity. Trimble Was Born
In The Year 1789 This Done
In The 18 Year of her Age. 1807.
N. A
S. T
C. T

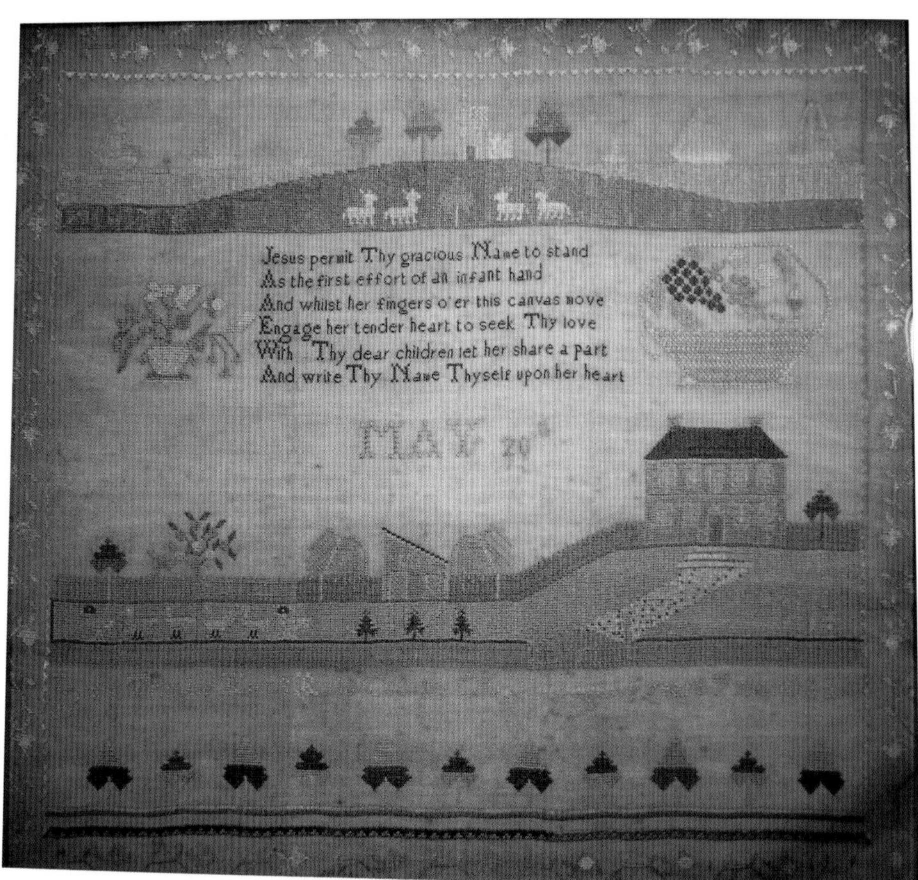

Fig. 112: Sampler of Lydia Trimble Kerns. 1843.
Size: 24" L x 26" W. Anonymous collector.

This large and beautifully stitched sampler was worked by a child named Lydia Trimble Kerns. Her canvas is inscribed more like a tombstone than a piece of needlework. Lydia says it was completed on "May 20th when she was aged 9 years, 7 months, and three days old"—a rather unusual way to sign a sampler.

This sampler has two seemingly unrelated perspective views. The top scene on the sampler shows us a wide panel of stitching with a castle atop a hill. The grassy lawn in the foreground provides a grazing pasture for four neatly stitched sheep. On either side of the castle overlooking the sea, sailing ships float on the blue water. The lower scene, with a fence stretching the width of the canvas and the large house on the hill, shows steps leading down to the pond in the foreground. In the pond is a string of ducks swimming neatly in a row. The building situated near the pond may be a springhouse. A complex sampler like this would have taken an enormous amount of patience for a nine-year-old to complete.

Lydia was born in Ohio in 1834, the oldest of four children born to Benjamin and Lydia Kerns. Early in the nineteenth century her paternal grandparents, Benjamin and Sarah (Winder) Kerns, came from Pennsylvania to Ross County, where Lydia's father was born in 1804. Young Benjamin and his family moved on to Marion County in central Ohio, where public records show he was a prosperous farmer. In May 1843, when Lydia finished this sampler, her family was living in Marion County, but she stitched "Ross County, Ohio" on her canvas. On August 1, 1843, Lydia's mother gave birth to a baby sister, Mary Emma. Lydia may have been sent to stay with relatives in Chillicothe, where she could attend school while her mother awaited the birth.

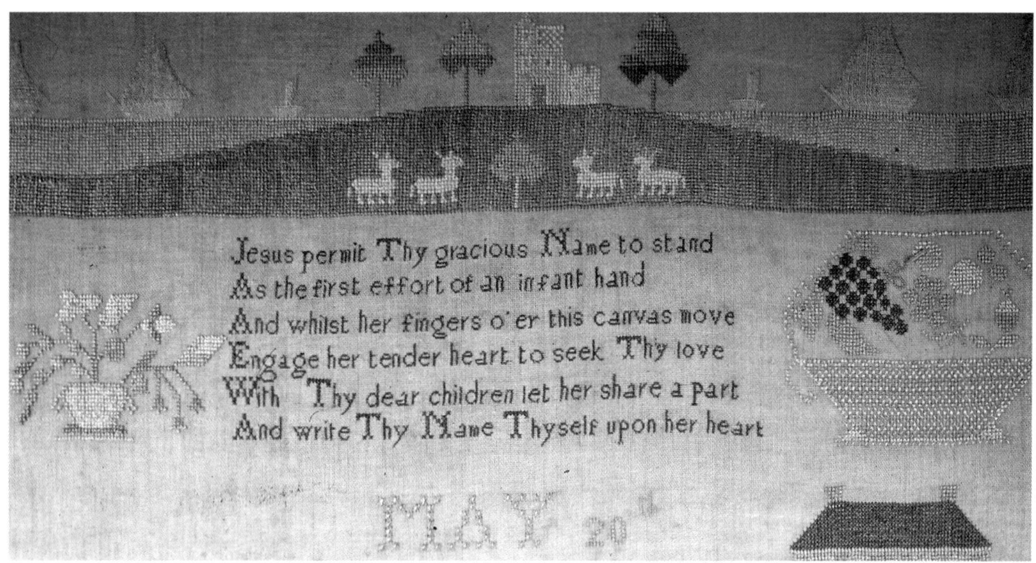

Fig. 113: Detail of Kerns Sampler.

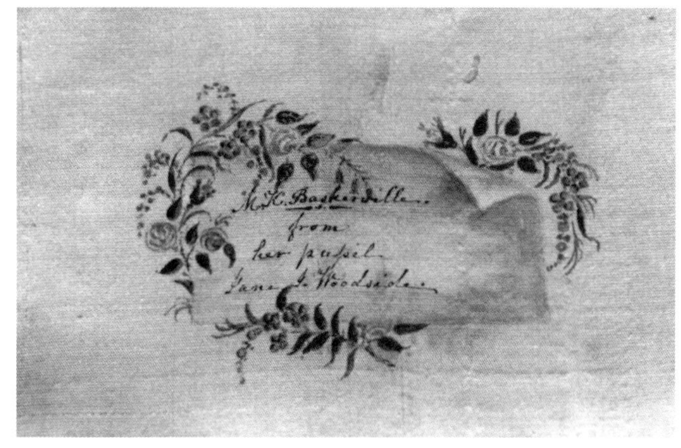

Fig. 114: Bristol Board Box. c. 1840.
Size: 7" L x 6" W x 2¾" D. Wool on bristol board.
Collection of Ross County Historical Society Museum.

Chillicothe's most celebrated teacher in its early days was without doubt Miss Mary K. Baskerville. Miss Baskerville came from Virginia and immigrated to Ohio in 1807 with her father, Colonel Samuel Baskerville. She was persuaded to come to Chillicothe about 1810, where she opened a school in a one-story frame house on West Second Street. She taught needlework and fine embroidery for many years and died in April 1856. History books describe her as a woman of determination and relate that she was very strict with students but was always held in great esteem by those who knew her as a stern taskmaster.[84]

Although no samplers from Mary Kay Baskerville's school have yet been documented, a delicate, hand-sewn bristol board box belonging to this teacher has been found. The lid is labeled "A Gift of Love," the inscription embroidered beneath a Berlin-work wreath of flowers. Inside the silk-lined lid is an artfully painted wreath of flowers encircling the inscription "M. K. Baskerville—from her pupil—Jane I. Woodside" (1824–1890).

Clermont County

Surprisingly, since the area was settled so early, only two samplers made in this county have been discovered. A great number of the pioneer settlers of Clermont County came to Ohio from Virginia, after first settling in Kentucky. When they felt the land north of the Ohio River was safe, they moved their families on to the Ohio Country. Clermont County was almost entirely within the Virginia Military Reservation Lands. After about 1804, large numbers of New Jersey settlers also arrived to purchase land in the area that was part of the Symmes Purchase. Clermont County attracted many abolitionists, and as the fleeing slaves arrived from Kentucky, they were rapidly sent on their way north, especially to the Quaker settlements in Clinton and Warren Counties.

Fig. 115: Sampler of Eliza Luin Kain. 1821.
Size: 16" L x 16¾" W. Collection of the Pioneer and Historical Society of Muskingum County.

Eliza Luin Kain completed four alphabets on her large marking sampler and clearly dated the canvas. She was born in Ohio c. 1816 to Major Daniel Kain and his second wife, Elenor (Nelly) Foster. James and Catherine Kain, Eliza's paternal grandparents, immigrated to the Ohio Country from Lancaster, Pennsylvania, and were among the first families to arrive in Columbia (Cincinnati) in the spring of 1792. By 1796, they purchased land in Clermont County and settled in Williamsburg, where they promptly opened Kain's Tavern. The Kain family was well known in the area, and their tavern became the most noted stopping place in pioneer times between Cincinnati and Chillicothe.[85]

Eliza's father Daniel, their oldest son, was about nineteen when the family came to Ohio. He was a tall, dark, fine-looking man and was commissioned a captain in 1801 in General Wayne's army. When the War of 1812 began, he served again, with the rank of major, and later as a colonel in the militia. After his illustrious military career, he held several offices in Clermont County, until his death in 1843.[86]

Morgan County

Sixteen years after Ohio's statehood was granted, Morgan County was organized. It was named to honor the Revolutionary War general Daniel Morgan. It is said that Morgan, one of the most successful leaders of the colonists, developed a long "Kentucky" rifle that could hit the redcoats at a great distance. A reflective glance into history leaves little doubt that the long rifle helped to suppress the Indians and open up the Northwest Territory.

The Muskingum River flows through the heart of this county, and it gave the first settlers easy access to the interior from the Ohio River at Marietta. McConnellsville, the county seat, is located on the Muskingum some thirty-six miles above Marietta, and this is where Margaret Vail's family was living when she stitched her sampler (fig. 116).

History books reveal nothing about the schools of this area, so we have no idea where Margaret Vail learned to stitch with such proficiency. Morgan County was sparsely populated and evidently did not have many schools. Even today, McConnellsville's population is less than two thousand. Perhaps Margaret received her needlework tutoring from a teacher working in neighboring Washington or Athens County.

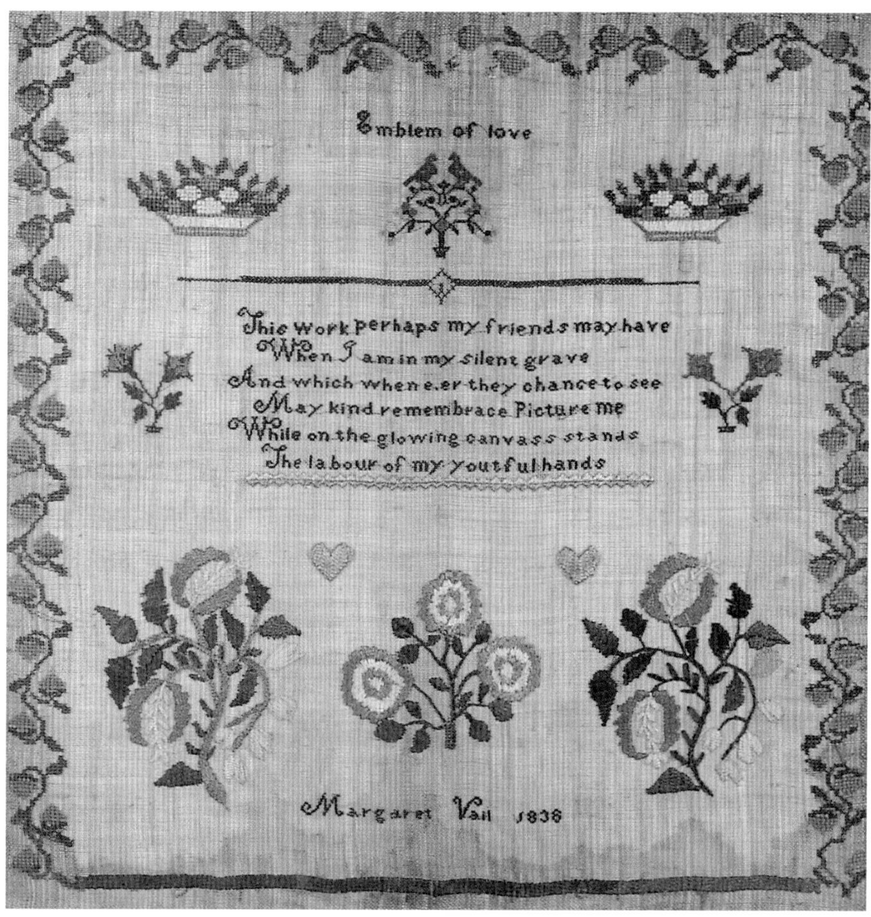

FIG. 116: SAMPLER OF MARGARET VAIL. 1836.
SIZE: 17½" L x 17½" W. COLLECTION OF MRS. THOMAS J. HANCOCK.

Margaret Vail's sampler exhibits a verse that is a favorite with many sampler collectors. It reads:

This work perhaps my friends may have,
When I am in my silent grave
And which whene'er they chance to see
May kind remembrance, picture me
While on the glowing canvass stands
The labour of my youthful hands.

Margaret was born on April 1, 1818. She made this sampler when she was eighteen years old. The daughter of Samuel and Margaret Grisell Vail, she spent her entire life in Morgan County. In 1842 she married James Blackburn McGrew.

This sampler is colorful, and the design elements symmetrically placed on the lower part of the canvas are compatible and pleasing. Margaret's fruit-filled baskets, the familiar design of the paired birds entitled "Emblem of Love," and the strawberry vine surrounding three sides of the canvas make this sampler very attractive. This young woman had been well taught and possessed considerable needlework skills.

FIG. 117: SAMPLER OF MARY CORNER. 1833.

SIZE: 9" L x 12½" W. COLLECTION OF ELIZABETH W. PETERS.

Mary Lowe Corner's simple marking sampler tells us that she completed her canvas when she was ten years old. Mary worked diligently to fit five different alphabets on her modest sampler, leaving barely enough room to tell us a little about herself. Her family lived in the small town of Malta, just across the Muskingum River from the county seat of McConnellsville. Mary was one of eight children born to George Lowe Corner and his wife, Sarah W. Hart. Both of Mary's parents were born in Washington County several years before Ohio achieved statehood. George was born in 1797, Sarah in 1800. Mary Lowe Corner was married in Malta on May 6, 1847, to Albert Clarke. She died in November 1866 at the age of forty-three. Her sampler is now owned by her great-granddaughter.

Gallia County

The first Ohio county of Washington, formed in 1788, was enormous and contained millions of acres. From that huge tract, land was soon taken to form other counties, and one of them was Gallia, whose southern border is formed by the Ohio River. Organized in 1803, the county was given the ancient name of France because it was first settled by Frenchmen.

News of the opening of the Northwest Territory had reached not only land speculators in the new country, but many Europeans as well. A group of men in Paris formed an association to arrange for purchase of land in this section of Ohio, and they bought about one and a half million acres. Situated on the Ohio River across from the mouth of the Kanawha, this land was represented to the French as a land of paradise. In reality the land was poor, hilly, and covered with trees and brush. Five hundred Parisians came to settle, most of them ill-fitted for such an enterprise. Guilders, carvers, artists, and coachmen were not prepared to clear a forest or construct a fortification against Indian attack. In fact, fewer than a dozen men in the group were farmers and laborers.[87] The French were deceived by two land speculators named Barlow and, ironically, Playfair!

Nonetheless, many of them stayed and there is a good chance that some of them may have been distant descendants of an old Norman French family originally named de Vezeay. By the seventeenth century however, the spelling had been changed to Veyssie, and at least one branch of the family had immigrated to the New World. Some settled in Virginia, and some in New York. Two centuries later, at least one family came to Gallipolis in Gallia County, Ohio. The Ohio 1850 Census of Springfield Township lists the following entry: "John B. Vessie, age 49—Farmer—$15.000—b. France; Frances Veyssie, Female age 38—b. France; Cecelia Veyssie, Female age 15—b. France; Lewis Veyssie, Male—age 12—b. Pennsylvania; Jane Harris, age 63—b. Virginia."[88] Based on this data, it is believed that the stitcher of the sampler shown in fig. 118 was Cecelia Veyssie.

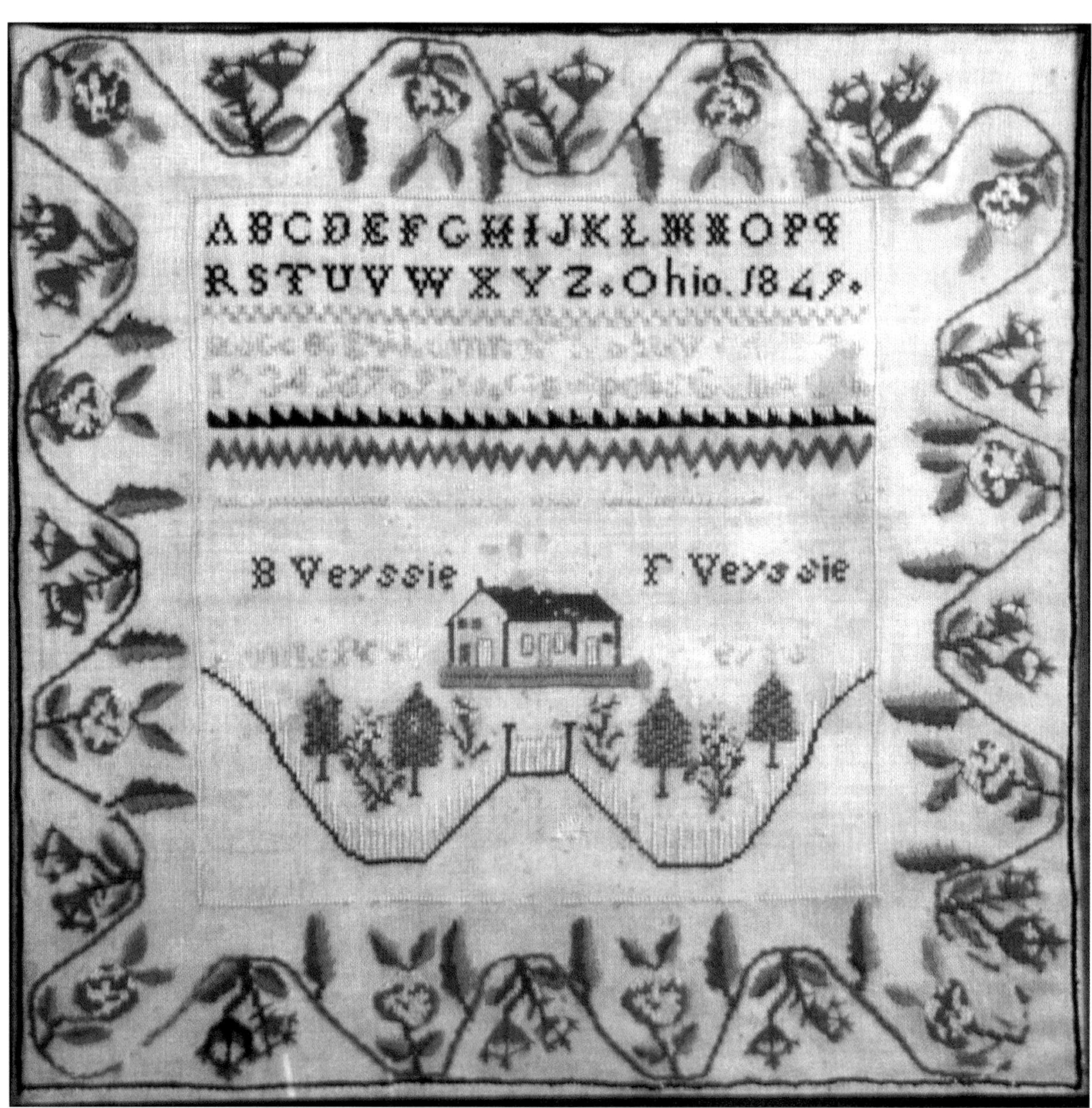

Fig. 118: Sampler of Cecelia Veyssie. 1849.
Size: 18" L x 17" W. Wool on linen.
Collection of Melvin and Connie Porcher.

Stitched in wool thread on a linen ground, this needlework is still in good condition. Although the stitcher did not give her name, of the five people in this family, Cecelia is the only one of an appropriate age to stitch a sampler, and the names "B. Veyssie and F. Veyssie" are those of her parents. Marked "Ohio—1849 Gallipolis—Gallia," the canvas exhibits an especially wide, beautiful border and a pleasing design.

Athens County

In 1805 land was taken from Ohio's first county, Washington, to form Athens County. The land in this area was poor for farming but rich in natural resources. It had coal, iron ore, salt, and an abundance of beautiful forest land. Even today impressive stands of timber comprise more than half of the county.

The men of the Ohio Company who had purchased and settled the land in Washington County were New Englanders, and many of them were well educated. They were quick to recognize the importance of establishing good schools, and in 1795 a tract of land was set aside for educational purposes.[89] Ohio University was founded in 1804 in Athens, the county seat. Appropriately, the town's name was taken from Athens, Greece, itself a center of learning.[90] This university holds the distinction of being the first institution of higher learning in all the territory northwest of the Ohio.

One of the first teachers to open a school in Athens County was Sarah Foster. She came from Massachusetts with her husband, Zadoc Foster, to Belpre (Washington County) in 1796, and by 1809 they had settled in Athens. Sarah began to teach after she was widowed in 1814 at the first schoolhouse on the town plat. It was a small brick building located just east of the Presbyterian Church. She taught for more than thirty years until her death in 1849.[91] Other teachers associated at one time with her school were Sally Jewett and Miss Haft.

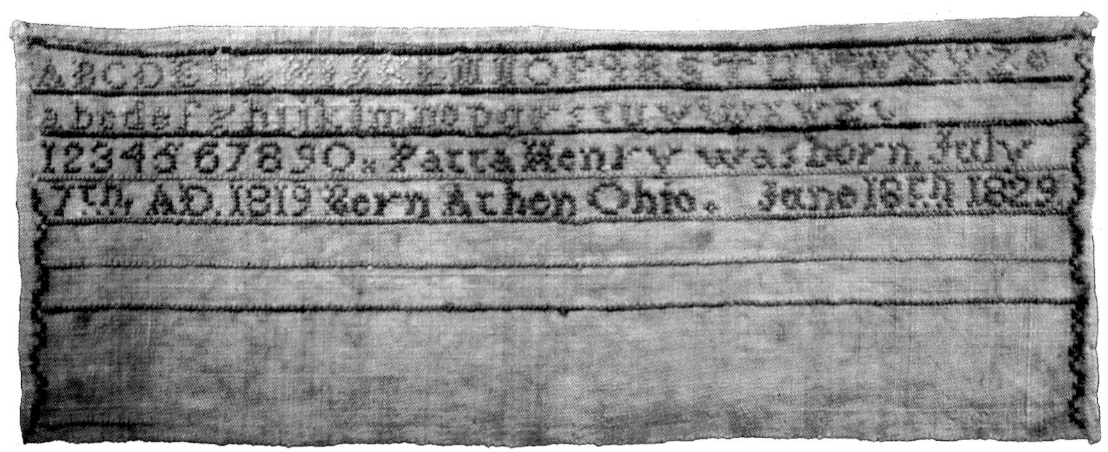

Fig. 119: Sampler of Martha Henry. 1829.

Size: 4" L x 12½" W. Collection of Martha Appel Burton.

Only two early pieces of needlework from Athens County have been discovered. Both are in good condition and charming. The small marking sampler of Martha Henry, done when she was ten years old, remains today with the stitcher's great-great-granddaughter and is a valued family memento. "Patty," the nickname she stitched on this practice sampler, was the child of John and Margaret McNutt Henry. Along with two alphabets and her numbers, she added that she was "born July 7th, A.D. 1819" and was living in "Bern" (township) in "Athen Ohio." Perhaps she tired of practicing her stitching, for she left the bottom of the canvas unfinished.

Patty's family lived on the "old Henry farm" bordering Washington County. Just before her nineteenth birthday in 1838, Patty married James Patterson, the oldest son of Jordan and Mary Lipsey Patterson. The couple spent their married lives in Amesville, Ohio, and had four daughters. Martha Henry Patterson died at the age of eighty-four on January 15, 1904.

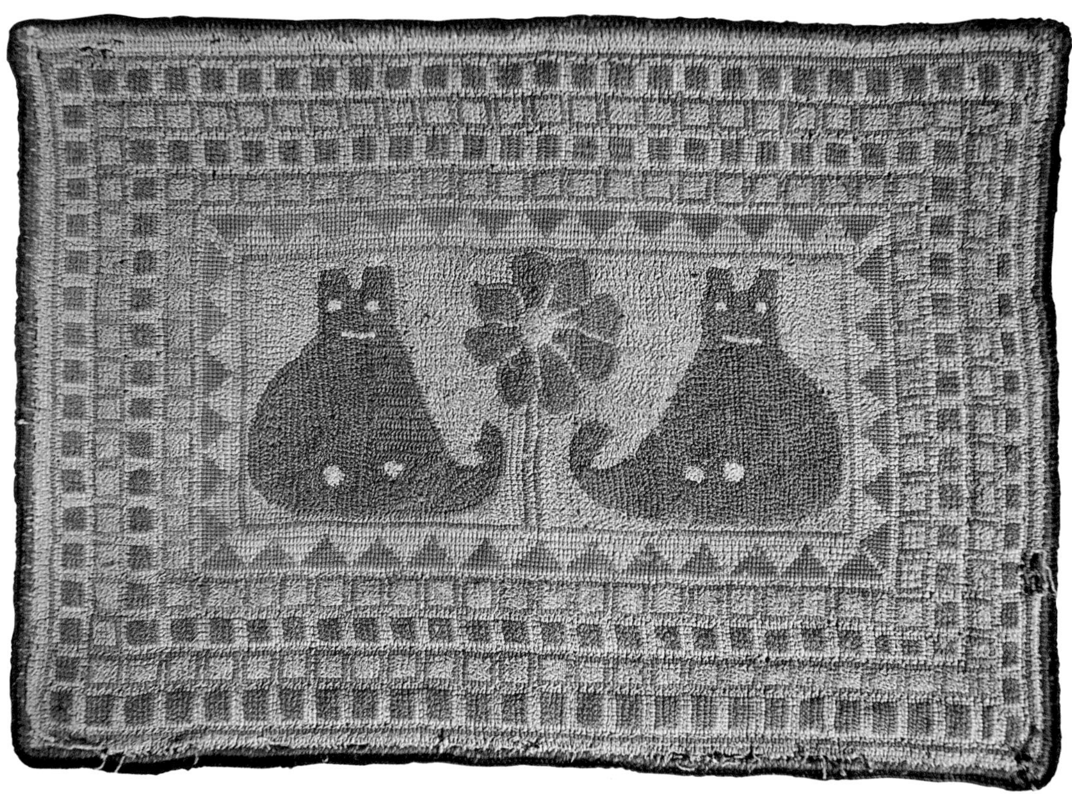

Fig. 120: Cross-Stitch Rug of Eunice Melona Rice. Undated.
Size: 31" L x 22" W. Wool on linen. Collection of Jane Collins.

This small cross-stitch rug is attributed to Eunice Melona Rice, the daughter of Sabinus and Pamela Hibbard Rice, who came to Ohio in 1799 from Poultney, Vermont. Her parents settled first near Marietta and in 1801 moved on to the village of Mudsock, now Amesville, Athens County, where the family farm was established on Federal Creek. Eunice was born there on March 2, 1833, one of eight children. She became a teacher and in the 1880s married the superintendent of the public school in Athens.[92] In her late seventies, Eunice wrote a lengthy and detailed account of her early family life. It documents well the importance of needlework in their lives: "We were taught to make all our own garments of every kind, shirts and trousers for men and all sorts of house linen and bed clothes. We pieced quilts and learned to quilt them and to make comforts and rag carpets. We learned to do hemstitching and other drawn work, some very fine and beautiful, to cross-stitch, tufted stitch, satin stitch, outline stitch and appliqué, and to make tatting and macramé work." Eunice also wrote about the making of this rug: "We made some rugs for two doors to match our mother's hearth rug. The little rugs were edged with fringe also, but the pattern of Sarah's rug was a pair of very life-like puppies done in tufted stitch, and the pattern on my rug was a pair of kittens."[93] The memoirs of Eunice Rice give a detailed account of how the family planted flax and spun and dyed threads and where she and her sister kept their sewing threads and needlework tools. Her words tell a great deal about the day-to-day life of the pioneer families who settled rural Ohio.

part two

CENTRAL OHIO

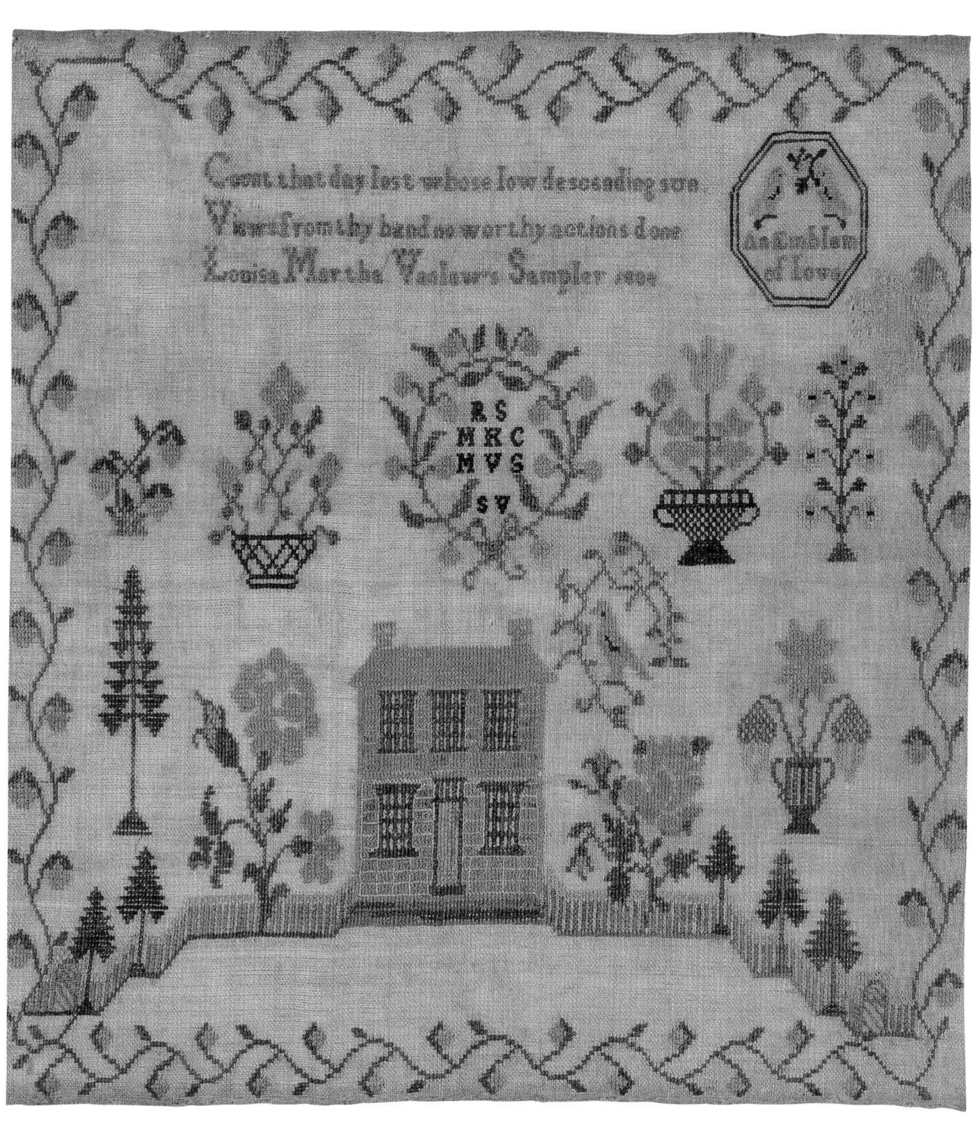

Clark County

During the Revolutionary War and the accompanying settlement of Kentucky in the 1780s, the area that became Clark County was very important. Most of the Indian raids on Kentucky settlements originated in this part of the Ohio Country. The fortified Shawnee Indian town of Picawillany was situated on the Mad River, just five miles west of present-day Springfield. General George Rogers Clark believed that once the strategic Ohio "Indian towns" of Old Chillicothe and Picawillany were destroyed, the white settlers in Kentucky would be safer from Indian attacks. The battle fought to destroy this Indian stronghold was an important turning point in the settlement of this wilderness land. Nearly forty years after that fearful battle of 1780, the county was formally organized in 1818. It seemed only fitting that it be named Clark. George Rogers Clark State Park is now situated on the high plains and rolling hills where the battle occurred.

During the ensuing years of settlement, several excellent schools were established. The *Western Pioneer* newspaper advertised on October 13, 1831: "Springfield Female Academy. Susan Voorhees respectfully informs the inhabitants of Springfield that she has, with the consent of the Trustees, taken charge of the Female Academy, and solicits a share of patronage. No boys will be hereafter admitted to the school, whose age exceeds six years. Terms of Tuition as heretofore."

One of the earliest teachers was Martha Mulford, a young widow who was teaching in Clark County in the 1820s.[1] She may have been the instructress of Mary A. Croft and Melissa Cory, whose samplers are seen in figs. 121 and 122.

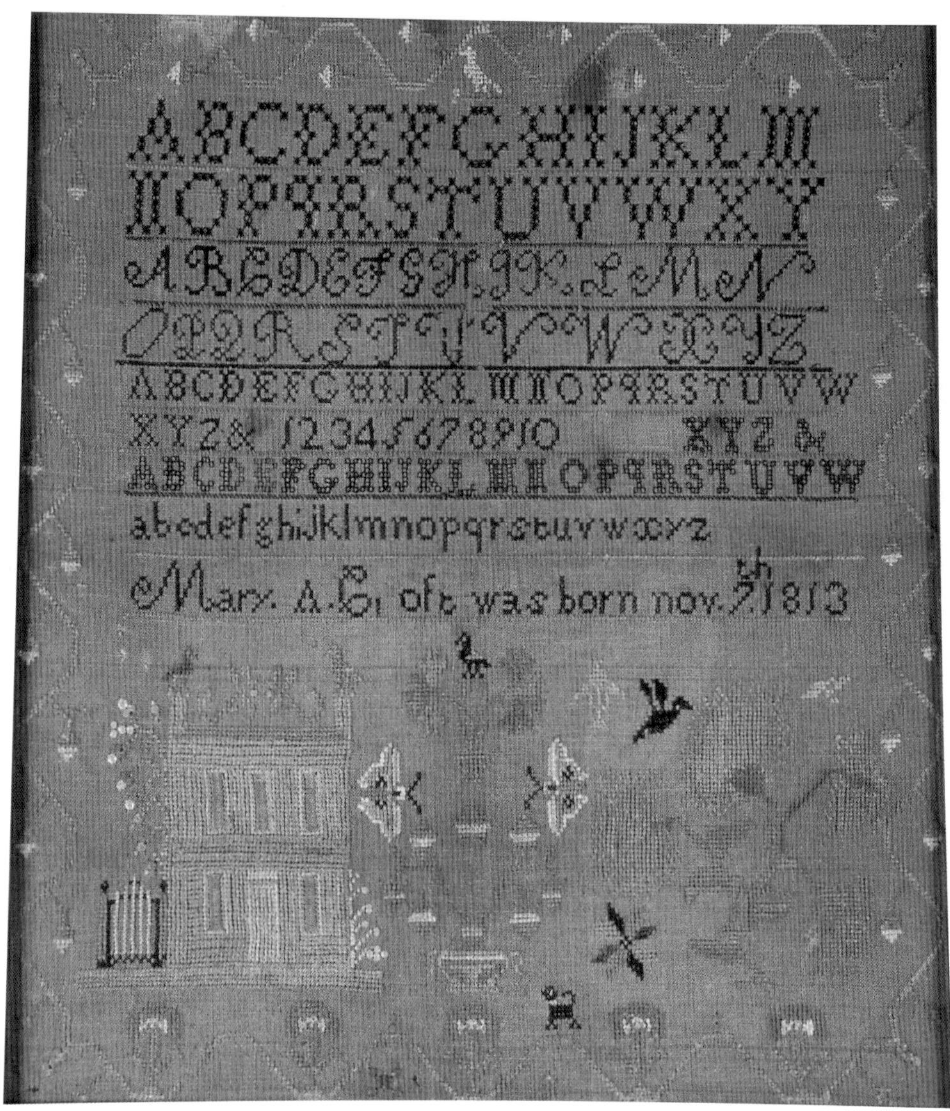

Fig. 121: Sampler of Mary A. Croft. c. 1824–25.
Size: 18" L x 16" W. Collection of Barbara and Tim Martein.

The needlework of Mary A. Croft is not dated but was probably executed when she was eleven or twelve years old. Her stitches tell us that she was "born November 7, 1813." Many of the design elements on this sampler, such as the hummingbird, the window and door surrounds, and the sprigs and birds on the chimney of the house, suggest that Martha Mulford designed this canvas.

Mary's family came to the area of Bethel Township near Springfield in 1804. She was the daughter of George and Mary (Critz) Croft. In 1830 Mary married James Leffel, who became a prominent industrialist. The couple had six sons and three daughters. She is described in an early history book as "an unpretentious motherly woman, charitable and generous, [who] is only spoken of in terms of kindness and esteem."[2]

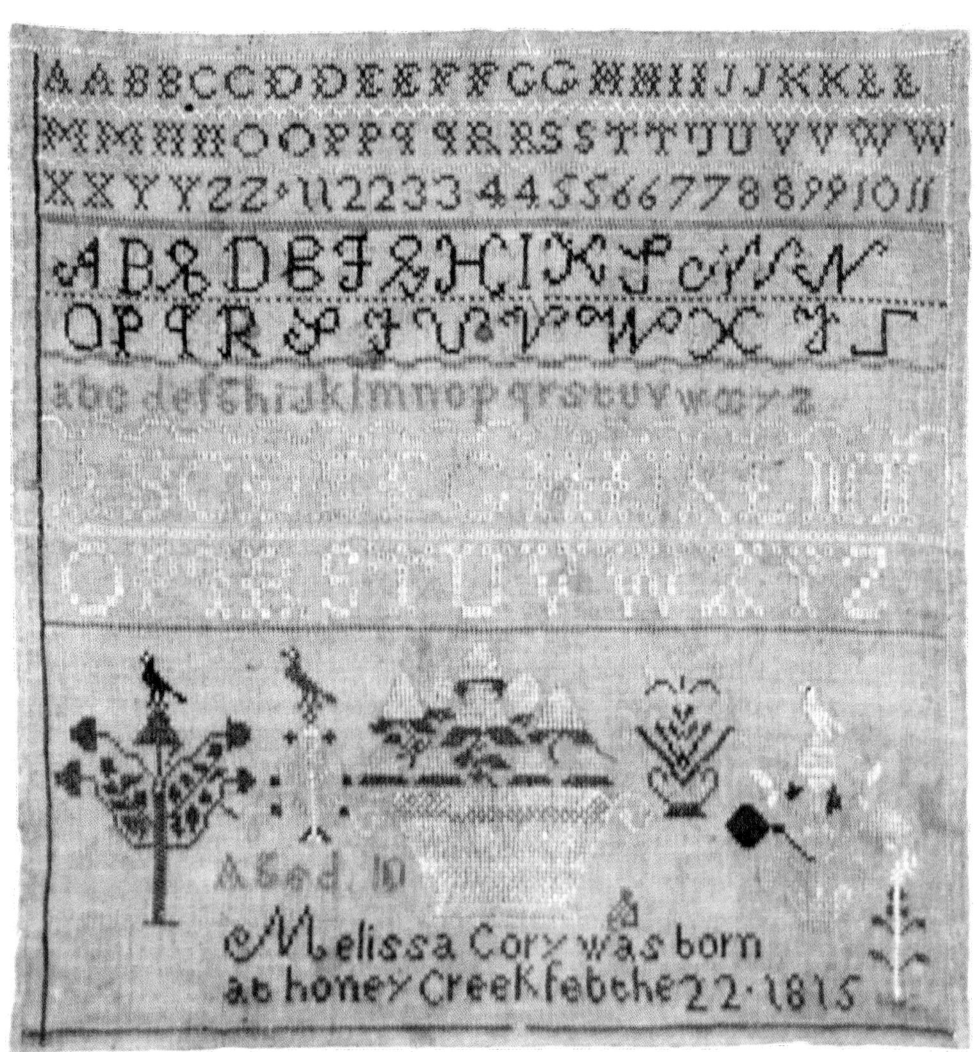

Fig. 122: Sampler of Melissa Cory. c. 1825.
Size: 16" L x 15" W. Collection of the Daughters of the American Revolution Museum, Washington, D.C.

Melissa Cory was one of the eleven children of Elnathan and Hannah (Jennings) Cory. She completed this rather naive but charming sampler c. 1825. Martha Mulford, who was teaching school in Springfield at the time this sampler was executed, married David J. Cory, Melissa's older brother. Melissa may well have been one of her students. Her canvas says she was "born on Honey Creek on February 22, 1815." Honey Creek is a picturesque creek still running through Bethel Township today. The stitcher's grandfather, Thomas Cory, came to Bethel Township from Essex County, New Jersey, in 1803, and the Cory Plat remains on the town map of New Carlisle.

Melissa married Samuel Stafford on May 12, 1834. She died in New Carlisle at age forty-five and is interred in the Stafford family plot in New Carlisle Cemetery.

Fig. 123: Sampler of Maria Wise. 1837. »

Size: 22" L x 18" W. Cotton on linen. Collection of Emma Anderson.

This Ohio sampler is a jewel and is certainly different from any others that have been discovered. Maria Wise must have been a loquacious young woman, and her needlework makes it easy to "bring her back to life." One can almost see this young girl, with needle and thread in her hands, giggling and visiting with her siblings. This sampler tells us many personal things about Maria if we study it carefully. Maria did not want to waste an inch of the canvas and stitched most everywhere she could fit something in. Design motifs like the tulips and "dutchy" hearts were passed from generation to generation, from the old country to the new. As is typical in German work, they are scattered around the canvas. The stitcher, who worked this sampler when she was sixteen years old, tells us: "Maria Wise is my name, Pike Township is my Station, Clark County is my dwelling place, and Christ is my Salvation."

Family initials are in the center of the canvas, probably those of her siblings. The large "J. W." and "C. W." are the initials of her parents, Jacob and Christina Wise. Maria married Simon Huffer in Montgomery County when she was twenty, and they had three children. Both families were members of the German Baptist (Dunkard) Church.

Maria Wise's work is typical of the samplers and hand towels that were stitched by girls of German descent. With the exceptions of the Moravians and perhaps some German girls living in urban areas like Cincinnati, German girls were educated at home, principally spoke German, and lived with their families on good farmlands. They worked hard and stayed mostly within their own close-knit societies. The Wise family lived on a farm, and Maria stitched many farm animals on her canvas. She shows us a turkey, a chicken, a lamb, and even a beguiling checkered goat.

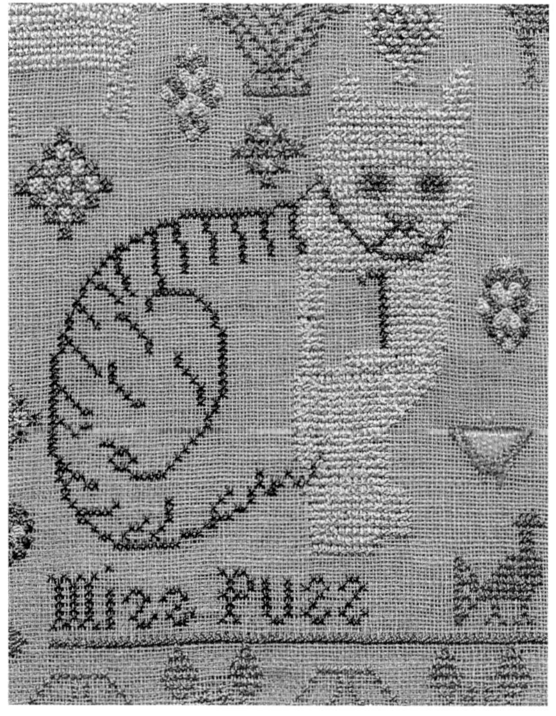

Fig. 125: Miss Puss.

Without doubt, the most important animal in Maria Wise's life was Miss Puss, whom she stitched as big as her house!

Fig. 124: Maria's Goat.

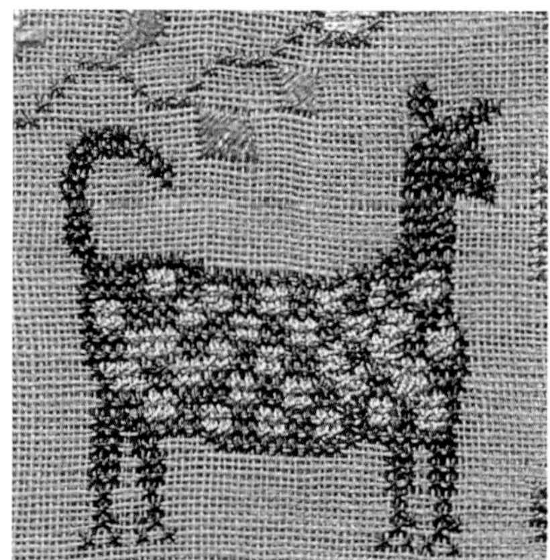

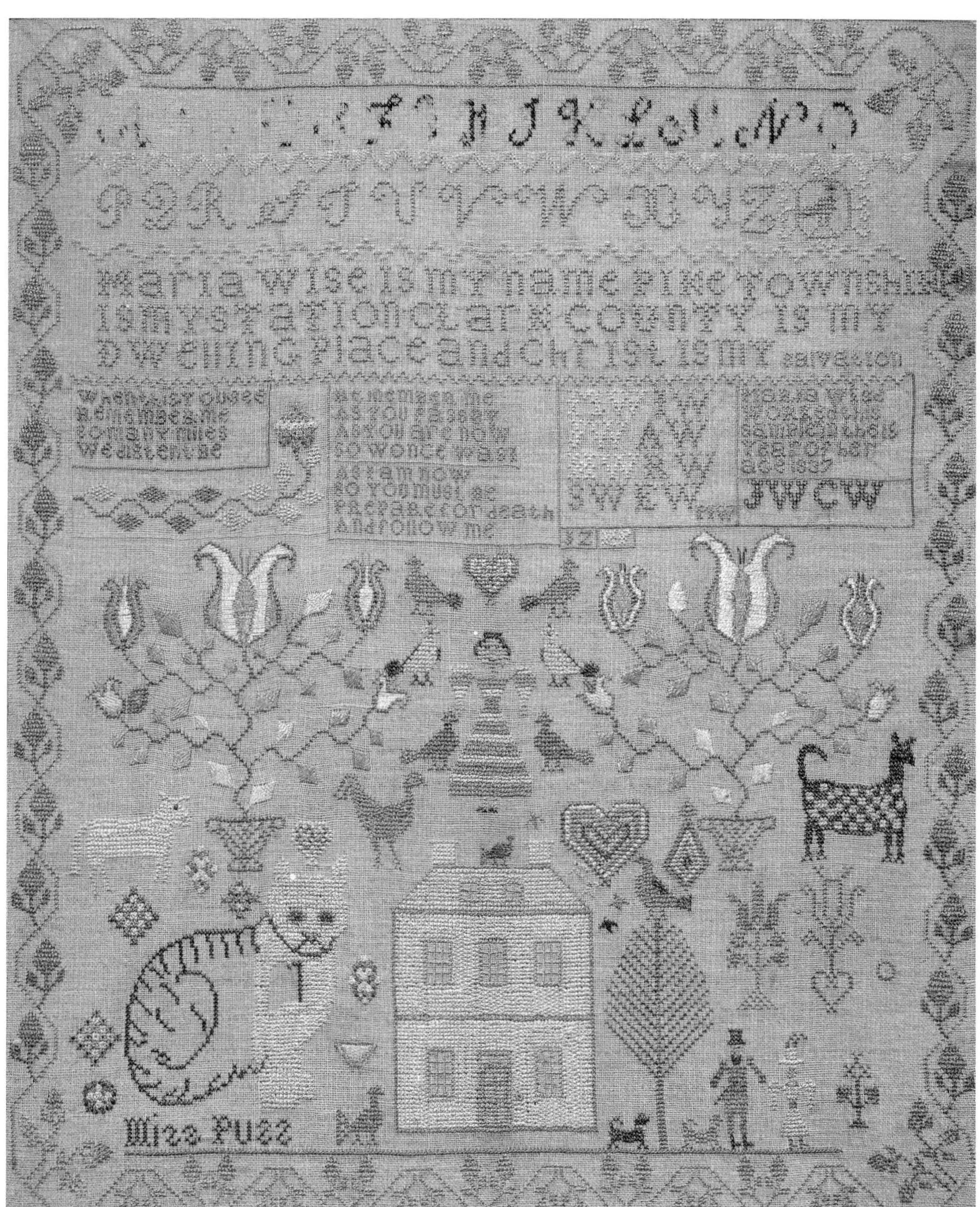

Maria's verse reads:

> *When this you see, remember me—Though many miles we distent be*
> *Remember me as you pass by—As you are now, so wonce was I*
> *As I am now so you must be—Prepare for death and follow me.*

Fig. 126: Sampler of Sarah M. Hupman. 1846. »

Size: 16¾" L x 17" W. Collection of Jane and George Harold.

The canvas of Sarah M. Hupman's genealogical sampler is filled to capacity. She stitched not only two poignant verses, but also four alphabets. We notice, however, that when she ran out of space to finish the alphabet done in the wide block Roman-style letters she ingeniously completed it by scattering *w, x, y,* and *z* in the outer border. Small mistakes like this make the sampler more appealing than it would be had it been executed perfectly.

John and Elizabeth Hupman came to Ohio from Virginia in 1835 and settled in Clark County. They may have encouraged their oldest daughter, Sarah, to embroider a Family Record sampler, the kind of needlework that often took the place of the family Bible for recording births, deaths, and marriages. Many major family events took place between 1839 and 1846, according to the sampler: Sarah's two older brothers, David and John, got married; her young brother Jacob died in 1842 at the age of twelve; and her baby niece, David's daughter Charlotte, died in 1843 at the sweet age of eight months.

The two verses Sarah chose to stitch are not common ones. One, for the marriage of her brothers, offered good advice:

In purest love, their souls unite,
That they, with Christian care,
May make domestic burden light,
By taking each their share.

The poem for the death records reads:

Lord, 'tis a Pleasant thing to stand,
In gardens planted by thy hand,
Let me within thy courts be seen,
Like a young cedar, fresh and green.

Needlework can be cathartic, and perhaps working on this sampler helped her cope with what had happened to her family.

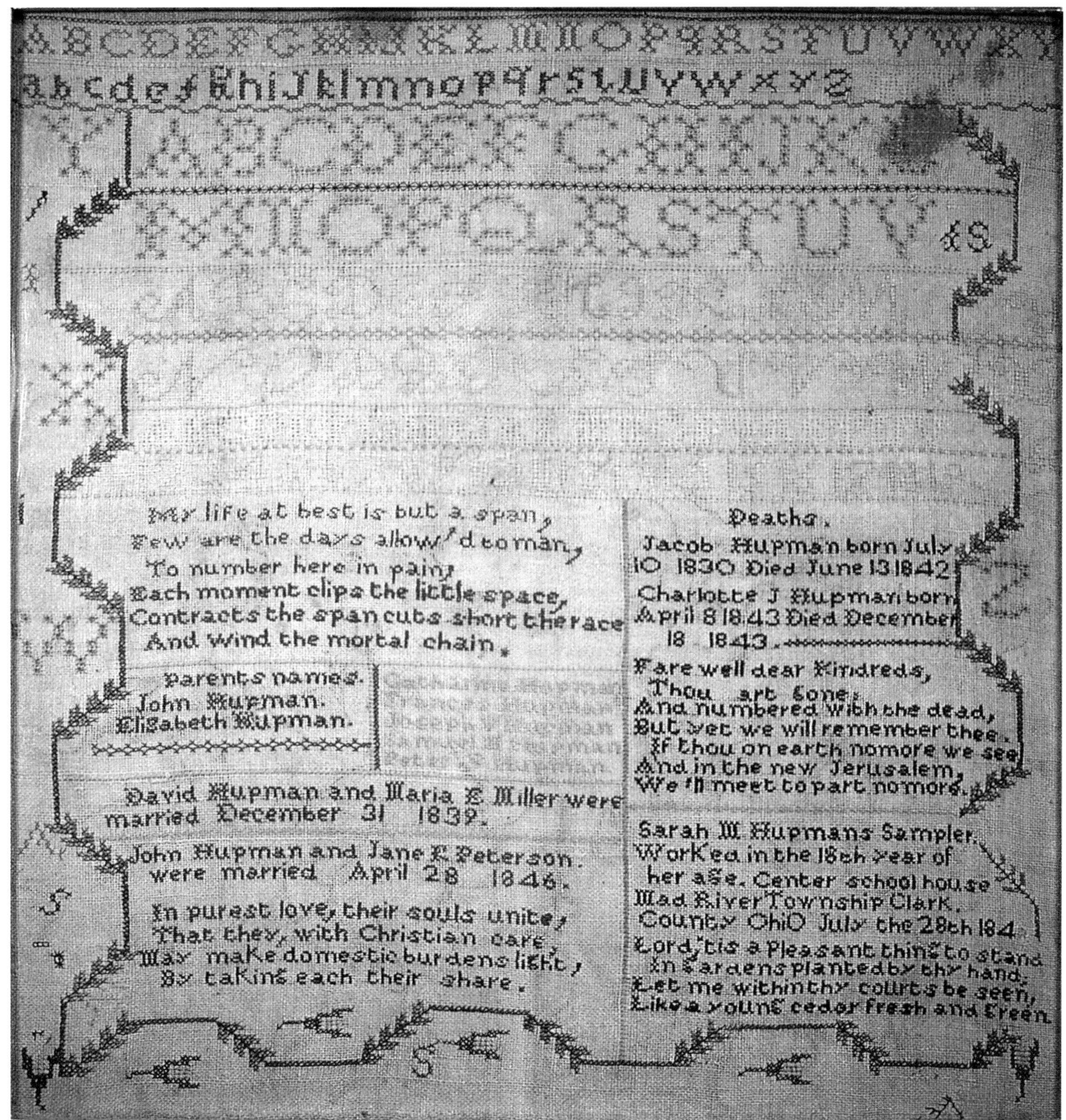

Sarah was born on July 13, 1828, though this information was not included on her canvas. She records that she was eighteen when she completed this work at Center Schoolhouse in Mad River Township, Clark County. In later years she picked out the date of 1846, the year she completed the canvas, to avoid giving away her age to everyone who viewed her sampler. Sarah M. Hupman died February 1, 1913, at the age of eighty-four.

Darke County

The site where the city of Greenville stands today was a point of major historical importance in Ohio's early history. It was here, in December 1793, that General Anthony Wayne built Fort Greenville. He located his sizable army at this fortification and remained there until midsummer the following year. In July, he and his men proceeded northward and engaged and defeated the Indians in a fearful battle at the Maumee River rapids, referred to as the Battle of Fallen Timbers. A year later in 1795, forced by this defeat, the Indians signed the famous Treaty of Greenville, making peace with eleven of the most powerful northwestern Indian tribes. This treaty resulted in a boundary line being drawn across the middle of the state, separating the Indian lands to the north from the American settlers.

But the Greenville Treaty did not entirely resolve the settlers' problems with the Indians. The great chief of the Shawnees, Tecumseh, traveled widely to organize the various tribes to continue their cause. At the battle at Fort Malden in Canada, in the War of 1812, Tecumseh, the leader of the allied Indian confederacy, was killed. Their spirit broken, the Delawares, Shawnees, Senecas, and Miamis then signed a second treaty in July of 1814. This opened up the remainder of the state for settlement.

Considered even today to be some of the best agricultural land in Ohio, Darke County's flat fertile ground attracted settlers long before the county was formally organized in 1817. Perhaps that was what brought the Zimmerman family from their home in Pennsylvania.

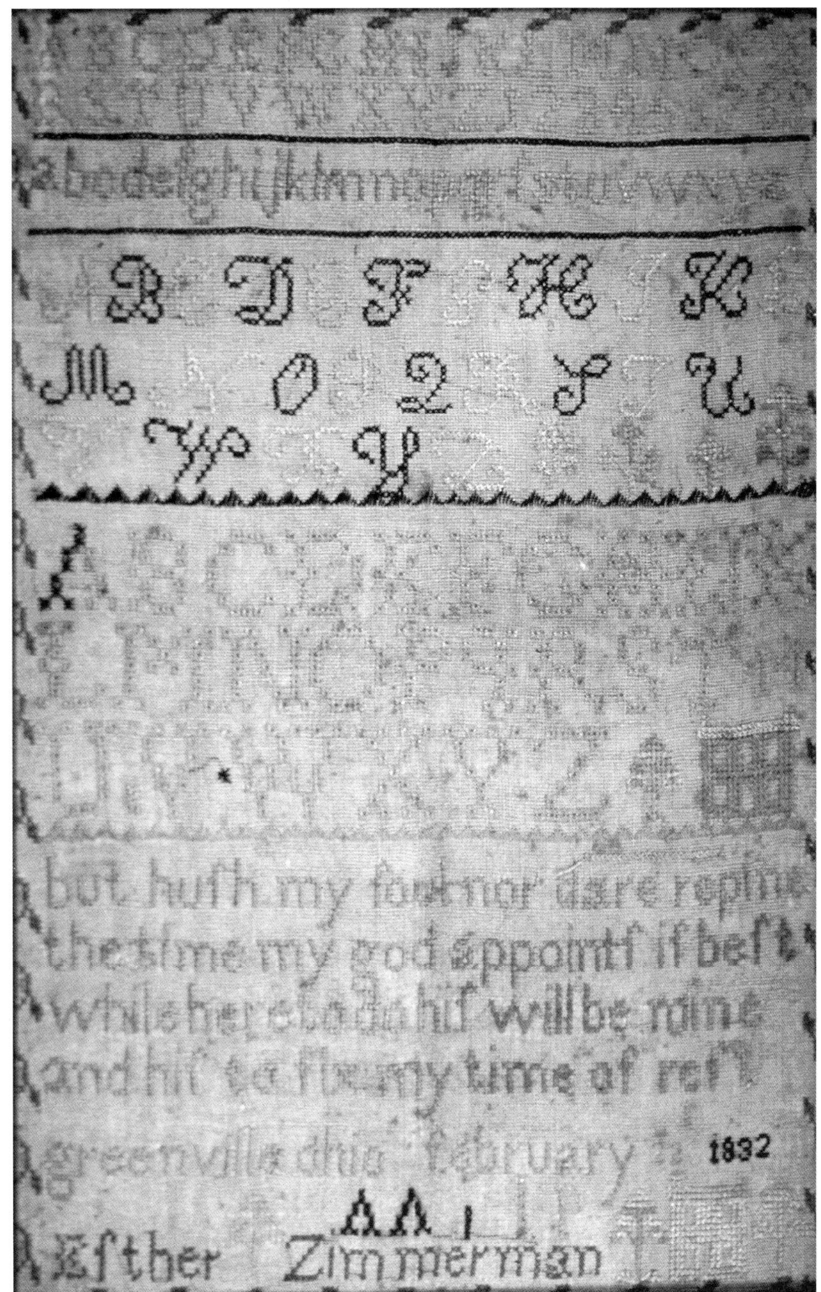

Fig. 127: Sampler of Esther Zimmerman. 1832.
Size: 16" L x 10" W. Collection of Judee and Phillip Harbaugh.

Esther Zimmerman's sampler is not very decorative, but it is clearly marked "was worked in Greenville Ohio." She was still using the old *f* for *s* in her words. It is likely that Esther was the daughter of Henry and Rebecca Zimmerman, who were the parents of nine children. Esther's name was not found in Ohio marriage records, so she may never have married. Her sampler holds the distinction of being the only Darke County sampler yet discovered.

Miami County

Even though the Treaty of Greenville had been signed in 1795, Indian attacks continued to discourage settlement of Miami County along the Great Miami River until well into the nineteenth century. The Indian towns of Upper and Lower Piqua were destroyed, but those Indians who were strongly allied with the British did not give up the fight. The great Chief Tecumseh organized many tribes to the west and north, and he and his warriors were well prepared by the British to prevent further white settlement. The story of their alliance and the War of 1812 is commemorated on a wonderful sampler (see fig. 220).

This was a critical time for the Indians who were friendly with the settlers, and they were in dire need of protection. In 1810, Colonel John Johnson was appointed by President James Madison to act as the Indian agent and assigned to attend to their needs. His large, handsome brick house was built at the Upper Piqua town and is maintained by the Ohio Historical Society. During the War of 1812, ten thousand peaceful Indians from various tribes gathered here. Most of them came from areas farther east, having been forced from their ancestral homes and hunting grounds. Colonel Johnson helped save many American lives, not only those of pioneer settlers, but also the lives of the friendly American Indians, to whom he offered food, clothing, and shelter. After the War of 1812 and the death of Tecumseh, Miami County and the surrounding lands were settled rapidly. Further encouragement for settlement of the county came with the completion of the Miami and Erie Canal in the 1830s.

Fig. 128: Sampler of Martha M. Telford. 1827.

Size: 17" L x 17½" W. Collection of Scherre Mumpower.

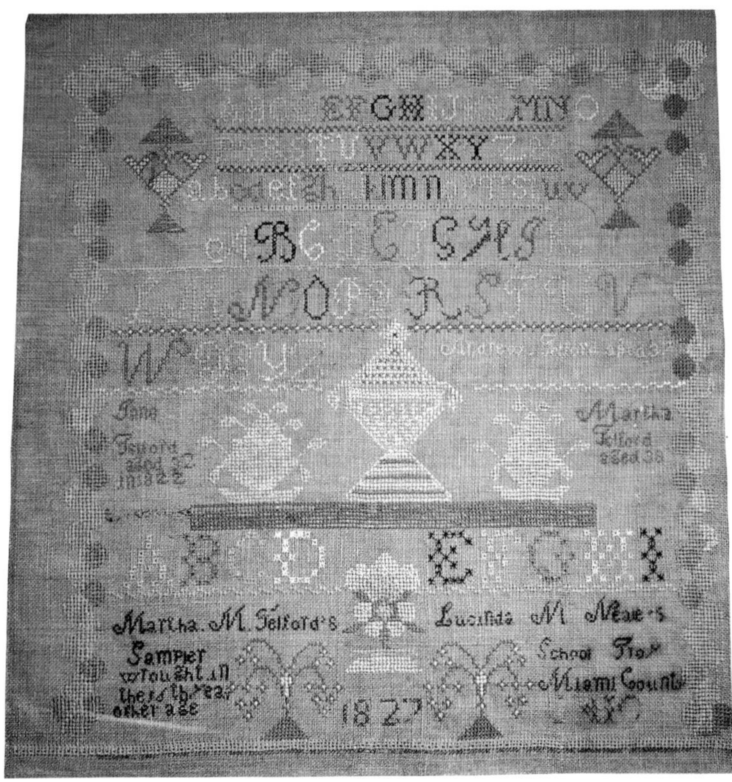

The sampler of Martha M. Telford has a great deal of genealogical information stitched on the canvas. The daughter of Andrew and Martha Telford completed this work when she was sixteen. Her needlework also allows us to document "Lucinda M. Neal's School [in] Troy, Miami County, Ohio." Martha filled her canvas with alphabets and surrounded three sides with a delicious blue-and-white "fruit" border. The dominant element on her work is the white, tiered vase in the center. It is geometric in design, as are each of the decorative motifs placed around the canvas. This is the only sampler that has been discovered from Lucinda Neal's School.

The Telford family was one of the first to settle in Miami County. Martha's grandfather, Alexander Telford, served in the Revolutionary War and emigrated from Virginia to Ohio in 1804. By 1806 Ohio Land Patents record that he and his second wife, Elizabeth McClung, were residing in Miami County with their family. Martha married Simeon French in Miami County on March 24, 1830. All of the family members listed on Martha's canvas are buried in Troy's Rose Hill Cemetery.

Until the Telford sampler was discovered, the existence of Lucinda M. Neal's school in Troy, the county seat, had not been recorded. *The History of Miami County* provides information about Lucinda Neal and her "tasteful residence." Not once, however, does it mention that she taught needlework.[3]

Lucinda Million Neal was the daughter of Francis and Jemima (Sweet) Million. She and her family immigrated to Monroe Township, Miami County, from Tennessee in 1808, and she spent her entire life there. In 1828 Lucinda married William Neal, whose family had also come from Tennessee to Miami County in 1808. Quaker records document that the Neals were active members of the Society of Friends. Lucinda and William Neal had seven children. The Beers 1881 history records that "Mr. Neal was 66 years of age at the time of his death and left a large estate." It continues: "Mrs. (Lucinda) Neal is among the eldest settlers now living in the county. . . . the home place is a lovely spot, and is carefully looked after. Mrs. Neal leaves her children a birthright of honesty and sociability."[4]

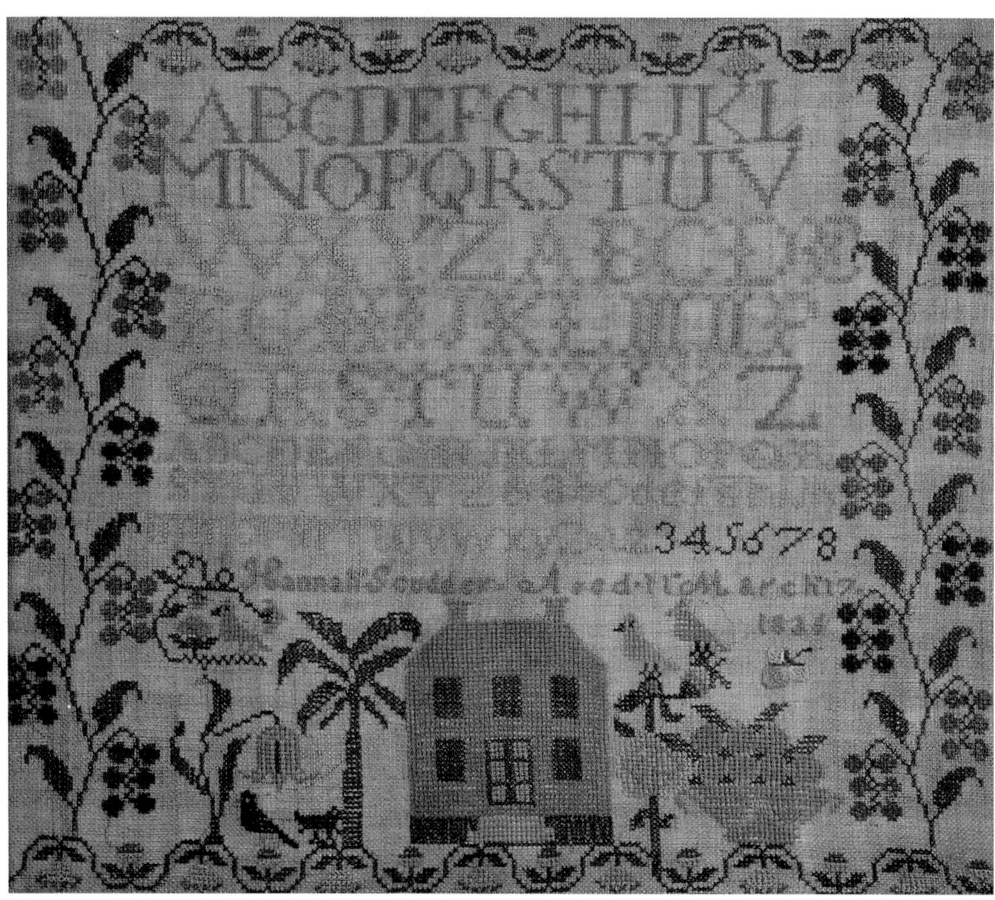

Fig. 129: Sampler of Hannah Scudder. 1836.
Size: 14½" L x 17½" W. Collection of the author.

Because this sampler shows so many similarities to that of Hannah Edmondson (see fig. 56), it is believed that this young girl was a student at Waynesville School in Warren County. Although Piqua, where this young lady lived, is quite a distance from Waynesville, it has been recorded that students from as far away as Indiana attended this school and boarded with local Quaker families. Hannah Scudder's sampler exhibits the typical wide block letters of the Quaker alphabet, and the grape border mirrors that stitched by Hannah Edmondson. Hannah Scudder stitched one motif that is an unusual one for an Ohio girl to place on her needlework: a neat palm tree beside the house. Perhaps her instructress used the palm tree because it was commonly seen on textiles and often found on the jacuard-woven coverlets so popular in Ohio.

Hannah was born in Piqua on March 17, 1825, to Cummings and Sarah (Sally) (Winans) Scudder, who came to Miami County from Rahway, New Jersey. Cummings Scudder, who is listed in 1850 Ohio Census records as a brick mason, began a long career as a builder. Several houses built by Scudder still stand in Piqua today. Hannah married James Johnston on October 20, 1840, and was the mother of five children. She was a devoted member of the Methodist Episcopal Church and spent her life in Miami County. She died March 1, 1887, and is interred at the Forest Hill Cemetery in Piqua.

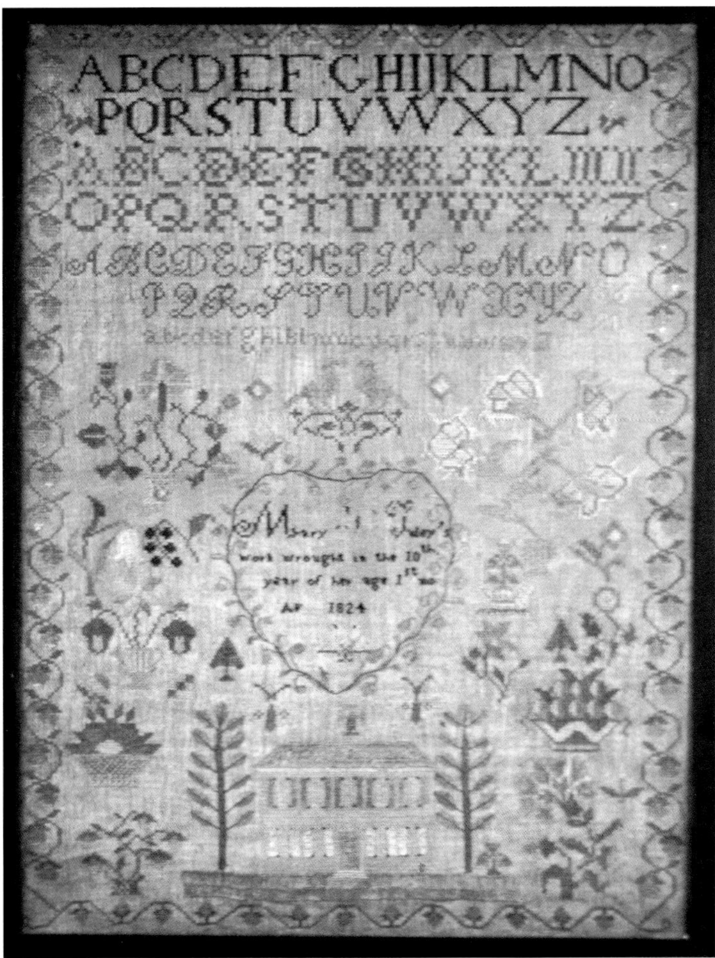

Fig. 130: Sampler of Mary J. Tuley. 1824.

Size: 22" L x 16¾" W. Collection of the Overfield Tavern Museum.

This needlework was completed when Mary J. Tuley was ten years old. The sampler, with its typical Quaker motifs, is attributed to the Waynesville School. The house and trees stitched at the bottom of the canvas resemble the sampler made ten years later by Mary Ann Edmondson from Dayton (fig. 55). The "W" basket motif is seldom omitted from canvases stitched at Waynesville School. Mary Tuley has filled her canvas, leaving just enough room in the heart-shaped vine cartouche in the center to stitch in her name. Unfortunately, the black silk threads that she so carefully stitched are beginning to disappear. Black threads were dyed with logwood or an iron mordant. Both were harmful to textiles, and the threads sometimes disintegrated.

Mary J. Tuley was born on January 24, 1814, in Burlington County, New Jersey. Her mother, Elizabeth Borden, was from a large Quaker family and married Thomas Tuley "out of unity" in June 1810. By 1820, when their daughter Mary J. was six years old, they moved their family to Warren County, Ohio, where they apparently enrolled her in the Waynesville School. About 1826, Thomas and Elizabeth Tuley moved farther north to Miami County, where on February 20, 1836, Mary married Solomon Jones. They were the parents of four children. Mary J. Tuley Jones lived a full life and died July 10, 1901, at the age of eighty-seven.

Fig. 131: Practice Sampler of Pamela Coleman. Undated.

Size: 9" L x 8½" W. Collection of the Overfield Tavern Museum.

Pamela Hale Coleman did not date either of the samplers that she stitched, but they were probably completed c. 1837–40. Her well-documented family is prominent in Miami County history.

Fig. 132: Sampler of Pamela Coleman. Undated. »

Size: 17¾" L x 17" W. Collection of the Overfield Tavern Museum.

Pamela Coleman stitched her name on her practice sampler (fig. 131), but only the initials PMC appear on her larger sampler. Her verse is the most common one found on samplers. It reads:

Jesus permit thy precious name to stand
As the first efforts of an infants hand
And while her fingers o'er the canvas move
Engage her tender heart to seek thy love.

Pamela did not finish the familiar verse, the last two lines of which are "With thy dear children let her share a part / And write thy name thyself upon her heart." There is enough open space in the lower part of the canvas that we can assume she tired of stitching and decided to finish the sampler with just her initials. The bouquets of flowers on either side of her initials are beautifully executed and tied with blue ribbon bows. An unusual geometric border on three sides of her sampler serves to frame her composition.

Pamela Coleman was born in Troy on July 4, 1827, one of eight children born to Dr. Asa Coleman and his third wife, Mary Keifer. Dr. Coleman came to Ohio from Connecticut in 1811. His service in the War of 1812 is documented in his letters, in which he gives eyewitness accounts of the war: "September 30, 1812—As to the effect the war has on the settlement of this country, it has put almost an entire stop to it, especially on the frontier part of the state. Most of the inhabitants of the county west of this [Darke] have moved off and a great many from this county."[5]

Pamela's grandfather, Dr. Asaph Coleman, who had served in the Revolution, followed his son to Troy. For well over a century, generation after generation of Dr. Colemans served the community. Pamela Hale Coleman married Henry Ware Allen in July 1853 and resided the rest of her life in Miami County. She died in 1915.

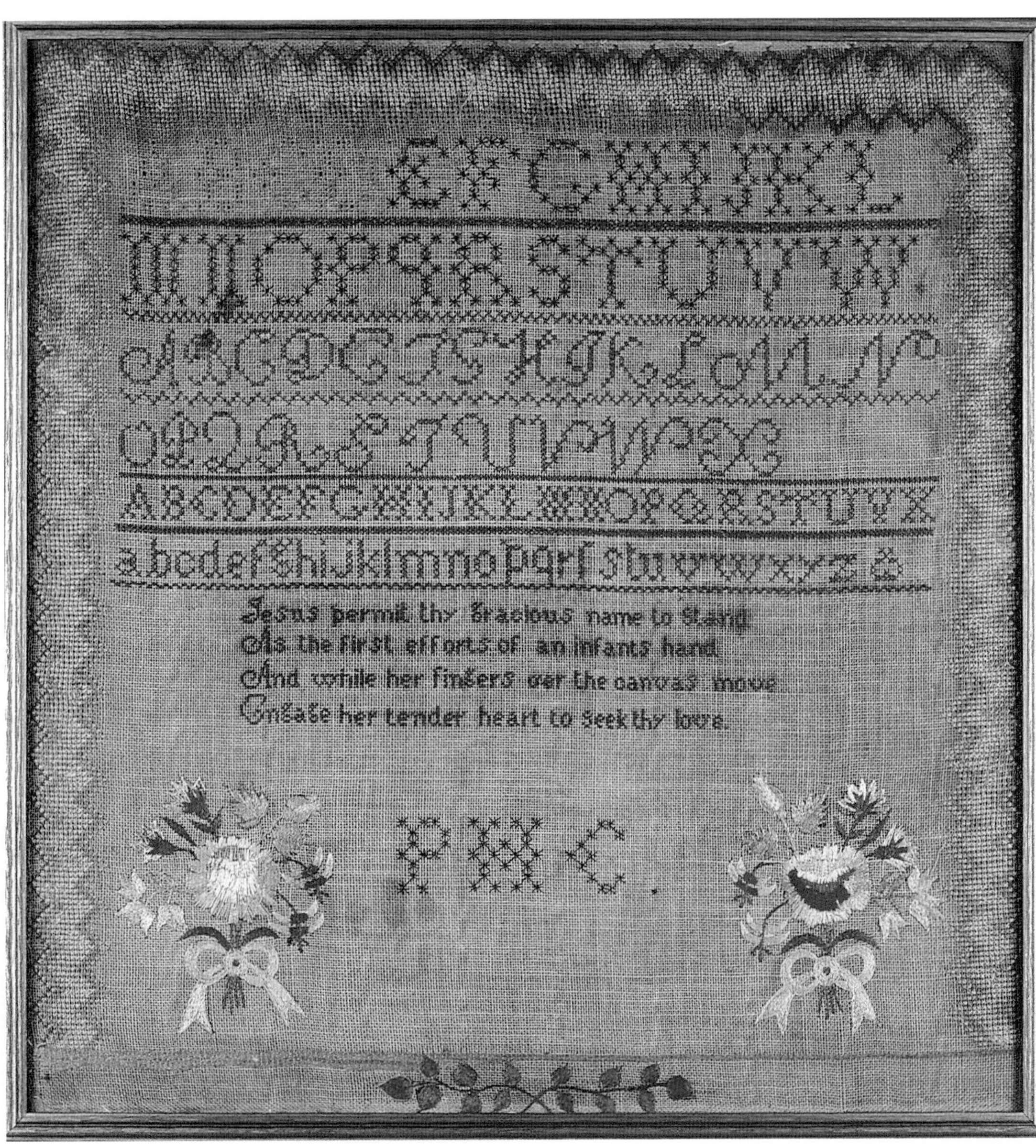
Jesus permit thy gracious name to stand
As the first efforts of an infants hand
And while her fingers oer the canvas move
Engage her tender heart to seek thy love.
P W C.

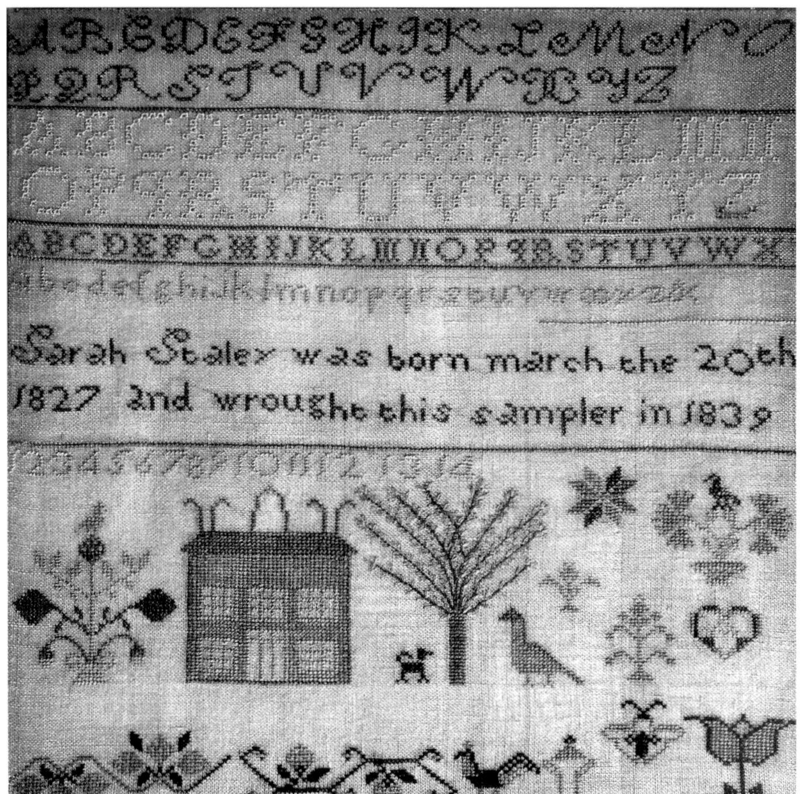

Fig. 133: Sampler of Sarah Staley. 1839.
Size: 15½" L x 17½" W. Collection of Carol J. Marker Mumford.

Sarah Staley was the daughter of Elias and Hannah Retter Staley. She stitched this needlework while living in the family's federal style brick house built in 1834. Elias served in the War of 1812 and came to Ohio from Maryland in 1816. Ten years later, he married Hannah Retter and the couple set up housekeeping in a simple log structure near the site where the brick house now stands. Sarah, the first of their seven children, was born on March 20, 1827, and executed this sampler at the age of twelve. She died at the homestead when she was nineteen, on September 5, 1846. The sampler is a special remembrance of her life because it remains in the home in which it was created.

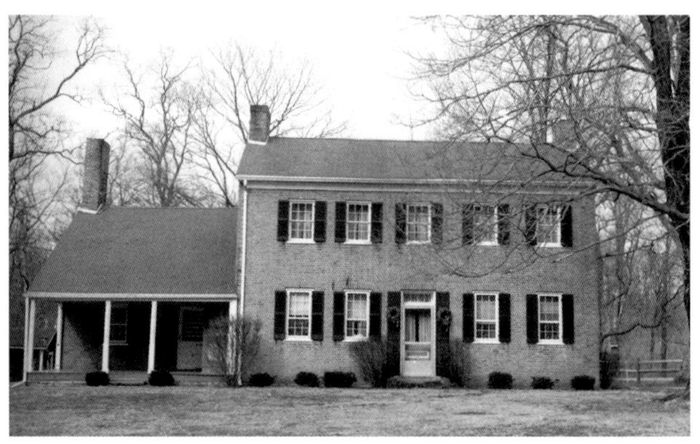

Fig. 134: Staley Homestead. 1834.

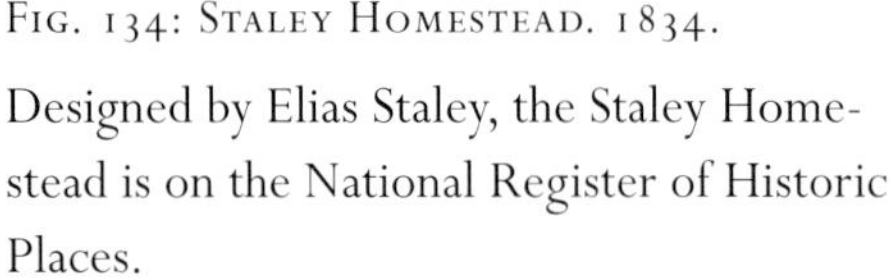

Designed by Elias Staley, the Staley Homestead is on the National Register of Historic Places.

Champaign County

Champaign County's earliest settlers were attracted to this area of the Ohio Country because of the vast tracts of prairie lands. Formed in 1805, the county still is primarily made up of fertile farmlands and has only one city, the county seat of Urbana.

Before white settlers arrived, the Shawnees roamed and hunted freely there. One of the most famous Indian fighters, Simon Kenton, eventually made his home near Urbana. Kenton was a legend in his own time, and tales of his escapades and cunning fill the history books. After the War of 1812, he came home to Champaign County, the land he knew so well, and eventually died there. The state of Ohio honored his memory by erecting a great monument over his grave at the Urbana Cemetery.

The day of the Indian fighter had ended by the time the Samuel Hitt family and the James Hunter family arrived about 1815. White settlers felt secure by this time, and the little town of Urbana beckoned them to stay.

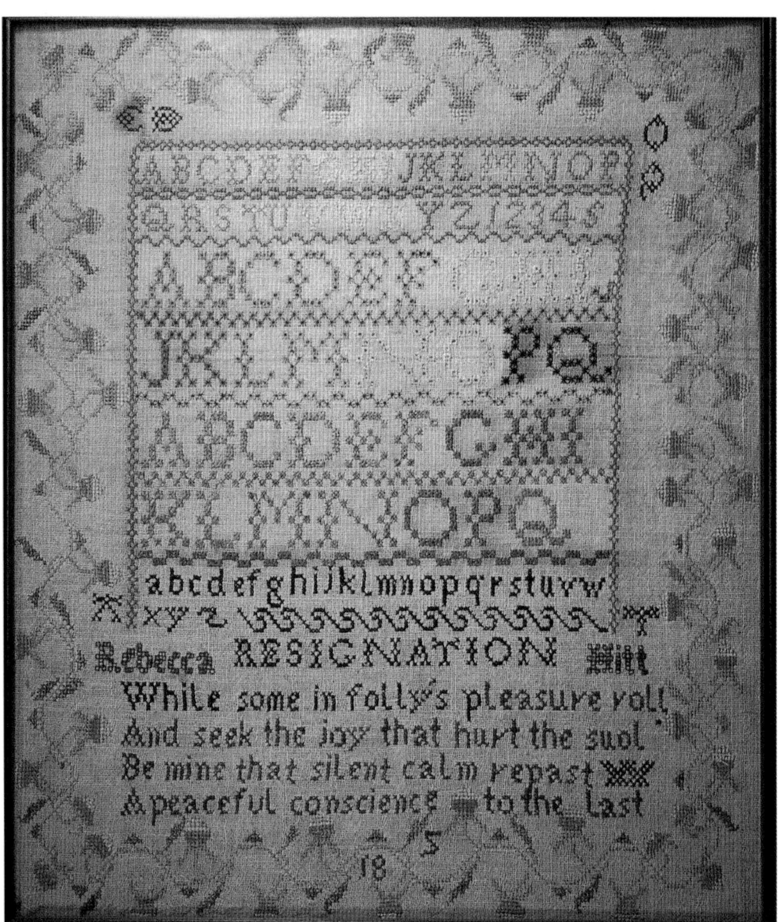

Fig. 135: Sampler of Rebecca Hitt. Undated.
Size: 17⅝" L x 15⅜" W. Collection of Nancy Gardner Goff.

The colorful sampler of Rebecca Hitt was stitched in Urbana, but it is not dated. The sampler does have an *18* at the bottom, suggesting that the stitcher forgot to go back and fill in the date when the work was completed. Distinct in design, the loose, wide border on Rebecca's sampler is unlike that on any other sampler we have found. The possibility exists that she did the sampler while the family was still living in Kentucky, but because she was only eleven when she reached Urbana, it is more likely that she did this rather complicated sampler in Ohio. The verse reads:

Resignation
While some in folly's pleasure roll
*And seek the joy that hurt the suol [*sic*]*
Be mine that silent calm repast
A peaceful conscience to the last.

Rebecca was born in Bourbon County, Kentucky, in November 1804. Her parents were Samuel and Ann (Smith) Hitt, who brought their family of eight children to Ohio from Kentucky in 1815. After settling in Urbana, another son and daughter were born into the family.

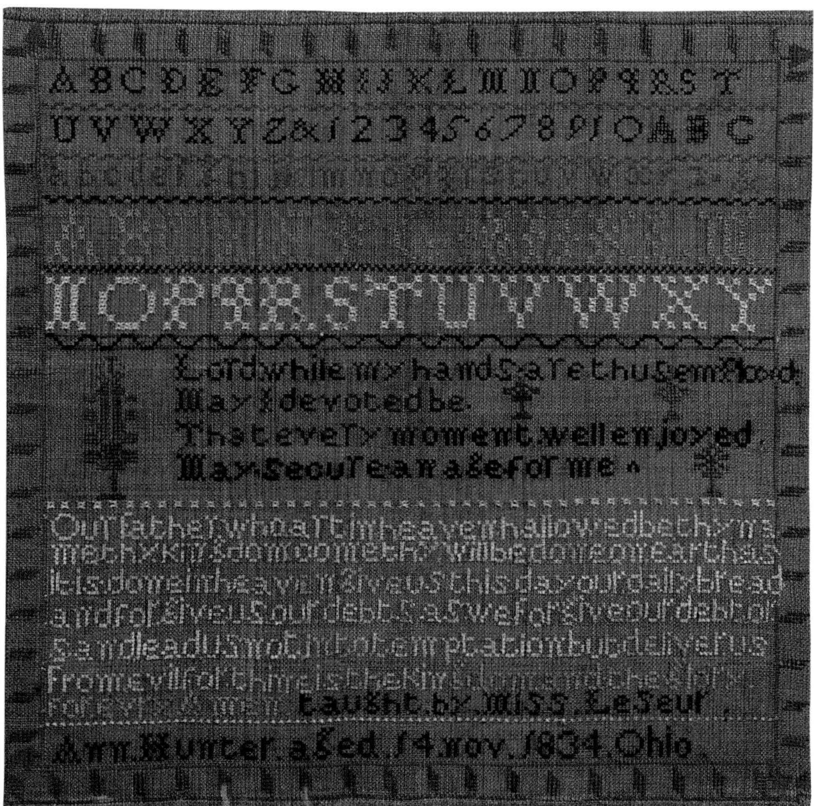

Fig. 136: Sampler of Ann Hunter. 1834.
Size: 17" L x 18" W. Collection of Melvin and Connie Porcher.

When fourteen-year-old Ann Hunter completed this large sampler, she marked it with her teacher's name and the word *Ohio*. Her parents, James and Eleanor Hunter, came to Champaign County sometime before 1815 from Loudoun in Frederick County, Virginia. They were active members of the Urbana Methodist Church. Ann was married to Silas N. Mathews in December 1839, and the couple had six children. She died in Urbana in 1871 at the age of fifty-one.

The name of Ann's teacher, Miss LeSeur, does not appear on any other Ohio needlework that has been discovered. An article that appeared in the *Urbana Daily Citizen* on May 3, 1910, about the history of the city noted Miss LeSeur's (spelled "Lazure") school. No records or advertisements have been found that can document how long her school operated. Ann's sampler is competently stitched but crowded. Including the Lord's Prayer was an ill-fated idea, for deciphering the words is difficult. Ann's other verse reads:

Lord while my hands are thus employed, may I devoted be,
That every moment well enjoyed, may secure an age for me.

Pickaway County

The picturesque Scioto River meanders through the middle of the vast plains of Pickaway County. The lands on either side of the river's bank are some of the most productive in Ohio. The original settlers of the area who saw the land's potential were principally from Virginia and Pennsylvania. Before their arrival, however, the Indians had also valued this "land of their fathers." Even so, after meeting together, the chiefs of the six allied Indian Nations agreed to a gradual peaceful settlement with the white man.

Under a huge elm tree, the English-speaking Mingo Indian Chief Logan acted as an eloquent spokesman for his comrades, and a Treaty of Peace was signed. Chief Logan, who had been baptized as a Christian by the Moravian missionaries in Pennsylvania years before, was held in great esteem.[6] The events of that fateful day in 1775 under the spreading branches of the old "Logan Elm" allowed central Ohio to be settled without bloodshed.

A stream of pioneers began to arrive long before the county was officially formed in 1810. The Scioto River flows directly into the Ohio, and it offered easy access to this central area of the new state. The village of Circleville was chosen as the county seat, and this is the town name Eliza Jane Melvin stitched on her canvas (fig. 137).

Fig. 137: Sampler of Eliza Jane Melvin. 1834.
Size: 13" L x 18" W. Collection of Kathryn Sandel.

Eliza Jane Melvin completed this rather plain sampler in 1834. Like many young stitchers, she did not plan ahead to leave space for all the alphabets she began. Eliza Jane did not fail, however, to tell us where she was living, and she centered well the words "Circleville. Ohio." Eliza Jane's teacher encouraged her to stitch some decorative blue-and-white flowers and leaves on the canvas to show that she had become an accomplished stitcher.

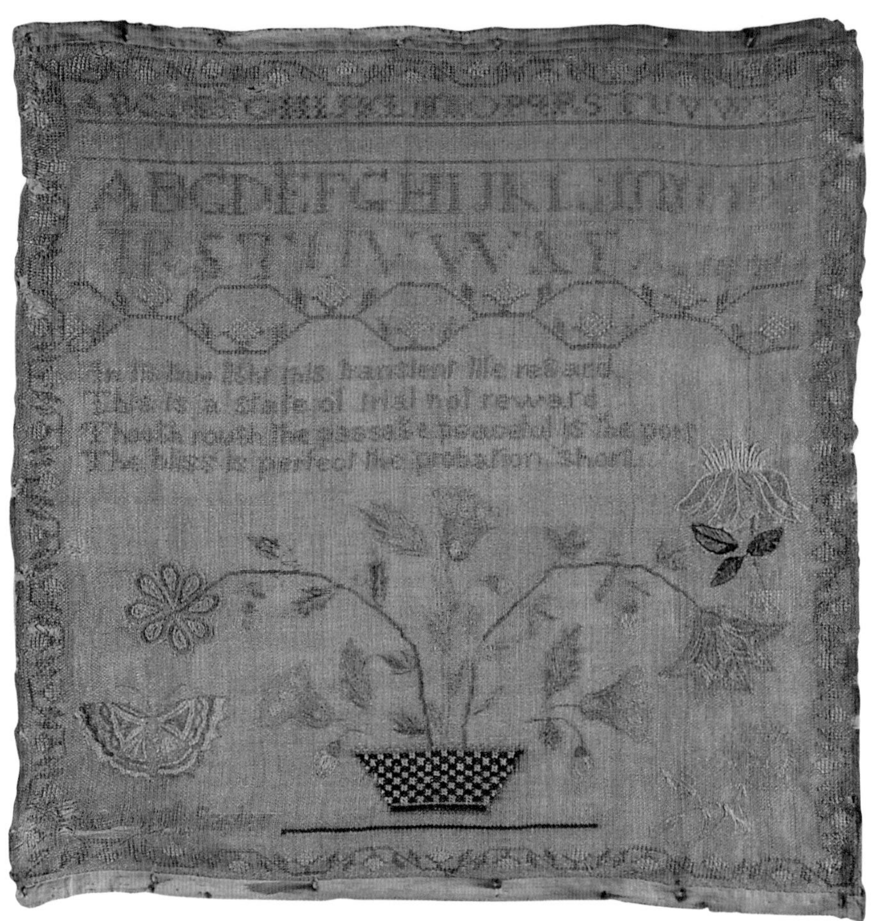

Fig. 138: Sampler of Margaret Sayler. 1841.
Size: 18" L x 18" W. Collection of Bill and Jan Rink.

Although the sampler of Margaret Sayler does not tell us where this young lady was living, sampler motifs and genealogical research indicate that she stitched this sampler in Pickaway County when she was sixteen years old. The sampler shares some of the same elements of design that Eliza Melvin's sampler (fig. 137) displays, though Margaret's sampler was stitched seven years later. It is possible that both girls attended the Circleville Female Academy, which was in operation during the time these young stitchers were making the samplers.

Margaret Sayler was the daughter of Elizabeth Ann (Betsey) Monnet (Monet) and Micah Sayler. The couple were early settlers of Pickaway County's Kinnikinnick Prairie. The Monnets were descendants of French Huguenots, who immigrated to America and settled in Maryland in the eighteenth century. The first member of the clan to move westward to Ohio arrived in Ross County about 1800.

Margaret was born October 2, 1825, in Pickaway County. In the autumn of 1842 she married a first cousin, Jacob Sayler. The young couple set up housekeeping in Hillsboro, where Jacob had already established a jewelry store. They spent their entire married lives there. Margaret had three children and was also active in civic affairs, taking up the cause of Temperance. Upon the occasion of her one hundredth birthday party, she commented, "I've lived long enough." She died in December of 1925, just two months after the celebration, and was buried with her family at Hillsboro, Highland County, Ohio.[7]

Franklin County

When the first pioneers to settle in Franklin County arrived in 1797, they chose to locate their homes on the west bank of the Scioto, where decades before the Wyandot Indians had had a thriving village. The settlers decided to name their new home Franklinton in honor of Benjamin Franklin. Six years passed until the county was organized, and the little town was designated as the county seat. The year was 1803, the same year that Ohio became the seventeenth state in the new nation.

The first Ohio Legislature met that year at Chillicothe, in Ross County, and continued to meet there until 1810. That year, the governing assembly removed to Zanesville for just two terms and then returned back to Chillicothe. The members of the legislature felt that a permanent state capital must be established and that it should be located in a central part of the state. After considering several sites, they voted that "the new State Seat of Government shall be located on the high ground opposite the town of Franklinton."[8]

Situated on land that was almost unbroken forest, the town of Columbus was formally laid out in June of 1812. Not a single human being was resident within its original limits.[9] That was soon to change, and by 1815 the new town had about seven hundred inhabitants. That figure increased steadily, and by 1826, when Miss Sarah Benfield and Miss Anna Treat decided to open a "female academy" on West Broad Street, Columbus had a population of more than two thousand. Girls from neighboring towns undoubtedly also patronized the school. It continued to operate successfully into the early 1830s. Miss Amy Rosalla Adams taught there as well but left after only two years and was employed by the newly established Columbus Female Seminary when it opened in 1828 on High and State Streets.[10]

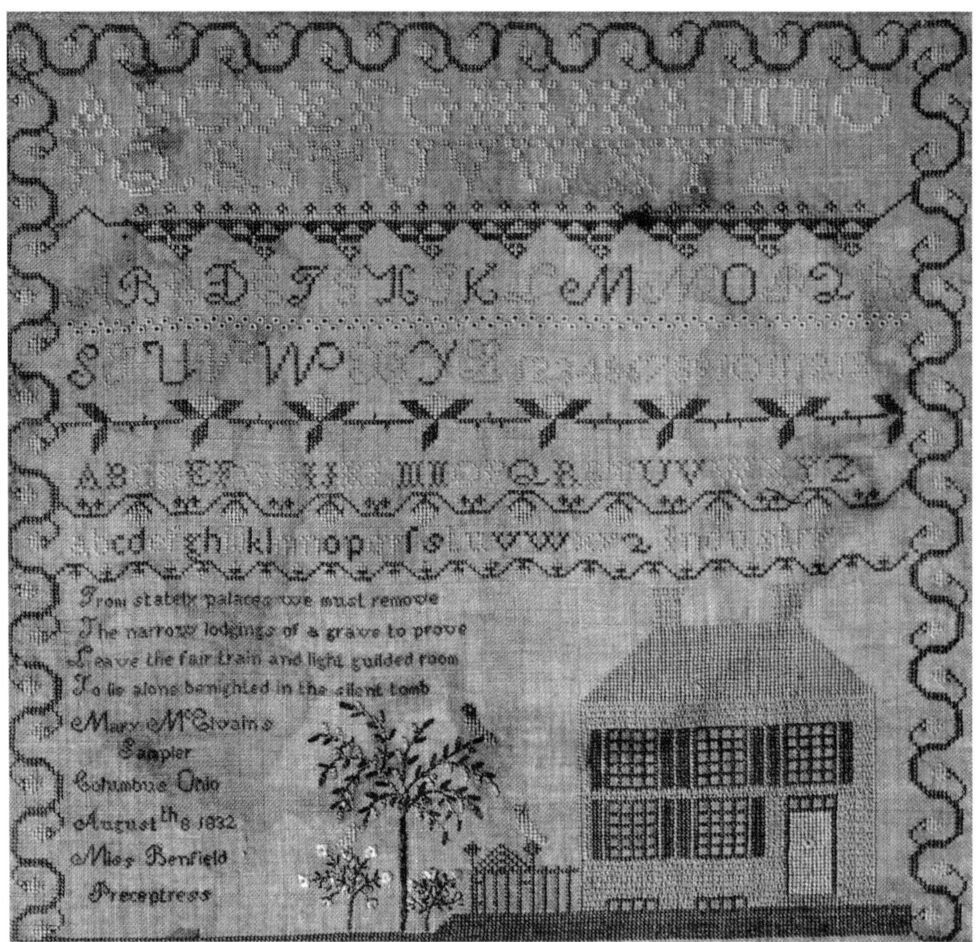

Fig. 139: Sampler of Mary McElvain. 1832.

Size: 17" L x 16" W. Collection of Andy and David Goss.

Two McElvain girls attended the "female academy" that the Misses Benfield and Treat established. Their engaging samplers were stitched six years apart. The work of Mary McElvain is beautifully executed and clearly says it was completed under the tutelage of "Miss Benfield—Preceptress—Columbus, Ohio—August 8, 1832." The canvas design is carefully planned and features a stately house that is architecturally distinctive. It has unusually large windows, and Mary has even stitched in the cellar windows. She used cross, satin, outline, and eyelet stitches as she filled this canvas and framed three sides with a tightly constricted strawberry border.

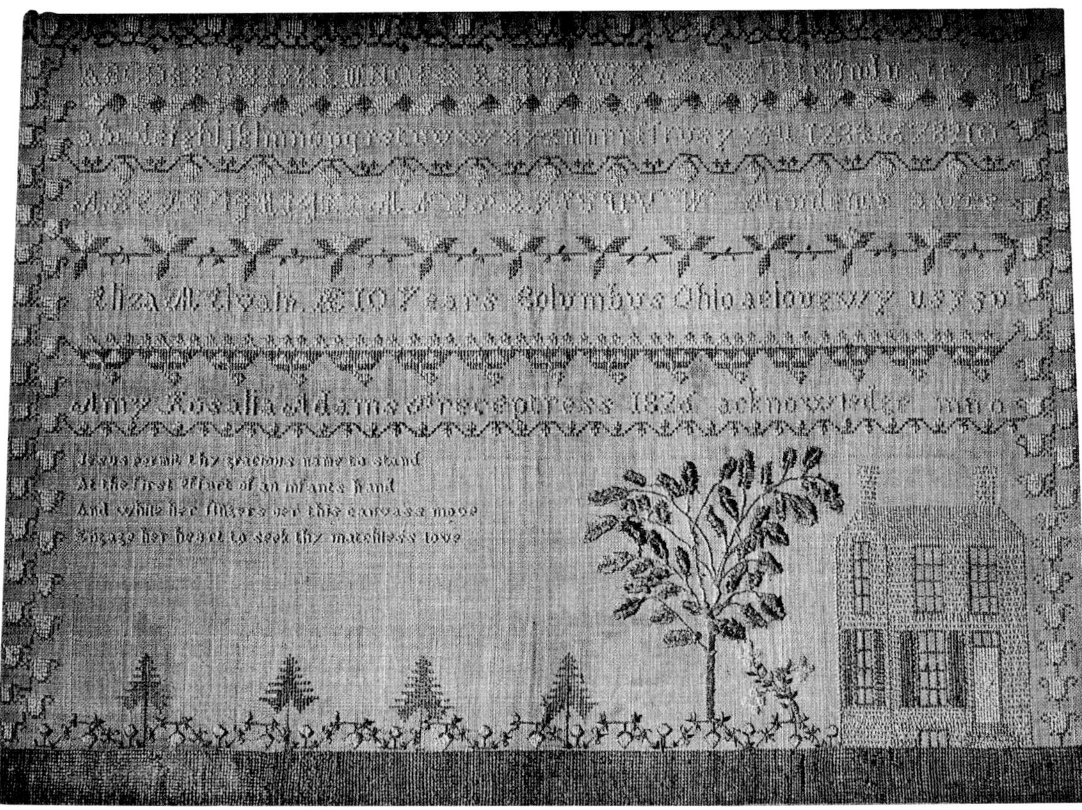

Fig. 140: Sampler of Eliza McElvain. 1826.

Size: 18" L x 24" W. Collection of Donald Jenkins.

Although the lower part of Eliza McElvain's canvas is unfinished, the stitcher has given us important information. She tells us the sampler was stitched when she was ten years old, in Columbus, Ohio, under the tutelage of Amy Rosalla Adams. The compositions of the McElvain girls' samplers indicate that they attended the same school, although they did not have the same teacher (see fig. 139). The samplers exhibit similar houses and trees and have unusual bands in the middle of the canvases. One of those distinctive bands looks like tiny windmill blades with a flower on top, and the other is made up of tiny triangles. Eliza stitched a political statement near the top of the canvas: WHIG INDUSTRY.

Mary and Eliza McElvain were probably sisters, the daughters of Colonel John and Lydia (Havens) McElvain. The McElvains were married on February 1, 1816, and 1830 Ohio Census records show them living in Montgomery Township of Franklin County with two daughters between the ages of ten and fifteen. Col. John McElvain served in the War of 1812 and afterwards began many years of public service. The *Ohio Plough-Boy,* a weekly newspaper published in Chillicothe, covered the elections held on October 31, 1828, and listed "John M'Elvain of Columbus, Franklin County," as seeking a seat as a representative in his congressional district.[11] McElvain was running on the same ticket with President Andrew Jackson.

Fig. 141: Sampler of Sophia Ann Naftel. 1845.
Size: 16" L x 16" W. Wool on linen. Collection of Marilyn Gale.

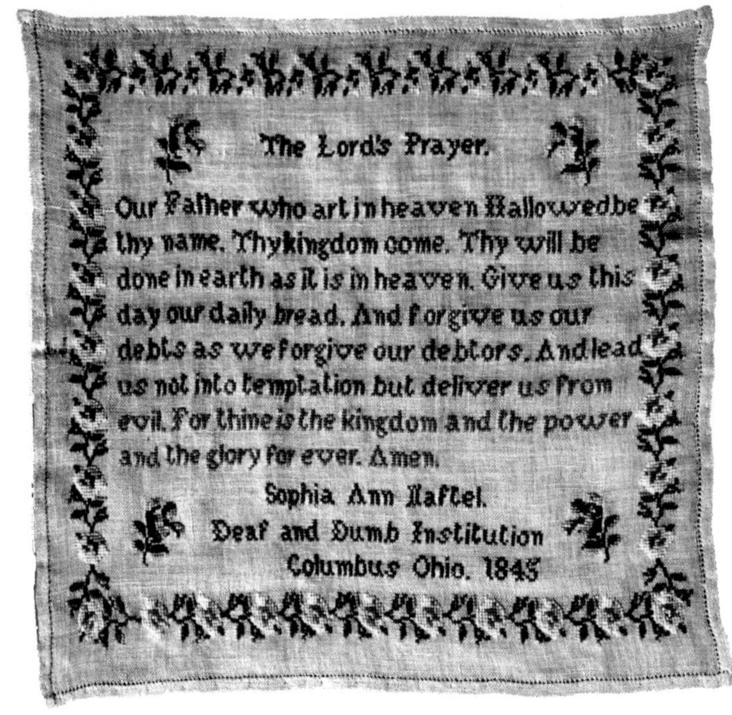

Sophia Naftel was an intelligent girl nearly thirteen years old when in the autumn of 1840 she left Cambridge and her father's care to attend the Institution for the Education of the Deaf and Dumb in Columbus. She stayed there for seven years. The object of the school was to "educate the mute and to fit pupils to occupy a position in the world where they will be of use to themselves and to others."[12] Sophia's sampler, completed when she was eighteen, gives evidence that she was taught plain and ornamental needlework. She may have communicated only with sign language, but she certainly could have *seen* the beauty she created with a needle and thread. Marked "Deaf and Dumb Institution—Columbus, Ohio," the colorful Berlin wool-work border is carefully executed, making an appropriate frame for the Lord's Prayer.

Sophia was the daughter of Thomas Naftel. In 1832, when she was four years old, she and her father immigrated to Cambridge, Guernsey County, from the Isle of Guernsey. Records make no mention of her mother, but other members of the Naftel family had arrived in the county as early as 1807. The Registry of Students for the school includes the following terse entry: "Sophia Ann Naftel—Pupil #187; from Cambridge, Guernsey Co.; Born Dec. 24, 1827; admitted Oct. 10, 1840; cause of deafness—fever; parents—Thomas Naftel. Discharged July, 1847."

Although the succinct list of students does not exude any great warmth for the "inmates," students often formed strong attachments to their teachers and other students. Sophia may well have felt a real sense of loss when she finally went back to Cambridge.

The Institution for the Education of the Deaf and Dumb opened in Columbus on October 16, 1829. By the time Thomas Naftel registered his daughter, a large new building had been erected on ten acres of land situated near the statehouse. In the "industrial department" of the school, the female students were taught to sew and make many necessary articles of wearing apparel, as well as to do all of the mending of "inmates'" clothes.[13]

Upon Sophia's return to Cambridge, the young woman went to live in the home of relative. Her father, a merchant who lived in a local inn, apparently had no home for her. She remained single until she was forty-five, when she married William K. Haworth in Greene County, Ohio. She lived her last years at the Ohio Home for the Aged and Infirmed Deaf and died without issue in 1913.

Delaware County

Even though Delaware County was not formally organized until 1808, hearty pioneers had begun to settle there by 1801. Two of the earliest, who came to survey and map this virgin land situated in the U.S. Military District, were Joseph Eaton and his young son James. They came in 1805, ready to work and eager to establish homes. Their hand-drawn survey maps and notes, as well as one of their surveying instruments, are valued relics that remain in the Delaware Historical Society Museum collection. This family's memorabilia also includes two beautiful pieces of needlework that were done by James Eaton's daughters, Laura Ann and Julia Ripley Eaton (figs. 142, 143, and 144).

(following page)

FIG. 142: SAMPLER OF LAURA ANN EATON. 1843.

SIZE: 16" L X 15½" W. WOOL ON LINEN. COLLECTION OF DELAWARE COUNTY HISTORICAL SOCIETY.

This Berlin wool-work sampler was meticulously stitched by Laura Ann Eaton in her thirteenth year. She boldly marked it "Delaware Ohio——1843," but failed to show that same confidence when stitched her name in tiny letters within the wreath of flowers at the bottom of the canvas. During the 1840s ornamental stitching and canvas designs began to change dramatically from those stitched in earlier decades. Laura's work would have been a stylish and decorative addition to any home of this period. The large parrots on either side of the canvas are particularly striking and colorful. Perhaps these bird designs were inspired by the work of the young pioneer artist, John James Audubon, who specialized in wildlife paintings. According to a March 25, 1820, advertisement in the *Cincinnati Gazette,* "Drawing and Painting" by Mr. Audubon was offered by Miss Deeds's Cincinnati school for "females of all ages." The by-then-famous painter traveled widely in Kentucky, Ohio, and Pennsylvania, and his work would have been familiar to Laura's teacher.

Born on November 10, 1830, Laura was the oldest daughter of James and Elizabeth (Caulkins) Eaton, early settlers of Berlin Township. The couple married in September 1822, in Delaware County, and spent their entire lives there.

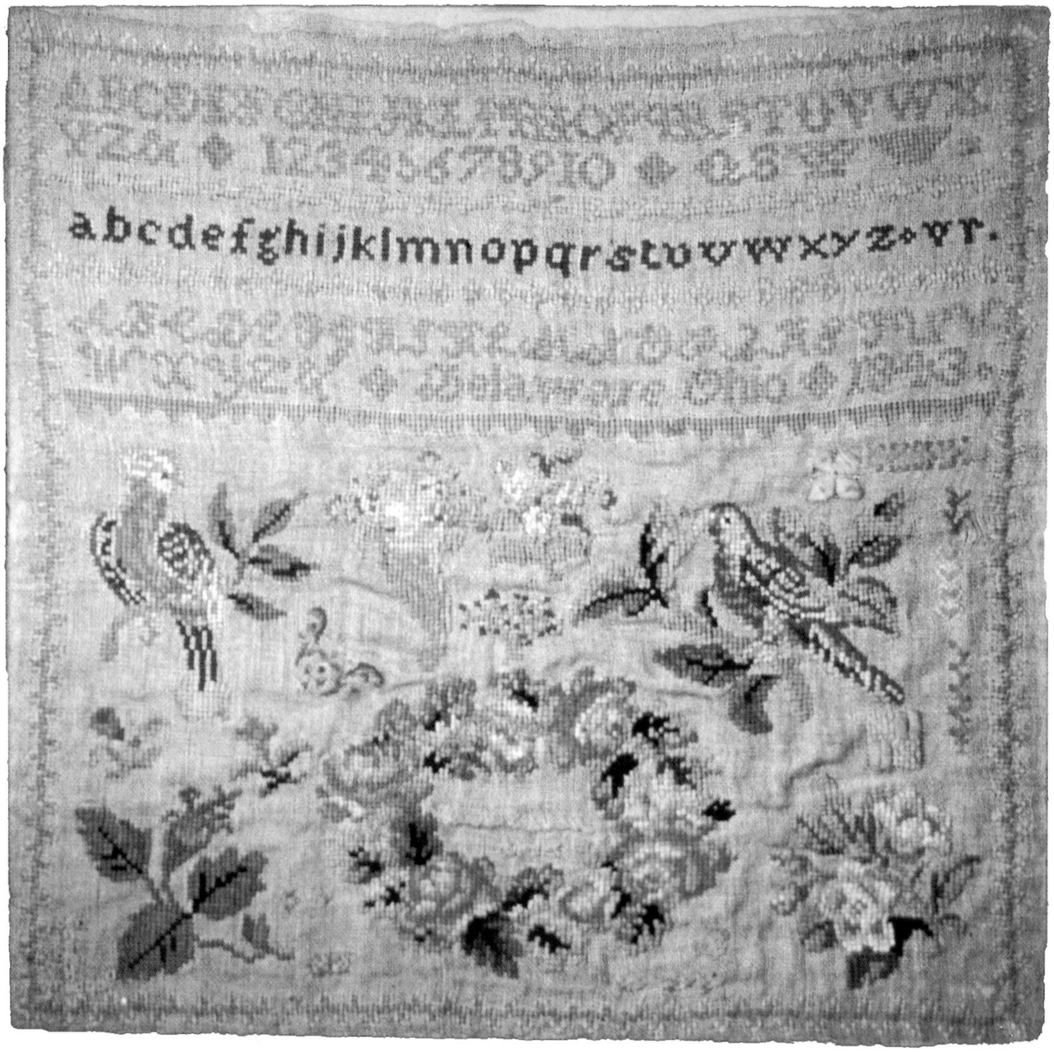

Fig. 142

Fig. 143: Oil Portrait of Laura Ann Eaton.

Laura Ann Eaton's portrait was painted about the time of her marriage to Tullius Clinton O'Kane in July 1853 when she was twenty-three years old. They had five children and were prominent in the Delaware community. Laura Ann Eaton O'Kane died in 1909. She is interred in the Delaware Oak Grove Cemetery.

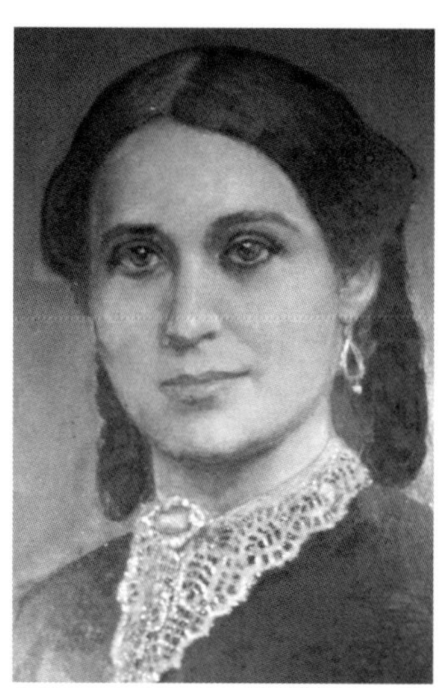

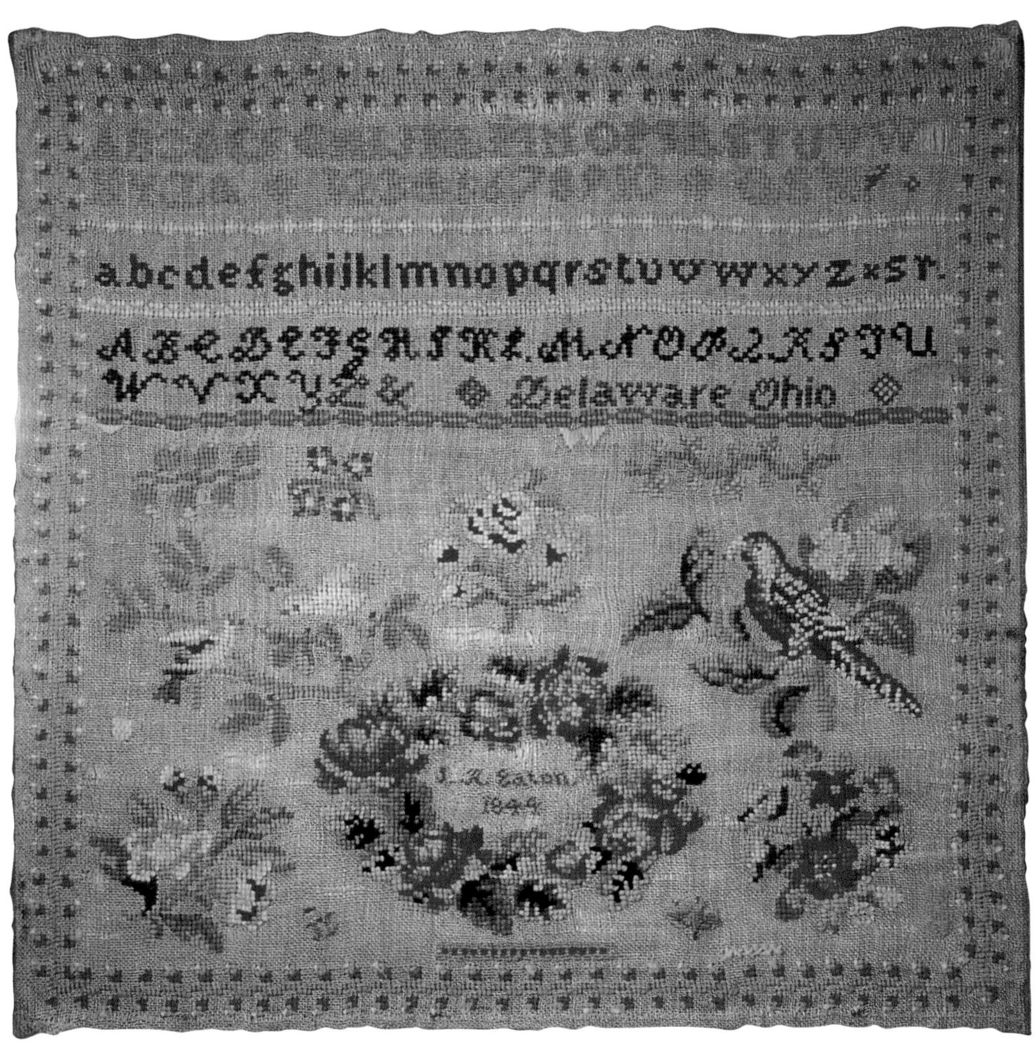

Fig. 144: Sampler of Julia Ripley Eaton. 1844.
Size: 16¾" L x 16" W. Wool on linen.
Collection of Delaware County Historical Society.

Julia Ripley Eaton was ten years old when she completed her sampler in 1844. Her older sister, Laura Ann, had finished her sampler the year before (fig. 142), and it is likely that young Julia wanted to emulate her sister's needlework. Julia Ripley Eaton did not marry. She died in Cincinnati at the age of twenty-six years in January 1859.

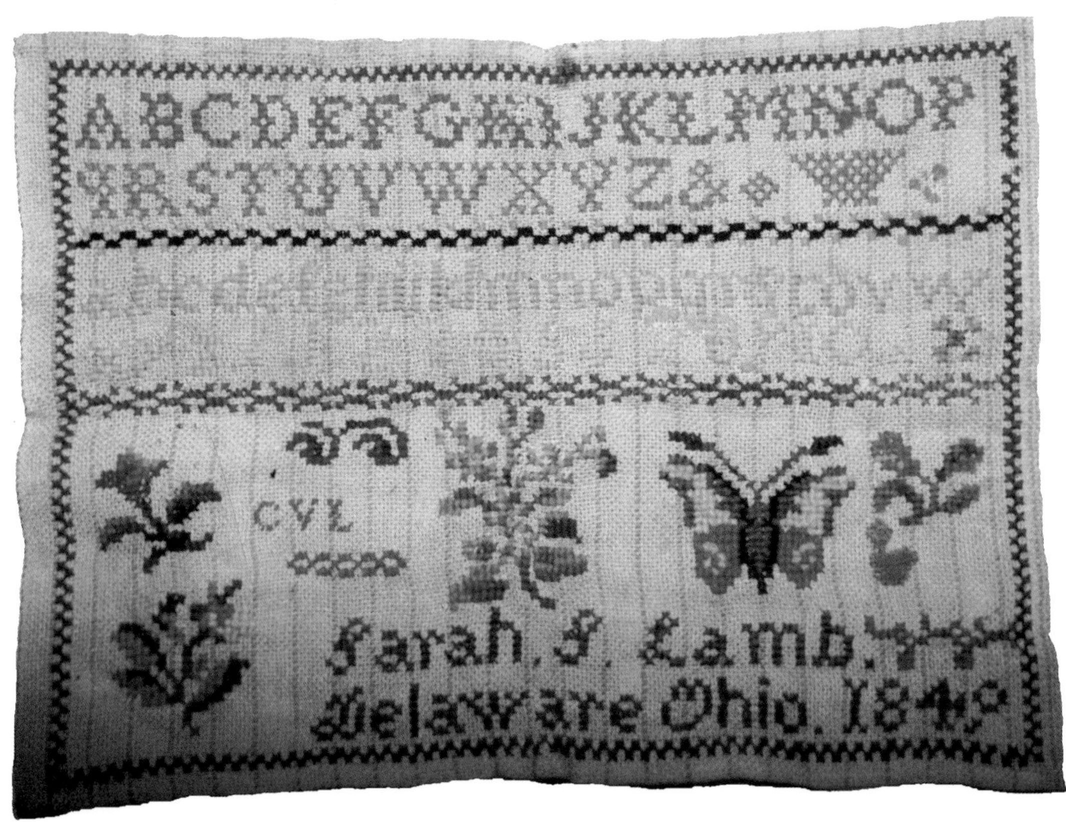

Fig. 145: Sampler of Sarah S. Lamb. 1849.
Size: 8" L x 12" W. Wool on linen. Collection of Charles Marlett.

This Berlin wool-work marking sampler was executed by Sarah S. Lamb. The linen canvas of Sarah's needlework (Penelope canvas) exhibits a blue thread running vertically to help guide the young girl's stitches. This guide thread is often seen on samplers of the early to mid-nineteenth century and was first produced in Germany. Sarah's work was undoubtedly done under the tutelage of the same teacher who taught the Eaton girls (figs. 142 and 144). The style of several of the letters in "Delaware, Ohio," matches perfectly with the Eaton samplers. We cannot be certain of the needlework teacher's identity, however, because there are no clues to it on any of the three samplers.

Mrs. Richard Murray, formerly Miss Joan Hills, may have been the Eaton girls' and Sarah S. Lamb's needlework teacher. She was, as one history book declared, a "born teacher," who first taught in her husband's school in Delaware in 1824 and 1825.[14] She taught for forty-four years, most of those years in classes she conducted in her home on Franklin Street. Many of the most cultivated ladies of the day were taught in her "unpretending, but admirable school."[15]

Union County

Union County was formed in 1820 from parts of the surrounding counties of Delaware, Franklin, Logan, and Madison. Good soil and large areas of prairie, free from trees, made this part of Ohio very inviting to early settlers. Decades earlier the Mingo Indians freely roamed and hunted these lands.

Pennsylvania and Virginia supplied the first pioneers for the southern part of the new county, where the little town of Homer was situated.[16] Later in the 1830s, a second migration of families from New England and New York arrived and became a driving force of business and social life in the village. Elisha Reynolds, whose daughter Martha Jane stitched a charming sampler (fig. 146), was a prominent member of this new group of settlers from the East.

When the railroad came through Union County in 1855 and established station stops, it bypassed Homer. No longer was the town a busy community of small manufactories, mills and stores. Residents began to move elsewhere as town lots were absorbed into farmlands. It is fortunate that Martha's needlework did not "fade away" as the small town did. Her sampler is an enduring reminder of a community that no longer exists.[17]

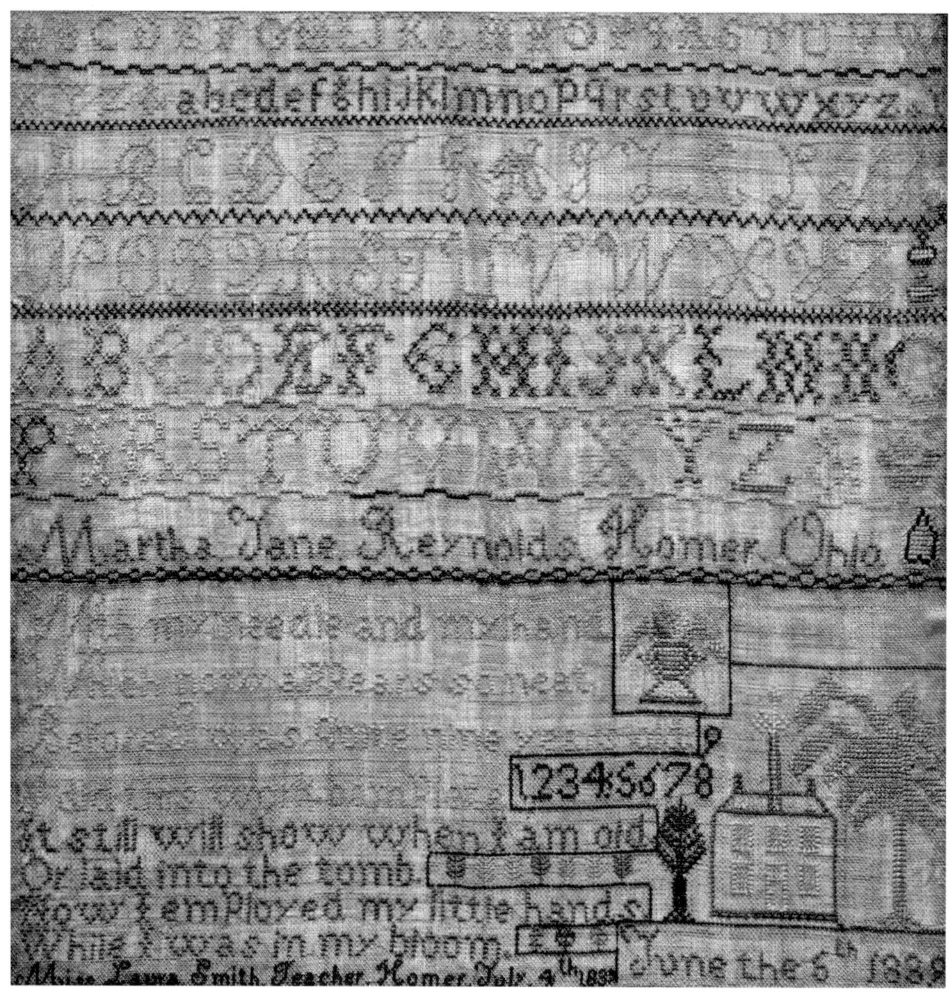

Fig. 146: Sampler of Martha Jane Reynolds. 1839.

Size: 18¾" L x 18" W. Collection of Nancy D. Wagner.

This beguiling sampler was executed by eight-year-old Martha Reynolds. She filled the canvas with stitches, leaving scarcely enough room at the bottom of her sampler to add "Miss Laura Smith—Teacher—Homer, Ohio."

Martha's verse conjures up an endearing young girl busily stitching away and enjoying the activity. It reads:

With my needle and my thread,
Which now appears so neat,
Before I was quite nine years old,
I did this work complete.
It still will show when I am old
Or laid into the tomb,
How I employed my little hands,
While I was in my bloom.

Licking County

Licking County's early settlers were primarily New Englanders. Also among the first arrivals to the county, which was formed in 1808, were many people from what are now the Canadian Maritime provinces of New Brunswick and the surrounding islands. During the Revolutionary War, anyone living in that area who offered support to the colonists lost his land and his home. Their procolonist stance made them very unpopular with the British and with most of their neighbors. After the Revolution ended, in a gesture of gratitude, the U.S. government set aside a large area, the "Refugee Tract," to reward them for their loyalty. Part of these central-Ohio lands were located in Licking County.

Newark

The town of Newark, which had been chosen for the county seat, was situated at the confluence of the three branches of the Licking River. It flourished and grew greatly with the completion of the Ohio and Erie Canal. When the monumental "ditch" was finished, more than three hundred miles of "river road" connected the village to the Ohio River to the south.[18] By going north, canal boats could reach Lake Erie. Newark was very nearly at the midpoint of the great canal. As early as 1827 the Ohio and Erie Canal was opened for boats, and families were coming from the East in considerable numbers. Among those arriving in 1836 were John W. Seymour, a merchant from Connecticut, his wife Caroline (Oliver) Seymour, and six-year-old Caroline Louisa (fig. 147).

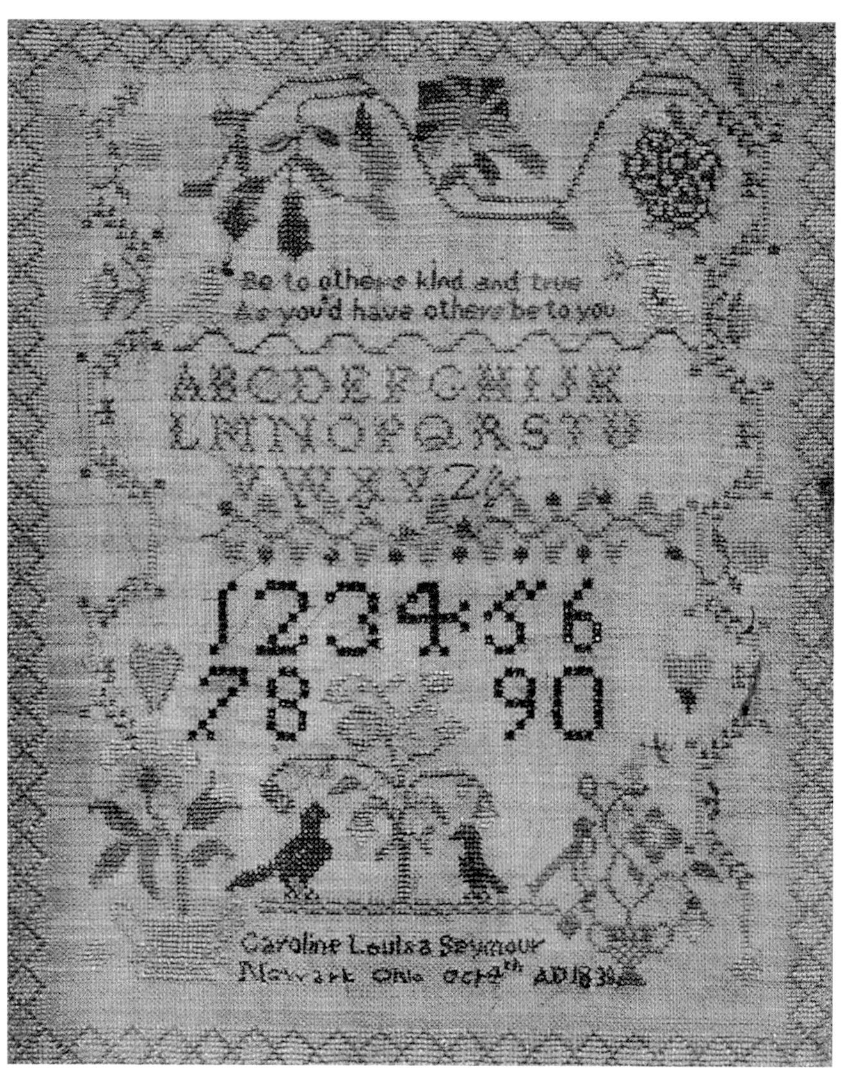

Fig. 147: Sampler of Caroline Louisa Seymour. 1838.

Size: 16" L x 13" W. Collection of Licking County Historical Society.

Caroline Louisa Seymour was eight when she followed her mother's instructions and completed this sampler in Newark. Caroline was born on January 14, 1830, in New Jersey, but the family lived in Hartford, Connecticut, just before coming west. Caroline's needlework shows a variety of stitches and has a strong relationship with that completed by her mother, Caroline Oliver Seymour, in 1824 (fig. 148). The overall design of the canvas, with the geometric diamond border, the asymmetric vine and flowers at the top, and the vase of flowers on the lower right side, came directly from her mother's sampler. Caroline Louisa grew up in Hartford, a village near Newark, and in 1848 became a teacher in the first Newark public schools. Never married, she died at age sixty-five in June 1895.

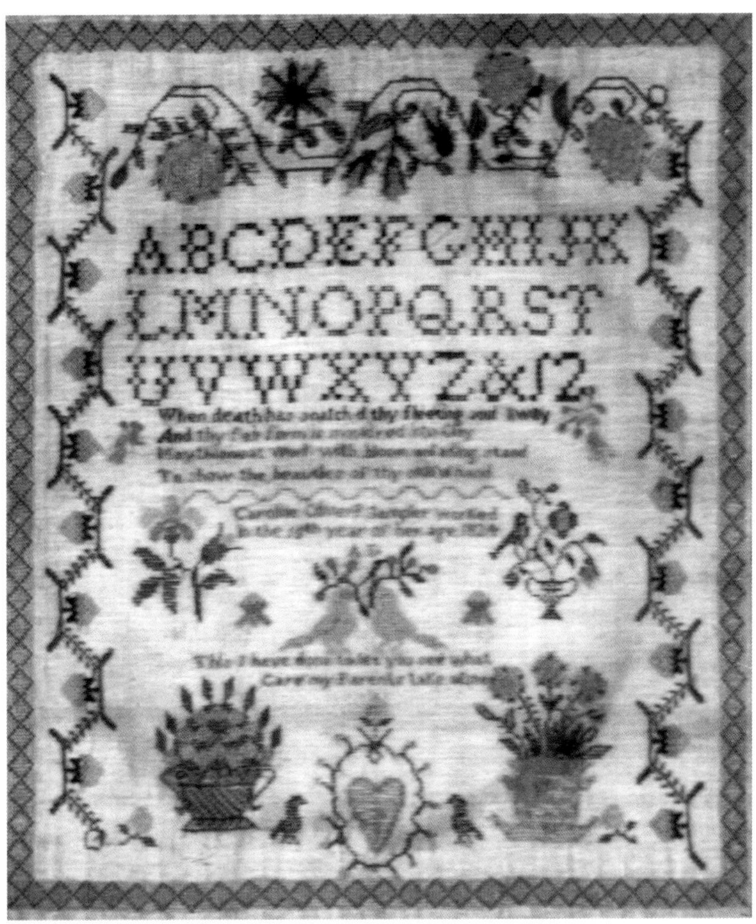

FIG. 148: SAMPLER OF CAROLINE OLIVER. 1824.
SIZE: 19" L x 16" W. COLLECTION OF LICKING COUNTY HISTORICAL SOCIETY.

This large sampler was not made in Ohio, but was brought here and later used by Caroline Oliver Seymour as an example for her students to copy. Many clues indicate that she was the needlework teacher who taught not only her daughter, Caroline Louisa, but other Newark students as well (see figs. 147 and 149). Mrs. Seymour did the sampler when she was fifteen. The verse is a common but pleasing one: "This I have done that you may see / What care my parents took of me." She failed to allow enough room to stitch her numbers, completing only the *1* and the *2*. Perhaps that is why she made sure her daughter's canvas had room for all of the numbers.

John W. and Caroline Oliver Seymour were not Quakers, but they were strong abolitionists and very active in the Congregational Church. The Congregationalists built a comfortable frame church about 1835 and opened it up for a "select school" for girls and boys in Newark. This is where Mrs. Seymour probably taught.

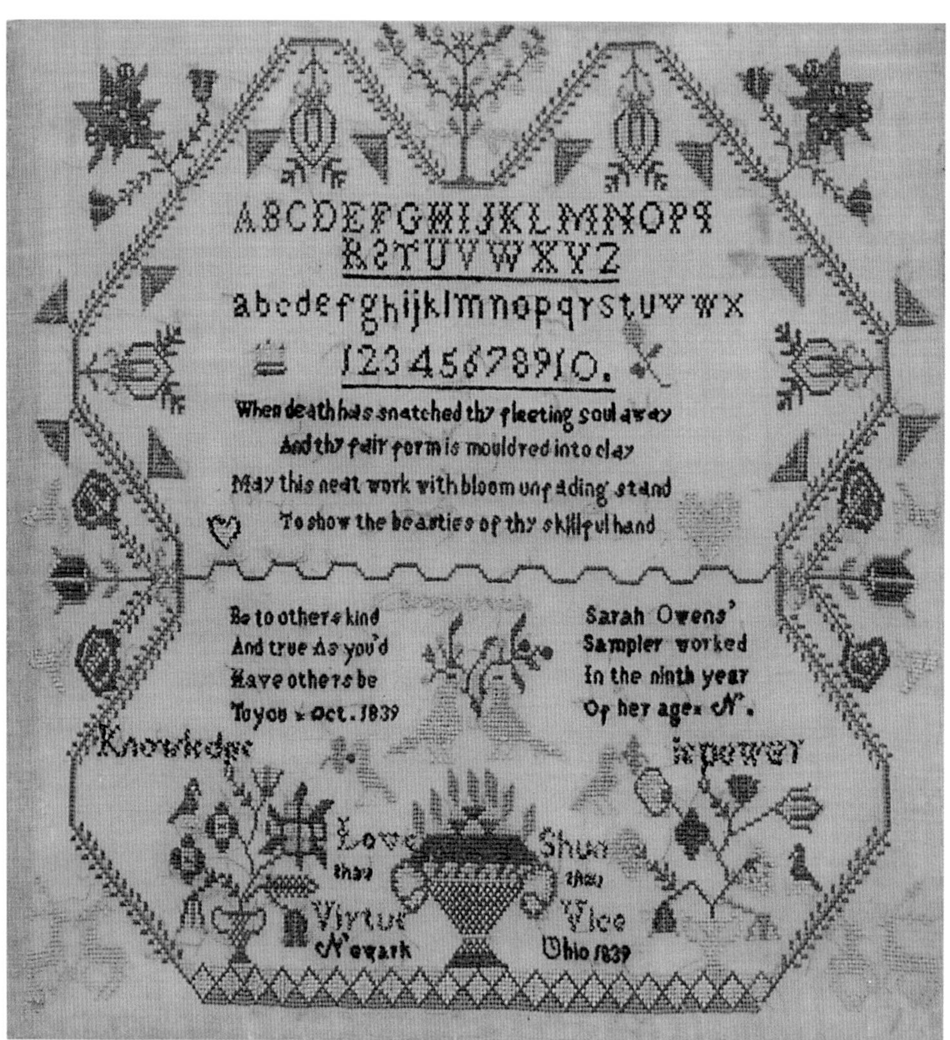

Fig. 149: Sampler of Sarah Owens. 1839.
Size: 17½" L x 17" W. Collection of the author.

The work of Sarah Owens, like that of Caroline Louisa Seymour (fig. 147), has "Newark Ohio" stitched on the canvas. Completed when she was nine years old, it has a different border design on three sides but the same geometric band along the bottom of the canvas. Several other elements tell us that Sarah Owens's teacher was probably Caroline Oliver Seymour (fig. 148), including Sarah's verse, which is also found on Caroline Oliver Seymour's sampler:

When death beds snatch thy fleeting soul away,
And thy fair form is moldering into clay,
May this neat work with bloom unfading stand,
To show the beauties of thy skillful hand.

The second verse, a paraphrase of the Golden Rule, reads: "Be ye to others kind and true / As you'd have others be to you."

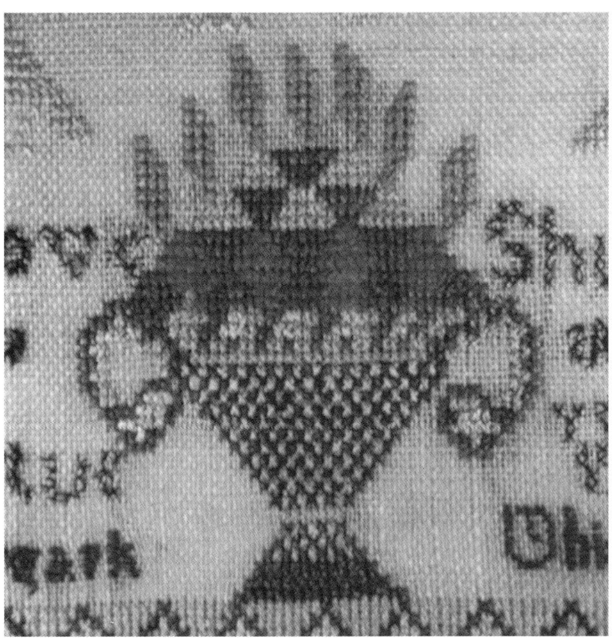

FIG. 150: DETAIL OF BASKET.
The unusual basket on Sarah Owens's sampler features distinctive leaves that stick straight up. It mirrors the basket design found on Caroline Oliver Seymour's sampler.

Granville

The town of Granville was founded in 1805 by a mass migration of New Englanders from Granby, Connecticut, and Granville, Massachusetts, who made up the Licking Company. In his reflections about Ohio, Henry Howe wrote in the 1850s that "Granville is perhaps the most peculiar, unique village in the State . . . an old-time New England village set down in central Ohio." He went on to write in glowing terms about the settlement: "At each end of the main street is a female seminary . . . while on a hill, overlooking all, stands Dennison University."[19]

Granville has been known from the beginning as a center for education. Located here first was the Granville Academy, established by the Congregational Church in 1827. In the first decades of the nineteenth century, at least five different Granville schools were established for female students. The schools changed their names several times as different teachers and religious denominations took charge.[20] These institutions are included in the list of Ohio pioneer teachers and schools beginning on page 277.

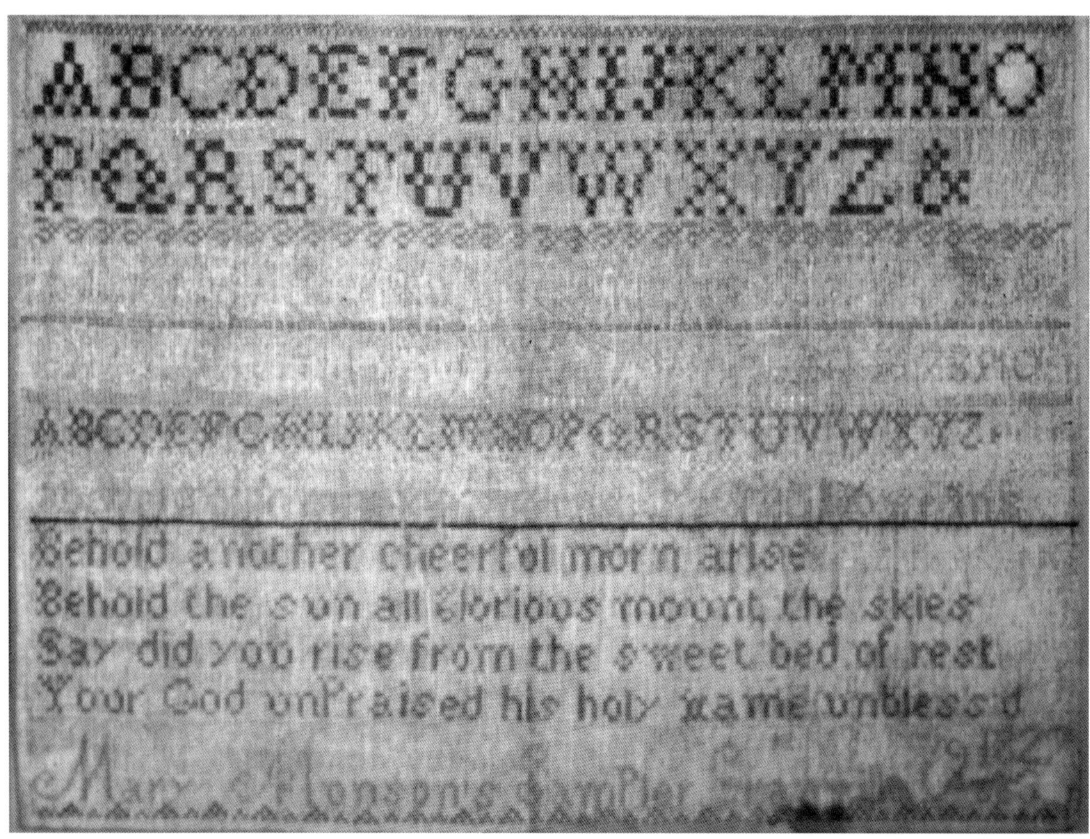

FIG. 151: SAMPLER OF MARY MUNSON. 1827.
SIZE: 11½" L x 15¾" W. COLLECTION OF AUDREY AND ORVILLE ORR.

The plain sampler stitched by Mary Munson is significant because it is the only one found from the well-known Granville Academy. Mary Munson marked her sampler with these words, though they are a bit difficult to read: "Mary Munson's Sampler Granville Ohio 1827 Miss Howe, Ins." Marianne Howe was the first to take charge of the "female department" when the school opened in 1827. In the beginning years, the school had both male and female students.[21]

The Munson family came to Granville early in the nineteenth century. Mary is listed as a student in the 1839–40 catalogue of the Granville Female Academy. There were two hundred forty-four students attending at that time, at least one hundred of whom were boarding students. The four-story building was apparently filled to capacity, not just with students from all over Ohio, but with girls from New York, Indiana, Massachusetts, Vermont, Michigan, and even Louisiana.

Fairfield County

The early history books about Ohio tell us that in 1790 one hundred Wyandot Indian wigwams were located on the Hockhocking River where Lancaster, Fairfield's county seat, now stands. By the Treaty of Greenville in 1795, the Wyandots ceded all of this area to the United States and lived peacefully among the white settlers. Settlement was steady, and was hastened considerably with the completion of Zane's Trace in 1797. Three years later, in 1800, Ebenezer Zane laid out the settlement of Zanesville at the point where the trail crossed the Hocking River.[22]

Several educational facilities were opened in Lancaster during the first decades of the nineteenth century, beginning with a log schoolhouse taught by Flora Butler. In 1820, a fine brick academy was built on Wheeling Street by a number of wealthy citizens. Among those who promoted this enterprise was Gottlieb Steinman, whose daughter Minerva stitched the sampler seen in fig. 152. When the academy closed sometime between 1834 and 1839, Professor Howe, who had been teaching there, opened Howe's Academy in a house he built on Mulberry Street. Professor Howe's Academy operated about ten years and was highly regarded. Some of the most prominent families patronized this "subscription school," for no public schools were available until 1838.[23]

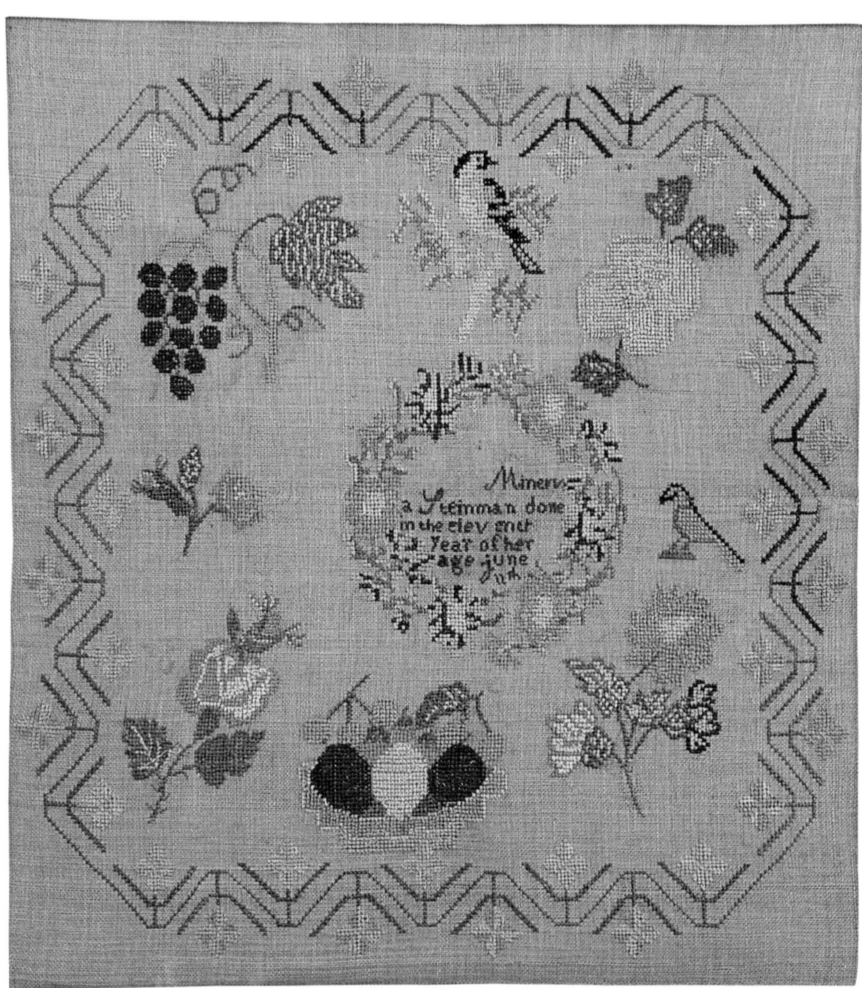

Fig. 152: Sampler of Minerva Steinman. 1834.

Size: 17" L x 16" W. Collection of Melvin and Connie Porcher.

Minerva Steinman of Lancaster completed this needlework in her eleventh year. The composition of the canvas is very unusual, and no other documented Ohio sampler seems to be related to it in form. Even the surrounding border is unique. Though the wreath of flowers is not centered on the canvas and the placement of the stitcher's name is a bit off balance, her sampler is well stitched and appealing.

Minerva was the daughter of Gottleib Steinman, who emigrated from Germany to Baltimore in 1811. He removed to Lancaster, Ohio, where he married Agnes Hubben in 1813. Minerva was born to the couple in Lancaster on April 25, 1823. Gottleib Steinman was a prominent early resident of Lancaster, and was the first proprietor of the Swan Hotel, which he established in 1820 on the corner of Main and Columbus Streets. By 1832, he was operating the Talmadge House, a popular stopping place for stagecoaches, and he soon owned the entire block. When the stables and hotel burned to the ground, he immediately rebuilt a new hotel, The Phoenix, on the same spot. Minerva's obituary tells us that she died unmarried on October 11, 1894. The Steinmans, members of the Lutheran Church, are all interred in the Elmwood Cemetery in Lancaster.[24]

FIG. 153: SAMPLER OF RACHEL R. ALLEN. 1839.
SIZE: 15½" L x 17" W. COLLECTION OF MRS. RALPH H. KRUEGER.

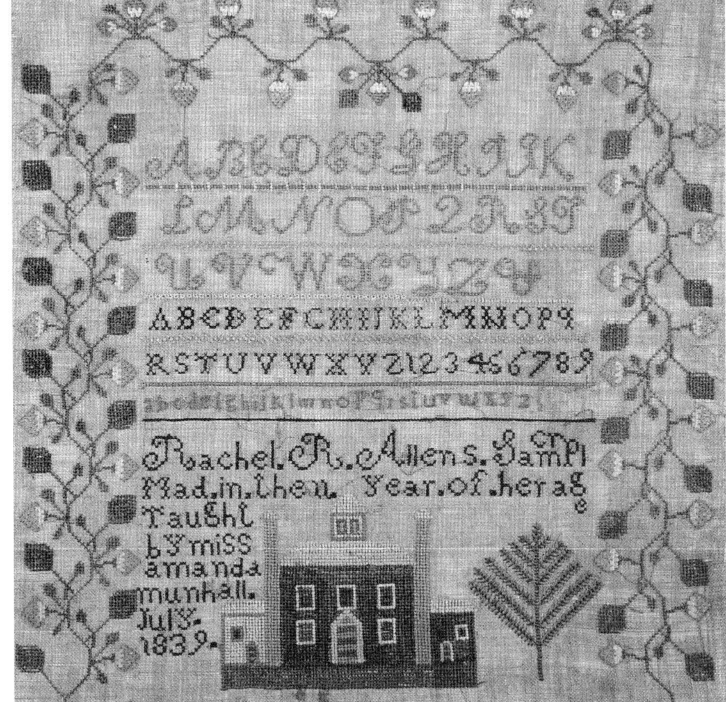

Rachel Rush Allen was born in Royalton, Fairfield County, and completed this needlework when she was eleven. The sampler is a beauty, with a canvas filled to capacity, a wide strawberry border surrounding three sides, and an impressive blue house. Her teacher, Amanda Munhall, expected her to use a variety of stitches, and Rachel executed them well. In 1845–46, Rachel attended the Methodist school, Worthington Female Seminary, in Franklin County. On November 10, 1846, eighteen-year-old Rachel married John W. Ball. Records reveal that she died in Davenport, Iowa, in 1899.

There were several subscription schools available in Lancaster where Rachel could have received instruction in needlework, and research did not reveal where her instructor, Amanda Munhall, was employed. One of the most important schools advertised in the *Lancaster Gazette* on July 5, 1838, with this lengthy notice:

> *Lancaster Institute for the instruction of young ladies, corner of Columbus and Mulberry streets, conducted by Mrs. And Mr. McGill, A. B. R. H. A.*
>
> *The principals beg leave to announce to their friends, and the people generally, that they have opened the above institution.*
>
> *The course of instruction comprises the Latin, French, and English languages: music, and singing on the Logerian system: drawing and the elements of perspective geometry; fruit, flower, figure and landscape painting: in oil and water colors; oriental painting on paper, satin, velvet and wood: Grecian and glass painting, Japanning; mezzotinting and transferring: orthography: reading: English grammar: composition and letter writing; history, ancient and modern: writing on a free, beautiful and easy system, in which legibility and elegance are combined: the ornamental hands; arithmetic and book keeping on an improved system, adapted to domestic accounts; geography: use of globes; construction of maps; astronomy; mythology and chronology; practical chemistry, as it relates to the useful arts dependent on that science: natural and moral philosophy: botany, with instructions for drawing and coloring plants, flowers, &c.: plain and ornamental needle and fancy work.*[25]

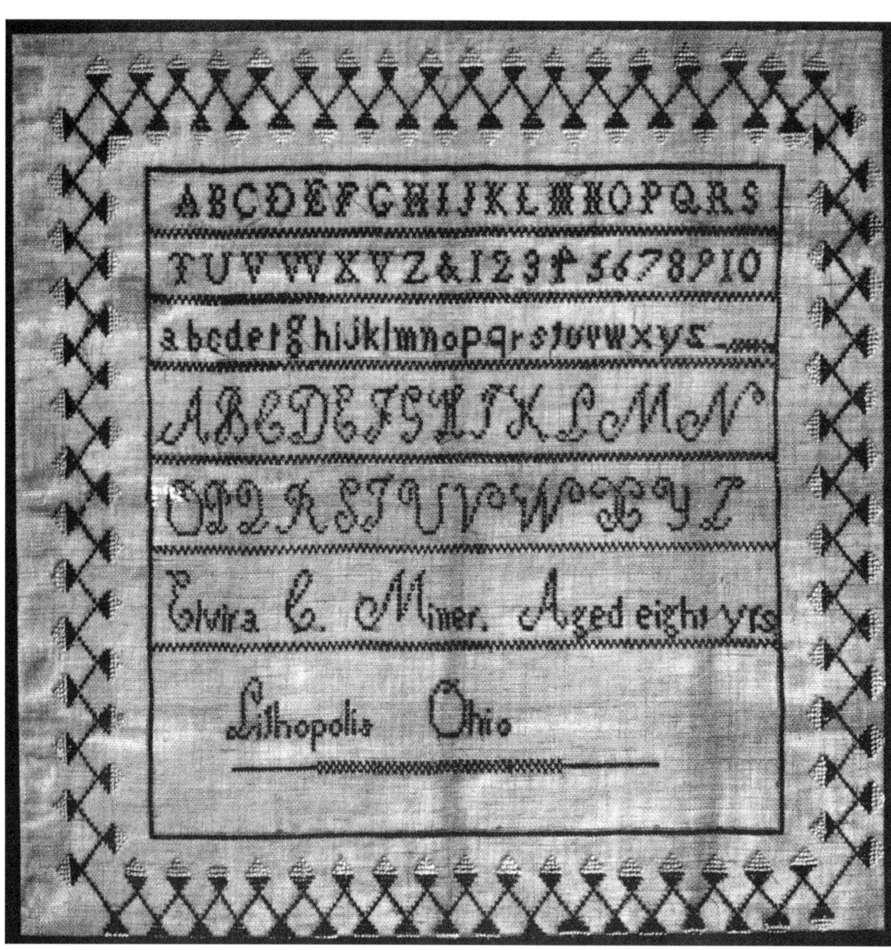

Fig. 154: Sampler of Elvira C. Miner. 1853.
Size: 18" L x 18" W. Collection of Nancy Conlon.

Elvira C. Miner's large, undated sampler was stitched in Lithopolis, a village southeast of Columbus. Born in 1845, she was the daughter of Dr. E. L. Miner and his wife Lucinda. Dr. Miner was prominent among the early settlers of the community and spent forty-five years of his professional life serving the small town. Lucinda was highly educated and was a teacher for a period of time before her marriage.[26] Both parents were active in the Presbyterian church, and Dr. Miner was instrumental in getting the Sabbath school organized. After his death, Lucinda Miner taught sewing in the Sabbath School, and it is likely that she taught Elvira sewing skills. The sampler Elvira produced was done mostly in cross-stitch and shows restraint in color and design. By the time this canvas was finished in 1853, the Victorian influences of bright wool yarns and complex Berlin patterns were very much in vogue, but Elvira's teacher wanted this child to make a typical marking sampler, something that children had been making in earlier times. Still, the sampler is not at all typical, and its wide geometric border makes it especially attractive.

Perry County

Four years after his victory in the Battle of Lake Erie, Commodore Oliver H. Perry was honored when Perry County was formally organized in central Ohio in 1817. The county was first settled by Pennsylvania Germans as early as 1802. Though the land was not particularly good for farming, it was rich in lumber and iron ore. Only one sampler from this county has been discovered, and it was stitched in New Lexington, the county seat of this sparsely populated area.

(following page)

Fig. 155: Sampler of Harriet Barnd. 1845.

Size: 17" L x 12" W. Wool on linen. Collection of Martha Lindsey Bowman.

Eleven-year-old Harriet Barnd completed this Berlin wool-work marking sampler in 1845. Although some thread loss has occurred, the canvas is still very readable. Harriet completed four alphabets and several decorative motifs before she clearly marked her name, the date, and her place of birth, "New Lexington." Her parents, Jacob and Julia Ann (Eckles) Barnd, came to Ohio in 1817 and were among the first settlers in the area. They came from Cumberland, Maryland, and built their home on Main Street, where Harriet was born ca. 1834. The pioneer home was eventually torn down, but Harriet remained in New Lexington, where she married William H. Goodin. Upon her death in 1918, her girlhood embroidery was passed on to her daughter.

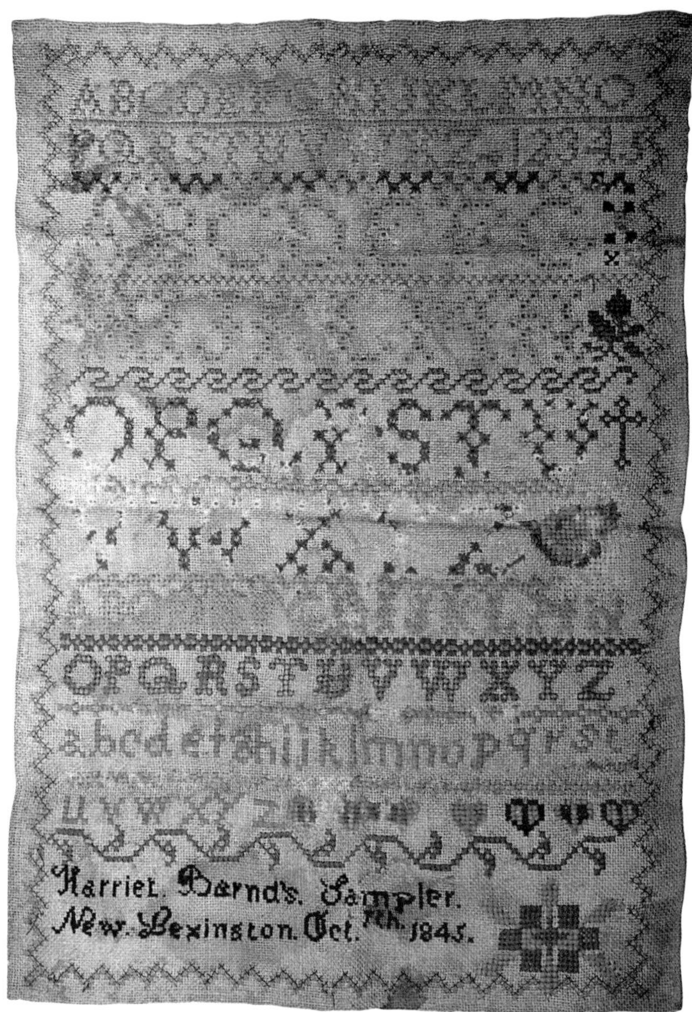

Fig. 155

This Ohio sampler lay forgotten in the bottom of an old trunk in an abandoned Perry County farmhouse for more than seventy-five years. A rusted straight pin held a scrap of paper to the canvas on which was written a note indicating that the maker's daughter had kept her mother's handwork and proudly displayed it at some long-ago Perry County fair. Upon the death of Harriet Barnd's granddaughter in 1997, the farmhouse's contents were consigned for auction, and Harriet's great-great-niece was thrilled to discover and purchase this lost scrap of needlework. It is once again a family treasure.

Knox County

Henry Knox distinguished himself as an able officer in the Revolutionary War, serving under General George Washington.[27] Knox County, Ohio, founded in 1808, was named in his honor. Because this was a time of intense patriotism, the county seat, Mount Vernon, was named after George Washington's home in Virginia. The new settlers of Ohio were among those most grateful for the opportunities that the War of Independence and its heroes offered them.

Knox County held great promise for those who wanted to establish homes on the rich farmlands. The first settlers began to arrive in 1805, and they judged the soil well, for today it is still primarily a productive agricultural county.

The residents of Knox County have always taken pride in Kenyon College, which was established in 1825 in Gambier, near Mount Vernon. The Reverend Philander Chase, who had served as the rector of Christ Church in Hartford, Connecticut, c. 1811, had come to Ohio by 1817, and first took charge of the Worthington Academy in Franklin County. He began in earnest to work for educational interests in Ohio and eventually purchased eight thousand acres in Knox County, where he established Kenyon College.[28] Early Ohio history books tell of the many accomplishments of Philander Chase, but, typically, only a bit about his wife: "Mrs. Chase entered with her whole soul into her husband's plans. She was a lady perfectly at home in all the arts and minutiae of housewifery; as happy in darning stockings for the boys as in entertaining visitors in the parlor . . . as in presiding at her dinner table, or dispersing courtesy in her drawing room."[29] Indeed, this anonymity of all women in early histories is a problem repeatedly encountered in researching samplers. Only one sampler from Knox County has been discovered, and the details that the stitcher, Elizabeth Davidson, sewed on the canvas are all we know about her.

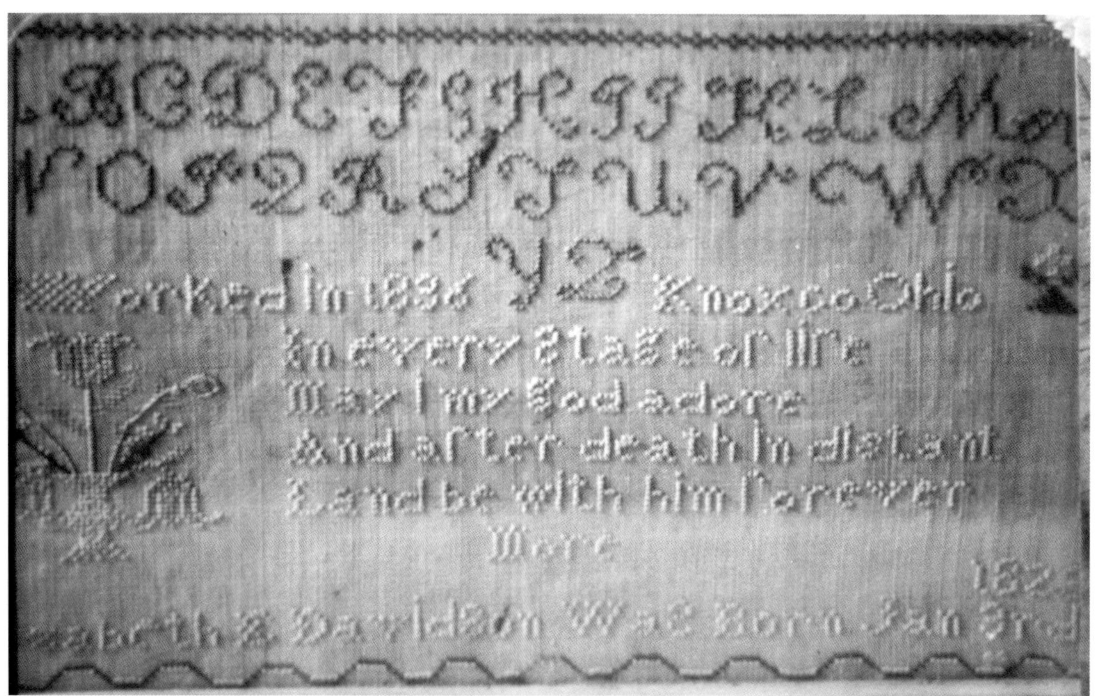

FIG. 156: SAMPLER OF ELIZABETH E. DAVIDSON (DETAIL). 1836.
SIZE: 17½" L x 17½" W. COLLECTION OF MELVIN AND CONNIE PORCHER.

Elizabeth E. Davidson's sampler tells us that she "was born on January 3, 1823" and completed this work in 1836. She neatly marked "Knox County, Ohio," on the sampler. Even with this information, we have been unable to further document the stitcher or her family. Her canvas, surrounded with a plain border, is competently worked and filled with four alphabets, a vase of flowers, and a somber religious verse (note: sampler is not pictured in its entirety):

In every stage of life
May I my God adore
And after death in distant
Land be with him forever more.

Holmes County

When most Americans think of the Amish, they think of the state of Pennsylvania and Lancaster County. Holmes County, Ohio, along with neighboring Wayne County, however, are the counties with the largest numbers of Old Order Amish in America. The settlement of Holmes County began early in the nineteenth century, and among the first pioneers to come to the area were the Amish of German and Swiss descent. Other "plain people," like the Dunkards and Mennonites, also immigrated to the area from Pennsylvania, Maryland, and Virginia. Almost all of these pioneer settlers held tenaciously to their Old World customs and German language. Travelers visiting the county today will find themselves sharing the roadways with the same kinds of horses and buggies that were in use almost two centuries ago.

The young girls of these communities learned how to create graphic quilt designs, mark their household linens, and stitch Germanic needlework motifs. Although Amish quilts are found in considerable numbers, very few examples of German samplers or show towels have been found in the Ohio search. When they are discovered, rarely do the pieces exhibit the same kind of pictorial elements that we have come to admire on other samplers. Perhaps the ornamental embroidery that was so much a part of the lives of young "English" (and German Moravian) girls was too worldly for these strict religious sects. With few exceptions, the embroidery done by the Amish, Mennonite, and Dunkard girls exhibits only small, scattered designs and is marked with little more than a young stitcher's name or initials and a date. This makes their work more difficult to identify and document. One piece of needlework that we *can* identify from Holmes County is that of Margaret Buchanan Tidball. A Presbyterian of Irish descent, she executed one of the most attractive samplers discovered in the search for early nineteenth-century Ohio needlework.

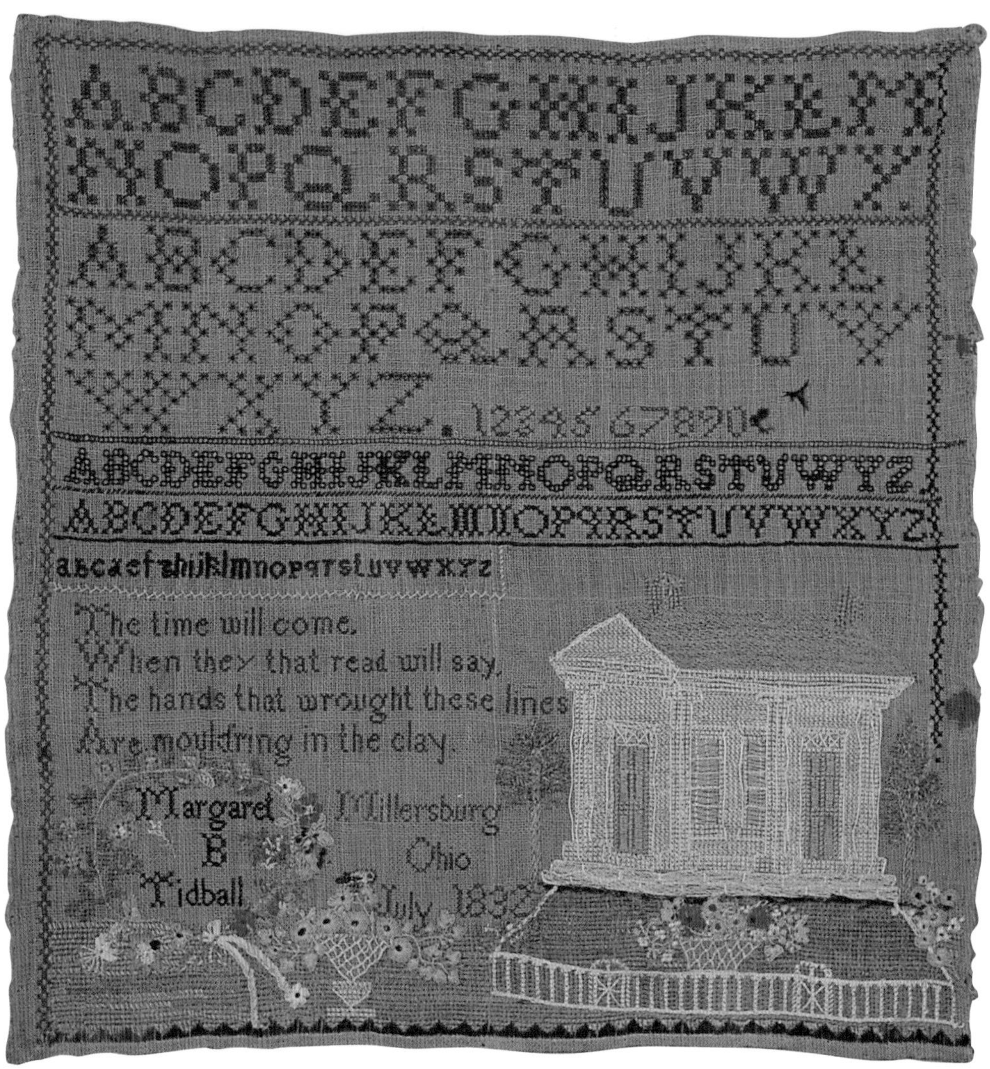

Fig. 157: Sampler of Margaret B. Tidball. 1832.
Size: 16" L x 16" W. Collection of Patricia McClelland Miller.

Margaret Buchanan Tidball completed her sampler when she was fifteen years old. The design of the lower half of the canvas is exceptional, and her skills with a needle and thread are apparent. Whoever designed the distinctive little Greek Revival building and its fanciful fenced lawn had an eye for detail, realism, and color. Few Ohio samplers show a more charming scene than this one. Her verse reads:

The time will come,
When they that read will say,
The hands that wrought these lines
Are moldring in the clay.

Beneath the verse Margaret marked her name and "Millersburg Ohio."

Margaret was the daughter of Brownhill and Lovely (Caldwell) Tidball. Brownhill Tidball originally came to Holmes County from Allegheny County, Pennsylvania. He married Lovely Caldwell in Wheeling (now in West Virginia) in 1814. Brownhill and Lovely Tidball first appear in Ohio in the 1830 census records, and they remained in Holmes County the rest of their married lives. Margaret, born December 30, 1817, was the couple's second child.

Brownhill Tidball's sister Mary Tidball was a needlework teacher in southwestern Pennsylvania. At least ten samplers have been discovered with Mary Tidball's name as the "instructress."[30] Family history suggests that Margaret Buchanan Tidball had a loving relationship with her Aunt Mary, but the sampler Margaret worked bears no resemblance to those designed by her aunt. We have no idea who tutored Margaret, and no other sampler has been discovered that seems related to this delightful needlework.

Margaret married Cicero Linn on November 3, 1836. Her needlework skills were sorely needed, for the couple eventually had thirteen children. Sadly, four of their children died in 1863, while their twenty-one-year-old son, Thomas Linn, was away fighting in the Civil War. Thomas's diary includes transcripts of his mother's letters telling him of the deaths of his siblings, sixteen-year-old Elizabeth Ann, three-year-old Casper (Cappie), and infant twins Albert and Allie. Two days after Allie died, Margaret wrote to Thomas:

> *Millersburg, Ohio, Sept. 20, 1863—*
> *Your father has told you of the death of our dear little twins. You cannot imagine how dear they were to us. I always looked on those children as a heritage from the Lord. They gave us so much pleasure before they took sick. Many people came to see them who were never in the house before. . . . Five of our family in heaven . . . what a nice little group. All them rest in the place "where prayer is heard and mercy found." What cause for praise. . . . Mother.*[31]

The last of her thirteen children, the twins were born when Margaret was forty-five years old. Like so many pioneer women who faced the death of a child, she relied on unwavering religious faith to cope with her grief. Margaret Tidball Linn died in April 1885 at the age of sixty-eight. She is buried in Hopewell Cemetery in Holmes County alongside other family members. Margaret's sampler remains in the family—it now belongs to her great-great-granddaughter.

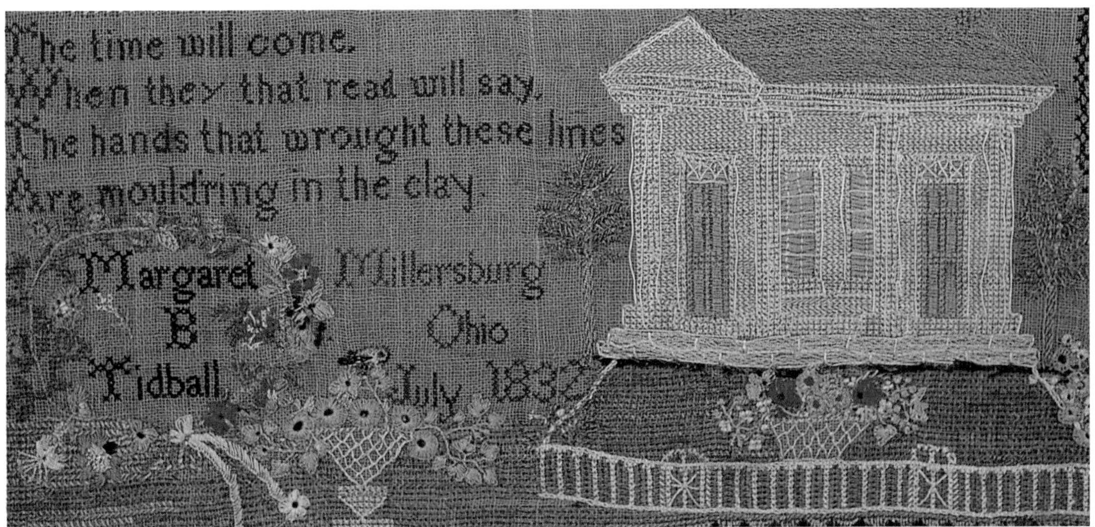

Fig. 158: Detail of Tidball Sampler.

Muskingum County

On May 1, 1796, Congress directed Ebenezer Zane, of Wheeling, Virginia, to open a road from Wheeling to the Ohio River, opposite the town of Limestone, now Maysville, Kentucky. In the following year, Zane, accompanied by his brother Jonathan and his son-in-law John McIntire, both experienced woodsmen, set out with enthusiasm to begin the task of marking the trail and cutting the new road through the difficult terrain.[32] When the trail was completed, Congress awarded Ebenezer Zane large sections of land at the crossing of the Muskingum, Hockhocking, and Scioto Rivers. His responsibilities included keeping ferries at all three crossings.

In 1799, with the completion of Zane's Trace, Ebenezer Zane and John McIntire laid out a town at the first crossing on the Muskingum, and Zane gave his son-in-law a large section of land there. John McIntire opened the first tavern and hotel and named the small village in honor of his father-in-law. Even though the town does not bear his name, John McIntire is considered the founder and patron of Zanesville. The village was rapidly settled, and both the town and its founder prospered. Transportation for the early pioneer families was less difficult now that they could travel westward by using the new trace. Newly arriving settlers eager to buy lands got a friendly, welcoming hand from John McIntire and the other citizens of the busy little town. Zanesville was named the county seat of Muskingum County in 1804, and from 1810 to 1812 the state capital was located there.[33]

John McIntire, who played such an important role in Ohio's development, is the father of one of the young stitchers in this book, Amelia McIntire (fig. 159). Her story is a fascinating and unusual one.

(following page)

Fig. 159: Needlework of Amelia McIntire. c. 1812.

Size: 19" L x 16½" W. Silk on silk. Collection of the Pioneer and Historical Society of Muskingum County.

This needlework picture was executed by Amelia McIntire of Zanesville. It is unique in the documented Ohio needlework search. Amelia's earliest schooling was at the first Zanesville school established in 1805 by Samuel Herrick. Young ladies, particularly from families of the "better sort" like the McIntires of Zanesville, were sometimes sent to out-of-state boarding schools. Their parents believed that these old established schools would give their daughters advantages not only in academic courses but in achieving poise and gentility. The schools of the Moravians were among those known for excellence, and they offered female students essentially the same subjects that boys were taught. Sewing remained, however, a very important part of a young girl's education. The Moravian School at Bethlehem, Pennsylvania, was known as one of the best, and that is where Amelia McIntire was sent when she was ten years old. Amelia's needlework is the only Moravian needlework found in Ohio.

Amelia's father, John McIntire, married Sarah Zane in 1789 in Wheeling. She was only fifteen years old, the second daughter of wealthy Ebenezer Zane. Her family was greatly dismayed by her determination to marry McIntire, who showed little promise and was a poor itinerant shoemaker twice her age. John spent a great deal of time at Zane's plantation, making shoes for the large Zane family and their slaves. He used some of that time to gain the affections of Sarah. Nothing the family said could influence the headstrong teenager to give him up. After a few years, however, McIntire, a handsome man with natural skills and address, succeeded in winning his father-in-law's respect. Ebenezer Zane called upon McIntire to accompany him to Ohio and McIntire accepted the challenge.

Once an outpost was established at Zanesville, John finally sent for Sarah to join him in the Ohio Country. She arrived by flatboat in May 1800, with all her household goods. The couple at this point had been married eleven years and had no children. Just one month later, on June 8, John presented her with a tiny baby girl. He announced that this was *his* little daughter, Amelia.

Sarah Zane McIntire's niece wrote in 1892:

> *No greater encomium on the kindly nature of the man (McIntire) could be written, than that his high spirited wife fully forgave his one, great dereliction. She adopted Amelia McIntire and raised her as her own daughter. Amelia was early sent to a seminary for young ladies at Bethlehem, Pennsylvania, where she was educated in all the accomplishments of the day designed to fit her for her future station in life. Samples of her fine embroidery are now in the McIntire Children's Home. She was always delicate in health, but was tenderly cared for by her foster mother. After her return from boarding school she entered into gay life with a zest—attending balls and parties, keeping late hours, fond of dress, receiving much attention from gentlemen.*
>
> *After Mrs. McIntire married Rev. David Young, his strict religious views interfered with her [Amelia's] gaiety. She would not be controlled, and left her once happy home—boarding first in Zanesville, and as her health failed, going to distant relatives in Wheeling. But missing the fostering care she had been accustomed to, she rapidly sank a victim to consumption and died at an early age.*[34]

John McIntire, by this time a wealthy man, died at age fifty-six in 1815. Amelia was fifteen when he died, and Sarah McIntire remarried not long thereafter. Amelia died in 1820, and she and her father are buried side by side in Zanesville, their graves protected by a large monument on the grounds that they donated for a school for the poor.

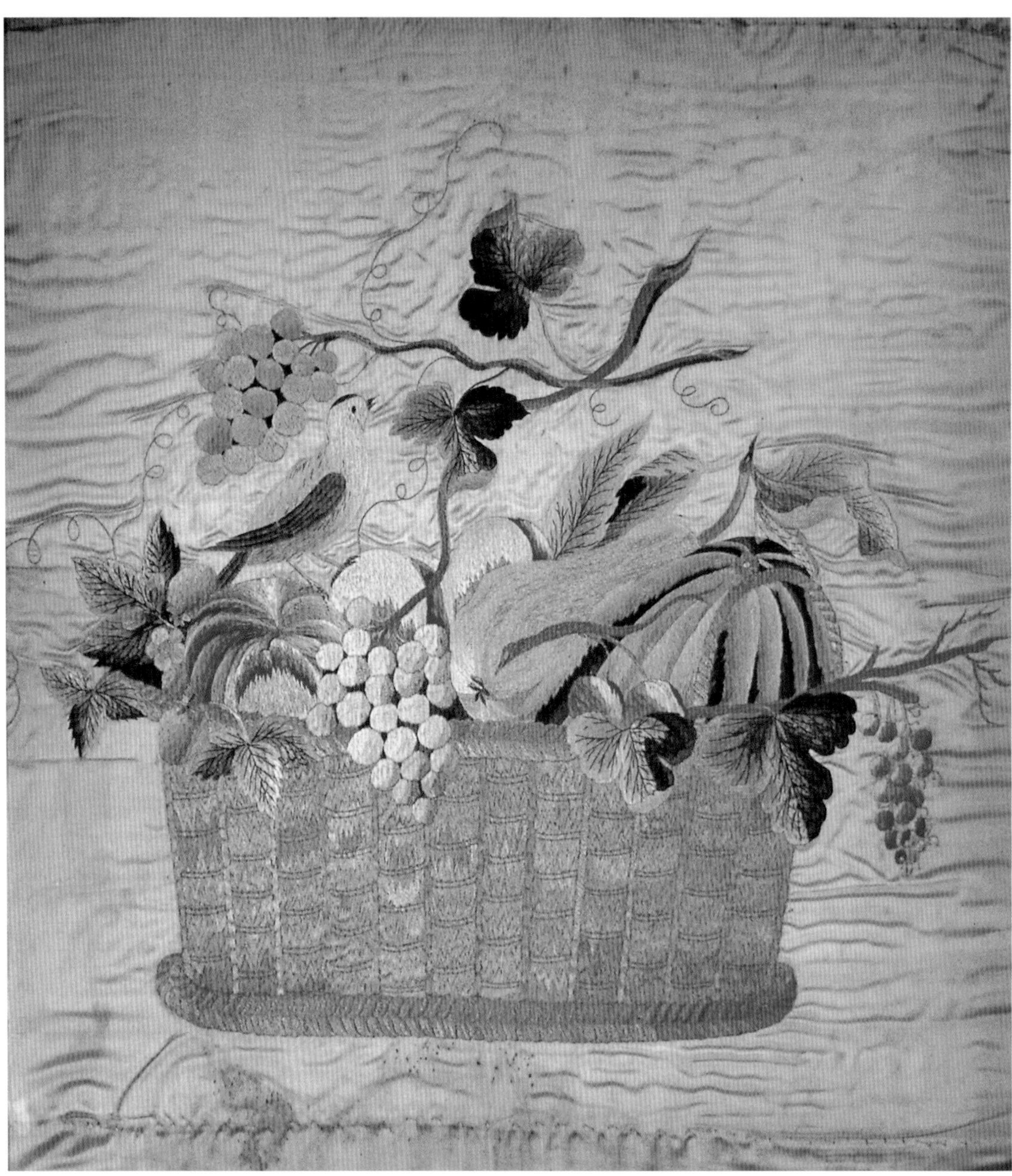

Fig. 159

Fig. 160: Detail of McIntire Needlework. »

To attempt to work successfully on a silk ground, a stitcher needed to have skill and confidence. Silk canvases were unforgiving; if an attempt was made to take out a mistake, a telltale hole would be visible on the canvas. When embroidering on linen, however, a young stitcher could rework a stitch until she had it "just right," and her canvas would not reveal the problems that had plagued her. It appears that Amelia McIntire did not have many problems with her needlework, for this piece was beautifully executed.

As it turns out, Amelia's birth mother was Liddy Zane, daughter of Andrew Zane and first cousin of Sarah Zane McIntire.[35] In John McIntire's last will and testament, dated August 4, 1815, he referred to his daughter as "Amelia McIntire, otherwise known as Amelia Messer," because Liddy later married a man by that name. As for Sarah Zane McIntire, she not only accepted their baby girl, but also helped to raise at least a dozen homeless and needy children during her lifetime. She never had any children of her own.

Before Amelia's death, a Moravian School was established in Zanesville, but how long it operated is unknown. The first notice of the school appeared in the *Zanesville Express* dated July 30, 1819. It read in part:

> *Female Education: Mr. and Mrs. Steinhauer, from Bethlehem, Pa., beg leave to inform their friends, and the public that they intend to open a school for the instruction of young ladies, in Zanesville, towards the end of August, upon a similar plan with the justly, celebrated establishment at Bethlehem, Pa.*
>
> *Mr. S., being a member of the church of the "Unitas Fratrum" (more generally known by the name of Moravians) is thoroughly acquainted with their approved mode of conducting their schools, the more so, as he has himself been engaged for many years in teaching, in one of the most respectable academies, in England. (The course of instruction, as usual, but specified.) Terms: Boarding per quarter . . . $30.00, Washing . . . 4.00.*

The following year, the Zanesville Seminary for the Education of Young Ladies published an even more complete description of the school that ran not only in the *Zanesville Express,* but in several newspapers in nearby counties. The "branches of education" offered included a wide range of academic courses, along with "plain needlework, Music, Drawing, Painting, and Ornamental needle work." The lengthy notice continued with persuasive arguments about why parents should enroll their young daughters: "In this flourishing region, highly favored with a healthy climate and enjoying all the blessings and conveniences of life, we flatter our selves, that with the patronage of the enlightened liberal public, the Young Ladies of the West, under a skillful and efficient cultivation may vie with those of the East in all the embellishments which exalt and adorn the female character."[36]

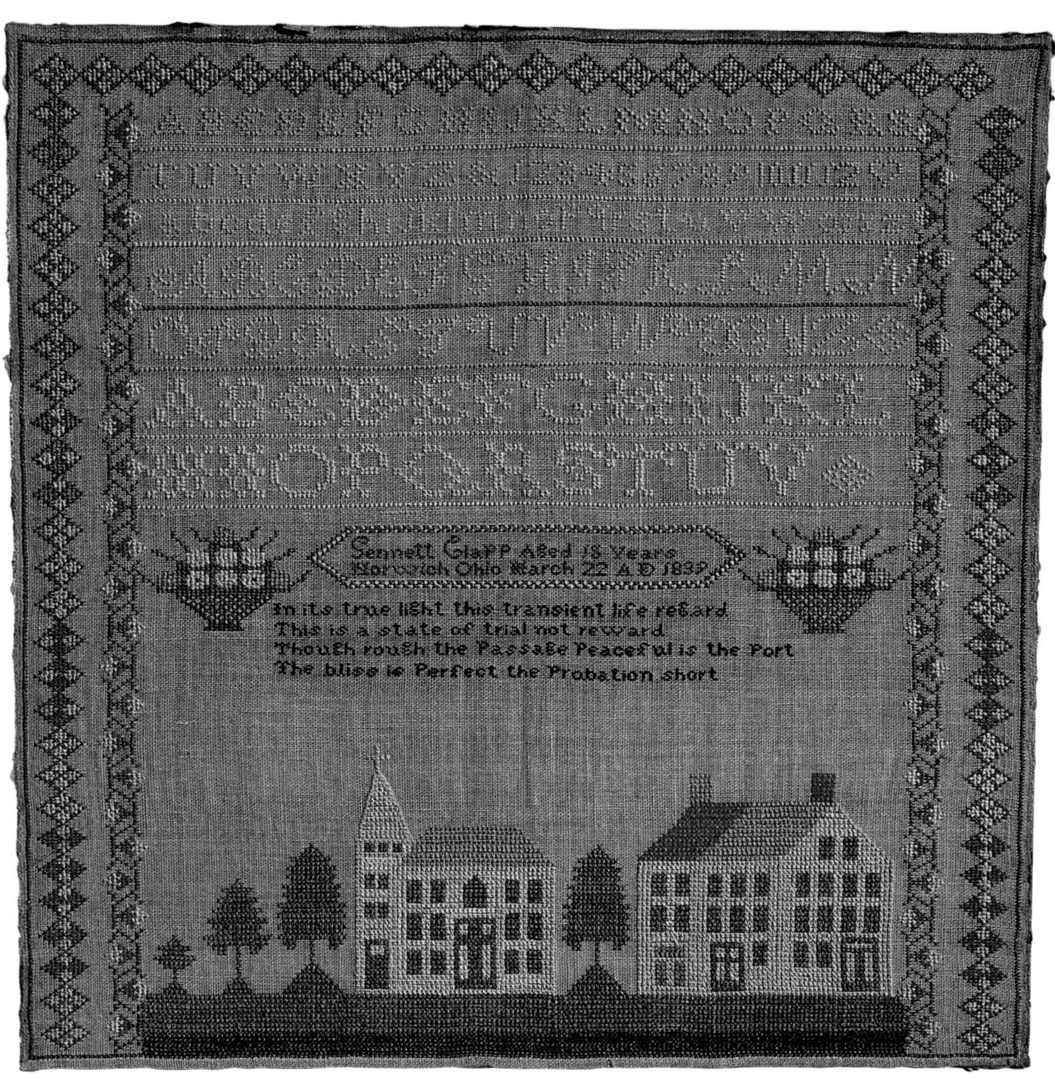

Fig. 162: Putnam Female Seminary. »

Several schools had been established in Zanesville by 1839, when Gennett Clapp stitched her sampler (fig. 161). Among the most celebrated was the Putnam Female Seminary, sketched here by Henry Howe in 1846. This school flourished from 1836 to 1846 and was a boarding school that could accommodate about one hundred students.[37] Pupils under fourteen years of age were received into the preparatory department, and those over that age were taught advanced academic subjects and offered an additional three-year course of study.

« Fig. 161: Sampler of Gennett Clapp. 1839.
Size: 18½" L x 17½" W. Anonymous collector.

Gennett Clapp was eighteen years old when this large sampler was completed in 1839. She has marked her canvas with the words "Norwich, Ohio," which was probably the location of her home rather than where she was attending school. Norwich is a tiny town in Muskingum County, and Gennett may well have attended school at Zanesville, where there were needlework teachers and boarding schools.

This sampler is one of the most attractive found, with the double geometric border on three sides and impressive buildings stitched at the bottom. The canvas is fully developed and sophisticated in design, indicating that Gennett worked under the guidance of a good instructor. Her verse reads:

In its true light this transient life regard
This is a state of trial not reward
Though rough the passage peaceful is the port
The bliss is perfect the probation short.

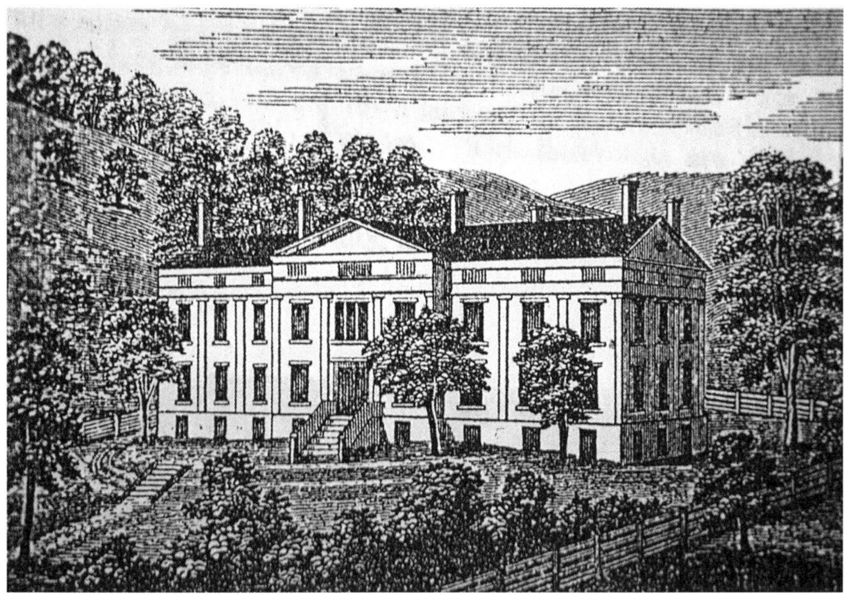

Guernsey County

Guernsey County was settled by several families who came from the Isle of Guernsey, a tiny island in the English Channel, located off the coast of France. The Sarchet family, a group of four brothers, was the first to purchase lots in the settlement of Cambridge when the town was laid out in 1806. Four years later, when the county was organized, Cambridge was named the county seat.

Four samplers have been discovered from Guernsey County, three of which are presented here.

Fig. 163: Sampler of Martha Clark. 1827. »
Size: 17¼" L x 12" W. Collection of Dr. John R. Ribic.

Martha Clark was one of six children born to Presbyterian minister Rev. Thomas Bader Clark and his second wife, Martha Wylie. Rev. Clark came from Hartford County, Maryland, and settled in Ohio in 1810. By 1817 the Clark family was living in Guernsey County.

Martha marked her sampler with her date of birth, May 10, 1820, and her considerable embroidery skills are evident. The canvas, surrounded by an attractive border, was completed when she was seven years old. Although she stitched four alphabets, clues indicate she may not have been literate. Stitched on the sloping front lawn, her verse is difficult to decipher: "O that my mind was so inclined to study wisdoms way / And as a dove to live in lov and never go astray."

Martha married James Ritchie on December 28, 1842, and the young couple made their home in Logan County, Ohio. She died in the little town of Belle Center.

1827
Othatmymindwasso
inclined to Study wisdoms
wayandasadove to live inLov,
Andnever Goastray
Martha Clark was born May th 10 A D 1820
abcdefghikl
mnoprstuwx
1234
56789

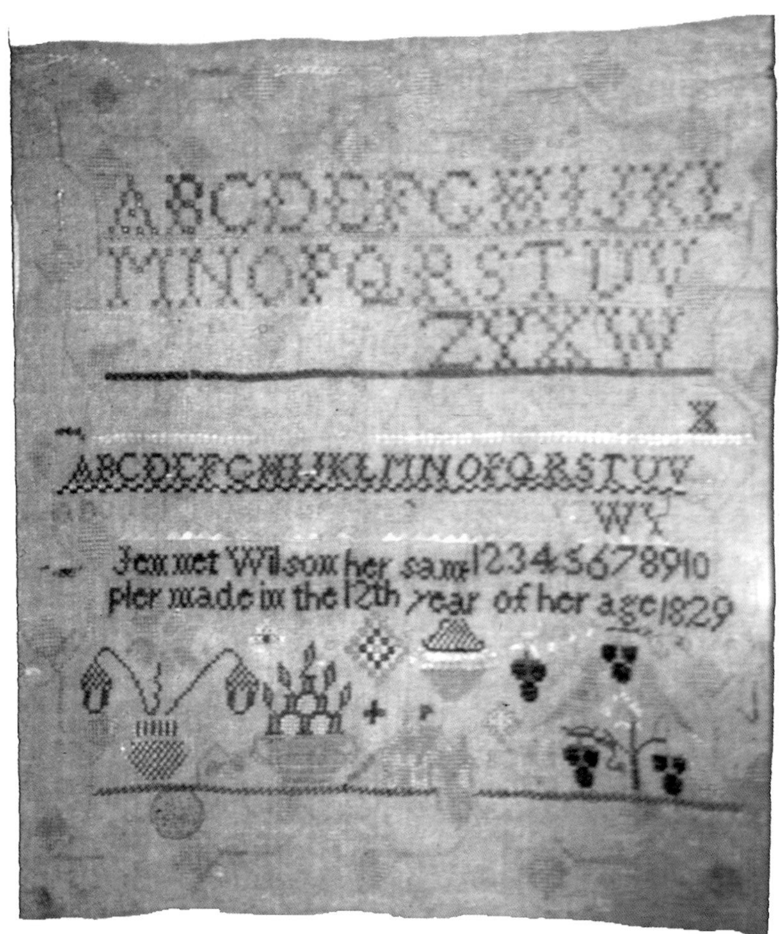

Fig. 164: Sampler of Jennet Wilson. 1829.

Size: 16" L x 16½" W. Collection of Glenn E. Warren.

Jennet Wilson plainly labeled this needlework "her sampler made in the 12th year of her age 1829." She was living in Guernsey County. The sampler is naïve in design, and, as is typical of many young stitchers, she had trouble fitting everything into place.

Born in 1817 in Cambridge Township, Jennet was the daughter of Josiah and Rebecca (Warden) Wilson, whose families had originally come from Ireland. When she was twenty-one, Jennet married Gabriel Glenn, and the couple settled on a farm in Westland Township, where they reared nine children. Oral history tells us that Johnny Appleseed, during his travels around the state, reserved seeds from the apple trees on the Glenn farm. Gabriel and Jennet were active members of the East Union Presbyterian Church, where they were married, and they donated land from the family farm for the church and adjoining cemetery. Jennet was interred there following her death on August 29, 1881.

This sampler has been handed down from generation to generation and is now in the possession of her great-grandson. Jennet could never have imagined that another of her great-grandsons, Ohio senator John H. Glenn Jr., would become a famous American hero. Like his ancestors who ventured into new territory, he ventured into space.

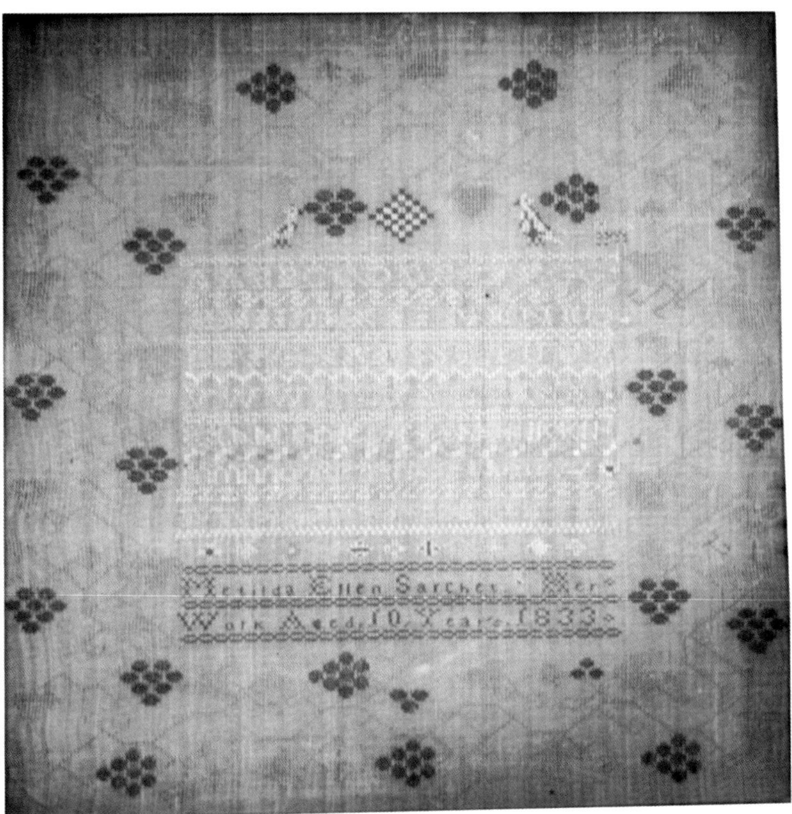

Fig. 165: Sampler of Metilda Ellen Sarchet. 1833.
Size: 17" L x 17½" W. Collection of Susan McFarland.

The family of Thomas B. and Anne Nancy (Bichard) Sarchet arrived in Ohio in 1806. They were among the first families who immigrated from the Isle of Guernsey, and their family name suggests that they were of French ancestry. The oldest son, Thomas, who was born on Guernsey Isle in 1790, was sixteen when the family arrived in the area. Three years later, in 1809, he and Catherine Marquard were married in Cambridge. They were the parents of ten-year-old stitcher Metilda Ellen Sarchet.

Metilda was one of nine children, six girls and three boys, all of whom were born in Guernsey County. Dated 1833, Metilda's sampler is faded and difficult to read. The wide border of stiff bunches of grapes, carefully scattered amid a maze of vines and leaves, is unique.

Monroe County

Although the first settlement of Monroe County began as early as 1791, the area growth rate was unhurried, and even today this hilly, heavily forested county remains sparsely populated. Bounded on the east by the Ohio River, the scenic county was not well suited to farming, though agricultural industries now include dairy farms and the raising of fine riding horses.

When Monroe County was cut from Washington County in 1815, the town of Woodsfield was chosen for the county seat. Mary Ann Kirtbride stitched the town name on her charming sampler (fig. 166). She and her family were residents of Center Township. Hers is the only sampler documented from this county.

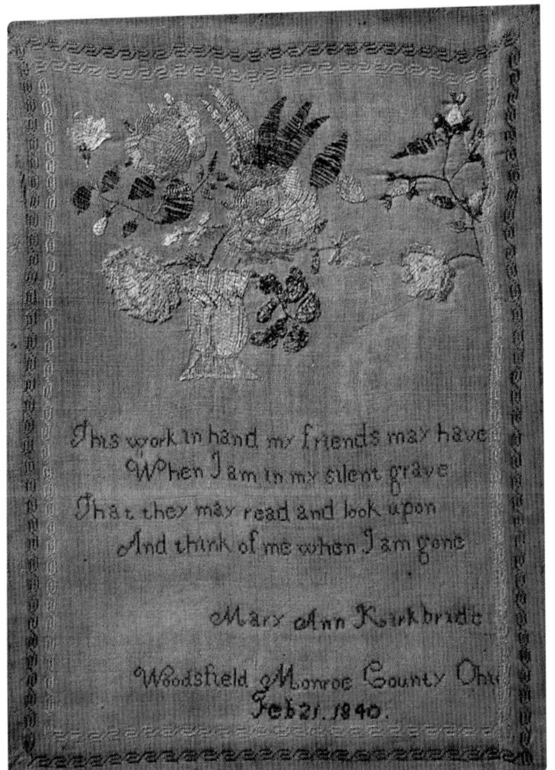

Fig. 166: Sampler of Mary Ann Kirtbride. 1840. Size: 18" L x 13½" W. Collection of Ross Trump.

Mary Ann Kirtbride completed this colorful and beguiling sampler in 1840. In the upper part of the canvas she carefully stitched an urn virtually brimming over with a bouquet of flowers. Unsuccessful at centering the design, she tried to balance the composition by placing a large sprig of flowers beside the vase. Mary Ann surrounded the canvas with a tight double-wave border. The often-used verse is a favorite of many collectors:

This work in hand my friends may have
When I am in my silent grave
That they may read and look upon,
And think of me when I am gone.

Belmont County

When the first pioneers arrived in Belmont County they were impressed with its natural beauty and impressive stands of timber. Like the neighboring counties of Jefferson and Monroe, Belmont County is bordered on the east by the wide Ohio River. Even though the county was organized in 1801, two years before Ohio achieved statehood, the settlement of this rural area was delayed because of many desperate encounters with the Indians. St. Clairsville, a small town situated on the newly opened Cumberland Trail, was laid out in 1801 and named the county seat.

Surprisingly, only two samplers have been found from this county. Both are attractive and well executed, but they look nothing alike. Since large numbers of Quaker families settled in the area early on, we would expect to discover some beautiful Quaker needlework. The St. Clairsville Monthly Meeting of the Society of Friends had nearly two hundred members and was a part of the large Stillwater Quarter, whose membership totaled nearly two thousand as early as 1826.[38] With a membership of this size, many Friends' schools may have existed, but we have documented just one Quaker sampler (fig. 167).

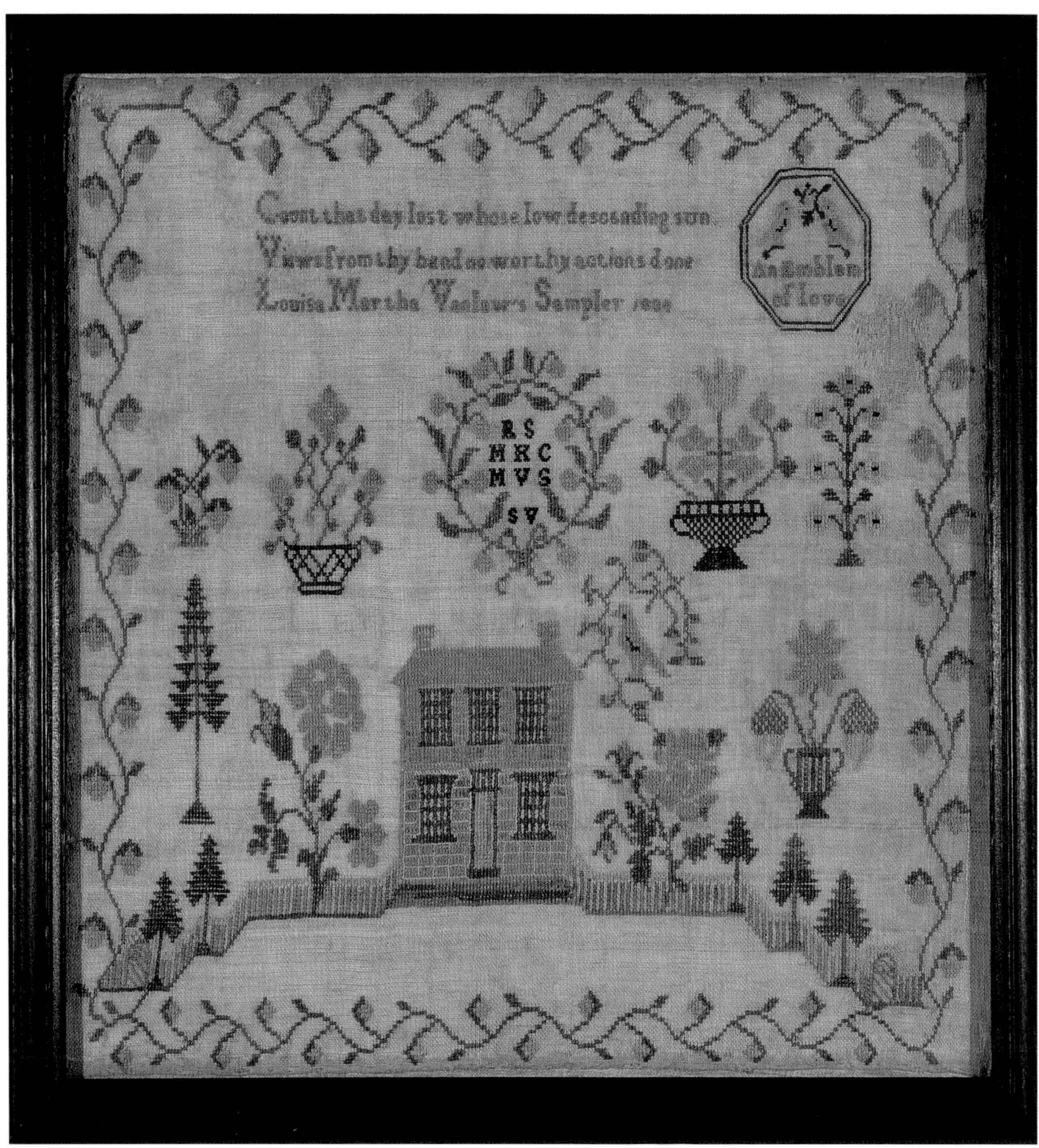
Count that day lost whose low descending sun
Views from thy hand no worthy actions done
An Emblem of Love
RS
MRC
MVS
SV

« Fig. 167: Sampler of Louisa Martha Vanlaw. 1834.
Size: 17½" L x 16½" W. Collection of William and Joyce Subjack.

Louisa Martha Vanlaw's sampler is a Quaker beauty in wonderful condition, but the overall design of the canvas does not resemble any other Ohio Quaker samplers. It has a variety of classic Quaker motifs, such as the cartouche enclosing the family initials centered in the canvas, but the plain leaf and vine that usually encircles them has been embellished with tiny flowers or berries. The familiar "Emblem of Love" motif with the paired birds framed in an octagonal medallion, the tall, thin evergreen tree made up of small dangling triangles, and the unusual terraced fence are all "new" elements for an Ohio Quaker sampler. Samplers like this reinforce the idea that Quaker teachers transferred motifs from one school to another, and from state to state, as they traveled westward. The inspiration for the fence on Louisa's needlework may well have been taken from the Quaker samplers produced in Burlington County, New Jersey, where the Vanlaw family lived before coming to the Ohio Country.

Research tells us that Louisa was a member of the large Stillwater Monthly Meeting. With a congregation of more than 360 members, the church most likely had an organized school. Louisa was born on April 22, 1818, in Belmont County, to John and Sarah (Sharp) Vanlaw. John Vanlaw came to Ohio c. 1805–10. He settled in Belmont County, where on March 29, 1812, he married Sarah Sharp. Sarah died in 1829, when she was thirty-five years old, leaving John with eleven-year-old Louisa and eight other young children to care for. The following year, he married Sarah Spencer. In 1843 Louisa Martha married James Doudna. She died in June of 1898 at the age of eighty.

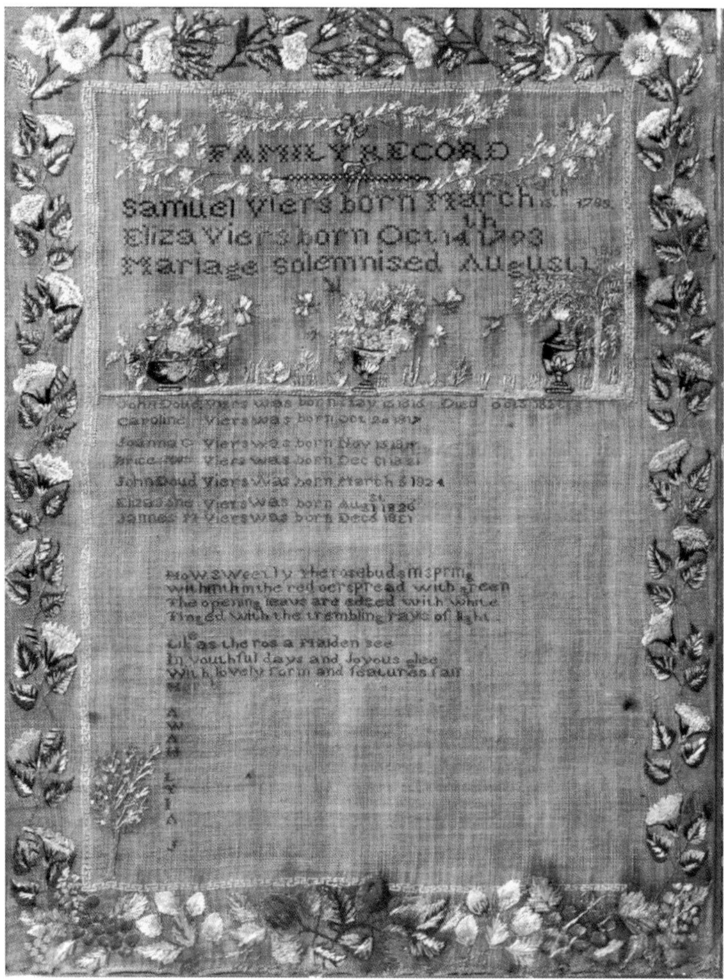

Fig. 168: The Viers Family Record. c. 1831.

Size: 24" L x 19" W. Collection of Nancy D. Wagner.

Morning glories, leaves, and vines form a tightly constricted, attractive border for the Viers Family Record. Attributed to Caroline, the youngest daughter, it was begun in 1831. Caroline was born in Ohio in October 1817, the second child of Samuel and Eliza Viers. The Vierses came from Pennsylvania to Ohio shortly after their marriage in 1815 and settled in Jefferson County. Caroline records their marriage date on the upper part of the canvas. After executing three flower-filled urns, she separated her composition into two sections and began to stitch the genealogical information.

The couple's first child, John Doud, was born in May 1816. The sampler records his death in October 1823 at the age of seven. Five months after his death, on March 6, 1824, Samuel and Eliza had another son. They named him John Doud, to honor the boy they lost. The last birth entry Caroline recorded was that of another son, James, in 1831. That year the Viers family moved to neighboring Belmont County.

Genealogical record samplers often took the place of the family Bible for recording the marriages, births, and deaths. When necessary, the decorative needlework record could be amended over time in much the same way. Although they are not often signed, such samplers were usually stitched by the oldest or the youngest daughter of the family.[39]

Jefferson County

Jefferson County, whose eastern border is delineated by the Ohio River, was settled just before the turn of the nineteenth century. The county was formed along a narrow strip of the Ohio Country that bordered what was then Virginia. In the 1780s, Fort Steuben was constructed on the banks of the river, but when it was no longer needed, and the Indians signed a treaty of peace, the fort was abandoned.

The town of Steubenville, established in 1798, was handsomely situated on an elevated plain above the Ohio. The settlement, almost from its inception, was a busy commercial town. Education was given a high priority, however, by the early families who settled the county. One of the largest and most successful schools for female students in the new state, the Steubenville Female Seminary, was established 1828–29.[40] It was built at the site of the old fort and had an expansive view of the river and surrounding hills.

Large numbers of Quaker families also came to this area early in the nineteenth century. The Society of Friends Short Creek Quarterly Meeting had over twenty-five hundred members by the 1820s. The influences of Quaker needlework teachers, among them those working at the large Steubenville Female Seminary, are found on the samplers discovered in this county.

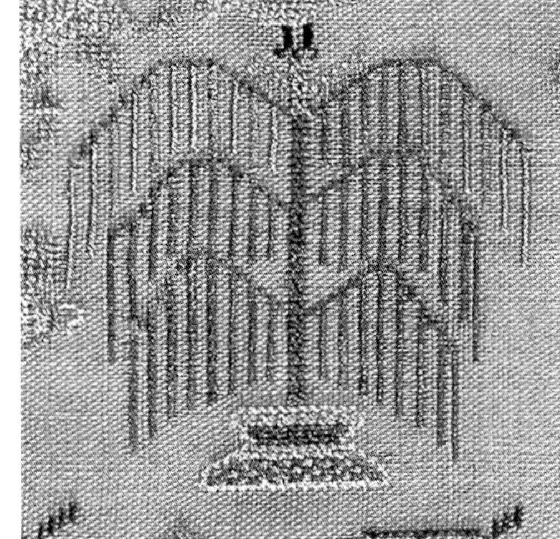

Fig. 169: The Distinctive Willow Tree Favored by Quaker Needlework Teacher Ann H. Thorn.

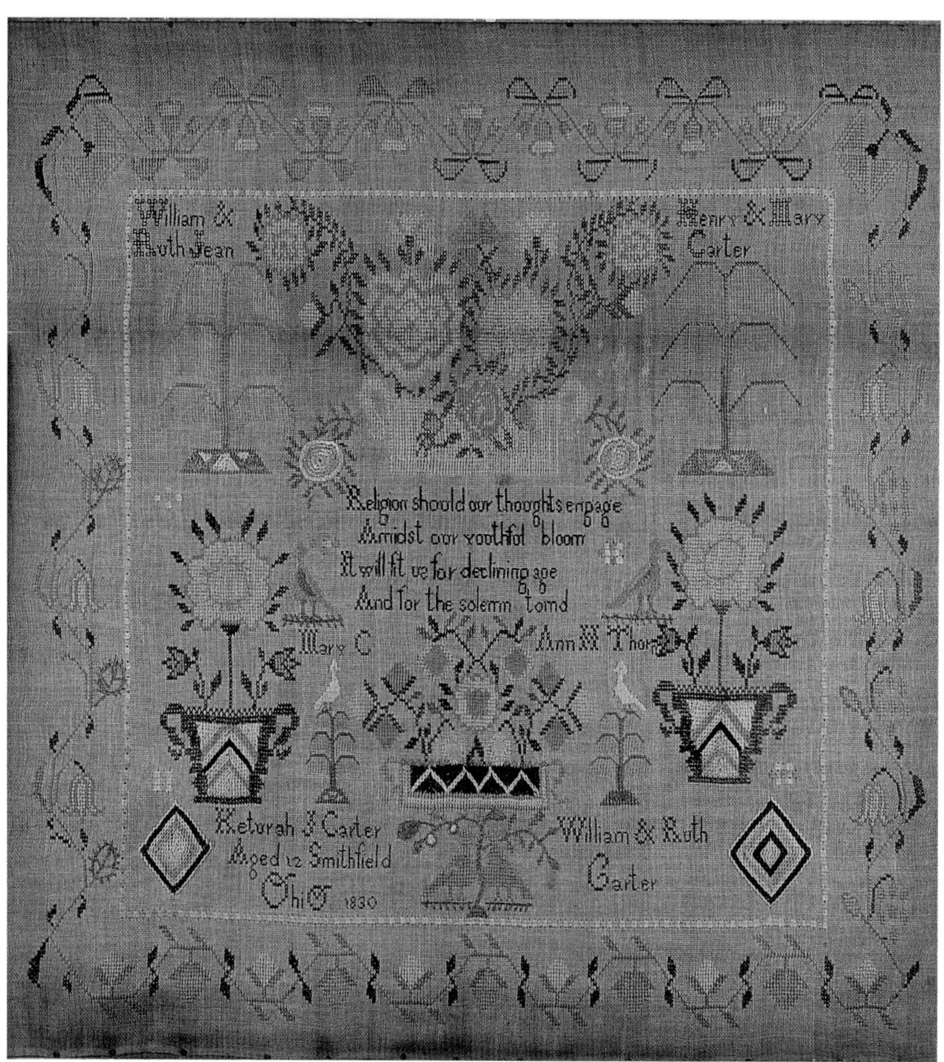

Fig. 170: Sampler of Keturah J. Carter. 1830.
Size: 22½" L x 21¾" W. Collection of Allan and Linda Cobourn.

The two young daughters of William and Ruth Jean Carter, Keturah and Achsah, worked beautiful samplers in 1830 in the small town of Smithfield, not far from Steubenville. Keturah was twelve and Achsah was ten when their canvases were completed. The girls not only had unusual names, but also produced extraordinary handwork. Both samplers credit preceptor Ann H. Thorn.

The definitive elements of design of this needlework allow us to identify other students whom Mrs. Thorn probably tutored. One of the most easily recognized signature motifs is the three-tiered weeping willow tree, sometimes topped with a bird. Another element she often used was a large flower blossom, tightly encircled with small, stiff leaves and usually placed in a square basket or decorated pot.

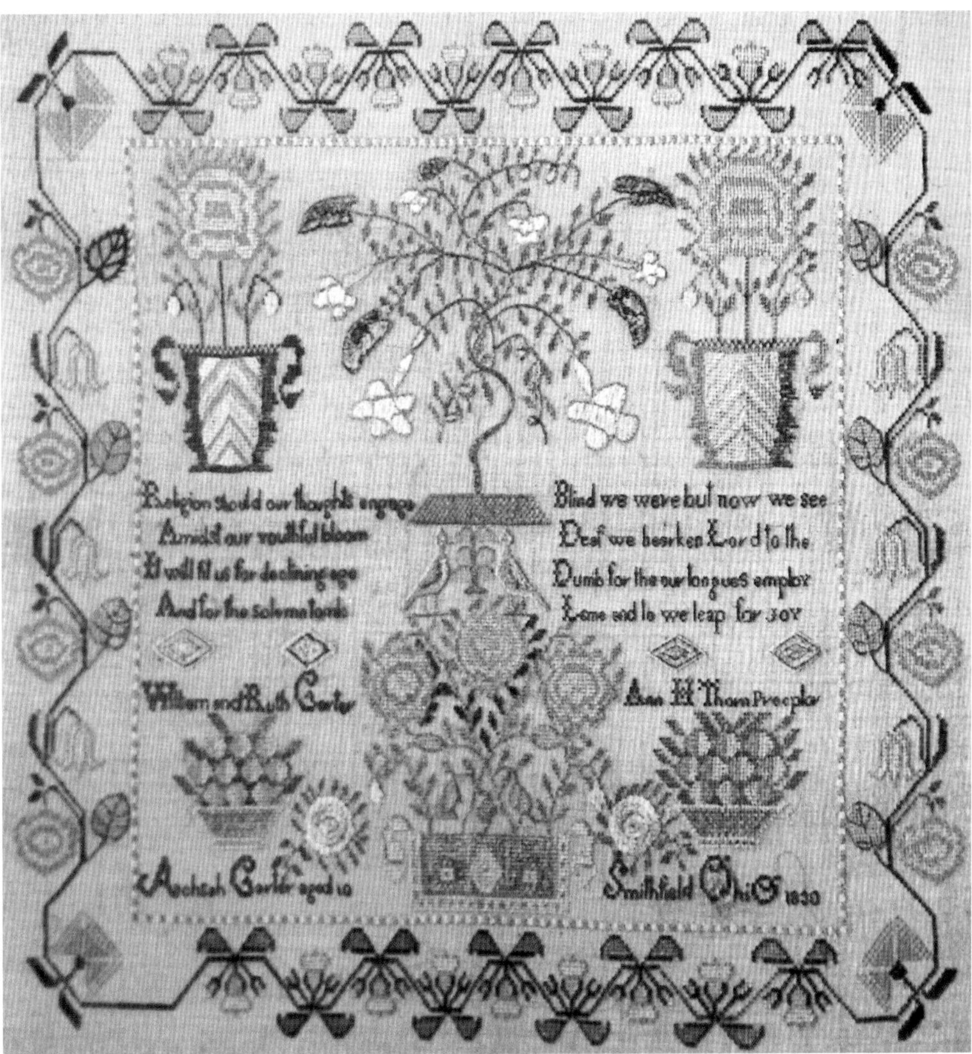

FIG. 171: SAMPLER OF ACHSAH CARTER. 1830.
SIZE: 22" L x 21" W. ANONYMOUS COLLECTOR.

Achsah Carter's canvas exhibits many of the same motifs that her sister worked, but the samplers are by no means identical. The chevron-decorated pots with the large blossoms mirror those stitched by Keturah, but the leafy center tree is different and unusual. Although two years younger, Achsah's needlework skills were no less impressive. Stitches include cross, satin, flat, outline, and queen.

Ann Thorn was the daughter of John and Levinah Gumery of Jefferson County. She was a member of Short Creek Quarterly Meeting, one of the first and largest of the four Quarterly Meetings established in eastern Ohio. Ann H. Thorn's students included both Quaker and non-Quaker girls, and she probably taught in a Quaker School setting rather than in her home. A fourth Ohio sampler, the work of Martha Judkin (1828, marked Steubenville), is also associated with Ann Thorn's tutelage.

Quaker records list that Ann Gumery married Thomas Thorn on May 29, 1811, at the West Grove Meeting House near Smithfield, in Jefferson County. In December 1829 she was disowned from Short Creek congregation because she joined the Hicksites.[41]

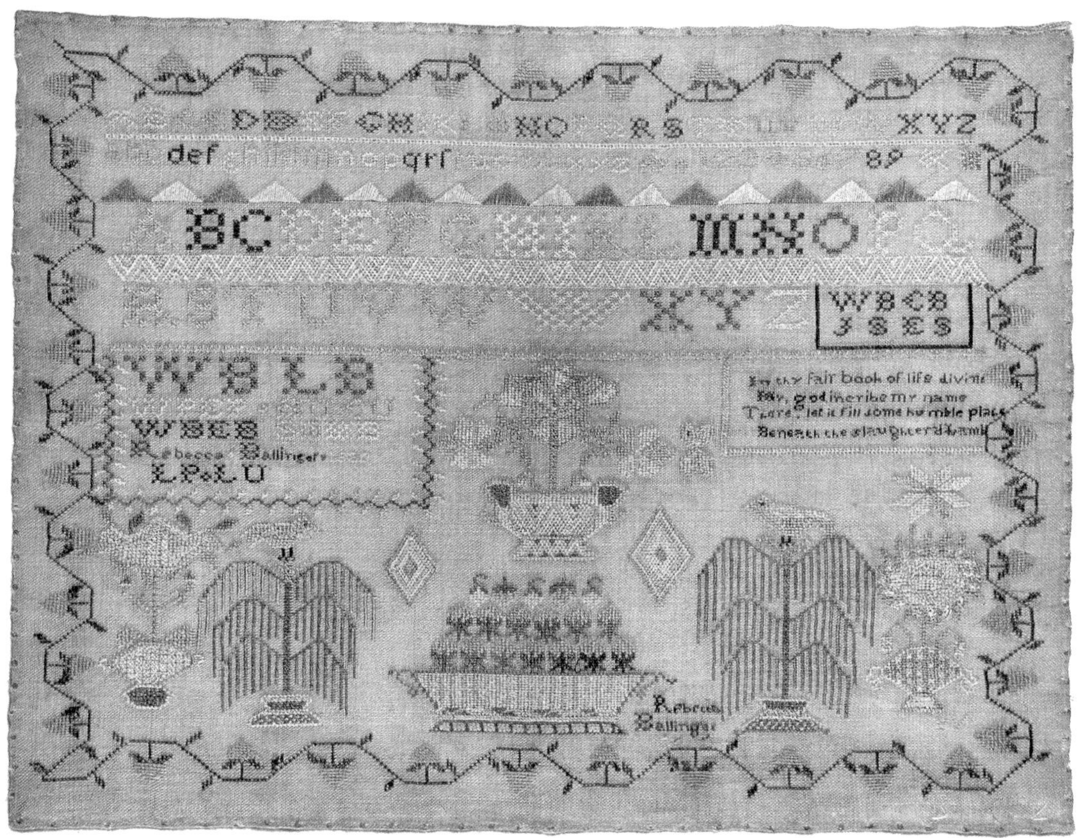

Fig. 172: Sampler of Rebecca Ballinger. 1830.
Size: 17" L x 23" W. Collection of Smithsonian Institution,
National Museum of American History, Behring Center, Washington, D.C.

Rebecca Ballinger was the daughter of William and Lydia (Smith) Ballinger, Quakers who came to Jefferson County from Carroll County, Maryland, in 1819. The canvas, completed when she was sixteen, is fully developed and filled with a myriad of designs, a verse, and initials of family members. Although Rebecca did not include the name of her needlework teacher, those droopy, angular weeping willow trees, the diamond-within-a-diamond motifs, the canvaswork band, and the decorated center pot are clues that Rebecca Ballinger worked under the guidance of Ann H. Thorn.

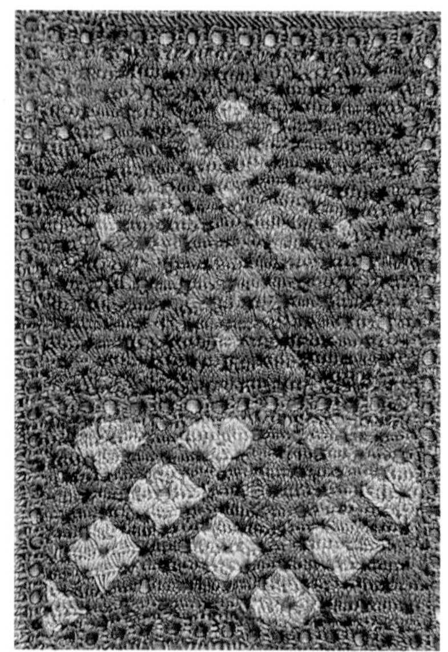

Rebecca was a member of the large Smithfield Monthly Meeting of Quakers, a congregation associated with the Short Creek Quarterly Meeting. According to church records, she married Thomas H. Terrell on April 22, 1863.

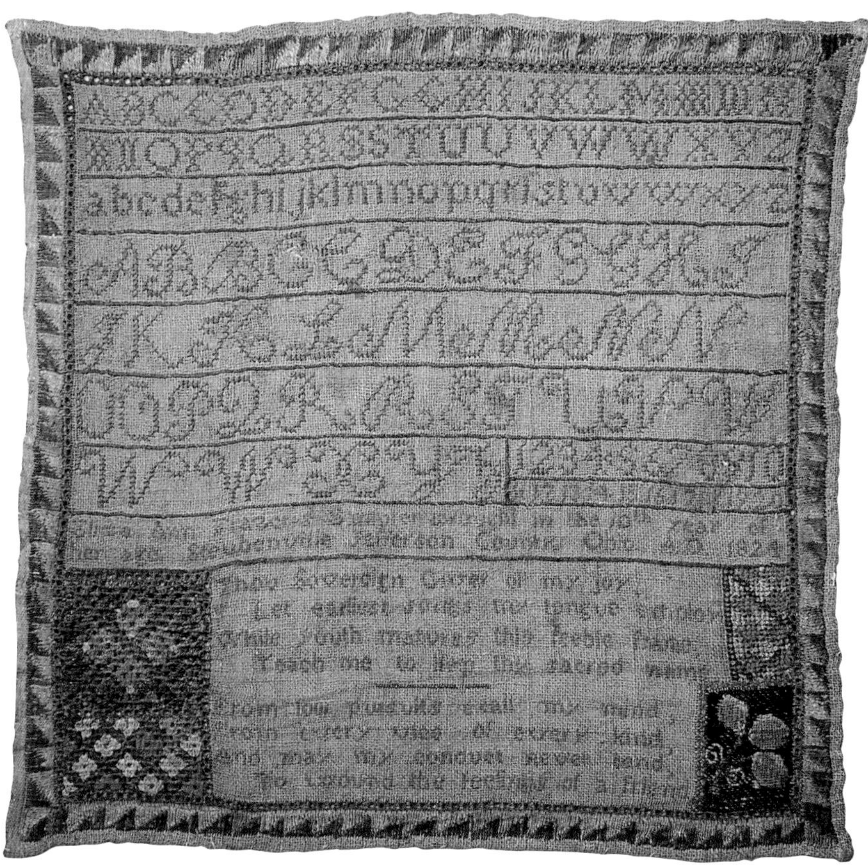

Fig. 173: Sampler of Eliza Ann Frazier. 1824.
Size: 12" L x 12" W. Collection of Larry and Sarah Mosteller.

The sampler of Eliza Ann Frazier is not large, but a great deal of information is stitched on the small canvas. It reads: "Eliza Ann Frazier's sampler wrought in the 10th year of her age Steubenville Jefferson County Ohio A.D. 1824." Eliza wasted none of the canvas and even used the corners to exhibit her needlework skills in executing difficult stitches (see fig. 174). She enclosed the canvas with a satin-stitch sawtooth border. The second part of the long verse Eliza stitched reads:

From low pursuits exalt my mind,
From every vice of every kind,
And may my conduct never tend,
To wound the feelings of a friend.

« Fig. 174: Detail of Frazier Sampler.

One of the colorful designs that Eliza Ann Frazier executed was done in the Queen stitch, also known as rococo stitch. It is easy to recognize because of the holes that are formed as the stitcher repeatedly goes in and out of the same hole to form the diamond-shaped stitch. It was the most time-consuming and complex of all the stitches and was generally used only as an accent.[42]

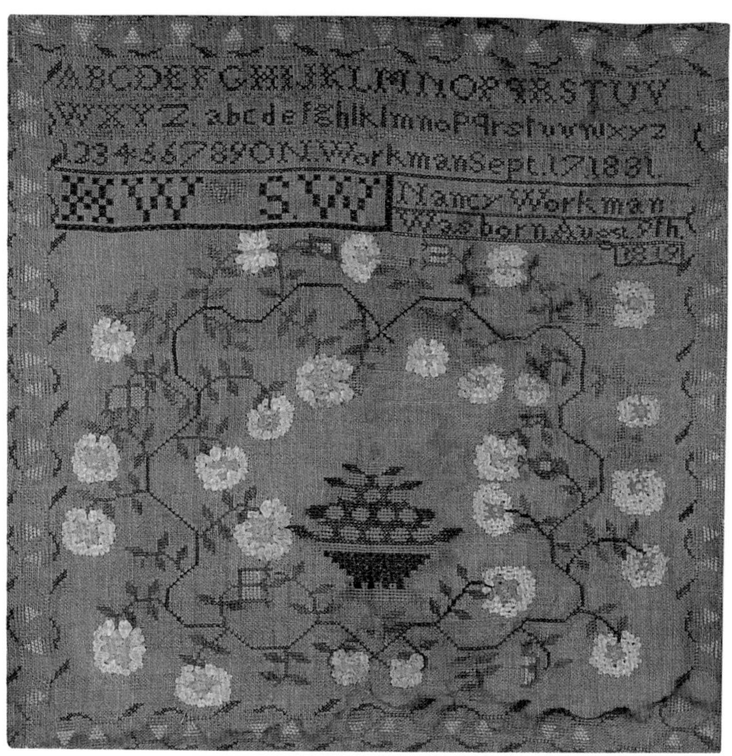

Fig. 175: Sampler of Nancy Workman. 1831.
Size: 17" L x 17" W. Collection of Eleanor McMinn.

Though Nancy Workman's large and pretty sampler is not marked with a location or school, it has been placed in Jefferson County because it shares many characteristics with another documented sampler that is marked with the town of Steubenville. It is possible that Nancy Workman was a boarding student at the Steubenville Female Seminary, for the school was patronized by many young ladies who were living in neighboring counties. Completed in 1831, the canvas design is distinctive with its wreath of small white flowers surrounding a basket of fruit. Nancy signed this work twice and tells us she was born on August 9, 1819. Her parents were Hugh and Sarah Workman, whose initials on the sampler are linked with a blue heart motif. Nancy married John Perkins in Chillicothe on September 24, 1840. She died four years later at the age of twenty-five.

Fig. 176: Steubenville Female Seminary.

In April 1829, the Reverend Charles C. Beatty and his wife, Hetty, formally opened the Steubenville Female Academy, shown here in an 1846 sketch by Henry Howe.[43] It was founded on the religious principals "of all Evangelical Protestants."The school flourished for many years and was considered one of the finest female seminaries in Ohio. Girls as young as ten were enrolled in the preparatory school, while the principal school, or young ladies' department, consisted of those students over the age of twelve.[44]

Carroll County

Carroll County is one of Ohio's smallest. Perhaps this is one reason we have found only two samplers from this area in the north-central part of the state. Carrollton is the county seat of government, and that location is stitched on Eliza Jane Combs's needlework. Both town and county were named in honor of Charles Carroll, who was the last surviving signer of the Declaration of Independence. He died in 1832, the year Carroll County was formed.

Fig. 177: Sampler of Eliza Jane Combs. 1844.
Size: 24" L x 16" W. Collection of Robert and Susan Pusecker.

Eliza Jane Combs's canvas is unusually large, and, although it does not exhibit any floral motifs, its plain and simple composition is pleasing. Eliza divided the four alphabets with narrow bands, each executed in a different stitch. She distinctly marked her name, her age (thirteen), the location, and the four important letters *o, h, i,* and *o*. In the 1840s, it was common, especially on a large sampler like this, to embroider with wool thread rather than silk. Wool-work would have taken less time, but the results would not have been as attractive. Using silk thread allowed Eliza to practice a variety of intricate stitches and to form alphabet letters that were precise and easy to read.

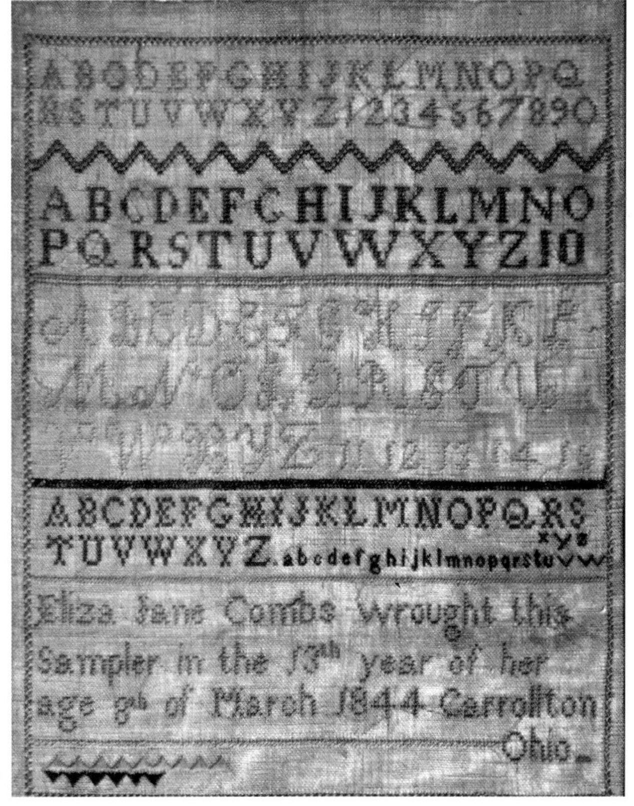

part three

NORTHERN OHIO

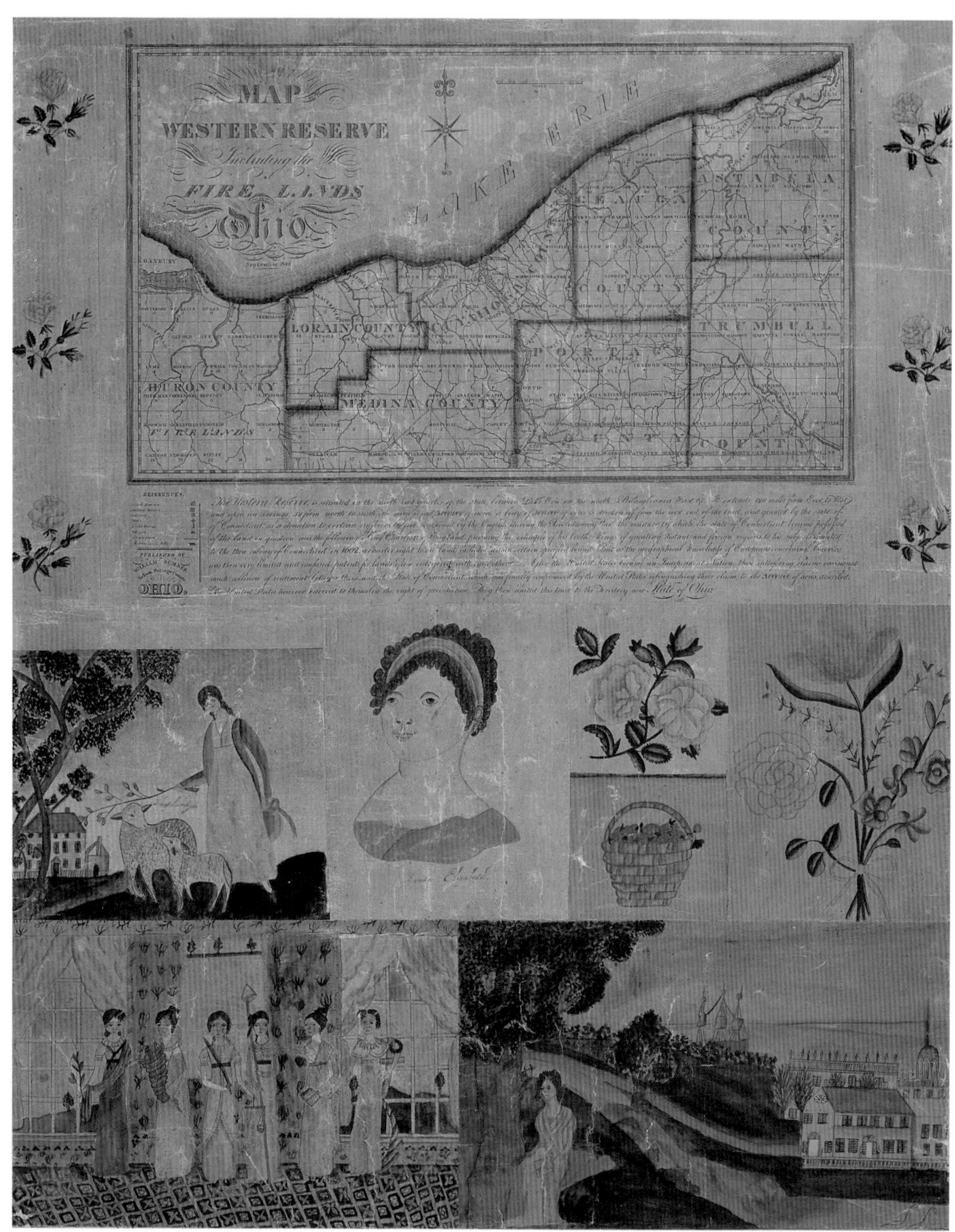

Map of the Western Reserve, Drawn by William Sumner. 1826.

Size: 35" L x 27" W. Collection of Dr. M. Donald Hayes.

Although this rare map probably served as a teaching tool in a female seminary, it displays the remarkable type of academic art that young female students might produce while attending a "select school." The curriculum advertised often included instruction in "painting from nature etc.," "plain and fancy needlework," and all the "ornamental branches." Sewing boxes and work tables sometimes received lavish decoration, but decorating a large scroll map with a variety of painted scene was far more creative and unusual.

Trumbull County

The entire area of the Connecticut Western Reserve began as Trumbull County in the year 1800. It was one of seventeen counties at the time of Ohio's statehood in 1803. Although there had been discussion about naming the area "New Connecticut," the county was named to honor Jonathan Trumbull Jr. At that time he was governor of Connecticut and had served with valor in the Revolution as aide-de-camp to George Washington.

The early settlers of the Western Reserve prided themselves on taming the wilderness lands. Even though they did not establish the first schools in Ohio, it did not take them long to bring teachers from the East to educate their children. Ten samplers from Trumbull County have been documented. The most unusual "Ohio" needlework from the Western Reserve was not executed in Ohio at all, but was done at school in Connecticut by Anna Maria Perkins (fig. 178).

Anna's father Simon had served as a general in the War of 1812. After the war, he eventually purchased a large tract of land in Summit County and laid out the town of Akron. The decision by General Perkins and his wife, Nancy, to send their daughter back East to school was not unusual. Like most of the families in the Western Reserve, they had relatives and strong ties there. Furthermore, the prevailing sentiment among most of those families was that schools in New England were better than those in Virginia or Pennsylvania. This was widely discussed in the literature of a century ago by specialists in the educational history of Ohio.[1]

Dr. James J. Burns wrote freely about how poor the teachers were in the southern part of the state: "The few schools established in this section were taught by cripples, worn-out old men, and women unable to scotch hemp and spin flax, or constitutionally opposed to the exercise." He continued: "they were regarded as a dependent on the bounty of the people, [people] whose presence was tolerated only because county infirmaries were not then in existence."[2] In contrast, he had this to say about those who were teaching in the Western Reserve: "The social status of the teacher was on an equal footing with that of the physician and the minister. Society welcomed him as an honored member. His periodic visit[s] to the homes of his pupils were regarded as quite an event by each household."[3]

Fig. 178: Mourning Picture of Anna Maria Perkins. c. 1822. »

Size: 17¾" L x 17¾" W. Silk on silk.

Collection of The Western Reserve Historical Society, Cleveland, Ohio.

The silk-on-silk mourning picture of Anna Maria Perkins is done in a distinctive style of embroidery called print-work. Anna Maria's stitches of black silk thread are so carefully sewn on the white silk ground that one can scarcely tell them from a pen-and-ink drawing. This classic memorial picture is encircled with a band of black velvet, and the tassels and bows around the border are painted directly on the silk canvas. Anna did this work when she was about fourteen years old (c. 1822) to commemorate the death of her baby sister, Martha, who died in 1817.

Anna Maria was born in 1807, the second of nine children born to Simon and Nancy (Bishop) Perkins of Warren, Ohio. Her first schooling was in the home of Miss Converse, but after a short period there, the Perkins children were sent to a school located near the old Warren Courthouse that was taught by Mrs. Lathrop.[4] In the summer of 1821, Nancy, Anna Maria's mother, decided that her daughter should be sent back East to Miss Sarah Pierce's School in Litchfield, Connecticut, "where students were taught geography, music and arts, and manners thought suitable for young ladies of good families." School records show she attended Miss Pierce's Female Academy through the winter quarter of 1823 and was a "Most excellent scholar and writer; stood at the head of the school, and bore off many prizes." In June 1822, her roommate wrote of her: "Anna Maria Perkins of Ohio also sleeps in the room with us. She is a very good companion and peculiarly amiable."[5] In November 1827, Anna Maria married John W. Allen, a promising young lawyer. She died of consumption the following year at the age of twenty-one.

Other writers were equally uncomplimentary about the teachers and the educational opportunities offered in the southern part of the state. In 1886, Jessie Cohen wrote about the problem: "In various settlements established early in Ohio, the educational aspect is widely different. In parts settled by the peoples from Connecticut and Massachusetts, intelligence became universal, while in those parts settled by those from Virginia and Pennsylvania, the evil results of the settlers' indifference remained discernible for years."[6]

Ohio girls, like Anna Maria Perkins (fig. 178), who studied at schools in the East often returned to Ohio and became successful teachers. The most notable example may be Irene Hiccox. In 1822 Miss Hiccox was persuaded by Mrs. John Andrews of Kinsman to study at Miss Pierce's academy in Connecticut. After completing training, she returned to Trumbull County and opened a select school in Mrs. Andrews's home. "Her school was probably in advance of any in the Western Reserve, and her fame drew students from Ashtabula, Austinburg, Hartford, New Lisbon, Poland, Youngstown, Hudson, Warren, and adjoining townships. Besides the usual subjects, painting in watercolors was offered and to work a sampler was indispensable."[7]

The excellent needlework created by early Ohio stitchers was produced by young girls all over the state. As many of their teachers came from the South as from the East, which may account for the incredible diversity of canvas designs and motifs that we find on Ohio samplers.

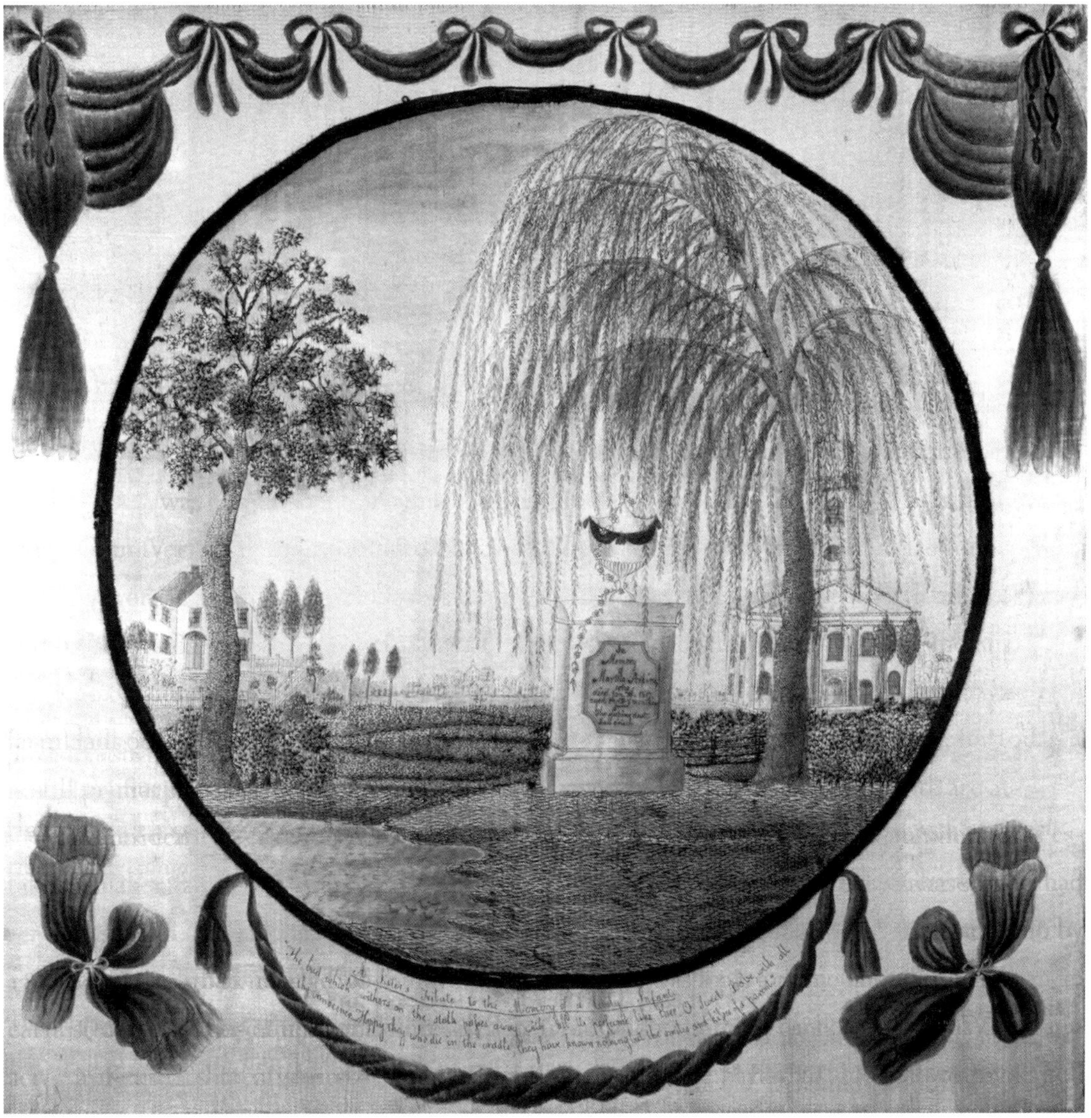

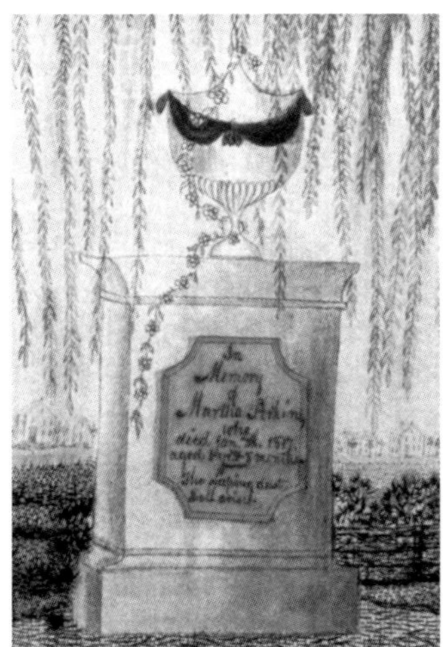

Fig. 179: Detail of Mourning Picture.

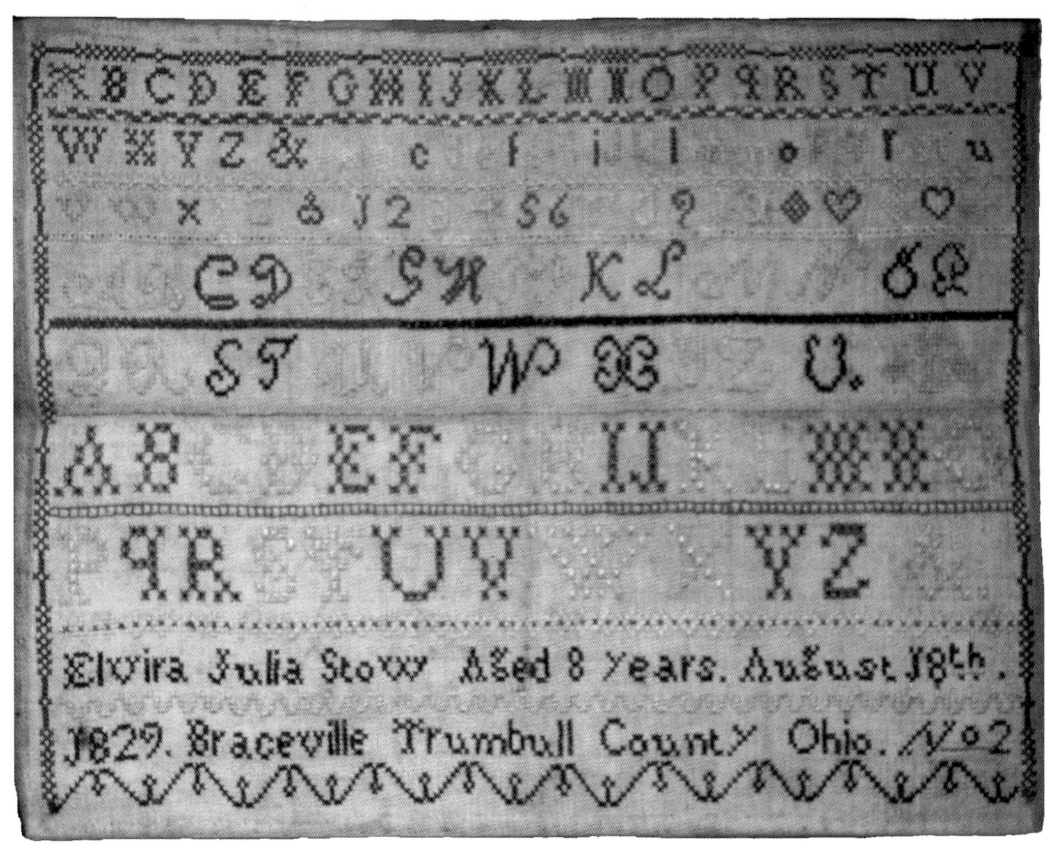

FIG. 180: SAMPLER OF ELVIRA J. STOW. 1829.

SIZE: 8½″ L x 11″ W. COLLECTION OF NANCY GARDNER GOFF.

The small sampler of Elvira Julia Stow is complete with four alphabets and a neatly stitched border. This eight-year-old boldly marked that she was living in "Braceville Trumbull County Ohio." At the end of that line she embroidered a few additional curious stitches: "No. 2." This marking must have been suggested, or perhaps even required, by her needlework teacher to indicate that this was the second needlework exercise that Elvira had completed.

At the time that this sampler was completed, several Stow families were living in Braceville Township, which is located in the southwestern part of Trumbull County. A large and prominent family, they came from Connecticut in 1810. As the decades passed, several members played significant roles in the area's early history. One of the first teachers in Braceville was Hervey Stow, who taught school there in 1812.[8] In fact, three early Braceville teachers were members of this large extended family and probably were closely related to Elvira. We do not know if any of them taught "plain and fancy needle work," but it is likely that needlework was a part of their school's curriculum.[9] It has not been determined who Elvira's parents were. Unfortunately, the only records of this young girl are this small sampler and her marriage record. She married Alexander Griffin in Trumbull County on July 14, 1843, when she was twenty-two years old.

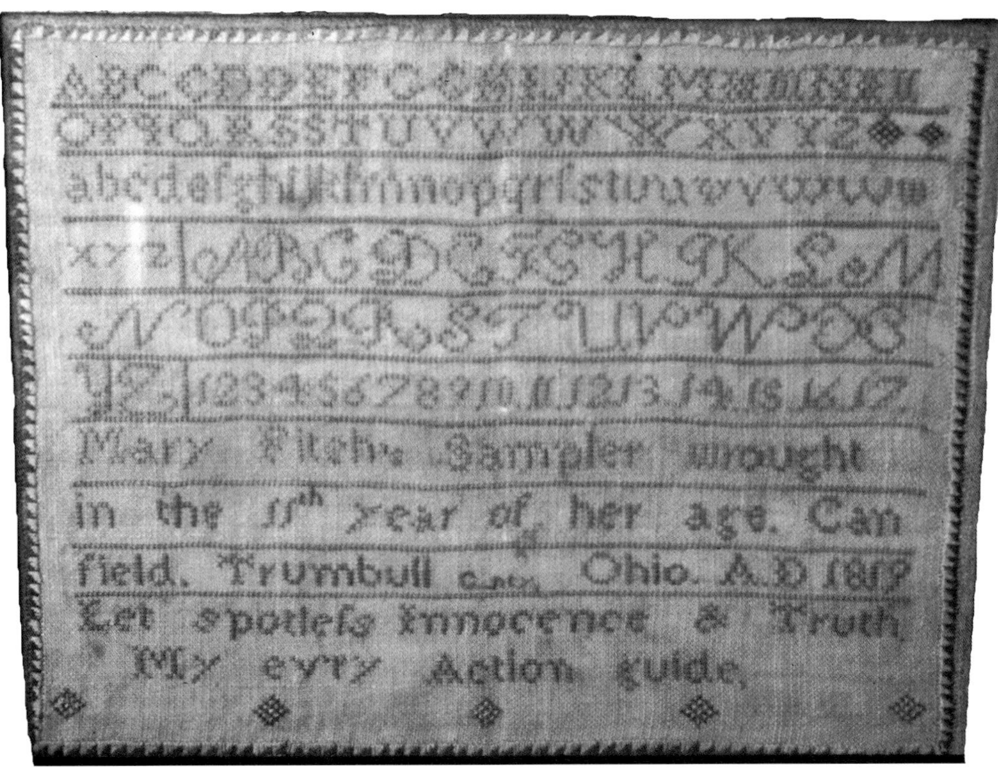

Fig. 181: Sampler of Mary Fitch. 1819.
Size: 12" L x 15½" W. Collection of Rebecca C. Bennett,
great-granddaughter of the stitcher.

The Fitch Family came to Trumbull County early in the nineteenth century and settled near the community of Youngstown. The Ohio census of 1820 lists Cook and Sarah (Bostwick) Fitch, whose daughter Mary stitched this plain sampler, as living in Canfield Township. This family, like many others, came to the Reserve from Connecticut.

Mary, who was born on January 23, 1808, stitched two samplers in 1819. Both have survived. This canvas, filled with three alphabets and a set of numbers, has the following inscription:

Mary Fitch's Sampler wrought in the 11th year of her age.
Canfield Trumbull County Ohio A.D. *1819*
Let spotless Innocence & Truth
My ev'ry Action guide

Mary used the old style of *f* for the letter *s*. This was common in the eighteenth century, but was dropped in the mid-nineteenth century. Her needlework was completed with five tiny diamond designs and a neat sawtooth border.

Mary's older sister, Thalia Rebecca Fitch (1806–26), married Henry T. Kirtland, son of Turhand Kirtland of Poland. When Thalia died in 1826, a year after their wedding, Henry was faced with the care of their little son, Cook Fitch Kirtland. After two years, the young widower resolved to marry again. He chose Mary, Thalia's younger sister, with whom he had three more sons. When Mary Fitch Kirtland died in 1877, she was buried in Poland beside her husband and sister.

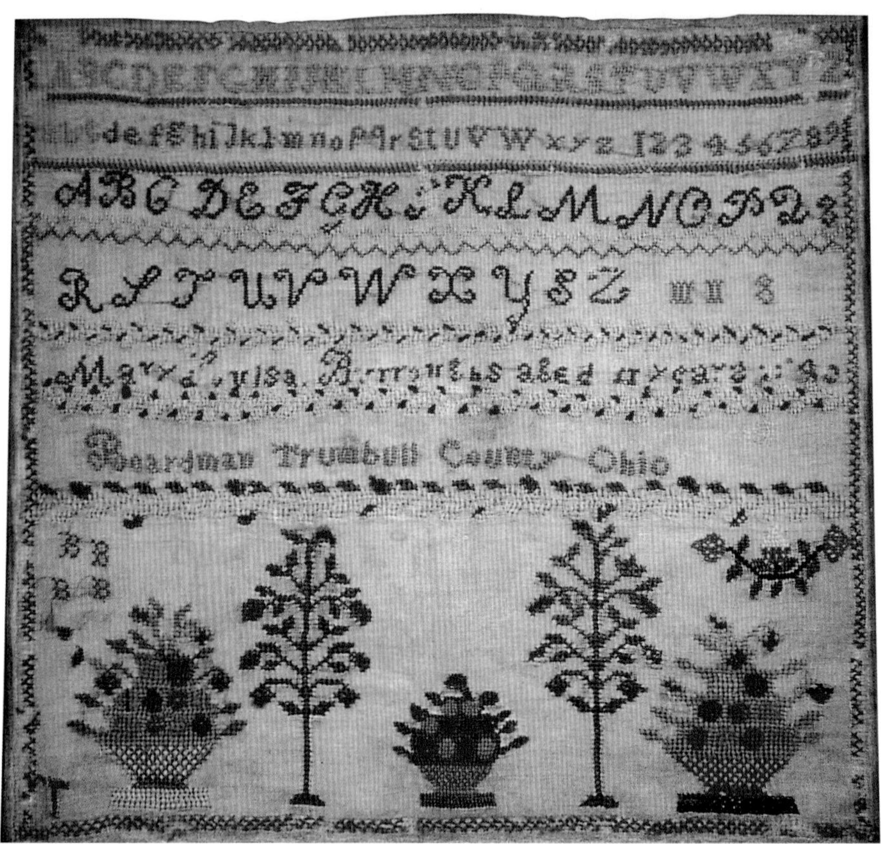

Fig. 182: Sampler of Mary Louisa Burroughs. 1840.
Size: 15½" L x 16½" W. Wool on linen. Anonymous collector.

Mary Louisa Burroughs clearly stitched her name and the words "Aged 11 years—1840 Boardman, Trumbull County Ohio" on her canvas. It is now difficult to read because some of the wool threads have been damaged by moths. The lower half of this colorful needlework is filled with three fruit-filled baskets, all stitched in a similar manner but of different sizes and colors. The sampler, with the decorative bands separating each section and the tall trees standing between the baskets, is well balanced and would have looked beautiful in the family's Victorian parlor.

Public records did not help in trying to identify Mary Louisa's parents. In fact, the Ohio Census Records for 1840 listed no families by the name of Burroughs living in Trumbull County, but they *did* list five families there by the name of Burrows. Even after genealogical researchers unraveled the misspelled name (census takers often listed surnames just as they sounded), Mary Louisa's parents remain unknown. In 1847 she married Asael E. Adams, a young man from a well-known Warren family. By 1860 the couple was recorded living in Cleveland where Asael E. Adams is listed as a merchant.

The Berlin yarn used in Mary's sampler probably came from the fleece of Merino sheep, a Spanish breed imported into the United States early in the nineteenth century. This wool was soft and angora-like, and was dyed in all shades of beautiful color-fast hues.[10] The presence of fuzzy, brightly colored Merino wool thread always means the piece was stitched in the nineteenth or twentieth century, not the eighteenth century.

FIG. 183: SAMPLER OF NANCY FAUNCE. 1828.
SIZE: 14" L x 14" W. ANONYMOUS COLLECTOR.

Nancy Faunce executed this sampler when she was twelve years old and living in the tiny settlement of Bazetta. Her parents were Alden Faunce and his second wife, Priscilla (Shurtliff) Faunce, who were married March 4, 1812. The couple came to the Western Reserve from Plympton (now Carver), Massachusetts, with their four children. Land records (c. 1826) show that Alden Faunce owned 415 acres in Trumbull County.

Nancy stitched the same sentimental verse that Eliza Frazier used on her sampler (fig. 173):

From low pursuits exalt my mind
From every vice of every kind
Nor may my conduct ever tend
To wound the feelings of a friend.

Teachers often provided stitchers with verses about friendship, virtue, death, idleness, and religion that imparted moral lessons to remember for a lifetime. Nancy's life was far too short, however, for she died in 1830 at age fourteen, about two years after the sampler was completed. Nancy and her mother, Priscilla Faunce, who died in April 1832, are interred side by side at Cortland Hillside Cemetery in Bazetta Township.

Columbiana County

Nine samplers have been documented from Columbiana County; certainly there are many more yet undiscovered. The county was settled early, starting in 1797, but not officially established until 1803. Trumbull and Columbiana Counties made up the entire Western Reserve when Ohio's statehood began. Families were eager to immigrate because the area was peaceful. It seemed free from the kind of conflicts with hostile Indians that settlers in the southern and central parts of the new state had to endure.

Many of the early settlers were members of the Society of Friends (Quakers), and several examples of their needlework have survived. Salem, located in the midst of agricultural country, was founded in 1806 by three Quaker families. Because there was strong sentiment by most of the town residents against slavery, the Western Anti-Slavery Society headquarters was located here. Long before the Civil War, the *Anti-Slavery Bugle,* a publication that was widely circulated, originated in Salem.[11]

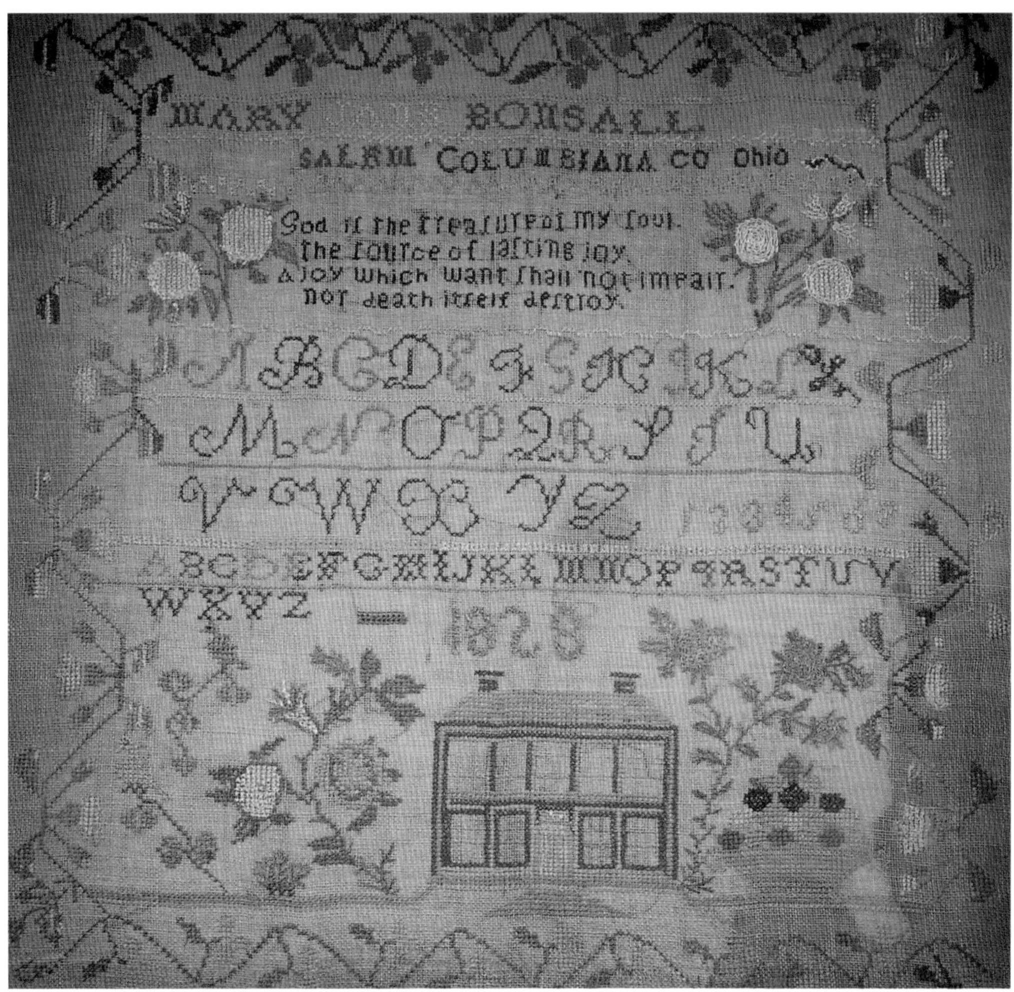

Fig. 184: Sampler of Mary Jane Bonsall. 1828.

Size: 18" L x 16" W. Collection of the Salem Historical Society, Inc.

A young Quaker girl named Mary Jane Bonsall completed this large and important sampler and clearly marked it with "Salem Columbiana Co. Ohio." We know very little about Mary, but we do know that several members of the Bonsall family immigrated to Columbiana County from Pennsylvania as early as 1807. Since her given name is a common one, we are not sure which Mary Bonsall stitched this beautiful needlework.

The canvas is stained but easily read. The wide border exhibits a profusion of color and form, surrounding all four sides of the sampler. The distinctive building with a chimney on each end and large windows is different from any other structure found on an Ohio sampler. Mary's verse reveals the importance of religion in her life:

God is the treasure of my soul,
The source of lasting joy,
A joy which want shall not impair,
Nor death itself destroy.

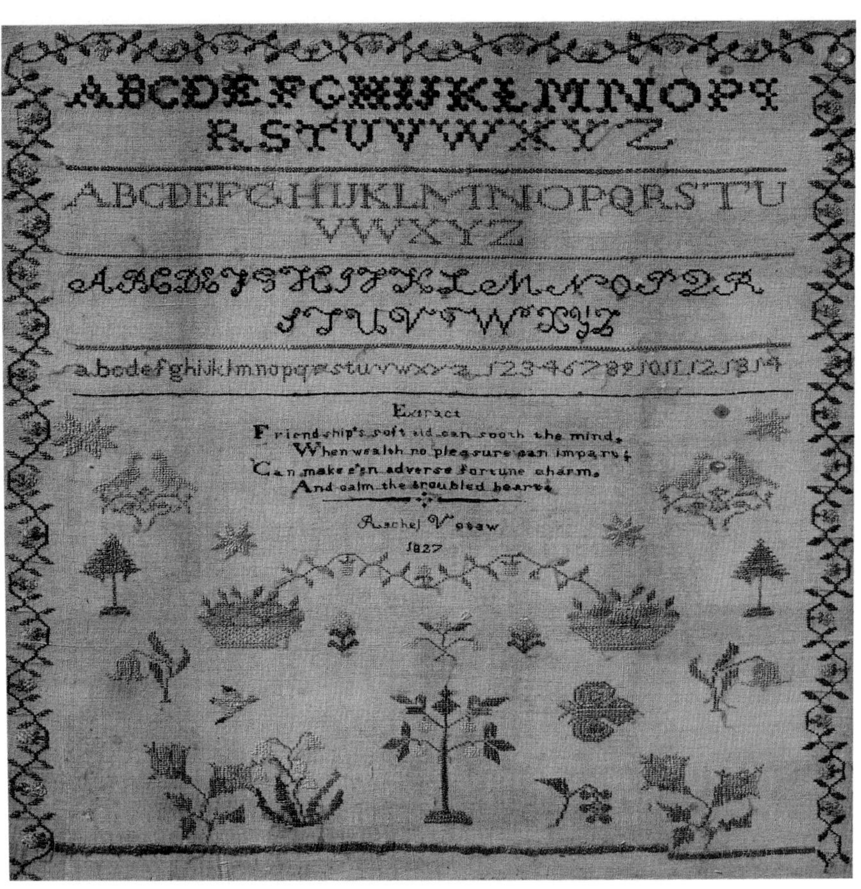

Fig. 185: Sampler of Rachel Votaw. 1827.

Size: 19½" L x 20" W. Collection of Jane and George Harold.

Rachel Votaw was born in Winona, Columbiana County, on February 26, 1811. She was the tenth of twelve children born to Moses and Mary (Brown) Votaw. Moses came from Loudoun, Virginia, and Mary's home was Washington County, Pennsylvania. Married in 1793, the young couple moved to Ohio in the autumn of 1803. Rachel's needlework displays many Quaker motifs, and records confirm that her family was a part of the Hicksite Branch of the Society of Friends.

Rachel completed this canvas in 1827 when she was sixteen years old. Two years later, on September 7, 1829, Rachel was found "Murdered—plain circumstances, say by James Courtney," according to the family Bible. Apparently, no one was ever tried or convicted of the crime.

Rachael's sampler serves as a memorial to a young girl who died an untimely death, before her life had really begun. Her grave is in Woodsdale Cemetery, near the family homestead in Winona.

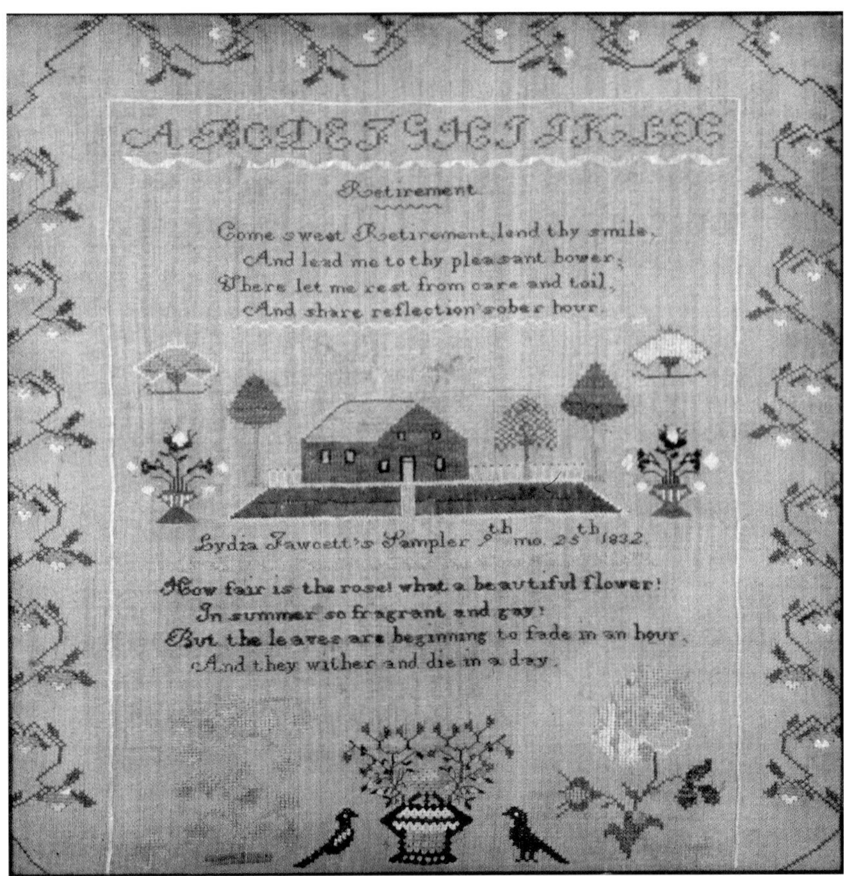

FIG. 186: SAMPLER OF LYDIA FAWCETT. 1832.

SIZE: 20" L x 20¼" W. COLLECTION OF GLEE KRUEGER.

A bright blue hipped-roofed building is nestled amongst moral sentiments on the 1832 sampler of Lydia Fawcett. She framed this large canvas with a strawberry vine on three sides and stitched several typical Quaker motifs. Lydia was the daughter of David and Hannah (Ball) Fawcett of Salem. Born on November 3, 1822, she was ten years old when her sampler was completed. In 1846, Lydia married Hutchins Satterthwaite, whose large extended family were also all members of the Society of Friends.

Her verse, entitled "Retirement," reads:

Come sweet Retirement, lend thy smile,
And lead me to thy pleasant bower;
There let me rest from care and toil,
And share reflection's sober hour.

Beneath the blue house she continues with:

How fair is the rose, what a beautiful flower!
In summer so fragrant and gay!
But the leaves are beginning to fade in an hour,
And they wither and die in a day.

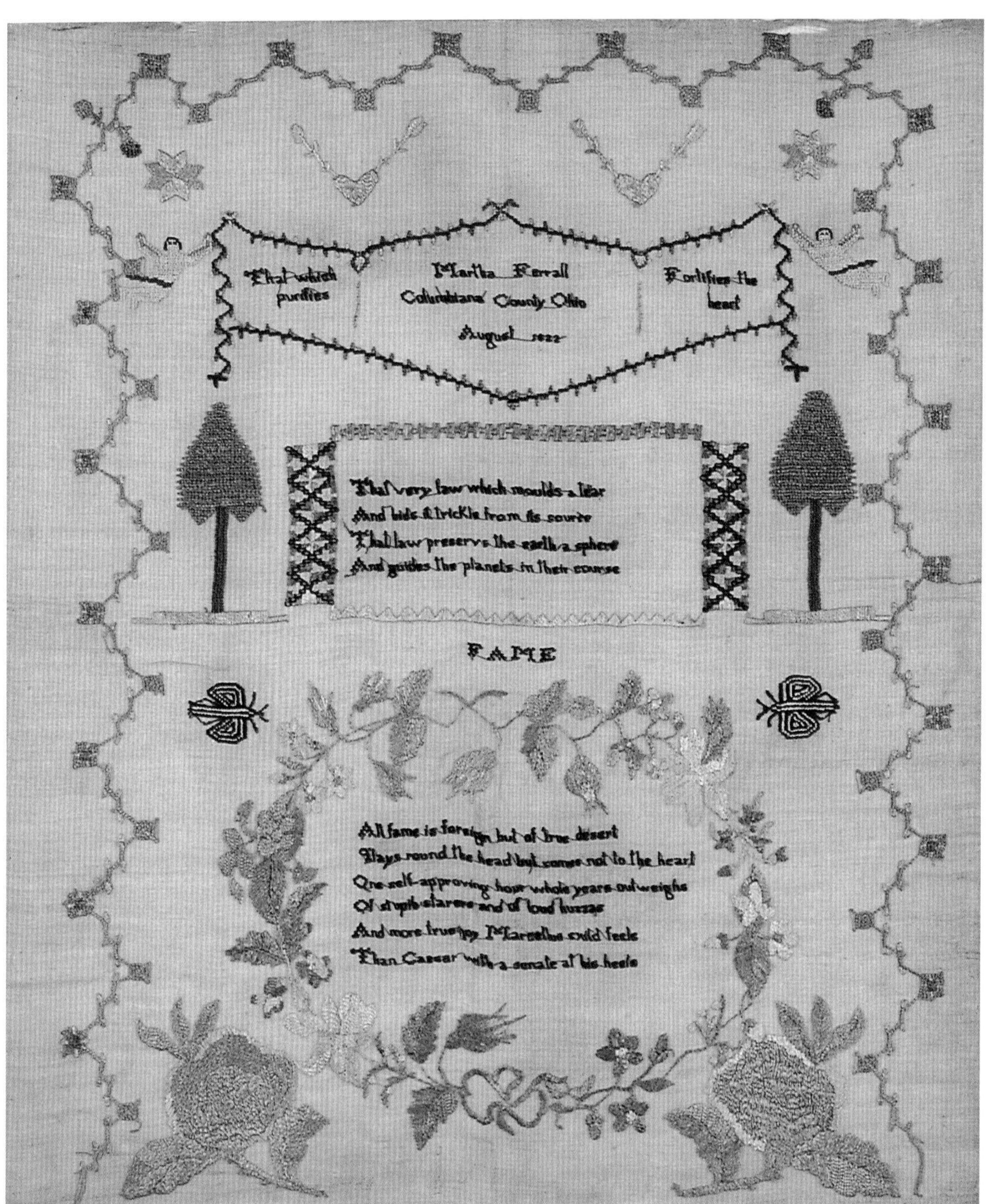

Fig. 187: Sampler of Martha Ferrall. 1822.
Size: 17" L x 16" W. Collection of Ann Bauer.

This sampler was completed in August 1822 by Martha Ferrall. Were the canvas not plainly marked "Columbiana County—Ohio," one would never guess where it was made. Its overall design is completely different from that of any other sampler discovered in Ohio. The basic design elements seem incongruous—the top half looks German, the bottom half Quaker. Blended together, however, the two parts combine into an especially attractive sampler. Martha's stitches are beautifully wrought on a closely woven canvas. They include satin and whip stitches and French knots.

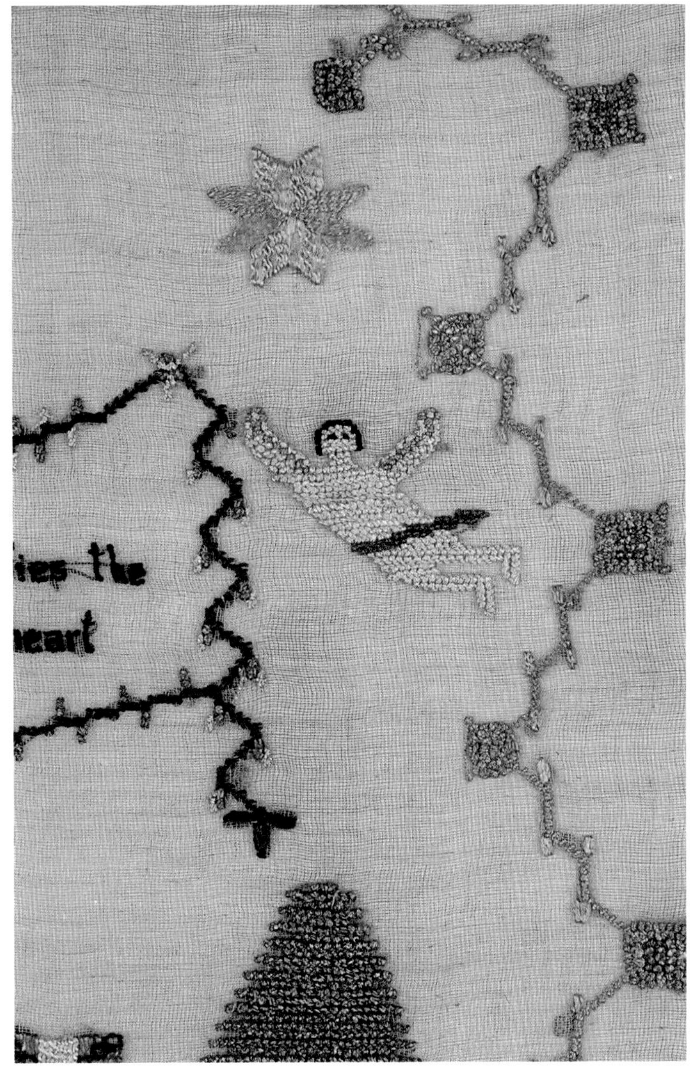

Fig. 188: Detail of Ferrall Sampler.

Near the top of Martha Ferrall's sampler, holding up the banner with her name, are two winged figures that are rarely found on needlework. They are reminiscent of the folk-art angel drawings that are occasionally seen on Pennsylvania German *fraktur schriften,* or frakturs.[12] Above the banner, Martha stitched Germanic hearts that are held with chains, another unusual design element.

The bottom half of the canvas exhibits typical Quaker motifs. The large moths or butterflies, the flower-and-vine cartouche with a bow at the bottom, and the sprigs of flowers are oft-used Quaker designs. An unusual arcaded border frames the canvas.

Martha and her sisters Lucy and Judith came with their mother, Mary Ferrall, from Pennsylvania to Columbiana County in 1814. Quaker records show they joined the Middleton Monthly Meeting of Friends. This congregation, founded in 1803, was situated in Middleton Township, which bordered Pennsylvania. It was a part of the large Salem Quarterly Meeting. Almost every Quaker Meeting operated a school in connection with their church. The Salem Friend's School was established in 1822, the year Martha Ferrell completed this sampler. The school's close proximity to the German communities in Pennsylvania, and to those Germans who crossed the Alleghenies to settle in Ohio, may account for the unusual flying angels on an American Quaker sampler.

Fig. 189: Needlework Picture of Abigail Mendenhall. 1817.
Size: 8½" L x 10½" W. Silk on silk. Collection of Melvin and Connie Porcher.

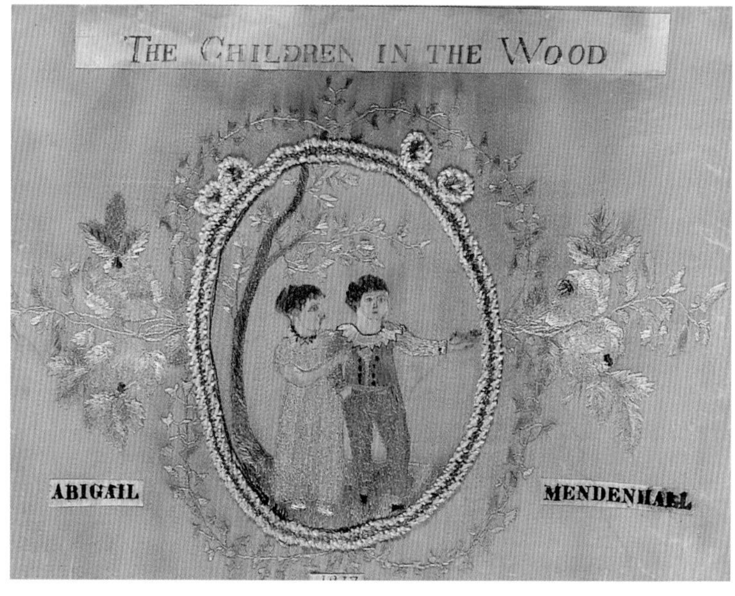

This rather naïve silk-on-silk embroidery picture stitched by fourteen-year-old Abigail Mendenhall is very unusual. Abigail applied her name, the title, and the date by printing them on paper and gluing them onto the silk ground. The design was inspired by a children's storybook called *The Children in the Wood*. The soft colors of the embroidery picture are worked in shades of green, beige, pale pink, yellow, and black, and the center medallion is framed by stitches of silk chenille threads.[13] The faces and arms of the children are drawn on the silk ground in pencil.

Abigail was born January 17, 1803, in Chester County, Pennsylvania. When she was five years old, her parents, Aaron and Lydia Register (Yarnall) Mendenhall, moved to Columbiana County and settled in New Garden. Abigail's parents were Quakers, and her needlework teacher was probably Jane Pierce, a young spinster who had learned to sew when she attended the Friend's Westtown School in Pennsylvania. By 1812, Miss Pierce moved from Pennsylvania to New Garden Monthly Meeting in Ohio. Abigail Mendenhall married Garrett Pim on January 30, 1843, and moved with him to Sandy Spring, near New Garden. The couple had four children. Abigail died in Columbiana County on December 28, 1884.

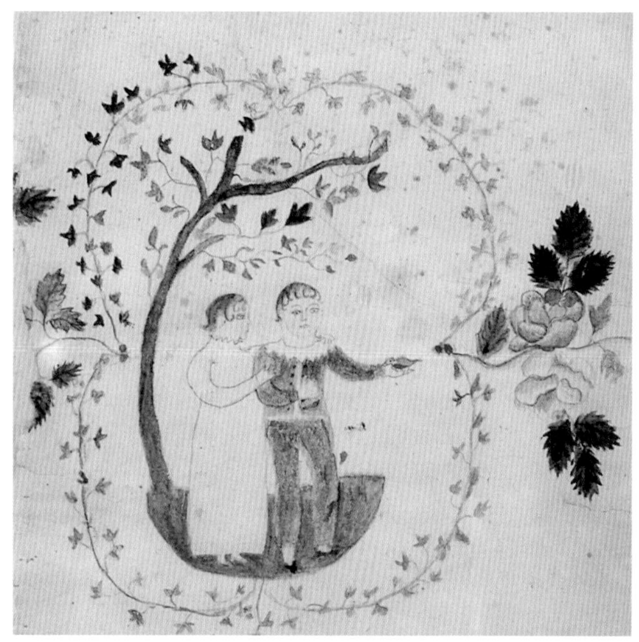

Fig. 190: Pattern for Mendenhall Embroidery.
Size: 9¾" L x 7¾" W. Watercolor on paper.

Not only is Abigail Mendenhall's needlework unusual, but, remarkably, the paper pattern that inspired her work still accompanies her embroidery picture. An old wallpaper-covered copybook, sewn together by hand, still holds the colorful pattern.

Geauga County

Although Geauga County was not formally organized and cut from Trumbull County until 1805, the area was beginning to fill with eager settlers much sooner. The 1798 Survey Map of the Connecticut Western Reserve by Seth Pease reveals that villages like Parkman, where sampler stitcher Betsey Converse (figs. 191 and 192) lived, had begun to spring up before the turn of the nineteenth century.[14]

Throughout the Western Reserve, the practical and systematic encouragement of agriculture was regarded as being of vital importance. The first agricultural fair and exhibition was held in 1823 in the village of Chardon. Accounts of that important autumn event are given in early Ohio history books. Cash awards were given not only to the men for the best horses, cattle, and sheep exhibited, but also to the most "accomplished" ladies who entered competition, including the following: "To Mrs. Sophia Howe, for the best piece of woolen cloth—$6.00; Mrs. Sarah French for the second best piece of woolen cloth—$3.00; Catherine Kerr, for the best piece of bleached linen—$5.00; Miss Caroline Baldwin, for best grass bonnet—$4.00." Learning the "art of housewifery" was indeed an important part of female education. These prizes represented tidy sums at that time.[15] The annual fair, which continued for many years, was an exciting and fun-filled occasion that provided a welcome respite from the duties that occupied early settlers from dawn to dusk.

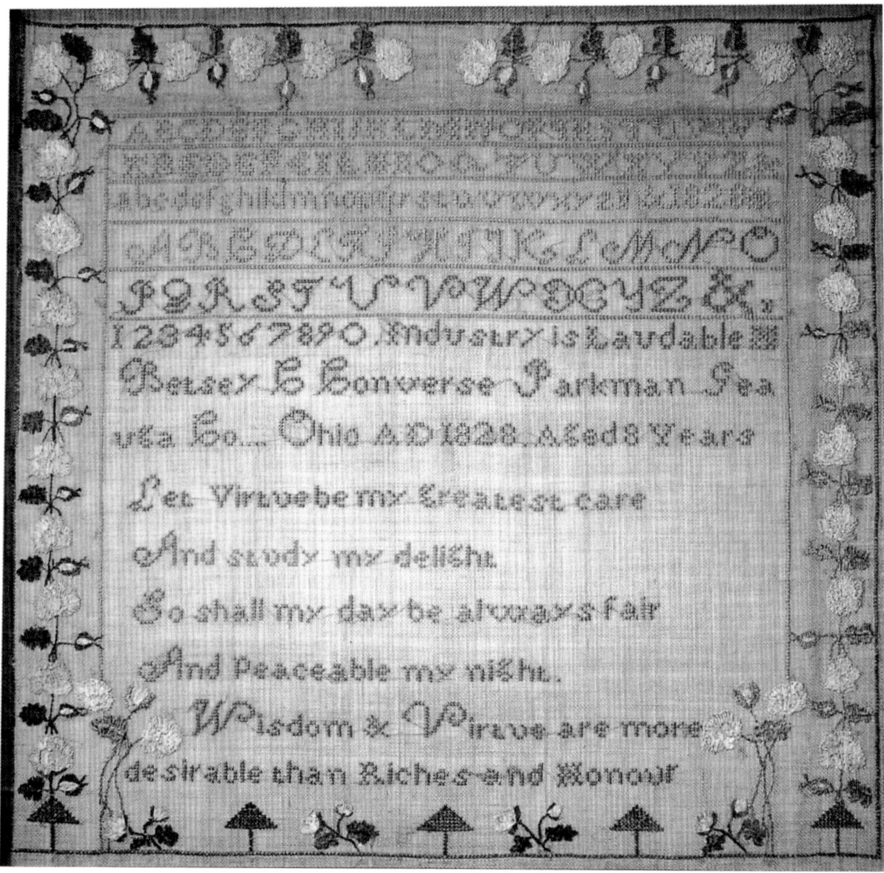

Fig. 192: Photograph of Betsey Converse Lyman. »

On October 26, 1847, Betsey married David Lyman in Parkman. She is shown here c. 1855 in a photograph with her young son, Henry Lyman, taken by Mathew B. Brady, the famous photographer best known for his photographs of the Civil War.[16]

Betsey's obituary reads:

> Parkman—Friend Converse: Our Christmas was not a merry one, but sad, oh, so sad! The saddest of the year; for, at 3 o'clock on that glorious morn, the soul of Mrs. B. C. Lyman passed to the arms of the Savior, whose birth we had prepared to celebrate. What a change from joy and gladness to sorrow and gloom! Although the event had been anticipated by some, the shock was not the less severe.
>
> Her loss is irreparable. A woman of rare intelligence and scholarly attainments, unsurpassed in her devotion to the sick and the afflicted, she occupied a grand sphere, peculiarly her own. No tinsel, no gauze, no aristocracy, except that noble aristocracy of the soul, which beamed with undimmed luster till the last moment of consciousness. . . . Wednesday, the body was laid by the side of her father, the late Judge Converse, in the old church-yard. Dec. 27, 1882.[17]

Betsey died on Christmas Day, her sixty-second birthday.

« Fig. 191: Sampler of Betsey C. Converse. 1828.

Size: 17" L x 16½" W. Collection of Larry and Sarah Mosteller.

Betsey C. Converse stitched her sampler in the southern part of the county, just a few miles east of the Cuyahoga River. The carefully rendered composition was worked when she was eight years old and marked "Parkman, Geauga Co., Ohio." Betsey completed three alphabets and her numbers and stitched a phrase of inspiration to begin the rest of her sampler: "Industry is Laudable." Her verse is a familiar one to sampler collectors:

Let Virtue be my greatest care
And study my delight
So shall my day be always fair
And Peaceable my night.
Wisdom & Virtue are more
desirable than Riches and Honour.

The design of this canvas is fully developed and well balanced. A tightly constricted border of white flowers, buds, and leaves frames three sides, while the bottom of the sampler is decorated with precise trees and sprigs.

Betsey C. Converse was born in December 1820 in the village of Parkman, the first child of John Phelps and Hannah (Parkman) Converse. She was named to honor the memory of John's first wife, Betsey Collins, who died in childbirth in 1817.

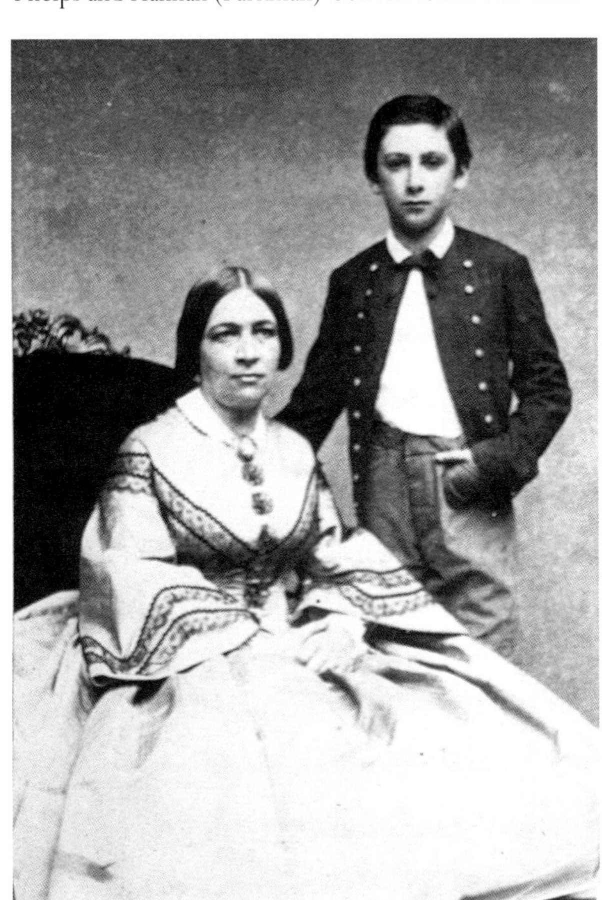

John Converse, the stitcher's father, was an important figure in the development of Geauga County and was involved in government and civic affairs all his life. A successful entrepreneur, he established several mills, including one for the manufacture of linseed oil, a valuable commodity. It provided a ready market for the flax seed grown in the county. He also operated the first mail routes in the area, served a term in the Ohio State Legislature, and became an associate judge in Geauga County.

Ashtabula County

Ashtabula County, defining the northeast corner of Ohio, is bounded on the east by Pennsylvania and on the north by Lake Erie. Settlers from the East began populating this part of the Connecticut Western Reserve before the turn of the nineteenth century. Land was taken from Trumbull and Geauga Counties to form this new county, which was organized in 1811. That is the year that Rev. Dr. Giles Hooker Cowles immigrated to Ohio from his home in Bristol, Connecticut, where he had served as the pastor of the Congregational Church for many years. He brought with him his wife, Sally (White) Cowles and eight children. The children ranged in age from seventeen-year-old Edwin to one-year-old Betsey. One of them was seven-year-old Polly, whose sampler appears here (fig. 193).

Even though settlement had begun more than a decade earlier, the population of the county was so small that itinerate ministers served the area. Rev. Cowles was the first settled minister in Ashtabula County, and by 1815 a new frame church had been erected by his congregation in Austinburg. Rev. Cowles, a Yale graduate, also made plans with other prominent leaders in the Reserve to establish the Western Reserve College in 1825.[18]

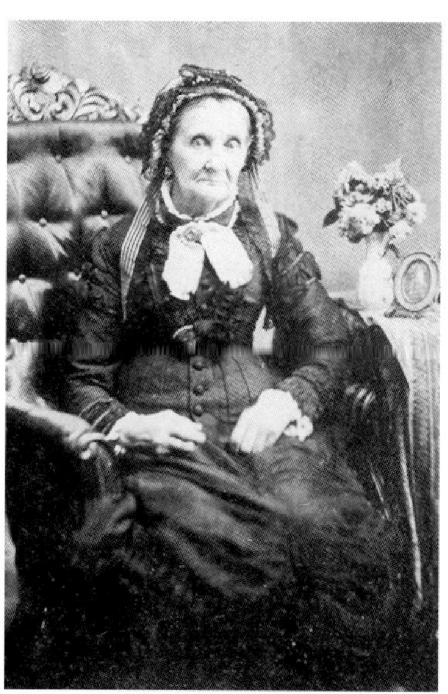

Fig. 194: Photo of Polly Cowles.

Martha (Polly) Hooker Cowles is seen here in later years. After her parents died, she quietly occupied the family homestead for many years, according to family history. Like Betsey and Cornelia, her two younger sisters, Polly never married. She is well remembered in the family for her "marvelously sweet soprano voice." Four of the children were blessed with beautiful voices and eagerly participated in the "singing meetings" that took place in their home.[19]

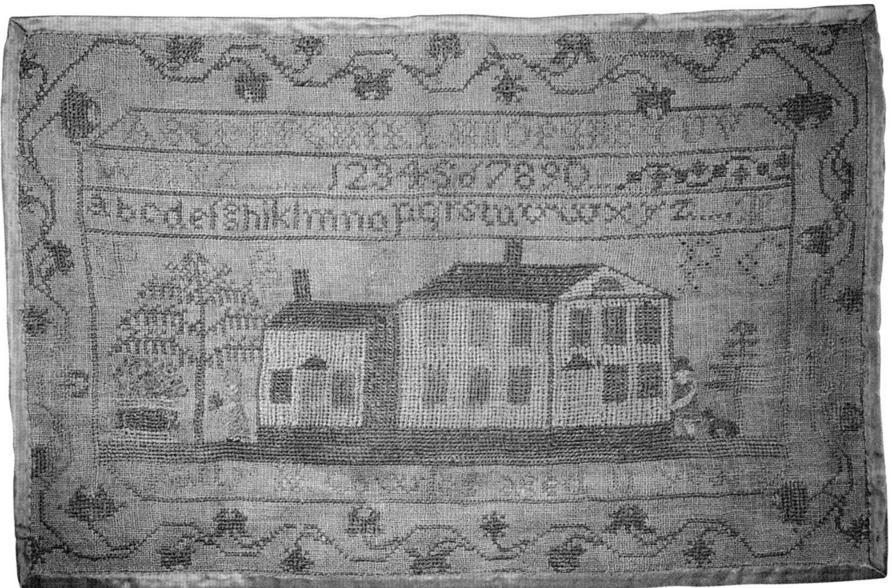

Fig. 193: Sampler of Polly Cowles. 1815.
Size: 9" L x 14" W. Collection of Margaret Cowles Ticknor.

Although time and light have taken a toll on the sampler by Martha (called Polly) Cowles, her canvas still provides us with an accurate picture of the Cowles family home, located at the edge of the little town of Austinburg. This embroidery was executed when Polly was eleven years old, the year the commodious family home was erected. Polly surrounded the canvas with a wide vine border trimmed with a blue silk ribbon. The sampler is now owned by Polly's great-great-niece.

Fig. 195: The Cowles Homestead. Built 1815.

This house, reminiscent of the New England homes that Rev. Cowles admired, stands today in its rural setting, and looks very much like it did when the Cowles family first moved in. This early sketch is not as accurate as Polly's sampler, however, for the rounded window near the peak of the roof on the main house has been omitted by the artist.[20]

The house is still occupied by descendants of the family. When Betsey Cowles died on July 25, 1876, at the age of sixty-six, she left an unusual condition in her will. It was her wish that the parlor in the old Cowles Homestead should remain as she had left it. Her wishes have been respected as generations of family members have occupied the old house. The large parlor was last redecorated in 1837. The strips of woven carpet, the set of Hitchcock chairs placed "at rest" around the perimeter of the room, the desk and papers, books, family portraits, and Polly's sampler are all there undisturbed.

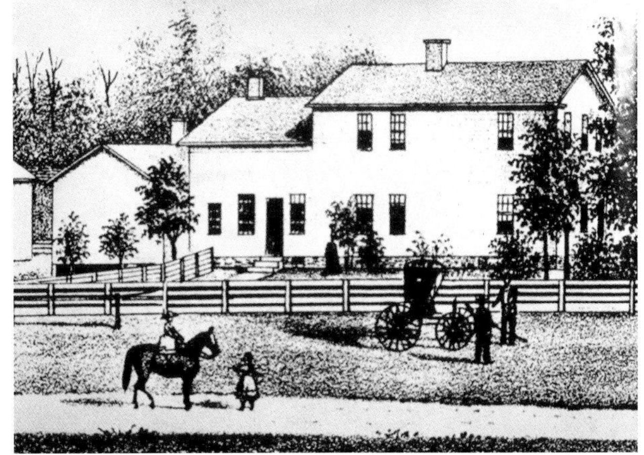

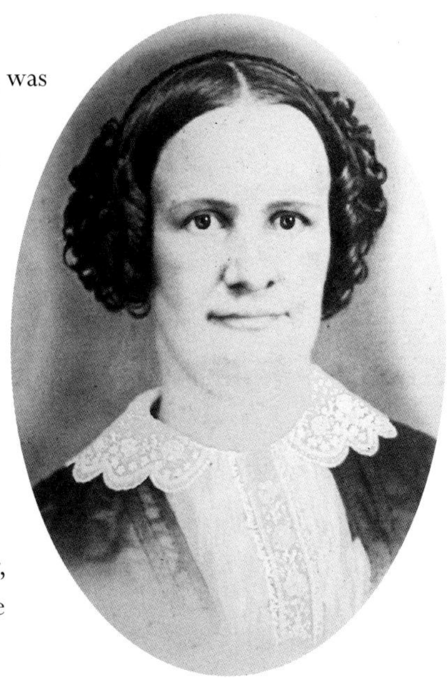

Fig. 196: Portrait of Betsey Cowles.

Betsey Mix Cowles, the sister of Polly Cowles (figs. 193 and 194), was one of the most influential and interesting women in Ohio's early history. Betsey did not leave us any of her needlework, but she left a wonderful legacy of forty years of teaching in early Ohio schools. After graduating from Oberlin College, she began teaching at a select school for girls at Portsmouth, in Scioto County. She remained there three years, then returned to Austinburg and succeeded Katharine Snow as the preceptress of Grand River Institute. About this time, she became acquainted with the leaders of the Abolitionist movement. She was so sympathetic to their cause that she traveled about giving anti-slavery lectures. In 1865, when Abraham Lincoln issued his emancipation proclamation, she read it and said, "The two great tasks of my life are ended together, my teaching is done, and the slaves are free."[21] In failing health, she returned to the old home in Austinburg.

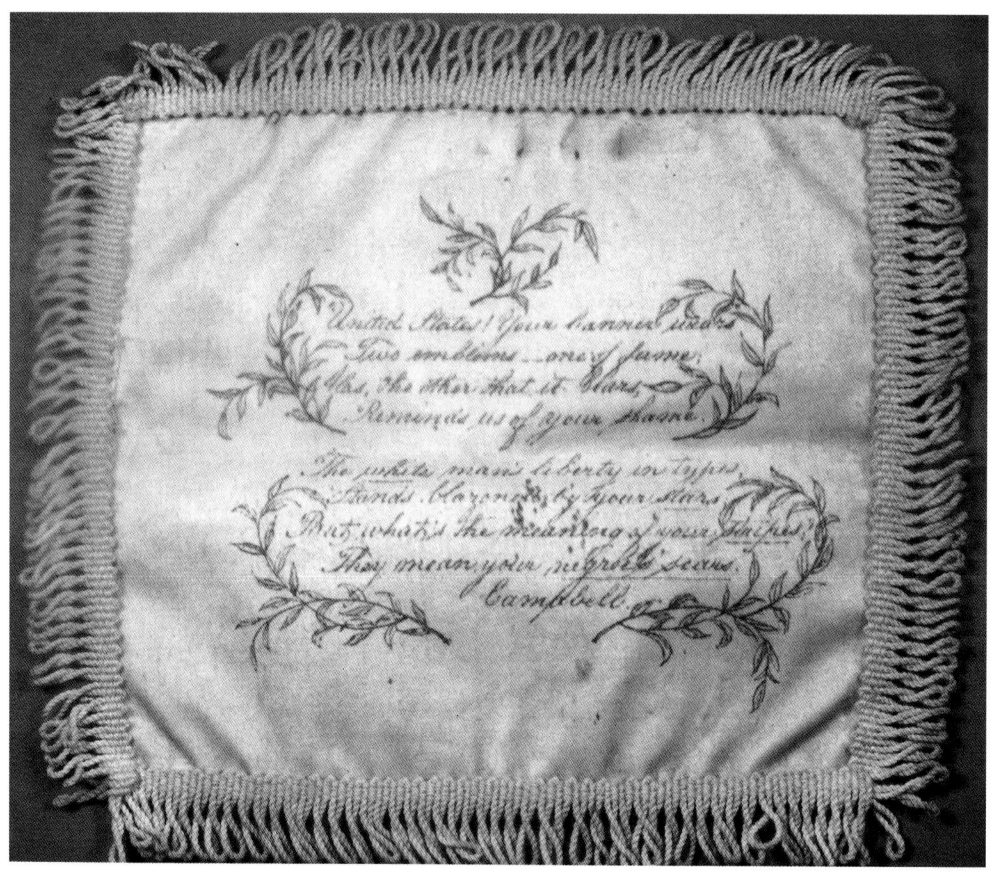

Fig. 198: Sampler of Hannah Wetmore. 1831.
Size: 10½" L x 10½" W.
Collection of The Western Reserve Historical Society, Cleveland, Ohio.

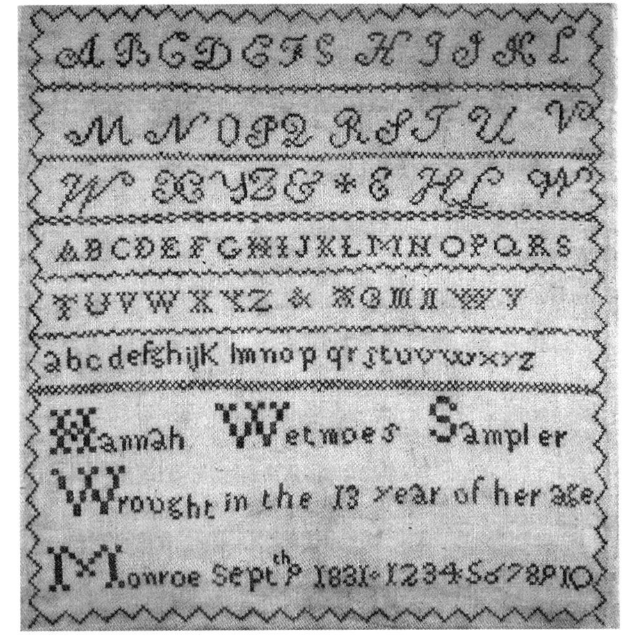

It is unusual to find the samplers of three sisters, but to find them still together today is remarkable. The samplers of Abigail and Margaret (not shown here) share many characteristics with this one done by Hannah Wetmore in 1831. All are plain in design and stitched with blue thread. These girls were the daughters of Benjamin and Thankful (Lucas) Wetmore, who came to Ohio from Middletown, Connecticut. Benjamin and Thankful arrived in the fall of 1820 with their family and a team of oxen and settled on a farm in Monroe Township, near Kelloggsville.[22] They were the parents of eight daughters and five sons.

Hannah's stitches of blue thread are precisely laid, and she framed her work with a simple zigzag border. Curiously, she misspelled her last name. The bottom of the small canvas is filled with these words: "Hannah Wetmoes Sampler—Wrought in the 13 year of her age—Monroe Sept 9th 1831."

« Fig. 197: Satin Pillow.
Size: Approx. 7" L x 7" W. Collection of Margaret Cowles Ticknor.

Her students presented Betsey Cowles (fig. 196) with this small satin pillow. A handwritten note that still accompanies the gift reads: "Dear Miss Betsey, do you know how well the children love you? . . . Do you see the invisible crown held by angel hands above you?"

The poem testifies about a very troubled time in America's history. It reads:

United States! Your banner wears
Two emblems, . . . one of fame;
Alas, the other that it bears
Reminds us of your shame.
The white man's liberty in types
Stands blazoned by your stars
But what's the meaning of your stripes?
They mean your negro's scars.

Campbell.

Wayne County

When Wayne County was formed in 1796, it covered a very large section of what was to become the new State of Ohio. By 1812, however, the county had been reduced in size to the boundaries that we know today. The excellent farmlands in this area, along with those of neighboring Holmes County, were particularly enticing to the Pennsylvania German families. Social historians tells us that these plain people seemed to be able to recognize intuitively where the most fertile ground was. Wooster, the county seat, was laid out in 1808. Four samplers have been discovered that were produced there.

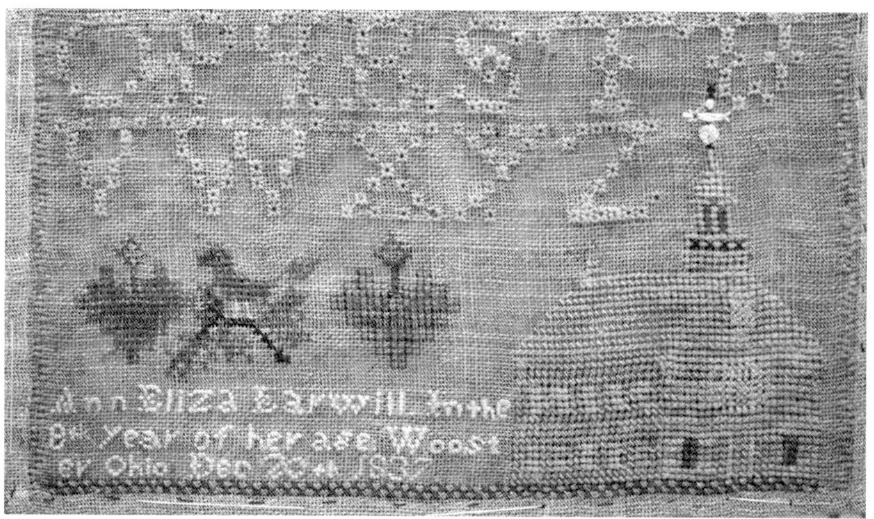

FIG. 199: SAMPLER OF ANN ELIZA LARWILL. 1837.
SIZE: 11¾" L x 12" W. COLLECTION OF PAUL AND ANNE LOCHER.

Ann Eliza Larwill's sampler reveals that she was eight years old and living in "Wooster Ohio" when she worked her canvas. After completing three alphabets, she stitched a large public building, probably a church, at the bottom of the canvas.

Ann Eliza was born in 1825, the first child of John and Ann (Straughan) Larwill. John and his two brothers, William and Joseph, came to Wayne County in 1807 from Pennsylvania and helped to lay out the town of Wooster the following year.[23]

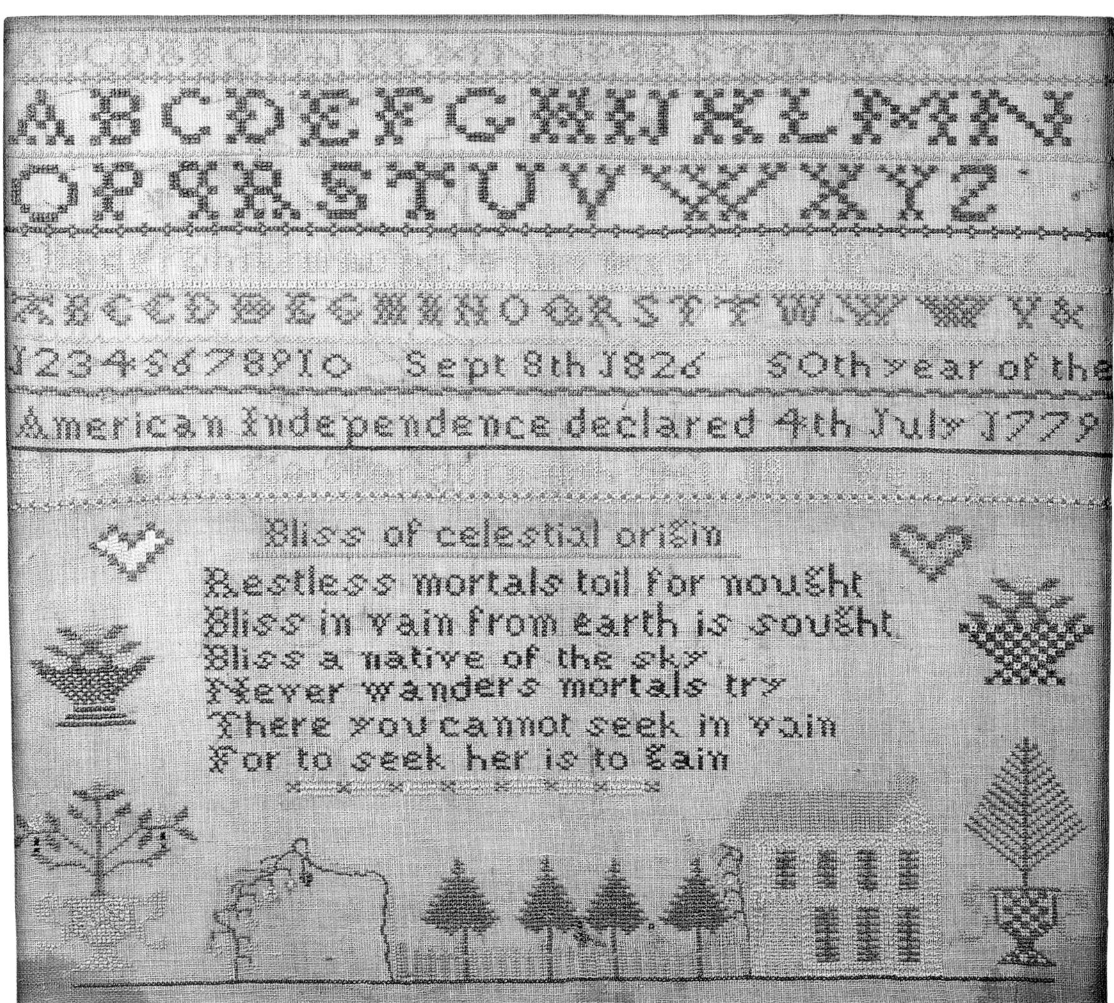

Fig. 200: Sampler of Elizabeth Keister. 1826.

Size: 17½" L x 19½" W. Collection of Dr. Jeffrey and Sharon Lipton.

The words that Elizabeth Keister stitched on her sampler are a reminder of a very important date in our country's history—the "birthday" of America. She begins: "Elizabeth Keister–born 4th October 18 . . . Penn. Wooster." The second line, however, tells of the pride she and her teacher felt in our young nation: "Sept. 8th 1826 50th year of the American Independence declared 4th July 1779." She apparently turned the canvas upside down as she worked, making *1776* into *1779*. Elizabeth's innocent mistake just adds to the charm, as well as the value, of her unusual sampler.

The two heart designs are distinctive in form, as are the four straight evergreen trees that stand in front of the picket fence in the naive scene at the bottom of the canvas. The same motifs are found on the 1827 sampler completed by Julia Ann Forbs (fig. 201).

It is probable that Elizabeth was the daughter of John Keister of Wooster, whose name appears in the 1830 Ohio census. She purposely left out the year of her birth. Ohio marriage records tell us that she married Joseph Hunter in East Union Township of Wayne County on September 2, 1834.

Fig. 201: Sampler of Julia Ann Forbs. 1827. »

Size: 17½" L x 17½" W. Collection of Dayton Art Institute.
Gift of the estate of Elmer R. Webster and Robert A. Titsch.

This charming sampler was worked by Julia Ann Forbs in 1827, a year after Elizabeth Keister completed her sampler (fig. 200). Both stitchers marked their needlework with the town of "Wooster," and although the overall compositions of the canvases are very different, other clues tell us that the girls had the same instructress. Julia added "Oh . . . io," but she had a difficult time getting those four important letters in the right places.

The large urns with distinctive handles, the trees and the picket fence, and the shuttered windows on the building Julia stitched are all identical to Elizabeth Keister's needlework. The focal point of Julia's sampler is the very tall girl picking a rose from the top of the building. The figure's face, painted directly on the canvas, suggests that Julia's teacher was not a talented artist. Painting the face of a figure on a *silk* canvas was often done, and painted *paper* faces were sometimes glued to the canvas. Painting a face on a *linen* ground, however, rarely worked out well. Julia did very precise work. Her stitches include satin, eyelet, fern, outline, and cross-stitch. Naïve designs fill every space on the canvas, and a pretty border frames all four sides. Her simple verse reads:

The rose is red
The leaves are green
The days are past
That I have seen.

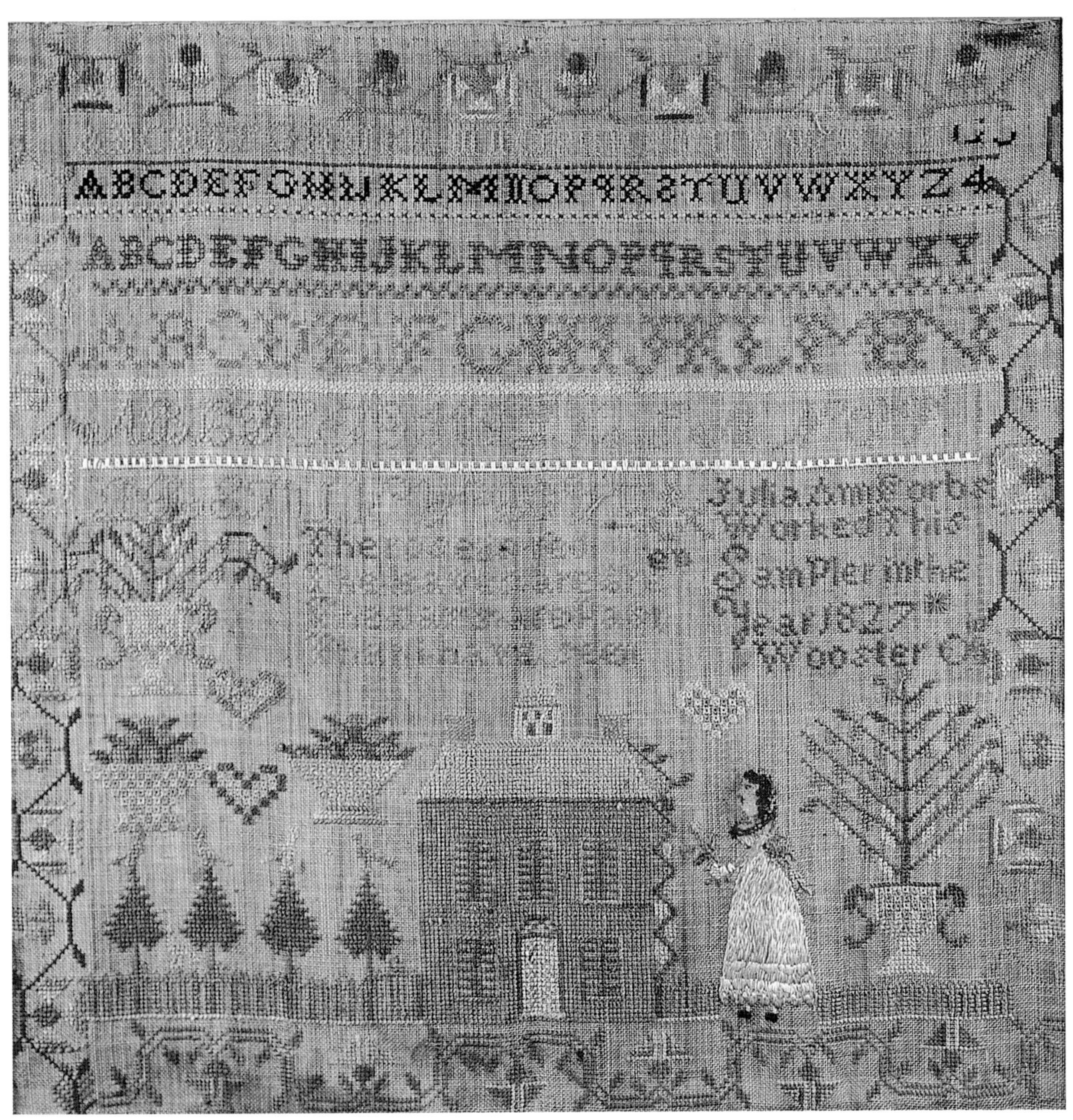
ABCDEFGHIJKLMNOPQRSTUVWXYZ
Julia Ann Forbes
Worked This
SamPler in the
Year 1827
Wooster O

Mahoning County

Mahoning County, formed in 1846, was one of the last counties to be organized in Ohio, even though the land had been surveyed and pioneer villages established as early as 1797. It was created from parts of Trumbull and Columbiana Counties. Youngstown, established by John Young in 1797, has always been the principal city. All of the samplers from this county were stitched many years before 1846, and they represent some of the earliest Ohio needlework to be documented.

The small marking sampler of Mary Beach Kirtland (fig. 202) is of special interest because her father was a key figure in the early history of the state.

Fig. 202: Sampler of Mary Beach Kirtland. 1806. »

Size: 11" L x 6" W. Collection of Mahoning Valley Historical Society, The Arms Museum.

Mary Beach Kirtland completed her marking sampler when she was eight years old. The third of seven children, she was born in 1798 in Wallingford, Connecticut, to Turhand Kirtland and his second wife, Mary (Polly) (Potter) Kirtland.

Turhand Kirtland was an agent and surveyor for the Connecticut Land Company and made his first trip to Ohio in 1797. He came to the Mahoning Valley the following year and assisted John Young in developing his purchase, known as Youngstown Township (now the city of Youngstown). As a surveyor, Kirtland had the opportunity to settle in a pleasant spot. He established his home in the neighboring area of Poland Township. The Kirtland family was one of Ohio's earliest, as indicated by their "address" on the old survey maps as Township 1, Range 1, of the Connecticut Western Reserve.[24]

In 1803, Turhand Kirtland returned to Connecticut to move his family, including five-year-old Mary, across the Allegheny Mountains to live with him in Poland. That same year he was appointed to serve as a judge of Trumbull County by territorial governor Arthur St. Clair, and he served as Ohio state senator from the county in 1815–16.

It has not been determined who taught Mary to embroider, but the decorative zigzag lines carefully stitched across the bottom of her canvas gives evidence that she and her first cousin Lucretia Kirtland (fig. 203) shared the same instructress.

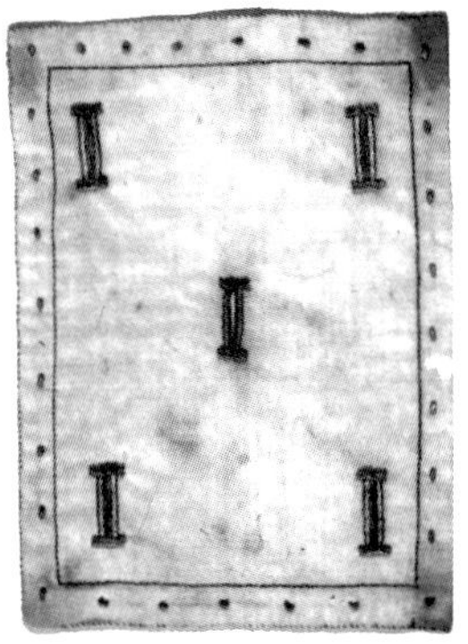

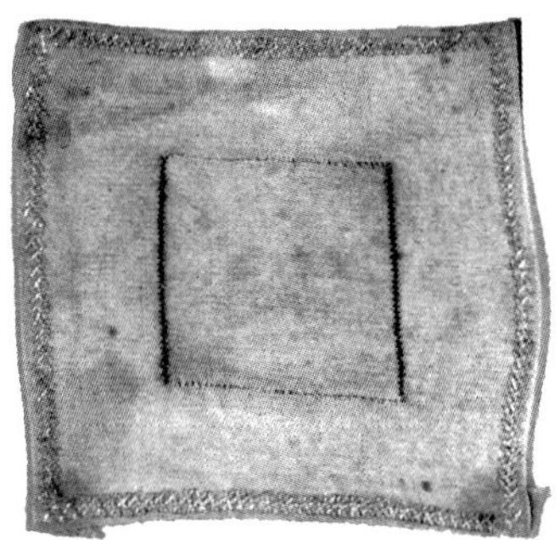

The Public Library of Cincinnati and Hamilton County.

Mary's teacher, who probably also taught Lucretia Kirtland (fig. 203), instructed her students in how to execute a variety of decorative stitches. Her tutoring would have included practice in seaming, buttonhole, and quilting techniques.

Fig. 203: Sampler of Lucretia Kirtland. 1808. »

Size: 14¼" L x 11½" W. Anonymous collector.

Lucretia Kirtland's sampler is extraordinary, and its design unique in the Ohio sampler search. Lucretia was the daughter of Jared and Lois Kirtland. Jared and Turhand Kirtland were brothers, and both settled their families in Poland, Ohio. Examples of darning inserts on samplers are often seen, but usually they stand alone and are not related to the ornamental motifs on the canvas. Lucretia and her teacher were very creative. At the top of the sampler Lucretia completed two alphabets before she stitched her name, the date, and her age. A zigzag flame-stitch band sets apart the large initials of her parents. This band is the same design found on her cousin Mary Beach Kirtland's marking sampler (fig. 202). Lucretia placed her family history and other details around the outside edges of her canvas:

Lucretia Kirtland—November 2nd 1807 Aged 10
Wallingford [Connecticut] is my native place
And English is my nation,
Poland is my dwelling place
And Christ is my salvation.
Jar. Kirtland is my Fat.'s name
& Lois K. is my mother
*Lucretia Kirtland is my name * 1808.*

The house, with the unusual flame-stitch, or Irish-stitch, arch above it, the picket fence and gate, the paired birds, and the sprigs of delicate flowers demonstrate that Lucretia was accomplished with the needle.

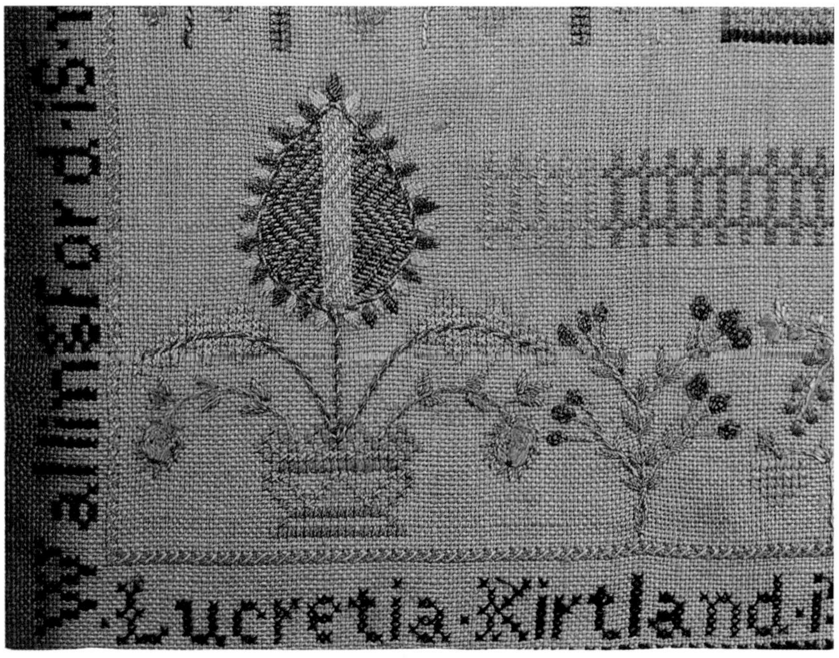

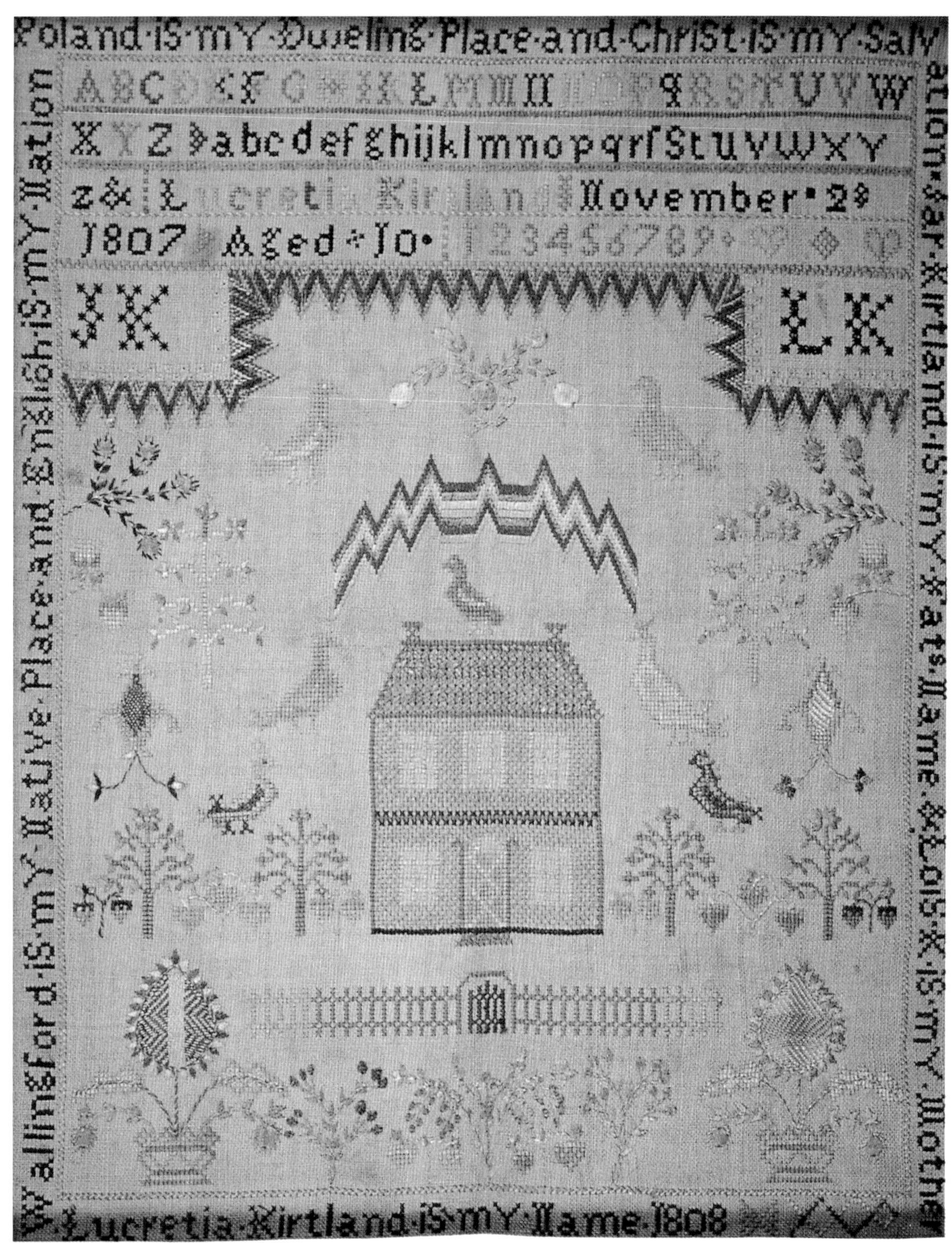

« Fig. 204: Detail of Lucretia Kirtland Sampler.

Each of the large urns at the bottom of Lucretia Kirtland's canvas contains an unusual flower worked in darning stitches. When darning inserts are included on samplers, and we do see them often, they are not usually incorporated in the other ornamental motifs.

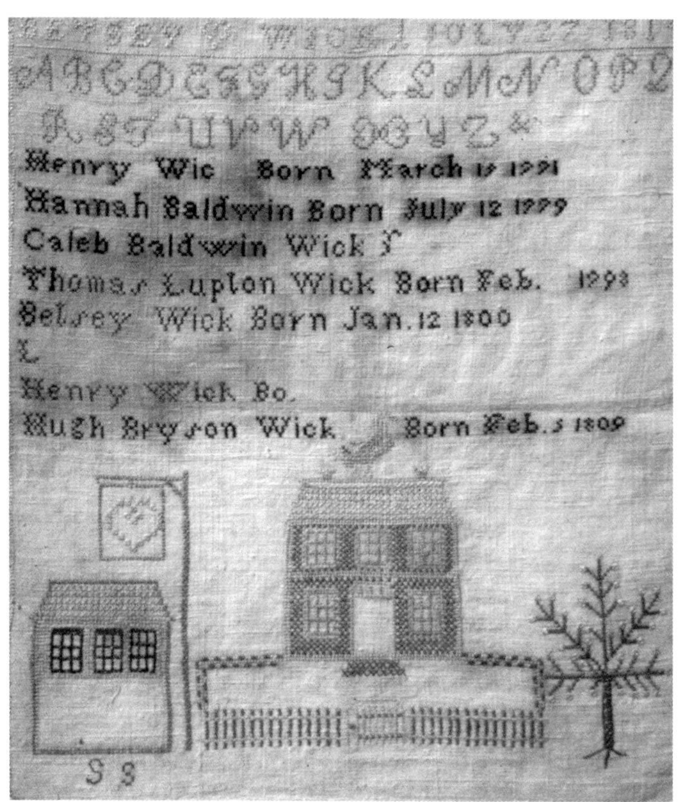

FIG. 205: SAMPLER OF BETSEY WICK. 1814.
SIZE: 14" L x 12" W. COLLECTION OF THE MAHONING VALLEY HISTORICAL SOCIETY, THE ARMS MUSEUM.

Fourteen-year-old Betsey Wick stitched at the top of her canvas the date that she began work on this genealogical sampler on July 17, 1814. After completing an alphabet, she proceeded to list all of the family names, beginning with her oldest brother, Henry Wick, and continuing with other siblings as the family grew in number.

Betsey's father, Henry Wick, was born on Long Island, New York, and moved with his family to Washington County, Pennsylvania, after the Revolutionary War. There he met and married Hannah Baldwin. The young couple, along with their four small children, made their way to Ohio in 1804, where Hannah's family had been living since about 1798.[25]

Henry and Hannah Wick established their home in Youngstown, near the Baldwins, and eventually had eight more children. Betsey did not leave room on her needlework to allow for additions to the family, instead filling the canvas with a quaint scene. The structure on the left was never completed, but she did not wait to hang the "heart" sign above it.

We have yet to discover who taught Betsey how to sew, but early family accounts tell us that Hannah Baldwin, Betsey's mother, also did fine embroidery work that was passed down to her granddaughters. Betsey may have been a student of Pheebe Wick, her cousin, who was one of the first teachers in Youngstown. Betsey Wick married Robert Leslie and died in her nineteenth year, five years after she began this genealogical record. In addition to her sampler, some of her sketches in India ink are preserved, along with her mother's embroidery.[26]

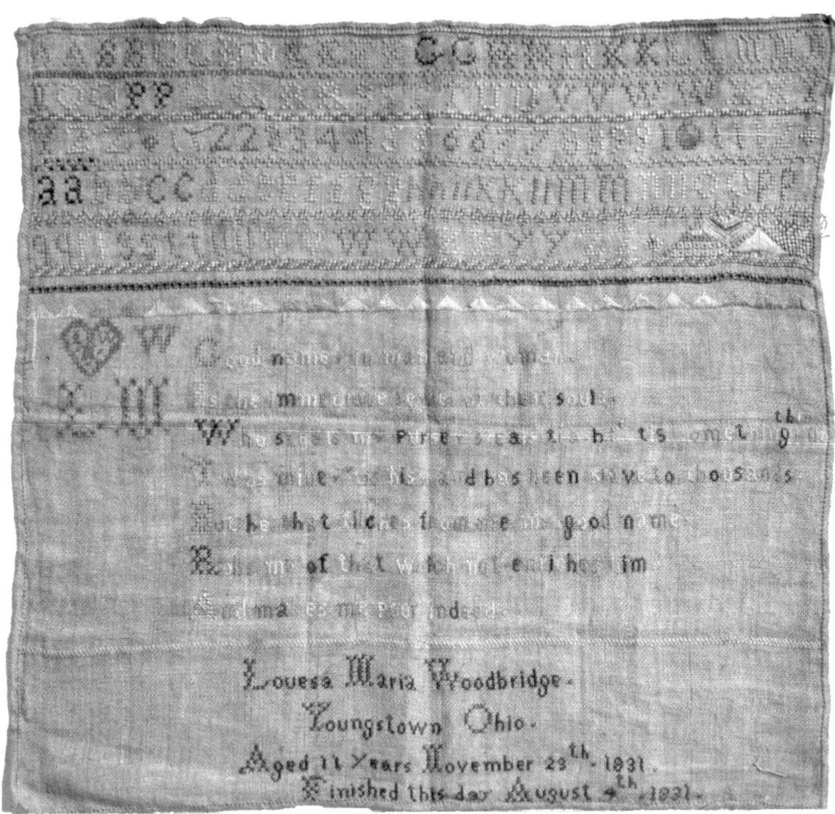

Fig. 206: Sampler of Louesa Maria Woodbridge. 1831.
Size: 16" L x 21" W. Collection of the Mahoning Valley Historical Society, The Arms Museum.

Louesa Maria Woodbridge chose to stitch each letter of the words in her verse in threads of alternating colors. Although this shows originality, it makes for difficult reading. In the lower part of the canvas she stitched, "Louesa Maria Woodbridge—Youngstown Ohio. Aged 11 years November 28th—1831. Finished this day August 4th—1831."

Louesa's parents, John Elliot and Mary (Horner) Woodbridge, came to the Mahoning Valley from Philadelphia in 1807. The men of prominent families like the Woodbridges contributed much to the written history of an area. Relatively little information is known about the women, however, beyond the samplers they stitched. Early accounts record only that Louesa married Robert W. Taylor c. 1840, and the couple made their home in Youngstown. They were married for twelve years and had seven children before Louesa's death in 1853.[27]

Stark County

Only two samplers have been discovered from Stark County. Organized in 1809, the county is situated in the eastern part of Ohio. Its abundance of good farmlands beckoned many Pennsylvania Germans to this area, but German-born John William Hamm did not come to farm. The inspiration and determination that brought Rev. Hamm to Ohio was a call to the ministry. His daughter Glorvinea stitched the sampler seen in fig. 207.

Fig. 207: Sampler of Glorvinea Elisabeth Hamm. 1839.
Size: 16 ½" L x 9" W. Wool on linen. Collection of Susan Paolano McKiernan.

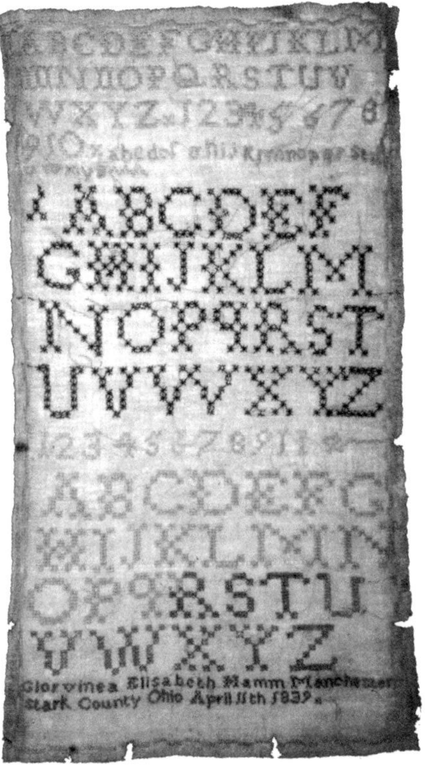

Glorvinea Elisabeth Hamm's marking sampler is plainly identified with her name and the words "Manchester—Stark County—Ohio—April 11th 1839." The stitcher used every part of her canvas to complete four alphabets and rows of numbers. Glorvinea's family was well known in the county, for her father, Rev. John Hamm, established churches in East Liberty, Green, and Uniontown, small towns close to Manchester. A few months after the sampler was completed, county boundaries were changed, with Manchester in the section that became part of Summit County in 1840.

Rev. Hamm was born in Germany in 1801. He immigrated to America and was first noted in the Ohio census in 1830. Associated with the Christian Reformed (Presbyterian) Church, he began his Manchester ministry in a log cabin. Rev. Hamm was known to preach in German as well as in broken English. His first wife, Glorvinea's mother Esther LeFever, died in1840. Stark County's largest school for young women, the Canton Female Institute, was founded in 1838, just when Glorvinea was learning to stitch. It soon became a flourishing institution, attracting students from the small surrounding villages. It is unlikely that Glorvinea's father enrolled his daughter there, however, since the Germans showed more attachment to schools where instruction was given in their native language. Ohio marriage records state that Glorvinea Hamm married Houston Sisler c. 1850.

Portage County

Time and again the early settlers of the West followed Indian trails as they made their way through the wilderness to establish a new home in Ohio. Portage County was formed from Trumbull in 1808 and was named for a particularly important trail. The old Portage Path trail lay between the Cuyahoga and Tuscarawas Rivers. By carrying their canoes for the eight-mile trek, the Indians could travel from the Great Lakes all the way to the Gulf of Mexico.

Emily Sheldon marked her sampler (fig. 208) with the town of Mantua, a settlement on the Cuyahoga, at the end of the Portage Path.

(following page)

Fig. 208: Sampler of Emily Sheldon. 1829.

Size: 12½" L x 12½" W. Collection of Robert and Charlotte Menker.

Emily Sheldon's small sampler is neatly marked. It reads:

Emily Sheldon—1829
Aged 8 years
Mantua Portage County Ohio
Flavia Spencer, Instructress

Emily Sheldon was born on April 5, 1821, in Twinsburg, Summit County, Ohio. She completed this colorful sampler when she was eight years old. Emily was the daughter of Simeon and Eunice (Harmon) Sheldon, who came to Ohio from Hartford, Connecticut, just before baby Emily was born. By the time the Ohio 1830 Census was taken, the young couple was living in Mantua, in Portage County. Emily married Carlton Hanchett after her twenty-third birthday, in April 1844.

The "instructress" listed on Emily's needlework was Flavia Spencer. The conspicuous display of her name would have attracted students as surely as would a notice in the local newspaper. It served as a clear advertisement to those who viewed Emily's canvas that Miss Sheldon was a very competent teacher. Needlework supplies for teachers and their students, however, were not always readily available. A history written about Portage County reiterates an account dated September, 1817:

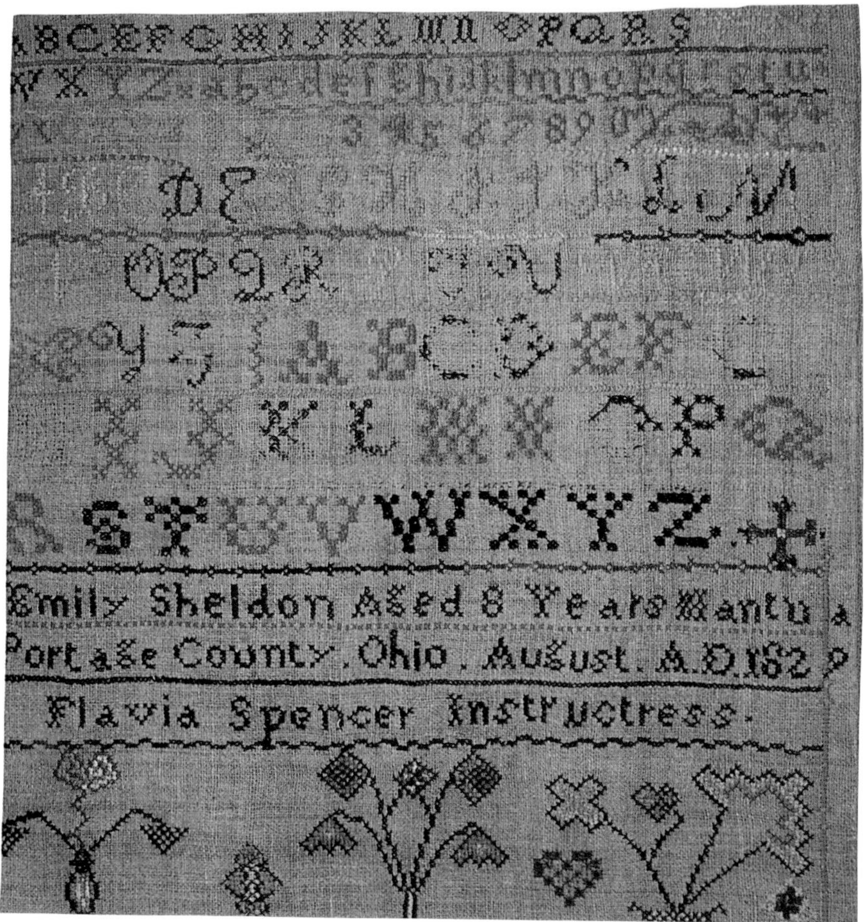

FIG. 208

At first the nearest place where pins, needles, thread, and a few other necessary articles could be purchased was at Pittsburg, about 100 miles distant, and later at Warren. And Windom was certainly a very prosperous township when a merchant, Isaac Clark, came. His wife acted as his buyer, making the trip to Pittsburg on horseback. His [store's] entry book listed:

> September, 1817.
> ½ lb tea @ $1.50 . . . $ .75
> ½ yd. Cambric @ 80c . . . 40
> ½ paper pins @ 25c . . . 12
> 5 ½ yds. calico @60c . . . 3.30
> 1 skein silk . . . 09
> 2 ½ yds. fulled cloth @1.75 . . . 4.37.[28]

Most needlework teachers were single. Once they married, they usually gave up teaching to become dutiful wives and mothers. Flavia Spencer's Ohio marriage records reveal that less than a year after Emily Sheldon finished her sampler, Miss Spencer married Rayner King in Portage County. No further mention of her school or teaching has been found.

Fig. 209: Sampler of Pamela Elvira Mills. c. 1829.
Size: 9" L x 9" W. Collection of the International Society of Daughters of Utah Pioneers.

Nine-year-old Pamela Elvira Mills confined the embroidery on her sampler to cross-stitch and finished the raw edges of her canvas with neat hem stitching. Her sampler is not large or colorful, but the story of her life is interesting. The familiar verse seems to fit her life perfectly:

Let virtue be my greatest care
And study my delight
So shall my day be always fair
And peaceable my night

Elvira, as she was called, was born in Nelson, Portage County, on March 1, 1820, to Robert and Rhoda (Hulet) Mills. Her father died in 1827, when she was seven years old. After his death, her mother's brother, Sylvester Hulet, helped his sister care for the farm and was like a father to young Elvira. He also assumed responsibility for another widowed sister and her child.

Sylvester heard about Joseph Smith and the Mormons, and after investigating he and his two sisters accepted the new religion. By 1833 they moved to Missouri with other followers of the church, but their happiness in this area was short-lived. They were driven from their new home and like many others, suffered for want of food, clothing, and shelter.

Elvira became the wife of Orville Sutherland Cox on October 3, 1838, and went with her new husband to Lima, Illinois. Joining with the "body of the Saints," the family eventually came to Utah, settling first in the town of Bountiful. Later they helped to colonize other communities in the southern part of that state. During this time Elvira's husband accepted the doctrine of plural marriage and took two other wives. While her husband helped survey roads and construct bridges, Elvira attended the affairs of their home and raised a family of eleven children. She died on February 18, 1903, two weeks before her eighty-third birthday, and was laid to rest beside her late husband.[29]

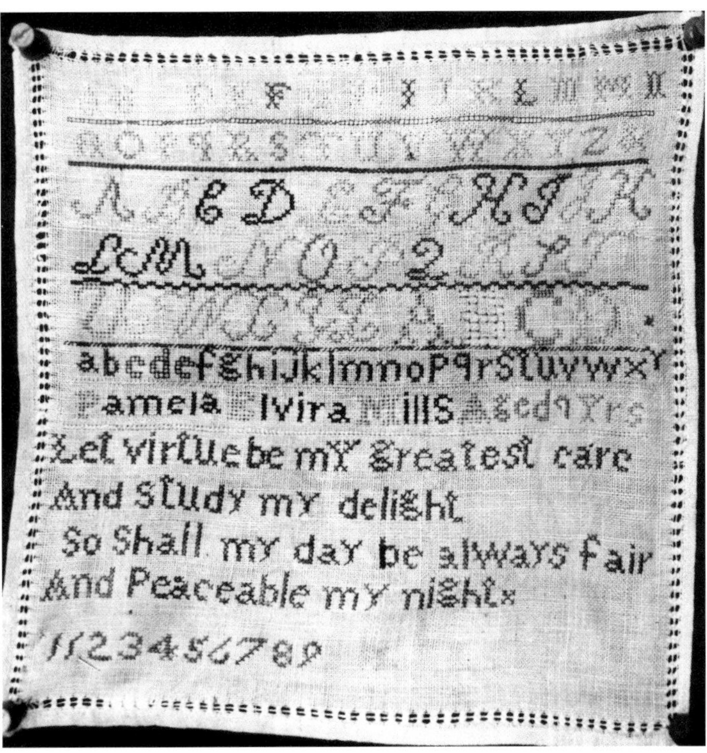

Summit County

When Cynthia Sackett stitched her small sampler in Tallmadge Township, this area was still part of Portage County (see fig. 210). The Sackett family came to the Western Reserve early in the nineteenth century, and Summit County was not formed until 1840. This section of the Reserve was situated at the highest point on the Ohio and Erie Canal route between Lake Erie and the Ohio River. The settlement of Tallmadge, located immediately east of Akron, was the county seat. The area enjoyed rapid growth in the 1830s because of the new "water highway."

At the time Cynthia Sackett was ready to begin formal schooling, several private or subscription schools were well organized and flourishing in Summit County. Although the Ohio Legislature had taken steps to levy taxes to support and provide for the building of public schools by 1825, many school districts did not provide enough funding to pay the full salaries of teachers. The balance was raised by an assessment on those attending the school.

Private schools advertised regularly for students. In Akron, for example, on July 27, 1836, Mrs. Susan E. Dodge announced in a local newspaper that "on the first day of August she will open a school at the corner of Main and Exchange Streets, for young ladies and misses, in which reading, writing and spelling will be taught for $2.50 a term of eleven weeks; grammar, geography and arithmetic, $3.50." A year and a half later, "Miss M. E. Hubble, of New York" announced that "on January 3, 1838, a select school will be opened at the corner of Middlebury and High Streets . . . where pupils will receive instruction in all branches usually taught in our eastern female seminaries. Tuition per quarter, $3.00 to $5.00, according to studies pursued. Music, including use of piano, $8.00."[30] Although Miss Hubble does not mention needlework instruction, it was very probably included in the "branches" offered.

Fig. 210: Sampler of Cynthia M. Sackett. c. 1832.

Size: 6½" L x 7" W. Collection of Susan S. Blashford.

Cynthia M. Sackett was seven years old when she completed this well-organized marking sampler. It was an ambitious task for a child so young to finish three alphabets.

Cynthia's parents were Clark and Laura (Aiken) Sackett. Clark Sackett was from Warren, Connecticut. When still a young man, he joined a colony of pioneer settlers who came to Summit County, driving their oxen teams and cutting a path through dense forests. The settlers purchased lands from the Connecticut Land Company, which controlled a large part of the Western Reserve. They soon established homes, and Mr. Sackett acquired one hundred acres in Talmadge Township. Upon the death of his first wife, Clark married Laura Aiken in the fall of 1822. The couple had eight children, of whom Cynthia was the first daughter. Cynthia married M. Luther Heath on November 7, 1849, in Summit County.

Cuyahoga County

Even before 1796, George Washington and Thomas Jefferson regarded the mouth of the Cuyahoga River on Lake Erie as a strategic harbor. It was not until after 1790 that the British relinquished it. When the first surveying party into the Connecticut Western Reserve arrived in May 1796, it was under the direction of Moses Cleaveland, a graduate of Yale and a bright lawyer. He was selected to serve as the principal agent for the Connecticut Land Company. As such he was given instructions to lay out a town at the mouth of the Cuyahoga and to subdivide the Western Reserve into townships. Among those accompanying Cleaveland were surveyors, civil engineers, mathematicians, and an astronomer.[31]

The settlement of Cleveland grew rapidly because it served as the major center for transportation of goods to the West. With the completion in 1825 of the New York–Erie Canal, new settlers and their belongings could more easily travel to the Reserve. No longer did eager pioneers have to endure the difficult trip to Ohio via rough roads and trails through the mountains of Pennsylvania.

Rufus and Jane Dunham were among those first settlers to establish a new life in the Western Reserve. They left their home in Mansfield, Massachusetts, in 1819, and records reveal that the young couple purchased nearly fourteen acres of land and began to farm. The Ohio samplers of their two daughters, Loretta and Caroline, survive today.

Fig. 212: Dunham Tavern »

After purchasing land in what was to become downtown Cleveland, Rufus Dunham, father of stitcher Caroline Sarah Dunham (fig. 211), built a log structure on his property that served as a home for the family. The north portion of the present structure was built in 1824. Later the main block of the house was added in front of this wing, and by 1832, the west wing completed the structure. After a time, Rufus decided to become a tavern keeper as well as a farmer, and he opened his home to travelers. The tavern soon became an important center of social and political life. It served as a stagecoach stop on the old Buffalo-Cleveland-Detroit Road. His busy establishment included a large tavern and waiting room on the first floor and sleeping rooms upstairs.

It is surprising that even though the Tavern is located in the busy urban setting of modern Cleveland, it remains on its original foundations. The Dunham Tavern Museum stands today, beautifully restored as a Cleveland landmark. It is registered as a National Historic Site.

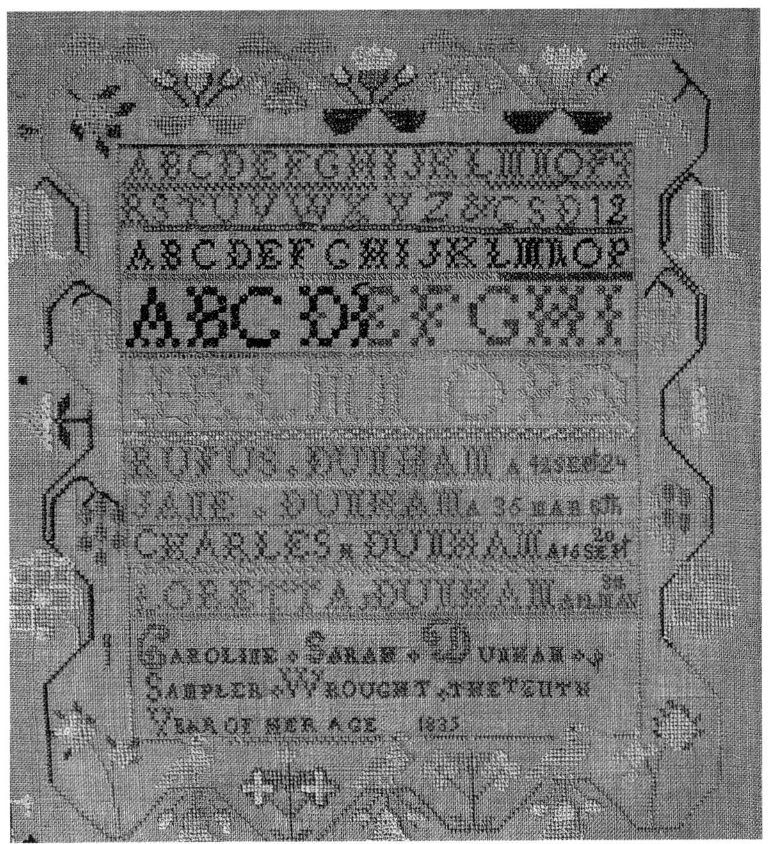

Fig. 211: Sampler of Caroline Sarah Dunham. 1835.
Size: 17 ½" L x 17 ½" W. Collection of the Dunham Tavern Museum, Inc.

Caroline Sarah Dunham completed this family record sampler in 1835. The youngest child of Rufus and Jane (Pratt) Dunham, Caroline tells us that her needlework was "Wrought in the Tenth Year of her age." Neatly stitched are the names of her sister, Loretta, age twelve, and her sixteen-year-old brother, Charles. The border framing the sampler is restrained, yet wide and decorative. Most of the embroidery is confined to cross-stitch, but several areas of eyelet practice stitches are randomly scattered on the canvas.

Caroline married James Welsh in 1853 and is buried in Cleveland's Lakeview Cemetery. Her needlework still hangs in the home in which it was carefully stitched, now the Dunham Tavern Museum.

The history of education in Cuyahoga County is a complex study that clearly reveals how important the establishment of schools was to the early settlers. Records document dozens of teachers who opened select or subscription schools in the county and taught successfully for many years. No information about who provided needlework instruction to Loretta and Caroline Dunham has been found, and the two samplers give no clues to her identity.

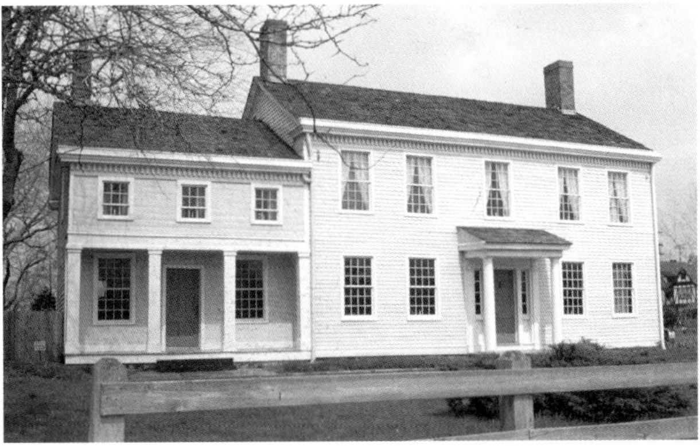

Medina County

When the pioneers arrived in the Western Reserve, they were confronted by dense forests of huge trees that had to be cleared before any settlement could begin to take hold. The first work, after locating the land that they purchased, was to chop away a few trees to build a cabin. Once this was completed, the Herculean task of clearing the forest commenced, so that crops could be planted. This scenario occurred in nearly every rural area of the Ohio Country. The backcountry of Medina County was no exception. The staggering task of clearing a single acre of forest of hard wood trees could take one man three to four weeks.

Medina County, formed in 1818, was blessed with rich farmlands, but marketing their agricultural products was difficult. Thousands of bushels of wheat could at one time be bought for less than twenty-five cents per bushel. Cases occurred where ten bushels were offered for a single pound of tea, and refused. One account tells of a man who brought an oxen-wagon filled with corn eight miles from Granger to the county seat of Medina, where he happily exchanged his load for three yards of "satinet."[32] It was not until the opening of the Ohio and Erie Canal that the settlers had a market for their products, and fortunes began to rise in the county.

The Hiram Hatch family of Granger Township may have been one of the more fortunate families who felt that prosperity build. Their daughter, Lucinda, almost certainly was tutored at a local school when she produced her decorative sampler (fig. 213).

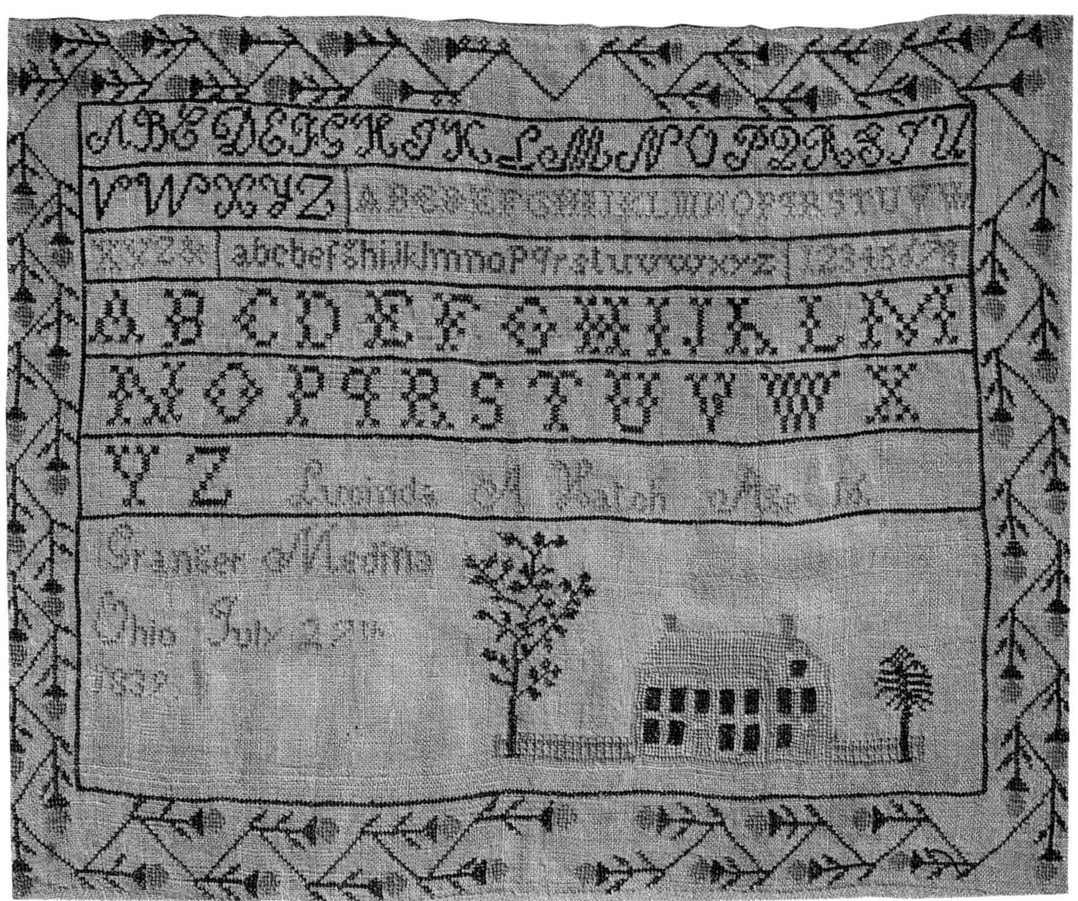

Fig. 213: Sampler of Lucinda A. Hatch. 1839.
Size: 12½" L x 16" W. Collection of Ross Trump.

Lucinda A. Hatch, daughter of Hiram and Amanda Hatch, completed this sampler when she was sixteen years old. She marked the canvas "Granger—Medina—Ohio July 17th 1839." The horizontal shape of the canvas is typical of this period, in contrast to the vertical composition that was favored earlier in the nineteenth century. The angular, stiff double strawberry vine that surrounds the needlework, although not particularly artistic, is unique. Lucinda's sampler is the only schoolgirl embroidery from Medina County documented in our Ohio search. Lucinda married Charles Williams. She died in 1851, when she was twenty-eight years old.

Lorain County

Bordered by the shores of Lake Erie, the settlement of Lorain soon became a flourishing port town and is the county's largest city today.

Not far south, the town of Oberlin and Oberlin College were founded in Lorain County in 1833. The college was the first in the country to admit women on the same status as men. At least six female graduates of Oberlin are listed in the Ohio pioneer teachers and schools section of this book.[33] This institution also became well known as a center of the American Anti-Slavery Society. Because of its easy access to Lake Erie, Oberlin was a major station for the Underground Railroad that led hundreds of runaway slaves to freedom in Canada.[34] Samuel Morgan, the father of Celestia Morgan, whose sampler is seen in fig. 214, is described in the early history of the county as a leader of the abolitionist movement in this area.[35]

Fig. 214: Sampler of Celestia Morgan. c. 1840.
Size: 7" L x 9" W. Wool thread on bristol board.
Collection of Ted and Virginia T. Seifert.

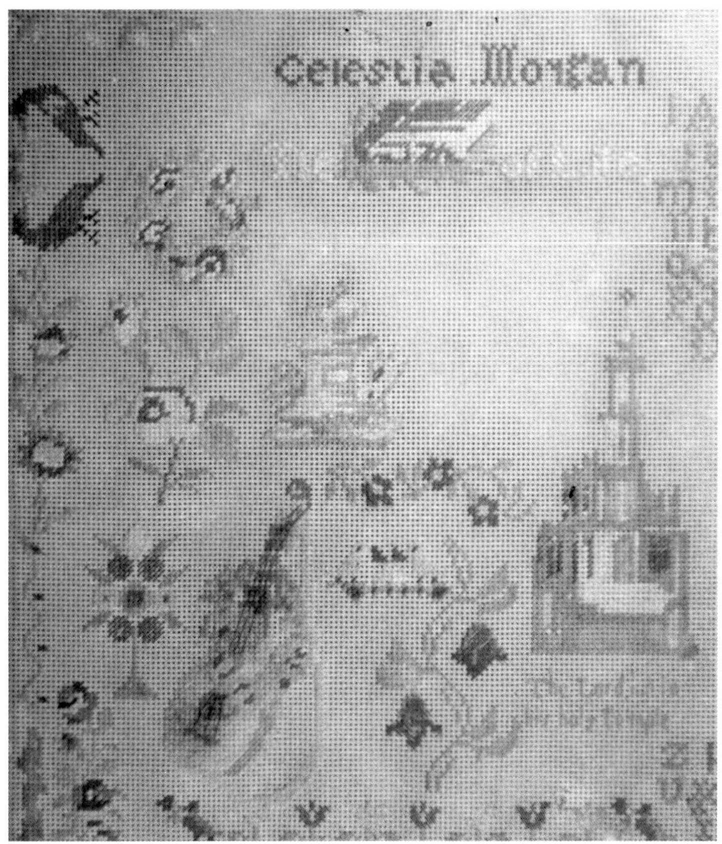

Celestia Morgan, the youngest of four children of Samuel and Amy (Allen) Morgan, did not date this embroidery, but it was executed about 1840. Records show that Celestia was born on April 12, 1828, in New York. According to the Ohio census, the Morgans moved to Ohio prior to 1840 and settled in Camden County, within a few miles of Oberlin. Celestia, at the age of fourteen, was baptized and united with the Baptist Church of Camden and remained an active member all her life.

Celestia's needlework was stitched not on a canvas of linen but on a perforated paper called bristol board. The stiffened paper had regularly spaced holes and could be purchased in varying thicknesses and hole sizes. It allowed even a stitcher who was not particularly talented with the needle to make even stitches. Wool thread was most often used, but, if the bristol board had very small holes, cotton or silk thread also worked well. This type of needlework became wildly popular during the 1840s, and the craze did not diminish until about three decades later. The stitches show little diversity, but Celestia used a variety of motifs as she scattered her work around the canvas. Patterns could be readily purchased for these Victorian designs. Wreaths of flowers, birds, and musical instruments were popular selections. Beneath the stitcher's name are a picture of a book and the words "The [Book] of Life." Stitched below the church are the words "The Lord is in his holy temple."

Celestia married Andrew Jackson Hinman in Lorain County on April 30, 1849. In 1851, Andrew left Celestia with their infant son, Andrew Floyd, and went to California to seek his fortune. Celestia looked forward to his return in the autumn of 1852, but she waited in vain. Word finally came that Andrew had died of smallpox. Celestia remained a widow for sixty years, devoting herself to the care of her son and her elderly parents. She is buried in the Camden Cemetery beside the members of her family.

Crawford County

Crawford County was formed from old Indian territory, and as late as 1819 no white families had yet settled in this backcountry region. The privations the first pioneers faced are well recorded, but cheap, rich land soon enticed farmers to the county. Bucyrus, established in 1822, was the only town of size, and it became a prosperous community. This is where stitcher Elmira (Almira) Jane Espy's family settled and where she, her sister Maggie, and her mother taught school.

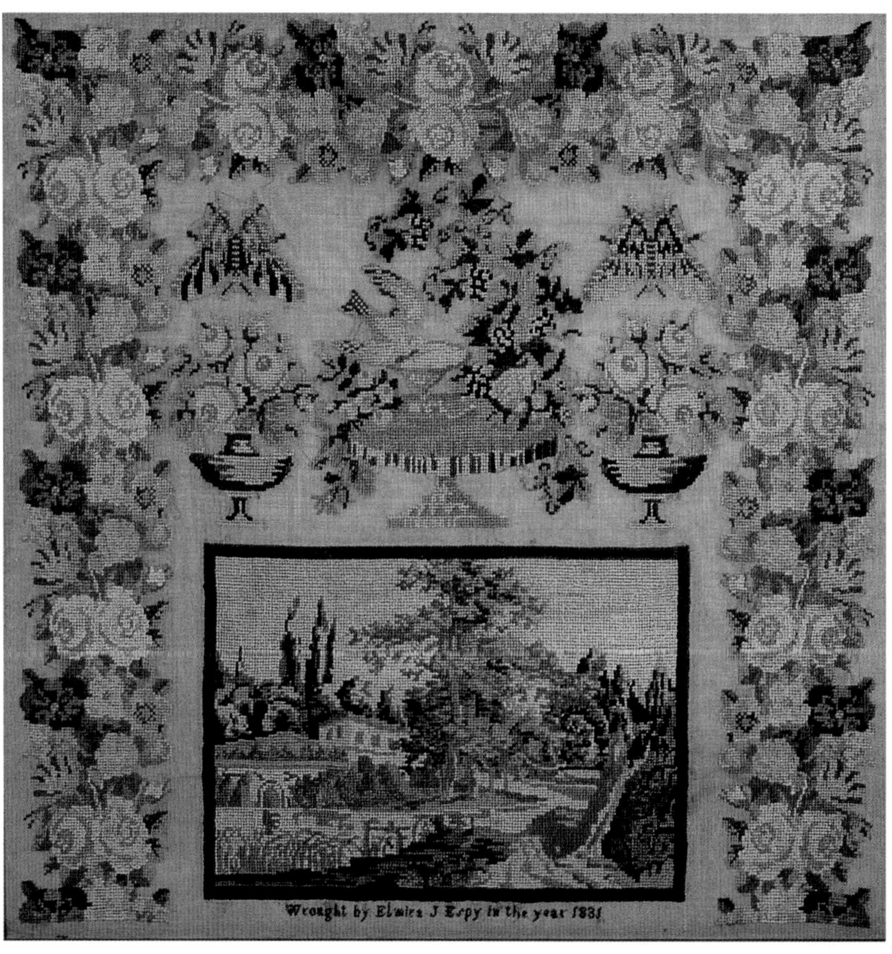

Fig. 216: Detail of Espy Sampler

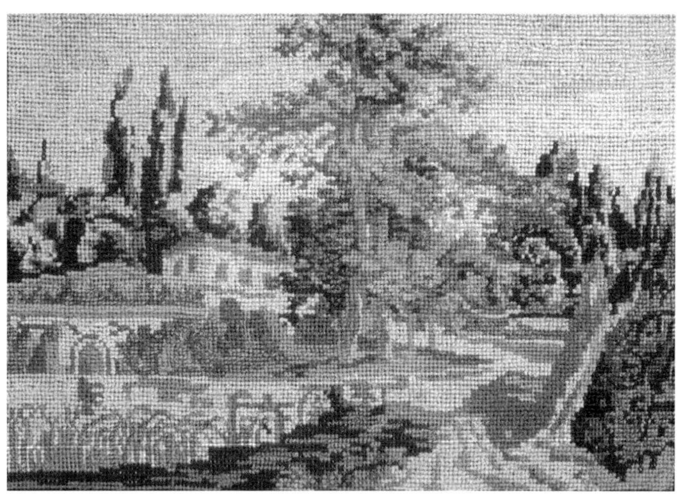

« Fig. 215: Sampler of Elmira Jane Espy. 1831.
Size: 21 H" L x 21 H" W. Collection of Gerry and Eunice Espey.

Public records indicate that Elmira Jane Espy's family was in Ohio well before 1831, when she stitched the sampler. Ohio census records, however, do not record the family until 1840. Elmira was born in Gettysburg, Adams County, Pennsylvania, the first daughter of John and Mary (Polly) (Dunwoody) Espy. Her parents had baby Elmira christened on October 6, 1815, in Gettysburg's Rock Creek Congregational Church, where they had been united in marriage a year and a half before. Records document that John was a fifth-generation American whose ancestors came from Ireland to Lancaster County, Pennsylvania, in 1725.

Elmira was sixteen years old when she completed this fashionable needlework in 1831. The work is executed in silk cross-stitches. Some areas are worked with double strands of thread, which tend to give a textured effect to the canvas. The overall design and the motifs used are very sophisticated for 1831. They were taken from Berlin work patterns that were very popular a decade or so later in America. *Godey's Lady's Book,* published the same year Elmira completed her needlework picture, described Berlin patterns with these words: "Paper patterns, covered with black cross lines, to represent the threads of canvass, and painted on the squares in the proper colours, may be bought at the worsted-shops."[36] As a rule, we think of these patterns as being used later and always embroidered with wool thread. Elmira chose to work them with silk. Patterns were relatively inexpensive and could sometimes be returned or traded for other patterns. The border of large roses and the detailed small landscape scene that Elmira chose to use are characteristic of the pattern designs that were favored. On March 19, 1840, Elmira married William J. Clugston of Crawford County.

John Espy, Elmira's father, died in Ohio before his wife and daughters moved to Crawford County. This loss of support is likely the reason the three women began teaching school. The fine needlework that Elmira executed may have been used as an example for her students.

The first brick building in town was erected in 1826. It served as a courthouse, town hall, school, and church meetinghouse for all the denominations in the town. After several years, this brick schoolhouse could not contain all the children, and in 1830 other schools were established around the town. In 1840, a two-story frame building, fitted with a belfry and a fine bell, was built. It opened in October of that year, with Maggie Espy as one of the first teachers.[37]

Ashland County

Ashland County was not formally organized in northern Ohio until 1846, although settlers had begun to come to the area at a much earlier date. Numbers of pioneers who came to claim land there were from Pennsylvania. They included a large number of German Baptists, commonly called Dunkards. These people were primarily farmers, and they seemed quickly to recognize and purchase the very best farming land in the area.

The county seat, located about fifty miles southeast of Cleveland, also had the name of Ashland. Laid out in 1815, it soon became a thriving community.

Mary Jane Short's is the only sampler in our survey of Ohio needlework that has been documented from Ashland County.

FIG. 217: SAMPLER OF MARY JANE SHORT. 1846. »
SIZE: 14½" L x 8" W. COLLECTION OF THE AUTHOR.

Although Mary Jane Short's sampler is naïve in design, the trees and flowers stitched in lower part of the canvas have a pleasing folk-art quality. The large center tree, reminiscent of the type of drooping willow that was often stitched decades earlier on silk-on-silk mourning embroideries in New England, is rather incongruous on a marking sampler.

Mary Jane was the daughter of James and Margary Short of Milton Township. James was born in Pennsylvania in 1784, and came to Ashland County sometime before 1827. He and his wife had five children, all born in Ohio. The Ohio 1850 Census lists James as a farmer. Tax records indicate that his land holdings were valued at six thousand dollars, a sizable amount for the time.

Pinned to Mary Jane's sampler when it was found was an old handwritten note that was not dated or signed. It said, "This sampler was made by Aunt Mary Short Woods. It was made in 1846. The samplers are precious as they show how girls learned to sew in the early days."

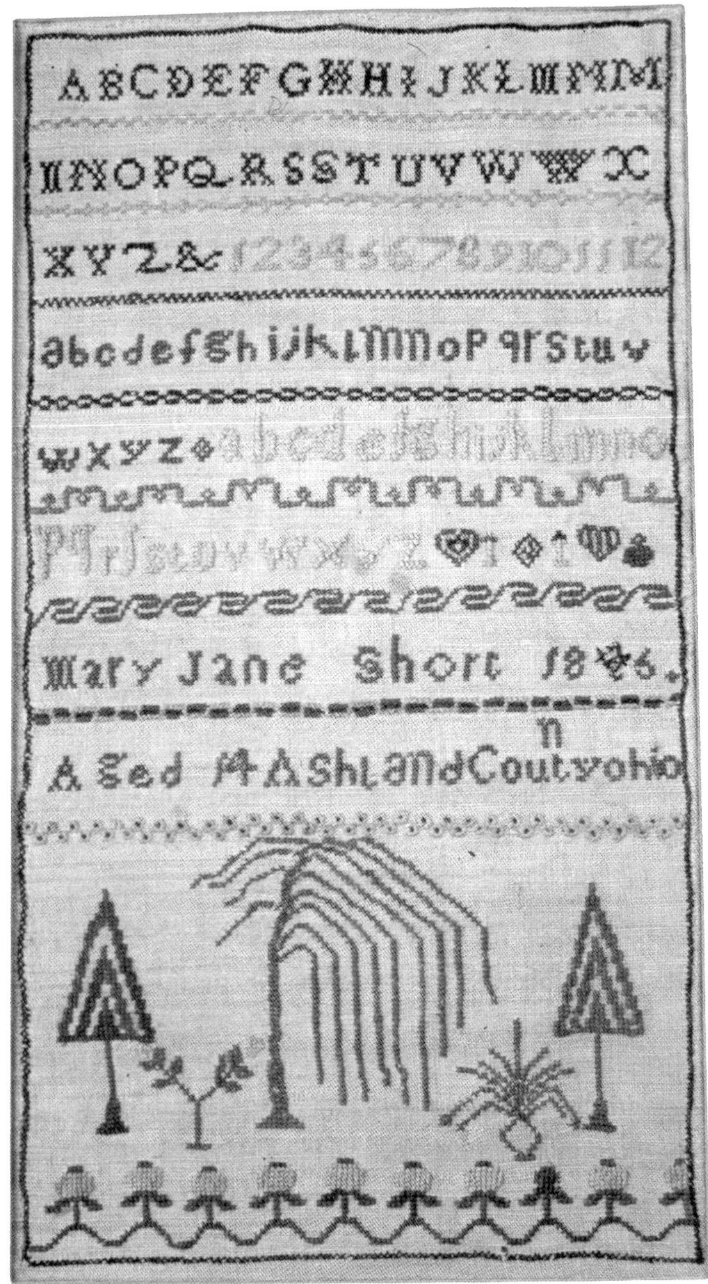

The decorative bands that separate the alphabets and numbers demonstrate that Mary Jane was a proficient stitcher. Her sampler, dated 1846, is plainly marked with her name and county. Little mistakes on a sampler add to their charm, and Mary Jane's later addition of an "n" to the spelling of "County" is one of the first things that catches the eye. She also makes us smile when we see that she was sensitive about her age as she grew older and decided to cross out part of the date when the sampler was completed.

Erie County

The settlement of Milan was laid out in 1816 along the banks of the Huron River in the Firelands area of the Western Reserve. The site had been a wilderness Indian village less than a decade before. The Huron and the Sandusky Rivers were the two waterways that opened the area for rapid growth, and as the decades passed Milan became a busy grain port and ship building center. Sandusky, a few miles north, was considered to be the best and largest port on the Great Lakes at this time. As prosperity grew, so did the need for self-government, and Erie County was formed in 1838.

A commodious brick academy building was built in Milan in 1832, and about one hundred and fifty students were enrolled each year.[38] By 1840, the town was a bustling settlement of more than fifteen hundred inhabitants. This was the year that eleven-year-old Marion Edison (fig. 219) arrived with her family from Canada to begin a new life in the United States.

Fig. 218: The Edison Homestead.

Courtesy of Edison Birthplace Association, Inc.

Samuel and Nancy Elliott Edison built this home in 1841. Marion Edison was twelve when the family moved into the new home. This is the birthplace of Thomas Alva Edison and where Marion was married. Her sampler hangs today in the front parlor of the family home where it was stitched more than a century and a half ago.

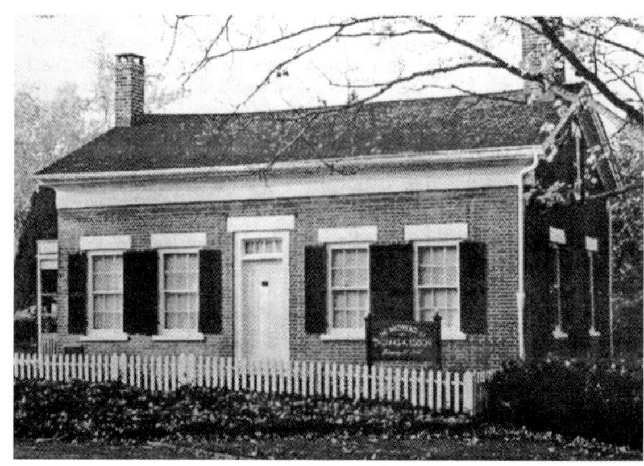

The years passed and Thomas Edison's fame grew. His many patents made him one of America's greatest inventors. Marion had a true sense of history, for she purchased the old family home in 1894, after it had been out of family ownership for forty years. She moved into the house after her husband's death and lived there much of the remainder of her life. Tucked away on a quiet street in historic Milan, the home is on the National Register of Historic Places.

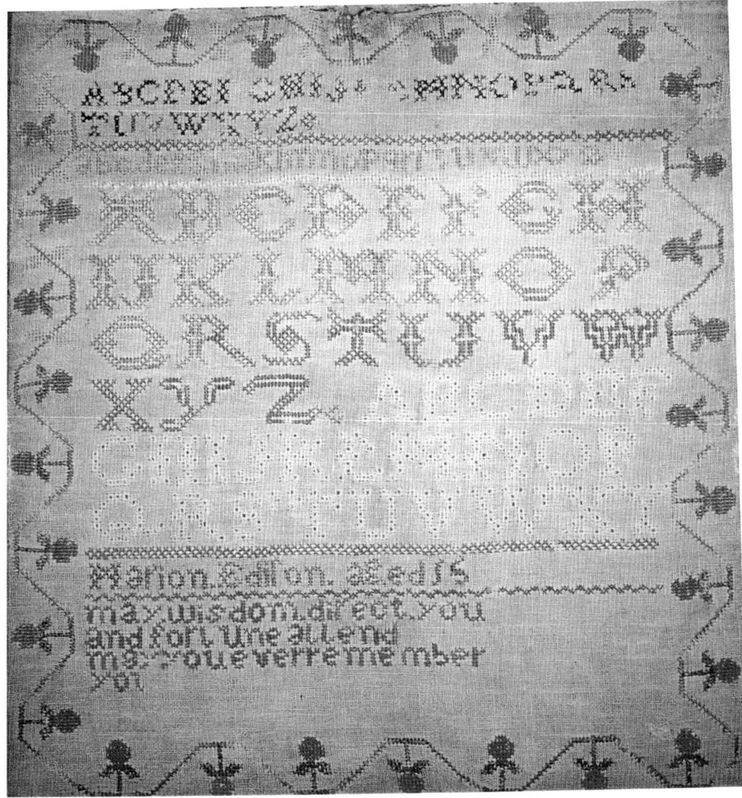

FIG. 219: SAMPLER OF MARION EDISON. 1844.
SIZE: 16½" L x 16" W. WOOL ON LINEN. COLLECTION OF EDISON BIRTHPLACE MUSEUM.

Marion Edison, the oldest daughter of Samuel Ogden and Nancy (Elliott) Edison, was born on September 15, 1829, when the family was living in Canada. She executed this sampler at the age of fifteen, surrounding the canvas with a neatly stitched arcaded strawberry vine border. Her verse was left unfinished.

Marion was one of seven children. She was eighteen when her brother Thomas Alva Edison was born. When she and Homer Page were married in the Edison home the week before Christmas in 1849, Thomas was two years old. Historians tell us that Marion and Homer lived on a beautiful farm in Milan Township, and often had young Tom out for visits. Before long, Homer and Marion had two children of their own, Isabel Marion and Harry. Marion died on January 31, 1900, and was interred with her husband in the Milan Cemetery.

John Edison, the paternal great-grandfather of Marion and Thomas Alva Edison, settled in New Jersey about 1730. He was a large landholder, but remained loyal to the British cause in the Revolution. When his land was confiscated at the end of the war, he moved his family to Nova Scotia. His son Captain Samuel Edison shared his father's political sympathies and served with the British in the War of 1812.[39]

Samuel O. Edison, Marion's father, married twenty-year-old Nancy Elliott in 1830 in Canada. From Stonington, Connecticut, she was the daughter of Captain Ebenezer Elliott, who served for seven years in the Revolutionary War in Washington's army. Politics do not appear to have had a detrimental effect upon the young couple's life. After ten years, Samuel O. Edison determined that he would bring his family back to the United States. They chose to settle in the thriving little town of Milan.[40]

Wood County

No region of Ohio was more important in determining the future of the state and the Northwest Territory than the area of the Maumee Valley. In October 1794, the Americans were victorious over the British and Indians at the Battle of Fallen Timbers on the north side of the Maumee River. This victory resulted in the Treaty of Greenville in 1795, allowing safe settlement of all of Ohio except the northwest quadrant, which bordered what is now Indiana.

This peace was to last for eighteen years until the War of 1812, when the valley once again became a critical theater of operations. It is not surprising that Eliza R. Johnson stitched "Fort Meigs" on her sampler (fig. 220). This American fort, located at Perrysburg and commanded by General William Henry Harrison, withstood two sieges by a combined force of five thousand British and Indian allies.

In October of 1813, Harrison assembled an army of battle-hardened soldiers and carried out an assault on the British at Fort Malden on the Canadian side of Lake Erie. His troops were escorted by the fleet of the bold and impulsive Commodore Oliver Hazard Perry, who had soundly defeated the British on Lake Erie a month earlier.

General Harrison's men were victorious, and with the death of the great Indian chief Tecumseh in this battle, the will of the allied Indian Nations was finally broken. A Treaty of Peace ending the War of 1812 was signed. Settlement of the rest of Ohio, and the Northwest Territories, was now possible.

FIG. 220: SAMPLER OF ELIZA R. JOHNSON. 1840.
SIZE: 17½" L x 17½" W. COLLECTION OF MELVIN AND CONNIE PORCHER.

Oh lonely is our old green fort,
Where oft in days of old,
Our soldiers bravely fought
Gainst savage allies bold.

Little is known about Eliza R. Johnson, the young girl who stitched this sampler, but her verse speaks volumes about the history of Ohio. It reveals the sentiments that were still being taught to the children of Perrysburg long after the historic battles had been fought. The town had been named in honor of the commodore of the navy, Oliver Perry, and tales of his victories at sea had been recited many times. When Eliza Johnson stitched this beautiful and large sampler, the village had just over a thousand residents. The old fort, now empty of soldiers, held a very significant place in the hearts of those who lived nearby.[41]

The border of Eliza's sampler demonstrates her considerable skill with needle and thread. It exhibits a profusion of color, with artfully arranged small-scale flowers, buds, leaves, and berries. Stitches include satin, cross, outline, and whip. Eliza's sampler is the only needlework documented from Wood County, and the verse she used is unique.

part four

VICTORIAN IMPULSES

Selected Needlework after 1850

Although the Ohio needlework search was limited to those pieces executed before 1850, young women did not put their sewing baskets away after that date. They continued to do the same plain and fancy work that their grandmothers and mothers had done earlier, but the fashion of the day dictated that their handwork take on a new look. Girls living in Ohio, particularly in the urban areas, sought to keep up with new needlework fashions, and evidence suggests that they succeeded.

With few exceptions, by the 1850s little girls were no longer pressured to sit in schools and learn to perform intricate stitches, nor were all parents eager to pay tuition to a private needlework teacher. Anne Hulme Price, a widow supporting herself and two young daughters, writes about her small private school in Cincinnati. Ann corresponded with relatives in New Jersey over a period of twelve years. Her earliest letters, written before her husband's death in 1832, are filled with optimism, but as a widow, Ann's life had become much more difficult. She wrote to her brother in April of 1834, "My school is small at present to what it was; every body hates to send to pay schools, as they call any but Free or District Schools."[1]

Later that year she wrote to her brother again: "I have but 7 schollars. I have went and got some sewing at a clothing store hoping to get some flannel and c, thereby but I find it impossible to sew constantly. I stood it well the two first weeks, but last week I spent several sleepless nights in consequence of straining my eyes. The Girls do all they can but they are not well."[2]

The last of her letters is dated July 12, 1836, and her plight seems not to have eased. She was not well enough to support herself as a seamstress, nor did her work as a teacher seem promising. The number of her students has been diminished by competition from "free" schools and larger private "female seminaries."

> *I have been preparing the clothes of one of my little boarders to go to a Boarding school in Kentucky. Tomorrow she leaves us and were it not that I shall miss her Board I could heartily rejoice; she has been to me a great trouble. . . . [H]er little sister will stay a little longer with me. . . . [N]either have I given up my Six Schollars. . . . [B]ut I fear I shall have to, last week was very oppressive. I have not heard of any cases of Cholera but much sickness among Children.*[3]

At this time Ann Price was forty-four years old. Perhaps she remarried later, but a search of the Ohio records has been inconclusive.[4]

In the beginning years of the nineteenth century, the primary role of young women was still that of homemaker, nurturing mother, and teacher of moral lessons. By mid-century, however, girls were expected to learn more important things than just the art of housewifery. Public schools were in most towns of size in Ohio. A child's hours in the public schoolroom were spent with more academic subjects, and sewing lessons were not usually a part of the organized curriculum. There were many exceptions to this, however, especially when we consider private schools operated by religious societies such as the Catholic Church. For example, four samplers dating from 1850 to 1869 have been documented from Cleveland's Urseline Convent, which was founded in 1845. As late as 1904, the Akron Sacred Heart Academy, under the direction of the Sisters of St. Dominic, still offered "needle work and embroidery."[5]

Parental pressure to do ornamental needlework may have been relieved, but for those girls who really *enjoyed* sewing and liked to show off their needlework skills, embroidery had changed. It was no longer necessary to have custom drawn patterns, because appealing printed and hand-colored patterns were readily available at the local stores. An enormous variety of subjects were offered by pattern makers from several European countries. Because the Berlin printmaker L. W. Wittich was one of the first to produce them and was the most successful, the new patterns came to be known as Berlin patterns. He first went into production about 1810, but the Wittich patterns were not popular in England until the 1820s. Wittich was a resourceful businessman. He hired trained artists to copy famous paintings and reduce them to the squares of point paper. This allowed him to make more complicated and detailed patterns than had ever before been available for needlework. Elaborate landscape scenes, sometimes with people, were perhaps his most popular subjects, but he did not often make patterns of floral borders and bouquets of the type stitched on Rhoda Warwick's sampler (fig. 221). His patterns were painted so that needleworkers did not have to decide the colors that were most suitable.[6] They could "stitch by number" as people sometimes paint by number today.

By the 1840s the Berlin work fad held full sway with American needleworkers, and its popularity lasted in Ohio well into the 1870s. The canvases of silk or finely woven cotton that had first been used in Europe and England were now replaced with a more loosely woven wool, cotton, linen, or punched paper canvas. These canvases allowed stitchers to use the beautiful worsted Berlin wool threads for their handwork. Instead of executing a variety of stitches with a fine silk thread, girls now confined their work to one or two kinds of stitches done in wool thread. With wool thread a young lady could fill the canvas much more quickly and easily than she could ever have done with fine silk thread. Adding to their appeal, the soft wool threads were available in lasting shades of every color.

This mechanical stitching attracted women young and old. It was the forerunner to the needlepoint that decorated the walls and chair seats in the parlors of almost every late Victorian home. Berlin wool work changed needlework all over America. With the arrival of printed patterns, bristol board, or point-paper canvases, and thick wool thread began an age of decline in the creative, intricate, and artfully stitched samplers of Ohio.

(following page)

Fig. 221: Sampler of Rhoda Jane Warwick. 1850.

Size: 18½" L x 18½" W. Wool on linen. Collection of Mr. and Mrs. Robert Jeffery.

This sampler was worked in 1850 and remains with the stitcher's family today. Rhoda Jane Warwick, born on January 21, 1833, was the daughter of Josiah and Clarissa (Wood) Warwick of Warren County. The young couple first resided in neighboring Butler County for several years but had removed to Warren County by the time Rhoda did this colorful needlework. She was almost eighteen when the work was executed.

Rhoda Jane completed three alphabets at the top of this large canvas before she began to stitch the decorative and intricate patterns that are so beautifully combined on her sampler. Her canvas-work stitches are precisely done and show a myriad of Victorian patterns that were very popular in this era. A curving spray of full-blown flowers, the floral wreath, sprigs of blossoms, baskets, and birds, and the cornucopia are artistically scattered. The scene is completed with a tight strawberry border on all four sides. In the reserve area, Rhoda stitched the following verse:

'Twill save us from a thousand snares
To mind religion young
Grace will preserve our following years
And make our virtue strong.

Rhoda was married on March 17, 1853, to William Jeffery. She is interred in the Jeffery lot at the Miami Cemetery in Corwin.

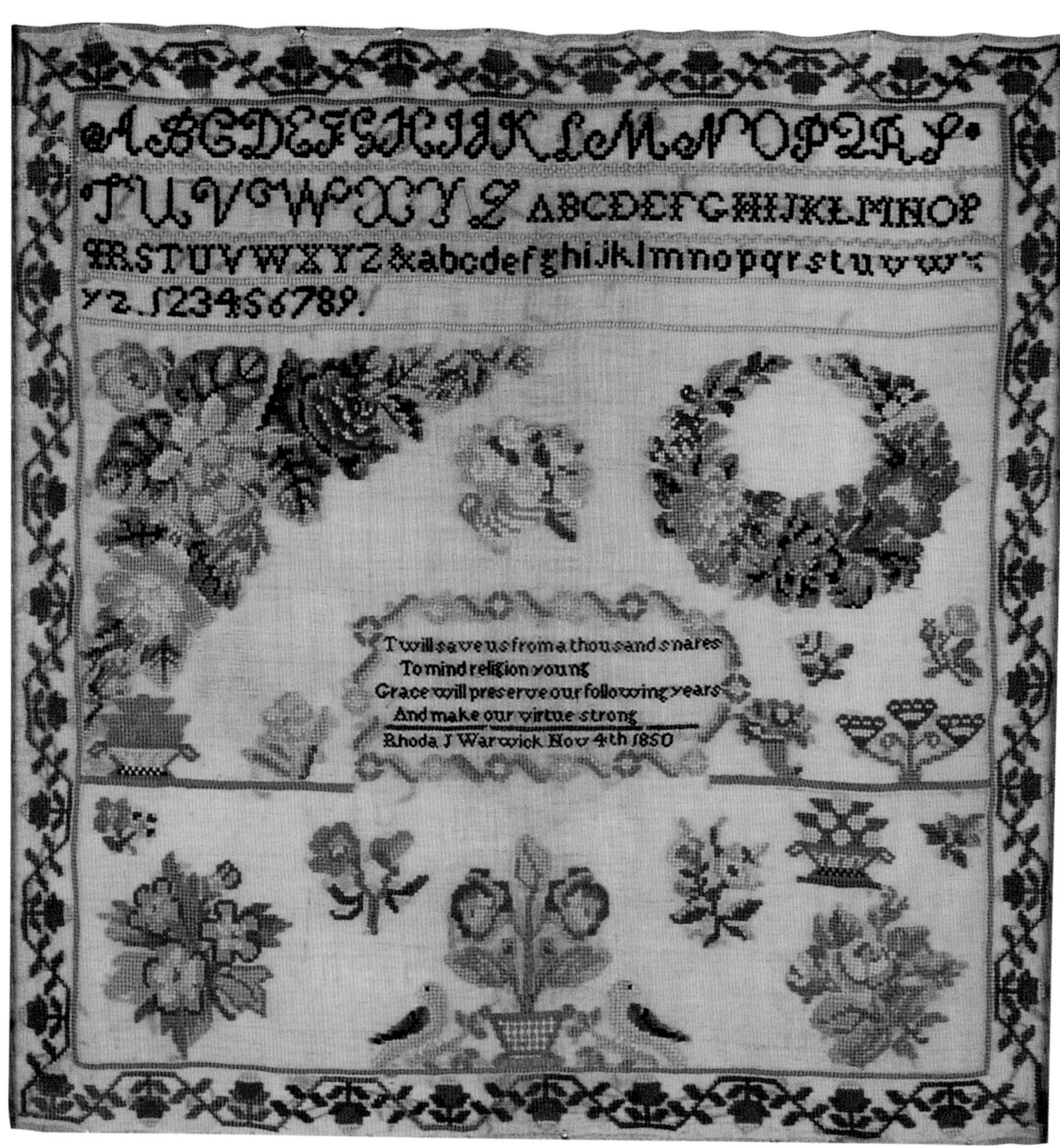
Twill save us from a thousand snares
To mind religion young
Grace will preserve our following years
And make our virtue strong
Rhoda J Warwick Nov 4th 1850

Fig. 221

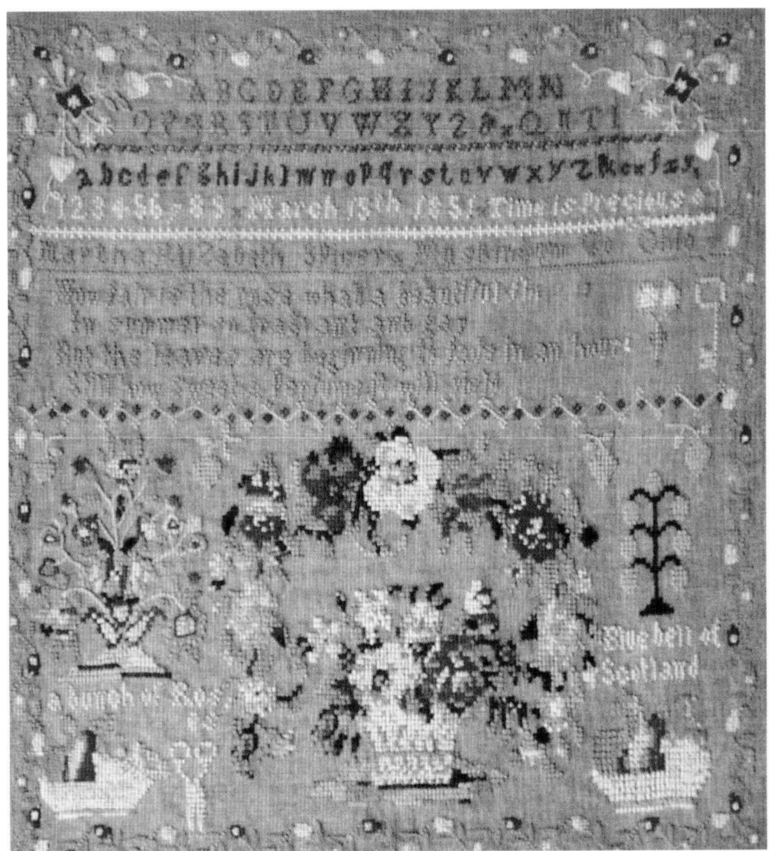

Fig. 222: Sampler of Martha Elizabeth Spicer. 1851.
Size: 17½" L x 16" W. Wool on linen. Anonymous collector.

The canvas of Martha Elizabeth Spicer is dated March 15, 1851, and marked "Muskingum Co. Ohio." Her work is confined primarily to a simple cross-stitch. She attempted to achieve a bit of diversity by introducing a satin stitch on some flower petals. After the completion of two alphabets, a row of numbers, and the date, Martha's teacher probably suggested that the phrase "Time is Precious" would fill the line perfectly.

Any verse in praise of the rose was a good choice, and Martha used a variation of one written by Rev. Isaac Watts, *Moral Songs III,* "The Rose."[7] It reads:

> How fair is the rose, what a beautiful flower
> In summer to treasure and feel
> For the leaves are beginning to fade in an hour
> Still how sweet a perfume it will yield.[8]

With that sentiment in mind, she stitched roses everywhere and labeled them, for good measure, "a bunch of Roses." On the right side of the canvas she determined that perhaps she should also label the tiny "Bluebells of Ireland," to balance the composition of her needlework. Small baskets fill the bottom corners. Martha even stitched pair of scissors, a nice addition to this very busy sampler. It is clear that the Victorian attitude of "more is better" had influenced Martha and her instructress.

Typical of girls doing wool work at this time, Martha used a rainbow of colors and stitched with Merino wool twisted thread.

Fig. 223: Sampler of Sarah Jane Pownall. 1854. »

Size: 18" L x 22" W. Wool on bristol board. Collection of Doris A. Lucas.

"Unique" is a word that has seldom been used in describing a sampler, but it is the first word that comes to mind when we examine the complex needlework of Miss Sarah Jane Pownall of Adams County, Ohio. Stitched on very small gauge bristol board, Sarah's Berlin work was meticulously executed with a fine wool thread.

Sarah Jane was the daughter of George C. and Asenith (Scott) Pownall who were living in Adams County before 1830. George and Senith (Asenith or Asenath) Pownall were married in January 1833, and Sarah Jane was born to the couple on February 19, 1835. The Pownalls, a large clan of several families, settled near each other on a high bluff known as Ginger Ridge overlooking the Ohio River. A small log house still stands, a tangible reminder of this pioneer family. Several yards away, the small Pownall family cemetery is nestled in a quiet grove of trees close to banks of the river.

Sarah was nineteen years old when this sampler was stitched in 1854. It is likely that she was a teacher rather than a student at the large West Manchester School, the red building shown just above Miss Pownall's name. About 1854 an impressive new school building with a large cupola was erected on the hill above the village. Miss Pownall's needlework, with the school so prominently stitched on the canvas, would have been a marvelous example for students to admire. Not only was the needlework expertly stitched, it provided a view of West Manchester that students could study in detail.

The village of Manchester, established in 1790, was the first white settlement in the Virginia Military Reservation. It was situated along the banks of the Ohio, about twelve miles upriver from Maysville (formerly Limestone), Kentucky. Sarah carefully stitched an accurate rendition of the old town, showing the village as it looked in 1854.[9] Additional lots were platted in 1849 to make up the section of West Manchester near where the Pownall families lived. Sarah has duplicated the original town plat map, showing each lot with its correct number. Situated beside the large school building is a peculiar symmetrical hill with a tree at the top. The hill was an ancient Indian burial mound that no longer exists.

Most of Manchester's citizens were involved in one way or another with the river. Sarah certainly must have intently watched the packet boats and big steamboats come and go at the landings, anxious to see what or who might be arriving or departing. The river was the lifeblood of the town, and her needlework tells us it was a busy place indeed. Large ships, small ships, all with captains at the front, smoke "dots" of steam coming from the tall stacks, and flags flying in the river breeze—Sarah saw it all and felt compelled to stitch it on her canvas. Her imaginative flair took over when she stitched the creatures that might be in the wide river. With precise stitches, she created fish of all sizes, a turtle, and a large, menacing snake or eel with its mouth open, ready to snatch up her turtle.

Miss Sarah Jane Pownall remained single until she was thirty years old. On August 17, 1865, Sarah married James Hook, a widower with four sons, who was sixteen years her senior. The couple's first child, a girl named after Sarah's mother, Asinath, was born the following year. This little girl died when she was three years old, but four other children survived to adulthood. Sarah died at the age of eighty-two.

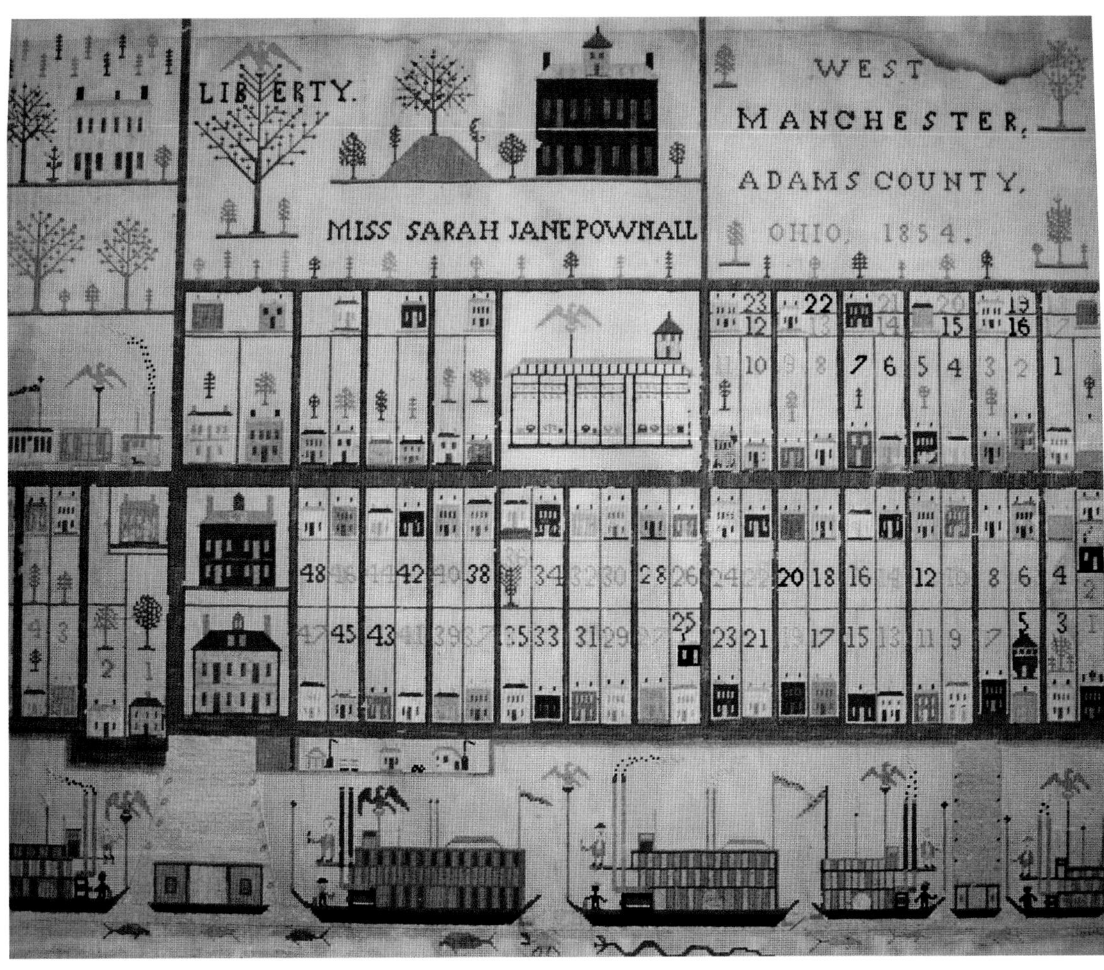

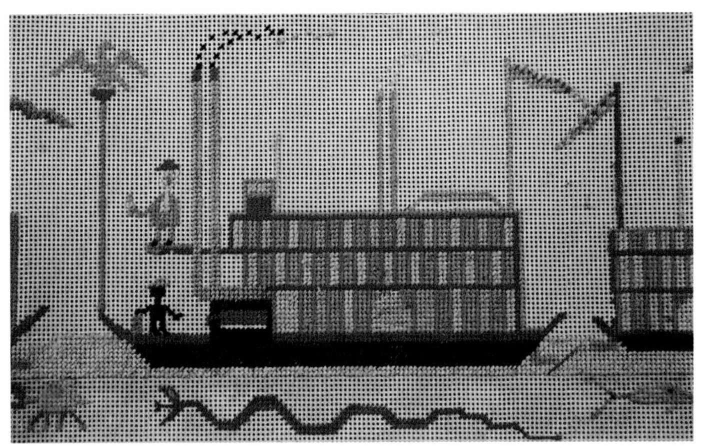

Fig. 224: Detail of Steamboat.

A steamboat pulls up to the landing in Sarah Jane Pownall's unusual sampler.

« Fig. 225: Detail of the School/Name.

Miss Sarah Jane Pownall proudly signed her work beneath a rendition of the West Manchester School.

epilogue

EVERYTHING OLD IS NEW AGAIN

Needlewomen of today are not interested in an antique sampler just as a collectible—many are eager to recreate the look of an early sampler and to work the old stitches with proficiency. This fascination with handwork of the past is nothing new. *Harper's New Monthly Magazine* (October 1880) pointed out,

> The needle has come into fashion again, and the needle, too, of our grandmothers. All the old samplers are being hunted up. This subject, Art Needlework, is one that has been rising to great importance since the Centennial Exhibition. Even before that time there were some embroiderers among us who had begun to create designs of their own with the needle, and to show the possibility of producing with it artistic effects. It is no wonder then, that the whole matter has passed into a sort of "rage." Decorative Arts societies and schools of Art needlework are starting up in our cities; the summer months at the watering-places are spent in lessons in art-embroidery from skilled teachers; every lady, young or old has her "sampler," and learns the South Kensington stitch, and is asking how she will get her designs on her material, and where, too, she shall look for her designs. This is a sudden change to bring the needle again into favor. The sewing machines had flung this little instrument [the needle] into disrepute. They did not diminish the quantity of work necessary, for ruffles and flounces increased as fast as the sewing-machines. But they banished sewing from the parlor, away among the machines and machine-work. How could one sit and listen to the reading of a play of Shakespeare by the busy whir of a sewing-machine! Or what sort of a gay talk could go on by the side of the click-click of the most noiseless sewing-machine ever patented?

The author of the article conceded that this new invention did have some value in relieving young stitchers from having to do much "plain needlework, with which they spend their solitary days, setting stitch by stitch in long seams of sheets and shirts."

> Nowadays we are finding more active occupations for women. In public life and private there is more varied work for them to do, and the modern inventions with the sewing-machine are relieving them from the necessity of spending many hours over the long seams. But plain sewing can not be given up. The sewing machines can not yet do it all. Nor can our young girls learn by nature how to sew. They have to begin each of them separately to learn how to hold a needle, how to use a thimble, how to take small stitches. Especially they have to learn not to fall into bad habits, not to get into bad ways, which can seldom be unlearned. For it is almost as hard for our young girls to learn how to sew as for the first great-great-granddaughter of Eve, who had a thorn put into her hand for the purpose, and they are about as awkward as that young woman must have been![1]

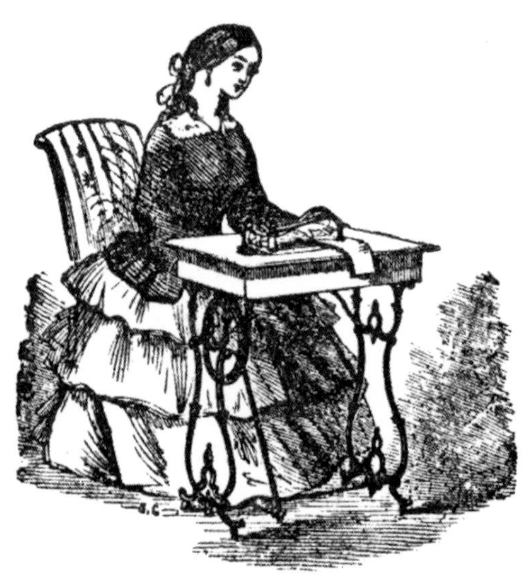

documented ohio samplers

Note: Figure numbers refer to figures in this volume. Material in quotes is taken directly from the sampler.

Adams, Mary W. C. 1833. Milan, Erie County. Collection of Milan Historical Museum.

Allen, Harriet. 1827. Cincinnati, Hamilton County. Collection of Joyce and William Subjack. "Cincinnati—in her 10th year"

Allen, Rachel R. 1839. Worthington, Franklin County. Collection of Glee Krueger. Fig. 153. "taught by Miss Amanda Munhall"

Anderson, Anna A. [Augusta]. 1835. Miami Township, Montgomery County. Collection of Colleen Dignan. Fig. 58.

Anonymous. 1852. Cincinnati, Hamilton County. Collection of Harry Lockwood. "work Performance in Rebecca W. Bodley's School" "Cincinnati—Ohio"

Ashton, Leah Jane. 1833. Dayton, Montgomery County. Collection of Jon and Sue Airey. Fig. 53. "Mrs. R. A. Cooper's School—Dayton"

Ashton, Leah Jane. 1833. Dayton, Montgomery County. Collection of Jane R. Bourne. Fig. 53.

Baggott, Alice. 1831. Cincinnati, Hamilton County. Anonymous collector. "St. Peter's School—Cincinnati"

Ballinger, Rebecca. 1830. Jefferson County. The Textile Collection, Smithsonian Institution National Museum of American History, Behring Center, Washington, D.C. Fig. 172.

Ballinger, Sarah. 1830. Preble County. Anonymous collector. Fig. 101. "done in her 11th year"

Barcalow, Lydia. 1825. Warren County. See Ethel Stanwood Bolton and Eva Johnston Coe, *American Samplers.*

Barnd, Harriet. 1845. New Lexington, Perry County. Collection of Martha Lindsey Bowman. Fig. 155. "New Lexington"

Barnett, Susannah Wilson. 1834. Lemon Township, Butler County. Collection of Hugh Barnett. Fig. 88.

Bartholomew, Minerva. 1817. Franklin County. Collection of Worthington Historical Society. "Worthington Academy" "Miss Barker, Preceptress"

Bashore, Celia Jane. C. 1835. New Antioch, Clinton County. Collection of Karen Buckley. Fig. 82.

Battin, Ann. 1815. Sandy Spring, Columbiana County. Collection of Marion Ackerman. "Sandy Spring—Ohio" "Parents names—John and Ann Battin"

Belangee, Ann Elizabeth. C. 1844. Cincinnati, Hamilton County. Anonymous collector. "Age 13 years"

Billings, Sarah. C. 1834. Cincinnati, Hamilton County. Collection of Marjorie Brown, great-granddaughter of stitcher.

Bone, Susan Harvey. 1838. Warren County. Collection of Frances Glass.

Bonsall, Mary Jane. 1828. Salem, Columbiana County. Collection of Salem Historical Society, Inc. Fig. 184. "Salem—Columbiana County Ohio"

Borton, Lydia Ann. 1829. Salem, Columbiana County. Collection of Salem Historical Society, Inc. "Salem"

Borton, Mary Ann. C. 1829. Warren County. Anonymous collector. "in her 12th year"

Borton, Mary Ann. 1832. Warren County. Anonymous collector.

Boughton, Jerusha [Ann]. C. 1830. Canfield, Trumbull County. Collection of Donald C. Stone. "Jerusha Ann B." "Canfield—Trumbull"

Brouse, Eleanor. 1816. Hillsboro, Highland County. See Ethel Stanwood Bolton and Eva Johnston Coe, *American Samplers.*

Brown, Priscilla. 1833. Israel Township, Preble County. Collection of Preble County Historical Society, Eaton.

Brown, Ruth. C. 1810. Union Shaker Village, Warren County. Collection of Philadelphia Museum of Art.

Bruen, Eliza Ann. 1828. Dayton, Montgomery County. Collection of Ohio Historical Society, Glendower Home, Lebanon. "Dayton—Ohio"

Bull, Huldah. 1819. Franklin County. Collection of Worthington Historical Society. "Worthington Academy—Miss Barker—Preceptress"

Burnham, Ireana. 1830. Centerville, Montgomery County. Collection of Centerville Historical Society. Fig. 60. "made in her 17 year—January 28th, 1830"

Burroughs, Mary Louisa. 1840. Boardman, Trumbull County, now Mahoning County. Anonymous collector. Fig. 182. "aged 11 years" "Boardman Trumbull County Ohio"

Campbell, Mary Jane. 1820. Steubenville, Jefferson County. Collection of Larry and Sarah Mosteller. "born June 28, 1811" "Steubenville, Ohio 1820"

Carter, Achsah. 1830. Smithfield, Jefferson County. Anonymous Collector. Fig. 171. "Smithfield—Ohio" "Ann H. Thorn, Preceptress"

Carter, Keturah J. 1830. Smithfield, Jefferson County. Collection of Allan and Linda Cobourn. Fig. 170. "Smithfield—Ohio" "Ann H. Thorn"

Cary, Anna. 1829. Warren County. Collection of Warren County Historical Society, Lebanon.

Chaddock, Lydiann. 1861. Montgomery County. Collection of Western Reserve Museum, Cleveland. "Montgomery County, Ohio U.S."

Clapp, Gennett. 1839. Norwich, Muskingum County. Anonymous collector. Fig. 161. "Norwich, Ohio"

Clark, Martha. 1827. Guernsey County. Collection of Dr. John R. Ribic. Fig. 163. "Born May 10, 1820"

Clevenger, H. 1834. Turtle Creek Township, Warren County. Collection of Mr. and Mrs. John P. Sackett.

Coleman, Pamela. Undated. Troy, Miami County. Collection of Overfield Tavern Museum, Troy. Fig. 132. "P.M.C"

Coleman, Pamela. Undated. Troy, Miami County. Collection of Overfield Tavern Museum, Troy. Fig. 131.

Combs, Eliza Jane. 1844. Carrollton, Carroll County. Collection of Robert and Susan Pusecker. Fig. 177. "Carrollton—Ohio"

Conover, Hannah. C. 1809. Warren County. Collection of Ohio Historical Society, Glendower Home, Lebanon.

Converse, Betsey C. 1828. Parkman, Geauga County. Collection of Larry and Sarah Mosteller. Fig. 191. "Parkman—Geauga County—Ohio aged 8 years"

Corner, Mary. 1833. Malta, Morgan County. Collection of Elizabeth W. Peters, great-granddaughter of stitcher. Fig. 117. "worked in her 10th year of age—Malta"

Corwin Mourning Embroidery. C. 1818. Attributed to Elvira Corwin. Lebanon, Warren County. Collection of Warren County Historical Society, Lebanon. Fig. 29.

Cory, Melissa. C. 1825. New Carlisle, Clark County. Collection of Daughters of the American Revolution Museum, Washington, D.C. Fig. 122. "born February 22, 1815 on Honey Creek"

Cowles, Polly [Martha]. 1815. Austinburg, Ashtabula County. Collection of Margaret Cowles Ticknor, great-niece of stitcher. Fig. 193. "aged 11 years"

Croft, Mary A. C. 1824–25. Bethel Township, Clark County. Collection of Barbara and Tim Martien. Fig. 121. "Mary A. Croft was born Nov. 7th, 1813"

Davidson, Elizabeth E. 1836. Knox County. Collection of Melvin and Connie Porcher. Fig. 156. "was born January 3, 1823 Knox County—Ohio"

Demarest, Maria. 1834. Dayton, Montgomery County. Collection of Debra Elizabeth Schaffer. "wrought in the 10th year of her age"

Demarest, Sarah Ann. C. 1835. Dayton, Montgomery County. Collection of Nancye Schooley. "wrought in the 8th year of her age"

Devoe, Sarah Alice. Undated. Hamilton County. Collection of Linda Gottschalk. Fig. 16. "Catholic School in Cincinnati"

Doan, Phebe. 1834. Clinton County. Collection of Nancy Geer Austin. Fig. 72. "Clinton County, Ohio"

Dodge, Mary Wing. 1826. Marietta, Washington County. Collection of Larry and Sarah Mosteller. Fig. 1. "in the 12th year of her age" "Marietta, Ohio"

Doolittle, Philena. 1837. Centerville, Montgomery County. Collection of M. Rolander. Fig. 67. "I was born July 30th, 1823" "Centreville, Ohio"

Dorn, Martha Ann. 1847. Cincinnati, Hamilton County. Collection of Frank W. Stout. Fig. 23. "Aged 9 years" "A present to grandmother"

Doty, Hannah. 1831. Butler County. Collection of Jane K. Martin.

Dresbach, Maria Louisa. 1829. Circleville, Pickaway County. Collection of Susan Randolph. "Circleville—Ohio"

Dubois, Phoebe Jane. 1834. Carlisle, Warren County. Collection of Warren County Historical Society, Lebanon.

Dunham, Caroline Sarah. 1835. Cleveland, Cuyahoga County. Collection of Dunham Tavern Museum, Inc., Cleveland. Fig. 211. "Wrought in the tenth year of her age—1835"

Dunham, Elizabeth. 1838. Newark, Licking County. Collection of Robbins Hunter Museum, Granville. "In the 10th year of age" "Newark—Ohio"

Dunham, Elizabeth. 1849. Wayne County. Collection of Larry and Sarah Mosteller.

Dunham, Loretta. C. 1835. Cleveland, Cuyahoga County. Collection of Glee Krueger. "Ae 12"

Eaton, Julia Ripley. 1844. Delaware, Delaware County. Collection of Delaware County Historical Society. Fig. 144. "13 years of age"

Eaton, Laura Ann. 1843. Delaware, Delaware County. Collection of Delaware County Historical Society. Fig. 142. "13 years of age"

Edison, Marion. 1844. Milan, Erie County. Collection of Edison Birthplace Museum, Milan. Fig. 219. "Aged 15 years"

Edmondson, Hannah. 1833. Dayton, Montgomery County. Collection of the Daughters of the American Revolution Pennsylvania House Museum, Springfield, Ohio. "Dayton—Ohio"

Edmondson, Hannah. 1834. Dayton, Montgomery County. Collection of the Daughters of the American Revolution Pennsylvania House Museum, Springfield, Ohio. Fig. 56. "Dayton—Ohio"

Edmondson, Mary Ann. 1834. Dayton, Montgomery County. Collection of Ohio Historical Society, Columbus. Fig. 55. "Dayton—Ohio"

Edmondson, Mary Ann. 1834 (miniature sampler). Dayton, Montgomery County. Collection of the Ohio Historical Society. "A.M. 1834 M.E."

Edmondson, Ruth Anna. 1842. Dayton, Montgomery County. Collection of Natalie Ruth Dall. Fig. 57.

Endly, Elizabeth Ann. 1829. Washington, Guernsey County. Anonymous collector. "in the 13th year of her age" "Washington—Guernsey County, State of Ohio"

Espy, Elmira Jane. 1831. Crawford County. Collection of Gerry and Eunice Espey. Fig. 215.

Espy, Isabella Marion. 1836. Columbus, Franklin County. Collection of Barbara Dua and Doug Harton. "Columbus, Ohio"

Essex, Sarah Ann. Undated. Licking County. Anonymous collector.

Evans, Antoinette. 1839. Ripley, Brown County. Collection of Nancy Antoinette Noland DeCamp, great-granddaughter of stitcher. Fig. 107. "Ripley"

Farquhar, Rebecca. 1828. Springboro, Warren County. Collection of Larry and Sarah Mosteller. "Springborough"

Faunce, Nancy. 1828. Bazetta, Trumbull County. Anonymous collector. Fig. 183. "Aged 12 years—Bazetta"

Fawcett, Lydia. 1832. Salem, Columbiana County. Collection of Glee Krueger. Fig. 186.

Ferrall, Martha. 1822. Columbiana County. Collection of Ann Bauer. Fig. 187. "Columbiana County—Ohio"

Finkle, Catharine A. M. 1818. Franklin, Warren County. Collection of Dr. John R. Ribic. Fig. 44. "C. V. B. Schenck's School—Franklin, Ohio"

Fitch, Mary. C. 1819. Canfield Township, Trumbull County. Anonymous Collection. "Mary Fitch born January 23, 1808"

Fitch, Mary. 1819. Canfield, Trumbull County. Collection of Rebecca Gibson Bennett, great-grandaughter. Fig. 180. "wrought in her 11th year" "Canfield Trumbull County Ohio"

Flinn, Agnes. 1828. Cincinnati, Hamilton County. Collection of Mrs. A. M. Kinney Jr, great-granddaughter of stitcher. "was born the first of June in the year 1817" "Worked this sampler during the summer of 1828"

Forbs, Julia Ann. 1827. Wooster, Wayne County. Collection of Dayton Art Institute. Gift of the estate of Elmer R. Webster and Robert A. Titsch. Fig. 201. "Wooster—Ohio"

Frank, Ammalia Louise. 1841. Cincinnati, Hamilton County. Collection of Nancy Koch Holterhoff. Fig. 20. "Aged 15 years"

Frazier, Eliza Ann. 1824. Steubenville, Jefferson County. Collection of Larry and Sarah Mosteller. Fig. 173. "wrought in the 10th year of her age" "Steubenville, Jefferson County, Ohio"

Frazier, Rebecca T. 1833. Clinton County. Collection of Margaret C. Smith.

Frazier, Rebecca T. 1835. Wilmington, Clinton County. Anonymous collector. Fig. 78. "Wilmington"

Fundenburg, Anna. 1828. Jefferson Township, Montgomery County. Collection of Eldon Studebaker. Fig. 64.

Fundenburg, Anna. 1836 (hand towel). Jefferson Township, Montgomery County. Author's collection.

Fundenburg, Anna. 1837 (hand towel). Jefferson Township, Montgomery County. Collection of Eldon Studebaker. Fig. 63.

Galbraith, Caroline. 1814. Steubenville, Jefferson County. Collection of Larry and Sarah Mosteller. "wrought in Steubenville Nov. 22, 1814" "In the 9th year of her age"

Garretson, Phebe. 1825. Springboro, Warren County. Collection of Annette Anderson Quebe. Fig. 51. "Springborough"

Garwood, Anna. 1822. Warren County. Collection of Victoria A. Kramb, Ph.D. Fig. 38. "In Ohio . . . In Warren . . ."

Gause, Martha P. [Pierce]. 1832. Warren County. Collection of Miriam Rosell.

Gilmore, Sarah H. March 9, 1849. Preble County. Collection of Preble County Historical Society, Eaton. Fig. 100. "Aged 19 years"

Gray, Rachel. 1825. Dayton, Montgomery County. Anonymous collector. "Dayton"

Greene, Sarah E. 1829. Newport, Washington County. Collection of Ohio Historical Society, Campus Martius Museum, Marietta. "Newport"

Gregg, Amanda. 1821. Springboro, Warren County. Collection of Warren County Historical Society, Lebanon. Fig. 50.

Griffeth, Eleanor Maria. C. 1833. Mesopotamia, Trumbull County. Collection of Mr. and Mrs. William Puckstein. "Born Feb. 21, 1820 Aged 13 years Mesopotamia—Trumbull County, Ohio"

Hagerty, Sarah Ann. 1849. Zanesville, Muskingum County. Anonymous collector. "Age 9 Mrs. Gates School Zanesville"

Hamm, Glorvenia Elisabeth. 1839. Manchester, Stark County. Collection of Susan Paolano McKiernan. Fig. 207. "Manchester Stark County Ohio"

Harris, Martha. 1832. Clarksville, Clinton County. Collection of Ohio Historical Society, Glendower Museum, Lebanon. "Aged 11 years Clarksville Clinton County Ohio"

Hartley, Margarette. 1833. Circleville, Pickaway County. Collection of Pickaway County Historical Society, Clarke-May Museum, Circleville.

Harvey, Lydia. 1847. Wayne Township, Warren County. Collection of Warren County Historical Society, Lebanon.

Hatch, Lucinda A. 1839. Granger, Medina County. Collection of Ross Trump. Fig. 213. "Granger—Medina, Ohio Age 16"

Hatfield, Charlotte. 1833. Montgomery County. Anonymous collector.

Hatfield, Cynthia Ann. 1833. Montgomery County. Anonymous collector.

Heagen, Henrietta. 1834. Dayton, Montgomery County. Collection of Tim and Barbara Martien. "Dayton—Ohio"

Henry, Martha [Patty]. June 18, 1829. Bern Township, Athens County. Collection of Martha Appel Burton. Fig. 119. "was born July 7th 1819" "Bern Athen Ohio June 18th 1829"

Hitt, Rebecca. Undated. Champaign County. Collection of Nancy Gardner Goff. Fig. 135.

Holliday, Lavina Caroline. C. 1829. Eaton, Preble County. Collection of Preble County Historical Society, Eaton. "was born 15 February 1820"

Holloway, Margaret. 1807. Waynesville, Warren County. See Ethel Stanwood Bolton and Eva Johnston Coe, *American Samplers.* "Waynesville School"

Holmes, Martha Anne. 1832. Cincinnati, Hamilton County. Collection of Cincinnati Art Museum. "Cincinnati"

Homan, Mary Martha. 1833. Preble County. Collection of Brookville Historical Society, Brookville, Ohio.

Hoover, Esther. 1838. Harrisburg, Stark County. Collection of Marion Ackerman. "Harrisburg Stark County Ohio"

Horn, Susanna. 1819. Cincinnati, Hamilton County. Collection of Cincinnati Museum Center. Fig. 17. "Cincinnati"

Houston, Eliza Jane. 1828. Dayton, Montgomery County. Collection of William and Joyce Subjack. "aged 7 years Dayton Ohio"

Howe, Elvira. 1818. Barlow, Washington County. Collection of Delores and Lowell Klaber. Fig. 6. "Aged 12 Barlow, Washington County" "State of Ohio"

Howe, Lucy. 1812. Barlow, Washington County. Collection of Jane and George Harold. "Aged 12"

Howe, Lucy. 1819. Barlow, Washington County. Collection of Linda Gardner Gant. "Aged 17 years Feb. 16, 1819" "Barlow, Washington County, Ohio"

Howell, Huldah. 1820. Champaign County. Collection of Donald and Patricia Clegg. "Champaign County Ohio"

Hunter, Ann. 1834. Urbana, Champaign County. Collection of Melvin and Connie Porcher. Fig. 136. "Aged 14, Nov. 1834 Ohio taught by Miss LeSeur"

Hupman, Sarah M. 1846. Mad River Township, Clark County. Collection of Jane and George Harold. Fig. 126. "Worked in the 18th year of her age" "Center Schoolhouse Mad River Township, Clark County, Ohio"

Hussey, M. [Mary Ann]. 1807. Waynesville, Warren County. Collection of Mr. and Mrs. Richard Johnson. Fig. 35. "Waynesville School"

Huston, Jennet. 1819. Mt. Healthy, Hamilton County. Collection of Mt. Healthy Historical Society. "was born Feb. 11. 1802" "completed this work in 1819 Aged 17"

Inglish, Mary. 1824. Chillicothe, Ross County. Collection of Ross County Historical Society, Chillicothe.

Irwin, Nancy. 1834. Lemon Township, Butler County. Collection of Warren County Historical Society, Lebanon. Fig. 85.

Jackson, Eupellia G. 1820. Geauga County. Collection of Bedford Historical Society, Bedford, Ohio. "was born on 24 July in the year 1810"

Jackson, Jane White. 1834. Xenia, Greene County. Collection of Shari L. Knight. Fig. 104. "Xenia"

Jenkinson, Elizabeth. 1824. Butler County. Collection of Tim and Barbara Martien. Fig. 95. "worked in the 12 year of her age"

Johns, Rhoda E. [Emily]. C. 1834. Waynesville School (Indiana boarding student). Collection of Monroe County Historical Society Museum, Bloomington, Indiana. Fig. 36. "R.E. Johns was born Sept. 6, 1824"

Johnson, Eliza R. 1840. Perrysburg, Wood County. Collection of Melvin and Connie Porcher. Fig. 220. "Fort Meigs Perrysburg Ohio"

Judkin, Martha. 1828. Steubenville, Jefferson County. Collection of Nancy Gardner Goff. "Steubenville"

Kain, Eliza Luin. 1821. Clermont County. Collection of the Pioneer and Historical Society of Muskingum County, Zanesville. Fig. 115.

Keely, Elizabeth. C. 1844. Butler County. Collection of Larry and Sarah Mosteller. Fig. 97. "in memory of W. H. Keely"

Keely, Mary J. 1827. Butler County. Collection of Larry and Sarah Mosteller. "born August 29, 1811—Aged 16"

Keister, Elizabeth. 1826. Wayne County. Collection of Dr. Jeffrey and Sharon Lipton. Fig. 200. "the 50th year of American Independence"

Kellogg, Clarissa. Undated. Monroe Township, Ashtabula County. Collection of Ashtabula County Historical Society.

Kelly, Mary. 1807. Warren County. Collection of Michael McAfee. Fig. 34. "Waynesville School"

Kemper, Isabella. 1830. Cincinnati, Hamilton County. Collection of The National Society of Colonial Dames of America in the State of Ohio, Cincinnati. Fig. 12.

Kerns, Lydia Trimble. 1843. Chillicothe, Ross County. Anonymous collector. Fig. 112. "Aged 9 yrs, 7 months, 3 days" "Ross County, Ohio"

Kiler, Ann. 1831. Montgomery County. Collection of Mrs. John O. Perka.

Kiler, Rebeccah. 1831. Montgomery County. Collection of Mrs. John O. Perka. "born 15 January 1820"

Kinney, Elizabeth. 1835. Portsmouth, Scioto County. Collection of Scioto County Historical Society, Portsmouth. Fig. 108.

Kirtbride, Mary Ann. 1840. Woodsfield, Monroe County. Collection of Ross Trump. Fig. 166. "Woodsfield, Monroe County—Ohio"

Kirtland, Emma O. Otillia. 1848. Plymouth, Richland County. Collection of Firelands Historical Society, Norwalk. "aged 9 years—Plymouth, Ohio"

Kirtland, Lucretia. 1808. Poland, Mahoning County. Anonymous collector. Fig. 203. "Poland—aged 10"

Kirtland, Mary Beach. 1806. Poland, Mahoning County. Collection of Mahoning Valley Historical Society, Youngstown. Fig. 202. "Aged 8"

Ladd, Ann Maria. Jan. 14, 1829. Franklin, Warren County. Collection of Doris and Kyle Fuller. Fig. 45. "in the 13th year of her age—Franklin, Ohio"

Lamb, Sarah S. 1849. Delaware, Delaware County. Collection of Rebecca Slisher and Charles Marlett. Fig. 145. "Delaware, Ohio"

Larwill, Ann Eliza. 1837. Wooster, Wayne County. Collection of Paul and Anne Locher. Fig. 199. "8th year of her age—Dec, 20th" "Wooster, Ohio"

Larwill, Martha. C. 1837. Wooster, Wayne County. Collection of Wayne County Historical Society, Wooster.

Layton, Hester. 1825. Clark County. Collection of Jan Panning. "was born August 26, 1809"

Lindsly, Martha G. C. 1830. Montgomery County. Collection of Evangeline Lindsley. "was born the 25th day of April, 1819" "Montgomery County—Ohio"

Lockwood, Priscilla. 1840. Franklin, Warren County. Collection of Mrs. Carl (Jenny) Withers. "Aged 7—Fraklin Ohio"

Looker, Harriet G. 1834. Cincinnati, Hamilton County. Collection of Allan and Linda Cobourn. Fig. 15. "St. Peter's Female Academy" "Cincinnati, Ohio"

Love, Sarah F. 1823. Rushville, Fairfield County. Collection of Sharon Kohler. "Rushville—Ohio Aged 14"

Malin, Elizabeth M. 1826. Steubenville, Jefferson County. Collection of Nadine Maitland. "born Dec. 24th, 1805 Steubenville"

Mason, Betsey. 1805. Marietta, Washington County. Author's collection. Fig. 5.

Mast, Mary. 1850. Holmes County. Collection of the German Culture Museum, Walnut Creek.

Matthews, Mary. 1846. Warren County. Collection of Ohio Historical Society, Glendower Museum, Lebanon.

McClellan, Martha. 1831. Lemon Township, Butler County. Anonymous collector. Fig. 89. "Eleven"

McCracken, Anna Mary. 1840. Centerville, Montgomery County. Collection of Centerville-Washington Township Historical Society, Centerville. Fig. 66. "Centreville Ohio"

McElvain, Eliza. 1826. Columbus, Franklin County. Collection of Donald B. Jenkins. Fig. 140. "Amy Rosalla Adams, Preceptress Columbus—Ohio"

McElvain, Mary. 1832. Columbus, Franklin County. Collection of David Goss. Fig. 139. "Miss Benfield—Preceptress" "Columbus—Ohio"

McGuire, Mary. C. 1838. Cincinnati, Hamilton County. Anonymous collector. Fig. 19. "Nazareth Academy" (Kentucky)

McIntire, Amelia. C. 1812. Zanesville, Muskingum County. Collection of Pioneer and Historical Society of Muskingum County, Zanesville. Fig. 159.

McKeag, Sarah. 1830. Cincinnati, Hamilton County. Collection of Larry and Sarah Mosteller. Fig. 13. "Cincinnati, Ohio"

McMeachan, Margaret. 1819. Hamilton, Butler County. Collection of Preble County Historical Society, Eaton. Fig. 83. "at age 13 years—Hamilton"

Megie, Catherine. 1832. Lemon Township, Butler County. Collection of Mrs. Thomas J. Hancock. Fig. 93.

Melvin, Eliza Jane. 1834. Circleville, Pickaway County. Collection of Kathryn Sandel. Fig. 137. "Circleville—Ohio"

Mendenhall, Abigail. 1817. Columbiana County. Collection of Melvin and Connie Porcher. Fig. 189.

Mendenhall, Elizabeth. 1832. Clinton County. Collection of Randolph County Historical Society, Winchester, Indiana. Fig. 70. "Clinton County, Ohio"

Merrit, Garthary. 1840. Miami County. Collection of Piqua Historical Society, Piqua.

Miller, Agnes Maria. 1833. Madisonville, Hamilton County. Anonymous collector. "Madisonville, Hamilton County—Ohio"

Mills, Pamela Elvira. C. 1829. Portage County. Collection of the International Society of Daughters of Utah Pioneers, Salt Lake City, Utah. Fig. 209.

Miner, Elvira C. 1853. Lithopolis, Fairfield County. Collection of Nancy Conlon. Fig. 154. "Lithopolis—Ohio"

Moleux, Miss C. [Celia]. 1850. Brown County. Collection of William and Joyce Subjack. "Ursuline Academy—Brown County—Ohio"

Moore, Mary Ann. 1833. Clinton County. Collection of Susan Hazard Douglass and Rebecca Hazard Rauch. Fig. 74. "Letitia M. Heston" (teacher)

Moore, Mary Ann. 1835. Clinton County. Collection of Susan Hazard Douglass and Rebecca Hazard Rauch. Fig. 73.

Moore, Mary F. 1847. Union Township, Butler County. Collection of Mrs. Laverne Rumer. Fig. 49. "Union Township—Butler County—Ohio"

Morgan, Celestia. C. 1840. Lorain County. Collection of Ted and Virginia T. Seifert. Fig. 214.

Morlan, Lydia. 1824. Middleton Township, Columbiana County. Collection of Allan and Linda Cobourn. "Middleton Township—Columbiana County" "State of Ohio—Aged 15 years"

Morrison, Rebecca A. 1837. Deerfield Township, Warren County. Anonymous collector. Fig. 47. "Deerfield Township—Warren County" "State of Ohio"

Mulford, Martha. 1824. Clark County. Collection of Mary Jaene Edmonds. "was born June First. 1796 Ohio"

Munson, Mary. 1827. Granville, Licking County. Collection of Audrey and Orville Orr. Fig. 151. "Granville Miss Howe—Ins."

Naftel, Sophia Ann. 1845. Columbus, Franklin County. Collection of Marilyn Gale. Fig. 141. "Deaf & Dumb Institution" "Columbus—Ohio"

Oliver, Caroline. 1824. Collection of Licking County Historical Society. Fig. 148.

Owens, Sarah. 1839. Newark, Licking County. Author's collection. Fig. 149. "in her 9th year—Newark—Ohio"

Page, Matilda. 1831. Jefferson, Ashtabula or Wayne County. Collection of Mary R. Yarton. "Jefferson, Ohio"

Patterson, Elcey. 1845. Warren County. Collection of Larry and Sarah Mosteller. Fig. 31. "Born in Lemon Tws, Butler County" "State of Ohio—April 17, 1803"

Patterson, Mary Ann. C. 1820. Miami County. Collection of Jane R. Bourne. "Wrot in the 11 year of her age"

Patton, Elizabeth. C. 1828. Lemon Township, Butler County. Collection of the Overfield Tavern Museum, Troy. Fig. 91.

Perkins, Anna Maria. C. 1822 (mourning embroidery). Warren, Trumbull County. Collection of Western Reserve Historical Society, Cleveland. Fig. 178.

Pinkerton, Lydia Ann. C. 1846–47. McConnellsville, Morgan County. Collection of Robert Andrews. "L.A.P."

Pollard, Sally D. 1839. Neville, Clermont County. Anonymous collector. "Neville, Ohio"

Pownall, Sarah Jane. 1854. Manchester, Adams County. Collection of Doris A. Lucas. Fig. 223. "West Manchester—Ohio"

Pratt, Sarah M. 1842. Marietta, Washington County. Collection of Ohio Historical Society, Campus Martius Museum, Marietta. Fig. 10. "aged 11 years"

Pugh, Leah. 1811. Waynesville, Warren County. Collection of Ohio Historical Society, Glendower Museum, Lebanon. "Waynesville School"

Pyle, Sarah. C. 1837. Warren County. Collection of Margaret Cowden.

Ramsey, Martha Agnes. 1849. Preble County. Anonymous collector. Fig. 98. "Hopewell Church"

Rand, A. J. 1846. Vienna, Trumbull County. Collection of Shari L. Knight. "Vienna—Trumbull County—Ohio"

Rankin, Julia D. [Doak]. 1837. Ripley, Brown County. Collection of Ohio Historical Society, Rankin House State Memorial, Ripley. Fig. 105. "Ripley—Ohio"

Reckard, Eliza Ann. 1823. Marietta, Washington County. Collection of Mrs. Ardis Postle. Fig. 8.

Reynolds, Eliza Ann. 1834. Mesopotamia, Trumbull County. Collection of Richard Raymond, great-grandson of stitcher. "wrought in the 14th year of her age" "Mesopotamia—Trumbull County—Ohio" "Instructress Emellene Ella Murray—aged 19 yrs."

Reynolds, Martha Jane. 1839. Homer, Union County. Collection of Nancy Wagner. Fig. 146. "aged 9 years" "Miss Laura Smith, Teacher Homer Ohio"

Rice, Eunice. Undated (cross-stitch rug). Athens County. Collection of Jane Collins. Fig. 120.

Ridgely, Phebe Ann. 1835. Zanesville, Muskingum County. Collection of Allan and Linda Cobourn. "Zanesville, Ohio"

Robenson, Hannah Susannah. C. 1840. Butler County. Collection of Melvin and Connie Porcher. Fig. 96. "born September 11, 1826"

Rothacker, Isabell. 1844. Carrollton, Carroll County. Collection of Western Reserve Historical Society, Cleveland. "Carrollton"

Ruckel, Sarah Ann. 1849. Medina County. Collection of Catherine Cauffield Nasca.

Russell, Abigail. C. 1820. North Union Shaker Village, Cuyahoga County. Collection of the Western Reserve Historical Society, Cleveland. "was born May 17, 1813—Warrensville"

Russell, Amanda. 1829. See Ethel Stanwood Bolton and Eva Johnston Coe, *American Samplers.* "Ohio"

Sackett, Cynthia M. C. 1832. Summit County. Collection of Susan Blashford. Fig. 210. "aged 7 years"

Sarchet, Metilda Ellen. 1833. Guernsey County. Collection of Susan McFarland. Fig. 165. "aged 10 years"

Satterthwaite, Eliza. 1830. Waynesville, Warren County. Anonymous collector. Fig. 39. "Waynesville"

Satterthwaite, Eliza. 1830. Waynesville, Warren County. Anonymous collector. Fig. 40. "Waynesville"

Sawyer (Swayer), Margaret. 1844. North Union Shaker Community, Cuyahoga County. Collection of Dr. John R. Ribic. "was born April 29, 1817—come here May 13, 1831"

Sayler, Margaret. 1841. Pickaway County. Collection of Bill and Jan Rink. Fig. 138.

Scank, Elizabeth Ann. 1846. Mt. Healthy, Hamilton County. Collection of Marilyn Jinks. Fig. 21. "Aged 15 years"

Schenck, Anna Cumming. 1821. Franklin, Warren County. Collection of Franklin Area Historical Society, the Harding Museum, Franklin. Fig. 43. "C.V.B. Schenck's School—Franklin, Ohio"

Scudder, Hannah. 1836. Piqua, Miami County. Author's collection. Fig. 129. "Aged 11"

Selby, Elizabeth. 1835. Butler County. Anonymous collector. "W.L.B.C. Age 16" "Inst'ss Gratla Webber"

Sellers, Martha. 1838. Warren County. Collection of Warren County Historical Society Museum, Lebanon.

Seymour, Caroline Louisa. 1838. Newark, Licking County. Collection of Licking County Historical Society, Webb House Museum, Newark. Fig. 147. "Newark—Ohio"

Sheldon, Emily. 1829. Mantua, Portage County. Collection of Robert and Charlotte Menker. Fig. 208. "Aged 8 years" "—Mantua, Portage County—Ohio" "Flavia Spencer, Instructress"

Sherwood, A. [Abigail]. 1838. Warren County. Collection of James and Helen Miller. Fig. 37.

Short, Mary Jane. 1846. Ashland County. Author's collection. Fig. 217. "Age 14 years Ashland County, Ohio"

Sintz, Susan. 1820. Springfield, Clark County. Collection of the Daughters of the American Revolution Pennsylvania House Museum, Springfield.

Skinner, Catharine Sophia. 1832. Lebanon, Warren County. Anonymous collector. Fig. 28. "Aged 11 years—completed at the Female Seminary—Lebanon, Ohio"

Smith, Elizabeth. 1830. Franklin, Warren County. Collection of Warren County Historical Society, Lebanon. "Franklin Warren County Ohio"

Spear, Betsey. 1826. Kinsman, Trumbull County. Anonymous collector. "Aged 12 years—Kinsman—September 1826"

Spencer, Ann. 1828. Steubenville, Jefferson County. Collection of Kathy Sandel. "Steubenville"

Spicer, Martha Elizabeth. 1851. Muskingum County. Collection of Ann St. Clair. Fig. 222. "Muskingum County, Ohio"

Staley, Sarah. 1839. Bethel Township, Miami County. Collection of Carol M. Mumford. Fig. 133. "born March the 20th, 1827"

Steinman, Minerva. 1834. Fairfield County. Collection of Melvin and Connie Porcher. Fig. 152. "done the 11th year of her age"

Stewart, Elizabeth. 1839. Franklin, Warren County. Collection of Dr. and Mrs. Kenneth Smith. "Franklin—Ohio"

Stites, Mary F. 1831. Hamilton County. Anonymous collector.

Stokes, Elizabeth Ann. 1828. Warren County. Collection of the Ohio Historical Society, Glendower Museum, Lebanon.

Stone, Melissa Barker. 1830. Belpre, Washington County. Collection of Larry and Sarah Mosteller. Fig. 3. "Belpre—Washington County—Ohio"

Stow, Elvira Julia. 1829. Braceville, Trumbull County. Collection of Nancy Gardner Goff. Fig. 180. "Aged 8 Aug. 18. 1829" "Braceville—Trumbull County—Ohio"

Swain, Eliza P. C. 1829. Dayton, Montgomery County. Author's collection. Fig. 54. "Aged eight years Dayton Ohio"

Taylor, Adaline. 1842. Germantown, Montgomery County. Author's collection. Fig. 61. "Aged 11 years Germantown Ohio"

Taylor, Elizabeth. 1807. Clinton County. Collection of Delores and Lowell Klaber. Fig. 80.

Taylor, Elizabeth. 1807 (second sampler). Clinton County. Collection of Delores and Lowell Klaber. Fig. 81.

Taylor, Elizabeth. 1810. Clinton County. Collection of Delores and Lowell Klaber.

Telford, Martha M. 1827. Troy, Miami County. Collection of Scherre Mumpower. Fig. 128. "wrought in the 16 year of her age" "Lucinda M. Neal's School—Troy, Miami County—Ohio"

Terwilleger, Sarah Lackey. 1839. Montgomery, Hamilton County. Collection of Robert Elliott McGowan. Fig. 25. "the 16th year of age"

Thatcher, Deborah. 1837. Clinton County. Collection of Janet E. Hiatt, great-granddaughter of stitcher. Fig. 77.

Thomas, Esther Ann. 1831. Springboro, Warren County. "aged 9 years."

Thomas, Hannah. 1832. Springboro, Warren County. Collection of Glee Krueger. Fig. 52. "Springborough"

Tidball, Margaret B. 1832. Millersburg, Holmes County. Collection of Patricia McClelland Miller, great-granddaughter of stitcher. Fig. 157. "Millersburg, Ohio"

Trimble, Charity. 1807. Chillicothe, Ross County. Collection of Emilie B. Savage. Fig. 111. "was born in 1789—This done in the 18 year of her age"

Tuley, Mary J. 1824. Troy, Miami County. Collection of Overfield Tavern Museum, Troy. Fig. 130. "Work wrought in the 10 year of age"

Turpin, Caroline M. [Matilda]. 1820. Newton, Hamilton County. Collection of Greater Milford Historical Society, Promont House Museum, Milford. "Newton"

Vail, Margaret. 1836. McConnellsville, Morgan County. Collection of Mrs. Thomas J. Hancock. Fig. 116.

Vail, Prudence. 1818. Franklin, Warren County. Anonymous collector. "C.V.B. Schenck's School—Franklin—Ohio"

Van Horne, Catharine Sophia. 1825. Piqua, Miami County. Collection of Dayton Art Institute. Gift of the estate of Elmer R. Webster and Robert A. Titsch. Fig. 26. "Piqua—Ohio Aged eight years"

Vanlaw, Louisa Martha. 1834. Belmont County. Collection of William and Joyce Subjack. Fig. 167.

Veyssie, Cecelia. 1849. Gallipolis, Gallia County. Collection of Melvin and Connie Porcher. Fig. 118. "Gallipolis—Gallia County—Ohio"

Viers, Caroline. C. 1831 (family record sampler). Belmont County. Collection of Nancy Wagner. Fig. 168.

Vogleson, Enora D. 1862. Columbiana County. Collection of the Historical Society of Columbiana, Fairfield Township, Columbiana. "aged 15 years Columbiana"

Voorheis, Sarah. 1830. Warren County. Collection of Ohio Historical Society, Glendower Museum, Lebanon.

Votaw, Rachel. 1827. Columbiana County. Collection of Jane and George Harold. Fig. 185.

Warren, Elizabeth. 1833. Madisonville, Hamilton County. Collection of William and Linda Gottschalk. "Madisonville, Hamilton County—Ohio"

Warwick, Rhoda Jane. 1850. Warren County. Collection of Mr. and Mrs. Robert Jeffery. Fig. 221.

Wead, Mary Jane. 1827. Beavercreek, Greene County. Collection of Montgomery County Historical Society, Dayton.

Wetmore, Abigail. Undated. Ashtabula County. Collection of Western Reserve Historical Society, Cleveland.

Wetmore, Hannah. 1831. Monroe Township, Kelloggsville, Ashtabula County. Collection of Western Reserve Historical Society, Cleveland. Fig. 198. "wrought in the 13 year of her age—Monroe" (township)

Wetmore, Harriet. 1827. Canfield, Trumbull County. Anonymous Collector. "Canfield" "Ohio"

Wetmore, Margaret. 1823. Monroe Township, Kelloggsville, Ashtabula County. Collection of Western Reserve Historical Society, Cleveland. "Monroe" (township)

Wheeler, S. E. 1840. Cincinnati, Hamilton County. Collection of William and Joyce Subjack. Fig. 24. "Medical College of Ohio"

Whinery, Esther. 1838. Clinton County. Collection of the Cleveland Museum of Art. Fig. 69. "E.B.M.—Clinton County, Ohio"

Wick, Betsey. 1814. Youngstown, Trumbull County (now Mahoning County). Collection of Mahoning Valley Historical Society, The Arms Museum, Youngstown. Fig. 205.

Wilgus, Angelina. 1823. Warren County. Collection of Stephen and Carol Huber.

Wilgus, Angelina. 1829. Warren County. Collection of Tim and Barbara Martien.

Williams, Martha. 1816 (mourning embroidery). Cincinnati, Hamilton County. Collection of Cincinnati Art Museum. Gift of Julia Sayre. Fig. 14. "Cincinnati"

Williams, Mary C. 1819. Dayton, Montgomery County. Collection of Ralph Pokluda. "Dayton—Ohio"

Williams, Rhoda Ann. 1829. Olive Township, Meigs County. Collection of Susan Anderson Withnell. "Olive Township—Meigs County" "State of Ohio—in the 14th year of life"

Wilson, Eleanor I. [Isabella]. 1829. Xenia, Greene County. Collection of Dr. John R. Ribic. Fig. 103. "Aged 8 years Xenia"

Wilson, Jennet. 1829. Guernsey County. Collection of Glenn E. Warren, great-grandson of stitcher. Fig. 164. "in the 12th year of her age"

Winner, Hannah. 1821. Franklin, Warren County. Collection of Warren County Historical Society, Lebanon. "C.V.B. Schenck's School Franklin—Ohio"

Winton, Eliza. 1819. Florence Township, Erie County. Collection of Mrs. Edith Anderson. "Florence"

Wise, Maria. 1837. Pike Township, Clark County. Collection of Emma Anderson. Fig. 123. "Pike Township—Clark County"

Woodbridge, Louesa Maria. 1831. Youngstown, Mahoning County. Collection of Mahoning Valley Historical Society, The Arms Museum, Youngstown. Fig. 206. "Youngstown"

Workman, Nancy. 1831. Jefferson County. Collection of Eleanor McMinn. Fig. 175. "born Aug. 9, 1819"

Wright, Mary Ann. 1823. Lebanon, Warren County. Collection of Metro Parks District of Toledo, Wildwood Manor House, Toledo. Fig. 27. "Lebanon W.C. Ohio Aged 11 years"

Yeazel, Sarah Ann. 1848. Clark County. Collection of Sarah Beard Love.

Zimmerman, Esther. 1832. Greenville, Darke County. Collection of Judee and Philip Harbaugh. Fig. 127. "Greenville—Ohio"

ohio pioneer teachers and schools

Hours of painstaking research went into this chart, but it is by no means a complete listing. It includes almost five hundred names of pioneer teachers and schools that were active in Ohio during the formative first half-century of settlement and statehood. Schools that are believed to have been for male students only were omitted.

Samplers did not always remain in the area where they were made. People migrated all over America, and samplers moved with them, a reminder of family ties and history. When one appears at an auction or is discovered packed away in an old trunk, this chart may help identify its Ohio origin, who stitched it, and who taught the girl to sew.

The sources used for this study are too numerous to mention or footnote. There were three main sources, the first two primary: First, any information stitched on a sampler canvas was taken to verify that that teacher or school existed, though further research was often necessary to determine the location. A second reliable source was early newspaper advertisements and notices of school activities. Many advertisements mention "the ornamental branches," and needlework may have been one of these "branches," even when it is not specifically mentioned.

The third major source of information for this chart was early history books and other written materials. Articles published through the years by the Ohio Archaeological and Historical Society have been especially helpful. The most valuable book for the northern part of Ohio was *Memorial to the Pioneer Women of the Western Reserve,* a four-volume set printed in 1896 on the occasion of the state's Centennial Celebration marking one hundred years of settlement. The book covers the years 1800 to 1850. An asterisk (*) in a chart listing indicates that the information is from this early book. The book was written under the auspices of the Woman's Department of the Cleveland Centennial Commission. Dozens of ladies from all over the Western Reserve helped with the project and became instant historians and writers. They often included facts about the families that are helpful to genealogists, and these bits of information are included in the chart. Genealogical information has not been verified by the author.

By Name

Teacher / School	*Location*	*Date*	*Additional Information and Associated Samplers*
Abbott, Miss M. A.	Shelby Co., Sidney	1843	*See* Sidney Male & Female Academy.
Adams, Miss Marion Ann	Lorain Co.	c. 1840–45	Came to Ohio from Mass. in 1823, taught at private school in Wellington until marr. to Rev. Charles Conklin.*
Adams, Miss Nancy	Huron Co., Peru Twp.	1812–17	Taught at 1st school in Macksville, 1817.*
Adams, Miss Amy Rosalla, Preceptress	Franklin Co., Columbus	1826	Taught in female academy run by Miss Sarah Benfield and Miss Anna Treat. Related samp.: Eliza McElvain—1826. In 1828 she taught at Columbus Female Seminary. *See* Columbus Female Seminary.
Adamson, Miss H. A.	Warren Co., Lebanon	1824	Opened school in Lebanon. Ref: *Western Star,* 24 July 1827: "Instructed in the following branches: . . . Plain & Variegated Needle Work."
Andrews, Hannah (Mrs. John)	Trumbull Co., Kinsman	c. 1802	Came to Ohio in 1802. Matron of small boarding school. First white woman settler of New Conn. *See* Hiccox, Miss Irene.
Andrews, Misses	Lorain Co., Grafton	c. 1830s	Family of John P. and Philanda (Newton) Andrews came from N.Y. Several daughters were teachers.*
(Mrs.) Ashley's Seminary for Young Women	Scioto Co., Portsmouth	1827	Needlework mentioned in curriculum. *See* Evans, *History of Scioto Co.*
Bailey, Misses	Hamilton Co., Cincinnati	c. 1800	Oldest female boarding school in Cincinnati (located on Broadway) kept by Misses Bailey, asstd. by Mr. F. Ecksteen.
Bailey, Eliza A.	Ashtabula Co., Morgan	1830s	Taught school 14 years.*
Baldwin, Harriet	Summit Co., Hudson	c. 1820	Daughter of Henry and Annie Mary (Hudson) Baldwin, she and her mother did exquisite needlework. Harriet taught little girls needlework before her death at 17.*

Teacher / School	Location	Date	Additional Information and Associated Samplers
Baldwin, Sylvia	Geauga Co., Montville	Early 1800s	First teacher in her township. Marr. I. N. Skinner. Her daughter taught also.*
Bankroft, Miss D. E.	Shelby Co., Sidney	1843	*See* Sidney Male & Female Academy.
Baptist, First Church School	Butler Co., Middletown, Lemon Twp.	1826–48	Converted church to school, operated until 1848.
Barker, Cynthia, Preceptress	Franklin Co., Worthington	c. 1810	From Montague, Mass. Taught at Worthington Academy Assoc. samplers: Minerva Bartholomew—1817; Hulda Bull—1819.
Barnesville Academy	Belmont Co., Barnesville	c. 1840	Co-ed, private boarding school operated until early 1860s.
Barney, Miss Mary	Miami Co., Troy	1838	Taught at select school for young ladies.
Barrett, Eliza	Ashtabula Co., Kingsville	1821	Taught at village school until 1821.*
Baron, Mr. and Mrs.; Lebanon Institute	Warren Co., Lebanon	1832	Ref: *Western Star,* 3 November 1832: "Taught girls of any age . . . will be taught plain needlework. $5.00."
Baskerville, Mary K.	Ross Co., Chillicothe	c. 1810	B. 9 June 1787 in Va. Came to Ohio in 1807 with father Col. Samuel Baskerville. Estab. school in a frame house on W. 2nd St. Taught needlework. and fine embroidery for many years. D. April 1856. Buried Grandview Cemetery, Ross Co.
Bateman, Jane	Warren Co., Springboro	c. 1850–52	Taught a select school with Caroline Smith (Quaker).
Beach Grove School (Academy)	Warren Co., Morrow	Bef. 1845	Soc. of Friends (Quaker). Robert Way, Director.
Beatty, Rev. Charles C. and Mrs. Hetty E. (Davis)	Jefferson Co., Steubenville	1828–29	*See* Steubenville Female Seminary / Academy.
Beck, Mrs. Mary (George)	Hamilton Co.	1829	Mary Beck taught in Baltimore 1795–98, then in Philadelphia 1798–1808, and in Lexington, Ky., bef. coming to Cincinnati.
Becker, Elizabeth	Wood Co.	c. 1835	Taught first school in Dist. 2.
Bedford, Harriet	Huron Co., Norwalk	1837	*See* Norwalk Female Seminary
Beecher, Misses Catherine and Harriet C.	Hamilton Co., Cincinnati	1832–33	Ref: *Western Star,* 17 February 1832, and *Ohio Argus,* 23 June 1832. Their school may never have opened in Lebanon, but they advertised for students there. Taught in Hartford (Conn.) Female Academy in 1827 before opening school in Cincinnati. *See Cincinnati Directory 1834.* Opened Western Female Institute (Seminary) at Sycamore and 4th Sts.
Beech Grove School	Hamilton Co., Cincinnati	Estab. 1837	*See* Mrs. Gooch.
Belmont School	Hamilton Co., Cincinnati	1826	A female seminary now used as the Taft Museum.
Benfield, Miss, Preceptress	Franklin Co., Columbus	1826	Miss Sarah Benfield and Miss Anna Treat opened a female academy in the Pike Bldg., W. Broad St. Amy Rosalla Adams also taught in 1826 Assoc. samplers: Mary McElvain—1832, Miss Benfield. Eliza McElvain—1826, Amy Rosalla Adams.
Bently, Miss Luette	Lake Co., Painesville	Bef. 1850	Graduate of Lake Erie Female Seminary, later became a teacher there.*
Bidwell, Miss Esther	Trumbull Co., Gustavus	c. 1813	Taught at first school.*
Birchard, Miss Mercy Anna	Trumbull Co., Braceville	1812	First teacher in Braceville.
(Miss) Blackwell's Boarding & Day School for Young Ladies	Hamilton Co., Cincinnati	1838	Ref: A flyer advertiser: "East Third Street, between Lawrence and Pike. . . . [P]lain and ornamental needlework. Twelve weeks to the quarter."
Blair, Misses	Lorain Co., Amherst	c. 1820–50	Daughters of Obadiah and Thompson Blair from Buffalo, N.Y. in 1818. All 7 were teachers. Daughter Sophronia Blair was 1st teacher in Amherst.*
Blakesly, Miss Eliza	Mahoning Co., Poland	1849	Taught in select school for young ladies. Later taught at Poland Academy.*
Bodley, Mrs. Rebecca W.	Hamilton Co., Cincinnati	c. 1836–37	Bodley, Mrs. Rebecca W., teacher, female school, Walnut and 12th Sts. *See Cincinnati Directory 1836–37.* Anon. sampler lists the school on the canvas.
Boll, Harry	Warren Co., Lebanon	c. 1843	Lebanon Female Seminary. *See Western Star,* 10 February 1843: "[T]o embrace as thorough and extensive course for education as any similar institution in the West. Boarding for pupils . . . with responsible families."
Booth, Miss Mary	Ashtabula Co., Conneaut	Bef. 1846	Taught in a fine classical academy with Mr. L. W. Savage, principal.
Bostwick, Miss	Trumbull Co., Warren Huron Co., Norwalk	c. 1816–17, 1826 c. 1830	Unclear if this is one teacher traveling from place to place or if there is more than one Miss Bostwick.*
Bostwick, Miss Getia	Mahoning Co., Canfield Twp.	c. 1806	Taught in unfinished room in house of Judson Canfield.
Bosworth, Mira	Cuyahoga Co., Strongsville	1843	Taught at 18 at a district school. B. 1825, d. 1859.*

Teacher/School	*Location*	*Date*	*Additional Information and Associated Samplers*
Boyden, Miss	Cuyahoga Co., Cleveland (West Side)	c. 1830	*See* Brooklyn Academy.
Branch, Mrs. Daniel	Geauga Co., Chester	1841	*See* Geauga Seminary (Chester Seminary).
Branch, Misses Eliza and Laura	Lorain Co., Russia Twp.	c. 1837	Sisters who graduated from Oberlin; taught in Russia Twp.*
Bronson, Prof.	Trumbull Co., Warren	c. 1844–45	Opened select school in basement of the old Methodist church on river bank. In 1844 tried to establish an Episcopal female seminary but failed.
Bronson, Miss Electa	Portage Co., Streetsboro and Summit Co., Hudson	1841	Taught school located over a store for 30 years.*
Bronson, Miss Salome	Summit Co., Hudson	1826–28	Taught 2 years before marr. to Fredrick Baldwin.*
Brooklyn Academy	Cuyahoga Co., Cleveland (west side)	c. 1826–30s	Teachers included: Mr. Merrill; Mrs. Asa Foote; Miss Caroline Buxton.*
Brown, Miss Alice	Ross Co., Frankfort	1847	Taught at an academy where she was in charge of the Primary Dept.
Browne, Misses Sarah and Mary Ann	Hamilton Co., Cincinnati	1804–5	Opened a "young ladies" school on Sycamore St. Ads in *Cincinnati Mercury* and *Liberty Hall:* "[W]here young ladies are taught sewing, Marking, and Embroidery. . . . Can accommodate a few boarders. Fine sewing work will be received."
Burnett, Perlyette	Geauga Co., Newbury	1840	Earned $1.50/week from public funds. School had 60 scholars.*
Burr, Mrs.	Warren Co., Franklin	c. 1831	Ref: *Western Star,* 23 April 1831: Franklin Female Seminary
Burton Academy	Geauga Co., Newbury	Estab. c. 1804	First schoolhouse burned, replaced in 1819. Sarah Russell from Middlefield, Mass. taught before 1825.*
Bushnell, Miss	Trumbull Co., Kinsman	1807	Taught with Eunice Allen and Lucy Andrews.*
Butler, Flora	Fairfield Co., Lancaster	c. 1812	Taught at the log schoolhouse on Main St.
Butternut Ridge School	Lorain Co., Eaton	1819	Teachers included: Julia Johnson; Mariah Terrel; Deborah Philips; Sarah and Mary Lawson.*
Buxton, Miss Caroline	Cuyahoga Co., Cleveland (west side)	c. 1830	Brooklyn Academy
Cambridge Female Academy	Guernsey Co.	Bef. 1850	
Canfield, Martha Miller	Geauga Co., Newbury	Early 1800s	In addition to teaching she earned $1.25 a week by spinning. Daughter Emma Miller also was a teacher.*
Canton Female Institute	Stark Co., Canton	1838	School had about 100 pupils. No information about curriculum.
Case, Melinda	Geauga Co., Huntsburg	Bef. 1850	Taught at private school.*
Cathcart, D.; Young Ladies Seminary	Hamilton Co., Cincinnati	1820	Ref: *Liberty Hall* and *Cincinnati Gazette,* 3 January 1820: Will admit females only; "he proposes to employ an assistant, well qualified to teach . . . Drawing, Painting, Embroidery &c."
Center Schoolhouse	Clark Co., Mad River Twp.	c. 1840s	Assoc. sampler: Sarah M. Hupman—1840—Family Record Sampler.
Chamberlain, Miss Mary	Geauga Co., Bainbridge Trumbull Co., Warren	c. 1830–40 c. 1844	Ref: *Western Reserve Chronicle,* 3 April 1844: School for Young Ladies and Misses; "a better location secured. . . . English Branches, from $2 to $4. French and Ornaments Branches, Extra."
Chapel, Betsy	Ashtabula Co., Colebrook Twp.	c. 1830	Began teaching at 15. Taught in each dist. of twp.*
Chappell, Julia	Ashtabula Co., Kingsville	c. 1836	Began teaching at 14. *See* Kingsville Academy.*
Chester Seminary	Geauga Co., Chesterland	Estab. 1842	Also known as Geauga Seminary.
Chillicothe Academy	Ross Co., Chillicothe	Estab. 1809	Located on W. Paint St. For children of all ages. Ref: *Scioto Gazette* 26 March 1809. By 1816 the head of the school was the pastor of the Presbyterian Reformed Church, Rev. John McFarland.
Chillicothe Female Seminary	Ross Co., Chillicothe	1832	Miss S. A. Stearns and Miss Smith opened a female school in rented quarters. Three years later, their academy had a building on 5th St. They were both former students of Mary Lyon (1797–1849), founder of Mount Holyoke Seminary and Ipswich Academy. Other teachers include: Miss Swift; Miss Fitch; Miss Nancy Tuck; Misses Clark; Miss Wheelock; Miss Phoebe Cook.
Cincinnati Female Academy	Hamilton Co., Cincinnati	1823	Opened by Dr. John Locke. Ref: *Cincinnati Directory 1836–37.* Needlework was included in the curriculum.
Cincinnati Female Institute	Hamilton Co., Cincinnati	1830s	Ref: *Cincinnati Directory 1836–37:* Messer Picket's Female Academy, SE corner of Vine and 5th Sts. Ref: "A CARD" "J. W. & A. PICKET announce . . . they have engaged an Instructress to superintend not only the manners and morals of *female pupils,* but also their instruction in the various *descriptions of needlework.*" John W. and Albert Picket first opened a school in NYC in the 1790s. In 1821 they opened a school in Baltimore.
Circleville Female Academy	Pickaway Co., Circleville	1835	

Teacher/School	Location	Date	Additional Information and Associated Samplers
Clapp, Miss Lucinda House	Medina Co., Chatham	Bef. 1850	Taught first school in the north part of town, in her own log house—73 scholars.*
Clark, Miss	Butler Co., Oxford	c. 1830s	Miss Clark and Miss Smith took over for Bethania Crocker at Oxford Female High School.
Clark, Mrs.	Lorain Co., Huntington	c. 1800	She first taught in Mass. Came to Ohio and taught in Hudson and Elyia.*
Clark, Mrs. Ansal R.	Summit Co., Hudson	1835	*See* Mr. Gross's school.*
Clarke, Laura Downs	Huron Co., Wakeman	c. 1810	The first school was taught in her home.*
Cleveland Academy	Cuyahoga Co., Cleveland	1822	*See* listings for the following teachers: Mary Dodge; Eliza McFarland; Louisa Snow; Miss Katie Welch; Miss Elijah Burton; Mrs. Thomas Crosly*; (Abigail Hollister); Miss Rebecca Sherman Pete.*
Cobb, Miss Mary W.	Warren Co., Lebanon	1830	Ref: *Western Star,* 14 May 1830 and 9 October 1830, "A Card." "This school taught in the brick house on Main Street. . . . Miss Cobb has taught almost five months (a misses school) and the undersigned says that there has no school been taught in Lebanon where more general satisfaction has been given etc.—Signed: A Subscriber to Miss Cobb's School."
Coe, Miss Sally	Summit Co., Tallmadge	c. 1810–16	B. Granville, Mass.; came to Charleston, Ohio, in 1810.
Colerick, Mrs. M.	Muskingum Co., Zanesville	1810	Ref: *Zanesville Express,* 28 October 1818: "Mrs. M. Colerick's Young Ladies' Seminary . . . on the SW corner of Market and Fourth Streets. The terms of tuition are as follows: Reading, Writing, Arithmetic, Grammar, Geography, Tambour and Emboidery, Cotton Work, Fringe, and Netting. Plain and Marking, $4.00 per quarter. . . . Mrs. M. Colerick."
Columbus Female Academy	Franklin Co., Columbus	1826	Estab. by Misses Sarah Benfield and Anna Treat. Located in Pike Bldg. on West Broad St. Amy Rosalla Adams also taught there for at least 2 years. Assoc. samplers: Eliza McElvain—1826, Mary McElvain—1832.
Columbus Female Seminary	Franklin Co., Columbus	1828	Estab. by Rev. Joseph Labaree. Located in the McCoy Bldg., NW corner of High and State Sts. Mr. Labaree was assisted by Emily Richardson, Miss Margaret Richardson, and Miss Amy Adams.
Columbus Female Seminary	Franklin Co., Columbus	1843–48	Estab. by Mr. and Mrs. E. Schenck, at Broad and High Sts.
Comstock, Misses Female Academy	Hamilton Co., Cincinnati	c. 1834–37	Ref: *Cincinnati Directory 1834, Cincinnati Directory 1836–37.* "Basement story Christ's Church, 4th St. between Sycamore and Broadway." *Cincinnati Directory 1834* lists the address on 6th St.
Conant, Miss Rebecca	Portage Co., Windham	Bef. 1820	Opened the first private school in Portage with Elizabeth Streator.*
Cone, Miss Mary	Muskingum Co., Zanesville	c. 1836–46	Miss Cone served as a Principal of The Putnam Female Seminary. In 1846 the school had about 100 students and 5 teachers. *See* Putnam Female Seminary.
(Newark) Congregational Church	Licking Co., Newark	c. 1835–40	Operated a select school for both male and female students in the church building. Mrs. John W. Seymour (Caroline Oliver) taught needlework there. Assoc. samplers: Caroline O. Seymour—1824; Caroline Louisa Seymour—1838; Sarah Owens—1839.
Cook, Miss Phoebe	Ross Co., Chillicothe	c. 1835	Taught a short time under Miss Stearns at the Chillicothe Female Seminary. Marr. Mr. McKell in 1836.
Cooper Female Institute (Seminary)	Montgomery Co., Dayton	Estab. 1844	Eliam E. Barney, school's first director. The Seminary was for older girls and may have taught academic courses only.
(Mrs. R. A.) Cooper's School	Montgomery Co., Dayton	1833	Assoc. samplers: Leah Jane Ashton—1833.
Cottage Hill Academy	Mahoning Co., Ellsworth	c. 1844	Ref: *Western Reserve Chronicle,* 20 March 1844: "The Ladies' department offers every facility for obtaining a thorough and useful education." Ellsworth, April 9, 1844.
Couch, Miss	Clark Co., Springfield	1841	Ref: *The Springfield Republic,* 17 December 1841: "Terms of tuition for twelve weeks: Reading, Spelling, Writing, . . . Improvement of the Mind—$3.00. Plain and Ornamental needle work."
Coulter, Mrs. Betsy (Rice)	Ashland Co., Perrysville	1815	Opened the first school in her home. Took spinning and weaving as part pay for tuition of students.
Cowgill, Matilda and Elizabeth	Highland Co., Hillsboro	1827	Ref: *Hillsboro Gazette,* 15 February 1827: "Matilda and Elizabeth Cowgill propose teaching and a Female School for Reading, Spelling, & writing—$4.00." "All kinds of Needle Work, Drawing & Painting—including the above—$5.00. They obligate themselves to give unremitting attention to the instruction of those who are placed under their care." In 1832–34, Elizabeth Cowgill is listed as teaching in Penn. at Westtown School.

Teacher / School	*Location*	*Date*	*Additional Information and Associated Samplers*
Cowles, Miss Betsey Mix	Ashtabula Co., Austinburg Scioto Co., Portsmouth Austinburg	c. 1830 c. 1838–41 c. 1841–42	Daughter of Rev. Giles H. and Sally (White) Cowles of Austinburg, she estab. an infant's school when still in her teens. After graduating from Oberlin College, she taught at Portsmouth Young Ladies Seminary for 3 years before returning to Austinburg. Taught at Grand River Institute and became first female principal of the Women's Dept. Betsey devoted her life to teaching and was an active leader for women's suffrage and the antislavery movement. D. 1876. *See* Grand River Institute; *see also* Cowles family story pp. 223–24.*
Cowles, Caroline Loomis	Summit Co., Twinsburg	1827	Taught the village school when she was 19 years old. She then marr. Justus T. Herrick.*
Crary, Stella	Lake Co., Kirtland	1811	Taught school near Painesville.*
Creel, Mrs. E.	Washington Co., Marietta	1850	Western Liberal Institute listed as teaching ornamental needlework, as well as instrumental music, drawing, and painting.
The Cress School	Montgomery Co., Butler Twp.	1807–08	The first subscription school in the upper Miami Valley.
Crocker, Bethania	Butler Co., Oxford	1830	*See* Oxford Female High School. Ref: *Western Star,* 2 March 1833: "Instruction will be given in Needlework in conjunction with any of the above branches, without any additional charge." School drew pupils from at least 3 states. Bethania marr. Rev. George Bishop.
Crocker, Miss Betsy	Cuyahoga Co., Dover	c. 1800	First teacher in a log school in District 2 on the lake shore. Her sister, Philena, assumed the job next.*
Crowell, Miss Martha R.	Shelby Co., Sidney	1843	*See* Sidney Male & Female Academy
Cummings, Miss M.	Scioto Co., Portsmouth	1838	Opened a school in the basement of the Methodist Church.
Curtiss, Miss	Geauga Co., Chester	1841	*See* Geauga Seminary*
Cushing, Misses	Ross Co., Chillicothe	c. 1831	Served as assist. under Miss Stearns at the Chillicothe Female Seminary. Taught the Primary Department.
Deaf and Dumb Institute	Franklin Co., Columbus	1829	Ref: *Western Star,* 17 October 1829: (this ad announced the school's beginning. Dr. Asa and Elizabeth Lord were superintendents. Assoc. sampler: Sophia Ann Naftel—1845.
(Miss) Deeds's School	Hamilton Co., Cincinnati	1820	Ref: *Western Spy,* 25 March 1820: "Informs the Ladies of Cincinnati that her school is open for the reception of females of all ages, where they will be instructed in the various branches of education, at $5.00 per quarter, French—$10.00, Drawing & Painting by Mr. Audubon."
Defiance Female Seminary	Defiance Co., Defiance	1850	This school later became Defiance College.
Delaware Girls Seminary	Delaware Co., Delaware	c. 1832	Two highly accomplished ladies from Ireland open a girls' seminary in the house of Col. Byxbe. Later assisted by Miss Meeker and Mrs. Sprague.
DeWolf, Miss Parnela	Lorain Co., Wellington	c. 1830–45	Came to Ohio from Mass. in 1820, unmarr. She taught school in Wellington and adjacent towns.
Dickenson, Sarah	Geauga Co., Huntsburg	Bef. 1850	Taught at a private school.*
(Mrs.) Dodge's Private School	Summit Co., Akron	1836	Ref: Ad in Akron newspaper, 20 May 1836: "Mrs. Susan E. Dodge announces a school in S. Akron where she will instruct a few young ladies. Also offered are classes in: Crayon, Mezzotinto, Pencil, Japanning, flower Painting, etc. Term 11 weeks." Needlework was not listed but may have been included at this private (subscription) school.
Dupuy, Miss	Scioto Co., Portsmouth	1829	Opened school at her mother's residence. "[T]aught ornamental needlework and painting on velvet."
Dutch Creek Schoolhouse	Clinton Co., Union Twp.	1813	Miss Catherine Saxton was a teacher there in 1813. (Quaker)
Dutton (Duton), Miss Mary	Hamilton Co., Cincinnati	1836	*See* Western Female Institute
Eaton, Amy	Trumbull Co., Weathersfield	Bef. 1850	Taught a select school in a two-story frame house she built with a schoolroom. Offered accomodations for boarders. Graduate of Granville Seminary.*
E. B. M.	Clinton Co., Wilmington	c. 1830s	Research cannot positively identify who "E. B. M." was, but it is probable that the initials stand for Elizabeth Mendenhall. *See* figure 70. Assoc. samplers: Eliza Satterthwaite—1830; Phoebe Doan—1834; Elizabeth Mendenhall—1832; Esther Whinery—1838; Rebecca Farquhar—1828; Deborah Thatcher—1837.
Edgerton, Miss Clarinda	Cuyahoga Co., Brecksville	1837	She came from Mass. and began to teach in 1837. In 1839 she marr. Isaac Oakes.*
Ellsworth, Miss E. B.	Summit Co., Hudson	1835	*See* Mr. Gross's School
Ely, Miss Elizabeth (Hall)	Ashtabula Co., Monroe	c. 1818–20	Came from Wilbraham, Mass. to Salem, then to Monroe Twp., where she taught the first school. "She was skilled in fine needlework and embroidery." Her 2 daughters were also teachers.*

Teacher / School	*Location*	*Date*	*Additional Information and Associated Samplers*
Espy, Mrs. John (Polly Dinwiddie), and daughters, Maggie and Elmira Jane	Crawford Co., Bucyrus	c. 1831–40	Mrs. Espy, with daughters Maggie and Elmira Jane, taught at the new brick schoolhouse built c. 1826. In 1840, Miss (Maggie) Espy was teaching in the new frame school that opened in Oct. 1840. Assoc. sampler: Elmira J. Espy—1831.
Estabrook, Miss	Trumbull Co., Warren	c. 1830	Taught a select school for young ladies assisted by Miss Dickinson.
Farmington Academy	Trumbull Co., Farmington	Bef. 1840	Founded by Rev. Daniel Miller (first teacher there). His daughter was Adeline Miller, also a Farmington teacher.*
Felicity Female Seminary	unknown	1848	Ref: Kathryn Kish Sklar, *History of Education in the Old NW, 1787–1880* (Ohio Univ. Press, 1987), p. 66.
Female Academy	Pickaway Co.	c. 1843	Ref: *Gazeteer,* 1843: records Pickaway Co. as having "1 academy, 15 students, 54 sch., 1,522 scholars."
(Delaware) Female Seminary	Delaware Co., Delaware	1820	
(Lebanon) Female Seminary; Mrs. Williams	Warren Co., Lebanon	1830	Ref: *Western Star,* 21 October 1833, 24 September 1831, 7 January 1832, 12 February 1831, 13 August 1830: "*Female Seminary*"— . . . Second Class: Reading, Writing, Arithmetic, Geography, History . . . Plain and Ornamental Work —$4.00. Young Ladies (not daily pupils) desirous to learn Ornamental Work, Marking, also Lace and Worsted Works, can attend on Wednesday when they will receive instruction in those branches. $1.25 per quarter. Assoc. sampler: Catherine Sophia Skinner—1832.
(Norwalk) Female Seminary	Huron Co., Norwalk	1837	Miss Harriet Bedford founded the Female Seminary in Dec. 1837. Teachers: Mary F. C. Wales; Louisa Snow.
Fisher, Miss Ellen	Lake Co., Painesville	Bef. 1850	For many years, a highly valued teacher for the Painesville Seminary.
Forman, Mrs. Catharine	Warren Co., Lebanon	1822–23	Ref: *Western Star,* 9 April 1822: "A CARD—Mrs. Catherine Forman announces . . . that her school will commence on Monday the 15th, in a convenient room of Mr. Samuel Nixon, on Broadway. . . . The terms of tuition for the present quarter: . . . For reading, writing, and arithmetic, $1.50 per scholar, for sewing and needle work $2.00."
Foster, Miss Lucy	Summit Co., Tallmadge	c. 1810	B. Hanover, N.H. in 1790. She taught at the first school in Tallmadge. Marr. Alpha Wright in 1811.*
Foster, Mrs. Sarah (Mrs. Zadoc)	Athens Co., Athens	c. 1815–49	Came with her husband in 1796 from Conn. First settled in Belpre, Wash. Co.; in Athens by 1809. Began to teach after she was widowed in 1814; taught until her death in 1849. Assoc. with her were Sallie Jewett and Miss Haft.
Frankenstein, Godfrey, Elizabeth and Marie.	Clark Co., Springfield	c. 1840s	Siblings who taught in the Springfield Female Academy
The Franklin Academy	Warren Co., Franklin	c. 1840s	E. P. Cole was the principal. This was a co-ed school located on 2nd and High Sts.
Franklin English and Classical School	Warren Co., Franklin	1835	Taught by Rev. and Mrs. Thomas E. Thomas, who formerly ran a school at Paddy's Run in Butler Co. in the 1820s.
Franklin Female High School	Warren Co., Franklin	1834	Ref: *Western Star,* 11 April 1834.
Franklin Female Seminary	Warren Co., Franklin	c. 1831	Ref: *Western Star,* 15 April 1831. The school was run by Presbyterian minister Rev. John Hudson.
Franklin Select Academy	Warren Co., Franklin	1836	Operated by George A. Gregg.
Franklin Seminary	Warren Co., Franklin	1822	Ref: *Western Star,* 18 June 1822: Run by Rev. Matthew G. Wallace. Boarding students accomodated. Classical subjects are offered.
Frazier, Miss Margaret	Warren Co., Lebanon	1823	Ref: *Western Star,* 3 May 1823: Advertised lace making only.
(Mr. Nathaniel) Furman's Academy	Butler Co., Middletown	1833	Operated an Academy for 15 years. Later, in 1835–36, he was listed as a teacher at the Hamilton-Rossville Female Academy. In 1833, Furman, his wife, and Lucretia Williams opened Middletown High School.
Geauga Co. Private School	Geauga Co., Huntsburg	Bef. 1850	Private school. Teachers: Esther Pritchard; Melinda Case; Miss Sarah Dickenson.*
Geauga Seminary	Geauga Co., Chester	1841	Estab. by Free-will Baptists. Teachers were: Mrs. Daniel Branch; Miss Curtiss; Miss Lucy Gilmore; Miss Humphrey; Miss Augusta M. Hawley; Miss Bettie Gillmore.*
Germantown Academy	Montgomery Co., Germantown	1840s	Estab. by Rev. Jacob Pentzer; a flourishing academy for both male and females.
Gillmore, Misses Lucy and Bettie	Geauga Co., Chester	1841	*See* Geauga Seminary.
Girard, Miss E. L. Grand	Highland Co., Hillsborough	c. 1827	Longtime teacher and head of the female dept. of a Hillsborough grammar school, under the direction of Rev. J. McD. Mathews.

Teacher / School	*Location*	*Date*	*Additional Information and Associated Samplers*
Goldthwaite, Miss	Washington Co., Marietta	1821	Ref: *Am. Friend* and *Marietta Gazette,* 3 December 1821: Muskingum Academy. Taught by Miss Goldthwaite, "recently from New England." Advertisement offered to teach young ladies; students could board nearby and study "drawing, painting, and embroidery."
Gooch, Mrs.	Hamilton Co., Cincinnati	1837	Ref: *Western Star,* 1 September 1837: "Beech Grove School for Young Ladies." Located 2 miles north of Cincinnati. Needlework was not separately listed but the school offered the ornamental branches and music, along with academic courses.
Goodspead, Miss Harriet	Scioto Co., Portsmouth	1831	Advertised a young ladies school.
Grand River Institute	Ashtabula Co., Austinburg	c. 1825	150 pupils, both male and female. Estab. by Rev. Thomas Tenney* c. 1840–41. Betsy M. Cowles taught and served as first female principle of women's department. The school closed in 1930; re-opened as private academy in 1934, and is currently a private school.
Granville Episcopal Female Seminary	Licking Co., Granville	Estab. 1838	Estab. by St. Luke's Episcopal Church, the seminary building was torn down in 1861. Historic St. Luke's Church, built in 1827, is restored and still in use.
Granville Female Academy	Licking Co., Granville	Estab. 1833	The Granville Female Academy was estab. by the Congregational Church. The female academy no longer exists, but the old academy building for male students is restored and stands. Assoc. sampler: Mary Munson—1827 (was a student in 1839–40).
Granville Female Seminary	Licking Co., Granville	1832	Founded by Charles Sawyer; later became Shephardson College. The name changed in 1840 to Episcopal Female Seminary; name changed in 1860 to Baptist Female Seminary; changed in 1867 to Granville Female Seminary (i.e., 4 name changes in 35 years).
Granville Select School	Licking Co., Granville	1827	Started by Rev. Jacob Little and his wife. The first teacher was Mary Ann Howe, one of his former pupils. Assoc. sampler: Mary Munson—1827.
Gravel Hill School	Warren Co., Waynesville	1838	By 1845, directors of Gravel Hill School had built a large building on S. Main St. and another building at 120 N. Fourth St.
Graves, Louisa	Ashtabula Co., Kingsville	1836	*See* Kingsville Academy.
Graves, Miss Sophia	Medina Co., Spencer	c. 1836–40	She taught the first district school and the first Sabbath school in the new frame schoolhouse.*
Graves, Miss Thankful	Scioto Co., Portsmouth	1838–39	Taught at the Fourth St. School. Students aged from 4 to 20, the boys and girls taught separately. There were 151 boys and 115 girls.
Grey, Lady Jane	Lorain Co., Grafton	Bef. 1850	From Burlington, Vt., a successful teacher who taught many years.*
Griswold, Miss Ursula	Ashtabula Co., Windsor	1804	She was sent back East to receive her education. Upon her return to Ohio she taught school in a pioneer church.
(Mr. H. H.) Gross's Academy ("Brick Academy")	Summit Co., Hudson	1835	Teachers: Mrs. Ansel R. Clark; Miss Harriet Snow; Mrs. E. B. Ellsworth; Miss Louisa Snow; Miss Smith; Miss Towne; Miss Strong. The school was the first academy in Hudson. It had a primary department, a boys' room, and a room for young ladies. Later 2 boarding schools for young ladies were well patronized.
Hair, Prof. Gilbert	Hamilton Co., Montgomery	c. 1817	*See* (Montgomery) Dames School and Academy.
Hall, Mrs. Lyman W.	Portage Co., Ravenna	c. 1835	Ran a select school in Ravenna.*
(Hamilton) Female Academy	Butler Co., Hamilton	1834	A flourishing female academy . . . on old Water St. at Stable St.
Hamilton-Rossville Female Academy	Butler Co., Hamilton	Estab. 1835	This academy was very successful. In 1836 it had 127 pupils. It continued until 1852. Mr. Nathaniel Furman occupied the building with his private school for the next 2 years. Teachers assoc. with the academy: Miss Marcia Drummond; Miss Georgietta Haven; Miss Amelia Looker; Miss Eliza Huffman; Mr. Nathaniel Furman.
Hamlin, Miss Louisa	Huron Co., Norwalk	1833	*See* Norwalk Seminary; Miss Eliza Ware.
Hammond, Rebecca	Ashtabula Co., Bath	Bef. 1850	Graduate of Miss Strong's School at Hudson. Taught at Galesburg. Her parents were Theodore and Nancy (Fisk) Hammond.*
Hammond, Rebecca (Farnum)	Ashtabula Co., Bath	Early 1800s	B. 1791 in Canan, Conn. She came with her parents to Hudson in 1800. In 1815 marr. Theodore Hammond and settled in Bath, where her home was a constant schoolhouse. Opened a select school at Hammond's Corner. D. age 33.
Hanchet, Emily Pardee	Medina Co., Wadsworth	Bef. 1850	Attended school at Granville. She came back to Wadsworth and organized a school of 25–30 little children.*
Harbison, Mary Eliza	Greene Co., Xenia	1851–52	Taught at Xenia Female Seminary.
(Lyman) Harding's Seminary for Girls	Hamilton Co., Cincinnati	1850–51	

Teacher / School	*Location*	*Date*	*Additional Information and Associated Samplers*
Hare's Academy	Warren Co., Franklin	c. 1830	Founded by Rev. J. M. Hare, a Presbyterian minister. Frances Baily was one of the teachers.
Harmar Female Academy	Washington Co., Harmar	Early 1800s	Opposite Marietta on the south bank of the Muskingum River.
(Miss) Harris's School	Cuyahoga Co., Cleveland (west side)	c. 1830	School was situated on Pearl St.
(Maria) Harrison's School for Young Ladies	Montgomery Co., Dayton	1832	
Hartford, Nancy M.	Greene Co., Xenia	1850	One of the first teachers at the Xenia Female Academy/Seminary.
Harveysburg Academy (Quaker)	Warren Co., Harveysburg	Bef. 1850	A classical academy (Quaker).
Harveysburg Free Black School	Warren Co., Harveysburg	c. 1830	Founded by Elizabeth (Burgess) Harvey. This was the first free black school in Ohio. The school was supported by the members of the Friend's Grove Meeting House (Quaker).
Hathaway, Julia McKay	Trumbull Co., Farmington	c. 1820–40	Taught a number of years in east Farmington.*
(Miss) Havens's School	Hamilton Co., Cincinnati	c. 1837	Ref: A letter of 29 September 1837 written by Amelia C. Hittell. Miss Hittell's letter can be found in John C. Cover's *Memoirs of the Miami Valley,* vol. 1 (1919), p. 109.
Hawley, Miss Augusta M.	Geauga Co., Chester	1841	*See* Geauga Seminary.
Hawley, Mrs. Caroline E.	Lake Co., Painesville	c. 1850–55	Taught in a large house on the corner of State and Erie Sts. *See* Lake Erie Female Seminary.
Heintz, Mrs. Caroline Lee	Hamilton Co., Cincinnati	1833	Had a popular school for a short time in Cincinnati. Ref: *Cincinnati Directory 1834,* listed as Mr. and Mrs. Heintz's Female Academy. It was located at Third St., east of Broadway.
Heston, Letitia M.	Clinton Co., Wilmington Warren Co., Springboro	1831 1840s	B. 1791 in Bucks Co., Pa. She came from Baltimore where she taught before coming to Ohio. Member of the (Quaker) Springborough MM in the 1840s. Marr. Zachariah Lownes. Assoc. sampler: Mary Ann Moore—1833.
Hiccox (Hickox), Miss Irene	Trumbull Co., Kinsman Warren	1822 1830	Studied at Mrs. Pierce's Litchfield (Conn.) Academy. She opened a select school in Kinsman at the home of Mrs. John Andrews. For more information about Miss Hiccox see p. 206 (Trumbull Co.). By 1830 Miss Hiccox was in Warren, Trumbull Co., at the Warren Academy.*
(Columbus) High School for Young Ladies	Franklin Co., Columbus	1838	
Hill, Harriet	Ashtabula Co., Kingsville	1836	*See* Kingsville Academy
Hillsborough Academy	Highland Co., Hillsboro	Incorp. 9 February 1829	Subscription school located on Main St. First located in the frame building that was used by John A Trimble. By 1831 Miss Ann Kemper of Walnut Hills, Cincinnati, was assisting in the female department.
Hoke, Mrs. Ann Eliza (Manley)	Lorain Co., Wellington	c. 1840	She was a daughter of Betsy Manley (*See* Manley, Betsy) and taught school in the Wellington District and village schools for many years.*
(N.) Holley's Female School	Hamilton Co., Cincinnati	c. 1834	Located on George St. Ref: *Cincinnati Directory 1834.*
Hollister, Abigail	Cuyahoga Co., Cleveland (east side)	Bef. 1850	Taught school at Collinwood. Instructed little girls in sewing.*
Hopewell Church School	Preble Co.	c. 1849	Founded by the Associate Reformed Presbyterian Church. Related samplers: Martha Agnes Ramsey—1849; Sarah Gilmore—1849.
(Mrs.) Hopwood's Female Academy	Hamilton Co., Cincinnati	c. 1836	Ref: *Cincinnati Directory 1836–37.* Walnut between 2nd and 3rd.
Howe, John M.	Muskingum Co., Zanesville	1836	Estab. Howe's Academy (private) on corner of North and Seventh Sts. John Howe later named principal of McIntire Academy. In 1842, the public Female Seminary was located in Howe's Academy building.
Howe, Miss Marianne	Licking Co., Granville	1827	Was in charge of the female department when the Granville academy (later called the Granville Female Academy) opened in 1827. Assoc. sampler: Mary Munson—1827.
Howe's Academy	Fairfield Co., Lancaster	c. 1838–48	Prof. Howe built a frame house on Mulberry St. and conducted school there for about 10 years. Many Lancaster young men and ladies attended this private academy.
Howlett, Miss M.	Lucas Co., Toledo	1841	Listed as having a school at the corner of Sycamore and Lagrange.
Hubble, Miss M. C.	Summit Co., Akron	1838	Ref: W. B. Doyle, *History of Summit Co., Ohio,* 1908, p. 174: 3 January 1838 ad: "A select school will be opened at the corner of Middlebury & High Streets, under the superintendence of Miss M. C. Hubble of N. York, where pupils will receive instruction in all branches usually taught in our eastern female seminaries."

Teacher / School	Location	Date	Additional Information and Associated Samplers
Hudson Female Seminary	Summit Co., Hudson	Bef. 1850	Two female seminaries were listed in Hudson by 1856. The town founder, David Hudson, had estab. a school and Congregational church there by 1802. *See* Harriet Baldwin.
Humphrey, Miss	Geauga Co., Chester	1841	*See* Geauga Seminary
Humphrey, Miss Emily B.	Trumbull Co., Braceville	1839	This may be the same teacher listed above, who taught at the Geauga Seminary.*
Humphrey, Miss Lucy	Trumbull Co., Braceville	c. 1815	Pioneer teacher who came from Canaan, Conn. She marr. Norman Stowe in 1818. Assoc. sampler: Elvira J. Stowe—1829.*
Hurlbert, Betsy	Ashtabula Co., Windsor	1820	She was a teacher and a tailor. Marr. Thompson Higley.*
Hurst's Boarding School Estab. by Eli P. Hurst	Warren Co., Springboro	1839	Ref: *Western Star,* 18 October 1839: "Hurst's Boarding School—For Males and Females" "Will be opened in Springboro, Warren Co., Ohio, 4 miles east of Franklin. The course of instruction comprises the following branches[:] . . . Reading, Plain & Ornamental Penmanship, Arithmetic, Geography . . . Painting, Drawing, and Needlework. . . . Eli P. Hurst." Assoc. teacher: Emily Welding.
Hutchinson, Miss Temprance	Portage Co., Randolph Summit Co., Hudson	1836 1806	Moved to Hudson, Ohio in 1806. Marr. Samuel Cheney. She taught school and was a famous spinner.*
Hutt, Mr. and Mrs. John	Ross Co., Chillicothe	1802	Opened a girls' school in a log house near the upper end of Bridge St. on Water St. He provided academic instruction while his wife taught the fine art of needle work.
Jackson, Sally	Cuyahoga Co., Mayfield	c. 1830	Teacher at Mayfield when the first female school was built at Mayfield Center in 1830.*
(Miss) Jacobs's School for Young Ladies	Hamilton Co., Cincinnati	1820	Ref: *Western Spy,* 29 April 1820.
Jaquith, Miss S.	Washington Co., Marietta	c. 1840	*See* Marietta Ladies Seminary.
Jenkins, Miss	Huron Co., Norwalk	1833	Teacher in the Norwalk Seminary. *See* Miss Eliza Ware
Jenks, Miss	Lucas Co., Toledo	1844	Listed as having a private school at the corner of Summit and Cherry.
Jewett, Miss Sallie	Athens Co., Athens	Bef. 1850	Taught at the first school located east of the Presbyterian church. *See* Sarah Foster
Johnson, Mrs. Dr.	Shelby Co., Sidney	1840	A school for girls in a building 2 doors above the NE corner of Main and Poplar Sts.
Jones, Roxanna	Ashtabula Co., Bath	c. 1825	Taught with her sister Phoebe, the first school of all ages and all grades. Roxanna was marr. in 1827 to Capt. Richard Howe.*
Joyce, M. and A. C.	Summit Co., Akron	1836	Ref: *Akron,* 20 May 1836: "M. and A. C. Joyce respectfully inform the inhabitants . . . have opened a school where they will instruct a few young ladies in Arithmetic, Orthography, History, etc." Also included in the listing of subjects is "Drawing in Crayon, Mezzotints, Pencil, India Ink, Japanning, Flower Painting, etc."
Kelsey, Mrs.	Scioto Co., Portsmouth	Bef. 1832	Had a Female Seminary. Mary Sharp announced in Nov. 1832 that she would be taking over for Mrs. Kelsey at the Female Seminary.
Kelsey, Miss Emma	Shelby Co., East Sidney	1848	Miss Kelsey taught with Martha Crowell at East Sidney in a small brick house at the foot of Orbison Hill.
Kemper, Mrs. Ann	Highland Co., Hillsboro	1829	Assisted the head of Female Department at Hillsboro Academy. *See* Hillsboro Academy.
(Old) Kingsville Academy	Ashtabula Co., Kingsville	1836	For a third of a century the leading school in NE Ohio. Mrs. Susan Osbourn: teacher and preceptress. Assoc. teachers: Nancy Loomis; Harriet Hall; Louisa Graves; Adelia Spencer; Martha Luce; Caroline Williams; Julia Chappell.*
Kinsman Academy	Trumbull Co., Kinsman	Estab. 1842–43	Estab. by the John Kinsman family in NE Trumbull Co.
Kirkpatrick, Misses Phoebe and Betsy	Mahoning Co., Youngstown	c. 1800	Taught at the first Presbyterian Church and school. Daughters of Betsy Baldwin Kirkpatrick. *See* Phoebe Wick. Assoc. sampler: Betsey Wick—1814.*
Lake Erie Female Seminary	Lake Co., Painesville	1856	Miss Caroline E. Hawley taught here. The school's founder and first teachers were from Mt. Holyoke Seminary at South Hadley, Mass.*
Lakey, Misses Caroline and Rowena	Warren Co., Lebanon	c. 1845	Teachers at the Lebanon Academy.
Lancaster Institute	Fairfield Co., Lancaster	1838	Opened by Mr. and Mrs. McGill. The school was for young ladies. *See* Fairfield Co., p. 171 for the full ad. "Plain and ornamental needle and fancy work."
Lancasterian Seminary	Montgomery Co., Dayton	1822	Ref: *Western Star,* 2 February 1822: "Benevolent Institution." "All persons in this town who are unable to pay for the education of their children, may have them taught gratis." (Male and female students.)

Teacher / School	*Location*	*Date*	*Additional Information and Associated Samplers*
Langford, Anna	Huron Co., Norwalk	1833	Teacher in the Norwalk Seminary. *See* Miss Eliza Ware.
Lanphear, Misses Female Academy	Hamilton Co., Cincinnati	c. 1836	Ref: *Cincinnati Directory 1836–37:* "6th between Walnut and Vine."
Lathrop, Miss	Trumbull Co., Warren	c. 1830	Early teacher in the primary department of Warren Academy.*
Lebanon Academy	Warren Co., Lebanon	Estab. 1845	Ref: 1845–46 Lebanon Academy Catalogue: both male and female students. Teachers, Primary Department: Misses Rowena and Caroline Lakey; Nancy R. Miller. *See* National Normal School. Alfred Hollbrook ran the school for 10 years and used the old academy building for his school.*
Lebanon Female Institute (Young Ladies Seminary)	Warren Co., Lebanon	1833–34	Ref: *Western Star,* 13 March 1834 and 21 October 1833: "Young Ladies Seminary—Mrs. Anne Mortimer respectfully informs . . . Patrons and Friends of her establishment that her school should be continued for a second year. Terms per Quarter of Twelve Weeks: Reading, Geography, Writing and Arithmetic—$3. English Grammar, . . . History, Composition, . . . &etc.—$4. French including the above branches—$6. Plain and ornamental Needlework will receive every attention, at stated hours, in addition to these studies. . . . Lebanon, March 13, 1834."*
Lebanon Institute; Mr. and Mrs. Baron	Warren Co., Lebanon	c. 1832	*See* Baron, Mr. and Mrs.
Le Seur, Miss	Champaign Co., Urbana	c. 1834	Ref: *Urbana Daily Citizen,* 3 May 1910: "Reminiscence" "Miss Lazure's and 'Bunty' Robinson's school." Assoc. sampler: Ann Hunter—1834.
Lewis, Mrs.	Geauga Co., Painesville	Bef. 1850	Conducted a school for girls.
Lindsley, Lavina	Huron Co., Norwalk	1828	Taught at the Norwalk Academy.
(Dr. John) Locke's Female Academy	Hamilton Co., Cincinnati	1823	Ref: *Cincinnati Directory 1836–37:* "East side Walnut St. between 3rd and 4th.
Loomis, Nancy	Ashtabula Co.	1836	*See* Kingsville Academy.
Lord, Dr. Asa D. and Elizabeth (Conant)	Lake Co., Kirtland	1830	Taught at the Western Reserve Seminary in Kirtland.*
Loveland, Mrs. Amelia (DeWolf)	Lorain Co., Brighton	1826	Taught the school in her home.*
Luce, Martha	Ashtabula Co., Kingsville	1836	*See* Kingsville Academy.*
Ludlow, Misses, School	Cuyahoga Co., Cleveland (west side)	Bef. 1850	School for young ladies; on Ontario St.*
Lyman, Miss Sophia	Ross Co., Chillicothe	c. 1830	Assisted Miss S. A. Stearns. *See* Chillicothe Female Seminary.
Lynch, Miss Rebecca	Warren Co., Springboro	1823	Taught village school. Member of the Quaker Church. Marr. Thomas Wilkins in 1824.
Manley, Mrs. Betsy (Webster)	Lorain Co., Wellington	c. 1821	After her husband's death she supported her family by teaching school and working as a tailoress. Betsy and her family came from Otis, Mass., in 1823.*
Mansfield Female Seminary	Richland Co., Mansfield	1849	
Marietta Institute of Education	Washington Co., Marietta	1830	Sometimes referred to as the Muskingum Academy, it had an infant school, primary school, ladies' seminary, and high school. In 1835 it was chartered as Marietta College.
Marietta Ladies Seminary	Washington Co., Marietta	c. 1830	Teachers: Miss Spalding from Ipswich, Mass. Successive teachers were: Mrs. D. P. Bosworth; Miss D. T. Wells; Miss C. M. Webster; Miss S. Jaquith; Miss L. Tenney; Mrs. E. Creel. (Mrs. E. Creel was listed as teaching ornamental needlework in 1850.) Mrs. L. Tenny (by 1850) had become superintendent.
Marsh, Clarissa (Rogers)	Medina Co., Spencer	c. 1830	Taught Sunday school and sewing in Spencer.*
Marsh, Mrs. Harriet (Stowe)	Trumbull Co., Braceville	Bef. 1850	A young widow who taught at Braceville. Assoc. sampler: Elvira J. Stowe—1829.*
Marsh, Miss Serepta	Franklin Co., Worthington	1839	Principal of Worthington Female Seminary.
Martin, Mrs. William T.	Franklin Co., Franklinton (Columbus)	1816–17	Taught with her husband at a school on Town St., ½ block east of High St.
Mather, Miss	Muskingum Co., Zanesville	1835	A "Miss Mather" was assistant to the principal of Putnam Female Institute in Oct. 1835. *See* Putnam Institute.*
McClelland, Miss	Hamilton Co., Cincinnati	c. 1833–36	Taught needlework. Ref: *Student sewing work book,* coll. Cincinnati Public Library.
McGill, Mrs. and Mr.	Fairfield Co., Lancaster	1838	Opened Lancaster Institute for young ladies.
McGookin, (McGoogan) Mrs.	Shelby Co., Sidney	1843	*See* Sidney Male & Female Academy.
McIlrath, Mrs. Sarah (Shaw)	Cuyahoga Co., Cleveland	Bef. 1830	She and her husband founded Shaw's Academy in East Cleveland.*

Teacher / School	Location	Date	Additional Information and Associated Samplers
McIntire Academy	Muskingum Co., Zanesville	c. 1836	School estab. by the will of John McIntire, founder of Zanesville. First principal was John M. Howe. Lower departments were taught by M. D. Martindale, T. H. Patrick, and 2 female assistants.
McLauren, Maria Carrington	Erie Co., Huron	Bef. 1850	She and her husband, S. H. McLauren, kept a private school.*
McMahan, Miss Elinore and Rev. Wm.	Warren Co., Lebanon	1819	Ref: *Western Star,* 27 July 1819: "Tuition" "The Rev. William M'Mahan proposes to meet the citizens of Lebanon and its vicinity, at the court house for purpose of making and entering a contract with them as a teacher. Miss Elinore M'Mahan, the daughter of the above named gentleman, will also make proposals. Miss M'Mahan will teach reading, writing, Arithmetic, English, English grammar, geography, Needlework, *embroidery,* etc. . . . They will, if properly encouraged, make Lebanon their residence for life. A Citizen."
McMechan, Miss Ellen A.	Butler Co., Hamilton	1819	Daughter of Rev. James McMechan (Presbyterian); opened a school at the NE corner of 3rd and Buckeye Sts. The first woman in Hamilton to engage in teaching. The school operated 8 years. Assoc. sampler: Margaret McMechan—1819.
McNeal, Miss	Trumbull Co., Warren	c. 1836	*See* Trumbull Co. teachers.
McQuillen, Patty	Miami Co., Conover in Brown Twp.	1818	Second teacher in Brown Twp. Taught in a house just south of Conover.
McQuirk, Mary E.	Greene Co., Xenia	1850	One of the first teachers at the Xenia Female Seminary.
Meeker, Miss	Delaware Co., Delaware	c. 1832–36	Assisted at the seminary opened by Mrs. Howson and her sister, Miss Johnson. Miss Meeker, c. 1834, started her own infant school.
Messenger, Miss	Delaware Co., Delaware	c. 1827–30	Attempted to establish a girls' seminary and taught a few terms. The effort eventually failed.
Methodist Female Collegiate Institute of Cincinnati	Hamilton Co., Cincinnati	c. 1842–43	Principal was Rev. Perlee B. Wilber, M. A.
Middletown High School	Butler Co., Middletown	1833	Nathaniel Furman, his wife, and Lucretia Williamson came in 1833 to Middletown and opened Middletown High School.
Miller, Clemence	Huron Co., Norwalk and New London	Bef. 1850	Was a student, then a teacher, at the female seminary in Norwalk. Taught several years. Marr. Bushnel Post.*
Miller, Emma	Geauga Co., Newbury	1830–40	Mrs. Stephen Miller (*see* Martha Canfield, her mother) was also an early Newbury teacher.*
Miller, Miss Nancy R.	Warren Co., Lebanon	c. 1845	*See* Lebanon Academy.
(Mrs.) Miller's Ladies' School	Clark Co., Springfield	1841	Ref: *Springfield Republic,* 3 September 1844: "Mrs. Miller will open a school for Young Ladies, in that well lighted and comfortable room lately occupied by Dr. Gillet. . . . Mrs. M. will teach all the various sorts of *Plain and Fancy Needle Work,* including *Rug Work* and *Embroidery.* Terms per quarter $3.00. August 27, 1841."
Monsow, Miss Lucy P.	Clark Co., Madison Twp.	c. 1830	On Friday afternoons, she gave female students lessons in sewing. They studied hard during other days, that they might have this privilege on Fridays. Operated a school on Franklin, near Williams St. until her marriage. Assoc. teacher: Mrs. Richard Murray (Joan Hills)—1826.
Montgomery Dames School and Academy	Hamilton Co., Montgomery	c. 1817	The academy was for male and female students. Prof. Gilbert Hair ran the school. It later became known as Hair's Academy.
Moore, Miss Sophia	Delaware Co., Delaware	1821	Operated a school on Franklin Street until her marriage. Assoc. teacher: Mrs. Richard Murray (Joan Hills).
Moravian School for Young Ladies	Muskingum Co., Zanesville	Estab. 1819	Ref: *Zanesville Express,* 30 July 1819: *see* advertisement on p. 183. School estab. by Mr. and Mrs. Steinhauer from Bethlehem, Pa.
Mortimer, Mrs. Anne	Hamilton Co., Cincinnati Warren Co., Lebanon	c. 1830 1833 to c. 1834	Ref: *Western Star,* 13 March 1834 and 21 October 1833. *See* Lebanon Female Institute. Mrs. Mortimer came from England to Philadelphia in 1820. After her husband died, moved to Cincinnati (c. 1830) and assisted at Mr. A. Truesdell's Female Academy. Moved to Lebanon in 1833 and opened her own school.
Mt. Auburn Young Ladies' Institute	Hamilton Co., Cincinnati	1856	Finishing school, estab. by Rev. E. A. Crawley.
Mt. Pleasant Friends Boarding School	Jefferson Co., Mt. Pleasant	Estab. 1837	Quaker school operated until 1875.
Mulford, Martha	Clark Co.	c. 1824	Assoc. samplers: Marth Mulford—1824 (made as example for her students); Mary A. Croft—1824; Melissa Cory—c. 1825.
Mulligan, Mrs.	Greene Co., Xenia	c. 1850	Taught at a school for young ladies that later became the Xenia Female Academy. Located on East Church St.
Munhall, Miss Amanda	Fairfield Co., Lancaster	c. 1839	Assoc. sampler: Rachel Allen—1839.
Muntz, Mary	Highland Co., Hillsboro	1847	*See* Amanda Wilson.

Teacher / School	*Location*	*Date*	*Additional Information and Associated Samplers*
Murray, Emmelene Ella	Trumbull Co., Mesopotamia	1834	Assoc. needlework: Eliza Ann Reynolds—1834; Eleanor Maria Griffith—c. 1833–34.
Murray, Miss Jennie	Shelby Co., Sidney	c. 1850–53	Taught at the Murray family home on Miami Ave., 2nd floor of Miss Jennie's father's wood-turning plant.
Murray, Mrs. Richard (Joan Hills)	Delaware Co., Delaware	c. 1824–68	Assoc. with Miss Moore c. 1825, then continued to teach her whole life.
Muskingum Academy	Muskingum Co., Marietta	c. 1821	*See* Miss Goldthwaite (teacher).
National Normal School	Warren Co., Lebanon	1855	Ref: Second Annual Catalog—1857. Estab. by Alfred Holbrook. This school was located in the building used earlier by the Lebanon Academy. When the Academy failed after 10 years, Holbrook's school took it over. *See* Lebanon Academy. The National Normal School offered, among "Optional Studies," "Painting and Embroidery."
Nazareth Academy	Bardstown, Kentucky	1814	Located south of Bardstown. Opened in 1814, it closed in 1966. Moved to present site in 1822. Many Cincinnati girls attended this Kentucky school. First teacher was Sister Ellen O'Connell. Assoc. sampler: Mary McGuire—1838.*
Neal, Mrs. Lucinda (Million)	Miami Co., Troy	c. 1827	Opened her own school. Marr. William Neal of Miami Co. on Oct. 23, 1828. Assoc. sampler: Martha N. Telford—1827.
Newark Seminary for Young Ladies	Licking Co., Newark	1837	
Newberry Quaker School	Clinton Co., Martinsville	c. 1816	Founded by Newberry MM—Quaker. Teachers: Elizabeth Wasson and Sarah Gibson.
New Hagerstown (Female) Seminary	Carroll Co., New Hagerstown	1839	
North Liberty Academy	Adams Co., Wayne Twp.	Estab. 1848–49	Began as select school taught by Rev. Jacob Foster (Associated Reform—United Presbyterian). In 1854, after the school changed locations several times, a large frame structure was built. Assoc. teachers: Rev. James Arbuthnot; James Wright; D. H. Harsha.
North, Misses Lucy, Ann, and Susan	Butler Co., Oxford	1835–40	*See* Oxford Female Academy.
Norton, Miss Clarissa	Trumbull Co., Warren	c. 1825–30	Taught at the Warren Academy. Marr. Gen. Curtis of Sharon.*
Norwalk Female Seminary (Norwalk Academy)	Huron Co., Norwalk	c. 1828	Founded by Elisha Whittlesey, who laid out the town in 1815. Housed in a three-story building, flourished 1830s and 1840s. Teachers: Getia Bostwick; Eliza Ware; Lavinia Lindsley.
Norwalk Presbyterian Female Seminary	Huron Co., Norwalk	1847–48	Located at 113 W. Main St.
Nutting, Prof. and Mrs. Rufus	Summit Co., Hudson	1827	Established first school for young ladies. Taught watercolor and embroidery.*
Oakland Female Seminary	Highland Co., Hillsboro	Estab. 1839	Estab. by Joseph McDowell Mathews, a Methodist minister. Came to Hillsborough in 1827 and opened the Hillsborough Academy for male and female students c. 1831. Assisted by Miss Ann Kemper of Cincinnati. His school contintued, assisted by Miss E. L. Girard, until 1846. In 1857, it became the Hillsborough Female College.
Olney Friends School	Belmont Co., Barnesville	1837	Founded by the Ohio Yearly Meeting of Quakers.
Oren, Ruth	Clinton Co., Gurneyville	Bef. 1850	Taught at a school located in Liberty Twp.
Oxford Female High School/ Oxford Academy	Butler Co., Oxford	1830	*See* Miss Bethania Crocker. Assoc. teachers: Misses Lucy and Ann North; Misses Smith and Clark. In 1856, the school became the female counterpart to Miami University.
Painesville Academy	Lake Co., Painesville		By 1857 it had become the Lake Erie Female Seminary. The Village of Painesville was founded in 1811, but estab. date of the academy is uncertain. Assoc. teachers: Ellen Fisher; Miss Pamelia Manter.*
Parker, Hannah	Trumbull Co., Kinsman	1853	Attended Willoughby Seminary and taught there. D. at age 18 in 1855.*
Parm, Mrs.	Warren Co., Lebanon	c. 1840	Ref: letter of Mrs. Thomas Corwin: "Mrs. Parm is teaching the girls in the basement of the Baptist church. Sally Ross is assisting her." Note: This may refer to Mrs. Sylvester Parmalee, who was principal of a ladies' seminary in the South.
Parmelee, Miss J. D.	Geauga Co., Chester	1830	B. Conn. Was a teacher and matron at the Geauga Seminary. Marr. Newton Barber in 1831.*
Parmalee, Mrs. William	Cuyahoga Co., Liverpool	1846	Came from Cazenovia, N.Y., to Ohio in 1842. Taught school and was a milliner after her husband's death. Mother of 2 daughters.*

Teacher / School	*Location*	*Date*	*Additional Information and Associated Samplers*
(Mrs.) Parshall's School	Warren Co., Lebanon	1836	Ref: Notice in *Western Star,* March 1836: Lecture being given in her school room.
Peck, Laura	Summit Co., Norton	c. 1820s	Had a select school and devoted herself to teaching. D. 1836.*
Peet, Miss Rebecca Sherman	Cuyahoga Co., Cleveland (east side)	Bef. 1850	Kept a private school in her house.*
Phelps, Eliza Griswald	Ashtabula Co., Windsor	1839	B. Ohio, but raised in Conn. For 14 years she was preceptress of a female seminary in Conn. before returning to teach in Ohio.
Pickaway Female Academy	Pickaway Co.	c. 1843	Ref: 1843 Gazeteer Records: "[H]ad 1 academy, 15 students, 54 schools, 1,522 scholars, and pop. 19,725."
Pickett, Messrs. John W. and Albert	Hamilton Co., Cincinnati	c. 1835	*See* Cincinnati Female Institute.
Poland Academy	Mahoning Co., Poland	Bef. 1850	Assoc. teacher: Miss Eliza Blakesly—1849.
Portsmouth Young Ladies Seminary	Scioto Co., Portsmouth	Estab. 1842	Estab. by Mr. A. (Aaron?) Williams. Assoc. teacher: Miss Betsey Cowles—1842.
Presbyterian Church	Cuyahoga Co., Cleveland (west side)	c. 1834	Located in a brick schoolhouse on Vermont St. Provided schools for those whose parents could not afford to send them to private schools.*
Price, Mrs. Ann Hulme	Warren Co., Lebanon Hamilton Co., Cincinnati	1824 1825–36	Ref: Letters sent back to relatives in N.J. *See* pp. 3, 30, 257. Coll: Ohio Hist. Soc. Archives.
Pritchard, Esther	Geauga Co., Huntsburg	1820	Taught in the private school.*
Pumrey, Rev. John	Ross Co., Chillicothe	1830	Started a female seminary.
Punderson, Betsey	Geauga Co., Newbury	1820–30	She attended school in New Haven, Conn. Taught at Painesville and Burton. Daughter of Mr. and Mrs. Lemuel Punderson, who came to Ohio from Conn. c. 1805.*
Putnam Classic Institute (Putnam Female Seminary)	Muskingum Co., Zanesville	1836	Opened Feb. 1836 in a building known as the Stone Academy. First principal was Miss L. A. Emerson of Newburyport, Mass. Early teacher: Miss Mather. Miss Mary Cone held this position c. 1846 (or earlier). Pupils under 14 years were received into the preparatory department. Those over 14 entered the upper department, a three-year course of study.
Ravenna Seminary (Female)	Portage Co., Ravenna	1839	
Rice, Miss Sally	Trumbull Co., Warren	1814	Ref: Teaching contract (8 June 1814): "We, the subscribers, to hereby mutually agree to hire Miss Sally Rice to teach school in the schoolhouse near Mr. William Smith's for the term of three months, to commence on the 9th day of June, instant. She is to commence school at the hour of 9 o'clock in the forenoon, and to keep until 12; and at the hour of 1 and continue until 4 o'clock. She is to teach reading and to instruct the young Misses in the art of sewing . . . and for which we agree to give her the sum of one dollar and twenty-five cents per week during the said term."
Richards, Clarissa	Summit Co., Tallmadge	c. 1810	Came from South Canaan, Conn., in 1810; became the second wife of Elizur Wright, and took care of his 5 daughters. She formed a child's sewing society.*
Ripley Female Seminary	Brown Co., Ripley	1832	In 1846 the school had 40 pupils under William C. Bissell and lady. Probable assoc. samplers: Julia Doak Rankin—1837; Antoinette Evans—1839.
Rouse, Bathsheba	Washington Co., Belpre	c. 1789	B. Mass. in 1769, the daughter of John Rouse. First woman teacher in the NW Territory. She opened her school at Belpre and later went to Farmer's Castle. Marr. Richard Greene. D. 1843. *See* p. 3.
Russell, Jerusha	Medina Co., Liverpool	1813–15	B. Windsor, Conn., 1784. Came to Warrensville with her parents. Taught c. 1814 in Newburgh before marriage to Moses Deming (his 3rd wife). He was also a teacher.*
(Mr. and Mrs.) Ryland's Female Academy	Hamilton Co., Cincinnati	1834	Ref. *Cincinnati Directories 1834* and *1836:* located on west side of Walnut, between 4th and 5th Sts.
Salem Friend's School	Columbiana Co., Salem	1822	Assoc. samplers: Mary Bonsall—1828; Lydia—Burton 1829.
Sandy Spring School	Columbiana Co.	1815	Society of Friends (Quaker). Assoc. sampler: Ann Batten—1815.
Sawyer, Cassandra	Ross Co., Chillicothe	c. 1830	*See* Chillicothe Female Seminary.
Saxton, Miss Catherine	Clinton Co., Union Twp.	1813	Teacher at the Dutch Creek Schoolhouse (Quaker). It was a co-ed one-room school. *See* Dutch Creek Schoolhouse.
Schenck, Mr. and Mrs. E.	Franklin Co., Columbus	Estab. 1843–48	*See* Columbus Female Seminary.
(Mrs.) Schenck's Female Seminary	Warren Co., Franklin	Bef. 1846	On West Second St. Estab. by Mrs. Isaac P. Schenck (Catherine DuBois).

Teacher / School	*Location*	*Date*	*Additional Information and Associated Samplers*
(C. V. B.) Schenck's School	Warren Co., Franklin	Estab. 1818	Opened by Catherine Van Brough Schenck, a Presbyterian minister's daughter. Family came from Long Island, N.Y., where she taught school at the Huntington Academy before coming to Ohio. The Franklin school was located in a house at the NE corner of Main and Second Sts. Assoc. samplers: Hannah Winner—1821; Catherine A. M. Finkle—1818; Prudence Vail—1818; Anna Cumming Schenck—1821; Eliza P. Swain—1829; Eliza Ann Bruen—1829; Rachel Gray—1825; Eliza Jane Houston—1828; Mary C. Williams—1819; Elizabeth Smith—1830.
Scoville, Miss Eunice	Trumbull Co., Vienna	1840s	Taught school in summer and worked as a tailoress in the winter.*
(Mrs.) Scranton's Select School	Cuyahoga Co., Cleveland	c. 1830*	
(Troy) Select School for Young Ladies	Miami Co., Troy	1838	Taught by Miss Mary Barney.
(Zanesville) Seminary for Young Ladies	Muskingum Co., Zanesville	1822–24	Rev. George Sedgwick taught a seminary for young ladies in a house which stood on the riverbank below the lower bridge.
Seymour, Caroline Oliver (Mrs. John W.)	Licking Co., Newark	c. 1836–40	Taught in the select school (both male and female students) opened in the Congregational Church. Assoc. samplers: Caroline Louisa Seymour—1838; Sarah Owens—1839.
Sharp, Miss Mary	Scioto Co., Portsmouth	Nov. 1832	Ref: Ad stating that she would be taking over for Mrs. Kelsey at the Young Ladies Seminary in Nelson W. Evans, *History of Scioto County, Ohio* (1903).
Shaw's (Academy)	Cuyahoga Co., Cleveland (east side)	Bef. 1850	Founded by Mrs. Sarah McIllrath and her husband.*
Shaw, Miss Mary A.	Franklin Co., Columbus	1838–39	Opened a school for young ladies in the lecture room of the First Presbyterian Church.
Sheldon, Miss	Geauga Co., Bainbridge	Bef. 1840	Taught 29 terms at Bainbridge and was the first teacher to allow sewing and drawing in the schools after lessons were completed.
Sheldon, Mrs. George (Harmony Ann Fobes)	Portage Co., Kent	1825	Rev. George Sheldon came to minister and she to open school. She taught common English branches, embroidery, and fine needlework to young ladies in their home, a handsome new house on the west side of the river, now known as the Parmalee homestead.
Sidney Male and Female Academy	Shelby Co., Sidney	1843	Estab. by Rev. William McGookin (McGoogan) in a brick house on Poplar St. Instructors include: Mrs. McGookin; Miss D. E. Bankroft; Miss Martha R. Crowell; Miss M. A. Abbott. Martha Crowell later took charge of McGookin's Academy.
Sisters of Notre Dame (Sixth Street Academy)	Hamilton Co., Cincinnati	1840	Eight members of the Order came to Cincinnati at the invitation of Bishop John B. Purcell. *See* Nazareth Academy.
Sisters of Notre Dame Female Educational Institute	Ross Co., Chillicothe	1850	
Sixth Street Academy	Hamilton Co., Cincinnati	1840	*See* Sisters of Notre Dame.
Skinner, Miss Sylvia	Cuyahoga Co., Mayfield	Bef. 1850	One of the first teachers in Mayfield at the school at Little Mountain.*
Smith, Miss	Summit Co., Hudson	1835	*See* Mr. Gross's School.
Smith, Miss A. M.	Butler Co., Oxford	c. 1827–30s	*See* Oxford Female Academy.
Smith, Caroline	Warren Co., Springboro	c. 1852	Taught a Springborough select school with Jane Bateman.
Smith, Mrs. David	Franklin Co., Columbus	1819	Wife of the editor of the *Monitor,* opened a school for girls on Front St.
Smith, Miss Laura	Union Co., Homer	c. 1839	Assoc. sampler: Martha Jane Reynolds—1839.
(Mr. Samuel) Smith's School	Clark Co., Springfield	c. 1812–25	40 to 50 students, both male and female. Assisted by his wife, who taught smaller children in their residence near the school.
Smith, Miss S. N.	Ross Co., Chillicothe	c. 1830	Taught at Mrs. Thurman's School. *See* Chillicothe Female Seminary.
Snow, Misses Harriet and Louisa	Cuyahoga Co., Cleveland (east side) Summit Co., Hudson	1835	*See* Cleveland Academy *See* Mr. Gross's School
Snow, Louisa	Cuyahoga Co., Brecksville	1830	B. 1812. Her family came from Maine. Her services were sought by people of Hudson and Cleveland. She taught at the Old Academy on St. Clair St. in Cleveland and at Norwalk the Seminary. Marr. Aquella Willett.*
Spaulding, Miss	Washington Co., Marietta	c. 1830	*See* Marietta Ladies Seminary.
Spaulding, Mother Catherine	Kentucky, Bardstown	1814	*See* Nazareth Academy.
Spencer, Adelia	Ashtabula	1836	*See* Kingsville Academy.
Spencer, Flavia	Portage Co., Mantua	1829	Assoc. sampler: Emily Sheldon—1829.

Teacher / School	*Location*	*Date*	*Additional Information and Associated Samplers*
Springborough School	Warren Co., Springboro	1816	Built in 1837 at SW corner of East and Market Sts. Had female students. No curriculum listed. Teacher: Robert C. Way.
Springborough School	Warren Co., Springboro	1833	*See* Emily Welding.
Springborough Boarding School	Warren Co., Springboro	1832–37	Ref: *Western Star:* No mention of needlework in the curriculum listed. Students were offered boarding at nearby recommended private homes. Teacher: Robert Way.
Springfield Female Academy	Clark Co., Springfield	1832	Ref: *Western Pioneer,* 6 October 1832: "Susan Voorhees respectfully informs the inhabitants of Springfield that she has . . . taken charge of the Female Academy, and solicits a share of patronage. No boys will be hereafter admitted in the school, whose age exceeds six years. Terms of Tuition as heretofore."
Springfield Female Seminary	Clark Co., Springfield	1849–71	Ref: Springfield Female Seminary Catalog 1855. A boarding school. Teachers included Godfrey, Elizabeth, and Marie Frankenstein. Along with academic subjects, the catalogue lists: "Ornamental Branches: Arrangements have been made for the best instruction in other ornamental branches."
St. Mary's Educational Institute	Montgomery Co., Dayton	1843	Eventually became Univ. of Dayton.
St. Mary Seminary	Perry Co., Somerset	1830	A school for young females. Many Protestant families also sent their daughters there.
St. Peter's Female Academy	Hamilton Co., Cincinnati	1829	Ref: *Cincinnati Directory 1836–37:* "For the support of female orphans, under the care of the Sisters of Charity." Assoc. samplers: Harriett Looker—1834; Alice Bagott—1831.
Stearns, Miss S. A.	Ross Co., Chillicothe	c. 1830	This teacher and her school were famous throughout Ohio and attracted many pupils. *See* Chillicothe Female Seminary. *See* Mrs. Thurman's School.
Steele, Thomas	Greene Co., Xenia	1816	Came from Ireland in 1812, to Xenia by 1816. Opened his first school in 1816 and taught for 32 years in Xenia. Male and female students.
Steinhauer (Steinour), Mr. and Mrs.	Muskingum Co., Zanesville Ross Co., Chillicothe	1819 1820–21–	For Zanesville, see Moravian School for Young Ladies. In Chillicothe the couple "began a boarding school for girls in a one-story house on the corner of Mulberry and Main, and afterwards in a brick building on east Main." (*Zanesville Express,* 13 March 1820).
Steubenville Female Seminary	Jefferson Co., Steubenville	Estab. 1828–29	Estab. by Rev. Charles C. and Hetty F. (Davis) Beatty. In 1829 it had 100 students, 12 teachers, 3 assistant teachers, and 3 assistant pupils. *See* fig. 200.
Stowe, Catherine and Harriet (Beecher)	Hamilton Co., Cincinnati	c. 1830–36	Kept a school on the site of St. John's Hospital. After Harriet marr., their father, Prof. Stowe, and Catherine became missionaries for female education in the West. Miss Mary Dutton, an assistant, then took charge, and after a time went back to N. H., where she maintained a school. *See* Western Female Seminary.
Streator, Miss Elizabeth	Portage Co., Windham	Bef. 1820	*See* Miss Rebecca Conant.
Strong, Miss	Summit Co., Hudson	1835	*See* Mr. Gross's School. She was originally from Ashtabula Co., in Bath, c. 1830.
Strong, Miss Eunice L.	Ross Co., Chillicothe	c. 1830	Teacher at Chillicothe Female Seminary. *See* Thurman's School.
Sugar Grove School	Warren Co., Waynesville	1814	Located SW of Waynesville. First building was a log structure, but was replaced in 1827 with a new brick school.
(Doinecia) Sullivan's Private School for Girls	Montgomery Co., Dayton	1815	Opened the first girls' school in Dayton in March 1815 on the west side of Main St., south of 3rd.
(Messrs.) Talbert's School	Hamilton Co., Cincinnati	Bef. 1850	On Fifth, between Vine and Race Sts. A monitorial or kindergarten for small children of both sexes.
(Mrs.) Tallant's Female Academy	Hamilton Co., Cincinnati	c. 1836	Ref: *Cincinnati Dir. 1836–37:* At Walnut between 3rd and 4th.
Tappan, Miss	Hamilton Co., Cincinnati	c. 1836	*See* Western Female Institute.
(Miss Sarah) Taylor's School for Young Ladies	Warren Co., Waynesville	1845	Ref: *Western Star,* June 1850: "Plain and Ornamental Needle work $4. Embroidery, Drawing and Painting—$5." Miss Taylor, a Quaker, located her school on N. Main St. She served also at the free school for Negroes that Elizabeth Harvey estab. in 1835.
Tenney, Mrs. L.	Washington Co., Marietta	c. 1830s	Listed as teaching at the Marietta Female Seminary, under Miss Spaulding. By 1850, Mrs. L. Tenney had become the superintendent of the seminary.
Tenny, Miss Roxena	Lake Co., Willoughby	1847	First principal of Willoughby Seminary.
Thayer, Miss	Portage Co., Kent	1817	Taught in the first building for use as a church and school.*

Teacher / School	*Location*	*Date*	*Additional Information and Associated Samplers*
Thomas, Rev. Thomas E. and Mrs.	Butler Co., Paddy's Run (now Shandon) Warren Co., Franklin	1820–27 c. 1835	Opened a school with academic subjects offered and taught needlework. By 1835, the Thomases had opened the Franklin English and Classical School in Warren Co.
Thompson, Miss Eliza T.	Delaware Co., Delaware	c. 1828–30	First female district schoolteacher; taught in a stone building at the corner of Franklin and Winter Sts. U.S. pres. Rutherford B. Hayes and his sister Fannie were students.
Thorn, Ann H. (Gumery) (Mrs. Thomas)	Jefferson Co., Steubenville Smithfield	c. 1828	Daughter of John and Levinah Gumery. Member and teacher at Short Creek Quarterly Meeting of Soc. of Friends (Quaker). M. Thomas Thorn, May 1811. Assoc. samplers: Achsah Carter—1830; Keturah Carter—1830; Martha Judkin—1828; Rebecca Ballinger—1830.
(Mrs. Pleasant) Thurman's School	Ross Co., Chillicothe	1824	Ref: Ad, 1820: "P. & M. G. Thurman . . . in association with Mrs. Wade and her daughters," began a boarding school for young ladies. The school offered academic subjects and "drawing, painting, embroidery on muslin and satin, wax-work, plain sewing, netting, music and French. Tuition—$5.00 per quarter, wax work was $10.00 extra. Boarding and washing offered at $2.00 per week." *See* Chillicothe Female Seminary.
Towne, Miss	Summit Co.	1835	*See* Mr. Gross's School.
Treat, Miss Anna	Franklin Co., Columbus	1826	Estab. with Miss Sarah Benfield a female academy in the Pike Bldg. on W. Broad St. It operated at least 6 years. Amy Rosalla Adams taught there until 1828, when she left to teach with Rev. Joseph Labaree at the Columbus Female Seminary. Assoc. samplers: Mary McElvain—1832; Eliza McElvain—1826.
Truesdell, Arnold and Lady	Hamilton Co., Cincinnati	c. 1830	"[B]y whom all the ornamental branches belonging to Female education are taught." Mrs. Anne Mortimer was "the lady" who assisted Mr. Trusdell. *See* Lebanon Female Institute.
Tucker, Sallie	Miami Co., Brown Twp. and Fletcher	1810	Taught in first schoolhouse. Her certificate states that "she was of good character, and could teach reading, writing, and arithmetic. Other branches could be taught if desired."
Twinsburg Institute	Summit Co., Twinsburg	1828	Estab. by Samuel Bissell, a Congregational minister. By 1840 the school had 7 teachers and more than 300 students from all over the Reserve.
Urbana Female Seminary	Champaign Co., Urbana	1824	
Ursuline Academy	Brown Co., St. Martin	Estab. 1845	Founded by French Ursuline (Catholic) sisters from St. Martin, France. This academy estab. for young women offered advanced academic subjects, music, drawing, and French embroidery. Assoc. needlework: Celia Moleux—1850.
Vincent, Miss Almeda	Cuyahoga Co., Chagrin Falls	1835	First teacher.
Vining, Mary	Huron Co., Townsend	1837	Taught a small school held in a room at the home of Mr. and Mrs. Arnold.*
Voorhees, Susan	Clark Co., Springfield	c. 1832	*See* Springfield Female Academy.
Wadsworth Academy	Medina Co., Wadsworth	Bef. 1850	"A fine academy for both sexes." No curriculum listed. Ref: Henry Howe, *Historical Collections of Ohio* (1856), p. 348.
Wales, Mrs. Adeline	Portage Co., Palmyra	1842	Taught the first select and boarding school. Taught grades 1 through 8 for 8 years.*
Wales, Mary F. C.	Huron Co., Norwalk	1835	Taught at the Female Seminary and at a private school for young ladies at her home. Marr. Hon. S. T. Worcester.*
Ware, Miss Eliza	Huron Co., Norwalk	1833	*See* Norwalk Female Seminary. She opened the school on Nov. 11, 1833 at the Methodist Episcopal Church. Other teachers: Miss Jenkins; Miss Louisa Hamlin; Miss Anna Langford. The seminary burned in 1836, and classes were held in the Baptist Church under the same teachers.
Warren Academy	Trumbull Co., Warren	c. 1820	A co-ed academy. Teachers included Miss Clarissa Norton and Miss Irene Hiccox.
Way, Robert	Warren, Clinton, and Highland Counties	c. 1813–65	Quaker minister and teacher. B. York Co., Penn. in 1788. He moved from place to place over a period of 60 years in the southern part of Ohio, devoting his life to education and teaching. He was schoolmaster at Dutch Creek School in 1813; moved to other Clinton Co. schools, then to Warren Co., opening the Springborough Boarding School in 1822. In 1827 he taught in Highland Co. *See* Beech Grove Academy.
Waynesville Academy	Warren Co., Waynesville	Estab. 1844	Founded by Dr. Sylvanus Fisher. Located on N. Main St., the academy for advanced students occupied a three-story building. It closed in 1857. *See* Rhoda Johns, fig. 43.

Teacher / School	*Location*	*Date*	*Additional Information and Associated Samplers*
Waynesville School	Warren Co., Waynesville	Estab. 1802–03	Founded by the Miami Monthly Meeting of the Society of Friends (Quakers). First teachers: Elizabeth and Susan Wright. *See* pp. 38, 39. Assoc. samplers: M. Hussey—1807; Margaret Holloway—1807; Mary Kelly—1807; Leah Pugh—1811; Mary J. Tuley—1824; Angelina Wilgus—1827; Sarah Demarest—1825; Eliza Satterthwaite—1830; Hannah Edmondson—1833 and 1834; Mary A. Edmondson—1834; H. Clevenger—1834; Henrietta Heagen—1834; Mary A. Borton—1832; Susan H. Bone—1838; Abigail Sherwood—1838; Ruth A. Edmondson—1842; Rhoda E. Johns—undated.
Webber, Gratia	Butler Co.	1835	Assoc. sampler: Elizabeth Selby—1835.
Webster, Miss C. M.	Washington Co., Marietta	1830–40	*See* Marietta Female Seminary.
Welding, Emily	Warren Co., Springboro	1833	Ref: *Western Star,* 15 March 1833: She advertises that the Springborough School (Quaker) will begin and offers to teach plain and ornamental needlework. Miss Welding probably lived at Eli Hurst's home for 3 years. *See* Hurst's Boarding School. After 1837 she returned to Philadelphia.
Wells, Miss	Washington Co., Marietta	c. 1830–40	*See* Marietta Ladies Seminary.
West Branch Friends School	Miami Co., West Milton	1808	The 1808 Meeting House was used as a school (Union Twp.). (Quaker)
Western Female Institute	Hamilton Co., Cincinnati	1836	Ref: *Cincinnati Directory 1836–37:* "[B]y Misses Dutton and Tappan. NW corner of Plum and 3d."
Western Female Seminary (or Institute)	Hamilton Co., Cincinnati	Early 1830s	Ref: *Cincinnati Directory 1834:* "Operated by Catherine and Harriet Beecher Stowe. Sycamore and Fourth Sts." *See* Stowe, Catherine and Harriet.
Western Liberal Institute	Washington Co., Marietta	1850 (or earlier)	Lists embroidery and needlework in all their various forms.
Western Reserve Academy	Summit Co., Hudson	1826	Founded as a co-educational prep school for grades 9–12 for Western Reserve College.
Western Reserve Normal School	Erie Co., Milan	c. 1846	Estab. at an early date and having 75 pupils by 1846.
Wheeler, Miss (and sister, Mrs. Amos P. Woodford)	Trumbull Co., Farmington	1813–14	Held classes every Saturday afternoon for all the girls in town, teaching embroidery, fine sewing, polite conversation, etc.*
Whinery, Esther	Clinton Co., Chester Twp.	c. 1841	Teacher at Chester Township's old brick school. Assoc. sampler: Esther Whinery—1838.
Wick, Phoebe (Pheebe)	Mahoning Co., Youngstown	c. 1800	The daughter of Rev. William Wick, who conducted the first religious service in the Western Reserve. The church was in use as a school for 30 years.*
Wiley, Miss Polly	Butler Co., Paddy's Run (Shandon); also called New London	1808	First teacher of a school opened by Welsh settlers, members of the Congregational Church. She taught 22 students.
Willey, Mrs. Fanny	Cuyahoga Co., Bedford	1830	Operated a select school at her church building that she had built.*
Williams, Mrs.	Hamilton Co., Cincinnati	c. 1802	Ref: *Western Spy:* "[T]hat she would teach sewing." Note: This may be the Mrs. Williams teaching in Lebanon in the 1830s.
Williams, Caroline	Ashtabula Co., Kingsville	1836	*See* Kingsville Academy.
(Mrs.) Williams's Lebanon Female Seminary	Warren Co., Lebanon	1830	She advertised her school over a three-year period in the *Western Star. See* Lebanon Female Seminary. Related sampler: Catherine S. Skinner—1832.
Williamson, Miss Jane	Adams Co., Manchester and West Union	c. 1835–43	B. in N. C. in 1803. Daughter of Rev. Williamson. Taught a select school. Left Adams Co., Ohio, in 1843 for missionary work with the Dakota Indians.
Williamson, Lucretia	Butler Co., Middletown	c. 1833	Assisted Mr. Nathaniel Furman and his wife. *See* (Nathaniel) Furman's Academy.
Willoughby Female Seminary	Lake Co., Willoughby	1847	The school had more than 100 students; it burned c. 1850. It was re-estab. as Lake Erie Seminary in Painesville. Hannah Parker attended the seminary and also taught.* *See* Miss Roxena Tenny.
Wilson, Amanda	Highland Co., Hillsborough	1847	No school name given. She served with David Herron as a teacher in a house on Walnut St., while Mary Muntz served as a teacher with William Herron at the old Main St. house. About 150 students enrolled.
Wood, Mrs.	Hamilton Co., Cincinnati	1828	Of London. Taught at finishing school in Belmont House, the present site of the Taft Museum.
(Mr. and Mrs.) Wood's Academy	Scioto Co., Portsmouth	1827	
Woodford, Eliza	Trumbull Co., Vienna	1820	Taught at the age of 16 in Hartford Twp. Later went to Hartford, Conn., and attended the school of Harriet Beecher Stowe.*
Woods, Mr. John	Butler Co., Hamilton	1832	*See* Hamilton-Rossville Academy.

Teacher / School	Location	Date	Additional Information and Associated Samplers
Woods, Miss R.	Warren Co., Franklin	1834	Ref: *Western Star,* 11 April 1834: Mentions her as a teacher at the Franklin Female High School.
(Mrs.) Woods's Female Academy	Hamilton Co., Cincinnati	1836	Ref: *Cincinnati Directory 1836–37:* "[A]t 4th between Walnut and Vine."
Wooster Female Seminary	Wayne Co., Wooster	Bef. 1850	"One female seminary in good repute."
Works, (Aunt) Mary	Trumbull Co., Bloomfield	1840	B. 1820. Never marr. She served as a teacher and tailoress.*
Worthington Academy	Franklin Co., Worthington	c. 1810	Opened by Mr. John Kilbourne, Principal. Cynthia Barker, Preceptress. The school became a college in 1819 but closed in 1823. Assoc. samplers: Minerva Bartholomew—1819; Hulda Bull—1819.
Worthington Female Seminary	Franklin Co., Worthington	1839	Founded by Methodist minister Rev. Jacob Young and Col. Kilbourne. Miss Serepta Marsh served as first principal. "The building is of brick, and stands in a pleasant green."
Wozencraft, Mrs.	Hamilton Co., Cincinnati	1811	Ref: *Liberty Hall,* 2 April 1811: "MRS. WOZENCRAFT, respectfully informs the public in general, that she has resumed her SCHOOL. At her dwelling house north west of the Academy. She hopes from her former care and attention to her pupils, to receive equal encouragement. To cultivate the mind, to mend the manners, and encourage the well inclined, has always been her aim, as well as to instruct and improve. She will teach: *Spelling, Reading, Writing, Plain Sewing, Embroidery, Tambouring, Lace work, Artificial, Drawing & Painting.* Plain Sewing and Flowering, will be executed in the neatest manner, and on the shortest notice. On the first Monday in May next, she intends removing her school to the corner of Fourth & Sycamore Sts., in the dwelling now occupied by Dr. C—y. Country produce will be taken in part pay, at the market price."
Wright, Elizabeth and Susan	Warren Co., Waynesville	1805	Sisters who were the first teachers of the Waynesville (Quaker) School. *See* Waynesville School, p. 38. Assoc. samplers: Leah Pugh—1811; Margaret Holloway—1807; Mary Ann Hussey—1807; Mary Kelly—1807.
(Mrs.) Wright's Female Academy	Hamilton Co., Cincinnati	1836	Ref: *Cincinnati Directory 1836–37:* "[A]t Walnut near 3d."
Wright, Mrs. Hannah (Lewis)	Greene Co., Xenia	c. 1840s	She and her husband operated a private boarding school that was known for excellence for several years. In 1851–52 she taught at the Xenia Female Seminary.
Xenia Female Academy	Greene Co., Xenia	Estab. 1850	Taught by Mrs. Mulligan and located on E. Church St. First teachers: Dr. Thomas S. Towler, Supt.; Nancy M. Hartford; Mary E. McQuirk; Mrs. Hannah Wright; Mary E. Harbison. Taken over by the Methodists in 1852.
Youngstown, First Presbyterian Church	Mahoning Co., Youngstown	c. 1800	Rev. William Wick used the church for 30 years, along with his daughter, Pheebe, as a school. Also teaching there: Pheebe Kirkpatrick; Betsey Kirkpatrick.*
Zanesville Female Seminary (Public)	Muskingum Co., Zanesville	Estab. 1842	In Sept. 1842 the public schools were divided into the Male Seminary and Female Seminary. The Female Seminary was located on Seventh St. in Howe Seminary.
Zanesville Seminary for Young Ladies	Muskingum Co., Zanesville	Estab. 1810	*See* Mrs. Colerick. Ref: *Zanesville Express,* 28 October 1818.

By County

Clark Co. Schools and Teachers

Springfield, bef. 1850:
Rev. Moore—1844, Boarding School; Samuel Smith's School; Mrs. Ann Warder's Female Academy—1832, Miss Armstrong, Asst.; Miss Eunice Strong with Miss Parsons, Asst.; Miss Elliott; Miss Mary Harrison; Miss Hannah Haas; Miss Catharine Hass; Mrs. Lowndes; Miss Lavinia Baird (taught in her own house); Misses Laura and Virginia Miller; Miss Vicroy; Miss Peet; Miss Emma Way; Mrs. Anna Foos; Mrs. Woodwar; Mrs. Donohue; Miss Finley; Miss Ebersole; Miss Doolittle; Miss Matilda Stout; Jane Reid; Miss Anna B. Johnson; Rev. Jonathan Edwards—c. 1849–52, Presbyterian select school for young women; Mrs. Menter—c. 1825; Mrs. Foster—c. 1825; Jane Reid, Miss Brown, and Miss Lee—c. 1840s.

*Cuyahoga Co. Teachers**

Bedford, bef. 1850:
Alzina Ames; Polly Allen; Lucy Baldwin; Miss Barnes; Julia Barnum; Linda Bassett; Arzelia Benedict; Harriet Boynton; Zeriah Burke; Roseamand Clark; Albina Cole; Caroline Hartshorn; Cornelia Knapp; Alvira Lambson; Sarah Neice; Julia Parshall; Hannah Jane Peck; Maria Peck; Fanny Robinson; Mary Ann Sill; Mrs. Smith; Julia Ann Tryon; Jemima Turner; Sally Warner; Eunice Waters.

Geauga Co. Teachers

Middlefield, c. 1810–20:
Paul Clapp; Mercy Tracy; Mary Bond; Ann Foote; Electa Clapp; Elvira Clapp; Phoebe Tracy; Electa Richmond; Phoebe Jarvis; Lucinda Grey; Olive Newcomb; Lucy Ann Grey.

Huntsburg, 1808–50:
Pioneer school teachers: Lucinda Walden; Electa Clapp; Miss Pitkin; Melissa Talbot; Mrs. H. M. R. Tracy; Mary Williams; Asenath Mastick.

Shelby Co. Teachers

Sidney, bef. 1850:
Includes: Rev. and Mrs. Samuel Cleland—c. 1848; Mrs. McKinley—1841; Miss Emma Kelsey—1848; Mrs. Dr. Johnson—1840; Miss Jennie Murray—1850–53. *See* Sidney Male & Female Academy above.

Trumbull Co. Teachers

Kinsman, 1822:
Miss Irene Hiccox (Hickox) had boarding school located (probably) in the home of Mrs. Hannah Andrews. Miss Hiccox, educated at Litchfield, Conn., opened the first school and attracted students from a large area. She offered painting, map drawing, and embroidery. Moved to Warren, then Cleveland. Marr. Joel Scranton. *See* Hannah Andrews.*

Vienna, 1805:
Mrs. Ira Bartholomew. The town sustained an academy for many years and a graded school at the center.*

Warren and Bloomfield, c. 1830:
Early Warren teachers included: Mrs. Dorcas Gaskill; Miss Lathrop; Miss McNeal (taught a primary school on Market St.); Miss Clarissa Norton; Miss Mary Case; Miss Bostwick; Miss Irene Hiccox. Early Bloomfield teachers included: Clarissa Howe; Elizabeth Huntington; M. Fisher; Julia and Almeda Ballard; Sophronia Otis; Samantha and Caroline Converse; Charlotte Kendall; Miss Atkins; Aurelia Howe; Julia Ann Wright; Almena Saunders; Adeline Warner.*

Weathersfield and Niles, 1844–49:
Dr. Eben Blachly and wife, Jane Trew, opened a popular boarding and day school in Niles.*

Warren Co. Teachers

Morrow, c. 1845–50:
Miss Sidney Thomas; Mrs. Mary Branigan; Mrs. Sharp; Miss Cox; Mrs. David Sanders; Miss N. B. Hart.

notes

Foreword

1. Florence Yoder Wilson, "Some Little Girls Enter the World of Art," *Needlecraft: The Magazine of Home Arts* 21 (Nov. 1929): 4.

2. See Kimberly Smith Ivey's *In the Neatest Manner: The Making of the Virginia Sampler Tradition*, Sue Studebaker's exhibit catalog *Ohio Samplers: Schoolgirl Embroideries 1803–1850*, and The Carter House, Franklin, Tennessee, exhibit catalog *Tennessee Stitches: Catalog to Accompany an Exhibit of 19th Century Williamson County Samplers*, as three exceptions to this.

3. Wilson, "Little Girls," p. 4.

Preface

1. Sue Studebaker, *Ohio Samplers: Schoolgirl Embroideries, 1803–1850*.

Introduction

1. Thomas Aquinas Burke, *Ohio Lands: A Short History*, pp. 14–15.
2. Henry Howe, *Historical Collections of Ohio*, v. 1, p. 131.
3. Burke, *Ohio Lands*, 5.
4. Howe, *Historical Collections of Ohio*, v. 1, p. 125.
5. Ibid.
6. Burke, *Ohio Lands*, 32.
7. Ibid., 13.
8. Howe, *Historical Collections of Ohio*, v. 1, p. 126.
9. Col. D. W. McClung, *Means and Ends or Self Training*.
10. Edward C. Biddle, *Young Lady's Own Book*, p. 195.

Southern Ohio

1. Henry Howe, *Historical Collections of Ohio*, v. 2, p. 797.

2. *American Friend*, Dec. 21, 1821, Ohio Historical Society (OHS), N 2784.

3. Williams Brothers, *History of Washington County, Ohio*, p. 513.

4. C. E. Dickson, *History of Belpre, Washington County Ohio*, p. 122.

5. Mary Eliza Mason, *Genealogy and History of the Family of Hugh Mason, William Mason, and Allied Families*, p. 258.

6. Susan Burrows Swan, *Plain and Fancy: American Women and Their Needlework, 1700–1850*, p. 231.

7. Pratt Family Files, Campus Martius Museum Archives, Marietta, Ohio. Personal handwritten letter by Sarah M. Pratt dated October 5, 1851. Letter written simply to "Dear C."

8. *Cincinnati: A Guide to the Queen City and Its Neighbors*, p. 161.

9. Howe, *Historical Collections of Ohio*, v. 1, p. 751.

10. Jane Sherzer, "The Higher Education of Women in the Ohio Valley Previous to 1840," p. 273.

11. William E. Smith, *History of Southwestern Ohio: The Miami Valleys*, v. 1, p. 383.

12. Ann Hulme Price Letters, Ohio Historical Society Archives. VFM 1947.

13. Queries for Ministers and Elders, Springfield Friends Meeting, p. 47.

14. D. C. Schilling, "Pioneer Schools and School Masters," p. 41.

15. Nazareth Academy School Records 1820–90 Catalogues, Archives, in Nazareth, Ky.

16. Nazareth Female Academy Catalogue (1858), Archives of Spaulding University, Louisville, Ky.

17. Howe, *Historical Collections of Ohio,* v. 1. (1856) p. 218.

18. *Indian Hill Living* (October 1986).

19. Elizabeth Collette, ed., *Journey to the Promised Land: Journal of Elizabeth Van Horne, 1807,* pp. 9–17.

20. Price, personal letters.

21. Ibid.

22. *Western Star,* April 10, 1830.

23. Ibid. Ads appeared regularly from April 10, 1830, through January 7, 1832.

24. Alfred Holcomb, *Lebanon Academy Catalogue of the Instructors and Pupils,* p. 3.

25. Sherzer, "Education," p. 3, quoting from Thwaites, *Early Western Travels,* vol. 4, pp. 184–85

26. Jane Sikes Hageman, *Ohio Pioneer Artists,* p. 114.

27. Collette, ed., *Journey,* p. 22.

28. Shaker samplers include: Elcey Patterson, 1846; Ruth Brown, undated; Abigail Russell, c. 1830; and Margaret Sawyer, 1844.

29. Sister Jennie M. Wells, unpublished personal letter to Mrs. J. C. Pillion, January 12, 1943.

30. Lindsay M. Brien, *Miami Valley Pioneers, Ohio: A Genealogical Index,* p. 141.

31. Union Village Shakers. Warren County Museum Archives. pp. 229–31.

32. The Wallace Hugh Cathcart Collection of Shaker Literature and Manuscripts. Western Reserve Historical Society. Reel 42 VB 254.

33. William W. Hinshaw, *Encyclopedia of American Quaker Genealogy,* v. 5, p. 18.

34. "Friends of the Landscape: A Preliminary Examination of the Society of Friends: Their Settlement and Architecture in Clinton, Highland, and Warren Counties, 1795–1860," p. vi.

35. Dennis Dalton, "Heighway to 1972: Traveling from W'ville 1797," p. 33.

36. Collection of Monroe County (Indiana) Historical Society.

37. Hinshaw, *Encyclopedia,* v. 5, p. 59

38. *Western Star,* Lebanon, Ohio, June 18, 1822. Advertisement for Franklin Seminary under Rev. Matthew G. Wallace, Superintendent. See entry in Pioneer Teachers and Schools section, page 000.

39. The Hazel Spencer Phillips Papers, "The First Schools."

40. Sarah Schenck Crane, *The Crane Family History*.

41. Sue Studebaker, *Ohio Samplers: Schoolgirl Embroideries, 1803–1850,* p. 2. See the entry for C. V. B. Schenck's School in the Pioneer Teachers and Schools section of this volume, page 289.

42. Dean F. Failey, *Long Island Is My Nation,* p. 189.

43. Donald Ross, "27 Stations to Libertyville."

44. Hinshaw, *Encyclopedia,* v. 5, p. 978.

45. Robert W. Steele, *Early Dayton, 1796–1896,* p. 133.

46. *Dayton Watchman,* Feb. 2, 1822.

47. Schilling, "Pioneer Schools," p. 40.

48. History accounts also mention the Butler County School at New London (now called Shandon) established by Reverend Thomas E. Thomas and his wife, Elizabeth Fisher Thomas. Mrs. Thomas trained the girls in "plain and ornamental sewing." Since she was "lately from England," undoubtedly some Dayton parents believed sending their daughters to Mrs. Thomas would ensure that they would receive the best training and learn the newest stitches.

49. Carl M. Becker, *The Village,* p. 10, fn. 63.

50. Studebaker, *Ohio Samplers,* p. 34. Abraham Shank, letter written to John and Margaret (Shank) Fundenburg, October 29, 1827. Private collection.

51. Jack Gieck, *A Photo Album of Ohio's Canal Era, 1825–1913,* p. 125.

52. Howard R. Houser, *A Sense of Place,* p. 59.

53. W. H. Beers, *History of Clinton County,* p. 307.

54. *Western Star,* Sept. 18, 1822. The curriculum listed advanced academic subjects. Instruction in needlework was not offered.

55. Hinshaw, *Encyclopedia,* v. 5, p. 540.

56. Margriet Hogue, personal consultation, Dayton, Ohio, August 9, 2001.

57. Beers, *History of Clinton County,* p. 916.

58. A stuffed-work toilette cover (c. 1821) made by Letitia Heston Lownes is in the collection of the Springboro Historical Society Museum, Springborough, Ohio. Miss Heston moved to Springborough in 1842 and married Zachriah Lownes.

59. Houser, *A Sense of Place,* p. 4. "The moral dilemma of existing slavery brought 18,000 Quakers into the Northwest Territory the first fifteen years of the nineteenth century."

60. Rebecca T. (Frazier) Bailey Schallenberger, "Biographical Notes Gathered by her Great-Granddaughters—Virginia Bailey Schallenberger and Lois Hunnicutt Joyce."

61. Swan, *Plain and Fancy,* p. 229.

62. For information on quilting techniques, see *Clues in the Calico* by Barbara Brackman, pp. 112, 113.

63. Howe, *Historical Collections of Ohio,* v. 1, p. 342.

64. Col. D. W. McClung, *The Centennial Anniversary of the City of Hamilton, Ohio,* p. 199.

65. Stephen Riggs Williams, *The Saga of "The Paddy's Run,"* pp. 147, 187.

66. *Western Star,* advertisement, Mar. 3, 1833.

67. Sherzer, "Education," p. 17.

68. Charles B. Galbreath, *History of Ohio,* p. 499.

69. George C. Crout, *Middletown U.S.A.: All-American City,* pp. 56–57.

70. Adjutant General of Ohio, *Roster of Ohio Soldiers in the War of 1812,* p. 132.

71. Swan, *Plain and Fancy,* p. 224.

72. Howe, *Historical Collections of Ohio,* vol. 2, p. 693.

73. Allan N. Eckert, *The Frontiersman,* p. 420.

74. Rebecca Galloway, diary.

75. M. A. Broadstone, *History of Greene County,* v. 1, p. 443.

76. "Rankin House State Memorial."

77. W. W. Boyd, *Secondary Education in Ohio Previous to 1840,* v. 25, p. 121; Howe, *Historical Collections of Ohio,* v. 1, p. 337.

78. Nelson N. Evans, *A History of Scioto County,* v. 1, p. 441.

79. Ibid. p. 487.

80. Ibid. p. 486.

81. Ibid.

82. Howe, *Historical Collections of Ohio,* v. 2, pp. 491–96.

83. Robert B. Casari, et al, *Chillicothe, Ohio, 1796–1996: Ohio's First Capital,* p. 44.

84. Rowland H. Rerick, *History of Ohio,* p. 155.

85. Byron Williams, *History of Clermont and Brown Counties, Ohio,* v. 1, pp. 84–85.

86. Ibid., p. 86.

87. Howe, *Historical Collections of Ohio,* v. 1, pp. 671–75.

88. Ohio Census of Springfield Township, Gallia County, 1850.

89. Walker, *History of Athens County, Ohio,* pp. 309–11.

90. C. J. Puetz, Ohio County Maps, p. 11.

91. Charles Manning Walker, *History of Athens County, Ohio,* pp. 220, 285, and 286.

92. Ibid., p. 220.

93. Eunice Rice, *Memoirs;* Studebaker, *Ohio Samplers,* fig. 14.

Central Ohio

1. Sue Studebaker, *Ohio Samplers: Schoolgirl Embroideries, 1803–1850,* fig. 16.

2. W. H. Beers, *History of Clark County, Ohio,* p. 869.

3. W. H. Beers, *History of Miami County, Ohio,* p. 660.

4. Ibid., p. 660.

5. Asa Coleman Letters.

6. Henry Howe, *Historical Collections of Ohio,* v. 1, p. 960.

7. Eugene Monnett, *History of the Monet Family in America.*

8. Howe, *Historical Collections of Ohio,* v. 1, p. 619.

9. Jacob H. Studer, *Columbus, Ohio: Its History, Resources and Progress,* p. 13.

10. Osman Castle Hooper, *History of the City of Columbus Ohio: From the Founding of Franklinton 1797 through the World War Period, to the Year 1920,* pp. 163–64.

11. *The Ohio Plough-Boy,* Aug. 26, 1828.

12. Howe, *Historical Collections of Ohio,* v. 1, p. 637.

13. Ibid., p. 637.

14. O. L. Baskin, *History of Delaware County and Ohio,* p. 362.

15. Ibid. p. 362.

16. Howe, *Historical Collections of Ohio,* v. 1, p. 714.

17. Ibid., p. 714.

18. Howe, *Historical Collections of Ohio,* v. 2, p. 71.

19. Howe, *Historical Collections of Ohio,* v. 2, p. 81.

20. Horace King, *Granville Buildings on the National Register of Historic Places.*

21. N. N. Hill, Jr., *History of Licking County Ohio,* p. 449.

22. Howe, *Historical Collections of Ohio,* v. 1, pp. 587–89.

23. W. H. Beers, *History of Fairfield and Perry Counties,* pp. 146–48.

24. *Lancaster Daily Eagle,* Oct. 15, 1894.

25. Beers, *Fairfield and Perry,* p. 151.

26. E. M. L. Wiseman, *Pioneer Period and Pioneer People of Fairfield County, Ohio,* pp. 211–12.

27. *Encyclopedia Britannica* (1968), v. 13, p. 433.

28. Howe, *Historical Collections of Ohio,* v. 1, pp. 988–89.

29. Ibid., p. 989. Mrs. Chase was born in February 1783 in Holland. Her maiden name was Sophia May Ingraham, and she married Rev. Philander Chase, the first bishop of all the Episcopal churches in Ohio, on July 4, 1819.

30. Stacey C. Hollander, *American Radiance: The Ralph Esmerian Gift to the American Folk Art Museum,* pp. 517–18.

31. Unpublished diary of Thomas Linn, Millersburg, Ohio. Private collection.

32. Howe, *Historical Collections of Ohio,* v. 2, pp. 328–30.

33. Norris Schneider, *Y Bridge City: The Story of Zanesville and Muskingum County, Ohio,* p. 46.

34. "Mr. and Mrs. M'Intire: A Graphic Biographic Sketch of Zanesville's Founder and His Wife," by granddaughter of Col. Ebenezer Zane and niece of Mrs. McIntire, *Zanesville Times Recorder,* Apr. 1892.

35. Howe, *Historical Collections of Ohio,* v. 2, p. 335; William W. Hinshaw, *Encyclopedia of American Quaker Genealogy,* v. 4, pp. 321, 337, 350.

36. *Zanesville Express,* Mar. 29, 1820; (Marietta) *American Friend; Columbus Monitor; Lancaster Eagle; Chillicothe Weekly Recorder and Scioto Gazette.*

37. Jane Sherzer, "The Higher Education of Women in the Ohio Valley previous to 1840," pp. 13–17.

38. The annotated "Map of the Meetings of Friends in Ohio Yearly Meetings: Salem School, 1826." The Stillwater Quarter included twelve Meetings (congregations).

39. Gloria Seaman Allen, *Family Record: Genealogical Watercolor and Needlework.*

40. Sherzer, "Education," pp. 13–17.

41. In 1828, differences in belief and ethics caused a separation in the Society of Friends. They were divided into the Orthodox Branch and the Hicksite Branch, the latter being the more liberal of the two.

42. Susan Burrows Swan, *Plain and Fancy: American Women and Their Needlework, 1700–1850,* p. 231.

43. Howe, *Historical Collections of Ohio,* v. 1, p. 970.

44. Sherzer, "Education," pp. 13–17.

Northern Ohio

1. Kenneth V. Lottich, *New England Transplanted,* p. 112.

2. James J. Burns, *Educational History of Ohio,* p. 21.

3. Burns, *Educational History,* p. 21. Many of these teachers were associated with the Congregational and Presbyterian Churches.

4. Mary Lou Conlin, *Simon Perkins of the Western Reserve,* p. 121.

5. Emily Noyes Vanderpoel, *More Chronicles of a Pioneer School from 1792 to 1833: The History of The Litchfield Female Academy Kept by Miss Sarah Pierce and her Nephew John Pierce Brace,* pp. 160, 236.

6. Jessie Cohen, "Early Education in Ohio," p. 118.

7. Gertrude Van Rensselaer Wickham, *Memorial to the Pioneer Women of the Western Reserve,* v. 3, p. 399.

8. H. Z. Williams, *History of Trumbull and Mahoning Counties,* v. 2, p. 465.

9. Wickham, *Memorial,* v. 2, pp. 241–42.

10. Susan Burrows Swan, *Plain and Fancy: American Women and Their Needlework, 1700–1850,* p. 222.

11. Henry Howe, *Historical Collections of Ohio,* v. 1, pp. 109, 448–49.

12. Frakturs are illuminated writings and drawings on paper, a type of German folk-art document that is collected with

great enthusiasm. They were usually done in pen and ink and then embellished with vigorous colors. They were made to commemorate special occasions such as births, baptisms, house blessings. etc. See *The Fraktur-Writings or Illuminated Manuscripts of the Pennsylvania Germans* by Donald A. Shelley, pp. 22, 93.

13. Swan, *Plain and Fancy*, p. 224. Chenille yarn, which originated in France, was a fuzzy silk yarn. It was used in American embroideries usually only for accents.

14. Thomas H. Smith, *The Mapping of Ohio*, p. 139.

15. Williams Brothers, *History of Geauga and Lake Counties*, p. 41.

16. *Encyclopedia Britannica* (1968), v. 4, p. 60.

17. Printed obituary, source unknown, accompanied sampler purchased at auction.

18. Williams Brothers, *History of Ashtabula County Ohio*, pp. 93–97.

19. Ibid., p. 96.

20. Ibid., p. 96.

21. Williams Brothers, *History of Ashtabula County, Ohio*, p. 101.

22. Harriet Taylor Upton, *History of the Western Reserve*, p. 1566.

23. Howe, *Historical Collections of Ohio*, v. 2, p. 832.

24. Wickham, *Memorial*, pt. 2, pp. 261–62.

25. Ibid., pt. 3, pp. 380–83.

26. Ibid., p. 383.

27. Ibid., p. 385.

28. Ibid., pt. 1, p. 15.

29. "An Enduring Legacy," pp. 99–100.

30. William B. Doyle, *Centennial History of Summit County Ohio*, pp. 174–75.

31. Margaret Manor Butler, *A Pictorial History of the Western Reserve*, p. 2.

32. Howe, *Historical Collections of Ohio*, v. 2, p. 201.

33. Eliza and Laura Branch; Betsey Cowles; Chloe Bradley Newton; Miss Parmalee; and Martha Wright. (Other teachers may also have attended Oberlin College, but the information was omitted in their listing.)

34. Butler, *Pictorial History*, p. 100.

35. Williams Brothers, *History of Lorain County, Ohio*.

36. Hope Hanley, *Needlework in America*, p. 71.

37. William H. Perrin, et al, *The History of Crawford County, Ohio*, pp. 401–3.

38. Howe, *Historical Collections of Ohio*, v. 1, p. 580.

39. Edison Birthplace Association, Inc. Publication (undated) Pamphlet. Milan, Ohio.

40. Ibid.

41. Howe, *Historical Collections of Ohio*, vol. 2, p. 878.

Victorian Impulses

1. Ann Hulme Price Letters.

2. Ibid.

3. Ibid.

4. Hamilton County records list Ann Eliza Price married Robert M. Moore on May 1, 1843. This Ann may be Ann Hulme Price, whose letters are quoted.

5. William B. Doyle, *History of Summit County*, p. 198.

6. Hope Hanley, *Needlepoint in America*, pp. 69 and 70.

7. Verses by Rev. Isaac Watts (1674–1748) were "quoted" on samplers more often than those by any other author. His most popular book for children, first printed in 1715, was entitled *Horæ Lyricæ and Divine Songs*.

8. *Encyclopedia Britannica* (1968), v. 5, p. 519.

9. J. A. Caldwell, *Atlas of Adams County, Ohio*.

bibliography

Published Works

Allen, Gloria Seaman. *Family Record: Genealogical Watercolors and Needlework.* Washington D.C.: DAR Museum, 1989.

"Amaranth." Nazareth Junior College and Academy Publication. Louisville, Ky., Spaulding University, Archives, 1926.

Andrews, Edward Deming. *The People Called Shakers.* 1953; rpt., New York: Dover, 1963.

Andrews, Israel Ward. *Washington County and the Early Settlement of Ohio.* 1877; rpt., Marietta: Washington County Historical Society, Inc., 1976.

"Art Needlework." *Harper's Monthly,* Oct. 1880.

Barney, E. E., et al. "Education of Girls in Dayton Cooper Seminary." Dayton: Cooper Seminary, n.d.

Baskin, O. L. *History of Delaware County and Ohio.* Chicago: O. L. Baskin Historical Publishers, 1882.

Becker, Carl M., Ph.D. *The Village: A History of Germantown, Ohio.* Germantown Historical Society Publication, 1976.

Beers, W. H. *History of Champaign County, Ohio.* Chicago, 1881.

———. *History of Clark County, Ohio.* 1881; rpt., Mt. Vernon, Ind.: Windmill Publications, 1994.

———. *History of Clinton County, Ohio.* 1882; rpt., Evansville, Ind.: Whipporwill Publication, 1989.

———. *History of Darke County, Ohio.* 1880; rpt., Evansville, Ind.: Unigraphic, 1970.

———. *History of Fairfield and Perry Counties.* Chicago, 1883.

———. *History of Madison County, Ohio.* Chicago: W. H. Beers & Co., 1883.

———. *History of Miami County, Ohio.* Chicago: W. H. Beers & Co., 1881.

———. *History of Warren County, Ohio.* Chicago: W. H. Beers & Co., 1881.

Biddle, Edward C. *Young Lady's Own Book.* Philadelphia: DeSilver, Thomas & Co., 1836.

"Birthplace of Thomas Alva Edison." Milan, Ohio: The Edison Birthplace Association, n.d.

Bogan, Dallas. "The Life of Washington LaFayette Schenck." (Lebanon) *Western Star,* Aug. 17, 1997.

Bolton, Ethel Stanwood, and Eva Johnston Coe. *American Samplers.* Boston: Massachusetts Society of Colonial Dames of America, 1921.

Boyd, W. W. "Secondary Education in Ohio Previous to 1840." *Ohio Archaeological and Historical Publication* 25 (Oct. 1916).

Brackman, Barbara. *Clues in the Calico.* EPM Publications, n.d.

Brien, Lindsay M. *Miami Valley Ohio, Pioneers: A Genealogical Index.* Dayton: Dayton Circle, Colonial Dames of America, 1970.

Broadstone, M. A. *History of Greene County, Ohio.* Indianapolis: B. F. Bowen & Co., 1918.

Burke, James L., and Donald E. Bensch. *Mount Pleasant and the Early Quakers of Ohio.* Columbus: Ohio Historical Society, 1975.

Burke, Thomas Aquinas. *Ohio Lands: A Short History.* Columbus: Auditor of State, State of Ohio, 1997.

Burns, James J. *Educational History of Ohio.* Columbus: Historical Publishing, 1905.

Butler, Margaret Manor. *A Pictorial History of the Western Reserve.* Cleveland: World Publishing Company for the Western Reserve Historical Society, 1963.

Caldwell, J. A. *Caldwell's Atlas of Adams County, Ohio.* Published by author, 1880.

Casari, Robert B., Luvada D. Kuhn, Patricia F. Medert, and William H. Nolan. *Chillicothe, Ohio, 1796–1996: Ohio's First Capital.* Chillicothe: Ross County Historical Society and Bicentennial Commission, 1996.

Cauffield, Joyce V. B., and Carolyn E. Banfield. *The River Book.* Cincinnati: Program for Cincinnati, 1981.

Cemetery Records of Clinton County, Ohio, 1798–1978. Wilmington, Ohio: Clinton County Historical Society, 1980.

Chambrun, de Clara Longworth. *Cincinnati: The Story of the Queen City.* New York: Scribner's Sons, 1939.

Che-Le-Co-The: Glimpses of Yesterday. Chillicothe, Ohio, 1896.

Chillicothe and Ross County. American Guide Series. 1938. [Federal Writers' Project.]

Cincinnati: A Guide to the Queen City and Its Neighbors. American Guide Series. Cincinnati: Wiesen-Hart Press, and the City of Cincinnati: 1943. [Compiled by the Writers' Program of the WPA in the State of Ohio.]

Cincinnati, Ohio: 1836, 1837, and 1840 Editions [Cincinnati Directory.]

Cist, Charles. *Sketches and Statistics of Cincinnati in 1851.* Cincinnati: William H. Moore & Co., 1851.

Cohen, Jessie. "Early Education in Ohio." *Magazine of Western History,* 3 (1886).

Collette, Elizabeth, ed. *Journey to the Promised Land: Journal of Elizabeth Van Horne, 1807.* Historical Society of Western Pennsylvania, 1939.

Collins, Lewis. *History of Kentucky.* Frankfort, Ky.: Kentucky Historical Society, 1966.

Combined Atlases of Warren County, Ohio, 1875, 1891, and 1903. Warren County Historical Society. Evansville, Indiana: Whipporwill Publications, 1984.

Cone, Stephen D. *Biographical and Historical Sketches: A Narrative of Hamilton and Its Residents.* 2 vols. Hamilton, Ohio: Republican Publishing Company, 1901.

Conlin, Mary Lou. *Simon Perkins of the Western Reserve.* Cleveland, Ohio: Western Reserve Historical Society, 1968.

Conover, Charlotte Reeve. *Dayton and Montgomery County Resources and People.* 4 vols. New York: Lewis Historical Publishing Company, 1932.

Corbin, Frank. *A Walking Tour of Old Worthington.* Worthington, Ohio: Worthington Historical Society Publication, n.d.

Cover, John C., et al. *Memoirs of the Miami Valley.* 3 Vols. Chicago: Robert O. Law Co., 1919.

Crane, Sarah Schenck. *The Crane Family History.* Cincinnati: Ebbert and Richardson Co, 1911.

Creamer, Sister Mary Michael, SCN. "Mother Catherine Spalding." *Filson Club History Quarterly,* (April 1989).

Crout, George C. *Middletown U.S.A: —All-American City.* Middletown, Ohio: Perry Printing Co., for the American Legion, 1960.

———. *Butler County: An Illustrated History.* Woodland Hills, Calif.: Windsor Publications, Butler County Historical Society, n.d.

———. "Special Schools for Young Ladies." *Middletown Journal,* Feb. 1987.

Dalton, Dennis E. "Heighway to 1972: Traveling from W'ville, 1797." *Miami Gazette,* 1972.

———. "Earnharts Now Live in a Home Once a Quaker School." (Lebanon) *Western Star,* 1966.

Dayton: A History in Photographs. Dayton, Ohio: Junior League of Dayton, 1976.

Dickson, C. E. *History of Belpre, Washington County, Ohio.* Parkersburg, W.V.: Globe Printing and Binding Co., for author, 1920.

Doyle, John H. *A History of Early Toledo.* Bowling Green, Ohio: C. S. Van Tassell, n.d.

Doyle, William B. *Centennial History of Summit County, Ohio.* 1908; Rpt., Mt. Vernon, Ind.: Windmill Publications, for Hudson Chapter of the Ohio Genealogical Society, 1993.

Eckert, Allan W. *The Frontiersman.* Boston and Toronto: Little, Brown & Co., 1967.

Edmonds, Mary Jaene. *Samplers and Samplermakers.* New York: Rizzoli, for Los Angeles Museum of Art, 1991.

Eldridge, Mabel, and Harriet E. Foley. *The History of Franklin in the Great Miami Valley.* 1982; rpt., Middletown, Ohio: Alliance Printing and Publishing, for The Franklin Area Historical Society, 1996.

Elliot, Celia. *Once Upon a Town and Township.* Centerville, Ohio: Centerville Historical Society, 1971.

Ellis, Alston. "Samuel Lewis, Progressive Educator in the Early History of Ohio." *Ohio Archaeological and Historical Publications* 25: (1917).

Encyclopedia Britannica, vols. 4 and 13. 1968.

"An Enduring Legacy." *Lessons for November 1978.* Salt Lake City, Utah: Daughters of Utah Pioneers.

Epoch of Blue Ball, Ohio. Blue Ball, Ohio: Blue Ball Historical Society, n.d.

Evans, Nelson W. *A History of Scioto County, Ohio.* 1903; rpt., Evansville, Ind.: Unigraphic, Inc., 1975.

Evans, Nelson W., and Emmons B. Stivers. *A History of Adams County, Ohio.* E. B. Stivers, 1900.

Everhart, J. F. *History of Muskingum County, Ohio.* 1882; rpt., Evansville, Ind.: Unigraphic, Inc., 1974.

Everts, L. H. *A Combination Atlas / Map of Montgomery County, Ohio, 1875.* Evansville, Ind.: Unigraphic, Inc., 1972.

Failey, Dean F. *Long Island Is My Nation.* Stauket, New York: Society for the Preservation of Long Island Antiquities, 1976.

Fleming, Miss Dora. "Annals of Our Neighborhood." *Franklin Chronicle,* Jan. 25, 1906.

Flowers, Olive. *The History of Oxford College for Women, 1830–1928.* Oxford, Ohio: Miami University Books, for the Miami University Alumni Association, 1949.

Foote, John P. *The Schools of Cincinnati and Its Vicinity.* New York: Arno Press and the New York Times, 1870.

Ford, Henry A., and Mrs. Kate B. Ford. *History of Hamilton County, Ohio.* Cleveland, Ohio: L. A. Williams and Company, 1881.

Frary, I. T. *Early Homes of Ohio.* Richmond, Va.: Garrett and Massie, 1936.

Galbreath, Charles B. *History of Ohio.* Chicago and New York: American Historical Society, 1925.

Gard, Willis L. "European Influence on Early Western Education." *Ohio Archaeological and Historical Publications* 25 (1915).

Genealogical and Biographical Record of Miami County, Ohio. Chicago: Lewis Publishing Company, 1900.

Gieck, Jack. *A Photo Album of Ohio's Canal Era, 1825–1913.* Kent, Ohio: Kent State University Press, 1988.

Goss, Rev. Charles Frederic. *Cincinnati: The Queen City, 1788–1912.* Chicago: S. J. Clarke Publishing Co., 1912.

Granville Female Academy (catalogue). Columbus, Ohio: Cutler and Wright, for Granville Female Academy, 1839–40.

Greve, Charles T. *Centennial History of Cincinnati,* vol. 1. Chicago: Biographical Publishing Company, 1904.

Hageman, Jane Sikes. *Ohio Pioneer Artists.* Cincinnati, Ohio: Ohio Furniture Makers, 1993.

Hager, Beth Ann. "Sara Jane's World: The West Manchester Sampler." *TimeLine* (Ohio Historical Society publication), Oct.-Nov. 1990.

Hanley, Hope. *Needlework in America.* New York: Charles Scribner's Sons, and Weathervane Books, 1969.

Hatcher, Harlan. *The Western Reserve: The Story of New Connecticut in Ohio.* Indianapolis and New York: Bobbs-Merrill, 1949.

Havighurst, Walter. *The Miami Years, 1809–1969.* New York: G. P. Putnam's Sons, 1969.

Heiser, Alta Harvey. *Quaker Lady: The Story of Charity Lynch and Her People.* Oxford, Ohio: Mississippi Valley Press, 1941.

Heisey, John W. *A Checklist of American Coverlet Weavers.* Williamsburg, Va.: Colonial Williamsburg Foundation, 1978.

Herr, Patricia T. *The Ornamental Branches: Needlework and Arts from the Lititz Moravian Girls' School, 1800–1865.* Virginia Beach, Va.: Donning Company, for The Heritage Center of Lancaster County, Inc., 1996.

Hill, N. N., Jr. *History of Licking County, Ohio.* Newark, Ohio: A. A. Graham & Co., 1881.

Hinshaw, William W. *Encyclopedia of American Quaker Genealogy.* 6 vols. Baltimore: Genealogical Publishing Company, 1973.

Historical Collections of the Mahoning Valley: An Account of the Two Pioneer Reunions. Youngstown, Ohio: Mahoning Valley Historical Society, 1876.

History and Biographical Cyclopaedia of Butler County, Ohio. Cincinnati: Western Biographical Publishing Co., 1882.

History of Butler County, Ohio. Cincinnati: Western Biographical Publishing Co., 1882.

Hollander, Stacey C. *American Radiance: The Ralph Esmerian Gift to the American Folk Art Museum.* New York: Harry N. Abrams, 2001.

Hooper, Osman Castle. *History of the City of Columbus, Ohio: From the Founding of Franklinton 1797 through the World War Period, to the Year 1920.* Columbus and Cleveland: Memorial Publishing Company, 1920.

Hoover, John C., et al. *Memoirs of the Miami Valley.* 3 vols. Chicago: Robert O. Law Co., 1919.

Houser, Howard R. *A Sense of Place.* Centerville, Ohio: Centerville Historical Society, 1977.

Howe, Henry. *Historical Collections of Ohio,* vols. 1 and 2. Norwalk, Ohio: Laning Printing Co., for The State of Ohio, 1896.

———. *Historical Collections of Ohio.* Cincinnati: Derby, Bradley & Co., for Author, 1847.

———. *Historical Collections of Ohio.* Cincinnati: E. Morgan & Co., 1856.

Ivey, Kimberly Smith. *In the Neatest Manner: The Making of the Virginia Sampler Tradition.* Williamsburg, Va.: The Colonial Williamsburg Foundation; and Austin, Tex.: Curious Works Press, 1997.

———. "The First Effort of an Infant Hand: An Introduction to Virginia Schoolgirl Embroideries, 1742–1850." *Journal of Early Southern Decorative Arts* 16, no. 2 (Nov. 1990).

Izant, Grace Goulder. *Hudson's Heritage.* Kent, Ohio: Kent State University Press, 1985.

Jackson, James S., and Margot Y. Jackson. *At Home on the Hill: The Perkins Family of Akron.* Akron, Ohio: Summit County Historical Society, 1983.

Kaufman, Stanley A., and Leroy Beachy. *Amish in Eastern Ohio.* Walnut Creek, Ohio: German Culture Museum, 1991.

Kemper, Willis Miller, and Harry Linn Wright. *Genealogy of the Kemper Family in the United States.* Chicago: George K. Hazlett and Co., 1899.

King, Horace. *Granville Buildings on the National Register of Historic Places.* Guide pamphlet. Granville, Ohio: Granville Preservation Association, n.d.

Kinnison, William A. *Springfield Clark County: An Illustrated History.* Northridge, Calif.: Windsor Publications, Inc., for Clark County Historical Society and Wittenberg University, 1985.

Knepper, George W. *Ohio and Its People.* Kent, Ohio: Kent State University Press, 1989.

Knight, Scott, and Robert McNemar. *Celebrating the Past, Claiming the Future: A History of the First One Hundred Years of Wilmington Yearly Meeting of The Religious Society of Friends.* Sabina, Ohio: Gaskin Printing, 1991.

Krueger, Glee F. *A Gallery of American Samplers: The Theodore H. Kapnek Collection.* Exhibition catalogue. New York: E. P. Dutton, 1978.

———. *New England Samplers to 1840.* Sturbridge, Mass.: Old Sturbridge Village, 1978.

Lottich, Kenneth V. *New England Transplanted.* Dallas: Royal Publishing Co., 1964.

MacKenzie, Donald Ralph. *Painters in Ohio, 1788–1860, With a Biographical Index.* Columbus: The Ohio State University, 1960.

Martin, William T. *History of Franklin County.* Columbus, Ohio: Follett, Foster & Co., 1858.

Martzolff, Clement L. "Land Grants for Education in the Ohio Valley States." *Ohio Archaeological and Historical Society Publications.* 25 (1917).

Mason, Mary Eliza. *Genealogy and History of the Family of Hugh Mason, William Mason, and Allied Families.* Marietta, Ohio: 1930.

Mattingly, Paul H., and Edward W. Stevens Jr. "*. . . schools and the means of education shall forever be encouraged": History of Education in the Old Northwest, 1787–1880.* Athens, Ohio: Ohio University Libraries, 1987.

McClung, Col. D. W. *Means and Ends or Self Training.* Boston: Marsh, Capon, Lyon & Webb, 1840.

———. *The Centennial Anniversary of the City of Hamilton, Ohio.* Hamilton, Ohio: Published by the author, 1892.

Medert, Patricia F. *Stories from Chillicothe's Past.* Chillicothe, Ohio: Published by the author, 1998.

Miller, E. Irene *History of Miami County, Ohio.* Tipp City, Ohio: The Miami County Historical Society, 1982.

Miller, Edward A. "History of the Educational Legislation in Ohio from 1803 to 1850" *Ohio Archaeological and Historical Publications* 27. Columbus, Ohio: Fred J. Heer, 1919.

Monnett, Eugene. *History of the Monet Family in America.* Published by the Author, 1911.

Mosteller, Larry. "Elcey Patterson and Her Union Village Sampler," *The Shaker Messenger* 13, no. 2 (June 1991).

Murdoch, Florence. "Summary of the Manuscript Recollections of Milo G. Williams." *Ohio State Archaeological and Historical Society Quarterly* 54 (April/June 1945).

Nelson, Narka. *The Western College for Women, 1853–1953.* Oxford, Ohio: Western College, 1954.

Perrin, William H., W. H. Battle, and Arthur G. Winston. *The History of Crawford County, Ohio.* Chicago: Baskin and Battey Historical Publications, 1881.

Piercy, Caroline B. *The Valley of God's Pleasure.* New York: Stratford House, 1951.

Pioneer and General History of Geauga County. The Historical Society of Geauga County, 1880.

Porcher, Connie M. "Miami County Sampler of Garthary Merrit." *Historical Register* 14, no. 2 (Piqua Historical Society) (Mar./Apr. 1991).

Private Independent Schools. Wallingford, Conn.: Bunting and Lyon, Inc., 1993.

Rae, Noel. *Witnessing America: The Library of Congress Book of Firsthand Accounts of Life in America, 1600-1900.* New York: Stonesong Press, Penguin Reference, 1996.

Randall, Emilius O., and Daniel J. Ryan. *History of Ohio: The Rise and Progress of an American State.* 6 vols. New York: Century History Company, 1915.

Reichel, William C. *History of the Bethlehem Female Seminary, 1785–1858.* Philadelphia: J. B. Lippincott & Co., 1858.

Reichel, William C., and William H. Bigler. *A History of the Rise, Progress, and Present Condition of the Moravian Seminary for Young Ladies at Bethlehem, Pennsylvania, With Its Catalogue of Its Pupils 1785–1858,* rev. and enl. Philadelphia: J. B. Lippincott, 1870.

Rerick, Rowland H. *History of Ohio.* Vol. 1. Madison, Wis.: Northwestern Historical Association, 1902.

Ring, Betty. *American Needlework Treasures.* New York: E. P. Dutton for The Museum of American Folk Art, 1987.

———. *Girlhood Embroidery: American Samplers and Pictorial Needlework, 1650–1850.* 2 vols. New York: Alfred A. Knopf, 1993.

Ronald, Bruce, and Virginia Ronald. *The Land Between the Miamis.* 2 Vols. Dayton, Ohio: Landfall Press, 1996.

Rose, Mary Lou, and Juanita Conklin. *History of Montgomery, Ohio, 1795–1995.* Montgomery, Ohio: Bicentennial Committee, 1995.

Rosenboom, Eugene H., and Francis P. Weisenburger. *A History of Ohio.* Columbus: Ohio Archaeological and Historical Society, 1953.

Ross, Donald. "27 Stations to Libertyville." *Historicalog* (Publication of Warren County Historical Society) (Apr./June 1998).

Roster of Ohio Soldiers in the War of 1812. Adjutant General of Ohio, 1916. Rpt. Baltimore: Genealogical Publishing Co., 1968.

Rowland, Nina E. "Three Pioneer Women in American Education in Washington County, Ohio." Thesis, Ohio University, Athens, May 1943.

Ruggles, Alice McGuffey. "A Buckeye Boarding-School in 1821." *Ohio Archaeological and Historical Quarterly* 53 (1944).

Rust, Orton G. *History of West Central Ohio.* 3 vols. Indianapolis: Historical Publishing Co., 1934.

Schiffer, Margaret B. *Historical Needlework of Pennsylvania.* New York: Charles Scribner's Sons, 1968.

Schneider, Norris. *Y-Bridge City: The Story of Zanesville and Muskingum County, Ohio.* Cleveland and New York: World Publishing Co., 1950.

Scott, Daniel. *A History of the Early Settlement of Highland County, Ohio.* Hillsboro, Ohio: Hillsborough Gazette, 1890.

Shelley, Donald A. *The Fraktur-Writings or Illuminated Manuscripts of the Pennsylvania Germans.* Allentown, Pa.: Schlechter's for The Pennsylvania German Folklore Society, 1961.

Sheppard, Dempsey O. *The Story of Barnesville, 1808–1940.* Barnesville, Ohio: F. J. Heer Printing Co., 1942.

Sherzer, Jane. "The Higher Education of Women in the Ohio Valley Previous to 1840." *Ohio Archaeological and Historical Publications* 25 (1906).

Shilling, D. C, "Pioneer Schools and School Masters." *Ohio Archaeological and Historical Publications* 7 (Oct. 1888–Apr. 1889).

Silberstein, Iola Hessler. *Cincinnati Then and Now.* Cincinnati: League of Women Voters of the Cincinnati Area, n.d.

Sklar, Kathryn Kish. "Female Teachers: 'Firm Pillars' of the West." In "*. . . schools and the means of education shall forever be encouraged:" History of Education in the Old Northwest 1787–1880.* Athens, Ohio: Ohio University Libraries, 1987.

Smith, William E., Ph.D. *History of Southwestern Ohio: The Miami Valleys.* New York and West Palm Beach: Lewis Historical Publishing Co., n.d.

Smith, Thomas H. *The Mapping of Ohio.* Kent, Ohio: The Kent State University Press, 1977.

Snyder, Marion. "Hurin, One of the Four Founders of Lebanon." (Lebanon) *Western Star,* Sept. 1979.

Stafford, Tom. "Springfield Female Seminary from 1849 to 1871." *Springfield* (Ohio) *News Sun,* Sept. 18, 2000.

Steele, Robert W. *Early Dayton, 1796–1896.* Dayton, Ohio: W. J. Shuey, 1895.

Storey, Russell M. "The Rise of the Denominational College." *Ohio Archaeological and Historical Publications* 25 (1917).

Strawser, Robert. *Yesterday: Historic Properties in Springboro: Property Sales and Transactions In Olde Springboro and Surrounding Lands, 1806–1915.* Springboro, Ohio: Springboro Historical Society, 1996.

Studebaker, Sue. *Ohio Samplers: Schoolgirl Embroideries, 1803–1850.* Exhibition catalog. Lebanon, Ohio: Warren County Historical Society, 1988.

———. "Sister Elsie's Sampler." (Worthington, Ohio) *Antique Review* (June 1991).

Studer, Jacob H. *Columbus, Ohio: Its History, Resources and Progress.* N.p., 1883.

Sullivan, Helena Louisa. "Mr. and Mrs. McIntire–A Graphic Biographical Sketch of Zanesville's Founder and His Wife." (Zanesville) *Times Recorder,* Apr. 1892.

Swan, Susan Burrows. *Plain and Fancy: American Women and Their Needlework, 1700–1850.* New York: Holt, Rinehart and Winston, 1977.

Taunton, Nerylla. *Antique Needlework Tools and Embroideries.* Woodbridge, Suffolk, England: Antique Collector's Club, Ltd., 1997.

Thomas, Thomas E. *Letters of Thomas E. Thomas to His Children and Others.* Cincinnati: Ebbert and Richardson Co., 1913.

Thwaites, Ruben G. *Early Western Travels.* Vol. IV. Cleveland: Arthur H. Clark Co., 1906.

Townsley, Gardner H. *Historic Lebanon . . . Beginning with Bedle's Station in 1795.* 1940; rpt. Lebanon, Ohio: Western Star, 1972.

Upham, Alfred H. *Old Miami: The Yale of the West.* Hamilton, Ohio: Republican Publishing Co., 1909.

Upton, Harriet Taylor. *History of the Western Reserve.* Chicago and New York: Lewis Publishing Co., 1910.

Vanderpoel, Emily Noyes. *More Chronicles of a Pioneer School from 1792 to 1833: The History of The Litchfield Female Academy Kept by Miss Sarah Pierce and her Nephew John Pierce Brace.* Cambridge, Mass.: The University Press, 1927.

Virkus, Frederick Adams. *The Compendium of American Genealogy.* Vol. 7. Baltimore: Genealogical Publishing Co., Inc., 1987.

Walker, Charles Manning. *History of Athens County, Ohio.* Cincinnati: R. Clark & Co., 1869.

Waynesville's First 200 Years. Waynesville, Ohio: The Waynesville Historical Society, 1997.

Weisenburger, Francis P. *The Passing of the Frontier.* Vol. 3 of *The History of the State of Ohio,* 6 vols. Columbus, Ohio: The Ohio State Archaeological and Historical Society, 1941–44.

Wickham, Gertrude Van Rensselaer. *Memorial to the Pioneer Women of the Western Reserve.* 4 parts. Cleveland: Cleveland Centennial Commission, Woman's Dept., 1896.

Williams Brothers. *History of Ashtabula County, Ohio.* Philadelphia: Lippincott & Co., 1878.

———. *History of Geauga and Lake Counties.* Philadelphia: J. B. Lippincott & Co., 1878.

———. *History of Lorain County, Ohio.* Philadelphia: Lippincott & Co., 1878.

———. *History of Ross and Highland Counties, Ohio.* Cleveland: W. W. Williams, 1880.

Williams, Byron. *History of Clermont and Brown Counties, Ohio.* 2 vols. 1913; rpt., Baltimore: Gateway Press, 1987.

Williams, H. Z. *History of Preble County, Ohio.* Cleveland: W. W. Williams, 1881.

———. *History of Trumbull and Mahoning Counties.* Vol. 1. Cleveland: H. Z. Williams and Bros., 1882.

Williams, Stephen Riggs. *The Saga of "The Paddy's Run."* Oxford, Ohio: Miami University, 1945.

Williams, William W. "Magazine of Western History." *Magazine Western History Company* 3 (Nov. 1885, Apr. 1886).

Wiseman, E. M. L. *Pioneer Period and Pioneer People of Fairfield County, Ohio.* 1901; rpt., Marceline, Mo.: Walsworth Publishing Co., 1984.

Wittke, Carl. *The History of The State of Ohio.* 6 vols. Columbus: Ohio Archaeological and Historical Society Publications, 1941-44.

Woody, Thomas. *A History of Women's Education in the United States.* 2 vols. New York and Lancaster, Pa.: Science Press, 1929.

Wright Descendants. *Aron and Mary Wright.* New York: Charles Francis Press, 1942.

Unpublished Works

Akin, Lewis. "The Kiphart Reunion" (family history). Warren Co., Ohio, Sept. 1, 1900.

Augspurger, R. E. "Education Progress in Warren County, Ohio, 1798–1948." Lebanon, Ohio, 1948.

Bogan, Dallas. "The Pioneer Writing of Josiah Morrow." Lebanon, Ohio, 1993.

Butterworth Family Papers. "A Quaker Biography of Nancy Wales Butterworth (1809–1909)." Lebanon, Ohio: Warren County Historical Society Museum Archives. N.d.

Cowles, Reverend Giles Hooker. "Personal Diary of the Trip to Ohio, 1811." Cowles Family Papers.

"Friends of the Landscape: A Preliminary Examination of the Society of Friends: Their Settlement and Architecture in Clinton, Highland, and Warren Counties, 1795–1860." Quaker Collection, Wilmington College Library, Wilmington, Ohio. 14 pp. N.d.

Galloway, Rebecca. Unpublished personal diary, c. 1840. Archives of Greene County Library, Xenia, Ohio.

Harper, "Nettie." Unpublished personal diary, 1867–76. Archives of the Preble County Historical Society, Eaton, Ohio.

"History of Lebanon Academy." Warren County Historical Society, Lebanon, Ohio. N.d.

Holcomb, Alfred. *Lebanon Academy Catalogue of the Instructors and Pupils,* 1845. Held at Warren County Historical Archives Library, Lebanon, Ohio.

Hough, Minerva. "History of Waynesville School." C. 1935. Archives of Mary L. Cook Library, Waynesville, Ohio.

Kiphart, Thomas J. "One Hundred Fifty Years of Cincinnati Monthly Meeting of Friends, 1815–1965." Archives of Wilmington College Library, Wilmington, Ohio.

Kramer, John Bartram, and Mabel C. Stevenson. "The Village: Memories of Lithopolis." Aug. 1836.

Letter of Margaret Tidball Linn to son Thomas Linn, Sept. 20, 1863, Millersburg, Ohio. Private collection.

Maineville Academy Minutes and History. Maineville, Ohio, May 30, 1857.

Peebles, Miss Charity. "Reminiscence of the Town of Springborough." New Vienna, Ohio, 1927. Archives of Warren County Historical Society, Lebanon, Ohio.

Phillips, Hazel Spencer. "Early Settlers in Springborough." Aug. 1915. Archives of Warren County Historical Society, Lebanon, Ohio.

———. "The First Schools." Lebanon, Ohio. N.d. Archives of Warren County Historical Society, Lebanon, Ohio.

Price, Ann Hulme. Personal letters, 1824–1836. Ohio Historical Society Archives (VFM-1947), Columbus.

"Proceeding—Centennial Anniversary: Miami Monthly Meeting, Waynesville, Ohio–10th Month, 16–17, 1903." Archives of Wilmington College, Wilmington, Ohio.

"Rankin House State Memorial." Ripley Heritage, Inc. Publication. N.d.

Rice, Eunice. "The Personal Memoirs of Eunice Rice." C. 1900. Private collection.

Rules and Regulations of Public School of Morrow. Morrow, Ohio: Tribune Print, 1899.

Schallenberger, Rebecca T. (Frazier) Bailey. "Biographical Notes Gathered by her Great Granddaughters—Virginia Bailey Schallenberger and Lois Hunnicutt Joyce," 7 pp., 1976.

Archives

Church of the Latter day Saints Library, Dayton and Fairborn, Ohio.

Cincinnati Historical Society Library, Cincinnati.

Cincinnati Public Library, Main Branch, Cincinnati.

Ohio Historical Society Library, Columbus.

Warren County Historical Society Library Archives, Lebanon, Ohio.

Western Reserve Historical Society Library Archives, Cleveland, Ohio.

Wilmington College Archives, The Quaker Collection, Wilmington, Ohio.

index

Note: References to illustrations are in italics.